Frommer's®
Scotland

POSTCARDS FROM

D0469264

The Scottish countryside, with its ancient stone walls, rolling hills, glens, and moors, is still a place where farmers make their living from the land. © Dewitt Jones/Robert Holmes Photography.

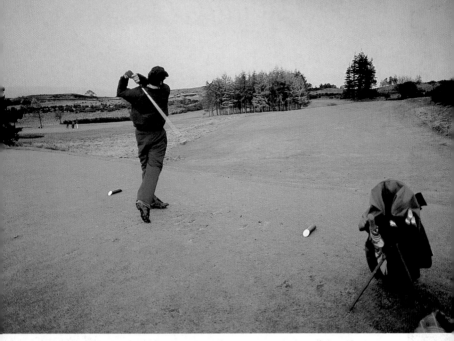

When in Scotland . . . do as the Scots do, and take a swing at one of the 400 courses. Gleneagles golfing center/sports complex is home to the King's and Queen's courses, which have hosted many championships, and which are considered to be among the finest in Europe. See chapters 3 and 9. © Macduff Everton Photography.

Rising mysteriously out of the mist along the banks of Loch Awe, Scotland's longest lake, stand the ruins of Kilchurn castle, once a stronghold of the Campbells of Glen Orchy. See chapter 7. © John Lawrence/Tony Stone Images.

Kelso Abbey (built in 1128) is the oldest and one of the largest of the Borders abbeys. It has lain in ruins since the 16th century, a testament to the long, bitter struggle with the English. See chapter 5. © *Andrea Pistolesi/The Image Bank.*

Edinburgh Castle rises above the city at the western end of the Royal Mile. Here, Mary Queen of Scots gave birth to James VI of Scotland. See chapter 4. © Kindra Clineff Photography.

The Royal Mile stretches through Edinburgh's Old Town from the Castle to the Palace of Holyroodhouse. See chapter 4. © Catherine Karnow Photography.

The Royal Highland Gathering is held the first Saturday of September, when Scots compete in bagpiping and dancing competitions, and contests of strength, like the hammer throw. See chapter 9. © Churchill & Klehr Photography.

Robert "Rob Roy" MacGregor (1671–1734), the Scottish hero of poems, stories, and film, is buried in the churchyard of Balquhidder Church near Callander. See chapter 8.

© Catherine Karnow Photography.

The thatch-roofed "black houses" are typical of Skye and the other Hebridean Islands. They are built without mortar, and though some houses have chimneys, smoke from the fires inside passes through the thatch, making it "black." See chapter 11. © Art Wolfe Photography.

Having "a wee dram" of whisky, blended or single malt, is a great Scottish tradition, enjoyed by George Grant, Chairman of the Glenfarclas Distillery at Ballindalloch. Grant's family has been producing the spirit since 1836. © Catherine Karnow Photography.

Rannoch Moor off Loch Laidon is a picturesque spot in the West Highlands, where the play of light on the land makes for a dramatic photo. © *Kindra Clineff Photography.*

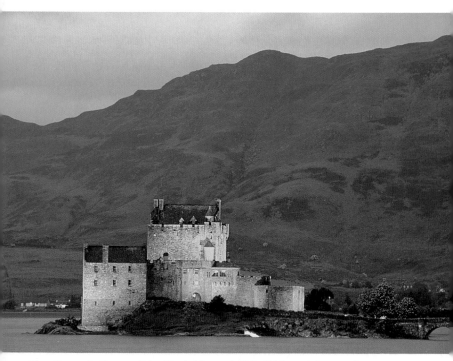

Eilean Donan Castle, near Kyle of Lochalsh, was built in 1214 as a defense against marauding Danes. In ruins for 200 years, it was restored in 1932 by Colonel MacRae of clan MacRae and is now a memorial and museum. See chapter 11. © *Catherine Karnow Photography.*

Scotland

8th Edition

by Darwin Porter & Danforth Prince

Here's what the critics say about Frommer's:

"Amazingly easy to use. Very portable, very complete."

—*Booklist*

"Detailed, accurate, and easy-to-read information for all price ranges."
—*Glamour Magazine*

"Hotel information is close to encyclopedic."

—*Des Moines Sunday Register*

"Frommer's Guides have a way of giving you a real feel for a place."
—*Knight Ridder Newspapers*

WILEY

Wiley Publishing, Inc.

About the Authors

Darwin Porter has covered Scotland since the beginning of his travel-writing career as author of *Frommer's England & Scotland.* Since 1982, he has been joined in his efforts by **Danforth Prince,** formerly of the Paris Bureau of the *New York Times.* Together, they've written numerous best-selling Frommer's guides—notably to England, France, and Italy.

Published by:

Wiley Publishing, Inc.

111 River St.
Hoboken, NJ 07030-5744

ISBN 0-7645-4126-9

Editor: Jennifer Moore
Production Editor: Ian Skinnari
Cartographer: Elizabeth Puhl
Photo Editor: Richard Fox
Production by Wiley Indianapolis Composition Services

Front cover photo: Eilean Donan Castle in Dornie
Back cover photo: Standing Stones of Callanish on the Isle of Lewis

For information on our other products and services or to obtain technical support, please contact our Customer Care Department within the U.S. at 800/762-2974, outside the U.S. at 317/572-3993 or fax 317/572-4002.

Wiley also publishes its books in a variety of electronic formats. Some content that appears in print may not be available in electronic formats.

Manufactured in the United States of America

5   4   3   2   1

Contents

5 The Borders & Galloway Regions 126

6 Glasgow & the Strathclyde Region 161

7 Argyll & the Southern Hebrides 210

12 The Orkney & Shetland Islands   400

Appendix: Scotland in Depth   431

Index   448

List of Maps

An Invitation to the Reader

In researching this book, we discovered many wonderful places—hotels, restaurants, shops, and more. We're sure you'll find others. Please tell us about them, so we can share the information with your fellow travelers in upcoming editions. If you were disappointed with a recommendation, we'd love to know that, too. Please write to:

Frommer's Scotland, 8th Edition
Wiley Publishing, Inc. • 111 River St. • Hoboken, NJ 07030-5744

An Additional Note

Please be advised that travel information is subject to change at any time—and this is especially true of prices. We therefore suggest that you write or call ahead for confirmation when making your travel plans. The authors, editors, and publisher cannot be held responsible for the experiences of readers while traveling. Your safety is important to us, however, so we encourage you to stay alert and be aware of your surroundings. Keep a close eye on cameras, purses, and wallets, all favorite targets of thieves and pickpockets.

Other Great Guides for Your Trip:

Frommer's Great Britain
Scotland For Dummies
Frommer's Britain's Best Bed & Breakfasts and Country Inns
Frommer's Britain's Best-Loved Driving Tours
Frommer's European Cruises & Ports of Call

Frommer's Star Ratings, Icons & Abbreviations

Every hotel, restaurant, and attraction listing in this guide has been ranked for quality, value, service, amenities, and special features using a **star-rating system.** In country, state, and regional guides, we also rate towns and regions to help you narrow down your choices and budget your time accordingly. Hotels and restaurants are rated on a scale of zero (recommended) to three stars (exceptional). Attractions, shopping, nightlife, towns, and regions are rated according to the following scale: zero stars (recommended), one star (highly recommended), two stars (very highly recommended), and three stars (must-see).

In addition to the star-rating system, we also use **seven feature icons** that point you to the great deals, in-the-know advice, and unique experiences that separate travelers from tourists. Throughout the book, look for:

Finds	Special finds—those places only insiders know about
Fun Fact	Fun facts—details that make travelers more informed and their trips more fun
Kids	Best bets for kids, and advice for the whole family
Moments	Special moments—those experiences that memories are made of
Overrated	Places or experiences not worth your time or money
Tips	Insider tips—great ways to save time and money
Value	Great values—where to get the best deals

The following **abbreviations** are used for credit cards:

AE	American Express	DISC	Discover	V	Visa
DC	Diners Club	MC	MasterCard		

Frommers.com

Now that you have the guidebook to a great trip, visit our website at **www.frommers.com** for travel information on more than 3,000 destinations. With features updated regularly, we give you instant access to the most current trip-planning information available. At Frommers.com, you'll also find the best prices on airfares, accommodations, and car rentals—and you can even book travel online through our travel booking partners. At Frommers.com, you'll also find the following:

- Online updates to our most popular guidebooks
- Vacation sweepstakes and contest giveaways
- Newsletter highlighting the hottest travel trends
- Online travel message boards with featured travel discussions

What's New in Scotland

Visitors justifiably flock to Scotland to revel in its traditions: medieval castles, dramatic countryside, world-class golf, and Highland Gatherings. But travelers will delight in this fair isle's new experiences, too, many of which incorporate the best of Scotland's past with the latest in entertainment, luxury, and style. Here are some of the latest developments:

EDINBURGH Accommodations Making waves is **The Edinburgh Residence,** 7 Rothesay Terrace (✆ **0131/ 226-3380**), a series of town house suites in beautifully restored Georgian buildings with grand staircases and accommodations that are the ultimate in luxury. In spite of the buildings' age, the interior comforts are as modern as the 21st century. In the shadow of Edinburgh Castle, the **Point Hotel,** 34 Bread St (✆ **0131/221-5555**), offers the most innovative contemporary interiors of any hotel in the city. Trading in tartan and Scottish antiques for neon and chrome, the exciting decor creates a dramatic minimalist effect. The capital's most offbeat, yet luxurious suites, are found at **The Witchery by the Castle,** Castlehill, along the Royal Mile (✆ **0131/ 225-5613**), an offshoot of its even more celebrated restaurant. *Cosmopolitan* and other media have hailed this as one of the "world's most wonderful places to stay." See "Where to Stay" for complete details.

Restaurants Fishers Bistro, 1 The Shore, Leith (✆ **0131/554-5666**), is attracting serious foodies from the center of Edinburgh to this old seaport. The bistro and seafood bar is celebrated for the quality of fresh fish dishes, including Loch Fyne oysters, acclaimed as Britain's finest. See p. 94.

Attractions Hidden beneath the City Chambers on the Royal Mile lies **The Real Mary King's Close** (Writer's Court, ✆ **0870/243-0160**), a newly opened archaeological wonder. Here you can tour a number of underground "Closes," originally very narrow walkways with houses on either side, some dating back centuries. See p. 99.

THE BORDERS Restaurants A former private manor house, **Edenwater House,** in the hamlet of Ednam near Kelso (✆ **01573/224-070**), has become a comfortable private hotel in one of the most tranquil settings in the Borders. Edenwater's elegant public rooms, welcoming guest rooms, and delicious cuisine make this small hotel a winner. See p. 136.

GLASGOW Accommodations Exciting new hotels continue to open in this Victorian city, notably **Langs,** 2 Port Dundas (✆ **0141/333-1500**). Outfitted in a trendy minimalist style with a diverse medley of guest rooms in various shapes, sizes, and configurations, Langs is the perfect place for guests seeking a taste of contemporary Japan in the heart of Glasgow. The aptly named **Theatre Hotel,** 25-27 Elmbank St. (✆ **0141/227-2712**), inhabits a 19th-century theater and dance hall. The hotel has retained traditional architectural details such as wood paneling and stained glass, but in all other ways this place is sleekly modern.

Restaurants Russian chefs have invaded Glasgow at **Café Cossachok,** 10 King St., Merchant City (© **0141/ 553-0733**), near the Tron Theatre. The kitchen turns out not only superbly prepared Russian fare (borscht and blinis, anyone?), but classics from other former Soviet republics, including Armenia, Georgia, and the Ukraine. An authentic Russian decor. The chic new place to dine in Glasgow is **Windows Restaurant,** on the 7th floor of the Carlton George Hotel, 44 West George St. (© **0141/353-6373**). Diners can feast their eyes on panoramic views from their tables while in the kitchen the chef skillfully prepares an innovative "Taste of Scotland" that might include seared West Coast scallops or grilled filet of Scottish beef with chanterelle mushrooms. See "Where to Dine," in chapter 6 for complete details.

Attractions McLellan Galleries. 270 Sauchiehall St. (© **0141/564- 4100**), came into prominence in 2003 when the Kelvingrove Art Gallery and Museum closed for a major restoration. Some of that gallery's most important oil paintings and sculpture, were temporarily (until 2006) transferred to this heretofore little-visited gallery. See p. 187.

FIFE & THE CENTRAL HIGHLANDS Accommodations The golfing capital of the world can finally boast its own premiere, government-rated five-star hotel: **St. Andrews Bay Golf Resort & Spa,** St. Andrews Bay, St. Andrews (© **01334/837-000**). It's the grandest hotel in Eastern Scotland, standing on a cliff overlooking the north Sean and the River Tay. Although golf is the main attraction—it is home

to two championship golf courses—guests also come here for the results first-class spa and health club (the latter of which number Prince William among its members). See p. 253.

ABERDEEN, THE TAYSIDE & THE GRAMPIAN REGIONS Accommodations Not to be outdone by the new St. Andrews Bay Golf Resort & Spa, Britain's premier golf hotel, **The Gleneagles Hotel,** Auchterarder (© **01764/662231**), has made vast improvements. In addition to adding a new annex with 59 deluxe rooms with private access, management has hired Andrew Fairlie, a Michelin-acclaimed star chef, to take over the superb cuisine served at this sprawling resort. See p. 294.

Restaurants Helping to overcome Dundee's reputation for lackluster cuisine, the **Het Theatercafe,** Tay Square (© **01382/206-699**), has arrived on the city's culinary scene. Sheltered under the roof of the Dundee Repertory Theatre, it offers diners the choice of eating in the cafe upstairs or in the excellent restaurant downstairs. Ideal for a pre-theater meal, it offers freshly prepared and good-tasting international food. Edinburgh-based Howies Restaurants has also contributed to the culinary revitalization of Dundee with its **Howies Dundee,** 25 Tay St. (© **01382/200-399**) the cuisine is called "Scottish with a twist." A self-styled "restaurant with rooms," the food is prepared with topnotch ingredients turned into tasty platters. See "Where to Dine" in Chapter 9 for details.

Another **Howies** (© **01224/639- 500**) has opened in Aberdeen to immediate success with its combination Scottish and international cuisine. Familiar fare such as Aberdeen Angus filet appears on the menu but it's given a modern flair, including lighter sauces.

1

The Best of Scotland

Scotland is permeated with legend and romance. Its ruined castles standing amid fields of heather and bracken speak of a past full of heroism and struggle and events that still ring across the centuries. Its two great cities—the ancient seat of Scottish royalty, Edinburgh, and even more ancient Glasgow, boasting Victorian splendor—are among Europe's most dynamic centers. Equally as thrilling is the country's awesomely beautiful outdoors, with Highlands, mountains, lochs, salmon-filled rivers, incomparable golf courses, and so much more.

1 The Best Travel Experiences

- **Checking Out the Local Pub:** You're in a Scottish pub, talking to the bartender and choosing from a dizzying array of single-malt whiskies. Perhaps the wind is blowing fitfully outside, causing the wooden sign to creak above the battered door, and a fire is flickering against the blackened bricks of the old fireplace. As the evening wanes and you've established common ground with the locals, you'll realize you're having one of your most authentic Scottish experiences. We list our favorite pubs in the destination chapters that follow.

- **Visiting Edinburgh at Festival Time:** The Edinburgh International Festival has become one of Europe's most prestigious arts festivals. During 3 weeks in August, a host of performers descends on the city, infusing it with a kind of manic creative energy. If you're planning to sample the many offerings, get your tickets well in advance, and make your hotel and flight reservations early. Call ② 0131/225-1188 or go to www.eif.co.uk to check schedules and

purchase tickets. See "Special Events & Festivals" in chapter 4.

- **Haunting the Castles:** The land of Macbeth numbers more castles than anywhere else in the world. Many are in evocative ruins, but dozens of the foreboding royal dwellings are intact and open to the public. Some of these castles, such as **Culzean** (p. 206), built by Robert Adam, are architectural masterpieces filled with paintings and antiques. Travelers who can't get enough of Scotland's castles should consider booking a night or two in one of the many relics that have been converted into comfortable, although sometimes drafty, hotels.

- **Horseback Trekking Through the Highlands & Argyll:** There's nothing like riding a sturdy pony through the Highlands' fragrant heather and over its lichen-covered rocks. One of Scotland's biggest stables is the **Highland Riding Centre,** Drumnadrochit (② 01456/450-220); see "Along Loch Ness" in chapter 10. For scenic equestrian treks across the moors, Highlands, and headlands

Scotland

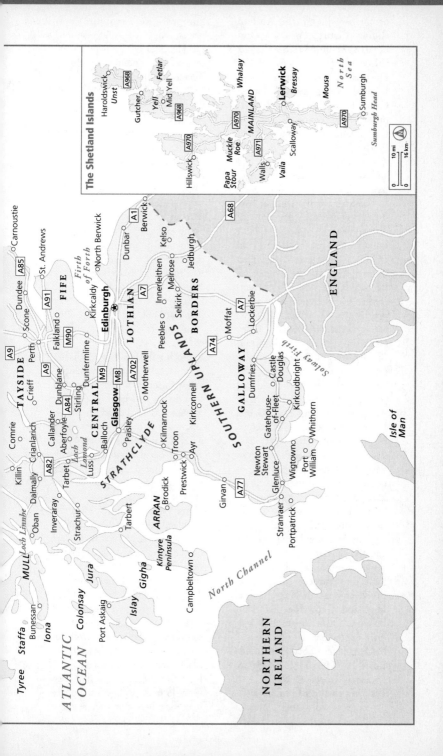

The Shetland Islands

North Sea

Haroldswick
Unst
A968
Fetlar
Gutcher
Yell
Mid Yell
A968
Whalsay
Lerwick
Bressay
Mousa
MAINLAND
A970
A970
Sumburgh
Sumburgh Head
Hillswick
A970
Muckle Roe
A971
Scalloway
Papa Stour
Walls
Vaila
Scalloway
10 mi
16 km

Carnoustie
Dundee
A85
St. Andrews
A91
FIFE
Firth of Forth
Scone
Perth
A9
Falkland
A9
Kirkcaldy
North Berwick
Dunbar
A1
Berwick
A68
Kelso
Jedburgh
Edinburgh
LOTHIAN
A7
Innerleithen
Melrose
Selkirk
Crieff
TAYSIDE
Dunblane
M90
Dunfermline
M9
A702
Peebles
BORDERS
A7
Lockerbie
ENGLAND
Comrie
Callander
A84
Stirling
CENTRAL
Glasgow
M8
Motherwell
SOUTHERN UPLANDS
Moffat
A74
Killin
Crianlarich
A82
Aberfoyle
Loch Lomond
Balloch
Luss
Paisley
Kilmarnock
Kirkconnell
Dumfries
GALLOWAY
Castle Douglas
Solway Firth
Dalmally
Tarbet
STRATHCLYDE
Troon
Ayr
Gatehouse-of-Fleet
Kirkcudbright
Oban
Inveraray
Strachur
Prestwick
Newton Stewart
Wigtown
Whithorn
Isle of Man
LOCH LINNHE
Brodick
ARRAN
Girvan
A77
Glenluce
Port William
MULL
Tarbert
Kintyre Peninsula
Stranraer
Portpatrick
Staffa
Bunessan
Iona
Jura
Campbeltown
North Channel
Tyree
ATLANTIC OCEAN
Colonsay
Islay
Gigha
Port Askaig
NORTHERN IRELAND

of the Argyll, try the **Ardfern Riding Centre,** Loch Gilphead (© **01852/500-632**). See the box titled "Seeing the Argyll on Horseback" in Chapter 7.

- **Cruising Along the Caledonian Canal:** In 1822, a group of enterprising Scots connected three of the Highlands' longest lakes (Lochs Ness, Lochy, and Oich) with a canal linking Britain's east and west coasts. Since then, barges have hauled everything from grain to building supplies without having to negotiate the wild storms off Scotland's northernmost tips. Now cabin cruisers tote a different kind of cargo along the Caledonian Canal: people seeking a spectacular waterborne view of the countryside that was tamed centuries ago by the Camerons, the Stewarts, and the MacDonalds. **Caley Cruisers,** based in Inverness (© **01463/236-328;** www.caleycruisers.co.uk), rents out skippered-cruisers by the week. See "Along Loch Ness" in chapter 10.

- **Attending a Highland Game:** Unlike any other sporting event, a Highland Game emphasizes clannish traditions rather than athletic dexterity, and the centerpiece is usually an exhibition of brute strength (tossing logs and the like). Most visitors show up for the men in kilts, the bagpipe playing, the pomp and circumstance, and the general celebration of all things Scottish. The best known (and most widely televised) of the events is Braemar's **Royal Highland Gathering,** held near Balmoral Castle in late August or early September. For details, call the Highlands of Scotland Tourist Board at © **01463/234-353.** See "Braemar" in chapter 9.

- **Ferrying to the Isle of Iona:** It's an otherworldly rock, one of Europe's most evocative holy places, anchored solidly among the Hebrides off Scotland's western coast. St. Columba established Iona as a Christian center in A.D. 563 and used it as a base for converting Scotland. You'll find a ruined Benedictine nunnery and a fully restored cathedral where 50 Scottish kings were buried during the early Middle Ages. Hundreds of Celtic crosses once adorned the island; today, only three of the originals remain. The island, now part of the National Trust, is home to the Iona Community, an ecumenical group dedicated to the perpetuation of Christian ideals. Reaching the island requires a 10-minute ferry ride from the hamlet of Fionnphort, on the island of Mull. See "Iona & Staffa: An Abbey & a Musical Cave" in chapter 11.

- **Exploring the Orkneys:** Archaeologists say the Orkneys, an archipelago with some 70 islands, contain the richest trove of prehistoric monuments in the British Isles— an average of three sites per square mile. Ornithologists claim that about 16% of all winged animals in the United Kingdom reside here, and linguists document an ancient dialect still using Viking terms. Northwest of the Scottish mainland, closer to Oslo than to faraway London, these islands are on the same latitude as St. Petersburg but much more exposed to the raging gales of the North Sea. The late-spring sunsets and the aurora borealis have been called mystical, and in midsummer the sun remains above the horizon for 18 hours per day. In winter, the islands are plunged into an equivalent twilight or total darkness. Only 19 of the Orkneys are inhabited; the others seem to float above primordial seas, drenched with rains and the weak sunlight of these northern climes. See "The Orkney Islands: An Archaeological Garden" in chapter 12.

2 The Best Golf

For full details about golfing in Scotland, see "Teeing Off: Golfing in Scotland," in chapter 3.

- **Turnberry Hotel Golf Courses** (Ayrshire; ☏ **01655/334-032**): Established in 1902, this is one of the world's most sought-after courses. It's not for the faint of heart—although some of the links are verdant, others are uncomfortably paired with the sands, the salt-resistant tough grasses, and the powerful winds blasting in from the nearby sea. See "Side Trips from Glasgow: The Best of the Strathclyde Region" in chapter 6.
- **Royal Troon Golf Club** (Ayrshire; ☏ **01292/311-555**): Laid out along lines paralleling the Firth of Clyde, this club fills a flat lowland terrain whose fairways are almost breathtakingly green despite their foundations on sandy soil. This is Lowland Scotland at its most seductive, a 7,097-yard (6,458m) course (one of Scotland's longest) with a par of 71. See "Side Trips from Glasgow: The Best of the Strathclyde Region" in chapter 6.
- **Old Course** (St. Andrews; ☏ **01334/466-666**): Sometime during the late 14th century, a group of bored aristocrats started batting a ball around the nearby meadows. By the time their activities were officially recorded in 1552, the bylaws of the game were well on the way to being part of Scotland's lore. The Old Course is the world's most legendary temple of golf, one whose difficulty is shaped by nature and the long-ago paths of grazing sheep. See "St. Andrews: The Birthplace of Golf" in chapter 8.
- **Carnoustie Golf Links** (Tayside; ☏ **01241/853-789**): Site of six British Opens, Carnoustie is much more difficult than most players anticipate at first glance. U.S. champions Tom Watson and Gary Player have referred to it as their favorite, and much of the town of Carnoustie was built because of the stream of world-class golfers who migrated here. See "Dundee & Glamis Castle" in Chapter 9.
- **Royal Dornoch Golf Club** (Sutherland; ☏ **01862/810-219**): This is the most northerly of the world's great golf courses, only 6° south of the Arctic Circle. Despite its northern isolation, Royal Dornoch enjoys a microclimate more akin to the fens around Norfolk, England, than to the Arctic. See "Sutherland: The Gem of Scotland" in chapter 10.

3 The Best Fishing

For more details about fishing in Scotland, see "Fishing" chapter 3.

- **The Borders & Galloway Regions:** Sea fishing is pure heaven in the Solway Firth; it's best near Port William and Portpatrick villages, in the vicinity of Loch Ryan, and along the shore of the Isle of Whithorn. The elusive salmon is best pursued along the River Tweed, and the lesser-known hill lochans are ideal for trout fishermen. Local tourist offices distribute two helpful guides: *A Comprehensive Guide to Scottish Borders Angling* and *Castabout Anglers Guide to Dumfries and Galloway.* See chapter 5.

- **Argyll & the Southern Hebrides:** This much-visited area in western Scotland is split in two by the long peninsula of Kintyre. It's definitely a northern Atlantic ecology, filled with open sea and loch and separated by the Firth of Clyde from the islands of the Inner Hebrides. There are some 50 prime sites on rivers and lochs for freshwater fishing, and some two dozen villages with fantastic sea fishing. See chapter 7.

- **Tayside:** The northeast section of Scotland is filled with major rivers—the Don, Dee, Ythan, and Deverson—plus smaller rivers like the Ugie, all ideal for salmon fishing. When estuary and loch fishing are considered, this becomes one of the country's best areas for game fishing. Local tourist offices keep abreast of all the details about boat rentals and permit prices, and some country hotels offer fishing packages. See chapter 9.

- **The Great Glen:** From all over the world, anglers flock to the Great Glen, with its many lochs and rivers, to cast their flies in search of Scottish trout and salmon. Sea angling from boat or shore is also permitted. Salmon season runs from February to September; brown trout season is mid-March to early October. Anglers can catch rainbow trout here year-round. See chapter 10.

- **Sutherland and the Northern Highlands:** There are endless possibilities for fishing here, since Sutherland is riddled with lochs. Trout fishing is the big lure, and local tourist offices will tell you all about boats and permits. Not only is the fishing great, but your hotel cook may also prepare your catch for you. See "Sutherland: The Gem of Scotland," in chapter 10.

- **The Orkney Islands:** These far northern islands are major fishing grounds. At least seven outfitters offer charters, and you can rent fishing equipment. Loch fishing is also a popular pastime in the Orkneys, especially in Loch of Stenness and Loch of Harray, where hopeful anglers go after salmon, trout, sea trout, and salmon trout, although porbeagle shark, cod, halibut, bass, hake, skate, and turbot also turn up. See "The Orkney Islands: An Archaeological Garden" in chapter 12.

4 The Best Countryside Drives

- **The Valley of the Tweed:** The waters originate in Scotland, define the border with England for part of their length, and are noted for some of Britain's best salmon fishing. Ruins of once-wealthy abbeys dot the landscape like beacons of long-lost power and prestige. Most travelers begin in Kelso and move west through Dryburgh, Selkirk, Melrose, Innerleithen, and Peebles. Although the total distance is less than 81km (50 miles), with a bit of backtracking en route, the many historic sites call for at least a full day's exploration. See chapter 5.

- **The Isle of Arran:** Anchored off Scotland's southwestern edge, Arran combines radically different climates and topographies into a relatively small space. You'll find a rich trove of prehistoric monuments, a red-sandstone pile beloved by medievalists, nostalgic ruins, and sweeping panoramas as far away as Northern Ireland. Its southern tier, warmed by the Gulf

Stream, contains lush, temperate vegetation, while the moors and hills of its northern edge are as wild and craggy as the Highlands. Allow half a day, not including stopover times, for the 90km (56-mile) circumnavigation of the island's coastal road. See "The Isle of Arran: Scotland in Miniature" in chapter 7.

- **The Lochs & Mountains South of Oban:** This area is lonely, but its drama includes views of the longest freshwater lake (Loch Awe), one of the longest saltwater fjords (Loch Fyne), some of the most historic buildings (Kilchurn Castle, Carnasserie Castle, and the Kilmartin Church), and one of the most crucial battlefields (the slopes of Ben Cruachan) in Scotland. Locals refer to it as the Hinterlands near Oban, but the 140km (87-mile) route follows an excellent network of highways along the jagged coast. Major towns you'll traverse en route are Dalmally, Inveraray, Lochgilphead, and Oban. See chapter 7.

- **The Trossachs:** At the narrowest point of the mainland, just north of Glasgow, the Trossachs have been famous for their scenery since Queen Victoria decreed them lovely in 1869. Mystery seems to shroud the waters of Lochs Lomond and Katrine. According to legend, the region's highest mountain, Ben Venue, is the traditional meeting point for Scotland's goblins. Ruled for generations by the MacGregor clan, this is the countryside of Sir Walter Scott's *Rob Roy* and *The Lady of the Lake*. A tour through the region, beginning at Callander and meandering through Aberfoyle, Stronachlacher, and Inversnaid, should take about half a day. Expect lots of traffic in summer, often from tour buses. See chapter 8.

- **The Road to the Isles (Hwy. A830):** It begins in Fort William, western terminus of the Caledonian Canal, and ends at Mallaig, the departure point for ferries servicing several offshore islands, including Mull, 74km (46 miles) northwest. En route, it passes the highest mountains in Britain. Along the way, you can see one of the Victorian Age's most dramatic engineering triumphs—Neptune's Staircase, a network of eight locks that raise the level of the canal 19m (64 ft.) in less than 455m (1,500 ft.). Although summer traffic can be dense, services en route are scarce, so start with a full tank of gas. See chapters 10 and 11.

5 The Best Bike Rides

For details on biking around the country, see "Biking, Walking, & Other Outdoor Pursuits" in chapter 3.

- **The Galloway Region:** Scotland's southwestern region is one of the least visited but one of the most beautiful. A land of fields, verdant forests, and mist-shrouded hills, Galloway offers endless biking possibilities. All tourist offices in the area carry *Cycling in Dumfries and Galloway,* which describes the best routes. A free leaflet published by the Scottish Forest Enterprise gives trail routes through the various forests. See chapter 5.

- **The Isle of Arran:** The largest of the Clyde Islands, Arran has been called "Scotland in miniature." If you don't have time to see the whole country, you can get a preview of its various regions by biking this island. The northern part is mountainous like the Highlands, but the southern part is more typically Lowland, like the scenery in the Borders. The full circuit around the island takes about 9 hours. The tourist office distributes the free *Cycling on Arran,* giving the best routes. See "The Isle of Arran: Scotland in Miniature" in chapter 7.

- **The Trossachs:** Scotland's most beautiful stretch for biking is the Trossachs (also the loveliest for driving or country walks), famed as Rob Roy MacGregor country. The best spot for biking is along Loch Katrine, 16km (10 miles) long and 3km (2 miles) at its widest. See chapter 8.
- **Glencoe:** Site of a famous 1692 massacre, Glencoe features stark and grandiose mountain scenery. Rent a bike in the village and set out on an adventure, although you're likely to get rained on, as some 100 inches of rain a year are recorded. But as one local said, "Biking through Glencoe in the rain is when it's at its most mystical—we Scots have done that for years." See "Around Loch Linnhe & Loch Leven" in chapter 10.
- **The Isle of Skye:** One of the most evocative of the Hebrides, Skye is the land of the Cuillins, a brooding mountain range you'll see at every turn as you pedal along. The most unusual place to bike is the 32km (20-mile) Trotternish Peninsula. It's known for its odd rock formations, and its coastal road passes an area of beautiful but often rocky seascapes, opening onto Loch Snizort and the Sound of Raasay. See "The Isle of Skye: Star of the Hebrides" in chapter 11.

6 The Best Hikes

- **The Southern Upland Way:** Rivaling the West Highland Way (see below), this is the second of Scotland's great walks. The footpath begins at Portpatrick and runs 341km (212 miles) on the southwest coast to Cockburnspath on the eastern coast. Along the way, it passes through some of the most dramatic scenery in the Borders, including Galloway Forest Park. Contact the **Edinburgh & Scotland Information Centre,** Deer Park Rd., Edinburgh (© **0131/ 473-3800**). See chapter 5.
- **East Neuk:** Directly south of St. Andrews lie some of Scotland's loveliest fishing villages, collectively known as East Neuk. The most enchanting walk is between the villages of Pittenweem and Anstruther. The day is likely to be breezy, with wind from the sea, so dress accordingly. The path begins at the bottom of West Braes, a cul-de-sac off the main road in Anstruther. See "East Neuk's Scenic Fishing Villages" in chapter 8.
- **The Trossachs:** The Trossachs Trail stretches from Loch Lomond in the west to Callander in the east and also from Doune to Aberfoyle and the Lord Ard Forest to the south. In the north, it's bounded by the Crianlarich Hills and Balquhidder, the site of Rob Roy's grave. Ever since Sir Walter Scott published *The Lady of the Lake* and *Rob Roy,* the area has attracted hikers in search of its unspoiled natural beauty. Our favorite start for walks is the village of Brig o' Turk, between Lochs Achray and Venachar at the foot of Glen Finglas. From here you can set out in all directions, including one signposted to the Achray Forest. There's also the Glen Finglas circular walk, and many hikers leave Brig o' Turk heading for Balquhidder via Glen Finglas. See chapter 8.

- **The West Highland Way:** This is one of Scotland's great walks. Beginning north of Glasgow in Milngavie, the footpath stretches for 153km (95 miles) north along Loch Lomond, going through Glencoe to Fort William and eventually to Ben Nevis, Britain's highest mountain. Even if you walk only part of this path, you need to make plans in advance. Contact the **Edinburgh & Scotland Information Centre,** Deer Park Rd., Edinburgh (✆ **0131/473-3800**). See chapter 8.

- **Ben Nevis:** Six kilometers (4 miles) southeast of the town of Fort William looms Ben Nevis, Britain's highest mountain at 1,342m (4,406 ft.). The snow-capped granite mass dominates this entire region of Scotland. This trip can be done in a day, but you'll need to massage your feet in the evening at a local pub. See the box labeled "Climbing Britain's Tallest Mountain" in chapter 10.

7 The Best Castles & Palaces

- **Edinburgh Castle** (Edinburgh): Few other buildings symbolize the grandeur of an independent Scotland as clearly as this one. Begun around A.D. 1000 on a hilltop high above the rest of Edinburgh, it witnessed some of the bloodiest and most treacherous events in Scottish history, including its doomed 1573 defense by Scottish patriot Grange in the name of Mary Queen of Scots. See p. 98.

- **Palace of Holyroodhouse** (Edinburgh): Throughout the clan battles for independence from England, this palace served as a pawn between opposing forces. In its changing fortunes, it has housed a strange assortment of monarchs involved in traumatic events: Mary Queen of Scots, Bonnie Prince Charlie, James VII (before his ascendancy to the throne), and French king Charles X (on his forced abdication after an 1830 revolution). The building's present form dates from the late 1600s, when it was rebuilt in a dignified neo-Palladian style. Today, Holyroodhouse is one of Queen Elizabeth's official residences. See p. 101.

- **Drumlanrig Castle** (Dumfries): Begun in 1679, this castle required 12 years to build and so much money that its patron, the third earl and first duke of Queensbury, complained to anyone who would listen how deeply he resented its existence. Later, it was embroiled in dynastic inheritance scandals worthy of a gothic novel. One of the most prestigious buildings in Scotland, it contains the antiques and artwork of four illustrious families. See p. 151.

- **Culzean Castle** (near Maybole): Designed for comfort and prestige, this castle was built in the late 1700s by Scotland's most celebrated architect, Robert Adam, as a replacement for a dark, dank tower that had stood for longer than anyone could remember. It was donated to the National Trust for Scotland just after World War II. A suite was granted to General Eisenhower for his lifetime use, in gratitude for his role in staving off a foreign invasion of Britain. See p. 206.

- **Stirling Castle** (Stirling): Stirling is a triumph of Renaissance ornamentation, a startling contrast to the severe bulk of many other

Scottish castles. Despite its beauty, after its completion in 1540 the castle was one of the most impregnable fortresses in the British Isles, thanks partly to its position on a rocky crag. See p. 258.

- **Scone Palace** (Scone): As early as A.D. 900, Scottish kings were crowned here, on a lump of granite so permeated with ancient magic the English hauled it off to Westminster Abbey in the 13th century, where it remained until 1995. The building you see today was rebuilt in 1802 from ruins that incorporated a 1580 structure and stones laid during the dim early days of Scottish and Pictish union. See chapter 9.

- **Glamis Castle** (Glamis): This castle's core was built for defense against rival clans during the 1400s, but over the centuries it evolved into a luxurious dwelling. The seat of the same family since 1372, Glamis is said to be haunted by the ghost of one of its former owners, Lady Glamis, who James V had burnt as a witch when she resisted his annexation of her castle. It figured into the ambitions of Macbeth, thane of Glamis, as well. See "Dundee & Glamis Castle," in chapter 9.

- **Crathes Castle & Gardens** (Grampian): Crathes evokes the severe luxury of a 15th- and 16th-century Scottish laird. The style focuses on high heraldry, with frequent references to the persistent Scottish hope of an enduring independence. The gardens contain massive yew hedges originally planted in 1702. See p. 287.

- **Balmoral Castle** (Ballater): Scotland offers far greater castles to explore, but Balmoral, the rebuilt castle of Prince Albert and Queen Victoria, draws the visiting hordes, hoping to get a glimpse of Prince William, no doubt. That's because it's still the Scottish residence of the queen. Although you can visit only its ballroom, the sprawling manicured grounds and gardens also await you. See p. 307.

- **Braemar Castle** (Grampian): Built by the earl of Mar in 1628 as a hunting lodge, Braemar was burned to the ground, and then rebuilt by Farquharson of Invercauld, the ancestor of the present owner. It's often photographed as a symbol of Scottish grandeur and the well-upholstered aristocratic life. See p. 311.

- **Cawdor Castle** (Cawdor): From its heavily fortified origins in the 1300s, Cawdor evolved into the Campbell clan's luxurious seat. According to legend and Shakespearean plot lines, three witches promised this castle to Macbeth to tempt him into the deeds that led to his destruction. See p. 347.

8 The Best Cathedrals

- **Melrose Abbey** (the Borders): If it weren't for the abbey's location in the frequently devastated Borders, this would be one of the world's most spectacular ecclesiastical complexes. Founded in the 1100s, Melrose acquired vast wealth and was the target of its covetous enemies; it was burned and rebuilt several times before the Protestant takeover of Scotland. Today, it's one of the world's most beautiful ruins, a site immortalized by Robert Burns, who advised people to visit it only by moonlight. See p. 138.

- **Cathedral of St. Kentigern** (Glasgow): In the 7th century, St. Mungo built a wooden structure here, intending it as his headquarters and eventual tomb. It burned down but was rebuilt in the 1300s. St. Kentigern is mainland

Scotland's only complete medieval cathedral, with a form based extensively on the pointed arch. In the 1600s, the Calvinists stripped it of anything hinting at papist idolatry, although a remarkable set of sculptures atop its stone nave screen, said to be unique in Scotland, still represent the seven deadly sins. See p. 189.

- **Dunfermline Abbey and Palace** (Fife): During the 1100s, in its role as Scotland's Westminster Abbey, Dunfermline became one of Europe's wealthiest churches. Three kings of Scotland were born here, and 22 members of the Scottish royal family were buried here. In the early 1800s, its ruined premises were partially restored to what you see today. Several years later, a different kind of benefactor, Andrew Carnegie, was born within the cathedral's shadow. See p. 240.

- **Dunblane Cathedral** (Fife): Partly because the site had been holy since the days of the Celts, David I founded a church here in 1150. Despite later alterations and additions, Dunblane is still one of the country's best examples of Gothic architecture from the 1200s. See p. 265.

- **St. Magnus Cathedral** (the Orkney Islands): The most spectacular medieval building in the Orkneys, St. Magnus features an odd imposition of the Norman Gothic style on a territory administered during the time of its construction (the 1100s) by the Norwegians. The bodies of St. Magnus, patron saint of the Orkneys, and his nephew Earl Rognvald, the church's builder, are buried inside. See "The Orkney Islands: An Archaeological Garden" in chapter 12.

9 The Best Ruins

- **Linlithgow Palace** (Lothian): These ruins brood over an island in a loch, an unhappy vestige of what was the most glamorous royal residence during Scotland's golden age of independence in the early 1500s. Mary Queen of Scots was born here, but tragedy seemed to permeate the palace, as roofs collapsed from lack of maintenance and early deaths in the royal family hastened an inevitable union of Scotland with England. In 1745, after it was occupied by Bonnie Prince Charlie and his troops, a mysterious fire swept over it. See p. 120.

- **Dryburgh Abbey** (the Borders): Begun in 1150 against a meandering curve of the River Tweed, Dryburgh was once home to thousands of monks who transformed the surrounding forests into arable fields and drained many local swamps. The abbey's position astride the much-troubled border with England resulted in its destruction in three episodes (1322, 1385, and 1544), the last of which included the burning of the nearby village (Dryburgh) as well. Today, the red-sandstone rocks are dim reminders of a long-ago monastic age. See p. 136.

- **Elgin Cathedral** (Grampian): This cathedral was built during the 1100s, and although many other churches were erected in Scotland at the time, Elgin was believed to have been the most beautiful. Burned and rebuilt twice (1290 and 1370), it deteriorated after the Reformation, along with many other Catholic churches, to the point that the belfry collapsed in 1711, shattering most of the roof and some of the walls. Efforts were begun to repair the damage, yet the place remains an evocative ruin. See "Speyside & the Malt Whisky Trail."

- **Skara Brae** (the Orkney Islands): Last occupied around 2500 B.C. and far humbler than the feudal castles you'll find on the Scottish mainland, this cluster of fortified stone buildings is the best-preserved Neolithic village in northwestern Europe. Buried beneath sand for thousands of years, they were uncovered by a storm as recently as 1850. See "The Orkney Islands: An Archaeological Garden" in chapter 12.

10 The Best Museums

- **National Gallery of Scotland** (Edinburgh): This museum boasts a small but choice collection whose presence in Edinburgh is firmly entwined with the city's self-image as Scotland's cultural capital. (Glaswegians will happily dispute that idea.) Highlights include works by Velázquez, Zurbarán, Verrocchio, del Sarto, and Cézanne. See p. 102.
- **National Museum of Scotland** (Edinburgh): In 1998, the collections of the Royal Museum of Scotland and the National Museum of Antiquities were united into a coherent whole. Here you'll find everything you ever wanted to know about Scotland, from prehistory to the Industrial Age, as represented by the unsparing views of life in the Saltmarket District of Glasgow. It's all here, from a milk bottle once carried by Sean Connery when he was a milkman to a 2.9 billion-year-old rock from the Isle of South Uist. See p. 102.
- **Burrell Collection** (Glasgow): The contents of this collection were accumulated through the exclusive efforts of Sir William Burrell (1861–1958), an industrialist who devoted the last 50 years of his life to spending his fortune on art. Set in a postmodern building in a suburb of Glasgow, it's one of Scotland's most admired museums, with a strong focus on medieval art, 19th-century French paintings, and Chinese ceramics. See p. 183.
- **Hunterian Art Gallery** (Glasgow): This museum owns much of the artistic estate of James McNeill Whistler, as well as a recreation of the home of Scotland's most famous designer, Charles Rennie Mackintosh. On display are grand oils by Whistler, Reubens, and Rembrandt, as well as one of the country's best collections of 19th-century Scottish paintings. See p. 186.
- **Aberdeen Art Gallery** (Aberdeen): A treasure trove of world art, this prestigious gallery has exhibits ranging from the 1700s to the present, from Hogarth and Reynolds to Picasso. The museum is also home to the most important temporary exhibits in northeast Scotland. See p. 278.

11 The Best Luxury Hotels

- **The Howard** (Edinburgh; © 0131/557-3500): Three adjacent Georgian-style town houses in an upscale neighborhood have undergone millions of pounds' worth of renovations, creating the most alluring accommodations in a city filled with fine hotels. A restaurant in one of the cellars serves meals inspired by Scotland's traditions. See p. 80.

- **Holyrood Hotel** (Edinburgh; ℂ 0131/550-4500): This deluxe charmer launched itself into the millennium when it was proclaimed "Hotel of the Year in Scotland." Near the new Scottish Parliament, it is a bastion of comfort with luxury furnishings. See p. 86.

- **The Malmaison** (Leith, outside Edinburgh; ℂ 0131/555-6868): Malmaison is at the port of Leith, about a 15-minute ride northeast of Edinburgh's center. Named after Joséphine's mansion outside Paris, it celebrates the Auld Alliance of France and Scotland and was created from a 1900 Victorian building. Malmaison once housed indigent seamen, but today is an oasis of chic. See p. 87.

- **Greywalls Hotel** (East Lothian; ℂ 01620/842-144): Although Sir Edward Lutyens designed dozens of opulent Edwardian homes throughout Britain, this is one of the few that's been converted into a hotel. Built in 1901 in what architects praise as perfect harmony with its setting, Greywalls features walled gardens designed by the doyenne of eccentric turn-of-the-20th-century landscape architects, Gertrude Jekyll. This national treasure, representing the Empire's most ostentatious days, is eccentric but eminently comfortable. See p. 123.

- **Knockinaam Lodge** (Portpatrick; ℂ 01776/810-471): Memories of Winston Churchill's clandestine meetings with General Eisenhower, a beacon of hope during the darkest days of World War II, pervade the Knockinaam. Today, the late-Victorian country house is as well upholstered and wryly sedate as you'd expect from a top-notch

hotel with such a pedigree. Its restaurant is always included in critics' lists of the best of Scotland. See p. 160.

- **One Devonshire Gardens** (Glasgow; ℂ 0141/339-2001): This is the best-groomed building in a neighborhood filled with similar sandstone-fronted town houses. Ring the doorbell and an Edwardian-costumed maid will answer, curtsy, and usher you inside as if you're an extra in a Merchant-Ivory film. This re-creation of a high-bourgeois, very proper Scottish home from the early 1900s boasts antique furnishings and discreetly concealed modern comforts. See p. 174.

- **St. Andrews Bay Golf Resort & Spa** (St. Andrews; ℂ 01334/837-000): This is the premier government-rated five-star hotel of Eastern Scotland, lying right outside "the home of golf," as the town of St. Andrews is so often called. Boasting two championship golf courses, the finest rooms and cuisine in the area, and a to-die-for spa and health club, the resort is the creation of two entrepreneurs from the southern U.S. state of Georgia. Did we mention that Prince William is a member of the health club? See p. 253.

- **Gleneagles Hotel** (Auchterarder; ℂ 01764/662-231): This is Britain's greatest golf hotel, a government-rated five-star resort that also offers such extras as a deluxe spa and hunting excursions. Better than ever after major renovations and expansion, it is also a gourmet citadel with one of Scotland's most awarded chefs, Andrew Fairlie, overseeing those pots and pans. See p. 294.

- **Kinnaird Estate** (Dunkeld; ℂ 01796/482-440): An 18th-century hunting lodge for the duke of Atholl, Kinnaird dominates an enormous estate—3,646 hectares (9,000 acres) of moor, mountain, and forest. You'll find all the accoutrements of a British country house in high-Edwardian style. The supremely comfortable interiors contrast dramatically with the tempests of the great outdoors, and the dining room is among the finest in the country. See p. 298.

- **Inverlochy Castle** (near Fort William; ☎ **01397/702-177**): This castle was built in 1863 by Lord Abinger in a style that set into stone the most high-blown hopes of Scottish Romantics. Today, lovers can follow in the footsteps of Queen Victoria amid the frescoed walls of this Scottish baronial hideaway. See chapter 10.
- **Culloden House** (Inverness; ☎ 01463/790-461): If you'd like to sleep where Bonnie Prince

Charlie did, head for this Adam-style Georgian mansion on 16 hectares (40 acres) of parkland. Scottish tradition appears at every turn, from the grand lounge to the sound of a bagpiper on the grounds. Dinner in the Adam Room is an elegant affair, with French culinary skills applied to the finest Scottish produce. See p. 340.

- **Carnegie Club at Skibo Castle** (Dornoch; ☎ **01862/894-600**): Andrew Carnegie called his glorious Highland castle and estate Heaven on Earth, and so it is. A private residential golf and sporting club, it stands on a 2835-hectare (7,000-acre) estate in one of Europe's last great wilderness areas. It was owned by the Carnegie family until the early 1980s and is one of the few places left where you can see how the privileged of the Gilded Age lived. See p. 353.

12 The Best Moderately Priced Hotels

- **Brasserie Malmaison** (Glasgow; ☎ 0141/572-1000): Linked to a hotel with the same name in Edinburgh (see above), this Malmaison dates from the 1830s, when it was built as a Greek Orthodox church. Now converted into one of the best of Glasgow's moderately priced hotels (though its prices are creeping up into the expensive range), it welcomes visitors with Scottish hospitality and houses them with quite a bit of style. See p. 173.
- **The ArtHouse** (Glasgow; ☎ 0141/221-6789): Unique to Glasgow, this stunner was converted from a 1911 Edwardian school building. Dramatically recycled, it offers first-class comfort and affordable prices, all part of a striking design. See p. 173.
- **Inn at Lathones** (St. Andrews; ☎ 01334/840-494): In the golf

capital of Scotland is this 2-century-old manor that has been lovingly restored with excellent accommodations. Scottish hospitality and tradition permeate the place, also known for its "Taste of Scotland" menu. See p. 255.

- **Polmaily House Hotel** (Drumnadrochit; ☎ 01456//450-343): While you search for Nessie, the Loch Ness Monster, you can lodge comfortably at this inn. The building dates from the 18th century and offers tasteful Edwardian-style living on a farm of mixed gardens and woodland. See p. 336.
- **The Cuillin Hills Hotel** (Portree, Isle of Skye; ☎ 01478/612-003): Built in the 1820s as a hunting lodge for the MacDonald clan, this manor house has been skillfully converted into a small hotel. It attracts nature lovers to its

nearby hills of heath and heather and offers lovely rooms and great food using some of the best Highland produce. See p. 369.

13 The Best Restaurants

- **The Tower** (Edinburgh; ✆ 0131/ 225-3003): The town's hot new dining ticket lies on the top floor of the Museum of Scotland, an unlikely venue for one of Edinburgh's best restaurants. Featuring fresh seafood and an innovative modern British cuisine, The Tower serves some of the city's tastiest fare based on the freshest of ingredients. See p. 92.
- **Martin Wishart** (Edinburgh; ✆ 0131/553-3557): Many food critics hail this newcomer as the best restaurant in Scotland. If not that, it ranks among the top five. Out in the port-bordering town of Leith in Greater Edinburgh, it serves a modern French cuisine— dishes composed with quality products and filled with flavor. See p. 94.
- **Ostlers Close** (Cupar, near St. Andrews; ✆ 01334/655-574): Chef Jimmy Graham is one of the finest in the St. Andrews area, and he's known to pick his own wild mushrooms. Golfers with discriminating palates flock to this modestly appointed place, which makes the best use of fish and seafood from the Fife Coast and ducks from a local free-range supplier. Everything is delectable. See p. 256.
- **The Cross** (Kingussie; ✆ 01540/ 661-166): Housed in a cleverly converted 19th-century tweed mill, The Cross is a lot more chic than you'd imagine. The menu items are a celebration of Scottish ingredients, prepared with modern international palates in mind. An example is the West Coast seafood salad with ultrafresh monkfish, scallops, prawns, and asparagus. See p. 318.
- **Inverlochy Castle** (near Fort William; ✆ 01397/702-177): Cherubs cavort across frescoed ceilings and chandeliers drip with Venetian crystal in a dining room created in the 1870s for a mogul. A Relais & Châteaux member, Inverlochy is likely to draw aristocrats and movie stars with a cuisine focusing on flavorful and natural interpretations of Scottish delicacies. See p. 329.

14 The Best Pubs

- **Café Royal Circle Bar** (Edinburgh; ✆ 0131/556-1884): The Café Royal Circle stands out in a city famous for its pubs. This longtime favorite, boasting lots of atmosphere and Victorian trappings, attracts a sea of drinkers, locals as well as visitors. See chapter 4.
- **Deacon Brodie's Tavern** (Edinburgh; ✆ 0131/225-6531): This is the best spot for a wee dram or a pint along Edinburgh's Royal Mile. It perpetuates the memory of Deacon Brodie, good citizen by day and robber by night, the prototype for Robert Louis Stevenson's *Dr. Jekyll and Mr. Hyde.* It's been around since 1806 and has a cocktail-lounge bar and a large, rowdy tavern. See p. 118.
- **Globe Inn** (Dumfries; ✆ 01387/ 252-335): In the Borders, this was Robert Burns's favorite *howff* (small, cozy room). Today, you can imbibe as he did in a pub that's been in business since 1610. He liked the place so much that

he had a child with the barmaid. A small museum is devoted to Burns. See p. 153.

- **Corn Exchange** (Glasgow; ℭ 0141/248-5380): There was a time when it took a bit of courage or a foolish heart to enter a Glasgow pub. Those bad old days are long forgotten at this reliable pub in the center. In the mid-1800s, the Corn Exchange was here (hence the name), but today it's a watering hole with good drinks and modestly priced bar platters. See p. 199.
- **Rabbie's Bar** (Ayr; ℭ 01292/262-112): Robert Burns didn't confine his drinking to Dumfries. Ayr was also one of his hangouts, and this favorite pub is a nostalgic reminder of another era. Bits of pithy verse by Burns adorn the walls, and the collection of imported beers is the best in the area. See "Side Trips from Glasgow: The Best of the Strathclyde Region" in chapter 6.
- **Dreel Tavern** (Anstruther; ℭ 01333/310-727): This 16th-century wood-and-stone coaching inn is now a pub where old salts from the harbor and other locals gather to unwind on windy nights. Try the hand-pumped Orkney Dark Island beer. Anstruther, 74km

(46 miles) northeast of Edinburgh, is a gem of a Scottish seaside town. See "East Neuk's Scenic Fishing Villages" in chapter 8.

- **Ship Inn** (Elie; ℭ 01333/330-246): Down at the harbor in this little port town, the Ship Inn is one of the best places along the east coast for a pint. The building dates from 1778, and the pub from 1830. In summer, you can enjoy your pint outside with a view over the water, but on blustery winter days, the blazing fireplace is the attraction. Stick around for dinner—the menu ranges from pheasant to venison to fresh seafood, not your typical pub grub. See "East Neuk's Scenic Fishing Villages" in chapter 8.
- **Prince of Wales** (Aberdeen; ℭ 01224/640-597): Furnished with church pews and antiques, the Prince of Wales features the city's longest bar counter. Oilmen from the North Sea join the regulars to ask for tap beers like Courage Directors and sample the chef's Guinness pie. You'll find real flavor and authentic atmosphere; it's a good place to mingle with the locals in a mellow setting. See "Aberdeen: The Castle Country" in chapter 9.

15 The Best Shopping

- **Celtic Jewelry:** Modern reproductions of Celtic jewelry are one of Scotland's most creative craft forms. Some pieces reflect early Christian themes, like the Gaelic cross so often displayed in Presbyterian churches. Others are pure pagan, and sometimes Nordic, rich with symbols like dragons, intertwined ovals, and geometrics that would gladden the heart of a Celtic lord. Another common theme commemorates the yearnings for a

politically independent country (Luckenbooths, entwined hearts surmounted by a monarch's crown). Clan brooches, kilt pins, and other jewelry are often adorned with the Highland thistle and sometimes rendered in fine gold, silver, or platinum.

- **Sheepskins:** Some of the rocky districts of Scotland contain more sheep than people. Tanned sheepskins are for sale in hundreds of shops, usually accompanied by advice from the sales staff on what to do with them once you return home. *Note:* Black sheepskins are much rarer than white ones.

- **Sweaters, Tartans, & Fabrics:** Sweaters come in every style and design, from bulky fishermen's pullovers to silky cashmere cardigans. Some factories pride themselves on duplicating the tartans of every Scottish clan; others stick to 50 or so of the more popular designs. A meter of fine tartan fabric sells for around £35 ($56). For a more authentic experience, buy your garment directly from whomever sewed or knitted it. You'll find ample opportunities at crofts and crafts shops around the countryside.

- **Liquor:** One of the most famous liquors in the world is named after the country that produces it: Scotch whisky (spelled without the "e") is distilled and aged throughout the country. Use your trip to Scotland as an opportunity to try new single malts (Laphroaig and MacCallan are our favorites) and bring a bottle or two home.

2

Planning Your Trip to Scotland

This chapter is devoted to the where, when, and how of your trip—the advance planning required to get it together and take it on the road. Because you may not know exactly where in Scotland you want to go or what surrounds the major city you want to see, we begin with a quick rundown on the various regions.

1 The Regions in Brief

Scotland is Great Britain's oldest geological formation, and is divided into three major regions: the **Southern Uplands,** smooth, rolling moorland broken with low crags and threaded with rivers and valleys, between the central plain and the English border; the **Central Lowlands,** where three valleys and the estuaries (firths) of the Clyde, Forth, and Tay rivers make up a fertile belt from the Atlantic Ocean to the North Sea; and the granite **Highlands,** with lochs (lakes), glens, and mountains, plus the hundreds of islands to the west and north. Each of these regions is then made up of smaller regions (see below).

Consult the map on p. 4 to visualize the areas described below.

EDINBURGH & THE LOTHIAN REGION

This area includes not only the country's capital but also West Lothian, most of Midlothian, and East Lothian. Half medieval and half Georgian, **Edinburgh** is at its liveliest every August at the International Arts Festival, but you can visit Edinburgh Castle and Holyroodhouse and walk the Royal Mile year-round. This is one of Europe's most beautiful capitals, and in 3 days you can do it royally, taking in the highlights of the Old Town and the New Town, which include some of the country's major museums. Edinburgh is surrounded by major attractions like the village of **Cramond,** the ancient town of **Linlithgow,** and **Dirleton,** the "prettiest village in Scotland."

THE BORDERS & GALLOWAY REGIONS

Witness to a turbulent history, the Borders and Galloway regions between England and Scotland are rich in castle ruins and Gothic abbeys.

Home of the cashmere sweater and the tweed suit, **Borders** proved a rich mine for the fiction of Sir Walter Scott. Highlights are **Kelso,** which Scott found "the most beautiful," and **Melrose,** site of the ruined Melrose Abbey and Scott's former home of Abbotsford. Ancient monuments include Jedburgh Abbey and Dryburg Abbey, Scott's burial place. At Floors Castle, outside Kelso, you can see one of the great mansions designed by William Adam.

Southwestern Scotland is known as the **Galloway region.** It incorporates much of the former stamping ground of Robert Burns and includes centers like **Dumfries, Castle Douglas,** and **Moffat.** Highlights are the artists' colony of **Kirkcudbright,** the baronial Threave Garden, Sweetheart Abbey outside Dumfries (the ruins of a Cistercian abbey from 1273), and the Burns Mausoleum at Dumfries.

GLASGOW & THE STRATHCLYDE REGION

A true renaissance has come to the once-grimy industrial city of **Glasgow,** and we recommend you spend at least 2 days in "the greatest surviving example of a Victorian city." Of course, part of the fun of going to Glasgow is meeting Glaswegians and, if only temporarily, becoming part of their life. But there are plenty of museums and galleries, too, notably The Burrell Collection, a wealthy ship-owner's gift of more than 8,000 items from the ancient world to the modern; and the Hunterian Art Gallery, with its array of masterpieces by everybody from Rembrandt to Whistler. The Kelvingrove Art Gallery and Museum, home of Britain's finest civic collection of British and European paintings, is closed for restoration until 2006, but highlights from the collection are on display at the McLellan Galleries.

Glasgow is at the doorstep of one of the most historic regions of Scotland. You can explore Robert Burns Country in the **Strathclyde region,** especially the district around Ayr and Prestwick, or visit a string of famous seaside resorts (including Turnberry, which boasts some of the country's greatest golf courses). An especially worthwhile destination in this region is **Culzean Castle,** overlooking the Firth of Clyde and designed by Robert Adam in the 18th century.

ARGYLL & THE SOUTHERN HEBRIDES

Once the independent kingdom of Dalriada, the **Argyll Peninsula** of western Scotland is centered at **Oban,** a bustling port town and one of Scotland's leading coastal resorts. Ace attractions here are **Argyll Forest Park,** actually three forests—Benmore, Ardgartan, and Glenbranter—covering some 24,300 hectares (60,000 acres). You can also visit **Loch Awe,** a natural moat that protected the Campbells of Inveraray from their enemies to the north, and explore some of Scotland's most interesting islands, including the **Isle of Arran,** called "Scotland in miniature." The **Isle of Islay** is the southernmost of the Inner Hebrides, with lonely moors, lochs, tranquil bays, and windswept cliffs. The **Isle of Jura,** the fourth largest of the Inner Hebrides, is known for its red deer, and it was on this remote island that George Orwell wrote his masterpiece *1984.* Finally, you can visit **Kintyre,** the longest peninsula in Scotland, more than 97km (60 miles) of beautiful scenery, sleepy villages, and sandy beaches.

FIFE & THE CENTRAL HIGHLANDS

The "kingdom" of **Fife** is one of the most history-rich parts of Scotland, evocative of the era of romance and pageantry during the reign of the early Stuart kings. Its most enchanting stretch is a series of fishing villages called **East Neuk.** And **Culross,** renovated by the National Trust, could well be the most beautiful village in Scotland. Opening onto the North Sea, **St. Andrews,** the "Oxford of Scotland," is the capital of golf and boasts many great courses. The area is rich in castles and abbeys, notably Dunfermline Abbey, burial place of 22 royal personages, and Falkland Palace and Gardens, where Mary Queen of Scots came for hunting and hawking. You can also visit **Stirling,** dominated by its castle, where Mary Queen of Scots lived as an infant monarch. **Loch Lomond,** largest of the Scottish lakes, is fabled for its "bonnie bonnie banks," and the **Trossachs** is perhaps the most beautiful area in Scotland, famed for its moors, mountains, and lakes.

ABERDEEN & THE TAYSIDE & GRAMPIAN REGIONS

Carved from the old counties of Perth and Angus, **Tayside** takes its name from its major river, the Tay, running for 192km (119 miles). One of the loveliest regions, it's known for salmon and trout fishing. Major centers are **Perth,** former capital of Scotland, standing where the Highlands meet the Lowlands; **Dundee,** an old seaport and royal burgh on the north shore of the Firth of Tay; and **Pitlochry,** a popular resort that's an ideal base for touring the Valley of the Tummel. The area abounds in castles and palaces, including Glamis, linked to British royalty for 10 centuries, and Scone, an art-filled palace from 1580. The great city of the north, **Aberdeen** is called Scotland's "granite city" and ranks third in population. It's the best center for touring "castle country." **Braemar** is known for its scenery as well as for being the site of every summer's Royal Highland Gathering, and Balmoral Castle at Ballater was the "beloved paradise" of Queen Victoria and is still home to the royal family. Finally, you can follow the **Whisky Trail** to check out some of Scotland's most famous distilleries, including Glenlivet and Glenfiddich.

INVERNESS & THE WEST HIGHLANDS

Land of rugged glens and majestic mountain landscapes, the Highlands is one of the great meccas of the United Kingdom. The capital is **Inverness,** one of the oldest inhabited localities in Scotland; another city of great interest is **Nairn,** old-time royal burgh and seaside resort. Top attractions are **Loch Ness,** home of the legendary "Nessie," and **Cawdor Castle,** the most romantic in the Highlands, linked with Macbeth. The **Caledonian Canal,** launched in 1803, stretches for 97km (60 miles) of manmade canal, joining the natural lochs. As you proceed to the north you can visit the **Black Isle,** a historic peninsula, before heading for such far northern outposts as **Ullapool,** an 18th-century fishing village on the

shores of Loch Broom (and for some, a gateway to the Outer Hebrides), and **John o' Groats,** the most distant point to which you can drive, near the northernmost point of mainland Britain, **Dunnet Head.**

THE HEBRIDEAN ISLANDS

The chain of the Inner Hebrides lies just off the west coast of the mainland. The major center is the **Isle of Skye,** a mystical island and subject of the Scottish ballad "Over the Sea to Skye." If you have time to visit only one island, make it Skye—it's the most beautiful and intriguing. However, the **Isle of Mull,** third largest of the Inner Hebrides, is also rich in legend and folklore, including ghosts, monsters, and the "wee folk." **Iona,** off the coast of Mull, is known as the "Grave of Kings," with an abbey dating from the 13th century. Those with time remaining can also explore the Outer Hebrides, notably **Lewis,** the largest and most northerly. Along with the island of **Harris,** Lewis stretches for a combined length of some 153km (95 miles). This is relatively treeless land of marshy peat bogs and ancient relics.

THE ORKNEY & SHETLAND ISLANDS

These northern outposts of British civilization are archipelagos consisting of some 200 islands, about 40 of which are inhabited. With a rich Viking heritage, they reward visitors with scenery and antiquities. Major centers of the Orkneys are **Kirkwall,** established by Norse invaders and the capital of the Orkneys for 9 centuries, and **Stromness,** the main port of the archipelago and once the last port of call before the New World. **Lerwick** is the capital of the Shetlands and has been since the 17th century. All these islands are filled with ancient monuments: The most outstanding are Midhower Broch (brochs are fortified structures, often called "castles of the Picts"); tombs on Rousay, dating from the Iron Age and called the "great ship of death"; Quoyness Chambered Tomb, on Sanday, a spectacular chambered cairn from 2900 B.C.; the Ring of Brodgar between Loch and Stenness, a stone circle of some 36 stones dating from 1560 B.C. and called the "Stonehenge of Scotland"; and Skara Brae, a Neolithic village joined by covered passages, last occupied about 2500 B.C.

2 Visitor Information

Before you go, you can get information from the **British Tourist Authority** (www.visitbritain.com). In the **United States:** 551 Fifth Ave., Suite 701, New York, NY 10176-0799 (© **800/462-2748,** or 212/986-2200 in New York; fax 212/986-1188). In **Canada:** 5915 Airport Rd., Mississagua, ON L4V 1T1 (© **888/VISIT-UK** in Canada; fax 905/405-1835 in Toronto). In **Australia:** Level 16, Gateway, 1 Macquarie Place, Sydney, NSW 2000 (© **02/9377-4400;** fax 02/9377-4499). In **New Zealand:** Fay Richwite Blvd., 17 Floor, 151 Queen St., Auckland 1 (© **09/303-1446;** fax 09/377-6965).

If you're in London and are contemplating a trip north, you can visit the **Scottish Tourist Board,** 19 Cockspur St., London SW1 Y5BL (© **020/ 7930-8661**); it's open Monday through Friday from 9:30am to 5:30pm and Saturday from noon to 4pm. Once you're in Scotland, you can stop by the **Edinburgh and Scotland Information Centre,** Waverley Market, 3 Princes St., Edinburgh EH2 2QP (© **0131/473-3800**). July and August, it's open Monday through Saturday from 9am to 8pm and Sunday from 10am to 8pm. May, June, and September, hours are Monday through Saturday from 9am to 7pm and Sunday from 10am to 7pm. From October to April, hours are Monday through Saturday from 9am to 6pm and Sunday from 10am to 6pm.

There are more than 170 **tourist centers** in Scotland, all well signposted in their cities or towns; some are closed in winter, however.

WHAT'S ON THE WEB? The most useful site was created by a very knowledgeable source, the British Tourist Authority itself, with U.S. visitors targeted. A wealth of information is tapped at **www.travelbritain.org**, which lets you order brochures online, provides trip-planning hints, and even allows e-mail questions for prompt answers. All of Great Britain is covered.

If you're surfing the Web for accommodations, a good site to browse is **www.visitscotland.com** (site of the Scotland Tourist Board).

Other useful websites include: **www.geo.ed.ac.uk/scotgaz/scotland. html**, a large database with information provided on Scottish villages that

---

(Tips Hot Line to Scotland

Travel information for the whole of Scotland is offered on Visit Scotland's national telephone hot line, available for inquiries from UK and overseas. Travel advisors are available to help you book accommodation throughout Scotland—whether hotels, guesthouses, or bed-and-breakfasts—or find out about special offers, events, and attractions to visit. You can order brochures as well. Advisors are available Monday to Friday 8am to 8pm and Saturday 9am to 5:30pm (UK time). In the UK, © **0845/225-5121;** from overseas, © **44-0-1506/832-222;** www.visitscotland.com.

Tips Passport Savvy

Allow plenty of time before your trip to apply for a passport; processing normally takes 3 weeks but can take longer during busy periods (especially spring). And keep in mind that if you need a passport in a hurry, you'll pay a higher processing fee. When traveling, safeguard your passport in an inconspicuous, inaccessible place like a money belt and keep a copy of the critical pages with your passport number in a separate place. If you lose your passport, visit the nearest consulate of your native country as soon as possible for a replacement.

range from the Borders to the Faraway Isles; **www.cntraveller.co.uk**, one of the largest Scottish resources, boasting nearly 10,000 detailed entries (The site for the famous magazine, *Condé Nast Traveler*, it provides general overview data, and is especially helpful with airport information.); and **www.travelscotland.co.uk**, which previews tours, itineraries, hotels, guesthouses, and even mountain walks from the Lowlands to the Highlands, with monthly features that bring you the latest in travel ideas for traversing Scotland.

3 Entry Requirements & Customs

ENTRY REQUIREMENTS

All U.S. citizens, Canadians, Australians, New Zealanders, and South Africans must have a passport with at least 2 months validity remaining. No visa is required. The immigration officer will also want proof of your intention to return to your point of origin (usually a round-trip ticket) and visible means of support while you're in Scotland. If you're planning to fly from the United States or Canada to the United Kingdom and then on to a country that requires a visa (India, for example), you should secure that visa before you arrive in Britain.

Your valid driver's license and at least 1 year of driving experience is required to drive personal or rented cars.

For information on how to get a passport, go to the Fast Facts section of this chapter—the websites listed provide downloadable passport applications as well as the current fees for processing passport applications. For an up-to-date country-by-country listing of passport requirements around the world, go the "Foreign Entry Requirement" web page of the U.S. State Department at http://travel.state.gov/foreignentryreqs.html.

CUSTOMS
WHAT YOU CAN BRING INTO SCOTLAND

Non-EU Nationals can bring in, duty-free, 200 cigarettes, 100 cigarillos, 50 cigars, or 250 grams of smoking tobacco. This amount is doubled if you live outside Europe. You can also bring in 2 liters of wine and either 1 liter of alcohol over 22 proof or 2 liters of wine under 22 proof. In addition, you can bring in 60 cc's (2.03 oz.) of perfume, a quarter liter (250ml) of eau de toilette, 500 grams (1 lb.) of coffee, and 200 grams (½ lb.) of tea. Visitors 15 and over may also bring in other goods totaling £145 ($232); the allowance for those 14 and under is £72.50 ($116). (Customs officials tend to be lenient about general merchandise, realizing the limits are unrealistically low.)

WHAT YOU CAN TAKE HOME FROM SCOTLAND

Returning **U.S. citizens** who have been away for at least 48 hours are allowed to bring back, once every 30 days, $800 worth of merchandise duty-free. You'll be charged a flat rate of 4% duty on the next $1,000 worth of purchases. Be sure to have your receipts handy. On mailed gifts, the duty-free limit is $200. With some exceptions, you cannot bring fresh fruits and vegetables into the United States. For specifics on what you can bring back, download the invaluable free pamphlet *Know Before You Go* online at **www.customs.gov**. (Click on "Know Before You Go!") Or contact the **U.S. Customs Service,** 1300 Pennsylvania Ave., NW, Washington, DC 20229 (✆ **877/287-8867**) and request the pamphlet.

For a clear summary of **Canadian** rules, write for the booklet *I Declare,* issued by the **Canada Customs and Revenue Agency** (✆ **800/461-9999** in Canada, or 204/983-3500; www. ccra-adrc.gc.ca). Canada allows its citizens a C$750 exemption, and you're allowed to bring back duty-free one carton of cigarettes, 1 can of tobacco, 40 imperial ounces of liquor, and 50 cigars. In addition, you're allowed to mail gifts to Canada valued at less than C$60 a day, provided they're unsolicited and don't contain alcohol or tobacco (write on the package "Unsolicited gift, under $60 value"). All valuables should be declared on the Y-38 form before departure from Canada, including serial numbers of valuables you already own, such as expensive foreign cameras. Note: The C$750 exemption can only be used once a year and only after an absence of 7 days.

The duty-free allowance in **Australia** is A$400 or, for those under 18, A$200. Citizens can bring in 250 cigarettes or 250 grams of loose tobacco, and 1,125 milliliters of alcohol. If you're returning with valuables you already own, such as foreign-made cameras, you should file form B263. A helpful brochure available from Australian consulates or Customs offices is *Know Before You Go.* For more information, call the **Australian Customs Service** at ✆ **1300/363-263,** or log on to www.customs.gov.au.

The duty-free allowance for **New Zealand** is NZ$700. Citizens over 17 can bring in 200 cigarettes, 50 cigars, or 250 grams of tobacco (or a mixture of all 3 if their combined weight doesn't exceed 250g); plus 4.5 liters of wine and beer, or 1.125 liters of liquor. New Zealand currency does not carry import or export restrictions. Fill out a certificate of export, listing the valuables you are taking out of the country; that way, you can bring them back without paying duty. Most questions are answered in a free pamphlet available at New Zealand consulates and Customs offices: *New Zealand Customs Guide for Travellers, Notice no. 4.* For more information, contact **New Zealand Customs,** The Customhouse, 17–21 Whitmore St., Box 2218, Wellington (✆ **04/473-6099** or 0800/ 428-786; www.customs.govt.nz).

⎛Tips Calling Scotland

To call Scotland from the United States, dial the **international prefix, 011;** then Scotland's **country code, 44;** then the **city code** (for example, **131** for Edinburgh and **141** for Glasgow—minus the initial zero, which is used only if you're dialing from within the United Kingdom); then dial the actual **phone number.**

4 Money

It's a good idea to exchange at least some money—just enough to cover airport incidentals and transportation to your hotel—before you leave home, so you can avoid lines at airport ATMs (automated teller machines). You can exchange money at your local American Express or Thomas Cook office or your bank. If you're far away from a bank with currency-exchange services, American Express offers travelers checks and foreign currency, though with a $15 order fee and additional shipping costs, at www.americanexpress.com or ℂ 800/807-6233.

POUNDS & PENCE

Britain's decimal monetary system is based on the pound Sterling (£), which is made up of 100 pence (written as "p"). Britons also call pounds "quid." Scotland issues its own pound notes, but English and Scottish money are interchangeable. There are £1 and £2 coins, as well as coins of 50p, 20p, 10p, 5p, 2p, and 1p. Banknotes come in denominations of £5, £10, £20, and £50.

As a general guideline, the price conversions in this book have been computed at the rate of £1 = $1.60 (U.S.). Bear in mind, however, that exchange rates fluctuate daily. For more exact ratios between these and other currencies, check an up-to-date source at the time of your arrival in Europe.

ATMS

The easiest and best way to get cash away from home is from an ATM (automated teller machine). The **Cirrus** (ℂ 800/424-7787; www.master card.com) and **PLUS** (ℂ 800/843-7587; www.visa.com) networks span the globe; look at the back of your bank card to see which network you're on, then call or check online for ATM locations at your destination. Be sure you know your personal identification number (PIN) before you leave home and be sure to find out your daily withdrawal limit before you depart. Also keep in mind that many banks impose a fee every time a card is used at a different bank's ATM, and that fee can be higher for international transactions (up to $5 or more) than for domestic ones (where they range from $1.50 to $3). On top of this, the bank from which you withdraw cash may charge its own fee. To compare banks' ATM fees within the U.S., use www.bankrate.com. For international withdrawal fees, ask your bank.

You can also get cash advances on your credit card at an ATM. Keep in mind that credit card companies try to protect themselves from theft by limiting the funds someone can withdraw outside their home country, so call your credit card company before you leave home.

TRAVELER'S CHECKS

Traveler's checks are something of an anachronism from the days before the ATM made cash accessible at any time. Traveler's checks used to be the only sound alternative to traveling

---

Regarding the U.S. Dollar, the British Pound & the Euro

You will not see Europe's newest currency, the euro (currently worth approximately $1.15), used in Great Britain, which steadfastly refuses to give up the British pound. As a result, all prices in this book are noted only in pounds and dollars at a rate of £1=$1.60. For up-to-the-minute exchange rates for all three currencies, check the currency converter website **www.xe.com/ucc**.

Tips **Small Change**

When you change money, ask for some small bills or loose change. Petty cash will come in handy for tipping and public transportation. Consider keeping the change separate from your larger bills so that it's readily accessible and you'll be less of a target for theft.

with dangerously large amounts of cash. They were as reliable as currency, but, unlike cash, could be replaced if lost or stolen.

These days, traveler's checks are less necessary because most cities have 24-hour ATMs that allow you to withdraw small amounts of cash as needed. However, keep in mind that you will likely be charged an ATM withdrawal fee if the bank is not your own, so if you're withdrawing money every day, you might be better off with traveler's checks—provided that you don't mind showing identification every time you want to cash one.

You can get traveler's checks at almost any bank. **American Express** offers denominations of $20, $50, $100, $500, and (for cardholders only) $1,000. You'll pay a service charge ranging from 1% to 4%. You can also get American Express traveler's checks over the phone by calling ✆ **800/221-7282;** Amex gold and platinum cardholders who use this number are exempt from the 1% fee.

Visa offers traveler's checks at Citibank locations nationwide, as well as at several other banks. The service charge ranges between 1.5% and 2%; checks come in denominations of $20, $50, $100, $500, and $1,000. Call ✆ **800/732-1322** for information. AAA members can obtain Visa checks without a fee at most AAA offices or by calling ✆ **866/339-3378. Master-Card** also offers traveler's checks. Call ✆ **800/223-9920** for a location near you.

Foreign currency traveler's checks are useful if you're traveling to one country, or to the euro zone; they're accepted at locations such as bed-and-breakfasts where dollar checks may not be, and they minimize the amount of math you have to do at your destination. **American Express** offers checks in Australian dollars, Canadian dollars, British pounds, euros, and Japanese yen. **Visa** checks come in Australian, Canadian, British, and Euro versions; **MasterCard** offers those four plus yen and South African rands.

If you choose to carry traveler's checks, be sure to keep a record of their serial numbers separate from your checks in the event that they are stolen or lost. You'll get a refund faster if you know the numbers.

CREDIT CARDS

Credit cards are a safe way to carry money, they provide a convenient record of all your expenses, and they generally offer good exchange rates. You can also withdraw cash advances from your credit cards at banks or ATMs, provided you know your PIN. If you've forgotten yours, or didn't even know you had one, call the number on the back of your credit card and ask the bank to send it to you. It usually takes 5 to 7 business days, though some banks will provide the number over the phone if you tell them your mother's maiden name or some other personal information. Your credit card company will likely charge a commission (1% or 2%) on every foreign purchase you make, but don't sweat this small stuff; for most purchases, you'll still get the best deal with credit cards when you factor in things like ATM fees and higher traveler's check exchange rates.

Places in England that accept credit cards take MasterCard and Visa and, to a much lesser extent, American Express. Diners Club trails in a poor fourth position.

5 When to Go

WEATHER

Weather is of vital concern in Scotland. It can seriously affect your travel plans. The Lowlands usually have a moderate year-round temperature. In spring, the average temperature is 53°F (12°C), rising to about 65°F (18°C) in summer. By the time the crisp autumn has arrived, the temperatures have dropped to spring levels.

In winter, the average temperature is 43°F (6°C). Temperatures in the north of Scotland are lower, especially in winter, and you should dress accordingly. It rains a lot in Scotland, but perhaps not as much as age-old myths would have it: The rainfall in Edinburgh is exactly the same as that in London. September can be the sunniest month.

Average Temperature & Rainfall in Scotland

City	Jan	Feb	Mar	Apr	May	June	July	Aug	Sept	Oct	Nov	Dec
Edinburgh												
Temp. (°F)	38	38	42	44	50	55	59	58	54	48	43	40
Temp. (°C)	3	3	6	7	10	13	15	14	12	9	6	4
Rainfall	2.2	1.6	1.9	1.5	2.0	2.0	2.5	2.7	2.5	2.4	2.5	2.4
Aberdeen												
Temp. (°F)	38	38	41	44	49	54	58	57	53	48	42	39
Temp. (°C)	3	3	5	7	9	12	14	14	11	9	6	4
Rainfall	2.5	2.0	2.1	1.9	2.1	2.0	2.8	2.8	2.5	3.0	3.1	2.9

WHEN YOU FIND BARGAINS

The cheapest time to travel to Scotland is off season: **November 1 to December 12** and **December 26 to March 14.** In the past few years, airlines have been offering irresistible fares during these periods. And weekday flights are cheaper than weekend fares, often by 10% or more.

Rates generally increase **March 14 to June 5** and in **October,** and then hit their peak in the high seasons from **June 6 to September 30** and **December 13 to 24.** July and August are when

---

Tips   Dear Visa: I'm Off to Edinburgh!

Some credit card companies recommend that you notify them of any impending trip abroad so that they don't become suspicious when the card is used numerous times in a foreign destination and your charges are blocked. Even if you don't call your credit card company in advance, you can always call the card's toll-free emergency number (see "Fast Facts," later in this chapter) if a charge is refused—a good reason to carry the phone number with you. But perhaps the most important lesson here is to carry more than one card with you on your trip; a card might not work for any number of reasons, so having a backup is the smart way to go.

most Britons take their holidays, so besides the higher prices, you'll have to deal with crowds and limited availability of accommodations.

Sure, in winter Scotland may be rainy and cold—but it doesn't shut down when the tourists leave. In fact, the winter season gives visitors a more honest view of Scottish life. Additionally, many hotel prices drop by 20%, and cheaper accommodations offer weekly rates (unheard of during peak travel times). By arriving after the winter holidays, you can take advantage of post-Christmas sales to buy your fill of woolens, china, crystal, silver, fashion, handicrafts, and curios.

In short, spring offers the countryside at its greenest, autumn brings the bright colors of the northern Highlands, and summer's warmth gives rise to the many outdoor music and theater festivals. But winter offers savings across the board and a chance to see Scots going about their everyday lives largely unhindered by tourist invasions.

HOLIDAYS

The following holidays are celebrated in Scotland: New Year's Day (January 1 and 2), Good Friday and Easter Monday, May Day (May 1), spring bank holiday (last Monday in May), summer bank holiday (first Monday in August), Christmas Day (December 25), and Boxing Day (December 26).

SCOTLAND CALENDAR OF EVENTS

You can get details of specific events at many of the festivals below by going to **www.edinburgh-festivals.com**.

January

Celtic Connections, Glasgow. During this celebration of the Celtic roots that combined with other cultures to form modern Scotland, concerts are staged in churches, auditoriums, and meeting halls throughout the city. A prime venue is the Old Fruit Market on Albion Street, drawing dance troupes from throughout Scotland, Wales, and Ireland. For tickets and details, call ☎ **0141/240-1111** or 0845/330-3501. Throughout January.

Burns Night, Ayr (near his birthplace), Dumfries, and Edinburgh. Naturally, during the celebrations to honor Robert Burns, there's much toasting with scotch and eating of haggis (spiced intestines), whose arrival is announced by a bagpipe. For details, call ☎ **01292/443-700** in Ayr, **0131/473-3800** in Edinburgh, or **01387/253-862** in Dumfries. January 25.

Up Helly Aa, Lerwick, in the Shetland Islands. The most northerly town in Great Britain still clings to tradition by staging an ancient Norse fire festival whose aim is to encourage the return of the sun after the pitch-dark days of winter. Its highlight is the burning of a replica of a Norse longboat. Call ☎ **01595/693-434.** Last Tuesday in January.

February

Aberdeen Angus Cattle Show, Perth. This show draws the finest cattle raised in Scotland. Sales are lively. Call ☎ **01738/626-183.** Early February.

March

Whuppity Scourie, Lanark. Residents of the Strathclyde get so tired of winter that they stage this traditional ceremony to chase it away. Call ☎ **01555/661-661.** March 1.

April

Edinburgh Folk Festival, at various venues, Edinburgh. For details on this feast of Scottish folk tunes, call ☎ **0131/473-3800.** Generally April 1.

Exhibitions at the Royal Scottish Academy, Edinburgh. Changing exhibits of international interest are offered here annually. Call ☎ **0131/473-3800.** Mid-April.

Kate Kennedy Procession & Pageant, St. Andrews. This historic university pageant is staged annually in the university city of St. Andrews, in eastern Scotland. Call ✆ **01334/472-021.** Second Saturday in April.

May

Scottish Motorcycle Trials, Fort William. The trials are run for 6 days at the beginning of the month, drawing aficionados from all over Europe. Call ✆ **01397/703-781.** Early May.

Highland Games & Gatherings, at various venues throughout the country, including Aberfeldy, Perth, Crieff, Ballater, Oban, and Portree on the Isle of Skye. Details are available from the Edinburgh and Scotland Information Centre (see "Visitor Information," earlier in this chapter). Early May to mid-September.

Pitlochry Festival Theatre, Pitlochry. Scotland's "theater in the hills" launches its season in mid-May. Call ✆ **01796/472-215;** www.pitlochry.org.uk. Mid-May to October.

June

Promenade Concerts, Glasgow. These concerts by the Scottish National Orchestra are given at the Glasgow Royal Concert Hall. Call ✆ **0141/353-8000.** Throughout June (sometimes into July).

Lanimer Day, Lanark. This week of festivities features a ritual procession around the town's boundaries, the election of a Lanimer Queen and a Cornet King, and a parade with floats, along with Highland dances and bagpipe playing. Call ✆ **01555/661-661.** The Thursday between June 6 and 12.

Guid Nychtburris (Good Neighbors), Dumfries. This age-old festival is an event similar to (but less impressive than) the Selkirk Common Riding (see below). Call ✆ **01387/253-862.** Mid-June.

Royal Highland Show, at the Ingliston Showground, outskirts of Edinburgh. This show is devoted to agriculture and commerce. For details, call ✆ **0131/473-3800.** Mid- to late June.

Selkirk Common Riding, Selkirk. This is Scotland's most elaborate display of horsemanship, remembering Selkirk's losses in the 1560 Battle of Flodden—only one Selkirk soldier returned alive from the battle to warn the town before dropping dead in the marketplace. Some 400 horses and riders parade through the streets, and a young unmarried male is crowned at the sound of the cornet, representing the soldier who sounded the alarm. Call ✆ **01750/200-54.** Mid-June.

Beltane Day, Peebles. A town "Cornet" rides around to see the boundaries are safe from the "invading" English, a young girl is elected Festival Queen, and her court is filled with courtiers, sword bearers, guards, and attendants. Children of the town dress in costumes for parade floats through the streets. Call ✆ **01721/720-138.** Mid-June.

Gay Pride, Edinburgh or Glasgow. Scotland's annual gay pride celebration alternates between Edinburgh and Glasgow. You'll see a quirky, boisterous parade through the heart of Glasgow or along Princes Street in Edinburgh. For details, call Glasgow's Gay Switchboard (✆ **0141/847-0447**) or Edinburgh's Gay Switchboard (✆ **0131/556-4049**). Sometime in June.

July

Glasgow International Jazz Festival, Glasgow. Jazz musicians from all over the world come together to perform at various venues around the city. Call ☎ **0141/204-4400;** www.jazzfest.co.uk. First week in July.

August

Lammas Fair, St. Andrews. Although there's a dim medieval origin to this 2-day festival, it's not particularly obvious. Temporary Ferris wheels and whirligigs are hauled in, cotton candy and popcorn are sold, palm readers describe your past and your future, and flashing lights and recorded disco music create something akin to Blackpool-in-the-Highlands. There's even an opportunity for bungee-jumping. Call ☎ **01334/ 472-021.** Second Monday and Tuesday of August.

World Pipe Band Championships, Glasgow. For this relatively new event (it's only 5 or 6 years old), bagpipe bands from around the world gather on the park-like Glasgow Green in the city's East End. From 11am to about 6pm, there's a virtual orgy of bagpiping, as kilted participants strut their stuff in musical and military precision. Call ☎ **0141/204-4400.** Mid-August.

Edinburgh International Festival, Edinburgh. Scotland's best-known festival is held for 3 weeks (see chapter 4, "Edinburgh & the Lothian Region" for more information). Called an "arts bonanza," it draws major talent from around the world, with more than a thousand shows presented and a million tickets sold. Book, jazz, and film festivals are also staged at this time, but nothing tops the Military Tattoo against the backdrop of spot-lit Edinburgh Castle. Contact the Festival Society, 21 Market St., Edinburgh, Scotland EH1 1BW (☎ **0131/473-2001;** www.eif.co.uk). Three weeks in August.

September

Ben Nevis Mountain Race, Fort William, in the Highlands. A tradition since 1895, when it was established by a member of the MacFarlane clan, it assembles as many as 500 runners who compete for the coveted MacFarlane Cup, a gold medal, and a prize of £50 ($80). Runners congregate at the base of Ben Nevis (Britain's highest peak) to tackle a course that takes them up narrow footpaths to the summit and back. Bagpipes rise in crescendos at the beginning and end of the experience. Call ☎ **01397/ 705-184;** www.visit-fortwilliam.co. uk. First Saturday in September.

Highland Games & Gathering, Braemar. The queen and many members of the royal family often show up for this annual event, with its massed bands, piping and dancing competitions, and performances of great strength by a tribe of gigantic men. Contact the tourist office in Braemar, The Mews, Mar Road, Braemar, Aberdeenshire, AB35 5YP (☎ **013397/416-00;** www.braemargathering.org). First Saturday in September.

Ayr Festival, Ayr. This is the major cultural event on the Ayr calendar, offering an array of film, theater, and music concerts. For exact dates, call ☎ **01292/678-100.**

Hamilton Flat Races, Hamilton, near Glasgow. The races take place over a period of 2 to 3 days. Call the Hamilton race course at ☎ **01698/ 283-806.**

October

Highland Autumn Cattle Show, Oban, in western Scotland. Since the days of Rob Roy, Oban has been a marketplace for the long-haired tawny cattle whose elongated horns have been associated with the toughness of the Highlands. For this show, buyers and

Tips Quick ID

A colorful ribbon or piece of yarn around your luggage handle, or a distinctive sticker on the side of your bag, will make it less likely that someone will mistakenly appropriate it. And if it does get lost, it will be easier to find.

sellers from Britain, as well as such cold-weather climes as Sweden, Norway, and Canada, come to buy cattle (either for stud or for beef purposes). Everything is rather businesslike (but still colorful) in the industrial-looking Caledonian Auction Mart, 5km (3 miles) south of Oban. Call ℭ **01631/563-122.** Mid-October.

November

Winter Antiques Fair, Edinburgh. This fair draws dealers and buyers from all over Europe and America. Call ℭ **0131/473-3800.** Third week in November.

Christmas Shopping Festival, Aberdeen. For those who want to shop early for Christmas. Call ℭ **01224/522-000.** Third week of November to December.

St. Andrews Week, St. Andrews. This annual festival of exhibits, concerts, sporting events, fireworks displays, and local foods takes place over the week leading up to St. Andrews Day on November 30. Call ℭ **01334/472-021.** The week ending November 30.

December

Flambeaux Procession, Comrie, Tayside. This torchlight parade takes place on New Year's Eve. For details, call ℭ **01764/652-578** in Crieff. December 31.

Hogmanay, Edinburgh. Hogmanay begins on New Year's Eve and merges into New Year's Day festivities. Events include a torchlight procession, a fire festival along Princes Street, a carnival, and a street theater spectacular. Call ℭ **0131/473-3800.** December 31.

6 Travel Insurance

Since Scotland for most of us is far from home, and a number of things could go wrong—lost luggage, trip cancellation, a medical emergency—consider the following types of insurance.

Check your existing insurance policies and credit-card coverage before you buy travel insurance. You may already be covered for lost luggage, cancelled tickets or medical expenses. The cost of travel insurance varies widely, depending on the cost and length of your trip, your age, health, and the type of trip you're taking.

TRIP-CANCELLATION INSURANCE Trip-cancellation insurance helps you get your money back if you

have to back out of a trip, if you have to go home early, or if your travel supplier goes bankrupt. Allowed reasons for cancellation can range from sickness to natural disasters to the State Department declaring your destination unsafe for travel. (Insurers usually won't cover vague fears, though, as many travelers discovered who tried to cancel their trips in October 2001 because they were wary of flying.) In this unstable world, trip-cancellation insurance is a good buy if you're getting tickets well in advance—who knows what the state of the world, or of your airline, will be in nine months? Insurance policy details vary, so read the fine print—and especially make sure that your airline or cruise line is on the list of carriers covered in case of bankruptcy. For information, contact one of the following insurers: **Access America** (© 866/807-3982; www.accessamerica.com); **Travel Guard International** (© 800/826-4919; www.travelguard.com); **Travel Insured International** (© 800/243-3174; www.travelinsured.com); and **Travelex Insurance Services** (© 888/457-4602; www.travelex-insurance.com).

MEDICAL INSURANCE Most health insurance policies cover you if you get sick away from home—but check, particularly if you're insured by an HMO. With the exception of certain HMOs and Medicare/Medicaid, your medical insurance should cover medical treatment—even hospital care—overseas. However, most out-of-country hospitals make you pay your bills up front, and send you a refund after you've returned home and filed the necessary paperwork. And in a worst-case scenario, there's the high cost of emergency evacuation. If you require additional medical insurance, try **MEDEX International** (© 800/527-0218 or 410/453-6300; www.medexassist.com) or **Travel Assistance International** (© 800/821-2828; www.travelassistance.com; for general information on services, call

the company's Worldwide Assistance Services, Inc., at © **800/777-8710**).

LOST-LUGGAGE INSURANCE On domestic flights, checked baggage is covered up to $2,500 per ticketed passenger. On international flights (including U.S. portions of international trips), baggage is limited to approximately $9.07 per pound, up to approximately $635 per checked bag. If you plan to check items more valuable than the standard liability, see if your valuables are covered by your homeowner's policy, get baggage insurance as part of your comprehensive travel-insurance package or buy Travel Guard's "BagTrak" product. Don't buy insurance at the airport, as it's usually overpriced. Be sure to take any valuables or irreplaceable items with you in your carry-on luggage, as many valuables (including books, money and electronics) aren't covered by airline policies.

If your luggage is lost, immediately file a lost-luggage claim at the airport, detailing the luggage contents. For most airlines, you must report delayed, damaged, or lost baggage within 4 hours of arrival. The airlines are required to deliver luggage, once found, directly to your house or destination free of charge.

7 Health & Safety

STAYING HEALTHY

You'll encounter few health problems while in Scotland. The tap water is safe to drink, the milk is pasteurized, and health services are good. The mad-cow crisis is over, but caution is always advised. (For example, it's been suggested that it's safer to eat British beef cut from the bone instead of on the bone.)

If you need a doctor, your hotel can recommend one, or you can contact your embassy or consulate. **Note:** U.S. visitors who become ill while in

England are eligible for free emergency care only. For other treatment, including follow-up care, you'll be asked to pay.

WHAT TO DO IF YOU GET SICK AWAY FROM HOME

If you need a doctor, your hotel can recommend one, or you can contact your embassy or consulate. Outside Edinburgh, dial © **100** and ask the operator for the local police, who will give you the name, address, and telephone number of a doctor in your area.

In most cases, your existing health plan will provide the coverage you need. But double-check; you may want to buy **travel medical insurance** instead. (See the section on insurance, above.) Bring your insurance ID card with you when you travel.

If you suffer from a chronic illness, consult your doctor before your departure. For conditions like epilepsy, diabetes, or heart problems, wear a **Medic Alert Identification Tag** (✆ 800/825-3785; www.medicalert.org), which will immediately alert doctors to your condition and give them access to your records through Medic Alert's 24-hour hot line.

Pack **prescription medications** in your carry-on luggage, and carry prescription medications in their original containers, with pharmacy labels—otherwise they won't make it through airport security. Also bring along copies of your prescriptions in case you lose your pills or run out. Don't forget an extra pair of contact lenses or prescription glasses. Carry the generic name of prescription medicines, in case a local pharmacist is unfamiliar with the brand name.

Contact the **International Association for Medical Assistance to Travelers (IAMAT)** (✆ 716/754-4883 or 416/652-0137; www.iamat.org) for tips on travel and health concerns in the countries you're visiting, and lists of local, English-speaking doctors. The United States **Centers for Disease Control and Prevention** (✆ 800/311-3435; www.cdc.gov) provides up-to-date information on necessary vaccines and health hazards by region or country. Any foreign consulate can provide a list of area doctors

who speak English. If you get sick, consider asking your hotel concierge to recommend a local doctor—even his or her own. You can also try the emergency room at a local hospital; many have walk-in clinics for emergency cases that are not life-threatening. You may not get immediate attention, but you won't pay the high price of an emergency room visit.

STAYING SAFE

Like all big cities, Edinburgh and Glasgow have their share of crime. Compared to most large cities of Europe, they are relatively safe, and violent crime against visitors is extremely rare. The same precautions prevail in these larger cities as they do elsewhere in the world. However, in rural Scotland you are relatively safe.

Crime, however, has increased over the past few years. Tourists are typically prey to incidents of pickpocketing; mugging; "snatch and grab" theft of mobile phones, watches, and jewelry; and theft of unattended bags, especially at airports and from cars parked at restaurants, hotels, and resorts.

Pickpockets target tourists, especially at historic sites, restaurants, on buses, trains, and the Underground (subway). Thieves often target unattended cars parked at tourist sites and roadside restaurants, looking for laptop computers and hand-held electronic equipment.

Visitors should take steps to ensure the safety of their passports. Visitors in Scotland are not expected to produce identity documents for police authorities and thus may secure their passports in hotel safes or residences.

8 Specialized Travel Resources

TRAVELERS WITH DISABILITIES

Many Scottish hotels, museums, restaurants, and sightseeing attractions have wheelchair ramps, less so in rural areas. Persons with disabilities are often granted special discounts at attractions and, in some cases, nightclubs. These are called "concessions" in Britain. It always pays to ask. Free information and advice is available from **Holiday Care,** Imperial Building, 2nd floor, Victoria Road, Horley, Surrey RH6 7PZ (© **01293/774-535;** fax 01293/784-647; www.holidaycare.org.uk).

Tripscope, The Courtyard, 4 Evelyn Rd., London W4 5JL (© **020/85807021;** www.justmobility.co.uk), which offers advice on travel in Britain and elsewhere for persons with disabilities.

Flying Wheels Travel (© **507/451-5005;** www.flyingwheelstravel.com) offers escorted tours and cruises that emphasize sports and private tours in minivans with lifts. **Rumpleduck Travel** (© **877/401-7736** or 310-850-5340) brings a personal touch to designing itineraries and specializes in trips to the U.K., Hawaii and Las Vegas. **Accessible Journeys** (© **800/846-4537** or 610/521-0339; www.disability travel.com) caters specifically to slow walkers and wheelchair travelers and their families and friends.

Organizations that offer assistance to travelers with disabilities include the **Moss Rehab Hospital** www.moss resourcenet.org), which provides a library of accessible-travel resources online; the **Society for Accessible Travel and Hospitality** (© **212/447-7284;** www.sath.org; annual membership fees: $45 adults, $30 seniors and students), which offers a wealth of travel resources for all types of disabilities and informed recommendations on destinations, access guides, travel agents, tour operators, vehicle rentals, and companion services; and the **American Foundation for the Blind** (© **800/232-5463;** www.afb.org), which provides information on traveling with Seeing Eye dogs.

For more information specifically targeted to travelers with disabilities, the community website **iCan** (www.icanonline.net/channels/travel/index.cfm) has destination guides and several regular columns on accessible travel. Also check out the quarterly magazine **Emerging Horizons** ($14.95 per year, $19.95 outside the U.S.; www.emerginghorizons.com); **Twin Peaks Press** (© **360/694-2462;** http://disabilitybookshop.virtualave.n et/blist84.htm), offering travel-related books for travelers with special needs; and *Open World Magazine,* published by the Society for Accessible Travel and Hospitality (see above; subscription: $18/year., $35 outside the U.S.).

GAY & LESBIAN TRAVELERS

Bars, clubs, restaurants, and hotels catering to gays are confined almost exclusively to Edinburgh, Glasgow, and Inverness. Call the **Lothian Gay and Lesbian Switchboard** (© **0131/556-4049**) or the **Glasgow Gay and Lesbian Switchboard** (© **0141/847-0447**) for information on local events.

Scotland doesn't boast much of a gay scene. Gay-bashing happens, especially in the grimy industrial sections of Glasgow, where neo-Nazi skinheads hang out. Although it's a crime, it's rarely punished. Open displays of affection between same-sex couples usually invite scorn in rural Scotland, although there's none of the fanatical homophobia so prevalent among the lunatic fringe in the United States.

The best guide is *Spartacus Britain and Ireland.* Although the third edition of *Frommer's Gay & Lesbian Europe* doesn't include Scotland, it does include London, and Brighton, in case you're heading to England before or after Scotland. For up-to-the-minute activities in Britain, we recommend *Gay Times* (London). These books and others are available from **Giovanni's Room,** 345 S. 12th St., Philadelphia, PA 19107 (© **215/923-2960;** www.giovannisroom.com).

The International Gay & Lesbian Travel Association (IGLTA) (© **800/448-8550** or 954/776-2626; www.iglta.org) is the trade association for the gay and lesbian travel industry, and offers an online directory of gay and lesbian–friendly travel businesses; go to their website and click on "Members."

Many agencies offer tours and travel itineraries specifically for gay and lesbian travelers. **Above and Beyond Tours** (© 800/397-2681; www.abovebeyondtours.com) is the exclusive gay and lesbian tour operator for United Airlines. **Now, Voyager** (© 800/255-6951; www.nowvoyager.com) is a well-known San Francisco–based gay-owned and operated travel service.

SENIOR TRAVEL

Many discounts are available to seniors. Be advised that in Scotland you often have to be a member of an association to get discounts. Public-transportation reductions, for example, are available only to holders of British Pension books. However, many attractions do offer discounts for seniors (women 60 or over and men 65 or over). Even if discounts aren't posted, ask if they're available.

If you're over 60, you're eligible for special 10% discounts on **British Airways (BA)** through its Privileged Traveler program. You also qualify for reduced restrictions on APEX cancellations. Discounts are also granted for BA tours and for intra-Britain air tickets booked in North America. **British Rail** offers seniors discounted rates on first-class rail passes around Britain. See "By Train from Continental Europe" in the "Getting There" section later in this chapter.

Don't be shy about asking for discounts, but carry some kind of identification that shows your date of birth. Also, mention you're a senior when you make your reservations. Many hotels offer seniors discounts. In most cities, people over the age of 60 qualify for reduced admission to theaters, museums, and other attractions, and discounted fares on public transportation.

Members of **AARP** (formerly known as the American Association of Retired Persons), 601 E St. NW, Washington, DC 20049 (© 800/424-3410 or 202/434-2277; www.aarp.org), get discounts on hotels, airfares, and car rentals. AARP offers members a wide range of benefits, including *Modern Maturity* magazine and a monthly newsletter. Anyone over 50 can join.

Many reliable agencies and organizations target the 50-plus market. **Elderhostel** (© 877/426-8056; www.elderhostel.org) arranges study programs for those aged 55 and over (and a spouse or companion of any age) in the U.S. and in more than 80 countries around the world. Most courses last 5 to 7 days in the U.S. (2–4 weeks abroad), and many include airfare, accommodations in university dormitories or modest inns, meals, and tuition. **ElderTreks** (© 800/741-7956; www.eldertreks.com) offers small-group tours to off-the-beaten-path or adventure-travel locations, restricted to travelers 50 and older.

Recommended publications offering travel resources and discounts for seniors include: the quarterly magazine *Travel 50 & Beyond* (www.travel50andbeyond.com); *Travel Unlimited: Uncommon Adventures for the Mature Traveler* (Avalon); *101 Tips for Mature Travelers,* available from Grand Circle Travel (© 800/221-2610 or 617/350-7500; www.gct.com); *The 50+ Traveler's Guidebook* (St. Martin's Press); and *Unbelievably Good Deals and Great Adventures That You Absolutely Can't Get Unless You're Over 50* (McGraw Hill).

FAMILY TRAVEL

If you have enough trouble getting your kids out of the house in the morning, dragging them thousands of miles away may seem like an insurmountable challenge. But family travel can be immensely rewarding, giving you new ways of seeing the world through smaller pairs of eyes.

When booking rooms, ask whether family suites are available. Accommodations in more rural areas sometimes let self-catering cottages or apartments, which might be an ideal solution for families trying to save some money and looking for a bit more space than a typical hotel room. Look also for our "Kids" icon, indicating attractions, restaurants, or hotels and resorts that are especially family friendly. Note that some castles and more private luxury accommodations do not accept young children as guests. Such instances are noted in all reviews.

Remember that for people 15 and under, a passport is valid for only 5 years, costing $40, whereas for those 16 and up, a passport is valid for 10 years, costing $60.

Familyhostel (© **800/733-9753;** www.learn.unh.edu/familyhostel) takes the whole family, including kids ages 8 to 15, on moderately priced domestic and international learning vacations. Lectures, fields trips, and sightseeing are guided by a team of academics.

You can find good family-oriented vacation advice on the Internet from sites like the **Family Travel Network** (www.familytravelnetwork.com); **Traveling Internationally with Your Kids** (www.travelwithyourkids.com), a comprehensive site offering sound advice for long-distance and international travel with children; and **Family Travel Files** (www.thefamilytravelfiles.com), which offers an online magazine and a directory of off-the-beaten-path tours and tour operators for families.

STUDENT TRAVEL

Students traveling outside of the U.S. would be wise to arm themselves with an **International Student Identity Card (ISIC),** which offers substantial savings on rail passes, plane tickets, and entrance fees. It also provides you with basic health and life insurance and a 24-hour help line. The card is available for $22 from **STA Travel** (© **800/781-4040,** and if you're not in North America there's probably a local number in your country; www.statravel.com), the biggest student travel agency in the world. If you're no longer a student but are still under 26, you can get a **International Youth Travel Card (IYTC)** for the same price from the same people, which entitles you to some discounts (but not on museum admissions). (*Note:* In 2002, STA Travel bought competitors **Council Travel** and **USIT Campus** after they went bankrupt. It's still operating some offices under the Council name, but it's owned by STA.)

Travel CUTS (© **800/667-2887** or 416/614-2887; www.travelcuts. com) offers similar services for both Canadians and U.S. residents. Irish

---

Tips **Farmhouse Holidays**

One way to understand the agricultural roots of Scotland is overnighting on a Scottish farm. **Scottish Farmhouse Holidays,** Renton Terrace, Eyemouth, Berwickshire TD14 5DF (© **0189/075-1830;** fax 0189/075-1831; www.scot farmhols.co.uk), will find you an appropriate croft. Only family-managed working farms are selected for the program, most within easy driving distance of at least a handful of historic sites. Many of the farmhouses are a century or so old and have been in the same family for several generations. Rates for bed-and-breakfast in rooms without a bathroom are from £20 ($32); rates for dinner, bed, and breakfast run from £28 ($45). Occupants of single rooms usually pay from £5 ($8) for a supplement.

students should turn to USIT (② 01/ 602-1600; www.usitnow.ie)

The Hanging Out Guides (www.frommers.com/hangingout), published by Frommer's, is the top student travel series for today's students, covering everything from adrenaline sports to the hottest club and music scenes.

9 Planning Your Trip Online

SURFING FOR AIRFARES

The "big three" online travel agencies, Expedia.com, Travelocity.com, and Orbitz.com sell most of the air tickets bought on the Internet. (Canadian travelers should try Expedia.ca and Travelocity.ca; U.K. residents can go for Expedia.co.uk and Opodo.co.uk.) Each has different business deals with the airlines and may offer different fares on the same flights, so it's wise to shop around. Expedia and Travelocity will also send you e-mail notification when a cheap fare becomes available to your favorite destination. Of the smaller travel agency websites, Side-Step (www.sidestep.com) has gotten the best reviews from Frommer's authors. It's a browser add-on that purports to "search 140 sites at once," but in reality only beats competitors' fares as often as other sites do.

Also remember to check airline websites, especially those for low-fare carriers such as Southwest, JetBlue, AirTran, WestJet, or Ryanair, whose fares are often misreported or simply missing from travel agency websites. Even with major airlines, you can often shave a few bucks from a fare by booking directly through the airline and avoiding a travel agency's transaction fee. But you'll get these discounts only by booking online: Most airlines now offer online-only fares that even their phone agents know nothing about. For the websites of airlines that fly to and from your destination, go to "Getting There," below.

Great last-minute deals are available through free weekly e-mail services provided directly by the airlines. Most of these are announced on Tuesday or Wednesday and must be purchased online. Most are only valid for travel that weekend, but some (such as Southwest's) can be booked weeks or months in advance. Sign up for weekly e-mail alerts at airline websites or check mega-sites that compile comprehensive lists of last-minute specials, such as Smarter Living (smarterliving.com). For last-minute trips, site59.com in the U.S. and lastminute.com in Europe often have better deals than the major-label sites.

If you're willing to give up some control over your flight details, use an opaque fare service like Priceline (www.priceline.com; www.priceline. co.uk for Europeans) or Hotwire (www.hotwire.com). Both offer rock-bottom prices in exchange for travel on a "mystery airline" at a mysterious time of day, often with a mysterious change of planes en route. The mystery airlines are all major, well-known carriers—and the possibility of being sent from Philadelphia to Chicago via Tampa is remote; the airlines' routing computers have gotten a lot better than they used to be. But your chances of getting a 6am or 11pm flight are pretty high. Hotwire tells you flight prices before you buy; Priceline usually has better deals than Hotwire, but you have to play their "name our price" game. If you're new at this, the helpful folks at BiddingForTravel (www.biddingfortravel.com) do a good job of demystifying Priceline's prices. Priceline and Hotwire are great for flights within North America and between the U.S. and Europe. But for flights to other parts of the world, consolidators will almost always beat their fares.

Frommers.com: The Complete Travel Resource

For an excellent travel-planning resource, we highly recommend **Frommers.com** (www.frommers.com). We're a little biased, of course, but we guarantee that you'll find the travel tips, reviews, monthly vacation giveaways, and online-booking capabilities thoroughly indispensable. Among the special features are our popular **Message Boards,** where Frommer's readers post queries and share advice (sometimes even our authors show up to answer questions); **Frommers.com Newsletter,** for the latest travel bargains and insider travel secrets; and **Frommer's Destinations Section,** where you'll get expert travel tips, hotel and dining recommendations, and advice on the sights to see for more than 3,000 destinations around the globe. When your research is done, the **Online Reservations System** (www.frommers.com/book_a_trip) takes you to Frommer's preferred online partners for booking your vacation at affordable prices.

For much more about airfares and savvy air-travel tips and advice, pick up a copy of *Frommer's Fly Safe, Fly Smart* (Wiley Publishing, Inc.).

SURFING FOR HOTELS

Shopping online for hotels in Scotland is fairly easy, although many of the smaller hotels and B&Bs—especially in the more rural areas—don't show up on websites at all. Of the "big three" sites, **Expedia** may be the best choice, thanks to its long list of special deals. **Travelocity** runs a close second. Hotel specialist sites **hotels.com** and **hoteldiscounts.com** are also reliable. An excellent free program, **TravelAxe** (www.travelaxe.net), can help you search multiple hotel sites at once, even ones you may never have heard of.

Priceline and Hotwire are even better for hotels than for airfares; with both, you're allowed to pick the neighborhood and quality level of your hotel before offering up your money. Priceline's hotel product even covers Europe and Asia, though it's much better at getting five-star lodging for three-star prices than at finding anything at the bottom of the scale. *Note:* Hotwire overrates its hotels by one star—what Hotwire calls a four-star is a three-star anywhere else.

SURFING FOR RENTAL CARS

For booking rental cars online, the best deals are usually found at rental-car company websites, although all the major online travel agencies also offer rental-car reservations services. Priceline and Hotwire work well for rental cars, too; the only "mystery" is which major rental company you get, and for most travelers the difference between Hertz, Avis, and Budget is negligible.

10 The 21st-Century Traveler

INTERNET ACCESS AWAY FROM HOME

Travelers have any number of ways to check their e-mail and access the Internet on the road. Of course, using your own laptop—or even a PDA (personal digital assistant) or electronic organizer with a modem—gives you the most flexibility. But even if you don't have a computer, you can still access your e-mail and even your office computer from cybercafes.

WITHOUT YOUR OWN COMPUTER

It's hard nowadays to find a city that *doesn't* have a few cybercafes. Although there's no definitive directory for cybercafes—these are independent businesses, after all—three places to start looking are at **www.cybercaptive. com**, **www.netcafeguide.com**, and **www.cybercafe.com**.

Aside from formal cybercafes, most **youth hostels** nowadays have at least one computer you can get to the Internet on. And most **public libraries** across the world offer Internet access free or for a small charge. Avoid **hotel business centers,** which often charge exorbitant rates.

Most major airports now have **Internet kiosks** scattered throughout their gates. These kiosks, which you'll also see in shopping malls, hotel lobbies, and tourist information offices around the world, give you basic web access for a per-minute fee that's usually higher than cybercafe prices. The kiosks' clunkiness and high price means they should be avoided whenever possible.

To retrieve your e-mail, ask your **Internet Service Provider (ISP)** if it has a web-based interface tied to your existing e-mail account. If your ISP doesn't have such an interface, you can use the free **mail2web** service (www. mail2web.com) to view (but not reply to) your home e-mail. For more flexibility, you may want to open a free, web-based e-mail account with **Yahoo! Mail** (mail.yahoo.com). (Microsoft's Hotmail is another popular option, but Hotmail has severe spam problems.) Your home ISP may be able to forward your e-mail to the web-based account automatically.

If you need to access files on your office computer, look into a service called **GoToMyPC** (www.gotomypc. com). The service provides a web-based interface for you to access and manipulate a distant PC from anywhere—even a cybercafe—provided your "target" PC is on and has an always-on connection to the Internet (such as with Road Runner cable). The service offers top-quality security, but if you're worried about hackers, use your own laptop rather than a cybercafe to access the GoToMyPC system.

WITH YOUR OWN COMPUTER

Major Internet Service Providers (ISP) have **local access numbers** around the world, allowing you to go online by simply placing a local call. Check your ISP's website or call its toll-free number and ask how you can use your current account away from home, and how much it will cost.

If you're traveling outside the reach of your ISP, the **iPass** network has dial-up numbers in most of the world's countries. You'll have to sign up with an iPass provider, who will then tell you how to set up your computer for your destination(s). For a list of iPass providers, go to www.ipass.com and click on "Reseller Locator." Under "Select a Country" pick the country that you're coming from, and under "Who is this service for?" pick "Individual." One solid provider is **i2roam** (www.i2roam.com; ✆ **866/811-6209** or 920/235-0475).

Wherever you go, bring a **connection kit** of the right power and phone adapters, a spare phone cord, and a spare Ethernet network cable.

Most business-class hotels throughout the world offer dataports for laptop modems, and a few thousand hotels in the U.S. and Europe now offer high-speed Internet access using an Ethernet network cable. You'll have to bring your own cables either way, so **call your hotel in advance** to find out what the options are.

USING A CELLPHONE IN SCOTLAND

The three letters that define much of the world's **wireless capabilities** are

GSM (Global System for Mobiles), a big, seamless network that makes for easy cross-border cellphone use throughout Europe and dozens of other countries worldwide. In the U.S., T-Mobile, AT&T Wireless, and Cingular use this quasi-universal system; in Canada, Microcell and some Rogers customers are GSM, and all Europeans and most Australians use GSM.

If your cellphone is on a GSM system, and you have a world-capable phone such as many (but not all) Sony Ericsson, Motorola, or Samsung models, you can make and receive calls across civilized areas on much of the globe, from Andorra to Uganda. Just call your wireless operator and ask for "international roaming" to be activated on your account. Unfortunately, per-minute charges can be high—usually $1 to $1.50 in Western Europe and up to $5 in places like Russia and Indonesia.

World-phone owners can bring down their per-minute charges with a bit of trickery. Call up your cellular operator and say you'll be going abroad for several months and want to "unlock" your phone to use it with a local provider. Usually, they'll oblige. Then, in your destination country,

pick up a cheap, prepaid phone chip at a mobile phone store and slip it into your phone. (Show your phone to the salesperson, as not all phones work on all networks.) You'll get a local phone number in your destination country— and much, much lower calling rates.

Otherwise, **renting** a phone is a good idea. (Even world-phone owners will have to rent new phones if they're traveling to non-GSM regions, such as Japan or Korea.) While you can rent a phone from any number of overseas sites, including kiosks at airports and at car-rental agencies, we suggest renting the phone before you leave home. That way you can give loved ones your new number, make sure the phone works, and take the phone wherever you go—especially helpful when you rent overseas, where phone-rental agencies bill in local currency and may not let you take the phone to another country.

Phone rental isn't cheap. You'll usually pay $40 to $50 per week, plus airtime fees of at least a dollar a minute. If you're traveling to Europe, though, local rental companies often offer free incoming calls within their home country, which can save you big bucks. The bottom line: Shop around.

Online Traveler's Toolbox

Veteran travelers usually carry some essential items to make their trips easier. Following is a selection of online tools to bookmark and use.

- **Visa ATM Locator** (www.visa.com), for locations of PLUS ATMs worldwide, or **MasterCard ATM Locator** (www.mastercard.com), for locations of Cirrus ATMs worldwide.
- **Intellicast** (www.intellicast.com) and **Weather.com** (www.weather.com). Gives weather forecasts for all 50 states and for cities around the world, including London.
- **Mapquest** (www.mapquest.com). This best of the mapping sites lets you choose a specific address or destination, and in seconds, it will return a map and detailed directions.
- **Universal Currency Converter** (www.xe.com/ucc). See what your dollar or pound is worth in more than 100 other countries.

Two good wireless rental companies are **InTouch USA** (© **800/872-7626;** www.intouchglobal.com) and **Road-Post** (www.roadpost.com; © **888/290-1606** or 905/272-5665). Give them your itinerary, and they'll tell you what wireless products you need. InTouch will also, for free, advise you on whether your existing phone will work overseas; simply call © **703/222-7161** between 9am and 4pm EST, or go to http://intouchglobal.com/travel.htm.

For trips of more than a few weeks spent in one country, **buying a phone** becomes economically attractive, as many nations have cheap, no-questions-asked prepaid phone systems. Stop by a local cellphone shop and get the cheapest package; you'll probably pay less than $100 for a phone and a starter calling card. Local calls may be as low as 10 cents per minute, and in many countries incoming calls are free.

11 Getting There

BY PLANE

Visitors will find frequent flights available from London to Scotland. **British Airways** (© 800/247-9297 or 08457/733377; www.britishairways.com) offers 22 nonstop flights daily from London's Heathrow Airport to both Edinburgh and Glasgow. British Airways can make a visit to Scotland cheaper than you might have expected. Ask about packages that include both airfare and discounted hotel accommodations in Scotland. **KLM UK** (© 0870/507-4077) flies from Stansted and London City airports to both Edinburgh and Glasgow daily. **Ryanair** (© 0871/246-0000) flies from Stansted outside London to Prestwick on the west coast of Scotland, and **British Midland** (© 0870/6070-555) flies from Heathrow to both Edinburgh and Glasgow.

Known for consistently offering excellent fares, **Virgin Atlantic Airways** (© 800/862-8621; www.virginatlantic.com) flies daily to either Heathrow or Gatwick from Boston; Newark, New Jersey; New York's JFK; Los Angeles; San Francisco; Washington's Dulles; Miami; and Orlando. **American Airlines** (© 800/433-7300; www.aa.com) offers daily flights to Heathrow from half a dozen U.S. gateways—New York's JFK (six times daily), Newark (once daily),

Chicago (three times daily), Boston (twice daily), and Miami and Los Angeles (each once daily).

Depending on the day and season, **Delta Air Lines** (© 800/241-4141; www.delta.com) runs either one or two daily nonstop flights between Atlanta and Gatwick. Delta also offers nonstop daily service from Cincinnati. **Northwest Airlines** (© 800/225-2525 or 800/447-4747; www.nwa.com) flies nonstop from Minneapolis and Detroit to Gatwick, with connections possible from other cities, such as Boston or New York.

Continental Airlines (© 800/231-0856; www.continental.com) has daily flights to London from Houston and Newark.

United Airlines (© 800/241-6522; www.united.com) flies nonstop from New York's JFK and Chicago to Heathrow two or three times daily, depending on the season. United also offers nonstop service three times a day from Dulles Airport, near Washington, D.C., plus once-a-day service from Newark and Los Angeles, and twice-a-day service from San Francisco and Boston.

For travelers departing from Canada, **Air Canada** (© 888/247-2262 in U.S. or 800/268-7240 in Canada; www.aircanada.ca) flies daily to London's Heathrow nonstop from

Vancouver, Montreal, and Toronto. There are also frequent direct flights from Calgary and Ottawa. **British Airways** (℡ 800/247-9297) has direct flights from Toronto, Montreal, and Vancouver.

For travelers departing from Australia, **British Airways** (℡ 800/247-9297) has flights to London from Sydney, Melbourne, Perth, and Brisbane. **Qantas** (℡ 131313; www.qantas.com) offers flights from Australia to London's Heathrow. Direct flights depart from Sydney and Melbourne. Some have the bonus of free stopovers in Bangkok or Singapore.

Departing from New Zealand, **Air New Zealand** (℡ 800/262-1234) has direct flights to London from Auckland. These flights depart daily.

Short flights from Dublin to London are available through **British Airways** (℡ 800/247-9297), with four flights daily into London's Gatwick airport, and **Aer Lingus** (℡ 800/FLY-IRISH; www.aerlingus.com), which flies into Heathrow. Short flights from Dublin to London are also available through **Ryan Air** (℡ 0870/156-9569; www.ryanair.com) and **British Midland** (℡ 0870/6070555; www.flybmi.com).

Some Scotland-bound passengers opt for flights into Manchester in England—it's closer than London to Scotland's Highlands and islands. British Airways offers frequent flights into Manchester, many nonstop, from various parts of the United States.

GETTING THROUGH THE AIRPORT

With the federalization of airport security, security procedures at U.S. airports are more stable and consistent than ever. Generally, you'll be fine if you arrive at the airport **1 hour** before a domestic flight and **2 hours** before an international flight; if you show up late, tell an airline employee and he or she will probably whisk you to the front of the line.

Bring a **current, government-issued photo ID** such as a driver's license or passport, and if you've got an e-ticket, print out the **official confirmation page;** you'll need to show your confirmation at the security checkpoint, and your ID at the ticket counter or the gate. (Children under 18 do not need photo IDs for domestic flights, but the adults checking in with them need them.)

Security lines are getting shorter than they were during 2001 and 2002, but some doozies remain. If you have trouble standing for long periods of time, tell an airline employee; the airline will provide a wheelchair. Speed up security by **not wearing metal objects** such as big belt buckles or clanky earrings. If you've got metallic body parts, a note from your doctor can prevent a long chat with the security screeners. Keep in mind that only **ticketed passengers** are allowed past security, except for folks escorting disabled passengers or children.

Federalization has stabilized **what you can carry on** and **what you can't.** The general rule is that sharp things are out, nail clippers are okay, and food and beverages must be passed through the X-ray machine—but security screeners can't make you drink from your coffee cup. Bring food in your carry-on rather than checking it, as explosive-detection machines used on checked luggage have been known to mistake food (especially chocolate, for some reason) for bombs. Travelers in the U.S. are allowed one carry-on bag, plus a "personal item" such as a purse, briefcase, or laptop bag. Carry-on hoarders can stuff all sorts of things into a laptop bag; as long as it has a laptop in it, it's still considered a personal item. The Transportation Security Administration (TSA) has issued a list of restricted items; check its website (www.tsa.gov) for details.

Travel in the Age of Bankruptcy

At press time, two major U.S. airlines were struggling in bankruptcy court and most of the rest weren't doing very well either. To protect yourself, **buy your tickets with a credit card,** as the Fair Credit Billing Act guarantees that you can get your money back from the credit card company if a travel supplier goes under (and if you request the refund within 60 days of the bankruptcy.) **Travel insurance** can also help, but make sure it covers against "carrier default" for your specific travel provider. And be aware that if a U.S. airline goes bust mid-trip, a 2001 federal law requires other carriers to take you to your destination (albeit on a space-available basis) for a fee of no more than $25, provided you rebook within 60 days of the cancellation.

In 2003, the TSA will be phasing out **gate check-in** at all U.S. airports. Passengers with e-tickets and without checked bags can still beat the ticket-counter lines by using **electronic kiosks** or even **online check-in.** Ask your airline which alternatives are available, and if you're using a kiosk, bring the credit card you used to book the ticket. If you're checking bags, you will still be able to use most airlines' kiosks; again call your airline for up-to-date information. **Curbside check-in** is also a good way to avoid lines, although a few airlines still ban curbside check-in entirely; call before you go.

BY CAR

If you're driving north to Scotland from England, it's fastest to take the **M1 motorway** north from London. You can reach M1 by driving to the ring road from any point in the British capital. Southeast of Leeds, you'll need to connect with **A1** (not a motorway), which you take north to Scotch Corner. Here **M1** resumes, ending south of Newcastle-upon-Tyne. Then you can take **A696,** which becomes **A68,** for its final run north into Edinburgh.

If you're in the west of England, go north along **M5,** which begins at Exeter (Devon). Eventually this will merge with **M6.** Continue north on M6 until you reach a point north of Carlisle. From Carlisle, cross into Scotland near Gretna Green. Continue north along **A74** via Moffat. A74 will

eventually connect with **M74** heading toward Glasgow. If your goal is Edinburgh, not Glasgow, various roads will take you east to the Scottish capital, including **M8,** which goes part of the way, as do **A702, A70,** and **A71** (all these routes are well signposted).

BY TRAIN

From England, two main rail lines link London to Scotland. The most popular and fastest route is **King's Cross Station** in London to Edinburgh, going by way of Newcastle and Durham. Trains cross from England into Scotland at Berwick-upon-Tweed. Fifteen trains a day leave London for Edinburgh between 8am and 6pm; night service is more limited, and you must reserve sleepers. Three of these trains go on to Aberdeen.

If you're going on to the western Highlands and islands, Edinburgh makes a good gateway, with better train connections to those areas than Glasgow.

If you're going via the west coast, trains leave **Euston Station** in London for Glasgow, by way of Rugby, Crewe, Preston, and Carlisle, with nearly a train per hour during the day. Most of these trains take about 5 hours to reach Glasgow. You can also take the *Highland Chieftain,* going direct to Stirling and Aviemore and terminating in Inverness, capital of the Highlands. There's overnight sleeper service from Euston Station to Glasgow, Perth,

Stirling, Aviemore, Fort William, and Inverness. It's possible to book a family compartment.

Scotland is served by other trains from England, including regular service from such cities as Birmingham, Liverpool, Manchester, Southampton, and Bristol. If you're in Penzance (Cornwall), you can reach Glasgow or Edinburgh directly by train without having to return to London.

Orient Express Trains & Cruises has launched its fifth train in Britain, the *Northern Belle*. You get great luxury, except for one oversight: There are no berths. Making about 20 departures a week, the *Northern Belle* carries 252 passengers and feeds them in six stately dining rooms evocative of a country home in Scotland. In addition to its runs in England, the train features weekend jaunts up to Scotland, with departures from Liverpool, Manchester, and York. What about taking a bath? Stays in hotels will be part of the plan. For reservations, call © **020/ 7805-5060** in the U.K., or 800/524-2420 in the U.S. You can also go to **www.orient-expresstrains.com**.

See "Getting Around Scotland," below, for information on rail passes.

BY TRAIN FROM CONTINENTAL EUROPE

Britain's isolation from the rest of Europe led to the development of an independent railway network with different rules and regulations from those observed on the Continent. That's all changing now, but one big difference that may affect you still remains: If you're traveling to Britain from the Continent, *your Eurailpass will not be valid when you get there.*

In 1994, Queen Elizabeth and President François Mitterand officially opened the Channel Tunnel, or Chunnel, and the *Eurostar* express passenger train began twice-daily service between London and both Paris and Brussels— a 3-hour trip. The $15 billion tunnel,

one of the great engineering feats of all time, is the first link between Britain and the Continent since the Ice Age.

So if you're coming to London from say, Rome, your Eurailpass will get you as far as the Chunnel. At that point, you can cross the English Channel aboard the *Eurostar,* and you'll receive a discount on your ticket. Once in England, you must use a separate BritRail pass or purchase a direct ticket to continue on to your destination.

Rail Europe (© **800/848-7245** in the U.S.; 800/361-RAIL in Canada; fax 800/432-1329; www.raileurope.com) sells direct-service tickets on the *Eurostar* between Paris or Brussels and London. A one-way fare between Paris and London costs $279 in first class and $199 in second class.

In London, make reservations for ***Eurostar*** by calling © **0870/530-0003;** in Paris, call © **01/44-51-06-02;** and in the United States, it's © **800/ EUROSTAR** (www.eurostar.com). *Eurostar* trains arrive and depart from London's Waterloo Station, Paris's Gare du Nord, and Brussels's Central Station.

BY BUS (COACH)

Long-distance buses, called "motorcoaches" in Britain, are the least expensive means of reaching Scotland from England. Some 20 coach companies run services, mainly from London to Edinburgh or Glasgow. The major operators are **National Express, Scottish Omnibuses, Western SMT, Stagecoach,** and **Eastern Scottish.** It takes 8 to 8½ hours to reach Edinburgh or Glasgow from London.

It's estimated that coach fares are about one-third of the rail charges for comparable trips to Scotland. Most coaches depart from London's **Victoria Coach Station.** If you're visiting between June and August, it's wise to make seat reservations at least 3 days in advance (4 or 5 days if possible). For timetables, available from London to Edinburgh, call **National Express**

(© **08705/808-080;** www.national express.com) or **Highland Country Buses** (© **01847/893-123**), or check on all other companies by calling © **08705/505-050.** Travel centers and travel agents also have details. Most travel agents in London sell coach seats and can make reservations for you.

If you're traveling by bus in the United Kingdom, consider purchasing a Britexpress Card, which entitles you to a 30% discount on National Express (England and Wales) and Caledonian Express (Scotland) buses. Contact a travel agent for details.

12 Getting Around Scotland

BY CAR

Scotland has many excellent roads, often "dual carriageways" (divided highways), as well as fast trunk roads, linking the Lowlands to the Highlands. In more remote areas, especially the islands of western Scotland, single-lane roads exist. Here caution in driving is most important. Passing places are provided.

However, many of the roads are unfenced, and livestock can be a serious problem when you're driving, either day or night. Drive slowly when you're passing through areas filled with sheep.

CAR RENTALS It's best to shop around, compare prices, and have a clear idea of your needs before you reserve a car. All companies give the best rates to those who reserve at least 2 business days in advance before leaving home and who agree to return the car to its point of origin, and some require drivers be at least 23 years old (in some cases 21). It's also an advantage to keep the car for at least a week, as opposed to 3 or 4 days. Be warned that all car rentals in the United Kingdom are slapped with a whopping 17.5% government tax known as VAT.

To rent a car in Scotland, you must present your passport and driver's license along with your deposit. No special British or international license is needed.

Rentals are available through **Avis** (© 800/331-1084; www.avis.com), **British Airways** (© 800/AIRWAYS; www.british-airways.com), **Budget**

(© 800/472-3325; www.budget.com), and **Hertz** (© 800/654-3001; www. hertz.com). **Kemwel Holiday Auto** (© 800/678-0678; www.kemwel. com) is among the cheapest and most reliable of the rental agencies. **Auto-Europe** (© 800/223-5555 in the U.S., or 0800/899893 in London; www. autoeurope.com) acts as a wholesale company for rental agencies in Europe.

Car-rental rates vary even more than airline fares. The price you pay depends on the size of the car, where and when you pick it up and drop it off, length of the rental period, where and how far you drive it, whether you purchase insurance, and a host of other factors. A few key questions could save you hundreds of dollars:

- Are weekend rates lower than weekday rates? Ask if the rate is the same for pickup Friday morning, for instance, as it is for Thursday night.
- Is a weekly rate cheaper than the daily rate? If you need to keep the car for 4 days, it may be cheaper to keep it for 5, even if you don't need it for that long.
- Does the agency assess a drop-off charge if you do not return the car to the same location where you picked it up? Is it cheaper to pick up the car at the airport compared to a downtown location?
- Are special promotional rates available? If you see an advertised price in your local newspaper, be sure to ask for that specific rate; otherwise you may be charged the

standard cost. The terms change constantly, and phone operators may not volunteer information.

- Are discounts available for members of AARP, AAA, frequent-flier programs, or trade unions? If you belong to any of these organizations, you are probably entitled to discounts of up to 30%.
- What is the cost of adding an additional driver's name to the contract?
- How many free miles are included in the price? Free mileage is often negotiable, depending on the length of your rental.
- How much does the rental company charge to refill your gas tank if you return with the tank less than full? Though most rental companies claim these prices are "competitive," fuel is almost always cheaper in town. Try to allow enough time to refuel the car yourself before returning it.

RENTAL INSURANCE Before you drive off in a rental car, be sure you're insured. Hasty assumptions about your personal auto insurance or a rental agency's additional coverage could end up costing you tens of thousands of dollars—even if you are involved in an accident that was clearly the fault of another driver.

U.S. drivers who already have their own car insurance are usually covered in the United States for loss of or damage to a rental car and liability in case of injury to any other party involved in an accident. But coverage probably doesn't extend outside the United States. Be sure to find out whether you are covered in England, whether your policy extends to all persons who will be driving the rental car, how much liability is covered in case an outside party is injured in an accident, and whether the type of vehicle you are renting is included under your contract. (Rental trucks, sport utility vehicles, and luxury vehicles such as the Jaguar may not be covered.)

Most **major credit cards** provide some degree of coverage as well—provided they are used to pay for the rental. Terms vary widely, however, so be sure to call your credit card company directly before you rent. But though they will cover damage to or theft of your rental, *credit cards will not cover liability* or the cost of injury to an outside party and/or damage to an outside party's vehicle. If you do not hold an insurance policy or if you are driving outside the United States, you may want to seriously consider purchasing additional liability insurance from your rental company. Be sure to check the terms, however: Some rental agencies only cover liability if the renter is not at fault.

Bear in mind that each credit card company has its own peculiarities. Most American Express Optima cards, for instance, do not provide any insurance. American Express does not cover vehicles valued at over $50,000 when new, such as luxury vehicles or vehicles built on a truck chassis. MasterCard does not provide coverage for loss, theft, or fire damage, and only covers collision if the rental period does not exceed 15 days. Call your own credit card company for details.

GASOLINE There are plenty of gas ("petrol") stations in the environs of Glasgow and Edinburgh. However, in remote areas they're often few and far between, and many are closed on Sunday. If you're planning a lot of Sunday driving in remote parts, always make sure your tank is full on Saturday.

Note that gasoline costs more in Britain than in North America, and to encourage energy saving the government has imposed a new 25% tax on gas.

DRIVING RULES & REQUIREMENTS In Scotland, *you drive on the left* and pass on the right. Road signs are clear and the international symbols are unmistakable.

It's a good idea to get a copy of the *British Highway Code,* available from almost any gas station or newsstand (called a "news stall" in Britain).

Warning: Pedestrian crossings are marked by striped lines (zebra striping) on the road; flashing lights near the curb indicate that drivers must stop and yield the right of way if a pedestrian has stepped out into the zebra zone to cross the street.

ROAD MAPS   The best road map, especially if you're trying to locate some obscure village, is *The Ordnance Survey Motor Atlas of Great Britain,* revised annually and published by Temple Press. It's available at most bookstores in Scotland. If you're in London and plan to head north to Scotland, go to W. & G. Foyle Ltd., 113 and 119 Charing Cross Rd. (© 020/7440-3225).

Other excellent maps include the *AAA Road Map of Scotland,* the *Collins Touring Map of Scotland,* and *Frommer's Road Atlas Europe.*

BREAKDOWNS   Membership in one of the two major auto clubs can be helpful: the **Automobile Association (AA)** at Norfolk House, Priestly Road, Basingstoke, Hampshire RG24 9NY (© 0870/600-0371), or the **Royal Automobile Club (RAC),** P.O. Box 700, Bristol, Somerset BS99 1RB (© 08705/722-722). You can join these clubs through your car-rental agent. (Members of AAA in the U.S. can enjoy reciprocity overseas.) There are roadside emergency telephone boxes about every mile along the motorways. If you don't see one, walk down the road for a bit to the blue-and-white marker with an arrow that points to the nearest box. The 24-hour number to call for the AA is © 0800/887-766; for the RAC, it's © 0800/828-282. In addition, you can call a police traffic unit that will contact either of the auto clubs on your behalf.

BY PLANE

The **British Airways Europe Airpass** allows travel in a continuous loop to between 3 and 12 cities on BA's European and domestic routes. Passengers must end their journey at the same point they began. If you book such a ticket (say, London to Manchester to Glasgow to Aberdeen to the Shetland Islands, with an eventual return to London), each segment of the itinerary costs about 40% to 50% less than if you'd booked it individually. The pass is available for travel to about a dozen of the most visited cities and regions of Britain, with discounted add-ons available to most of BA's destinations in Europe. It must be booked and paid for at least 7 days before departure from the States, and all sectors of the itinerary must be booked simultaneously. Some changes are permitted in flight dates (but not in the cities visited) after the ticket is issued. Check with BA (© 800/247-9297, or 08457/733-377 in the U.K.; www.britishairways.com) for full details.

Scotland's relatively small scale makes flights between many cities inconvenient and impractical. Although **British Airways** (see above) offers regular flights between Glasgow and Edinburgh, the excellent rail and

---

⌐Value Comparison Shop!

Many packages include airfare, accommodations, and a rental car with unlimited mileage. Compare these prices with the cost of booking airline tickets and renting a car separately to see if these offers are good deals.

Tips **Eurailpass Warning**

Note that your Eurailpass is *not* valid on trains in Great Britain.

highway connections usually deter most passengers from flying that route—unless their plane just happens to stop en route to other, more distant, points in Scotland. Frankly, except for visits to the far-distant Shetlands and Orkneys, we prefer to drive to all but the most inaccessible points. However, British Airways is by far the largest intra-Britain carrier since its recent merger with regional carriers Logan Airways and British Express. Aboard BA from Edinburgh, you can arrange flights to Inverness, Wick, Kirkwall (the Orkneys), and Lerwick (the Shetlands).

BY TRAIN

The cost of rail travel in Scotland can be quite low. Trains are generally punctual, carrying you across the country or at least to ferry terminals if you're exploring the islands. Timetables are available at all stations, and free timetables covering only certain regions are available at various stations. For £18 ($29), a **young person's rail card** (ages 16–25) is sold at major stations. Two passport-size photos are needed. It's estimated this card reduces all fares by one-third for 1 year.

If you plan to travel a great deal on the European railroads, it's worth securing a copy of the *Thomas Cook European Timetable of European Passenger Railroads.* It's available from **Forsyth Travel Library,** 44 S. Broadway, White Plains, NY 10601 (© **800/FORSYTH**), for $27.95 plus $4.95 priority airmail postage in the United States or plus $2 (U.S.) for shipments to Canada. You can also find the timetable at major travel bookstores.

The greatest rail guide in Scotland is aboard **The Royal Scotsman,** one of the most luxurious trains in the world—called "a country house hotel on wheels." The train passes by ancient mountains and mysterious lochs, through glens and across villages as you live in sumptuous surroundings. It's like being the guest at a private party. The train carries only a maximum of 36 guests at one time, each passenger enjoying plenty of space. Plush beds and opulent bathrooms are the order of the day. The classic tour calls for 4 nights aboard and is the most popular, as this journey goes from the panoramic Southern Highlands to the more rugged grandeur of the Western Highlands. A superb cuisine and a long list of fine wines and choice malt whiskies is another reason to hop aboard.

For information on rail travel in Scotland, contact **ScotRail,** Caledonian Chambers, 87 Union St., Glasgow G1 3TA, Scotland (© **0845/755-0033**).

BRITRAIL TRAVEL PASSES

If you're traveling anywhere in the United Kingdom, consider purchasing a **BritRail Classic Pass**. These passes allow you to travel for a consecutive number of days for a flat rate. In first class, adults pay £178 ($285) for 4 days, £253 ($405) for 8 days, £381 ($609) for 15 days, £481 ($769) for 22 days, and £572 ($915) for 1 month. In second class, fares are £118 ($189) for 4 days, £168 ($269) for 8 days, £253 ($405) for 15 days, £322 ($515) for 22 days, and £381 ($609) for 1 month. Senior citizens (60 and over) qualify for discounts in first class travel: It's £153 ($245) for 4 days, £216 ($345) for 8 days, £324 ($519) for 15 days, £412 ($659) for 22 days, and £487 ($779) for 1 month. Passengers under 26 qualify for a **Youth**

Pass: £97 ($155) for 4 days, £137 ($219) for 8 days, £178 ($285) for 15 days, £224 ($359) for 22 days, and £268 ($429) for 1 month. One child (5–15) can travel free with each adult or senior pass by requesting the BritRail Family Pass. Additional children pay half the regular adult fare.

BritRail Passes allow unlimited travel in England, Scotland, and Wales on any British rail scheduled train over the whole of the network during the validity of the pass without restrictions. **BritRail Euro Consecutive Pass** is ideal if you plan to hop on and off the train. A typical fare of 8 days of travel costs £253 ($405) in first class, £168 ($269) in standard class. The more versatile pass is **BritRail Europe FlexiPass** allowing you to travel where you want. It costs £324 ($519) for 8 days of travel in first class or £218 ($349) in standard class. Discounts are granted to seniors, and children (ages 5 to 15) pay half the adult fare. For the **BritRail Family Pass,** you can purchase any adult or senior BritRail Pass which allows one child (ages 5 to 15) to travel for free according to the same limitations as the adult fare.

To call BritRail in the United States, dial ✆ **877/677-1066.** The fax is 877/477-1066. On the web. BritRail Passes and vacation packages are presented at www.britrail.net and www.BritainSecrets.com.

TRAVELPASSES FOR SCOTLAND

If you plan to tour throughout the United Kingdom, one of the above BritRail passes might be appropriate. If you focus intensively on Scotland, however, a BritRail pass might not be adequate. The Scottish Tourist Authorities offer the **Freedom of Scotland Travelpass,** with unlimited transportation on trains and most ferries throughout Scotland and discounts for bus travel. It includes access to obscure bus routes to almost forgotten hamlets, free rides on ferries operated by Caledonian MacBrayne,

---

Getting Your VAT Refund

You can get a VAT refund if you shop at stores that participate in the Retail Export Scheme. (Signs are posted in the window.) When you make a purchase, show your passport and request a Retail Export Scheme form (VAT 407) and a stamped, pre-addressed envelope. Show the VAT form and your sales receipt to British Customs when you leave the country—they may also ask to see the merchandise. After Customs has stamped it, mail the form back to the shop in the envelope provided *before you leave the country.* Your VAT refund will be mailed to you.

Remember: Keep your VAT forms with your passport; pack your purchases in a carry-on bag so you'll have them handy; and allow yourself enough time at your departure point to find a mailbox.

Several readers have reported a VAT refund scam. You must get the refund forms from the retailer on the spot. (Don't leave the store without one.) Some merchants allegedly tell customers they can get a refund form at the airport on their way out of the country. *This is not true.* The form must be completed by the retailer on the spot, or you won't get a refund later.

For information, contact **Global Refund,** 707 Summer St., Stamford, CT 06901 (✆ **800/566-9828;** fax 203/674-8709; www.globalrefund).

and discounted fares with P&O Scottish Lines. The ferries connect to the Western Islands, the islands of the Clyde, and the historic Orkneys.

The Travelpass covers all the Scottish rail network and is usable from Carlisle on the western border of England and Scotland and from Berwick-upon-Tweed on the eastern Scottish border. In addition, if you have to fly into London and want to go straight to Scotland from there, a reduced rate is available for a round-trip ticket between London and Edinburgh or Glasgow for Travelpass holders.

The Travelpass is available for 4 days' travel over an 8-day period for £87 ($139); 8 days' travel over a 15-day period for £112 ($179); and 12 days' travel over a 15-day period for £137 ($219). When you validate the pass at the beginning of the journey, you'll get a complete packet of rail, bus, and ferry schedules. For more information, contact **BritRail** (see above).

BY BUS (COACH)

No doubt about it, the cheapest means of transport from London to Scotland is the bus (coach). It's also the least expensive means of travel within Scotland.

All major towns have a **local bus service,** and every tourist office can provide details about half- or full-day bus excursions to scenic highlights. If you want to explore a particular area, you can often avail yourself of an economical bus pass. If you're planning to travel extensively in Scotland, see the Freedom of Scotland Travelpass, described above.

Many adventurous travelers like to explore the country on one of the **postal buses,** which carry not only mail but also a limited number of passengers to rural areas. Ask at any local post office for details. A general timetable is available at the head post office in Edinburgh.

Scottish CityLink Coaches are a good bet. They link the major cities (Glasgow and Edinburgh) with the two most popular tourist centers, Inverness and Aviemore. Travel is fast and prices are low. For example, it takes only 3 hours to reach Aviemore from Edinburgh, and Inverness is just 3½ hours from Edinburgh. A direct Scottish CityLink overnight coach makes the run from London to Aviemore and Inverness at reasonable fares.

Coaches offer many other popular runs, including links between Glasgow and Fort William, Inverness and Ullapool, and Glasgow and Oban. For details, contact **Rapsons,** Farraline Park, Inverness (☎ **01463/710-555;** www.rapsons.co.uk), or **Scottish CityLink,** Buchanan Street Bus Station, Glasgow (☎ **08705/505-050;** www.citylink.co.uk).

BY FERRY

You can use a variety of special excursion fares to reach Scotland's islands. For the Clyde and Western Isles, contact **Caledonian MacBrayne** (☎ **01475/650-100,** or 01475/650-288 for brochures; www.calmac.co.uk); for the Orkneys and Shetlands, **NorthLink Orkney & Shetland Ferries,** Ferry Terminal, Stromness, Orkney (☎ **01856/851-144**).

Caledonian MacBrayne, operating 30 ferries in all, sails to 23 Hebridean and all Clyde Islands. The fares, times of departure, and even accommodation suggestions are in a special book, *Ferry Guide to 23 Scottish Islands.* There are reasonably priced fares for vehicles and passengers through a "Go As You Please" plan, a kind of island hopscotch program offering a choice of 24 preplanned routes at a discount off the cost of individual tickets. Tickets are valid for 1 month and can be used in either direction for one trip on each leg of the tour. Cyclists can take their bikes aboard free on some routes.

13 Recommended Books

TRAVEL   Since the Middle Ages, English writers have been fascinated by the idiosyncrasies of their northern neighbors. Without contest, the most influential (and perhaps the most curmudgeonly) of these was Samuel Johnson, whose usually negative impressions were recorded by Scottish-born James Boswell in *James Boswell's Journal of a Tour to the Hebrides with Samuel Johnson* (1773, reprinted by Littlefield, Adams in 1978). In the same vein is Donald E. Hayden's *Wordsworth's Travels in Scotland* (University of Oklahoma Press, 1988).

BIOGRAPHY   *Burns: A Biography of Robert Burns,* by James MacKay (Mainstream, 1993), is one of the best works devoted to Scotland's national poet (1759–96), in that it often relies on primary source materials and not previously published information. The life of Burns is portrayed against the historical framework of 18th-century Scotland. A Burns scholar, MacKay defends the author of *Tam o' Shanter* and *Auld Lang Syne* against previously published charges that he was a drunkard and a rake.

Today's most famous Scot is revealed in a biography, *Sean Connery: From 007 to Hollywood Icon,* by Andrew Yule (Fine, 1992), who traces the legendary actor's rise from humble origins in Edinburgh to later success "escaping bondage" in such films as *Rising Sun.* Like all true Scotsmen, Connery is said to have a fascinated interest in golf (playing it) and money (not spending it). Scottish-American readers may find the early years of growing up in Edinburgh during the Depression the most interesting.

Robert Louis Stevenson: A Biography, by Frank McLynn (Random House, 1994), a massive book of 576 pages, maintains that the frail adventurer and author of *The Strange Case of Dr. Jekyll and Mr. Hyde* was Scotland's greatest writer. The book documents the tragic life of the writer who suffered from "bloody jack" (a hemorrhaging consumption) and was to die at 44.

FICTION   *Morning Tide,* by Neil Gunn (republished by Walker, 1993), was actually written in the 1930s, and helps explain why Gunn (1891–1973) is considered perhaps the master of modern Scottish fiction. It's a straightforward account of a boy's coming of age in a small fishing village in Scotland in the last years of Victoria's reign.

MUSIC & LORE   The myth and lore of Scotland has always been best expressed in its oral and musical traditions. David D. Buchan's *The Ballad and the Folk* (Routledge and Kegan Paul, 1972) and John Pinkerton's *Select Scottish Ballads* (1783; edited and reprinted by AMS Publishers, 1982), both of which offer poetic and charming insights into a still-thriving art form. You might also consult Roger Fiske's *Scotland in Music* (Cambridge University Press, 1983). Also useful is George B. Douglas and Richard Dorson's *Scottish Fairy and Folk Tales* (a 1977 reprint by Ayer & Co. of a 1901 classic).

HUMOR   Scottish humor, whose innuendo was always credited for making life on the heath and Highlands more bearable, can be better understood through Julie Macdonald's *Scottish Proverbs* (edited by John and Jean Zug, and published in 1987 by Penfield), and W. B. Burnett's *Scotland Laughing* (Albyn Press, 1955). Broader in its scope and self-satire is Malcolm Lawson-Paul's *Clan Chowder: The MacTanistry Papers Embellished* (Putnam, 1983), a compilation of the kinds of jokes and lampoons that spread with Scottish emigrations throughout the British Empire.

HISTORY   *Scotland: The Story of a Nation,* by Magnus Magnusson (Atlantic Monthly, 2001), focuses on royalty and warfare, and attempts to depict Scotland from the Stone Age to the present millennium. It's a flawed work and much of it reads like a swashbuckling tale of great battles and heroes, but the book punctures a lot of myths, particularly those given wide publicity in Shakespeare's *Macbeth* and the film *Braveheart. Stone Voices: The Search for Scotland,* by Neal Ascherson (Hill & Wang, 2003), is a search for the national character of Scotland, although the author finds it hard to pin down. The book is a series of anecdotes and reflections. Ascherson draws some striking contrasts between England and Scotland. Good historical overviews of Scotland, beginning with its earliest prehistory, are Michael Jenner's *Scotland Through the Ages* (Viking Penguin, 1990), Rosalind Mitchison's *A History of Scotland* (Methuen, 1970), and W. Croft Dickinson and George S. Pryde's *A New History of Scotland* (Nelson, 1961). Also insightful, perhaps because of its authorship by a famous Scots novelist, is Alistair Maclean's *Alistair Maclean Introduces Scotland* (edited by Alastair Dunnett; McGraw Hill, 1972).

Dealing in detail with the famous personalities of the 16th century is Alison Plowden's *Elizabeth Tudor and Mary Stewart: Two Queens in One Isle* (B&N Imports, 1984). Antonia Fraser's *Mary, Queen of Scots* (Dell, 1984) is a highly readable biography. Also by Antonia Fraser is a short, very subjective, and exceedingly charming anthology, *Scottish Love Poems: A Personal Anthology* (Peter Bedrik Books, 1989).

Other historical eras are analyzed by Iain Moncreiffe in *The Highland Clans* (Potter, 1968), and by Richard B. Sher and Jeffrey R. Smitten in *Scotland and America in the Age of Enlightenment* (Princeton University Press, 1990). Also interesting is David Daiche's *A Hotbed of Genius: The Scottish Enlightenment 1730-1790* (Columbia University Press, 1987), and Henry Hamilton's *The Industrial Revolution in Scotland* (Littlefield, Adams, 1966).

James Kerr's *Fiction Against History: Scott as Storyteller* (Cambridge University Press, 1989) explores the fiction as well as the sense of historical destiny of Scotland's "national troubadour," Sir Walter Scott. In her book *Burns and Tradition* (University of Illinois Press, 1984), Mary Ellen Brown explores the values of Robert Burns and the influence upon him of Scotland's lore and history.

The more recent Scottish experience, particularly the events engendered by the flow of black gold from the North Sea, is carefully described in T. M. Lewis and J. H. McNicoll's *North Sea Oil and Scotland's Economic Prospects* (Crown Helm Publications, 1978). In the same vein is Charlotte Lythe and Madhavi Mamjudar's *The Renaissance of the Scottish Economy* (G. Allen & Unwin Co., 1982). Appropriate for anyone interested in European history just before, during, and after World War II is T. Christopher Smout's *A History of the Scottish People 1930-1950* (Yale University Press, 1986).

CLANS & THEIR SYMBOLS Finally, on a purely decorative and symbolic level, but with rich interest for anyone tracing genealogical roots, is Robert Bain's *The Class and Tartans of Scotland,* enlarged and reedited by Margaret MacDougall, with heraldic advice supplied by P. E. Stewart-Blacker and with dozens of illustrations (Fontana-Collins, 1985). Somewhat shorter and more succinct is *Tartans,* (edited and published by the Belvedere Editions of Rizzoli International, 1989).

FAST FACTS: Scotland

American Express There's an office at 139 Princes St. in Edinburgh (© 0131/225-7881); hours are Monday through Friday from 9am to 5:30pm and Saturday from 9am to 4pm. Another office is at 115 Hope St. in Glasgow (© 0141/226-3077); it's open Monday through Friday from 8:30am to 5:30pm, Saturday from 9am to noon (9am–4pm in June and July).

Area Codes The country code for Britain is **44**. The area code for Edinburgh is **0131**; for Glasgow **0141**.

Business Hours With many, many exceptions, business hours are Monday through Friday from 9am to 5pm. In general, stores are open Monday through Saturday from 9am to 5:30pm. In country towns, there is usually an early closing day (often on Wed or Thurs), when the shops close at 1pm.

Car Rentals See "Getting Around Scotland," earlier in this chapter.

Climate See "When to Go," earlier in this chapter.

Currency See "Money," earlier in this chapter.

Customs See "Entry Requirements & Customs," earlier in this chapter.

Documents Required See "Entry Requirements & Customs," earlier in this chapter.

Drug Laws Great Britain is becoming increasingly severe in enforcing drug laws. People arrested for possession of even tiny quantities of marijuana have been deported, forced to pay stiff fines, or sentenced to jail for 2 to 7 years. Possession of drugs like heroin and cocaine carries even more stringent penalties.

Drugstores In Britain, they're called "chemists." Every police station in the country has a list of emergency chemists. Dial "0" (zero) and ask the operator for the local police, who will give you the name of one nearest you.

Electricity British electricity is 240 volts AC (50 cycles), roughly twice the voltage in North America, which is 115 to 120 volts AC (60 cycles). American plugs don't fit British wall outlets. Always bring suitable transformers and/or adapters—if you plug an American appliance directly into a European electrical outlet without a transformer, you'll destroy your appliance and possibly start a fire. Tape recorders, VCRs, and other devices with motors intended to revolve at a fixed number of revolutions per minute probably won't work properly even with transformers.

Embassies & Consulates All embassies are in London. There's a **U.S. Consulate** in Edinburgh at 3 Regent Terrace (© 0131/556-8315), open Monday through Friday from 1 to 4pm. All other nationals have to use London to conduct their business: The **Canadian High Commission** is at MacDonald House, 1 Grosvenor Sq., London W1K 4AB (© 020/7258-6600), open Monday through Friday from 8am to 4pm. The **Australian High Commission** is at the Strand, London WC2B 4LI (© 020/7379-4334), open Monday through Friday from 9:30am to 3:30pm. The **New Zealand High Commission** is at New Zealand House, 80 Haymarket at Pall Mall, London SW1Y 4TQ (© 020/7930-8422), open Monday through Friday from 9am to 5pm. The **Irish Embassy** is at 17 Grosvenor Place, London SW1X 7HR (© 020/7235-2171), open Monday through Friday from 9:30am to 1pm and 2:15 to 5pm.

Emergencies For police, fire, or ambulance, dial ℂ **999.** Give your name, address, phone number, and the nature of the emergency. Misuse of the 999 service will result in a heavy fine (cardiac arrest, yes; dented fender, no).

Holidays See "When to Go," earlier in this chapter.

Information See "Visitor Information," earlier in this chapter, and the individual city/regional chapters that follow.

Legal Aid Your consulate, embassy, or high commission (see above) will give you advice if you run into trouble. They can advise you of your rights and even provide a list of attorneys (for which you'll have to pay if services are used), but they can't interfere on your behalf in the legal processes of Great Britain. For questions about American citizens arrested abroad, including ways of getting money to them, call the **Citizens Emergency Center of the Office of Special Consulate Services,** in Washington, D.C. (ℂ **202/647-5225**). Other nationals can go to their nearest consulate or embassy.

Liquor Laws The legal drinking age is 18. Children under 16 aren't allowed in pubs, except in certain rooms, and then only when accompanied by a parent or guardian. Don't drink and drive; the penalties are stiff. Basically, you can get a drink from 11am to 11pm, but this can vary widely, depending on the discretion of the local tavern owner. Certain licensed premises can have hours extended in some areas up to 4am, on a "local need" basis. Not all pubs are open on Sunday; those that are generally stay open from noon to 3pm and 7 to 10:30 or 11pm. Restaurants are allowed to serve liquor during these hours, but only to people who are dining on the premises. The law allows 30 minutes for "drinking-up time." A meal, incidentally, is defined as "substantial refreshment." And you have to eat and drink sitting down. In hotels, liquor may be served from 11am to 11pm to both guests and nonguests; after 11pm, only guests may be served.

Mail Post offices and sub-post offices are open Monday through Friday from 9am to 5:30pm and Saturday from 9:30am to noon.

Sending an airmail letter to North America costs 45p (70¢) for 10 grams (0.35 oz.), and postcards require a 40p (65¢) stamp. British mailboxes are painted red and carry a royal coat of arms. All post offices accept parcels for mailing, provided they are properly and securely wrapped.

Newspapers & Magazines Each major Scottish city publishes its own newspaper. All newsagents (newsstands) carry the major London papers as well. In summer, you can generally pick up a copy of the *International Herald Tribune*, published in Paris, along with the European editions of *USA Today, Time,* and *Newsweek*.

Passports **For Residents of the United States:** Whether you're applying in person or by mail, you can download passport applications from the U.S. State Department website at **http://travel.state.gov**. For general information, call the **National Passport Agency** (ℂ **202/647-0518**). To find your regional passport office, either check the U.S. State Department website or call the **National Passport Information Center** (ℂ **900/225-5674**); the fee is 55¢ per minute for automated information and $1.50 per minute for operator-assisted calls.

For Residents of Canada: Passport applications are available at travel agencies throughout Canada or from the central **Passport Office,** Department of Foreign Affairs and International Trade, Ottawa, ON K1A 0G3 (© 800/567-6868; www.dfait-maeci.gc.ca/passport).

For Residents of the United Kingdom: To pick up an application for a standard 10-year passport (5-yr. passport for children under 16), visit your nearest passport office, major post office, or travel agency or contact the **United Kingdom Passport Service** at © 0870/521-0410 or search its website at www.ukpa.gov.uk.

For Residents of Ireland: You can apply for a 10-year passport at the **Passport Office,** Setanta Centre, Molesworth Street, Dublin 2 (© 01/671-1633; www.irlgov.ie/iveagh). Those under age 18 and over 65 must apply for a €12 3-year passport. You can also apply at 1A South Mall, Cork (© 021/272-525) or at most main post offices.

For Residents of Australia: You can pick up an application from your local post office or any branch of Passports Australia, but you must schedule an interview at the passport office to present your application materials. Call the **Australian Passport Information Service** at © 131-232, or visit the government website at www.passports.gov.au.

For Residents of New Zealand: You can pick up a passport application at any New Zealand Passports Office or download it from their website. Contact the **Passports Office** at © 0800/225-050 in New Zealand or 04/474-8100, or log on to www.passports.govt.nz.

Pets Great Britain has finally eased a 100-year-old mandatory pet quarantine, but rigid requirements are still in place. Now pets need no longer fear a long separation from their Britain-bound families if they pass several tests and can wait long enough. The animal must also be coming from a country that is approved by Britain. All countries in the European Union such as Germany, Switzerland, Austria, Spain, Italy, and France are participants in the PETS program, but the United States is not. For information, check out www.defra.gov.uk/animalh/quarantine/index.htm.

Police The best source of help and advice in emergencies is the police. For non-life-threatening situations, dial "0" (zero) and ask for the police, or **999** for emergencies. If the local police can't assist, they'll have the address of a person who can. Losses, thefts, and other crimes should be reported immediately.

Restrooms Public toilets are clean and often have an attendant. Hotels can be used, but they discourage nonguests. Garages (filling stations) don't always have facilities for the use of customers. There's no need to tip, except to a hotel attendant.

Safety See "Staying Safe," earlier in this chapter.

Taxes There's no local sales tax. However, Great Britain imposes a standard value-added tax (VAT) of 17.5%. Hotel rates and meals in restaurants are taxed 17.5%; the extra charge will show up on your bill unless otherwise stated. This can be refunded if you shop at stores that participate in the Retail Export Scheme (signs are posted in the window); see "Getting Your VAT Refund," earlier in this chapter.

The departure tax for leaving Britain is £22 ($35) for passengers flying worldwide, including the United States, and £11 ($18) for flights within Britain and the European Union. This tax is accounted for in your ticket.

As part of an energy-saving scheme, the British government has also added a special 25% tax on gasoline ("petrol").

Telephone To call England from North America, dial **011** (international code), **44** (Britain's country code), the local area codes (usually three or four digits and found in every phone number we've given in this book), and the seven-digit local phone number. The local area codes found throughout this book all begin with "0"; you drop the "0" if you're calling from outside Britain, but you need to dial it along with the area code if you're calling from another city or town within Britain. For calls within the same city or town, the local number is all you need.

For **directory assistance** in London, dial **142;** for the rest of Britain, **192.**

There are three types of public pay phones: those taking only coins, those accepting only phonecards (called Cardphones), and those taking both phonecards and credit cards. At coin-operated phones, insert your coins before dialing. The minimum charge is 10p (15¢).

Phone cards are available in four values£2 ($3.20), £4 ($6.40), £10 ($16), and £20 ($32)—and are reusable until the total value has expired. Cards can be purchased from newsstands and post offices. Finally, the credit-call pay phone operates on credit cards—Access (MasterCard), Visa, American Express, and Diners Club—and is most common at airports and large railway stations.

To make an international call from Britain, dial the international access code **(00),** then the country code, then the area code, and finally the local number. Or call through one of the following long-distance access codes: **AT&T USA Direct** (📞 1800/CALLATT), **Canada Direct** (📞 0800/890016), **Australia** (📞 0800/890061), and **New Zealand** (📞 0800/890064). Common country codes are: USA and Canada, **1**; Australia, **61**; New Zealand, **64**; and South Africa, **27.**

For calling **collect** or if you need an international operator, dial **155.**

Caller beware: Some hotels routinely add outrageous surcharges onto phone calls made from your room. Inquire before you call! It'll be a lot cheaper to use your own calling-card number or to find a pay phone.

Time England follows Greenwich mean time (5 hours ahead of Eastern Standard Time), with British summertime lasting (roughly) from the end of March to the end of October. For most of the year, including summer, Britain is 5 hours ahead of the time observed in the eastern United States. Because of different daylight-savings-time practices in the two nations, there's a brief period (about a week) in autumn when Britain is only 4 hours ahead of New York, and a brief period in spring when it's 6 hours ahead of New York.

Tipping For **cab drivers,** add about 10% to 15% to the fare as shown on the meter. If the driver personally unloads or loads your luggage, add 50p (80¢) per bag.

Hotel **porters** get 75p ($1.20) per bag even if you have only one small suitcase. Hall porters are tipped only for special services. **Maids** receive £1

($1.60) per day. In top-ranked hotels, the **concierge** often submits a separate bill, showing charges for newspapers and the like; if he or she has been particularly helpful, tip extra.

Hotels often add a **service charge** of 10% to 15% to bills. In smaller B&Bs, the tip isn't likely to be included. Therefore, tip for special services, such as the waiter who serves you breakfast. If several people have served you in a B&B, a 10% to 15% charge will be added to the bill and divided among the staff.

In **restaurants** and **nightclubs**, a 15% service charge is added to the bill. To that, add another 3% to 5%, depending on the quality of the service. **Waiters** in deluxe restaurants and clubs are accustomed to the extra 5%, which means you'll end up tipping 20%. If that seems excessive, remember that the initial service charge reflected in the fixed price is distributed among all the help. **Sommeliers** (wine stewards) get about £1 ($1.60) per bottle of wine served. Tipping in **pubs** is not common, although in cocktail bars the waiter or barmaid usually gets about £1 ($1.60) per round of drinks.

Barbers and **hairdressers** expect 10% to 15%. **Tour guides** expect £2 ($3.20), but it's not mandatory. **Petrol station attendants** are rarely tipped. **Theater ushers** also don't expect tips.

Water Tap water is considered safe to drink throughout Scotland.

3

The Active Vacation Planner

If you're headed to Scotland to enjoy the outdoors, you can get guidance from the **Scottish Sports Council,** Caledonian House, South Gyle, Edinburgh EH12 9DQ (℃ **0131/317-7200;** fax 0131/317-7202), open Monday through Friday from 9am to 5pm. It can supply names of nature areas, playing fields, prices, and facilities, as well as send a copy of *Arena,* a bulletin packed with advice on sporting programs and facilities.

1 Teeing Off: Golfing in Scotland

Although golf has become Scotland's pride, the sport hasn't always been so well received. Monks around St. Andrews weren't applauded when they diverted themselves from a schedule of felling trees and praying to play *gowff,* and James I and James II rather churlishly issued edicts prohibiting its practice. Despite that, by the mid-1700s the game was firmly entrenched in Scotland and viewed as a bucolic oddity by Englishmen chasing after the hounds in the milder climes to the south.

Scotland has more than 440 golf courses, many of them municipal courses open to everyone. Some are royal and ancient (such as St. Andrews), others modern and hip. An example of a well-received relative newcomer is the Loch Lomond course in the Trossachs, established as a private club in 1993. Although they lie as far north as Sutherland, only 6 degrees south of the Arctic Circle, most courses are in the Central Belt, stretching from Stirling down to Edinburgh and Glasgow.

Fortunately, you don't need to lug a complete set of golf clubs across the Atlantic if you don't want to, because many courses rent full or half sets. If you're female or plan on playing golf with someone who is, be aware that some courses are restricted to men only, banning women completely or limiting them to designated days. Despite this tradition-bound holdover from another era, women's golf thrives in Scotland, with about 33,000 members in the Scottish Ladies Golfing Association. The Ladies British Open Amateur Championship was first held in 1893. (The U.S. equivalent was first held in 1895.) Contact Mrs. L. H. Park, Secretary, **Scottish Ladies Golfing Association** (for information on tournaments or finding women golf partners), or Ian Hume, Esq., Secretary, at the **Scottish National Golf Centre,** Drumoig, Leuchars, St. Andrews, Fife KY16 0DW (℃ **01382/549-500;** fax 01382/549-510). Sharing offices with the Scottish Ladies Golfing Association is the **Scottish Golf Union,** established in 1920 to foster and maintain a high standard of amateur golf in Scotland.

Any serious golfer who will be in Scotland for a long stay should consider joining a local club. Membership makes it easier to get coveted tee times, and attending or competing in a local club's tournaments can be both fun and sociable. If you won't be staying long, you might not bother, but remember to bring a letter from a golf club in your home country—it can open a lot of doors otherwise closed to the general public.

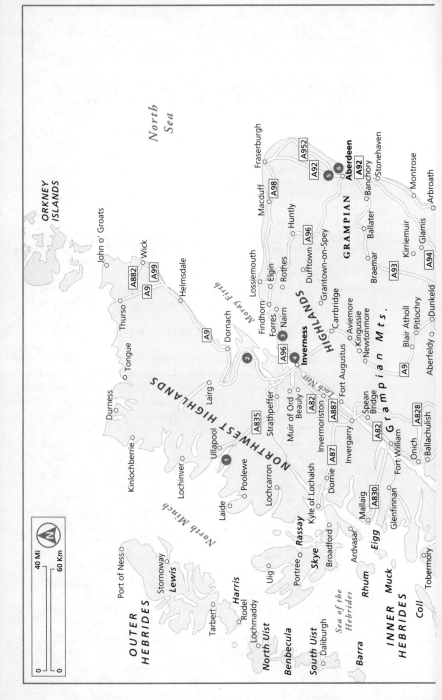

Access to many private clubs can be dicey, however, particularly those boasting so much tradition that waiting lists for tee-off times can stretch on for up to a year in advance. You can always stay in a hotel (Gleneagles or Turnberry) that has its own course, thereby guaranteeing the availability of tee times. Or you can arrange a golf tour (see below).

Abandon forever any hope of balmy tropical weather, azure skies, and lush fairways. Scotland's rains and fogs produce an altogether different kind of golf-related aesthetic, one buffeted by coastal winds, sometimes torn by gales and storms, and (in some places) accented only with salt-tolerant tough grasses and wind-blown stunted trees and shrubs like gorse and heather.

Knowing a term or two in advance might help in picking your golf course. The Scots make a strong distinction between their two types of courses: links and upland. **Links courses** nestle into the sandy terrain of coastal regions, and although years of cultivation have rendered their fairways and putting greens emerald colored, there's a vague sense that eons ago the terrain was submerged beneath the water. Links courses are among the famous names in Scotland and include Royal Troon, Turnberry, Prestwick, North Berwick, and Glasgow Gailes. All links courses are on or near the sea. **Upland courses,** by contrast, are based inland and invariably consist of hilly terrain. They're usually drier and less windy than links courses. Nonetheless, it rains a lot in Scotland, so a sweater and raingear are recommended for *all* courses. Examples of upland courses are Gleneagles, Loch Lomond, and Pitlochry.

GOLF TOURS

Access for nonmembers to the country's maze of golf courses hasn't always been possible. All that changed in 1988, however, with the establishment of **Golf International,** 14 E. 38th St., New York, NY 10016 (© **800/833-1389** or 212/986-9176; www.golfinternational.com), which maintains a branch office in St. Andrews, the ivy-clad *sanctum sanctorum* of the golfing world. The company caters to golfers from moderate to advanced levels and, against hitherto impossible odds, will guarantee its clients starting times at 40 or so of Scotland's most sought-after courses, including St. Andrews, Carnoustie, Royal Troon, Prestwick, and Gullane.

Potential clients, in self-organized groups of 2 to 12, produce a wish list of the courses they'd like to play. Starting times are prearranged (sometimes rigidly) with an ease that an individual traveler or even a travel agent would find impossible. Packages can be arranged for anywhere from 7 to 14 days (the average is about 7 days) and can include as much or as little golf, at as many courses, as you want. Weekly prices, including hotels, breakfasts, car rentals, greens fees, and the services of a greeter and helpmate at the airport on arrival, range from £1,538 to £3,347 ($2,461–$5,355) per person. Discounted airfares to Scotland can also be arranged.

Other companies specializing in golf tours are **Adventures in Golf,** 22 Greeley St., Suite 7, Merrimack, NH 03054 (© **603/424-7320**); **Classic Golf & Leisure,** 75706 McLachlin Circle, Palm Desert, CA 92211 (© **760/772-2560;** www.classic-golf.com); **ITC Golf Tours,** 4134 Atlantic Ave., Suite 205, Long Beach, CA 90807 (© **800/257-4981** or 562/595-6905; www.itcgolf-africatours.com/golftour.html); **Perry Golf,** 8302 Dunwoody Place, Suite 305, Atlanta, GA 30350 (© **800/344-5257** or 770/641-9696; www.perrygolf.com); and **Tayleur Mayde Golf Tours,** 21 Castle Street, Edinburgh EH2 3DA (© **800/847-8064;** www.tayleurmayde.com).

A Beginner's Warning

Neophytes unfamiliar with the rules of the game simply aren't allowed to play the country's most legendary golf courses. Many courses will want evidence of your familiarity with the game before you're allowed on the links. Depending on the setting and the season, this could include a letter from your club back home citing your ability and experience, or visual proof that you've mastered a basically sound swing and an understanding of golf-related etiquette.

THE CLASSIC COURSES

For more details on these fabled golf courses, refer to "The Best Golf" in chapter 1. In addition to the big names below, many additional courses are listed in the appropriate destination chapters that follow.

The **Carnoustie Golf Links,** Links Parade, Carnoustie, Angus (© **01241/ 853-789;** fax 01241/852-720), has a par of 72. This 6,941-yard (6,316m) championship course requires the use of a caddy, costing £34 ($54) for 18 holes. As with most championship courses, electric golf carts aren't allowed, but you can rent a trolley for £4 ($6.40) per round. Greens fees are £82 ($131), and club rentals, available at Simpson's Golf Shop, 6 Links Parade (© **01241/854-477**), cost £15 ($24).

The par-72 **Old Course, St. Andrews,** Golf Place, St. Andrews, Fife (© **01334/466-666**), is a 6,566-yard (5,975m) 18-hole course. Golf was first played here around 1400, and it's billed as the Home of Golf. This fabled course hosted the 2000 British Open, and witnessed history when Tiger Woods became the youngest golfer to complete a grand slam (and only the fifth golfer to ever perform the feat). Greens fees are £20 to £105 ($32–$168), a caddy costs £40 ($64) plus tip, and clubs rent for £20 to £30 ($32–$48) per round. Electric carts are not allowed, and you can rent a trolley on afternoons only between May and September for £3 ($4.80). Reservations must be made in advance.

The 18-hole **Royal Dornoch Golf Club,** Dornoch, Sutherland (© **01862/ 810-219**), 64.5km (40 miles) north of Inverness, has a par of 70. At this 6,185-yard (5,628m) course, the greens fees are £70 ($112) Monday through Saturday and £85 ($136) on Sunday (members only). Golf club and trolley rentals are £25 to £35 ($40–$56) and £4 ($6.40), respectively. Caddy service is available for £40 ($64) plus tip.

The par-71 **Royal Troon Golf Club,** Craigend Road, Troon, Ayrshire (© **01292/311-555;** fax 01292/318-204), has one of the largest courses in Scotland, with 7,097 yards (6,458m) of playing area. The greens fees of £170 ($272) for a day include a buffet lunch and two 18-hole sets. For one round of play, a trolley rents for £4.50 ($7.20) and a caddy £30 ($48); club rental is £25 ($40) per round or £40 ($64) per day.

The **Turnberry Hotel Golf Courses,** Ayrshire (© **01655/331-069;** fax 01655/331-706), gives priority at its 6,971-yard (6,344m) par-70 course to guests of the hotel. The greens fees—£105 ($168) for guests and £130 to £175 ($208–$280) for nonguests—include 18 holes on the Ailsa course and an 18-hole round on the less-desirable Arran course. For one round, clubs rent for £40 ($64) and caddy service costs £30 ($48) plus tip. If you're not staying here, call in the morning to check on any unclaimed tee times—but it's a long shot.

2 Fishing

Anglers consider Scotland a paradise. Its fast-flowing rivers harbor Atlantic salmon (the king of all game fish). The rivers and numerous pristine lochs allow you to enjoy some of Europe's most beautiful scenery, along with the marvelous hospitality extended by its innkeepers. Note that permits for fishing (often arranged by your hotel) can be expensive. For one of the grand beats on the River Tay, a week's permit could run into hundreds of pounds. However, there are many lesser-known rivers where a club ticket costs only pounds a day.

The **Tweed** and the **Tay** are just two of the famous Scottish salmon rivers. In Perthshire, the Tay is the broadest and longest river in the country. The **Dee** is the famous salmon-fishing river of Aberdeenshire. The royal family fishes this river, and the queen herself has been seen casting from these banks. Other anglers prefer to fish the **Spey,** staying at one of the inns along the Malt Whisky Trail. Certain well-heeled fishermen travel every year to Scotland to fish in the lochs and rivers of the **Outer Hebrides.**

In general, Scotland's season for salmon fishing runs from late February until late October, but these dates vary from region to region.

TYPES OF FISHING

Here's a breakdown of terms you're likely to hear even before you cast your first line into the country's glittering waters:

COARSE FISHING   This means going after any species of freshwater fish except salmon and trout. Especially prized trophies, known for putting up a spirited fight, are carp, tench, pike, bream, roach, and perch. Because few lochs actually freeze during winter, the sport can be practiced throughout the year. Local tourist boards all over the country can provide advice.

GAME FISHING   Salmon and trout (brown, rainbow, or sea) are the most desired of the game fish and the ones that have inspired the image of a fly fisherman whipping a lure and line in serpentine arcs above a loch. Many vacationers dream of donning bulky rubber waders up to their waists and trying their luck in streams and freshwater lochs. Fly-fishing for salmon and trout is subject to seasonal controls and sometimes requires a permit. For details on game fishing, contact the **Salmon & Trout Association (Scottish Branch),** 10 Great Stuart St., Edinburgh EH3 7TN (✆ **01577/861-116;** www.salmon-trout.org).

SEA FISHING   This simply means fishing from a beach, a rocky shoreline, or a pier. Inshore fishing involves dropping a line into ocean waters within 5km (3 miles) of any Scottish coastline; deep-sea fishing is off a boat more than 5k (3 miles) offshore in a style made popular by cigar-chomping tycoons and Hemingway clones. Offshore waters have produced several species of shark, including porbeagle, thresher, mako, and blue shark. For information on what to expect

---

Fun Fact **Death Chimes for the Fox Hunt**

Some old-time Scots are rolling over in their graves, but the Scottish Parliament in 2002 outlawed traditional fox hunting with dogs in Scotland. The passage of the Protection of Wild Mammals Bill brings to an end a hunting tradition of centuries. A last ditch demonstration by fox hunters failed. Heavy fines or a 6-month prison sentence will be imposed on violators.

from deep offshore waters, contact the **Scottish Tourist Board,** 23 Ravelston Terrace, Edinburgh EH14 3TP (℃ **0131/332-2433;** www.visitscotland.com).

FISHING CLUBS

Getting permits and information on worthwhile places to fish is easier if you join one of the more than 380 fishing clubs headquartered in Scotland. (The oldest angling club in the world, the Ellem Fishing Club, was founded in Scotland in 1829.) Each of its activities is supervised by the **Scottish Anglers National Association** (℃ **01577/861-116**), which firmly believes that newcomers should learn at the side of the more experienced. Courses in the fine art of fishing are offered in or around Scotland. For details, contact the Scottish Tourist Board (see above).

We've recently discovered a fishing guide service, **Highland Rod & Reels,** that's ideal for Americans. Their headquarters (℃ **0145/673-992**), is near Glasgow, even though the service they provide blankets Scotland. You tell the people here where you want to go fishing, and for how long, and they'll arrange everything for you, from the accommodations to the boat, from the hotel to the licenses and gear. Scotland's brown trout, sea trout, and salmon are waiting for you.

3 Biking, Walking & Other Outdoor Pursuits

BIKING

Scotland is one of the most gorgeous settings in Europe for a bike trip, but note that bicycles are forbidden on most highways and trunk roads and on what the British call dual carriageways (divided highways). May, June, and September are the best months for cycling in spite of the often bad weather. Many of the narrow and scenic roads are likely to be overcrowded with cars in July and August. For the best biking routes, see chapter 1.

Your first source of information should be the **Scottish Cyclists Union,** which provides an annual handbook and a regular newsletter for members. It's also one of the most potent lobbying groups in Scotland for the inauguration and preservation of cyclists' byways. It distributes maps showing worthwhile bike routes and supports the publication of technical material of interest to cyclists. Nonmembers are welcome for a small fee. Contact Jim Riach, Executive Office, Scottish Cyclists Union, The Velodrome, Meadowbank Stadium, London Road, Edinburgh EH7 6AD (℃ **0131/652-0187;** fax 0131/661-0474; www.scuonline.org).

Although based in England, the **Cyclists Tourist Club,** Cotterell House, 69 Meadrow, Godalming, Surrey GU7 3HS (℃ **0870/873-0060;** fax 0870/873-0064; www.ctc.org.uk), offers details on cycling holidays in Scotland. Membership is £28.50 ($46) a year for adults and £10 ($16) for those 17 and under. A family of three or more can get a membership for £46 ($74). This organization will give advice on where to rent or buy a bike; it also offers free legal advice to members involved in cycle-related accidents and information on available medical insurance for members.

You may take your bike without restrictions on car and passenger ferries in Scotland. There's almost no case where it's necessary to make arrangements in advance. However, the transport of your bike is likely to cost £2 to £8 ($3.20–$13), plus the cost of your own passage.

The best biking trips in Scotland are offered by **Bespoke Highland Tours,** The Bothy, Camusdarach, Inverness PH39 4NT (℃ **01687/450-272**), and

Scottish Border Trails, Drummore, Venlaw High Road, Peebles EH45 8RL (✆ **01721/720-336;** fax 01721/723-004).

U.S.-based **Backroads,** 801 Cedar St., Berkeley, CA 94710 (✆ **800/GO-ACTIVE** [462-2848] or 510/527-1555; www.backroads.com), offers a couple of weeklong biking tours through Scotland. Accommodations are in charming inns along the way, and fine food, all equipment, and van support are included.

Local rental shops offer a wide range of bicycles, from three-speeds to mountain bikes, and may offer organized trips, ranging from tours of several hours to full-fledged weeklong itineraries. We've listed the best local rental shops, with their rates, in the destination chapters that follow.

BIRD-WATCHING

The moors and Highlands of Scotland, partly because of their low population density, attract millions of birds. For reasons not fully understood by ornithologists, the Orkneys shelter absolutely staggering numbers of birds. Bird-watchers cite the Orkneys as even richer in native species than the more isolated Shetlands, with species like the hen harrier, short-eared owl, and red-throated diver (a form of Arctic loon) not frequently seen in the Shetlands.

Any general tour of the Orkneys will bring you into contact with thousands of birds, as well as Neolithic burial sites, cromlechs, dolmens, and other items with intriguing backgrounds and histories. A worthy tour operator is **Wild About,** 5 Clouston Corner, Stenness, Orkney KW17 3LD (✆ **01856/851-011**). Tour guides in minivans will help you spot the sites. The per-person cost is £23 ($37) for a full day, £16 ($26) for a half day. In summer, reserve in advance.

A bird-watching specialist is **Orkney Island Wildlife,** Shapinsay 12, Orkney KW17 2DY (✆ **01856/711-373**). Between May and November, it leads 5-day bird-watching tours that include full board, housing, and exposure to the fields, moors, and wetlands of Shapinsay and Orkney. Tours are conducted from a rustic croft or farmstead that was upgraded and enlarged into a center in 1990. Your hosts are Paul and Louise Hollinrake, both qualified wardens at the Mill Dam Wetlands Reserve and accredited by the Royal Society for the Protection of Birds. Tours depart every morning around 9am (allowing participants to either sleep late or embark on sunrise expeditions of their own). Lunches are box-lunch affairs. Touring is by minivan or by inflatable boat, allowing close-up inspection of offshore skerries (small islets without vegetation) and sea caves. No more than six participants are allowed on any tour. All-inclusive rates are £600 to £720 ($960–$1,152) per person for the 5-day/6-night experience.

During winter and early spring, the entire Solway shoreline, Loch Ryan, Wigtown Bay, and Auchencairn Bay areas are excellent locations for observing wintering wildfowl and waders. Inland, Galloway has a rich and varied range of bird life, including British barn owls, kestrels, tawnies, and merlins. Bird-watching fact sheets are available at tourist offices in Galloway.

CANOEING

Several canoe clubs offer instruction and advice. Supervising their activities is the **Scottish Canoe Association (SCA),** Caledonia House, South Gyle, Edinburgh EH12 9DH (✆ **0131/317-7314**). It coordinates all competitive canoeing events in Scotland, including slaloms, polo games, and white-water races. It also offers a handbook and a range of other publications, plus promotional material like its own magazine, *Scottish Paddler.* (An equivalent magazine published in England is *Canoe Focus.*)

HIKING & WALKING

Scotland is Valhalla for those who like to walk and hike across mountain and dale, coming to rest on the bonnie, bonnie banks of a loch.

In all Scotland, there are no finer long-distance footpaths than the **West Highland Way** and the **Southern Upland Way,** both previewed in chapter 1. One begins north of Glasgow in the town of Milngavie, the other in Portpatrick in Galloway. Information on these paths is provided by the **Scottish Tourist Board,** 23 Ravelston Terrace, Edinburgh EH4 3EU (© **0131/332-2433**). Nearly all bookstores in Scotland sell guides documenting these paths.

The **Borders** (see chapter 5, "The Borders & Galloway Regions") is one of the greatest places for walks. All tourist boards in the area provide a free guide, *Walking in the Scottish Borders,* detailing half-day scenic walks around the various towns. Scotland's longest footpath, the 341km (212-mile) **Southern Upland Way,** also extends through the Borders.

The magnificent coastline of **Galloway,** southwest of the Borders, is ideal for walks. Tourist offices distribute a free guide to 30 walks, *Walking in Dumfries and Galloway.* They also offer a helpful pamphlet called *Ranger-Led Walks and Events,* outlining scenic hikes through the forests of the southwest.

In central Scotland, the **Cairngorm region** offers the major concentration of ski resorts in the country, including Ben Macdui, the second highest peak in Britain at nearly 1,304m (4,300 ft.). In the Cairngorm Ski Area, Cairngorm Rangers offer guided walks through the forest to both skilled and beginning hikers. The **Glenmore Forest Park Visitors Centre** (© **1479/861-220**) dispenses information on great walks in the area. It's open daily from 9am to 5pm.

The best self-led tours of the Scottish Highlands and islands is offered by **Bespoke Highland Tours,** 14 Belmont Crescent, Glasgow (© **0141/334-9017**). It has devised a series of treks, lasting from 3 to 12 days, including the **West Highland Way,** that take in the finest scenery in Scotland. Their tours are reasonably priced, ranging from £90 to £400 ($144–$640).

John Fisher, The Old Inn, Strachur, Argyll (© **01369/860-712**), specializes in guided walking and hiking holidays. Most of them last 6 days, with 7 nights' accommodation at a cost of £575 to £775 ($920–$1,240). Groups are small, usually between four and eight persons. Highlights of these tours include treks across the isles of Mull and Iona. And with **North-West Frontiers,** 18A Braes, Ullapool (© **01854/612-628**), you can explore remote glens, magnificent mountains and lochs, and isolated islands and beaches. You're likely to see seals, deer, and many species of birds, including divers and golden eagles. Unlike Bespoke (see above), these tours are led by experienced hikers who know the countryside like their backyard.

Some of the most memorable walks in Scotland are along **Loch Lomond** and the **Trossachs.** At tourist centers and various bookstores in Scotland, you can purchase a copy of *Walk Loch Lomond and the Trossachs* to guide you on your way.

An organization that can put you in touch with like-minded hikers is the **Ramblers Association (Scotland),** Kingfisher, Auld Business Park, Milnathort, Kinross KY1 39DA (© **01577/861-222**). To book a rambling tour before you go to Scotland, contact the **English Lakeland Ramblers,** 18 Stuyvesant Oval, Suite 1A, New York, NY 10009 (© **212/505-1020;** www.ramblers.com).

Offering guided walking and hiking tours on a daily basis from Edinburgh, **Walkabout Scotland,** 2 Rossie Place, Edinburgh (© **0131/661-7168;** www. walkaboutscotland.com), specializes in jaunts through the Highlands. A different tour for each day of the week is offered, tackling different grades of walks. From backpackers to millionaires, the ages of clients range from 16 to 69. Longer walking holidays throughout Scotland can also be booked, including to such fabled spots as Glen Nevis, Glencoe, Loch Lomond, and the Isle of Arran.

C-N-Do Scotland (✆ **01786/445-703;** www.cndoscotland.com) has been organizing hiking tours since 1984. It knows the Scottish landscapes well, and hooks up its patrons with the best in hiking, good Scottish food, wildlife viewing, and what it terms (accurately) "a palette-full of panoramas."

English Lakeland Ramblers (✆ **800/724-8801;** www.ramblers.com) features a walking tour of Skye and the Outer Isles. The tour spends two nights on Skye, plus three on the Outer Hebridean Islands of Lewis and Harris. Passengers walk along hills and dales, mountain screes and grassy moors, and lakes and gushing waterfalls. Later they can explore old Scottish villages, stopping off perhaps at a pub for a wee dram of Scotch.

HORSEBACK RIDING & PONY TREKKING

Horseback riding and trekking through the panoramic countryside—from the Lowlands to the Highlands and through all the in-between lands—can be enjoyed by most everyone, from novices to experienced riders.

Although more adventurous riders prefer the hillier terrain of the Highlands, the Borders in the southeast (see chapter 5) is the best for horseback riding—in fact, it's often called Scotland's horse country. Its equivalent in the United States would be Kentucky. On the western coastline, Argyll (see chapter 7, "Argyll & the Southern Hebrides") is another great center for riding while taking in dramatic scenery. The Argyll Forest Park, stretching almost to Loch Fyne, encompasses 24,300 hectares (60,000 acres) and contains some of the lushest scenery in Scotland. It's trails lead through forests to sea lochs cut deep into the park, evoking the fjords of Norway.

Pony trekking across moors and dales is reason enough to come to Scotland. Pony trekking originated as a job for Highland ponies that weren't otherwise engaged in toting dead deer off the hills during deer-stalking season. Most treks last from 2½ hours to a full day, and most centers have ponies suitable for most age groups. You'll find operators in Kirkudbright and on Shetland, plus several in the Hebrides.

MOUNTAINEERING

Mountain climbing can range from fair-weather treks over heather-clad hilltops to demanding climbs up rock faces in wintry conditions of snow and ice.

The **Southern Uplands,** the **offshore islands,** and the **Highlands** of Scotland contain the best mountaineering sites. Regardless of your abilities, treat the landscape with respect. The weather can turn foul during any season with almost no advance notice, creating dangerous conditions. If you're climbing rock faces, you should be familiar with basic techniques and the use of such specialized equipment as carabiners, crampons, ice axes, and ropes. Don't even consider climbing without proper instruction and equipment.

Ben Nevis is the highest (but by no means the most remote) peak in Scotland. Despite its loftiness at 1,336m (4,406 ft.), it has attracted some daredevils who have driven cars and motorcycles to points near its top; one eccentric even arranged the transport of a dining table with formal dinner service and a grand piano.

If you want to improve your rock-climbing skills, consider joining a club or signing on for a mountaineering course at a climbing center maintained by the

Scottish Sports Council. Also contact the **Mountaineering Council of Scotland,** Perth (© **01738/638-227;** www.mountaineering-scotland.org.uk). Membership allows overnight stays at the club's climbing huts on the island of Skye (in Glen Brittle), in the Cairngorms (at Glen Feshie), and near the high-altitude mountain pass at Glencoe. True rock-climbing aficionados looking to earn certification might contact the **Scottish Mountain Leader Training Board,** at Glenmore, Aviemore, Inverness-shire PH22 1QU (© **01479/861-248;** www.mltuk.org).

SAILING & WATERSPORTS

Wherever you travel in Scotland, you're never far from the water. Windsurfing, canoeing, water-skiing, and sailing are just some of the activities available at a number of sailing centers and holiday parks. You'll find it easy to rent boats and equipment at any of the major resorts along Scotland's famous lakes.

4

Edinburgh & the Lothian Region

Edinburgh ★★★ (pronounced *edin*-burra) has been called one of Europe's fairest cities, the Athens of the North, and the gateway to central Scotland. You can use it as a base for excursions to the Borders, the Trossachs (Scotland's Lake District), the silver waters of Loch Lomond, and the Kingdom of Fife on the opposite shore of the Firth of Forth.

Edinburgh is filled with historic and literary association: John Knox, Mary Queen of Scots, Robert Louis Stevenson, Sir Arthur Conan Doyle, Alexander Graham Bell, Sir Walter Scott, and Bonnie Prince Charlie are all part of its past.

In modern times, the city has become famous as the scene of the ever-growing **Edinburgh International Festival,** with its action-packed list of cultural events. But remember that the treasures of this ancient seat of Scottish royalty are available all year—in fact, when the festival-hoppers have gone home, the pace is more relaxed, the prices are lower, and the people themselves, under less pressure, return to their traditional hospitable nature.

Built on extinct volcanoes atop an inlet from the North Sea (the Firth of Forth) and enveloped by rolling hills, lakes, and forests, Edinburgh is a city made for walking. Its Old Town and New Town sport elegant streets, cobbled alleys, lovely squares, and enough circuses and crescents to rival Bath in England; from every hilltop, another panoramic view unfolds. Edinburgh's sunsets are spectacularly romantic—Scots call the fading evening light the "gloaming."

Edinburgh was once the cultural capital of the north, but it has lost that position to Glasgow. However, the lively capital is trying its best to regain its old reputation. In fact, if you could visit only two cities in all Great Britain, we'd say make it London first and Edinburgh second. But you may want to budget some time for side trips, too. Notable attractions on the doorstep of Edinburgh are the royal burgh of Linlithgow, where Mary Queen of Scots was born at Linlithgow Palace; the port of North Berwick (today a holiday resort); and lovely Dirleton, with its 13th-century castle ruins.

1 Essentials

ARRIVING

BY PLANE Edinburgh is about an hour's flying time from London, 633km (393 miles) south. **Edinburgh Airport** (✆ 0131/333-1000) is 10km (6 miles) west of the center, receiving flights from within the British Isles and the rest of Europe. Before heading into town, you might want to stop at the **information and accommodation desk** (✆ 0131/473-3800); it's open Monday to Saturday 8am to 8pm and Sunday 9am to 4:30pm. A double-decker Airlink bus makes the trip from the airport to the city center every 15 minutes, letting you off near Waverley Bridge, between the Old Town and the New Town; the fare is £3.30 ($5.30) one-way or £5 ($8) round-trip, and the trip takes about 25 minutes.

A taxi into the city will cost £12 ($19) or more, depending on traffic, and the ride will be about 25 minutes.

BY TRAIN InterCity trains link London with Edinburgh and are fast and efficient, providing both restaurant and bar service as well as air-conditioning. Trains from London's Kings Cross Station arrive in Edinburgh at **Waverley Station,** at the east end of Princes Street (℃ **08457/484950** in London for rail info). Trains depart London every hour or so, taking about 4½ hours and costing about £40.50 to £90.50 ($65–$145) one-way. Overnight trains have a sleeper berth, which you can rent for an extra £35 ($56). Taxis and buses are right outside the station in Edinburgh.

BY BUS The least expensive way to go from London to Edinburgh is by bus, but it's an 8-hour journey. Nevertheless, it'll get you there for only about £27 ($43) one-way or £38 ($61) round-trip. Scottish CityLink coaches depart from London's Victoria Coach Station, delivering you to Edinburgh's **St. Andrew Square Bus Station,** St. Andrew Square (℃ **8705/808080** for information).

BY CAR Edinburgh is 74km (46 miles) east of Glasgow and 169km (105 miles) north of Newcastle-upon-Tyne in England. No express motorway links London and Edinburgh. The M1 from London takes you part of the way north, but you'll have to come into Edinburgh along secondary roads: A68 or A7 from the southeast, A1 from the east, or A702 from the north. The A71 or A8 comes in from the west, A8 connecting with M8 just west of Edinburgh; A90 comes down from the north over the Forth Road Bridge. Allow 8 hours or more for the drive north from London.

VISITOR INFORMATION

Edinburgh & Scotland Information Centre, Fairways Business Park, Deer Park Road, at the corner of Princes Street and Waverley Bridge (© **0131/473-3800;** fax 0131/473-3881; www.edinburgh.org; Bus: 3, 331, or 69), can give you sightseeing information and also help find lodgings. The center sells bus tours, theater tickets, and souvenirs of Edinburgh. It's open year round, Monday through Saturday from 9am to 8pm. There's also an information and accommodations desk at Edinburgh Airport.

CITY LAYOUT

Edinburgh is divided into a New Town and an Old Town. Chances are, you'll find lodgings in the New Town and visit the Old Town only for dining, drinking, shopping, and sightseeing.

New Town, with its world-famous **Princes Street,** came about in the 18th century in the Golden Age of Edinburgh. Everybody from Robert Burns to James Boswell visited in that era. The first building went up here in 1767, and by the end of the century, classical squares, streets, and town houses had been added. Princes Street is known for its shopping and also for its beauty, as it opens onto the Princes Street Gardens with panoramic views of the Old Town.

North of and running parallel to Princes Street is the New Town's second great street, **George Street.** It begins at Charlotte Square and runs east to St. Andrew Square. Directly north of George Street is another impressive thoroughfare, **Queen Street,** opening onto Queen Street Gardens on its north side. You'll also hear a lot about **Rose Street,** directly north of Princes Street—it boasts more pubs per square block than any other place in Scotland and is filled with shops and restaurants.

Seemingly everyone has heard of the **Royal Mile,** the main thoroughfare of the **Old Town,** beginning at Edinburgh Castle and running all the way to the Palace of Holyroodhouse. A famous street to the south of the castle is **Grassmarket,** where convicted criminals were once hanged on the dreaded gallows.

THE NEIGHBORHOODS IN BRIEF

The Old Town This area is where Edinburgh began. Its backbone is the **Royal Mile,** a medieval thoroughfare stretching for about 1.6km (1 mile) from Edinburgh Castle running downhill to the Palace of Holyroodhouse. It's composed of four connected streets: Castlehill, Lawnmarket, High Street, and Canongate. "This is perhaps the largest, longest, and finest street for buildings and number of inhabitants in the world," or so wrote English author Daniel Defoe. The same might be said of the street today.

The New Town Lying below the Old Town, the New Town burst into full bloom between 1766 and 1840 and became one of the largest Georgian developments in the world. It takes in most of the northern half of the heart of the city, covering some 320 hectares (790 acres). With about 25,000 residents, it's the largest conservation area in all Britain. The New Town is made up of a network of squares, streets, terraces, and circuses, reaching from Haymarket in the west to Abbeyhill in the east. The New Town also goes from Canonmills on the northern perimeter down to Princes Street, its main artery, along the southern tier.

Marchmont About 1.5km (1 mile) south of High Street, this suburb was constructed between 1869 and 1914 as a massive building program of new housing for people who could no longer afford to live in the New Town. It borders a public park, the Meadows. This has no tourist interest. Sometimes visitors go here seeking an affordable B&B in one of the little homes that receive guests.

Bruntsfield This suburb to the west is named for Bruntsfield Links. Now a residential district, it was the ground on which James IV gathered the Scottish army he marched to its defeat at Flodden in 1513. Plague victims were once brought here for burial; now suburban gardens have grown over those graves. Many low-cost B&Bs are found in this area.

Churchill Churchill is known as "holy corner" because of the wide array of Scottish churches within its borders at the junctions of Colinton, Chamberlain, and Bruntsfield roads. These churches are primarily for local worshipers and not of artistic interest.

Leith The Port of Leith lies only a few kilometers north of Princes Street and is the city's major harbor, opening onto the Firth of Forth. The area is currently being gentrified, and visitors come here for the restaurants and pubs, many of which specialize in seafood. The port isn't what it used to be in terms of maritime might; its glory days were back when stevedores unloaded cargoes by hand.

Newhaven Newhaven is the fishing village adjacent to Leith. Founded in the 1400s, this former little harbor with its bustling fish market was greatly altered in the 1960s. Many of its "bow-tows" (a nickname for closely knit, clannish residents) were uprooted, like the Leithers, in a major gentrification program. Now many of the old houses have been restored, and the fishwife no longer goes from door to door hawking fish from her basket. The harbor is today mostly filled with pleasure craft instead of fishing boats. If your time is limited, you can skip this area, as its attractions are limited.

Tips **Finding an Address**

Edinburgh's streets often follow no pattern whatsoever, and both names and house numbers seem to have been created purposely to confuse. First, the city is checkered with innumerable squares, terraces, circuses, wynds, and closes, which will jut into or cross or overlap or interrupt whatever street you're trying to follow, usually without the slightest warning.

Then the house numbers run in sequences of odds or evens or run clockwise or counterclockwise as the wind blows—that is, when they exist at all. Many establishments don't use street numbers. (This is even truer when you leave Edinburgh and go to provincial towns.) Even though a road might run for one or two kilometers, some buildings on the street will be numbered and others will say only "Kings Road" or whatever, giving no number. Before heading out, get a detailed map of Edinburgh and ask for a location to be pinpointed; locals are generally glad to assist a bewildered foreigner. If you're looking for an address, try to get the name of the nearest cross street.

2 Getting Around

Because of its narrow lanes, wynds, and closes, you can only explore the Old Town in any depth on foot. Edinburgh is fairly convenient for the visitor who likes to walk, as most of the attractions are along the Royal Mile, Princes Street, or one of the major streets of the New Town.

BY BUS

The bus will probably be your chief method of transport. The fare you pay depends on the distance you ride, with the **minimum fare** 80p ($1.30) for 3 stages or less and the **maximum fare** £1 ($1.60) for 44 or more stages. (A stage isn't a stop but a distance of about .8km/½ mile with a number of stops.) Children age 5 to 15 are charged a flat rate of 50p (80¢), but teenagers age 13 to 15 must carry a **teen card** (available where bus tickets are sold—see below) as proof of age, and children age 4 and under ride free. Exact change is required if you're paying your fare on the bus.

A **family ticket** for two adults and four children goes for £6 ($9.60) a day and another for £1.60 ($2.55) operates 6:30pm onward. The **Edinburgh Day Saver Ticket** allows 1 day of unlimited travel on city buses at a cost of £1.50 to £2.50 ($2.40–$4) adults and £1.80 ($2.90) children.

For daily commuters or die-hard Scottish enthusiasts, a **RideCard** season ticket allows unlimited travel on all buses. For adults, the price is £11 ($18) for 1 week and £33 ($53) for 4 weeks; tickets for children cost £7 ($11) for 1 week and £21 ($34) for 4 weeks. Travel must begin on Sunday.

You can get these tickets and further information in the city center at the **Waverley Bridge Transport Office,** Waverley Bridge (© **0131/554-4494;** Bus: 3, or 31), open Monday to Saturday 8:30am to 6pm and Sunday 9:30am to 5pm, or at the Hanover Street office (Bus: 3, or 31), open Monday to Saturday 8:30am to 6pm. For details on timetables, call © **0131/555-6363.**

> **Tips   Look Both Ways!**
>
> Remember, you're in Great Britain, and cars drive on the left. Always look both ways before stepping off a curb. Lots of new arrivals practically commit suicide crossing the street because they forget which way to look for traffic.

BY TAXI   You can hail a taxi or pick one up at a taxi stand. Meters begin at £2 ($3.20) and increase £2 ($3.20) every 1 km (½ mile). Taxi ranks are at Hanover Street, North St. Andrew Street, Waverley Station, Haymarket Station, and Lauriston Place. Fares are displayed in the front of the taxi and charges posted, including extra charges for night drivers or destinations outside the city limits, and a call-out is charged at 60p (95¢). You can also call a taxi. Try **City Cabs** at © **0131/228-1211** or **Central Radio Taxis** at © **0131/229-2468.**

BY CAR   Don't think about driving in Edinburgh—it's a tricky business, even for natives. Parking is expensive and difficult to find. Metered parking is available, but you'll need the right change and have to watch out for traffic wardens who issue tickets. Some zones are marked PERMIT HOLDERS ONLY—your vehicle will be towed if you have no permit. A yellow line along the curb indicates no parking. Major parking lots (car parks) are at Castle Terrace, convenient for Edinburgh Castle and the west end of Princes Street; at Lothian Road, near the west end of Princes Street; at St. John Hill, convenient to the Royal Mile, the west end of Princes Street, and Waverley Station; and at St. James Centre (entrance from York Place), close to the east end of Princes Street.

You may want a rental car for touring the countryside or for heading onward. Many agencies grant discounts to those who reserve in advance (see chapter 2, "Planning Your Trip to Scotland," for more information). Most will accept your U.S. or Canadian driver's license, provided you've held it for more than a year and are over 21. Most of the major car-rental companies maintain offices at the Edinburgh airport should you want to rent a car on the spot. Call **Avis** (© **0131/333-1866**), **Hertz** (© **0131/333-1019**), or **Europcar** (© **0131/333-2588**).

BY BICYCLE   Biking isn't a good idea for most visitors because the city is constructed on a series of high ridges and terraces. You may, however, want to rent a bike for exploring the flatter countryside around the city. Try **Central Cycle Hire,** 13 Lochrin Place (© **0131/228-6333;** Bus: 10), off Home Street in Tollcross, near the Cameo Cinema. Depending on the type of bike, charges average around £15 ($24) per day. A deposit of £100 ($160) is imposed. June to September, the shop is open Monday to Saturday 9:30am to 6pm and Sunday noon to 7pm; October to May, hours are Monday to Saturday 10am to 5:30pm.

FAST FACTS: Edinburgh

American Express The office is at 139 Princes St. (© **0131/225-7881;** Bus: 3, 39, or 69), 5 blocks from Waverley Station. It's open Monday through Friday from 9am to 5:30pm and Saturday from 9am to 4pm; on Thursday, the office opens at 9:30am.

Babysitters The most reliable services are provided by Guardians Baby Sitting Service, 13 Eton Terrace (© **0131/337-4150**), and Care Connections, 45 Barclay Place (© **01506/856-106**).

Business Hours In Edinburgh, banks are usually open Monday through Wednesday from 9:30am to 3:45pm and Thursday and Friday from 9:30am to 5 or 5:30pm. Shops are generally open Monday through Saturday from 10am to 5:30 or 6pm; on Thursday, stores are open to 8pm. Offices are open Monday through Friday from 9am to 5pm.

Currency Exchange Try the **Clydesdale Bank** at 5 Waverley Bridge and at Waverley Market.

Dentists If you have a dental emergency, go to the **Edinburgh Dental Institute,** 39 Lauriston Place (© **0131/536-4900;** Bus: 23 or 41), open Monday through Friday from 9am to 3pm.

Doctors You can seek help from the **Edinburgh Royal Infirmary,** 1 Lauriston Place (© **0131/536-1000;** Bus: 23 or 41). Medical attention is available 24 hours.

Embassies & Consulates See "Fast Facts: Scotland," in chapter 2.

Emergencies Call © **999** in an emergency to summon the police, an ambulance, or firefighters.

Hospitals See "Doctors," above.

Internet Access The **International Telecom Centre,** 52 High St. (© **0131/559-7114;** Bus: 1 or 6), charges £1 ($1.50) for 15 minutes. Open daily from 9am to 10pm.

Laundry/Dry Cleaning For your dry cleaning needs, go to **Johnson's Cleaners,** 23 Frederick St. (© **0131/225-8095;** Bus: 23 or 41), open Monday through Friday from 8:30am to 5:30pm and Saturday from 8am to 4pm.

Luggage Storage/Lockers You can store luggage in lockers at **Waverley Station,** at Waverley Bridge (© **0131/550-2333**), open Monday through Saturday from 7am to 11pm and Sunday from 8am to 11pm.

Newspapers Published since 1817, *The Scotsman* is a quality daily newspaper. Along with national and international news, it's strong on the arts.

Pharmacies There are no 24-hour drugstores (called chemists or pharmacies) in Edinburgh. The major drugstore is **Boots,** 48 Shandwick Place (© **0131/225-6757;** Bus: 3 or 31), open Monday through Friday from 8am to 9pm, Saturday from 8am to 6pm, and Sunday from 10am to 4pm.

Police See "Emergencies," above.

Post Office The Edinburgh Branch Post Office, St. James's Centre, is open Monday through Friday from 9am to 5:30pm and Saturday from 9am to noon. For postal information and customer service, call © **0845/722-3344.**

Restrooms These are found at rail stations, terminals, restaurants, hotels, pubs, and department stores. Don't hesitate to use the system of public toilets, often marked wc, at strategic corners and squares throughout the city. They're perfectly safe and clean, but likely to be closed late in the evening.

Safety Edinburgh is generally safer than Glasgow—in fact, it's one of Europe's safest capitals for a visitor to stroll at any time of day or night. But that doesn't mean crimes, especially muggings, don't occur. They do, largely because of Edinburgh's shockingly large drug problem.

Weather For weather forecasts and road conditions, call © **0845/300-0300.** This number also provides weather information for Lothian, the Borders, Tayside, and Fife.

3 Where to Stay

Edinburgh offers a full range of accommodations throughout the year. However, it should come as no surprise that during the 3-week period of the Edinburgh International Festival in August, the hotels fill up; if you're coming at that time, be sure to reserve far in advance.

The **Edinburgh & Scotland Information Centre,** Waverley Shopping Centre, 3 Princes St., at the corner of Princes Street and Waverley Bridge (© **0131/473-3800;** fax 0131/473-3881; www.edinburgh.org; bus: 3, 7, 14, 31, or 69), compiles a lengthy list of small hotels, guesthouses, and private homes providing a bed-and-breakfast for as little as £18 ($29) per person. A £3 ($4.80) booking fee and a 10% deposit are charged. Allow about 4 weeks' notice, especially during summer and during the festival weeks. Hours are Monday to Saturday 9am to 8pm and Sunday 10am to 8pm; May, June, and September, hours are Monday to Saturday 8am to 7pm and Sunday 9am to 5pm; October to April, hours are Monday to Saturday 9am to 6pm and Sunday 10am to 6pm.

If you have an early flight out and need a hotel convenient to the airport, consider the 244-unit **Edinburgh Marriott,** 111 Glasgow Rd. (© **0131/334-9191**), off A8 on Edinburgh's western outskirts. It offers doubles for £140 to £170 ($224–$272), including breakfast. Facilities include an indoor pool, gym, sauna, and restaurant.

THE NEW TOWN
VERY EXPENSIVE

Balmoral Hotel ✦✦✦   This legendary place opened in 1902 as the grandest hotel in the north of Britain. After a $35-million restoration, it reopened in 1991 under a new name, the Balmoral. Almost directly above the Waverley Rail Station, it features a soaring clock tower that many locals consider one of their city's landmarks. Kilted doormen and a bagpiper supply the Scottish atmosphere. Furnished with reproduction pieces, the guest rooms are distinguished and rather large—a graceful reminder of Edwardian sprawl. Each unit comes with a commodious bathroom with combination tub/shower. Dining options include the elegant No. 1 Princes Street (see "Dining," later in this chapter) and the more convivial brasserie Hadrian's. Afternoon tea is served in the high-ceilinged Palm Court. Foremost among the several bar areas is N.B.'s, a Scottish pub with an entrance directly on Princes Street.

1 Princes St., Edinburgh EH2 2EQ. ✆ **800/223-6800** in the U.S., or 0131/556-2414. Fax 0131/557-3747. www.thebalmoralhotel.com. 188 units. £220–£330 ($352–$528) double; from £450 ($720) suite. AE, DC, MC, V. Valet parking £15 ($24). Bus: 50. **Amenities:** 3 restaurants; 2 bars; indoor pool; health club; spa; sauna; concierge; business center; 24-hr. room service; dry cleaning/laundry service. *In room:* A/C, TV, fax, dataport, minibar, hair dryer, safe.

The Bonham ✦✦   One of Edinburgh's newest and most stylish hotels occupies three connected town houses that functioned since the 19th century as a nursing home and as dorms for the local university. In 1998, all that changed when a team of entrepreneurs poured millions of pounds into its refurbishment, pumped up the style level, and outfitted each high-ceilinged guest room in a hip blend of old and new. Each has an individual theme, plush upholsteries, and a TV with a keyboard hooked up to the Internet—the first setup of its kind in Europe. Bathrooms are cutting edge, with checkered floors, Molton Brown toiletries, and combination tub/showers. The Restaurant at the Bonham is reviewed under "Dining," later in this chapter.

35 Drumsheugh Gardens, Edinburgh EH3 7RN. ✆ **0131/226-6050.** Fax 0131/226-6080. www.thebonham. com. 48 units. £190–£235 ($304–$376) double; £335 ($536) suite. Rates include continental breakfast. AE, DC, DISC, MC, V. Bus: 23 or 27. **Amenities:** Restaurant; 24-hour room service. *In room:* TV w/Internet, dataport, minibar, coffeemaker, hair dryer, iron/ironing board, trouser press.

Caledonian Hilton Edinburgh ✦✦   Completely renovated in 1991, the hotel remains one of the city's landmarks and offers commanding views over Edinburgh Castle and the Princes Street Gardens. The public rooms are reminiscent of Edwardian splendor, and the guest rooms (many of which are exceptionally spacious) are conservatively styled with reproduction furniture. The fifth-floor rooms are the smallest. Bathrooms come with combination tub/showers. Although the accommodations are superior to those of many first-class hotels in Edinburgh, the Caledonian lacks the leisure facilities of its major competitor, the Balmoral. The hotel contains a traditional pub, Henry J. Beans, and Chisholms Bar. More formal meals are served in Pompadour Restaurant (see "Dining," later in this chapter). A traditional tea is featured in the high-ceilinged lounge.

Princes St., Edinburgh EH1 2AB. ✆ **0131/222-8888.** Fax 0131/222-8889. www.caledonian.hilton.com 249 units. £275–£380 ($440–$608) double; from £340 ($544) suite. Children age 15 and under stay free in

Edinburgh Accommodations & Dining

ACCOMMODATIONS ■

A Haven Townhouse **2**
Balmoral Hotel **34**
The Bank Hotel **52**
The Bonham **15**
Caledonian Hilton Hotel **20**
Carlton Highland Hotel **33**
Channings Hotel **18**
Crown Plaza **31**
The Edinburgh Residence **18**
41 Heriot Row **7**
4 Forres Street **6**
George Inter-Continental **13**
The Glasshouse **40**
Greenside Hotel **39**
Holyrood Hotel **41**
The Howard **4**
The Malmaison **38**
Mansfield House **11**
Mount Royal
  Ramada Jarvis **19**
19 St. Bernard's Crescent **5**
Old Waverley Hotel **15**
Point Hotel **24**
Prestonfield House **46**
Roxburghe Hotel **17**
The Scotsman **29**
7 Danube Street **5**
Sheraton Grand Hotel **23**
16 Lynedoch Place **18**
Teviotdale House **44**
Thrums Private Hotel **45**
Walton Hotel **10**
The Witchery by
  the Castle **26**

To Leith

| Church
(i) Information
— Railway

0   1/10 mi
0   0.1 km

N

Annandale St.
East London St.
Broughton Street
Union Street
Elm Row
Brunswick Road
Montgomery Street
Montgomery Street
Albany Street
York Place
Union Place
Hillside
Crescent
London Road
Royal Terrace
W. Register St.
Elder St.
Leith Street
Waterloo Place
CALTON HILL
Lincoln Monument
Nelson Monument
REGENT GARDENS
Regent Terrace
Abbey Hill
Regent Road
Burns Monument
Calton Road
Holyroodhouse
Waverley Station
North Bridge
Waverley Bridge
Market St.
The Royal Mile
(see Attractions map)
† Canongate Church
John Knox House
Jeffrey Street
High St.
Canongate
Huntly House
CANONGATE
Holyrood Road
St. Mary's St.
Museum of Childhood
South Bridge
High Kirk of St. Giles
Cowgate
■ National Library
Chambers St.
George IV Bridge
Bristo Place
National Museum of Scotland
College St.
Drummond St.
Nicolson St.
Pleasance
HOLYROOD PARK
The Queen's Drive
McEwan Hall
George Square
Potterrow
Buccleuch Street
West Richmond
Buccleuch Place
Crosscauseway
St. Leonard's St.
Middle Meadow Walk
THE MEADOWS
Meadow Lane
Clerk St.
Melville Drive
S. Clerk St.
Dalkeith Road
East Preston St.

DINING ◆

The Atrium **21**
Baked Potato Shop **28**
Blue Bar Café **22**
Café Saint-Honoré **9**
Channings **18**
Cosmo Ristorante **8**
Dome Bar & Grill **14**
Dubh Prais **25**
Duck's at Le Marché Noir **3**
Far Pavilions **1**
Fishers Bistro **37**
Haldanes Restaurant **35**
Henderson's Salad Table **12**
Iggs **32**
Jackson's Restaurant **27**
Malmaison Brasserie **38**
The Marque **43**
Martin's **16**
Martin Wishart **36**
No. 1 Princes Street **34**
Pompadour Restaurant **20**
Prestonfield House **46**
Restaurant at the Bonham **18**
The Tower **42**
Vinter's Room **36**
Witchery by the Castle **26**
Zinc Bar & Grill **37**

79

parent's room. AE, DC, MC, V. Bus: 33. Parking £8 ($13). **Amenities:** 2 restaurants; bar; indoor pool; exercise room; 24-hr. room service; laundry/dry cleaning service. *In room:* TV, dataport, minibar, hair dryer, iron/ironing board, trouser press.

Carlton Highland Hotel *Kids*   A century ago, this was one of Edinburgh's leading department stores, with 4 of its 10 stories below sidewalk level. In 1984, the baronial pile was converted into a plush hotel. Its Victorian turrets, Flemish gables, and severe gray stonework rise from a corner on the Royal Mile, near Waverley Station. The Paramount investment group substantially improved this hotel with an influx of pounds. Some bedrooms were done away to make the units larger and more comfortable, with private bathrooms with tub and shower. Furnishings are tasteful with a subdued modern simplicity. In spite of its overhaul, some of the architectural charm of 1900 still remains. Offering more facilities than the landmark Caledonian, the Carlton is known for its topnotch service and both formal and informal dining venues.

19 North Bridge, Edinburgh, Lothian EH1 1SD. ℭ **0131/472-3000.** Fax 0131/556-2691. 189 units. £180–£195 ($288–$312) executive double. Children age 14 and under stay free in parents' room. AE, DC, MC, V. Parking £6 ($9.60). Bus: 55 or 80. Pets. **Amenities:** Restaurant; bar; indoor pool; health club; Jacuzzi; sauna; limited room service; babysitting; squash courts. *In room:* TV, coffeemaker, hair dryer, iron, safe.

The Edinburgh Residence ✦✦✦   If Robert Burns, who liked his luxuries, were checking into a hotel in Edinburgh today, he no doubt would be booked in here. It's one of the finest luxury hotels in Scotland, a series of elegant town house suites installed in a trio of architecturally beautiful and sensitively restored Georgian buildings. As you enter, grand staircases and classic wood paneling greet you. A stay here is like finding lodging in an elegant town house from long ago, although with all the modern conveniences. This hotel is on the same level or better than its sibling, The Howard, Bonham, and Channings. Accommodations are the ultimate in local comfort, with a trio of classic suites having their own private entrances. All units are spacious.

7 Rothesay Terrace, Edinburgh EH3 7RY. ℭ **0131/226-3380.** Fax 0131/226-3381. www.theedinburgh residence.com. 29 units. £150–£265 ($240–$424) suite; £260–£395 ($416–$632) apt. AE, MC, V. Free parking. Bus: 19 or 37. Rates include continental breakfast. **Amenities:** Bar; 24-hr. room service. *In room:* TV, minibar, hair dryer, iron/ironing board.

George Inter-Continental ✦   Designed by famed architect Robert Adam and only yards from St. Andrew Square, the city's financial center, the George opened in 1755 and was turned into a hotel in 1972. The public rooms have retained the style, elegance, and old-fashioned comfort of a country house. The guest rooms come in various sizes and have undergone frequent refurbishments. The best units, opening onto views, are those on the fourth floor and above in the new wing. The Carver's Table, with some of Adam's design still intact, has for almost a century fed diners on prime Scottish beef, lamb, and pork. Le Chambertin is the choice for gourmet French fare.

19–21 George St., Edinburgh EH2 2PB. ℭ **800/327-0200** in the U.S., or 0131/225-1251. Fax 0131/226-5644. www.Edinburgh.intercontinental.com. 195 units. £190–£275 ($304–$440) double; from £460 ($736) suite. AE, DC, MC, V. Bus: 41 or 42. Limited free parking. **Amenities:** 2 restaurants; bar; concierge; 24-hr. room service; babysitting; laundry/dry cleaning service. *In room:* TV, dataport, minibar, coffeemaker, hair dryer, iron/ironing board, safe.

The Howard ✦✦✦   Dubbed the most discreet government-rated five-star hotel in the city, this lovely hotel is composed of a trio of Georgian terraced houses that once were private homes of rich burgers. The landmark is more expensive and a more refined version of its sibling, Channings (see later in this chapter). Service is a hallmark of the Howard, with a dedicated butler tending to your needs, even unpacking your luggage if you desire. Some of the aura of a private home remains in much of the buildings. Accommodations are midsize to spacious, each individually and rather elegantly decorated, with some of the best bathrooms in town, featuring power and double showers and, in some, a Jacuzzi. The decor is traditional and modern, using both antiques and reproductions. Three of the units are terraced suites, and the accommodations are named after Edinburgh streets. To sum up, an oasis of Georgian charm and class.

34 Great King St., Edinburgh EH3 6QH. © 0131/557-3500. Fax 0131/557-6515. www.thehoward.com. 18 units. £180–£275 ($288–$440) double; £270–£360 ($432–$576) suite. Rates include breakfast. AE, DC, MC, V. Bus: 13, 23, 27, or C5. **Amenities:** Restaurant; 24-hr. room service; laundry/dry cleaning service. *In room:* TV, dataport, hair dryer.

The Scotsman 𝓐𝓐𝓐   Located on the historic North Bridge, only minutes from the Royal Mile and Princes Street, this is one of the brightest and most stylish hotels to open in Edinburgh in many a year. Its name honors the famous newspaper that was published here for nearly a century. One reviewer noted when it opened: "Think native son Sir Arthur Conan Doyle getting a reverent makeover from Gucci's Tom Ford." Traditional styling and cutting-edge design are harmoniously wed in the 1904 baronial limestone pile, a city landmark since it was first constructed. Guest rooms, in honor of their former roles as newspaper offices, are categorized by size and given masthead ranks such as assistant editor, editor, or publisher. They include state-of-the-art bathrooms and such extras as two-way service closets, which means your laundry is picked up virtually unnoticed. Our favorite retreat here is Room 399, a cozy bar named for its number of single-malt whiskies.

20 N. Bridge, Edinburgh EH1 1DF. © 0131/556-5565. Fax 0131/652-3652. www.thescotsmanhotel.co.uk. 68 units. £180–£265 ($288–$424) double; from £375 ($600) suite. AE, DC, DISC, MC, V. Bus: 7, 8, 21, 31, or 33. **Amenities:** 2 restaurants; bar; indoor pool; health club; spa; sauna; salon; 24-hr. room service; massage; babysitting; laundry/dry cleaning service. *In room:* TV, dataport, minibar, coffeemaker, hair dryer, iron/ironing board, safe.

Sheraton Grand Hotel 𝓐𝓐   This former railway siding, a short walk from Princes Street, is now a six-story postmodern structure housing a glamorous hotel and an office complex. The hotel is elegant, with soaring public rooms and carpeting in tones of thistle and mauve. Boasting a central location and a well-chosen staff, this is the most appealing modern hotel in the capital. The spacious, well-furnished guest rooms have double-glazed windows; glamorous suites are available, as are rooms for nonsmokers and travelers with disabilities. The castle-view rooms on the top three floors are the best. The main restaurant, with views of the Festival Square Fountain, presents well-prepared meals and a lavish Sunday buffet. The plushly modern cocktail bar is a favorite rendezvous for locals.

1 Festival Sq., Edinburgh, Lothian EH3 9SR. © 800/325-3535 in the U.S. and Canada, or 0131/229-9131. Fax 0131/228-4510. www.sheraton.com 260 units. June–Sept £190–£260 ($304–$416) double, from £300 ($480) suite; off season £115 ($184) double, £215 ($344) suite. AE, DC, MC, V. Bus: 4, 15, or 44. **Amenities:** 3 restaurants; 2 bars; indoor and outdoor pools; exercise room; spa; sauna; concierge; 24 hr. room service; massage; babysitting; laundry/dry cleaning service. *In room:* A/C, TV, dataport, minibar, coffeemaker, hair dryer, iron/ironing board, trouser press.

EXPENSIVE
The Glasshouse 𝓐 *Finds*   A newly built property, this unique hotel is not only one of the most modern but among the best so-called boutique hotels of

Edinburgh. It uniquely combines the old and the new. At the foot of Carlton Hill, within walking distance of Princes Street, if offers both an impressive church façade, which is the actual entrance to the hotel, coexisting in amazing harmony with a modern glass structure. The well-furnished bedrooms open onto panoramic views of Edinburgh. A special feature is the residential rooftop bar. The bedrooms are as modern as tomorrow, with sleek, well-styled furnishings, the beds closed off from the sitting area by wood panels.

2 Greenside Place, Edinburgh EH1 3AA. © 0131/525-8200. Fax 0131/525-8205. www.theetoncollection. com/hotels/glasshouse. 65 units. £175–£195 ($280–$312) double; £225–£295 ($360–$472) suite. AE, DC, MC, V. Parking £13 ($21). Bus: 10, 11, 15, 16, 17, or 22. **Amenities:** Restaurant; bar; health club; concierge; 24-hr. room service; babysitting; laundry/dry cleaning service. *In room:* A/C, TV, dataport, minibar, coffeemaker, hair dryer, safe, trouser press.

Mount Royal Ramada Jarvis ⭐   The Mount Royal, a remake of an 1860s hotel, is right in the middle of Princes Street. A modern world emerges as you climb the spiral staircase or take an elevator to the second floor, with its reception rooms and lounges and floor-to-ceiling windows opening onto views of the Old Town and the castle. There aren't a lot of frills, but the comfort is genuine in the streamlined guest rooms. Be aware this is a tour-group favorite. The lounge, with views of the Scott Memorial and Princes Street, provides a wide range of savory and sweet snacks and beverages throughout the day.

53 Princes St., Edinburgh EH2 2DG. © 0131/225-7161. Fax 0131/220-4671. www.ramadajarvis.co.uk. 158 units. £150–£180 ($240–$288) double; £180–£250 ($288–$400) suite. AE, DC, MC, V. Bus: 15 or 100. Pets accepted. Parking. **Amenities:** Restaurant; bar; 24-hr. room service; laundry/dry cleaning service. *In room:* TV, coffeemaker, hair dryer, trouser press.

Old Waverley Hotel ⭐   Opposite Waverley Station, the Old Waverley dates from 1848, when the seven-floor structure was built to celebrate the then-newfangled railroads. The lounges have been given a contemporary look. The recently refurbished guest rooms are well maintained and comfortable; some look onto Princes Street and the castle. Each unit comes with a combination tub/shower. The hotel also has a good carvery-style restaurant.

43 Princes St., Edinburgh EH2 2BY. © 0131/556-4648. Fax 031/557-6316. www.paramount-hotels.co.uk. 66 units. £124 ($198) double. Rates include breakfast. AE, DC, MC, V. Parking £8 ($13) for 24 hr. Bus: 15 or 100. **Amenities:** Restaurant; bar; spa; sauna; concierge; room service (7am–9pm); laundry/dry cleaning service. *In room:* TV, dataport, hair dryer, coffeemaker.

Roxburghe Hotel ⭐   The heart of the Roxburghe is a stately graystone–Robert Adam town house on a tree-filled square, a short walk from Princes Street. The atmosphere is traditional, reflected in the drawing room with its ornate ceiling and woodwork, antique furnishings, and tall arched windows. In 1999, the hotel was enlarged into two neighboring buildings, tripling the original number of guest rooms, which vary in size. The largest are in the original building and maintain features like their imposing fireplaces. The new rooms have more recent furnishings and more up-to-date plumbing. The elegant Consort Restaurant is a good place to congregate for drinks.

38 Charlotte St.. (at George St.), Edinburgh EH2 4HQ. © 0131/240-5500. Fax 0131/240-5555. www. macdonaldhotels.co.uk. 197 units. £140–£180 ($224–$288) double; from £230 ($368) suite. AE, DC, MC, V. Parking £10.50 ($17). Bus: 100. **Amenities:** Restaurant; bar; indoor pool; health club; sauna; 24-hr. room service; laundry/dry cleaning service. *In room:* TV, minibar, coffeemaker, hair dryer, iron/ironing board, trouser press.

MODERATE

A-Haven Townhouse *(Kids*   A-Haven is a semi-detached gray-stone Victorian, a 15-minute walk or a 5-minute bus ride north of the rail station in an up-and-coming neighborhood. The guest rooms are of various sizes (the biggest on the second floor) and outfitted with traditional furnishings and shower-only bathrooms. Some units in back overlook the Firth of Forth, and those in front open onto views of Arthur's Seat. Some units are large enough to accommodate family bedrooms with cots, and a playground is available for children. Ronnie Murdock extends a Scottish welcome in this family-type place. He has a licensed bar (for guests only), but breakfast is the only meal served.

180 Ferry Rd., Edinburgh, EH6 4NS. © 0131/554-6559. Fax 0131/554-5252. www.a-haven.co.uk. 14 units. £60–£99 ($96–$158) double. Rates include breakfast. AE, MC, V. Free parking. Bus: 1, 6, 7, 11, 14, 25, C3, 17, 14A, 25A, or 55. **Amenities:** Bar; children's playground. *In room:* TV, dataport, hair dryer, coffeemaker, trouser press.

41 Heriot Row This stone-fronted town house was built in 1806 on what was then one of Edinburgh's most prestigious residential streets. Today, it's the home of Erlend and Hélène Clouston, who make an event out of breakfasts and are especially proud of the fenced-in park across the street (guests can gain access to it); its decorative pond is said to have inspired Robert Louis Stevenson while he was writing *Treasure Island.* The furnishings are attractive and upscale, with unusual prints, exposed flagstone floors, and antique rugs and furnishings. The guest rooms have brass headboards and a sampling of unusual books. One room comes with a shower-only bathroom and the other has a shower and tub combination.

41 Heriot Row, Edinburgh EH3 6ES. © and fax **0131/225-3113.** www.edinburghaccommodation.org.uk. 2 units. £95–£110 ($152–$176) double. Rates include gourmet breakfast. No credit cards. Bus: 4. *In room:* Coffeemaker, hair dryer, no phone.

4 Forres Street Behind a granite facade in the commercial heart of town, a 2-minute walk from Princes Street, this cozy B&B dates back to 1825. A sweeping staircase leads up to the Yellow, Cream, and Pink Rooms, high-ceilinged and very large. (The Cream Room has the largest bathroom, with its own Jacuzzi.) Less spacious, but still comfortable, are the Blue and Green Rooms. Unlike many other Edinburgh guesthouses, this one welcomes kids over 10. No smoking is permitted.

4 Forres St., Edinburgh EH3 6BJ. © © **0131/220-5073.** www.aboutscotland.co.uk/edin/forres.html. 5 units. £90–£120 ($144–$192) double. Rates include breakfast. MC, V. Bus: 82. *In room:* TV, coffeemaker, iron.

19 St. Bernard's Crescent One of the city's most appealing guesthouses occupies the grand home of William Balfour, owner of Edinburgh's Theatre School of Dance and Drama. It was built as an architectural showplace in the early 1800s by the son of Sir Henry Raeburn, one of Scotland's most prominent portraitists. It has grand Doric pillars, a magnificent sandstone staircase, and a distinguished collection of 18th- and 19th-century furniture. Guests enjoy access to the salons and sitting rooms (site of a grand piano). The midsize guest rooms are comfortably appointed, often with four-poster beds (most with shower only). No smoking is permitted.

19 St. Bernard's Crescent, Edinburgh EH4 1NR. © and fax **0131/332-6162.** www.aboutscotland.com/ edin/stbernards.html. 3 units. £100 ($160) double. Rates include continental or full Scottish breakfast. V. Bus: 24 or 34. No children. *In room:* No phone.

Point Hotel With one of the most dramatic contemporary interiors of any hotel in Edinburgh, this is a stylish place in the shadow of Edinburgh Castle. The decor has appeared in a book detailing the 50 premier hotel designs in the world, with a great emphasis on color and innovation, including a black stone floor at the front that's marked by "dusty footprints." In one place red neon spots blue walls in different shades of brilliant light to create an optical fantasy. Sometimes for a dramatic minimalist effect, a lone armchair and sofa will occupy 1,000 square feet of space. Bedrooms are spacious and attractively furnished. Most of the guest rooms have views of the castle; however, those in the rear do not, so be duly warned. If you like stainless steel, laser projections, and chrome instead of Scottish antiques, this might be an address for you. Standard rooms are a bit small, the premium rooms more comfortable and spacious.

34 bread St., Edinburgh EH3 9AF. ℂ 0131/221-5555. Fax 0131/221-9929. www.point-hotel.co.uk. 139 units. Summer £105–£160 ($168–$256) double, £350 ($560) suite; off season 68–£88 ($109–$141) double, £115 ($184) suite. Rates include English breakfast. AE, DC, MC, V. Bus: 4 or 31. **Amenities:** Restaurant; bar; limited room service; laundry/dry cleaning service. *In room:* TV, dataport (executive rooms only), hair dryer, iron.

7 Danube Street ✦   This 1825 B&B, run by Fiona and Colin Mitchell-Rose, is in Stockbridge, a stylish residential neighborhood a 10-minute walk north of the commercial center. It was designed by architect James Milne and was once the home of painter Horatio McCulloch. The public rooms and spacious guest rooms boast artfully draped chintzes. The most desirable room has a four-poster bed and direct access to the garden. All units are well stocked with such sundries as perfumed soaps, adapters, dental floss, and nail files. A lavish breakfast in the formal dining room may include venison sausages, omelets made from free-range eggs, homemade scones, and jams and marmalades put up by Fiona. No smoking is permitted.

7 Danube St., Edinburgh EH4 1NN. ℂ **0131/332-2755.** Fax 0131/343-3648. www.aboutedinburgh.com/ danube.html. 5 units. £90–£110 ($144–$176) double. Rates include breakfast. MC, V. Free parking nearby. Bus: 28. **Amenities:** Laundry. *In room:* TV, dataport, coffeemaker, hair dryer.

16 Lynedoch Place   This stone-fronted 1821 Georgian row house, run by affable hosts Andrew and Susie Hamilton, has a flower-filled front garden, unusual for a house of this type. Inside are high ceilings with deep cove moldings, a cantilevered staircase illuminated by a glassed-in cupola, and family antiques. The midsize guest rooms are cozy and decorated with charm (three with shower only and one with bath only). The elaborate breakfasts are served in a formal dining room. Andrew is an expert in planning itineraries through the Highlands, thanks to the time he spent there as a member of the elite Black Watch Infantry.

16 Lynedoch Place, Edinburgh EH3 7PY. ℂ **0131/225-5507.** Fax 0131/226-4185. www.16lynedochplace. co.uk. 4 units. £60–£100 ($96–$160) double. Rates include breakfast. MC, V. Bus: 19. Pets accepted. *In room:* TV, no phone.

INEXPENSIVE

Greenside Hotel   Behind a chiseled sandstone facade on the back side of Carlton Hill, this four-story Georgian, although recently renovated, has retained such features as its high ceilings, cove moldings, and elaborate trim. Guests access their rooms via a winding staircase, illuminated by a skylight. The rooms are so large that 10 of them contain a double bed and two singles. All have shower-only bathrooms. The Firth of Forth, the yacht *Britannia*, and the dramatic Forth Road Bridge are visible from the uppermost front floors; a sloping tiered garden, with a patio at the bottom, is visible from the rear windows. Breakfast is served in a formal dining room.

9 Royal Terrace, Edinburgh EH7 5AB. ℂ and fax 0131/557-0022. www.townhousehotels.co.uk. 16 units. £46–£92 ($74–$147) double. Rates include breakfast. AE, MC, V. Bus: 4, 15, or 44. **Amenities:** Restaurant; bar. *In room:* TV, coffeemaker, hair dryer.

(Kids) Family-Friendly Hotels

A-Haven Townhouse (p. 82)   With some guest rooms large enough to accommodate families, and a playground for children, any family should feel right at home here.

Carlton Highland Hotel (p. 80)   Kids will love the indoor pool. Parents will love the availability of extra large units and the fact that kids 14 and under stay free in parents' room.

Thrums Private Hotel (p. 87)   This hotel takes its name from J. M. Barrie's fictional name for his hometown of Kirriemuir. Barrie is known to children as the author of *Peter Pan*. Kids are made especially welcome here and are housed in family rooms with their parents.

Teviotdale House (p. 87)   Some enthusiastic visitors rate this place the best B&B in Edinburgh. Three rooms are large enough for families with up to four members. A great value.

Mansfield House   Well located in the New Town, this friendly gay guesthouse offers individually decorated rooms of reasonable size. The best rooms, numbers 9 or 10, are two superior king-size units with sumptuous beds. Bathrooms contain showers only. The hotel is within walking distance of all the gay bars, clubs, and restaurants. It's always busy, so early booking is advised.

57 Dublin St., Edinburgh EH3 6NL. ℂ 0131/556-7980. Fax 0131/466-1315. www.mansfieldguesthouse.com. 9 units, 6 with private bathroom. £50 ($80) double without bathroom; £60–£70 ($96–$112) double with bathroom. Rates include continental breakfast. MC, V. Bus: 19 or 39. *In room:* TV, fridge (in some), coffeemaker, iron, no phone.

Walton Hotel ❀ *(Finds)*   A real discovery, this little hotel lies right in the heart of Edinburgh and in a well-restored 200-year-old town house. A complete refurbishment and renovation has maintained the essential Georgian character and elegant features, but have revitalized and modernized the entire hotel. Bedrooms are midsize, cozy, comfortable, and tranquil. In the morning you're served a superior breakfast. The location is only a few minutes walk to Princes Street.

79 Dundas St., Edinburgh EH3 6SD. ℂ 0131/556-1137. Fax 0131/557-8367. www.waltonhotel.com. 10 units. Summer £89–£120 ($142–$192) double off season £79 ($126) double. Rates include breakfast. MC, V. Bus: 23 or 27. Free parking. In room: TV, coffeemaker, hair dryer.

THE OLD TOWN
VERY EXPENSIVE

The Witchery by the Castle ❀❀❀ *(Finds)*   An offbeat offshoot of a famous Edinburgh restaurant (p. 93), this is a sumptuous, theatrically decorated secret address of Gothic antiques and elaborate tapestries along The Royal Mile. *Cosmopolitan* and other media have hailed this place as one of the "world's most wonderful places to stay." Each lavishly decorated suite features splendid furnishings—"fit for a lord and his lady"—and such extras as books, mood lighting, chocolates, a Bose sound system, and a free bottle of champagne. All the hype about the suites at this hotel are true—"the perfect lust-den," "Scotland's most romantic hotel," "a jewel-box setting," and "one of the 50 best places in the world for honeymooners." Each suite has its own individual character.

Expect a huge roll-top bath built for two. The building is 17th century, filled with open fires, opulent beds, luxurious sitting areas, a galley kitchen, and wall-to-wall luxury. Before your arrival, the beds were broken in by the likes of Michael Douglas, Catherine Zeta-Jones, Pierce Brosnan, and Andrew Lloyd Webber.

Castlehill, The Royal Mile, Edinburgh, EH1 2NF. ℂ **0131/225-5613.** Fax 0131/220-4392. www.thewitchery. com. 6 suites. From £225 ($360) double. AE, DC, MC, V. Rates include continental breakfast. Bus 1 or 6. **Amenities:** 2 restaurants. *In room:* A/C, TV, fridge, coffeemaker, hair dryer, iron/ironing board, safe.

EXPENSIVE

The Bank Hotel ★ *Value*   This imposing hotel offers better value than many of its competitors in this congested neighborhood beside the Royal Mile. Until around 1990, it was a branch of the Royal Bank of Scotland, and the past is still evident in its Greek Temple design. High ceilings, well-chosen furnishings, and king-size beds provide comfort; all but one guest room has shower and tub bathrooms. Each bedroom celebrates the work of a famous Scot, including rooms dedicated to Robert Burns, Robert Louis Stevenson, and Alexander Graham Bell.

Royal Mile at 1 S. Bridge St., Edinburgh EH1 1LL. ℂ **0131/622-6800.** Fax 0131/622-6822. www.festival-inns. co.uk. 9 units. £110–£140 ($176–$224) double with bathroom; £100 ($160) double without bathroom. Rates include breakfast. AE, MC, V. Nearby parking £6.50 ($10). Bus: 4, 15, 31, or 100. **Amenities:** Bar; laundry service. *In room:* TV, coffeemaker, hair dryer, trouser press.

Crown Plaza ★   This is the best major hotel in the old city close to "Royal Edinburgh." This restored and mellow old brick building lies midway along the Royal Mile, halfway between Edinburgh Castle and Holyrood Palace. In spite of the antique geography, the hotel is thoroughly modernized and offers first-class facilities, though lacking the old world charm of some of Edinburgh's grand dame hotels. It's also one of the best-equipped hotels in the area, with such luxuries as a leisure club with a jet stream pool and undercover parking. Most of the bedrooms are spacious and well-decorated; bathrooms contain tub and showers and heated floors for those chilly Scottish mornings. Most of the accommodations are nonsmoking.

80 High St., Edinburgh EH1 1TH. ℂ **0131/557-9797.** Fax 0131/557-9789. www.crowneplazaed.co.uk. 238 units. £100–£230 ($160–$368) double; £260–£330 ($416–$528) suite. AE, DC, DISC, MC, V. Bus 1 or 6. Parking £7.50 ($12). Pets accepted. **Amenities:** Restaurant; bar; indoor pool; health club; sauna; concierge; business center; 24-hr. room service; massage; laundry/dry-cleaning service. *In room:* TV, dataport, minibar, coffeemaker, hair dryer, iron/ironing board, trouser press, safe.

Holyrood Hotel ★★★   We prefer this deluxe charmer to the grand palace hotels of Edinburgh. Holyrood launched itself into the millennium by being proclaimed "Hotel of the Year for Scotland" by Automobile Association. This impressive and exceedingly stylish hotel stands near the Scottish Parliament, the Palace of Holyroodhouse, and Dynamic Earth, and is only 5 minutes from Princes Street. Bedrooms are luxurious, with deluxe furnishings and elegant toiletries. The Club Floor is one of the best retreats in Edinburgh for luxury-minded guests: It has its own private elevator, lounge, and library along with butler and business services.

Holyrood Rd., Edinburgh EH8 8AU. ℂ **0131/550-4500.** Fax 0131/550-4545. www.macdonaldhotels.co.uk. 157 units. £150–£250 ($240–$400) double, from £325 ($520) suite. Rates include buffet breakfast. AE, DC, MC, V. Bus: 25. **Amenities:** Restaurant; bar; indoor pool; health club; sauna; 24-hr. room service; laundry/dry cleaning service; club-level rooms. *In room:* A/C, TV, fax, dataport, minibar, coffeemaker, hair dryer, iron/ironing board, trouser press, safe.

BRUNTSFIELD
EXPENSIVE

Thrums Private Hotel *(Kids)*   About 1.6km (1 mile) south of Princes Street, Thrums is a pair of connected antique buildings, one a two-story 1820 Georgian and the other a small inn (ca. 1900). The hotel contains high-ceilinged guest rooms with contemporary (in the inn) or reproduction antique (in the Georgian) furnishings. Children are especially welcome here, and some accommodations are set aside as family rooms. Six rooms come with a shower-only bathroom, the rest are equipped with combination tub and shower. The Thrums restaurant serves set-price and a la carte menus of British food; there's also a bar and a peaceful garden.

14–15 Minto St., Edinburgh EH9 1RQ. *©* **0131/667-5545.** Fax 0131/667-8707. www.thrumshoteledinburgh. com. 15 units. £65–£85 ($104–$136) double; £90–£120 ($144–$192) family room. Rates include breakfast. MC, V. Free parking. Bus: 3, 7, 8, 31, 81, or 87. **Amenities:** Restaurant; bar; laundry service. *In room:* TV, coffeemaker, hair dryer.

Teviotdale House *(★★)* *(Kids)* *(Value)*   Some visitors rate this three-story 1848 house—10 minutes by bus from Princes Street, Waverley Station, and Edinburgh Castle—as the finest B&B in Edinburgh. Elizabeth and Willy Thiebaud's attention to detail has earned them an enviable reputation. The house is completely no smoking and is furnished with antiques. The three largest can accommodate up to four beds. The home-cooked breakfast may be the highlight of your day's dining, and can include smoked salmon, kippers, and home-baked bread and scones.

53 Grange Loan, Edinburgh EH9 2ER. *©* and fax **0131/667-4376.** teviotdale.house@btinternet.com. 7 units. £56–£90 ($90–$144). AE, MC, V. Bus: 42. *In room:* TV, coffeemaker, hair dryer.

LEITH

The Malmaison *(★★)*   This is Leith's most stylish boutique hotel, lying in the dockyard district, a few steps from Leith Water. It was converted from an 1883 seamen's mission/dorm and is capped by a stately stone clock tower. Its owners have created a hip, unpretentious place with a minimalist decor. The color schemes vary by floor; the purple-and-beige floor has been favored by rock bands who have stayed here during concert tours. Rooms are average in size but well equipped. The facilities are sparse, but you'll find the Malmaison Brasserie (see "Where to Dine," later in this chapter) and a cafe and wine bar favored by locals.

1 Tower Place, Leith, Edinburgh EH6 7DB. *©* **0131/555-6868.** Fax 0131/468-5002. www.malmaison.com. 100 units. £125 ($200) double; £160 ($256) suite. AE, DC, MC, V. Free parking. Bus: 16 or 22. **Amenities:** Restaurant; bar; exercise room. *In room:* TV, dataport, minibar, coffeemaker, hair dryer.

PRESTONFIELD
EXPENSIVE

Prestonfield House *(★★)*   The Prestonfield, rising in Jacobean splendor above 5.3 hectares (13 acres) of grounds and a 5-minute drive from the center, is more celebrated as a restaurant than as a hotel. It was designed by Sir William Bruce, who also designed Holyroodhouse. Guests appreciate the traditional atmosphere and 1680s architecture as well as the peacocks and Highland cattle that strut and stroll across the grounds. The spacious bedrooms are decorated in country-house style and open onto a view of Arthur's Seat, a golf course surrounding the hotel, and the gardens. In 1997, the five rooms in the main house were supplemented by a three-story annex that matches the original structure;

these up-to-date rooms get lots of sun thanks to the large windows. The hotel has one of the city's finest dining rooms (see "Where to Dine," later in this chapter).

Priestfield Rd., Edinburgh EH16 5UT. ℰ 0131/668-3346. Fax 0131/668-3976. www.prestonfieldhouse.com. 31 units. £155–£235 ($248–$376) double; from £345 ($552) suite. Rates include breakfast. AE, DC, MC, V. Free parking. Bus: 21 or 33. Pets accepted. **Amenities:** Restaurant; 2 bars; concierge; secretarial service; 24-hr. room service; babysitting; laundry/dry cleaning service. *In room:* TV, dataport, coffeemaker, hair dryer, iron/ironing board.

DEAN VILLAGE

Channings 🏵🏵   Five Edwardian terrace houses combine to create this hotel, 7 blocks north of Dean Village in a tranquil residential area. Although it's a 5-minute drive from the city center, it maintains the atmosphere of a Scottish country house, with oak paneling, ornate fireplaces, molded ceilings, and antiques. The guest rooms are in a modern style; the front units get the views, but the rear ones get the quiet. The most desirable rooms are the "Executives," most of which have bay windows and wingback chairs. Even if you're not a guest, consider a meal here, as Channings offers some of the best hotel food in Edinburgh (see "Where to Dine," below).

South Learmonth Gardens 15, Edinburgh EH4 1EZ. ℰ **0131/315-2226.** Fax 0131/332-9631. www.channings. co.uk. 46 units. £170 ($272) double; £250 ($400) suite. Rates include breakfast. Children age 14 and under £25 ($40) extra. AE, DC, DISC, MC, V. Bus: 18, 19, 41, or 81. **Amenities:** 2 restaurants; bar; 24-hr. room service; laundry/dry cleaning service. *In room:* TV, dataport, coffeemaker, hair dryer, iron/ironing board, trouser press.

4 Where to Dine

Rivaled only by Glasgow, Edinburgh boasts the finest restaurants in Scotland, and the choice is more diverse now than ever before. Even if you don't care for some of the more exotic regional fare, like haggis (spicy intestines), you'll find an array of top French dining rooms along with other foreign cuisines, especially Indian. And you'll find more and more restaurants catering to vegetarians. But we advise you go native and sample many of the dishes Edinburgh is known for doing best, like fresh salmon and seafood, game from Scottish fields, and Aberdeen Angus steaks. What's the rage at lunch? Stuffed potatoes (baked potatoes with a variety of stuffings). Many Scots make a lunch out of just one of these.

Some restaurants have sections reserved for nonsmokers; others don't. If smoking and dining (or nonsmoking and dining) are very important to you, inquire when making your reservation.

Note: For the locations of the restaurants below, see the "Edinburgh Accommodations & Dining" map, on p. 78.

THE NEW TOWN
EXPENSIVE

The Atrium 🏵   MODERN SCOTTISH/INTERNATIONAL   Since 1993, this has been one of the most emulated restaurants in Edinburgh. No more than 60 diners can be accommodated in the "deliberately moody" atmosphere that's a fusion of Argentinean hacienda and stylish Beverly Hills bistro. Flickering oil lamps create shadows on the dark-colored walls while patrons enjoy dishes prepared with taste and flair. Although offerings vary according to the inspiration of the chef, our favorites include grilled salmon and roasted sea bass, the latter with Dauphinois potatoes, baby spinach, charcoal-grilled eggplant, and baby fennel. The desserts are equally superb, especially the lemon tart with berry soulis and crème fraîche.

10 Cambridge St. (beneath Saltire Court in City Center, a 10-min. walk from Waverly Train Station). C 0131/228-8882. Reservations recommended. Fixed-price meal £15–£18 ($24–$29) at lunch; main courses £15–£19 ($24–$30) at dinner. AE, DC, MC, V. Mon–Fri noon–2pm and 6:30–10pm; Sat 6:30–10pm. Closed for 1 week at Christmas. Bus 11 or 15.

Channings ✦ SCOTTISH/INTERNATIONAL   This is the main dining room of an Edwardian charmer of a hotel, offering traditional decor and elegant service from a well-trained staff. The exemplary cuisine allows the natural flavors of the superior-quality Scottish ingredients to shine through. The chefs know, for example, to go to the "Baines of Tarves" for his free-range Aberdeen chickens, or to Iain Mellis for his cheese. For dinner, you might opt for the terrine of seared tuna, potatoes, and slow-roasted tomatoes. To finish, try the hot banana and butterscotch soufflé with honeycomb ice cream. The restaurant is proud of its extensive wine list, which incorporates the old standards and newer, more exciting choices.

A less formal brasserie, with a log fireplace and a casual atmosphere, serves bar meals, light lunches, and dinners.

In Channings Hotel, 15 S. Learmonth Gardens. C 0131/315-2225. Reservations recommended. Fixed-price lunch £16 ($26) for 2 courses, £19 ($30) for 3 courses. AE, MC, V. Tues–Sat noon–3:30pm and 7–10pm; Sun 7–10pm. Closed Dec 26–29. Bus: 41 or 42.

Cosmo Ristorante ✦ ITALIAN   Even after more than 30 years in business, Cosmo is still one of the most popular Italian restaurants in town, where courtesy, efficiency, and good cooking draw in the crowds. The soups and pastas are always reliable. The kitchen is known for its *saltimbocca* (veal with ham) and Italian-inspired preparations of fish. This isn't the greatest Italian dining in Scotland, but you'll certainly have a good, filling meal.

58A N. Castle St. C 0131/226-6743. Reservations required. Main courses £14.50–£21.90 ($23–$35). AE, MC, V. Mon–Fri 12:30–2:15pm; Mon–Sat 7–10:45pm. Bus: 31 or 33.

Dome Bar & Grill ✦ INTERNATIONAL   In a restored Georgian building with an elaborate domed ceiling, this bar and grill is part of the Dome entertainment complex. Throughout are elaborate columns, pedimental sculptures, and marble mosaic floors. The menu is ambitious and creative, with dishes like duck liver pâté with Cumberland sauce and oat cakes, king prawn brochettes, mullet with horseradish mash, and vegetable risotto.

14 George St. C 0131/624-8624. Reservations required for lunch and dinner. Main courses £9–£20 ($14–$32) at lunch; £10–£21 ($16–$34) at dinner; fixed-price dinner menu £30 ($48). AE, DC, MC, V. Restaurant daily noon–10pm; bar Sun–Thurs 10am–11pm, Fri–Sat 10am–1am. Bus: 3, 21, 26, 31, or 85.

Duck's at Le Marché Noir ✦ SCOTTISH/FRENCH   This place's cuisine is more stylish, and more tuned to the culinary sophistication of London, than many other restaurants in Edinburgh. A handful of dishes honor the traditions of Scotland—for example, the baked haggis in phyllo pastry on a bed of turnip purée. More modern dishes include breast of duck with a lentil bean casserole flavored with blackberry juice. A classic favorite is Angus beef with a red onion confit and port *jus*.

2–4 Eyre Place. C 0131/558-1608. Reservations recommended. Set-price lunch £9.90 ($16) for 2 course, £13.50 ($22) for 3 courses; dinner main courses £9.50–£20.50 ($15–$33). AE, DC, MC, V. Tues-Fri noon–2:30pm and daily 7–10:30pm. Bus: 23 or 27.

Oh, Give It a Try!

Haggis, the much-maligned national dish of Scotland, is certainly an acquired taste. But you've come all this way—why not be brave and give it a try? **Macsween of Edinburgh Haggis** is a long-established family business specializing in haggis. Macsween haggis includes lamb, beef, oatmeal, onions, and a special blend of seasonings and spices cooked together. There's also an all-vegetarian version. Both are sold in vacuum-packed plastic bags that require only reheating in a microwave or regular oven. You can find this company's product at food stores and supermarkets throughout Edinburgh. Two central distributors are **Peckham's Delicatessen,** 155–159 Bruntsfield Place (© **0131/229-7054**), open daily from 8am to 8pm, and **Jenner's Department Store,** 2 East Princes St. (© **0131/ 260-2242**), open Monday through Saturday from 9am to 6pm and Sunday from noon to 5pm.

Haldanes Restaurant ⚜ SCOTTISH   Set in the cellar of the Albany Hotel building, in a pair of royal blue and gold dining rooms, Haldanes serves dinners that are conducted like meals in a private country house, with polite and deferential service. In nice weather, you can sit in the verdant garden. The chef applies a light touch to innovative dishes, including haggis in phyllo pastry with tatties (roasted potatoes) and whisky sauce; and a pavé of lamb with mint-flavored herb crust, wild mushrooms, and zucchini. One of the local favorites is a baked filet of monkfish with cream spinach served with a crayfish and brandy bisque.

39A Albany St. © **0131/556-8407.** Reservations recommended. Dinner main courses £15.95–£22.50 ($26–$36). DC, MC, V. Daily 6–9:30pm. Bus: 15.

Martin's ⚜ SCOTTISH   Owners Gay and Martin Irons and their trio of top chefs are deeply committed to wild and organically grown foods and include them on the menu when they can. Although the setting is unlikely, off Edinburgh's pub street and down an unpromising alley, the restaurant's celadon-green rooms are now a landmark. The menu changes daily to take advantage of the freshest ingredients, and Martin's father provides herbs from his own garden. The best of the country's venison, fish (especially salmon), and shellfish appear regularly; wild mushrooms are a particular favorite. You might try pan-fried filet of sea trout with caramelized fennel, or roast loin of wild venison in a red wine *jus.*

70 Rose St., North Lane. © **0131/225-3106.** Reservations required. Lunch main courses £7–£18 ($11–$29), 2-course lunch £13.50 ($22); dinner main courses £17–£23 ($27–$37), 3-course dinner £25 ($40). AE, DC, MC, V. Tues–Fri noon–2pm; Tues–Sat 7–10pm. During festival in Aug Mon–Sat 6:30–11pm. Closed Dec 24–Jan 23, 1 week in May/June, and 1 week in Sept/Oct. Bus: 2, 4, 15, 21, or 44. No children under 8 allowed.

No. 1 Princes Street ⚜ SCOTTISH/CONTINENTAL   This is the Balmoral's premier restaurant, an intimate, crimson-colored enclave whose walls are studded with Scottish memorabilia. You can sample the likes of pan-seared Isle of Skye monkfish with saffron mussel broth, or perhaps roulade of Dover sole with langoustine, oyster, and scallop garnish. Dessert brings a variety of sorbets, cheeses, and more exotic choices like mulled wine parfait with a cinnamon sauce. There's a separate vegetarian menu and a wide-ranging wine list with celestial tariffs.

In the Balmoral Hotel, 1 Princes St. © **0131/556-2414.** Reservations recommended. Main courses £19.50–£22.95 ($31–$37); fixed-price lunch £14.50 ($23) for 2 courses; fixed-price dinner £38.50 ($62) for 3-courses, £52.50 ($84) for 6 courses. AE, DC, MC, V. Sun–Thurs 7–10pm; Fri–Sat 7–10:30pm.

Pompadour Restaurant ⭐ SCOTTISH/FRENCH   On the mezzanine of the Caledonian Hilton Edinburgh, the Pompadour is one of Edinburgh's best. The restaurant has been refurbished in a Louis XV decor. The chef blends cuisine moderne with traditional menus, and his daily offerings reflect the best available from the market, with Scottish salmon, venison, and other game often included. The menu also features fresh produce from local and French markets—items like goose liver with wild mushrooms, lamb with spinach and rosemary, and charlotte of marinated salmon filled with seafood. The wine list is lethally expensive.

In the Caledonian Hilton Edinburgh, Princes St. ℂ **0131/222-8888**. Reservations required. Fixed-price lunch menu £15.50–£18.50 ($25–$30); main courses £15–£25 ($24–$40). AE, DC, MC, V. Tues–Fri 12:30–2pm; Tues–Sat 7:30–9:30pm. Bus: 4, 15, or 44.

MODERATE

Blue Bar Café INTERNATIONAL   In the building containing the Traverse Theatre, this attractive bistro is the less expensive sibling of The Atrium (see above). You'll find a mostly white, minimalist decor (with touches of blue); solid oaken tables; and a cheerful staff. The sophisticated menu might feature delectable seared scallops; succulent breast of duck with a compote of figs and apple jus; and a perfect charcoal-grilled tuna with basil-flavored noodles or bubble and squeak.

10 Cambridge St. ℂ **0131/221-1222**. Reservations recommended. Set-price lunch £7.95–£13.95 ($13–$22); main courses £10.95–£14.95 ($18–$24). AE, DC, MC, V. Mon–Sat noon–3pm and 6–11pm. Bus: 10, 11, 16, or 27.

Café Saint-Honoré FRENCH/SCOTTISH   This French-inspired bistro is a deliberately rapid-paced place at lunchtime, then becomes much more formal at dinner. The menu is completely revised each day, based on what's fresh and what the chefs feel inspired to cook. An upbeat and usually enthusiastic staff serves a combination of Scottish and French cuisine that includes venison with juniper berries and wild mushrooms, local pheasant in wine and garlic sauce, or lamb kidneys with broad beans.

34 NW Thistle St. Lane. ℂ **0131/226-2211**. Reservations recommended. Main courses £8–£24 ($13–$38) at lunch, a fixed-price meal £16–£30 ($26–$48) at dinner. AE, DC, MC, V. Mon–Fri noon–2:15pm; Mon–Fri (pre-theater meal) 5:30–7pm; Mon–Sat 7–10pm and sometimes 11pm. Bus: 3, 16, 17, 23, 27, or 31.

(*Moments*   **Tea for Two**

If you're looking for a bit of refreshment while sightseeing, try **Clarinda's Tea Room**, 69 Canongate (ℂ **0131/557-1888**), for the very British experience of afternoon tea. This cubbyhole of a tearoom is only steps from Holyroodhouse and decorated in the manner you'd expect, with lace tablecloths, bone china, and antique Wedgwood plates on the walls. There are plenty of teas from which to choose, plus a long list of tempting sweets. Homemade soup, lasagna, baked potatoes with cheese, salads, and similar dishes are also offered. It's open Monday to Saturday 9am to 4:45pm and Sunday 10am to 4:45pm.

Another choice is **Ryan's Bar**, 2 Hope St. (ℂ **0131/226-6669**), near the northwestern corner of the West Princes Street Gardens. It serves tea daily 10:30am to 1am. If you want a more formal tea ceremony, try the Palm Court at the **Balmoral Hotel**, Princes Street (ℂ **0131/556-2414**), serving tea daily noon to 3pm.

The Marque ⭐ SCOTTISH/INTERNATIONAL   The Marque is ideally located for the theater and offers reasonably priced pre- and post-theater dinners. Owned by Lara Kearney, John Rutter, and Glyn Stevens, all formerly of The Atrium, this is a fast-growing, popular place. The bold yellow walls and black-and-white floor give this converted antiques shop a unique, contemporary look. The cuisine is ambitious and seductive. Main courses include halibut roasted in olive oil, char-grilled tuna, and chicken and foie gras terrine with onion jam. The rhubarb crumble with tamarind ice cream is a great way to end an enjoyable meal.

19–21 Causewayside. ✆ 0131/466-6660. Reservations recommended. Main courses £11.50–£16.95 ($18–$27); set-price lunch and pre- and post-theater dinner £11.50–£14 ($18–$22) for 2 courses. AE, MC, V. Tues–Thurs 11:45am–2pm and 5:30–10pm; Fri 11:45am–2pm and 5:30–11pm; Sat noon–2pm and 5:30–11pm. Bus: 42.

Restaurant at the Bonham ⭐⭐ SCOTTISH/CONTINENTAL   The setting at one of Edinburgh's most charming restaurants marries 19th-century oak paneling and deep ceiling coves with modern paintings and oversized mirrors. Chef Michel Bouyer has greatly improved the cuisine here, creating a stimulating menu in his own style. Though classically trained in Paris, he adds his own creative touches to favorites such as char-grilled tuna with a lime and mint couscous; wild mushroom, lentil, and tarragon ravioli with a green bean and artichoke salad; and pan-fried halibut with a carrot and cumin purée and candied lemons.

In The Bonham Hotel, 35 Drumsheugh Gardens. ✆ 0131/623-9319. Reservations recommended. Main courses £15–£18.50 ($24–$30). AE, DC, MC, V. Daily 12:30–2:30pm and 6:30–10pm. Bus: 23 or 27.

The Tower ⭐⭐ SEAFOOD/MODERN BRITISH   This is the town's hot new dining ticket, set at the top of the Museum of Scotland. The chef uses local ingredients to create some of the capital's tastiest fare. The inventive kitchen will regale you with hearty portions of steak, roast beef, and excellent seafood. We still remember fondly the smoked haddock risotto with a poached egg and shavings of Parmesan cheese. The sea bass was perfectly seasoned and grilled, and there's even sushi on the menu.

⌒Kids Family-Friendly Restaurants

Mr. Boni's Ice Cream Parlour   Mr. Boni's is at 4 Lochrin Bridge (✆ 0131/ 229-2740). Every kid comes away loving Mr. Boni, who makes the best homemade ice cream in Edinburgh, plus sandwiches, jumbo hot dogs, and beef burgers with french fries.

Henderson's Salad Table   Edinburgh's leading vegetarian restaurant has an array of nutritious salads, followed by some of the most delectable homemade desserts in the city. Located at 94 Hanover St. (✆ 0131/ 225-2131).

Baked Potato Shop   Children delight in being taken to this worker's favorite lunch spot, where they can order flaky baked potatoes with a choice of half a dozen hot fillings along with all sorts of other dishes, including chili and 20 kinds of salads. It's cheap, too. 56 Cockburn St. (✆ 0131/225-7572).

In the Museum of Scotland, Chambers St. ℂ **0131/225-3003.** Reservations required. Lunch main courses £9–£17.95 ($14–$29). Dinner main courses £13.95–£24.95 ($22–$40). AE, DC, MC, V. Daily noon–11pm. Bus: 3, 7, 21, 30, 31, 53, 69, or 80.

INEXPENSIVE

Far Pavilions INDIAN/CONTINENTAL   Established in 1987, this Indian restaurant offers finely tuned service. You might appreciate a drink in the bar before confronting the long menu, with dishes from the former Portuguese colony of Goa and the northern Indian province of Punjab. Highly recommended is the house specialty, Murgi Massala, concocted with tandoori chicken that falls off the bone thanks to slow cooking in a garlic-based butter sauce.

10 Craighleith Rd., Comely Bank. ℂ **0131/332-3362.** Reservations recommended. Lunch main courses £8–£15.95 ($13–$26), lunch buffet £6.95 ($11) per person, dinner main courses £8–£15.95 ($13–$26). AE, MC, V. Mon–Fri noon–2pm and Mon–Sat 5:30pm–midnight. Bus: 19, 39, 55, 81, or X91.

THE OLD TOWN
EXPENSIVE

Dubh Prais ⭐ SCOTTISH   Dubh Prais (Gaelic for "The Black Pot") conjures up an image of old-fashioned Scottish recipes bubbling away in a stewpot above a fireplace. In dining rooms adorned with stenciled thistles, you'll be served time-tested and not at all experimental meals that are flavorful nonetheless. Examples include smoked salmon; saddle of venison with juniper sauce; and a suprême of salmon with grapefruit-flavored butter sauce.

123B High St., Royal Mile. ℂ **0131/557-5732.** Reservations recommended. Lunch main courses £6.50–£9.50 ($10–$15); dinner main courses £12.50–£16.50 ($20–$26). AE, MC, V. Tues–Fri noon–2pm and Tues–Sat 6–10:30pm. Bus: 11.

Iggs ⭐ SPANISH/SCOTTISH   Just off the Royal Mile in Old Town, this Victorian-style establishment is the domain of a dynamic chef, Andrew McQueen, who is not afraid to experiment but also seems well grounded in the classics. Dinner here is made more charming by the attention from the waitstaff, clad in black polo shirts. For a main course you might choose the more traditional rack of Highland lamb with spring vegetables; if you want to go more exotic, opt for the loin of veal on a truffle and Gruyère risotto given extra flavor by a Madeira sauce. After you think you've had every dessert in the world, along comes a honey-roasted butternut-squash cheesecake with a caramel sauce.

15 Jeffrey St. ℂ **0131/557-8184.** Reservations recommended. Main courses £13.50–£19 ($22–$30); fixed-price lunch £15.50 ($25) for 3 courses. AE, DC, MC, V. Mon–Sat noon–2:30pm and 6–10:30pm. Bus: 1 or 35.

Jackson's Restaurant ⭐ SCOTTISH   Serving a cuisine described as "Scottish with a French flair," this bustling restaurant is in the stone cellar of a 300-year-old building. Choose your drink from almost 40 kinds of Highland malts, and then select from a menu featuring dinners made from local ingredients. The charming staff will help you translate such items as "beasties of the glen" (haggis with rosemary-and-garlic sauce) and "kilted salmon" pan-fried in green ginger-and-whisky sauce.

209 High St., Royal Mile. ℂ **0131/225-1793.** Reservations recommended. Main courses £11–£18 ($18–$29); fixed-price dinner £25 ($40). AE, DC, MC, V. Daily noon–2:30pm and 6–10:45pm. Bus: 35.

Witchery by the Castle ⭐ SCOTTISH/FRENCH   This place bills itself as the oldest, most haunted restaurant in town, and the Hellfire Club was supposed to have met here during the Middle Ages. The building has been linked with witchcraft since the period between 1470 and 1722, when more than 1,000 people were burned alive on Castlehill; one of the victims is alleged to haunt the Witchery. The chef uses creative flair to create classy Scottish food, such as Angus beef, Scottish lobster, and Loch Fyne oysters. Such well-prepared old-time favorites as confit of wild rabbit with bacon appear on the menu, as does pan-roasted monkfish with a thyme and lemon risotto or seared seabream with pumpkin and potato *rôsti* flavored with a rosemary cream. One restaurant critic called the vast slabs of bloody beef and venison politically incorrect—that and the cigar smoke.

352 Castlehill, Royal Mile. © 0131/225-5613. Reservations recommended. Main courses £13–£20 ($21–$32). AE, DC, MC, V. Daily noon–4pm and 5:30–11:30pm. Bus: 1 or 6.

LEITH

In the northern regions of Edinburgh, the old port town of Leith opens onto the Firth of Forth. After decades of decay, it has become an arty neighborhood with a collection of restaurants, wine bars, and pubs.

EXPENSIVE

Martin Wishart ★★★ MODERN FRENCH   Several gourmet associations claim this is the "Scottish restaurant of the year." Chef and owner Martin Wishart takes it all in stride and continues to improve the quality of his establishment in a fashionable part of the Leith docklands. The minimalist decor features white walls and modern art. The menu is short but sweet, taking advantage of the best of the season. The gratin of sea bass arrives aromatically with a soft, herby crust. Many dishes are simply prepared, the natural flavors coming through; others show a touch of fantasy, as in the partridge breast with black truffle and foie gras. Where can you get a good pot roast pig's cheek if not here? After eating the glazed lemon tart with praline ice cream on white raspberry coulis, the day is yours.

54 The Shore, Leith. © 0131/553-3557. Reservations required. Main courses £18.50–£23.50 ($30–$38). Set lunch £18.50 ($30) (3 courses). Tues–Fri noon–2pm; Tues–Thurs 6:30–10pm; Fri–Sat 6:30–10:30pm. Bus: 7 or 10.

Vintner's Room ★ FRENCH/SCOTTISH   This stone-fronted building down by the waterfront was constructed around 1650 as a warehouse for barrels of Bordeaux (claret) and port that came in from Europe's mainland. Near the entrance, beneath a ceiling of venerable oaken beams, a wine bar serves platters and drinks beside a large stone fireplace. Most people, however, head for the dining room, decorated with elaborate Italianate plasterwork and lit with flickering candles. The menu might feature such robust cuisine as seafood salad with mango mayonnaise, pigeon-and-duck terrine, and venison in a bitter-chocolate sauce.

The Vaults, 87 Giles St., Leith. © 0131/554-6767. Reservations recommended. Main courses £10–£13 ($16–$21) at lunch; dinner main courses £14.50–£19 ($23–$30). AE, MC, V. Mon–Sat noon–2pm and 7–10:30pm. Closed 2 weeks at Christmas. Bus: 7 or 10.

MODERATE

Fishers Bistro ★   This place is noted for its outstanding seafood and its setting at a 17th-century windmill with a panoramic view of the harbor at Leith. It's well known among the locals who praise it for its selection of seafood and the quality of its fresh fish. You can dine in the main restaurant or at a specialty seafood bar. Naturally, a nautical aura prevails with fish nets, pictures of the sea, and various marine memorabilia. The Miller family founded the restaurant in the early 90s, and their chefs offer such enticing appetizers as fresh Loch Fyne oysters, acclaimed as among Britain's finest. For your main course, sample the tasty baked *Finnan Haddie* (smoked haddock) topped with roasted peppers and vine-ripened tomatoes or the king scallops with a wild asparagus "caviar." One of the most commendable main courses is roast Scottish wild salmon filet with yogurt.

1 The Shore, Leith. ⟨✆⟩ 0131/554-5666. Reservations required. Main courses £11–£20 ($18–$32). AE, MC, V. Mon–Sat noon–4pm and 5–10pm; Sun noon–4pm and 5–10:30pm. Bus: 22.

Malmaison Brasserie TRADITIONAL FRENCH   In the previously recommended hotel, this unpretentious brasserie is charming enough to merit a trip out from Edinburgh. The setting is simple, with lots of polished wood and wrought iron. The bistro-inspired menu includes fried steak with *pommes frites* (french fries), sea bass with vinaigrette, and sole meunière with rosemary potatoes. Everyone's favorite dessert is the crème brûlée. Regrettably, the restaurant doesn't have a view of the harbor but faces a side street.

In the Malmaison Hotel, 1 Tower Place, Leith. ⟨✆⟩ 0131/555-6868. Reservations recommended for dinner. Fixed-price menu £12.95–£15.95 ($21–$26). AE, DC, MC, V. Daily noon–2:30pm and 6–11pm. Bus: 6, 16, or 22A.

INEXPENSIVE

Zinc Bar & Grill   INTERNATIONAL. No one does modern chic better than Sir Terence Conran as you'll soon see if you dine at this entrepreneur's latest offering. You'll dine off metal tables while enjoying (perhaps) the abstract wall hangings. The restaurant is part of the £120 million leisure resort, called Ocean Terminal, which opened in 2001, with a cinema, bars, dining choices, and shops. To reach Zinc, take the escalator upstairs.

This brasserie-grill opens onto vast picture windows with a view of the harbor. For warm days, there is an outdoor terrace. It's a good choice for lunch, while visiting the Royal Yacht Britannia. Food is prepared to order, and it includes an array of burgers, roast lamb, grilled chicken, fried sole or salmon, along with tender Scottish steaks made from Angus beef. You might opt for such good-tasting dishes as poached salmon with couscous, or else a tender sirloin steak. Pasta fans might gravitate to the spaghetti with a lemon basil sauce and pine nuts.

Unit 42, Ocean Terminal. Leith. ⟨✆⟩ 0131/553-8070. Reservations recommended. Main courses £7.50–£10.50 ($12–$17) lunch; £9.50–£15.50 ($15–$25) dinner. 2-course lunch or dinner £12 ($19), 3-course lunch or dinner £15 ($24). AE, DC, MC, V. Mon–Thurs noon–11pm; Fri–Sun noon–midnight. Bus: 22.

PRESTONFIELD
EXPENSIVE

Prestonfield House ⊛ BRITISH   Hidden amid 5.3 hectares (13 acres) of private parkland and gardens, 5km (3 miles) south of Edinburgh's center, this elegant restaurant often hosts locals celebrating special occasions. It's an old-fashioned choice, certainly, but it still offers the same fine quality as always. Menu items include grilled salmon with braised leeks and gazpacho, baked lamb in phyllo with tomatoes and wild mushrooms, and marinated smoked pigeon with avocado-and-raspberry salad.

Priestfield Rd., Edinburgh EH16 5UT. ⟨✆⟩ 0131/668-3346. Reservations preferred. Main courses £14.50–£19.25 ($23–$31); table d'hôtel menu £19 ($30) lunch. AE, DC, MC, V. Daily noon–2pm and 7–9:30pm. Bus: 2, 14 or 31.

5 Exploring the City
ALONG THE ROYAL MILE

Old Town's **Royal Mile** ⊛⊛⊛ stretches from Edinburgh Castle all the way to the Palace of Holyroodhouse and bears four names along its length: Castlehill, Lawnmarket, High Street, and Canongate. Walking along, you'll see some of the most interesting old structures in the city, with turrets, gables, and towering chimneys. Take bus no. 1, 6, 23, 27, 30, 34, or 36 to reach it.

Edinburgh Attractions

Britannia **22**
Burns Monument **24**
Calton Hill **21**
Calton Old Cemetery **19**
Dean Gallery **4**
Dean Village **3**
Dynamic Earth **30**
Edinburgh Castle **10**
Edinburgh Zoo **2**
Georgian House **6**
Gladstone's Land **15**
High Kirk of St. Giles **17**
Huntly House **28**
John Knox House **25**
Lincoln Monument **20**
Museum of Childhood **26**
National Gallery
  of Scotland **9**
National Museum
  of Scotland **16**
Nelson Monument **23**

To Leith **22**

| 0 | 1/10 mi |
| 0 | 0.1 km |

✝ Church
ⓘ Information
— Railway

Annandale St.

Brunswick Road

Elm Row

East London St.

Union Street

Montgomery Street   Montgomery Street

Broughton Street

Hillside   Crescent

London Road

Albany Street

Union Place

Royal Terrace

York Place

Elder St.

CALTON HILL 20   **21 REGENT GARDENS**

W Register St.

Leith Street

Waterloo Place

19

23

Regent Terrace

Regent Road

Abbey Hill

North Bridge

Calton Road   **24**

Canongate Church   **29 Holyroodhouse**

Waverley Station

Waverley Bridge

Market St.

Jeffrey Street

27   The Royal Mile

Canongate   **28**   **30**

18 The Royal Mile   **25**   High Street   **26**   **CANONGATE**

South Bridge   St. Mary's St.

Holyrood Road

17

Holyrood Road

H O L Y R O O D

P A R K

Cowgate

■ **National Library**

George IV Bridge

Chambers St.

College St.

Drummond St.

Pleasance

Nicolson St.

Bristo Place

Potterrow

31

West Richmond

The Queen's Drive

■ **McEwan Hall**

George Square

Buccleuch Street

Crosscauseway

Buccleuch Place

St. Leonard's St.

Middle Meadow Walk

Meadow Lane

Clerk St.

Dalkeith Road

THE MEADOWS

Melville Drive

S. Clerk St.

32

East Preston St.

Edinburgh Castle ★★   No place in Scotland is filled with as much history, legend, and lore as Edinburgh Castle, one of the highlights of a visit to this little country. It's believed the ancient city grew up on the seat of a dead volcano, Castle Rock. The early history is vague, but it's known that in the 11th century, Malcolm III (Canmore) and his Saxon queen, later venerated as St. Margaret, founded a castle on this spot. The only fragment left of their original castle—in fact, the oldest structure in Edinburgh—is St. Margaret's Chapel, built in the Norman style, the oblong structure dating principally from the 12th century. After centuries of destruction, demolitions, and upheavals, the buildings that stand today are basically those that resulted from the castle's role as a military garrison in the past two or three centuries.

You can visit the State Apartments, particularly Queen Mary's Bedroom, where Mary Queen of Scots gave birth to James VI of Scotland (later James I of England). Scottish Parliaments used to convene in the Great Hall. The highlight is the Crown Chamber, housing the Honours of Scotland (Scottish Crown Jewels), used at the coronation of James VI, along with the scepter and sword of state of Scotland. The French Prisons were put to use in the 18th century, and these great storerooms housed hundreds of Napoleonic soldiers in the early 19th century. Many of them made wall carvings you can see today. Among the batteries of cannons that protected the castle is Mons Meg, a 15th-century cannon weighing more than 5 tons.

Castlehill (✆) **0131/225-9846**. Admission £8.50 ($14) adults, £2 ($3.20) children age 15 and under. Apr–Sept daily 9:30am–5:15pm; Oct–Mar daily 9:30am–4:15pm. Bus: 1 or 6.

Outlook Tower and Camera Obscura   The 1853 periscope at the top of the Outlook Tower throws a revolving image of nearby streets and buildings onto a circular table. Guides point out the landmarks and talk about Edinburgh's fascinating history. In addition, there are several entertaining exhibits, all with an optical theme, plus a well-stocked shop selling books, crafts, and CDs.

Castlehill. (✆) **0131/226-3709**. Admission £5.75 ($9.20) adults, £4.60 ($7.35) seniors and £3.70 ($5.90) children. Open Apr–Oct Mon–Fri 9:30am–6pm, Sat–Sun 10am–6pm, until 7:30pm in July and 7pm in Aug; Nov–Mar daily 10am–5pm. Bus: 1 or 6.

Scotch Whisky Heritage Centre   This center is privately funded by a conglomeration of Scotland's biggest distillers. It highlights the economic effect of whisky on both Scotland and the world, and illuminates the centuries-old traditions associated with whisky making. You get to see a 7-minute audiovisual show and ride an electric car past 13 sets showing historic moments in the whisky industry. A tour entitling you to sample five whiskies and take away a miniature bottle costs £11.95 ($17.95) per person.

354 Castlehill (10-min. walk from Waverley Train Station). (✆) **0131/220-0441**. Admission £6.50 ($10) adults, £5.50 ($8.80) seniors, £4.50 ($7.20) students with ID, £3.95 ($6.30) children age 5–17, children age 4 and under free. Daily 10am–5pm.

Gladstone's Land ★   This 17th-century merchant's house has been furnished and kept in its original style. On the ground floor is a reconstructed shop booth displaying replicas of goods of the period, and an upstairs apartment is furnished as it might have been in the 17th century. It's worth a visit on your journey along the Royal Mile, if only to get the impression of how confined living conditions were, even for the reasonably well off, before the construction of New Town.

477B Lawnmarket (10-min. walk from Waverley Train Station). (✆) **0131/226-5856**. Admission £3.50 ($5.60) adults, £2.50 ($4) students and seniors, £1 ($1.60) children. Apr–Oct Mon–Sat 10am–5pm, Sun 2–5pm. Closed other months.

Frommer's Favorite Edinburgh Experiences

Contemplating the City & Environs from Arthur's Seat. At 250m (823 ft.) atop Arthur's Seat (which you reach by climbing up Holyrood Park), you'll see the Highlands in miniature—the view is magical. Scots congregate here to await the solstice.

Visiting Dean Village. About 30m (100 ft.) below the level of the rest of the city, Dean Village is an 800-year-old grain-milling town on the Water of Leith. Come here to soak up local color and enjoy a summertime stroll on the path by the river; it makes for great people-watching.

Shopping Along Princes Street. This is the main street of Edinburgh, the local equivalent of New York's Fifth Avenue. Flower-filled gardens stretch along the street's whole south side. When not admiring the flowers, you can browse the country's finest merchandise, everything from kilts to Scottish crystal.

Downing a Pint in an Edinburgh Pub. Sampling a pint of McEwan's real ale or Tennent's lager is a chance to soak up the special atmosphere of Edinburgh. Our favorites are the Abbotsford (p. 118) and the Bow Bar (p. 118).

Writers' Museum   This 1622 house is a treasure trove of portraits, relics, and manuscripts relating to three of Scotland's greatest men of letters: Robert Burns (1759–96), Sir Walter Scott (1771–1832), and Robert Louis Stevenson (1850–1894). The Burns collection includes his writing desk, rare manuscripts, portraits, and many other items. Also on display are some of Sir Walter Scott's possessions, including his pipe, chess set, and original manuscripts. The museum holds one of the most significant Stevenson collections anywhere, including personal belongings, paintings, photographs, and early editions.

In Lady Stair's House, off Lawnmarket (10-min. walk from Waverley Train Station). ℂ **0131/529-4901.** Free admission. Mon–Sat 10am–4:45pm.

High Kirk of St. Giles ★★   Built in 1120 a short walk downhill from Edinburgh Castle, this church is one of the most important architectural landmarks along the Royal Mile. It combines a dark and brooding stone exterior with surprisingly graceful flying buttresses. One of its outstanding features is Thistle Chapel, housing beautiful stalls and notable heraldic stained-glass windows.

High St. ℂ **0131/225-9442.** Free admission, but £1 ($1.60) donation suggested. Easter–Sept Mon–Fri 9am–7pm, Sat 9am–5pm, Sun 1–5pm; Oct–Easter Mon–Sat 9am–5pm, Sun 1–5pm. Sun services at 8, 10, and 11:30am and 6 and 8pm. Bus: 23 or 27.

The Real Mary King's Close *Finds*   Beneath the City Chambers on the Royal Mile lies Old Town's deepest secret, a warren of hidden streets where people lived and worked for centuries. This new attraction allows you to go back into the turbulent days of plague-ridden Edinburgh in the 17th century. Today's visitors can see a number of underground "Closes," originally very narrow walkways with houses on either sides, some dating back centuries. When the Royal Exchange (now the City Chambers) were constructed in 1753, the top floors of the buildings of the Close were torn down, although the lower sections were left standing and used as the foundations of the new building, leaving a number of dark and mysterious passages intact. In April of 2003, guided parties were allowed to visit these dwellings for the first time. Subtle lighting and audio effects add to the experience. You can visit everything from a grave digger's family stricken with the plague to a grand 16th-century town house. The haunted Shrine room is the best surviving 17th-century house in Scotland.

Writers' Court, off the Royal Mile. © 0870/243-0160. Admission £7 ($11) adults, £5 ($8) children, £21 ($34) family ticket. Nov–Mar daily 10am–4pm; Apr–Oct daily 10am–9pm. Bus: 1 or 6.

John Knox House   Even if you're not interested in the reformer who founded the Scottish Presbyterian church, you may want to visit his late-15th-century house, with its timbered gallery, as it's characteristic of the "lands" that used to flank the Royal Mile. The Oak Room is noteworthy for its frescoed ceiling and for its Knox memorabilia. Born into a prosperous East Lothian peasant family, John Knox is acknowledged as the first Moderator of the Presbyterian Church of Scotland, the tenets of which he established in 1560. He's regarded as the prototype Puritan, but actually started his professional life as a Catholic priest and was renowned for his sharp wit and sarcasm. Knox lived at a time of great religious and political upheaval, and although he escaped execution, he spent 2 years as a galley slave in France for agitating against papal authority. On his release, he worked tirelessly with the English crown to ensure Protestant victory in Scotland, then closely aligned to Catholic France. Knox was also a writer/historian—his *History of the Reformation* was his greatest literary achievement, but he's better known for the inflammatory treatise *The Monstrous Regiment* [Government] *of Women,* largely inspired by his opposition to the reign of Mary Queen of Scots. However, the title did very little to endear him to Mary's cousin Elizabeth I, who insisted his particular brand of crusading zeal remain north of the border.

43–45 High St. (5-min. walk from Waverley Train Station.) © 0131/556-9579. Admission £2.25 ($3.60) adults, £1.75 ($2.80) seniors and students, 75p ($1.20) children. Mon–Sat 10am–4:30pm (July–Aug also Sun noon–4:30pm).

Museum of Childhood *(Kids*   The world's first museum devoted solely to the history of childhood stands just opposite the John Knox House. Contents of its four floors range from antique toys to games to exhibits on health, education, and costumes, plus video presentations and an activity area. Not surprisingly, this is usually the noisiest museum in town.

42 High St. © 0131/529-4142. Free admission. Mon–Sat 10am–5pm; during the Edinburgh Festival, also Sun noon–5pm.

For Fans of Mr. Hyde

Near Gladstone's Land is **Brodie's Close,** a stone-floored alleyway. You can wander into the alley for a view of old stone houses that'll make you think you've stepped into a scene from a BBC production of a Dickens novel. It was named in honor of the notorious Deacon Brodie, a respectable councilor by day and a thief by night (he was the inspiration for Robert Louis Stevenson's *The Strange Case of Dr. Jekyll and Mr. Hyde,* although Stevenson set his story in foggy London town, not in Edinburgh). Brodie was hanged in 1788. The mechanism used for the hangman's scaffolding had previously been improved by Brodie himself—for use on others, of course. Across the street is the most famous pub along the Royal Mile: **Deacon Brodie's Tavern,** 435 Lawnmarket (© 0131/225-6531).

The People's Story If you continue walking downhill along Canongate toward Holyroodhouse (see below), you'll see one of the handsomest buildings on the Royal Mile: Built in 1591, the Canongate Tolbooth was once the court-house, prison, and center of municipal affairs for the burgh of Canongate. It now contains this museum, which celebrates the social history of the inhabitants of Edinburgh from the late 18th century to the present, with an emphasis on the cultural displacements of the Industrial Revolution.

163 Canongate. © 0131/529-4057. Free admission. Mon–Sat 10am–5pm. Bus: 1.

Huntly House Across from the Canongate Tolbooth is this fine example of a restored 16th-century mansion, whose builders preferred a bulky, relatively sim-ple design that suited its role as a secular, rather than an ecclesiastical, building. Today, it functions as Edinburgh's principal museum of local history. Inside are faithfully crafted reproductions of rooms inspired by the city's traditional indus-tries, including glassmaking, pottery, wool processing, and cabinetry.

142 Canongate. © 0131/529-4143. Free admission. Mon–Sat 10am–5pm (during the Edinburgh Festival, also Sun noon–5pm). Bus: 35.

Palace of Holyroodhouse ★★ James IV built this palace in the 16th cen-tury adjacent to an Augustinian abbey David I had established in the 12th cen-tury. The nave of the abbey church, now in ruins, still remains, but only the north tower of James's palace is left. Most of what you see today was built by Charles II after Scotland and England were united in the 17th century. The palace suf-fered long periods of neglect, but it basked in glory at the ball thrown by Bon-nie Prince Charlie in the mid–18th century, during the peak of his feverish (and doomed) optimism about uniting the Scottish clans in their struggle against the English. Queen Elizabeth II and Prince Philip stay here whenever they visit Edinburgh; when they're not in residence, the palace is open to visitors.

The old wing was the scene of Holyroodhouse's most dramatic incident. Mary Queen of Scots's Italian secretary, David Rizzio, was stabbed 56 times in front of her eyes by her jealous husband, Lord Darnley, and his accomplices. A plaque marks the spot where he died on March 9, 1566. And one of the more curious exhibits is a piece of needlework done by Mary depicting a cat-and-mouse scene. (Her cousin, Elizabeth I, is the cat.)

Highlights of the palace are the oldest surviving section, King James Tower, where Mary Queen of Scots lived on the second floor, with Lord Darnley's rooms below. Some of the rich tapestries, paneling, massive fireplaces, and antiques from the 1700s are still in place. The Throne Room and other drawing rooms are still used for state occasions. In the rear of the palace is the richly fur-nished King's Bedchamber. The Picture Gallery boasts many portraits of Scot-tish monarchs by Dutch artist Jacob De Witt, who in 1684 signed a contract to turn out one potboiler portrait after another at the rate of one a week for 2 years. However, don't take all the portraits too seriously: Some of these royal figures may have never existed, and the likenesses of some aren't known, so the portraits are from the artist's imagination.

Behind Holyroodhouse begins **Holyrood Park,** Edinburgh's largest. With rocky crags, a loch, sweeping meadows, and the ruins of a chapel, it's a wee bit of the Scottish countryside in the city, and a great place for a picnic. If you climb up Holyrood Park, you'll come to 250m-high (823-ft.) **Arthur's Seat,** from which the panorama is breathtaking. (The name doesn't refer to King Arthur, as many people assume, but perhaps is a reference to Prince Arthur of Strathclyde or a corruption of *Ard Thor,* Gaelic for "height of Thor." No one knows for sure.) If you visit on a winter morning, you'll think you're in the heart of the Highlands. Arthur's Seat dates from prehistoric times; you can see clusters of cultivated terraces from the Dark Ages, especially on the east flank of the hill, both above and below Queen's Drive.

Canongate, at the eastern end of the Royal Mile. ℂ **0131/556-7371.** Admission £7.50 ($12) adults, £6 ($9.60) seniors, £4 ($6.40) children age 15 and under, £19 ($30) families (up to 2 adults and 2 children). Daily 9:30am–5:15pm. Closed 2 weeks in May and 3 weeks in late June and early July (dates vary). Bus: 1 or 6.

THE TOP MUSEUMS & MONUMENTS

Dean Gallery ★ *Finds*   Across from the Scottish Gallery of Modern Art, the Dean Gallery opened mainly to house the larger museum's vast collection of Dada and Surrealism. A lot of this showcase came from the collection of Edinburgh-born sculptor, Sir Eduardo Paolozzi, who gave an extensive body of his private collection to the National Galleries of Scotland, including prints, drawings, plaster maquettes, and molds. The works of Salvador Dalí, Max Ernst, and Joan Miró overflow, as does a large selection of the Paolozzi's own sculpture. The artist's mammoth composition of the robotic Vulcan dominates the entrance hall. In the gallery is a re-creation of Paolozzi's London studio. The gallery also hosts traveling or changing exhibitions.

73 Belford Rd. ℂ **0131/624-6200.** www.nationalgalleries.org. Free admission to permanent collection; variable prices to special exhibitions. Fri–Wed 10am–5pm; Thurs 10am–7pm. Closed Dec 25–26. Bus 13.

National Gallery of Scotland ★★★   In the center of Princes Street Gardens, this gallery is small as national galleries go, but the collection has been chosen with great care and expanded considerably by bequests, gifts, and loans. A recent major acquisition was Giulio Romano's *Vièrge à la Légende.* Other important Italian paintings are Verrocchio's *Ruskin Madonna,* Andrea del Sarto's *Portrait of a Man,* Domenichino's *Adoration of the Shepherds,* and Tiepolo's *Finding of Moses.* There are also works by El Greco and Velázquez.

The duke of Sutherland has lent the museum two Raphaels, Titian's two Diana canvases and *Venus Rising from the Sea,* and Nicolas Poussin's *The Seven Sacraments.* On loan from the queen is an early Netherlandish masterpiece historically linked to Edinburgh, Hugo van der Goess's *Trinity Altarpiece.* Notable also are Rubens's *The Feast of Herod* and *The Reconciliation of Jacob and Esau* and Rembrandt's *Woman in Bed,* as well as superb landscapes by Cuyp and Ruisdael. In 1982, the gallery made one of its most prized acquisitions, Pieter Saenredam's *Interior of St. Bavo's Church, Haarlem,* his largest and arguably finest painting.

The most valuable gift to the gallery since its foundation, the Maitland Collection, includes one of Cézanne's *Mont St-Victoire* series, as well as works by Degas, van Gogh, Renoir, Gauguin, and Seurat. In 1980, two rare works were added: an early Monet, *Shipping Scene—Night Effects,* and a stunning landscape, *Niagara Falls, from the American Side,* by 19th-century American painter Frederic Church. In the new wing (opened in 1978), Henry Raeburn is at his best in the whimsical *The Rev. Robert Walker Skating on Duddingston Loch.*

2 The Mound. ℂ **0131/624-6200.** www.nationalgalleries.org. Free admission. Fri–Wed 10am–5pm (extended hours during the festival); Thurs 10am–7pm. Closed Dec 25–26. Bus: 3, 21, or 26.

National Museum of Scotland (NMS) ★★★   In 1998, two long-established museums, the Royal Museum of Scotland and the National Museum of Antiquities, were united into this single institution 2 blocks south of the Royal Mile. The museum showcases exhibits in the decorative arts, ethnography, natural history, geology, archaeology, technology, and science. Six modern galleries distill billions of years of Scottish history, a total of 12,000 items ranging from rocks dating back 2.9 billion years found on the island of South Uist to a Hillman Imp, one of the last 500 cars manufactured at the Linwood plant near Glasgow before it closed in 1981. One gallery is devoted to Scotland's role as an independent nation before it merged with the United Kingdom in 1707. Another gallery, devoted to industry and empire from 1707 to 1914, includes exhibits on shipbuilding, whisky distilling, the railways, and such textiles as the tartan and paisley.

Chambers St. ⓒ 0131/225-7534. www.nms.ac.uk. Free admission. Mon and Wed–Sat 10am–5pm; Tues 10am–8pm; Sun noon–5pm. Walk south from Waverley Station for 10 min. to reach Chambers St. or take bus no. 3, 7, 21, 30, 31, 53, 69, or 80.

Scott Monument ⊛
Looking more like a church spire than a monument to a writer, the Gothic-inspired Scott Monument is Edinburgh's most famous landmark, completed in the mid–19th century. In the center of the over 60m (200 ft.) spire is a large seated statue of Sir Walter Scott and his dog, Maida, with Scott's heroes carved as small figures in the monument. You can climb 287 steps to the top for a spectacular view. From here, you can also see the **Burns Monument,** dedicated to Robert Burns and designed by Thomas Hamilton in 1830, clearly visible along Regent Road.

In the East Princes St. Gardens. ⓒ **0131/529-4068.** Admission £2.50 ($4). Mar–May and Oct, Mon–Sat 9am–6pm, Sun 10am–6pm; June–Sept, Mon–Sat 9am–8pm, Sun 10am–6pm; Nov–Feb, Mon–Sat 9am–4pm, Sun 10am–4pm. Bus: 1 or 6.

Scottish National Gallery of Modern Art ⊛
Scotland's national collection of 20th-century art occupies a gallery converted from an 1828 school set on 4.8 hectares (12 acres) of grounds, a 15-minute walk from the west end of Princes Street. The collection is international in scope and quality, despite its modest size. Major sculptures outside include pieces by Henry Moore and Barbara Hepworth. Inside, the collection ranges from Braque and Picasso to recent works by Paolozzi. English and Scottish art are strongly represented, and you'll also find artists from Europe and America, notably Matisse, Miró, Kirchner, Ernst, Balthus, Lichtenstein, and Hockney. The cafe sells light refreshments and salads.

Belford Rd. ⓒ **0131/556-8921.** www.nationalgalleries.org. Free admission, except for some temporary exhibits. Fri–Wed 10am–5pm; Thurs 10am–7pm. Closed Dec 25–26. Bus: 13 stops by the gallery but is infrequent; nos. 18, 20, and 41 pass along Queensferry Rd., a 5-minute walk up Queensferry Terrace and Belford Rd. from the gallery.

Scottish National Portrait Gallery ⊛
Housed in a red-stone Victorian Gothic building designed by Rowand Anderson, this portrait gallery gives you a chance to see what the famous people of Scottish history looked like. The portraits, several by Ramsay and Raeburn, include everybody from Mary Queen of Scots to Flora Macdonald to Sean Connery.

1 Queen St. ⓒ **0131/624-6200.** www.nationalgalleries.org. Free admission, except for some temporary exhibits. Fri–Wed 10am–5pm; Thurs 10am–7pm. Closed Dec 25–26. Bus: 18, 20, or 41.

Tips A Note on Museum Hours

Be aware that many museums that are usually closed on Sunday *are* open on Sunday during the Edinburgh Festival. Some museums that open only in summer are also open on public holidays.

The Father of Dr. Jekyll & Mr. Hyde

Robert Louis Stevenson (1850–94) was a complex, often mysterious character. Some saw him as a poet of intellect and sensitivity like Dr. Jekyll, and others as a debauched scoundrel like Mr. Hyde. Born in Edinburgh, he spent much of his life restlessly roaming the world. He has been alternately hailed as Scotland's greatest writer and dismissed as a creator of tall tales for children with limited brain capacity.

Stevenson was the son of Robert Stevenson, the famed Scottish civil engineer. He was a sickly child and, not surprisingly, a big disappointment to his father. When at age 22 he announced he was an agnostic, his father declared, "My son has rendered my whole life a failure." The meager allowance he received from his father drove the promising author to abandon his parents' respectable upper-class neighborhood and live cheaply among Scotland's lowliest dock areas and bordellos. Determined to roam ("I shall be a nomad"), he traveled to France and wrote early works like *An Inland Voyage* (1878) and *Travels with a Donkey in the Cevennes* (1879).

In 1876, he met a married American, Fanny Osborne, who found him an enticing enigma. Fanny divorced her husband by Christmas 1879 and wed Stevenson the following May. She proved a poor critic of his work: She didn't like *The Sea-Cook* (1881), which became the ever-popular *Treasure Island*. That was followed by *Kidnapped* (1886), which Stevenson set in the moorland and wilderness of western Scotland. But his most famous work was *The Strange Case of Dr. Jekyll and Mr. Hyde* (1886). (By the way, Jekyll should be pronounced *jee*-kill, according to the author.) Fanny's criticism of the first version of this book caused Stevenson to burn it, but he later felt this version was better than the one he published.

Eventually Stevenson and Fanny settled in Samoa, where he bought 122 hectares (300 acres), hoping to find a climate that would suit his tuberculosis-damaged lungs. The Samoans loved Stevenson—they called him Tusitala ("Teller of Tales")—but not Fanny. (The Samoan servants labeled her the "Witch Woman of the Mountain.") While here, Stevenson worked on his masterpieces *The Ebb-Tide* (1894) and the unfinished *Weir of Hermiston* (published posthumously in 1896) and translated one of his tales into Samoan. However, his happiness didn't last long, for on December 3, 1894, he suddenly collapsed at only age 43.

More than 200 grieving Samoans dug a road up Mt. Vaea so he could be buried on the mountain he loved. Carved on his grave is his famous requiem:

> *This be the verse you grave for me:*
> *Here he lies where he longed to be;*
> *Home is the sailor, home from the sea,*
> *And the hunter home from the hill.*

ADDITIONAL ATTRACTIONS

Dynamic Earth ★ *Kids*   This former brewery has been converted into a stone amphitheater capped by a futuristic translucent tent. Its galleries celebrate the natural diversity of the physical earth, with emphasis on the seismological and biological processes that led from the Big Bang to the world we know today. The presentation has been called "physical evolution as interpreted by Disney"—audio and video clips; buttons you can push to simulate earthquakes, meteor showers, and views of outer space; replicas of the slimy green primordial soup where life began; time capsules winding their way back through the eons; and a series of specialized aquariums, some with replicas of primordial life forms, some with actual living sharks, dolphins, and coral. You'll wander through simulated terrains like polar ice caps, tundras, deserts, and grasslands. The most dramatic is a tropical rainforest where skies darken at 15-minute intervals, and torrents of rainfall and creepy-crawlies appear underfoot. Hands down the most fun is the exhibit in which you can jump up and down on a monitored platform and your movements are amplified to duplicate an earthquake; seismic instruments record what it would have registered on the Richter scale. On the premises are a restaurant, a cafe, a children's play area, and a gift shop. Plan to spend at least 1½ hours here.

Holyrood Rd. (10-min. walk from Waverley Train Station.) ✆ **0131/550-7800.** www.dynamicearth.co.uk. Admission £8.45 ($14) adults, £4.95 ($7.90) students, £4.95 ($7.90) seniors and children age 14 and under, family ticket £15 ($24). Easter–Oct daily 10am–6pm; Nov–Easter Wed–Sun 10am–5pm.

Britannia: The People's Yacht

In case Queen Elizabeth II never invited you to sail aboard her 125m (412-ft.) yacht, you still have a chance to board this famous vessel since the gangplank has been lowered for the public. The luxury ***Britannia*** ★ was launched on April 16, 1953, sailed more than a million miles, and was decommissioned on December 11, 1997. Today, the ship rests at anchor in the port of Leith, 3km (2 miles) from Edinburgh's center. You reach the vessel by going through a visitor center designed by Sir Terence Conran. Once on board, you're guided around all five decks by an audio tour. You can walk the decks where Prince Charles and Princess Diana strolled on their honeymoon, visit the drawing room and the Royal Apartments, and explore the engine room, the galleys, and the captain's cabin.

All tickets should be booked as far in advance as possible by calling ✆ **0131/555-5566.** The yacht is open daily except Christmas, with the first tour beginning at 10am, the last tour at 3:30pm. Lasting 90 to 120 minutes, each tour is self-guided with the use of a headset lent to participants. Adults pay £8 ($13), seniors £6 ($9.60), and children ages 5 to 17 £4 ($6.40); those age 4 and under visit for free. A family ticket, good for two adults and up to two children, is £20 ($32). From Waverley Bridge, take either city bus (Lothian Transport) X50, or else the Guide Friday tour bus, which is marked all over its sides with the words BRITANNIA.

Edinburgh Zoo ★★ *Kids*   Scotland's largest animal collection is 10 minutes from Edinburgh's city center on 32 hectares (80 acres) of hillside parkland offering unrivaled views from the Pentlands to the Firth of Forth. It contains more than 1,500 animals, including many endangered species: snow leopards, white rhinos, pygmy hippos, and others. The zoo boasts the largest penguin colony in Europe, with four species, plus the world's largest penguin enclosure. From April to September, a penguin parade is held daily at 2pm.

134 Corstorphine Rd. ⓒ **0131/334-9171.** Admission £7.50 ($12) adults, £4.50 ($7.20) seniors, £3.80 ($6.10) children, £20–£27 ($32–$43) families. Apr–Sept daily 9am–6pm; Oct–Mar daily 9am–5pm. Parking £2 ($3.20). Bus: 2, 26, 69, 85, or 86.

Georgian House   The most architecturally-interesting district of New Town is the north side of Charlotte Square, designed by Robert Adam. Together with his brother, James, he developed a symmetrical but airy style with an elegant reworking of Greek and Roman classical motifs. The Adams' influence was widespread in Britain and the United States, especially in the American South. Georgian House has been refurbished and opened to the public by Scotland's National Trust. The furniture is mainly Hepplewhite, Chippendale, and Sheraton, all from the 18th century. A sturdy old four-poster with an original 18th-century canopy occupies a ground-floor bedroom. The dining room table is set with fine Wedgwood china and the kitchen stocked with gleaming copper pots and pans.

7 Charlotte Sq. ⓒ **0131/225-2160.** Admission £5 ($8) adults, £3.75 ($6) children, students, and seniors, £13.50 ($22) per family. Apr–Oct daily 10am–5pm; Nov–Dec 24 daily 11am–3pm. Bus: 2, 12, 26, or 31.

Royal Observatory Visitor Centre   This center, in a public park on Edinburgh's south side, displays Scotland's largest telescope, antique instruments, and images of astronomical objects. An exhibit called *The Universe* uses photographs, videos, computers, and models to take you on a cosmic whirlwind tour from the beginning of time to the farthest depths of space in a couple of hours. The balcony affords a panoramic view of the city, and the astronomy shop is well stocked.

Blackford Hill. ⓒ **0131/668-8405.** Admission £2.60 ($4.15) adults, £1.85 ($2.95) students, seniors, and children age 5–16, free for children age 4 and under. Mon–Sat 10am–5pm; Sun noon–5pm. Bus: 40 or 41.

Sir Jules Thorn Exhibition of the History of Surgery/Dental Museum Edinburgh's rich medical history and associations make the Exhibition of the History of Surgery well worth a visit. On the upper floors of a 19th-century town house in a tucked-away square, you can chart the development of surgery from 1505 to the 20th century. The sometimes macabre exhibits include such gems as a pocketbook made from the skin of the notorious body snatcher William Burke. The Dental Museum, its gleaming glass cases full of every conceivable dentistry tool, is certainly not for the squeamish or those experiencing dental problems!

9 Hill Sq. ⓒ **0131/527-1649.** Free admission. Mon–Fri 2–4pm. Bus: 31 or 33.

THE MONUMENTS ON CALTON HILL

Calton Hill ★★★, rising 106m (350 ft.) off Regent Road in the eastern sector, is often credited with giving Edinburgh a look somewhat like that of Athens. It's a hill of monuments; when some of them were created, they were called "instant ruins" by critics. People visit the hill not only to see its monuments but also to enjoy the panoramic views of the Firth of Forth and the city spread beneath it.

The "Parthenon" was reproduced in part on this location in 1824. The intention of the builders was to honor the brave Scottish dead killed in the Napoleonic wars. However, the city fathers ran out of money and the monument (often referred to as "Scotland's shame") was never finished.

The **Nelson Monument** (© **0131/556-2716**), containing relics of the hero of Trafalgar, dates from 1815 and rises more than 30m (100 ft.) above the hill. A time ball at the top falls at 1pm Monday through Saturday. The monument is open April to September, Monday from 1 to 6pm and Tuesday through Saturday from 10am to 6pm; and October to March, Monday through Saturday from 10am to 3pm. Admission is £2 ($3.20). Take bus no. 26, 85, or 86.

For Americans, the curiosity here is the **Lincoln Monument,** which Edinburghers erected in 1893. It was dedicated to the thousands of American soldiers of Scottish descent who lost their lives in America's Civil War. Below Waterloo Place, on the flatter slope of Calton Hill, you can walk through the **Calton Old Cemetery,** dating from the 1700s. Many famous Scots were buried here, often with elaborate tombs honoring their memory (notably the Robert Adam–designed tomb for philosopher David Hume).

DEAN VILLAGE 𝕒

Beautiful Dean Village is one of the city's most photographed sights. This former grain-milling center dating from the 12th century occupies a valley about 30m (100 ft.) below the level of the rest of Edinburgh. It's located few minutes from the West End, at the end of Bells Brae off Queensferry Street, on the Water of Leith You can enjoy a celebrated view by looking downstream under the high arches of Dean Bridge (1833), designed by Telford.

The village's old buildings have been restored and converted into apartments and houses. You don't come here for any one particular site but to stroll around, people-watch, and enjoy the village as a whole. You can also walk for kilometers along the Water of Leith, one of the most tranquil strolls in the greater Edinburgh area.

GARDENS

The **Royal Botanic Garden** 𝕒𝕒𝕒, Inverleith Row (© **0131/552-7171**), is one of the grandest in Great Britain. Sprawling across 28 hectares (70 acres), it dates from the late 17th century, when it was originally used for medical studies. In spring, the rhododendrons alone are reason enough to visit Scotland. Admission is by donation. It's open daily: Admission is by voluntary donation. It's open daily: January to February 10am to 4pm, March 10am to 6pm, April to September 10am to 7pm, October 10am to 6pm, and November to December 10am to 6pm.

As New Town grew, the city fathers decided to turn the area below Edinburgh Castle into the **Princes Street Gardens,** now one of the city's main beauty spots. The area was once Nor Loch, a body of water in the city center, but it was drained to make way for a railway line. (When it was still a bog, the great philosopher David Hume fell into it, couldn't remove himself, and called for help from a passing woman. She recognized him, pronounced him an atheist, and wouldn't offer her umbrella to pull him out of the mire until he recited the Lord's Prayer.)

ORGANIZED TOURS

For a quick introduction to the principal attractions in and around Edinburgh, consider the tours offered from April to late October by **Lothian Region**

Transport, 14 Queen St. (© **0131/555-6363**). You can see most of the major sights of Edinburgh, including the Royal Mile, the Palace of Holyroodhouse, Princes Street, and Edinburgh Castle, by double-deck motor coach for £7.50 ($12) for adults, £6 ($9.60) for seniors and students, and £2.50 ($4) for children. This ticket is valid all day on any **LRT Edinburgh Classic Tour bus,** which allows passengers to get on and off at any of the 15 stops along its routes. Buses start from Waverley Bridge every day beginning at 9:40am, departing every 15 minutes in summer and about every 30 minutes in winter, then embark on a circuit of Edinburgh, which if you remain on the bus without ever getting off will take about 1 hour. Commentary is offered along the way.

Tickets for any of these tours can be bought at LRT offices at Waverley Bridge, or at 14 Queen St., or at the tourist information center in Waverley Market. Advance reservations are a good idea. For more information, call © **0131/555-6363,** 24 hours a day.

McEwan's Literary Pub Tour (© **0131/226-6665**) follows in the footsteps of such literary greats as Robert Burns, Robert Louis Stevenson, and Sir Walter Scott. The *Edinburgh Evening News* has hailed this tour (and we concur) as "vivid, erudite, and entertaining." The tour goes into the city's famous or infamous taverns and *howffs* (Scottish pubs) highlighting such literary events as tales of Dr. Jekyll and Mr. Hyde or the erotic love poetry of Burns. Tours depart from the Beehive Pub on Grassmarket in the Old Town, going along the Royal Mile. The 2-hour tour costs £8 ($13) for adults or £6 ($9.60) for children. From June to September tours leave nightly at 7:30pm; April, May and October Thursday to Sunday at 7:30pm; and November to March Friday at 7:30pm. Reservations are recommended.

The Witchery Tours (© **0131/225-6745**) are filled with ghosts, gore, and witchcraft, enlivened by "jumper-outers"—actors who jump out to scare you. Two tours—Ghost & Gore and Murder & Mystery—are a bit similar and overlap in parts. Scenes of many horrific tortures, murders, and supernatural happenings in the historic Old Town are visited, all under the cloak of darkness. The ghost tour departs daily at 7pm and 7:30pm, with the murder tour leaving daily at 9pm and again at 10pm year round. Tours last 1 hour and 15 minutes, costing £7 ($11) or £4 ($6.40) for children. Departures are from outside The Witchery Restaurant on Castlehill. Reserve early for the tour.

Mercat Tours (© **0131/557-9933**) conducts the best walking tours of Edinburgh, covering a wide range of interests from "Secrets of the Royal Mile" to a "Haunted Underground Experience." Tours meet outside the Tourist Office on Princes Street. The Secrets of the Royal Mile Tour leaves daily at 10:30am with a Grand Tour departing at 10am daily. The Hidden Vaults tour runs hourly from May to September 11am to 4pm; off season daily at noon, 2pm and 4pm. The cost of these tours begins at £6 ($9.60) for adults or £4 ($6.40) for children. Reservations are recommended for these 1 ½-hour tours.

Guide Friday (© **0131/556-2244**) is good for a quick overview. You can later follow up with more in-depth visits. You're taken around the city in one of the company's fleet of open-top, double-decker buses, with informed and often amusing running commentaries. Highlights include the Royal Mile, Princes Street, Holyrood Palace, and Edinburgh Castle, as well as the New Town. Tours run between 9:20am and dusk, costing £8.50 ($14) for adults or £2.50 ($4) for kids ages 5 to 15. Reservations are recommended. Departures are from Waverly Bridge, with tours lasting 1 hour.

6 Special Events & Festivals

Hogmanay begins on New Year's Eve and merges into New Year's Day festivities. It's celebrated throughout Scotland with the ritual kissing of everyone in sight, followed by the time-honored practice of "first footing" with a lump of coal, a bun, and (needless to say) a drop of the hard stuff. In 1993, the Edinburgh City Council began a 3-day festival that now features street theater, lively processions illuminated by firebrands, and the burning of a long boat. By 1997, the crush to attend Europe's largest winter festival forced the city to limit numbers; you now have to get tickets to enter the city center after 8pm on New Year's Eve. For details, call ⓒ **0131/473-3800.**

January 25 is **Burns Night,** *the* night when Scots the world over gather to consume the traditional supper of haggis, *neeps* (turnips), and *tatties* (potatoes), accompanied by a wee dram of whisky, while listening to recitals of the works of Scotland's Bard, Robert "Rabbie" Burns, whose birthday is being celebrated. Burns suppers are held all over town.

By far, the highlight of Edinburgh's year comes in the last weeks of August during the **Edinburgh International Festival.** Since 1947, the festival has attracted artists and companies of the highest international standard in all fields of the arts, including music, opera, dance, theater, poetry, and prose. One of the festival's most exciting spectacles is the **Military Tattoo** on the floodlit esplanade in front of Edinburgh Castle, high on its rock above the city. First performed in 1950, the Tattoo features the precision marching of not only the British Army's Scottish regiments but also performers from some 30 countries, including bands, dancers, drill teams, gymnasts, and motorcyclists—and even horses, camels, elephants, and police dogs. The music ranges from ethnic to pop and from military to jazz. Schedules are released each year about 6 months before the festival, but they're subject to change. Mail-order bookings are available from the Edinburgh Military Tattoo, Tattoo Office, 32 Market St., Edinburgh EH1 1QB (ⓒ **0131/225-1188**). You can check schedules and buy tickets online at **www.eif.co.uk**.

Running simultaneously with the festival but less predictable in quality is the **Edinburgh Festival Fringe,** an opportunity for anybody—professional or non-professional, an individual, a group of friends, or a whole company—to put on a show wherever they can find an empty stage or street corner. Late-night revues, outrageous contemporary drama, university theater presentations, even full-length opera—Edinburgh gives them all free rein. As if that weren't enough, Edinburgh has a **Film Festival,** a **Jazz Festival,** a **Television Festival,** and a non-annual **Book Festival** at the same time.

Ticket prices vary from £4 ($6.40) to £6 ($9.60). You can get information from **Edinburgh International Festival,** The Hub, Castle Hill, Edinburgh EH1 7ND (ⓒ **0131/473-2000;** fax 0131/473-2002), open Monday through Friday from 9:30am to 5:30pm. Other sources of information are the **Edinburgh Festival Fringe,** 180 High St., Edinburgh EH1 1BW (ⓒ **0131/226-5257**); **Edinburgh Book Festival,** Scottish Book Centre, 137 Dundee St., Edinburgh EH11 1BG (ⓒ **0131/228-5444**); and **Edinburgh Film Festival,** 88 Lothian Rd., Edinburgh EH3 9BZ (ⓒ **0131/228-4051**).

The most convenient but slightly more expensive way to order tickets for the festival is to purchase them before you leave home from **Global Tickets, Inc.,** 234 W. 44th Street, Suite 100, New York, NY 10036 (ⓒ **800/223-6108**).

7 Spectator Sports & Outdoor Pursuits

SPECTATOR SPORTS

HORSE RACING   Place your bets at the **Musselburgh Racecourse,** Musselburgh Park (© **0131/665-2859**), about 6.5km (4 miles) east of Edinburgh. In summer, the races are on a flat circular track, but in winter, the more elaborate National Hunt format challenges horses and riders to a series of jumps and obstacle courses of great technical difficulty. Admission is £10 to £15 ($16–$24).

RUGBY   Home of the National Rugby Team of Scotland, **Murrayfield Stadium,** Murrayfield (© **0131/346-5000;** www.sru.org.uk), is about 1.6km (1 mile) west of Edinburgh. The sport is played from September to April, usually on Saturdays. Some of the most passionate matches are those among teams from the five-nation bloc comprising Scotland, Wales, England, Ireland, and France. These matches occur only between January and March, when sports enthusiasts in Scotland seem to talk about little else. Ticket prices range from £23 to £35 ($37–$56).

SOCCER   You might quickly get swept up in the zeal of Edinburghers for their local soccer (referred to as "football") clubs. Both teams, when not battling each other, challenge other teams from throughout Europe. The home of the Edinburgh Hearts (more formally known as the Heart of Midlothian Football Club) is **Tynecastle Park,** Gorgie Road (© **0131/337-7004**); the home of the Hibs (short for the Hibernians) is **Easter Road Park,** Easter Road (© **0131/661-2159**). The traditional playing times are Saturday afternoons, when games are likely to be televised in pubs throughout Scotland. Tickets range from £10 to £22 ($16–$35).

OUTDOOR ACTIVITIES

GOLF   Note that none of the following courses has caddy service.

The par-74 **Silverknowes Golf Course,** Silverknowes Parkway (© **0131/336-3843**), is a 6,202-yard (5,644m) course. Greens fees for 18 holes are £12 ($19) Monday through Friday and £14.50 ($23) Saturday and Sunday, with club and cart rentals costing £15 ($24) and £2 ($3.20), respectively.

The par-67 **Craigentinny,** Craigentinny Gold, Fillyside Road (© **0131/554-7501**), 5km (3 miles) east of Edinburgh, features 5,413 yards (4,926m) of playing area. Clubs rent for £15 ($24) per round and carts for £2 ($3.20). Greens fees for 18 holes are £11.50 ($18) Monday through Friday and £13.50 ($22) Saturday and Sunday.

The par-67, 5,306-yard (4,828m) **Liberton Golf Course,** Kingston Grange, 297 Gilmerton Rd. (© **0131/664-8580**), requires 2 days' notice if you want to rent clubs, the price of which is included in the greens fees of £20 ($32) Monday through Friday for 18 holes. On Saturday and Sunday, fees are £30 ($48). Carts can be rented for £2 ($3.20).

The par-70 **Braids,** Braid House Golf Course, Approach Road (© **0131/447-6666**), is 5km (3 miles) south of Edinburgh's city center. The greens fees at this 5,731-yard (5,215m) course are £14 ($22) Monday through Friday and £16 ($26) Saturday and Sunday. Clubs rent for £15 ($24) including deposit; carts go for £2 ($3.20) plus a £15 ($24) deposit per 18 holes of play.

The par-66 **Swanston Golf Course,** Swanston Road (© **0131/445-4002**), is an 18-hole, 4,825-yard (4,391m) course located 15km (9 miles) southwest of

Edinburgh. Clubs go for £10 ($16) and trolleys for £2 ($3.20); greens fees are £15 ($24) per round Monday through Friday and £25 ($40) Saturday and Sunday. The per-day rates are £15 to £25 ($24–$40).

The **Portobello,** Stanley Street (℃ **0131/669-4361**), is a 9-hole course with a par of 64. The greens fees at this 2,410-yard (2,193m) course are £3.50 to £10 ($5.60–$16) Monday through Friday and £7 to £12 ($11–$19) Saturday and Sunday. A deposit of £10 ($16) is required for club rental, costing £7 ($11). Carts go for £2 ($3.20) plus a £10 ($16) deposit.

Carrick Knowe, Glen Devon Park (℃ **0131/554-7501**), is one of Scotland's larger courses, featuring 6,229 yards (5,668m) of playing area. Eight kilometers (5 miles) west of Edinburgh, this 18-hole, par-71 course was redesigned in 1998 and offers club rentals at £15 ($24) and trolleys at £2 ($3.20). The greens fees for 18 holes are £2 ($3.20) Monday through Friday and £14.50 ($23) Saturday and Sunday.

The par-66 **Torphin Hill Golf Course,** Torphin Road (℃ **0131/441-1100**), is a 4,648-yard (4,230m), 18-hole course, offering no club rentals or trolleys. The greens fees are £15 ($24) per round Monday through Friday and £20 ($32) per day Saturday and Sunday.

SAILING   Visit the Firth of Forth firsthand by contacting the **Port Edgar Sailing Centre,** Port Edgar, South Queensferry (℃ **0131/331-3330**), about 15km (9 miles) west of the city center. Between Easter and mid-October, it offers instruction in small-craft sailing, canoeing, and powerboating, as well as half-day rentals. The rate for a dinghy, suitable for four adults, is £27.70 ($44) for 2 hours. April through September, the center is open daily from 9am to 7:30pm, and boats can be hired to 9pm. In winter, it's open daily from 9am to 4:30pm.

TENNIS   Reservations are necessary for the courts at the **Craiglockhart Sports Centre,** 177 Colinton Rd. (℃ **0131/444-1969**), which also has badminton courts and a gym. Indoor courts cost £7.40 to £10 ($12–$16) per hour for adults and £3.40 ($5.45) for children; they're available daily from 7am to 10:30pm. The outdoor courts cost £4.50 to £9.50 ($7.20–$15) per hour for adults and £4.50 ($7.20) for children; these are available daily from 7am until 10:30pm. They're closed when the weather turns cold. Racquet rental is free of charge. More convenient and sometimes more crowded are a handful of concrete-surfaced **public tennis courts** behind George Square, on the north side of the public park known as the Meadows.

8 Shopping

New Town's **Princes Street** is the main shopping artery. **George Street** and Old Town's **Royal Mile** are also major shopping areas. The best buys are in tartans and woolens, along with bone china and Scottish crystal.

Shopping hours are generally Monday through Saturday from 9am to 5 or 5:30pm and Sunday from 11am to 5pm. On Thursdays, many shops remain open to 7 or 8pm.

BOOKS

James Thin, Ltd.   Edinburgh's most respected bookstore is a vast resource for virtually every academic discipline imaginable, yet also stocks a hefty number of counterculture and pop fiction titles, including a section on gay literature. 53 South Bridge. ℃ **0131/556-6743.** Bus: 1.

BRASS RUBBINGS

Scottish Stone and Brass Rubbing Centre   You can rub any of the brass or stones on display here to create your own wall hangings, or buy them ready made. Those commemorating King Robert the Bruce are particularly impressive. The brass you choose is covered in white or black paper, silver wax is used to outline the brass, and then you fill it in with different colors of wax. You can visit the center's collection of replicas molded from ancient Pictish stones, rare Scottish brasses, and medieval church brasses. Trinity Apse, Chalmers Close, near the Royal Mile. ✆ **0131/556-4364.** Bus: 1.

CRYSTAL

Edinburgh Crystal   This place is devoted to handmade crystal glassware. The visitor center (open Mon–Sat 9am–4:30pm, Sun 11am–4:30pm) contains the factory shop where the world's largest collection of Edinburgh Crystal (plus inexpensive factory seconds) is on sale. Although Waterford is the more prestigious name, Edinburgh Crystal is a serious competitor, its most popular design being the thistle, symbolizing Scotland. It can be traced back to the 17th century, when the glassmaking art was brought here by the Venetians. The center also has a gift shop and a coffee shop specializing in home baking. Thirty-minute tours of the factory to watch glassmakers at work are given Monday to Friday 10am to 4pm; April to September, weekend tours are given 10am to 2:30pm. Tours costs £3.50 ($5.60) for adults, £2.50 ($4) for children, £9.50 ($15) for a family ticket. Eastfield, Penicuik (16km/10 miles south of Edinburgh, just off A701 to Peebles). ✆ **01968/675-128.** Bus: 37, 37A, 62 (Lowland), 64 or 65 (green), or 81 or 87 (red) Waverly bus link.

DEPARTMENT STORES & A MALL

Debenham's   Old reliable Debenham's is still perhaps the best department store in Edinburgh, with a wide array of Scottish and international merchandise displayed in a marble-covered interior. 109–112 Princes St. ✆ **0131/225-1320.** Bus: 3, 31, or 69.

Jenners   Everyone in Edinburgh has probably been to Jenner's at least once. Its neo-Gothic facade, opposite the Scott Monument, couldn't be more prominent. The store's array of Scottish and international merchandise is astounding. Jenner's sells much the same merchandise as Debenham's, but it boasts a wider selection of china and glassware, and has a well-known food hall with a wide array of products, including heather honey, Dundee marmalade, and a vast selection of Scottish shortbreads and cakes. 48 Princes St. ✆ **0131/225-2442.** Bus: 3, 31, or 69.

Princes Mall   There's something for everyone at this tri-level mall. You can browse through some 80 shops selling fashions, accessories, gifts, books, jewelry, beauty products, and a wide selection of Scottish arts and crafts. Unique handmade items are sold in the crafts center. The food court has tempting snacks, while the food hall boasts top-quality produce. Next to Waverley Station, Princes St. ✆ **0131/557-3759.** Bus: 3, 31, or 69.

⌜Tips Bring That Passport!

Take along your passport when you go shopping in case you make a purchase that entitles you to a **VAT (value-added tax)** refund. For details, see "Getting Your VAT Refund" under "Fast Facts: Scotland," in chapter 2.

DOLLS

Doll Hospital (Geraldine's of Edinburgh)   Lined with glass-fronted cases, this is a basement showroom for Edinburgh's only doll factory, with more than 100 dolls on display. Each of the heirloom-quality dolls requires about 10 full days' labor to create and has a hand-painted porcelain head and sometimes an elaborate coiffure. Also available are fully jointed, all-mohair teddy bears that any child will love. 35A Dundas St. ✆ 0131/556-4295. Bus: 23, or 27.

FASHION

Bill Baber   Ten to fifteen highly creative craftspeople work here, creating artfully modernized adaptations of traditional Scottish patterns for both men and women. Expect to find traditional Scottish jacquard-patterned knits spiced up with strands of Caribbean-inspired turquoise or aqua; rugged-looking blazers, jackets, and sweaters suitable for treks or bike rides through the moors; and tailored jackets a woman might feel comfortable wearing to a glamorous cocktail party. 66 Grassmarket, near the Royal Mile. ✆ 0131/225-3249. Bus: 2, or 12.

Corniche   Designer Nina Grant operates the most sophisticated boutique in Edinburgh. If it's the latest in Scottish fashion, expect to find it here, even "Anglomania kilts" designed by that controversial lady of fashion herself, Vivienne Westwood. Relative newcomer Jackie Burke has made a splash with her fur-trimmed Harris tweed riding jackets. 2 Jeffrey St. ✆ 0131/556-3707. Ten minute walk from Waverley Train Station.

Edinburgh Woollen Mill Shop   One of about 30 such shops throughout the United Kingdom, the Edinburgh Woollen Mill Shop sells good Scottish woolens, knitwear, skirts, gifts, and travel rugs. Note, however, that most of the merchandise is made in England. 139 Princes St. ✆ 0131/226-3840. Bus: 3, 31, or 69.

Ragamuffin   The staff here sells what is termed "wearable art" created by some 150 fashion designers from all over the U.K. Along the Royal Mile, Lesley Robertson and her staff sell what they amusingly call "clothes for clowns" in jazzy, bright, and bulky knits, many of which contain Celtic motifs. This is one of the most unusual designer label shops in Edinburgh. The apparel here is unique. Canongate, Royal Mile. ✆ 0131/557-6007. Bus 1 or 6.

Schuh   Schuh has the latest in unique footwear, specializing in the yellow, red, and blue plaid boots made famous by the local rugby team. Expect fierce, funky finds. 6 Frederick St. ✆ 0131/220-0290. Bus: 11, 15, 16, or 25.

Shetland Connection   Owner Moira-Ann Leask promotes Shetland Island knitwear, and her shop is packed with sweaters, hats, and gloves in colorful Fair Isle designs. She also offers hand-knitted mohair, Aran, and Icelandic sweaters. Items range from fine-ply cobweb shawls to chunky ski sweaters in high-quality wool. A large range of Celtic jewelry and gifts makes this shop a top-priority visit. 491 Lawnmarket. ✆ 0131/225-3525. Bus: 1.

GIFTS

Ness Scotland   Along the Royal Mile, Ness Scotland is filled with whimsical accessories searched out by Gordon MacAulay and Adrienne Wells. They have scoured the country from the Orkney Islands to the Borders for that unique item. You'll see hand-loomed cardigans, tasteful scarves, and charming Dinky bags made during the long winters on the Isle of Lewis. 367 High St. ✆ 0131/226-5227. A 5 minute walk from Waverley Train Station.

JEWELRY

Alistir Tait This is one of the most charming jewelry stores in Edinburgh, with a reputation for Scottish minerals like agates; Scottish gold; garnets, sapphires, and freshwater pearls; and estate jewelry. Ask to see the artful depictions of Luckenbooths. Fashioned as pendants, usually as two entwined hearts capped by a royal crest, they're associated with the loves and tragedies of Mary Queen of Scots and often accessorized with a baroque pearl. They come in subtle hues of petal, orange, brown, and (most desirable and rare) purple. Prices for Luckenbooths are £28 to £250 ($45–$400). 116A Rose St. ℂ 0131/225-4105. Bus: 3, 31, or 69.

Hamilton & Inches Since 1866, the prestigious Hamilton & Inches has sold gold and silver jewelry, porcelain and silver, and gift items. You'll find everything you'd want for an upscale wedding present, all sorts of jewelry, and two memorable kinds of silver dishes—weighty plates copied from items found in the Spanish Armada wrecks during Elizabeth I's reign and endearingly folkloric *quaichs* (drinking vessels). The quaichs originated in the West Highlands as whisky measures crafted from wood or horn and were later gentrified into something like silver porringers or chafing dishes, each with a pair of lugs (ears) fashioned into Celtic or thistle patterns. 87 George St. ℂ 0131/225-4898. Bus: 41, or 42.

LINENS & BEDS

And So To Bed The danger of popping into this store is you might make a much larger investment than you'd intended when you see the fine-textured sheets and pillowcases. Most feature Italian and British cotton (not linen), usually in white and cream. There's also a beautiful collection of ornate brass, iron, and wooden beds you can order in several sizes and have shipped anywhere. 30 Dundas St. ℂ 0131/652-3700. Bus: 23, or 27.

MUSIC

Virgin Megastore Here you'll find one of the biggest selections of records, CDs, videos, and tapes in Scotland. The shop has a special strength in traditional and Scottish music. The staff is charming and eager to share their love of Scottish music with interested visitors. 125 Princes St. ℂ 0131/220-2230. Bus: 3, 31, or 69.

TARTANS & KILTS

Anta Some of the most stylish tartans are found at Anta, where Lachian and Anne Stewart, the creative design team behind Ralph Lauren's home tartan fabrics, present a series of tartans newly invented in unique styles. The woolen blankets with hand-purled fringe are woven on old-style looms. 32 High St. ℂ 0131/557-8300.

Clan Tartan Centre This is one of the leading tartan specialists in Edinburgh, regardless of which clan you claim as your own. If you want help in identifying a particular tartan, the staff will assist you. 70–74 Bangor Rd., Leith. ℂ 0131/553-5100. Bus: 7, or 10.

Geoffrey (Tailor) Highland Crafts This is the most famous kiltmaker in the Scottish capital. Its customers have included Sean Connery, Charlton Heston, Dr. Ruth Westheimer, members of Scotland's rugby teams, and Mel Gibson (who favors the tartan design Hunting Buchanan and wore his outfit when he received an award from the Scottish government after filming *Braveheart*). Expect a delay of 4 to 8 weeks before your costume can be completed. The company sets up sales outlets at Scottish reunions and Highland Games around the world and maintains a toll-free number (℅ **800/566-1467**) for anyone who calls from the United States or Canada and wants to be outfitted. It stocks 200 of Scotland's best-known tartan patterns and is revolutionizing the kilt by establishing a subsidiary called 21st Century Kilts, which makes them in fabrics ranging from denim to leather.

Geoffrey is also one of the few kiltmakers to actually weave the object, and you can watch the process at the **Edinburgh Old Town Weaving Company,** 555 Castlehill (℅ **0131/557-0256;** Bus: 1), Monday through Friday from 9am to 5pm. Note that the factory doesn't sell kilts directly to visitors. 57–59 High St. ℅ 0131/557-0256. Bus: 1.

James Pringle Woolen Mill   The mill produces a large variety of top-quality wool items, including cashmere sweaters, tartan and tweed ties, travel rugs, tweed hats, and tam o' shanters. In addition, it boasts one of Scotland's best Clan Tartan Centres, with more than 5,000 tartans accessible. A free audiovisual presentation shows the history and development of the tartan. You can visit for free, and there's even a free taxi service to the mill from anywhere in Edinburgh (ask at your hotel). 70–74 Bangor Rd., Leith. ℅ 0131/553-5161. Bus: 7, or 10.

Tartan Gift Shops   Tartan Gift Shops has a chart indicating the place of origin (in Scotland) of family names, accompanied by a bewildering array of hunt and dress tartans for men and women, sold by the yard. There's also a line of lambswool and cashmere sweaters and all the accessories. 54 High St. ℅ 0131/558-3187. Bus: 1.

Tracing Your Ancestral Roots

If you have a name beginning with Mac (which simply means "son of") or one of the other Scottish names, you may have descended from a clan, a group of kinsmen claiming a common ancestry. Clans and clan societies have their own museums throughout Scotland, and local tourist offices will have details about where to locate them. Bookstores throughout Scotland sell clan histories and maps.

Scotland's densest concentration of genealogical records is at the **General Register Office,** New Register House, 3 W. Register St., Edinburgh EH1 3YT (℅ **0131/334-0380;** Bus: 3, 26, 33, or 86). Opened in 1863 in a black-brick Victorian headquarters, it contains hundreds of thousands of microfiche and microfilm documents and a computerized system that tells you where to begin looking for whatever records interest you. The strictly self-service system is open Monday through Friday from 9am to 4:30pm; it gets crowded in summer. The fee you pay for a full day's access to the records is £19 ($30); if you enter after 1pm, you'll pay £12 ($19).

The house has on record details of every birth, marriage, and death in Scotland since 1855. There are also old parish registers, the earliest dating from 1553, listing baptisms, marriages, and burials, but these older records are far from complete. It also has census returns for every decade from 1841 to 1891 and such data as the foreign marriages of Scots, adopted children's registers, and war registers.

Tartan Weaving Mill & Exhibition   This is both a shopping venue and an attraction. You can view powerlooms blending together different wools, and can also see a display of Highland dress down through the centuries. At this outlet you can also look up your clan tartan and buy the appropriate kilt right on the spot. 55 Castlehill, Royal Mile. © **0131/226-1555.** Bus 1 or 6.

9 Edinburgh After Dark

Every year in late August, the **Edinburgh International Festival** brings numerous world-class cultural offerings to the city, but year-round there are plenty of choices, whether you prefer theater, opera, ballet, or other diversions. The waterfront district, featuring many jazz clubs and restaurants, is especially lively in summer, and students flock to the pubs and clubs around Grassmarket. Discos are found off High and Princes streets, and in the city's numerous pubs you can often hear traditional Scottish folk music for the price of a pint.

For a thorough list of entertainment options during your stay, pick up a copy of *The List,* a free biweekly paper available at the tourist office. Before you leave home, you might want to check *Time Out* (www.timeout.com/edinburgh) for the latest listings.

THE PERFORMING ARTS

THEATER   Edinburgh has a lively theater scene. In 1994, the **Festival Theatre,** 13–29 Nicolson St. (© **0131/662-1112** for administration, 0131/529-6000 for tickets during festival times with an additional phone line (© **0131/473-2000**) that's operational during the August festival; bus: 3, 31, or 33), opened in time for some aspects of the Edinburgh Festival. Set on the eastern edge of Edinburgh, near the old campus of the University of Edinburgh, it has since been called "Britain's de facto Dance House" because of its sprung floor, its enormous stage (the largest in Britain), and its suitability for opera presentations of all kinds. Tickets are £6 to £60 ($9.60–$96).

Another major theater is the **King's Theatre,** 2 Leven St. (© **0131/529-6000;** bus: 10 or 11), a 1,600-seat Victorian venue offering a wide repertoire of classical entertainment, including ballet, opera, and West End productions. The **Netherbow Arts Centre,** 43 High St. (© **0131/556-9579;** bus: 1), has been called "informal," and productions here are often experimental and delightful—new Scottish theater at its best.

Moments   **A Wee Dram for Fans of Malt Whisky**

It requires a bit of an effort to reach it (take bus 10A, 16, or 17 from Princes Street to Leith), but for fans of malt whisky, the **Scotch Malt Whisky Society** has been called "The Top of the Whisky Pyramid" by distillery-industry magazines in Britain. It's on the second floor of a 16th-century warehouse at 87 Giles St., Leith (© **0131/554-3451**), and was originally designed to store Bordeaux and port wines from France and Portugal. All you can order are single-malt whiskies, served neat, usually in a dram (unless you want yours watered down with branch water), and selected from a staggering choice of whiskies from more than 100 distilleries throughout Scotland. Hours are Monday to Wednesday 10am to 5pm, Thursday to Saturday 10am to 11pm, and Sunday 12:30 to 10pm.

The resident company of **Royal Lyceum Theatre,** Grindlay Street (✆ **0131/ 248-4848;** bus: 11 or 15), also has an enviable reputation; its presentations range from the works of Shakespeare to new Scottish playwrights. The **Traverse Theatre,** Cambridge Street (✆ **0131/228-1404;** bus: 11 or 15), is one of the few theaters in Britain funded solely to present new plays by British writers and first translations into English of international works. In a modern location, it now offers two theaters under one roof: Traverse 1 seats 250 and Traverse 2 seats 100.

BALLET, OPERA & CLASSICAL MUSIC   The **Scottish Ballet** and the **Scottish Opera** perform at the **Playhouse Theatre,** 18–22 Greenside Place (✆ **0870/606-3424;** bus: 7 or 14), which, with 3,100 seats, is the town's largest theater. The **Scottish Chamber Orchestra** makes its home at the **Queen's Hall,** Clerk Street (✆ **0131/668-2019;** bus: 3, 33, or 31), also a major venue for the Edinburgh International Festival.

FOLK MUSIC & CEILIDHS   Folk music is presented in many clubs and pubs in Edinburgh, but these strolling players tend to be somewhat erratic or irregular in their appearances. It's best to read notices in pubs and talk to the tourist office to see where the ceilidhs will be on the night of your visit.

Some hotels regularly feature traditional Scottish music in the evenings. You might check with the **George Hotel** 19–21 George St. (✆ **0131/225-1251;** bus: 3, 31, or 33). **Jamie's Scottish Evening** is presented daily at the King James Hotel on Leith Street (✆ **0131/556-0111;** bus: 7 or 14) Tuesday through Sunday at 7pm, costing £43.50 ($70) for a four-course dinner, wine, and show.

THE CLUB & MUSIC SCENE

The Cavendish   This isn't necessarily where you go to hear the next Oasis or Blur, but who knows? A rock legend might be born here every Friday or Saturday, when live bands take the stage. The bar is open Wednesday through Sunday from 10pm to 3am. Note: No tennis shoes or jeans allowed. 3 W. Tollcross. ✆ 0131/228-3252. Cover £6 ($9.60) Fri–Sat Bus: 11, 15, or 23.

Club Mercado   The glamorous Club Mercado, once the headquarters of the Scottish branch of British Rail, hangs suspended over the rail tracks behind the city's main station. On Friday, the action kicks off with no-cover TFIS, which stands for a somewhat saltier version of "Thank God It's Friday"; it runs from 5 to 10pm and caters to youngish workers who indulge in cut-price drinks. Other special nights are alternate-Saturday Viva (eclectic music attracting all sorts from toughs to drag queens) and Eye Candy (basically a rave featuring the latest house music). Open daily from 10:30pm to 3am. 36–39 Market St. ✆ 0131/226-4224. Cover £3–£10 ($4.80–$16), depending on what's on. Bus: 1.

Po Na Na   Po Na Na is the Edinburgh branch of the most successful chain of clubs in Britain. The theme is a Moroccan casbah, thanks to wall mosaics, brass lanterns, and artifacts shipped in from Marrakech. You'll dance to a mix of house and funk in the cellar of a transformed 19th-century building, beneath a tented ceiling illuminated with strobes. Po Na Na isn't specifically gay, but does draw a strong gay following. Open daily from 8pm to 3am. 43B Frederick St. ✆ 0131/226-2224. Cover £2–£3 ($3–$4.50). Bus: 80.

Revolution   Popular with an under-25 crowd, this is Edinburgh's largest club, with a capacity of 1,500. Mainstream dance music (plus five bars) attracts the crowds, and there are theme and student nights as well. Open Wednesday through Sunday from 10:30pm to 2am. 31 Lothian Rd. ✆ 0131/229-7670. Cover £3–£10 ($4.80–$16). Bus: 11, or 15.

The Venue   Behind the main post office and Waverley Station is the Venue, the principal stage for live music. Some of the biggest bands in the United Kingdom perform here. 15 Calton Rd. ✆ 0131/557-3073. Bus: 26.

Whynot   In the basement of the Dome Bar & Grill (see "Where to Dine," earlier in this chapter), Whynot is a hot entertainment complex that opened in the former Bank of Scotland building. It has low ceilings with veil-like curtains above the dance floor and lots of seating coves tucked away for privacy. The club swings Thursday through Sunday from 10pm to 3am. On Thursday, there's dancing to the music of the 1960s, 1970s, and 1980s; Friday features mainstream pop; and Saturday brings the best in contemporary dance music. 14 George St. ✆ 0131/624-8633. Cover £5–£7.50 ($8–$12). Bus: 41, or 42.

PUBS & BARS

The Abbotsford   Near the eastern end of Rose Street, a short walk from Princes Street, the Abbotsford has served stiff drinks and oceans of beer since 1887. The gaslight era is alive here, thanks to a careful preservation of the original dark paneling, battered tables, and ornate plaster ceiling. The beers on tap change about once a week, supplementing the roster of single malts. Drinks are served Monday through Saturday from 11am to 11pm. Platters of food are dispensed from the bar Monday through Saturday from noon to 3pm and 5:30 to 10pm. 3 Rose St. ✆ 0131/225-5276. Bus: 3, 31, or 33.

Bow Bar   Near Edinburgh Castle, the Victorian Bow Bar is arranged around a series of tall beer pulls, antique phonographs, pendulum clocks, and as many as 140 single-malt whiskies from virtually every corner of the country. The only food offerings are simple snacks like steak or minced pie. Open Monday through Saturday from noon to 11:30pm and Sunday from 12:30 to 11pm. 80 West Bow. ✆ 0131/226-7667. Bus: 2, or 12.

Café Royal Circle Bar ⭐   This is Edinburgh's most famous pub. One part is now occupied by the Oyster Bar of the Café Royal, but life in the Circle Bar continues as usual, still with the opulent trappings of the Victorian era. Hours for the bar are Monday through Wednesday from 11am to 11pm, Thursday from 11am to midnight, Friday and Saturday from 11am to 1am, and Sunday from 12:30 to 11pm. The restaurant is open Sunday through Wednesday from noon to 2pm and 7 to 10pm (Thurs to midnight, Fri and Sat to 1am). 17 W. Register St. ✆ 0131/556-1884. Bus: 3, 31, 33.

Deacon Brodie's Tavern ⭐   Opened in 1806, Deacon Brodie's is the neighborhood pub along the Royal Mile. It perpetuates the memory of Deacon Brodie, good citizen by day and robber by night. The tavern and wine cellars offer a traditional pub setting and lots of atmosphere. The tavern is open Sunday through Thursday from 10am to midnight and Friday and Saturday from 10am to 1am. Light meals are served in the bar from 10am to 10pm; in the restaurant upstairs, more substantial food is served from noon to 10pm. 435 Lawnmarket. ✆ 0131/225-6531. Bus: 1.

Guildford Arms   This place got a face-lift back to the mauve era of the 1890s, although a pub has stood here for 200 years. The Victorian Italianesque pub has seven arched windows with etched glass and an ornate ceiling. It's large, bustling, and at times a bit rough, but has plenty of character. Upstairs is a fish-and-chips shop run by the same company. Place your order at the upstairs bar. At festival

Booked aisle seat.

Reserved room with a view.

With a queen – no, make that a king-size bed.

With Travelocity, you can book your flights and hotels together, so you can get even better deals than if you booked them separately. You'll save time and money without compromising the quality of your trip. Choose your airline seat, search for alternate airports, pick your hotel room type, even choose the neighborhood you'd like to stay in.

Visit www.travelocity.com or call 1-888-TRAVELOCITY

time, folk music is presented nightly. Open Monday through Thursday from 11am to 11pm, Friday and Saturday from 11am to midnight, and Sunday from 12:30 to 11pm. 1–5 W. Register St. ℭ **0131/556-4312.** Bus: 3, 31, or 33.

GAY BARS & CLUBS

The heart of the gay community is centered on **Broughton Street** around the Playhouse Theatre (take bus 8, 9, or 19). Be sure to check "The Club & Music Scene" (see above) for the heavily gay crowd at **Po Na Na.**

C. C. Bloom's   Named after Bette Midler's character in *Beaches,* C. C. Bloom's is one of Edinburgh's most popular gay spots. The upstairs bar offers drinks and camaraderie; on Thursday and Sunday at 11pm, there's karaoke, and Sunday afternoons heat up with a male stripper. The downstairs club offers dancing to a wide range of music, with no cover. Open Monday through Saturday from 6pm to 3am and Sunday from 3pm to 3am.

Next door is **Habana,** 22 Greenside Place (ℭ **0131/556-4349**), drawing a mixed gay crowd daily from noon to 1am. 23–24 Greenside Place. ℭ **0131/556-9331.**

New Town Bar   Adjacent to the corner of Queen Street is the New Town Bar, a street-level pub where everyday blokes clad in everything from jeans to suits gather for a pint of lager. It's open daily from noon to 2am. If you're looking for something a bit less conventional and it happens to be Wednesday through Sunday between 10pm and 2am, head into the basement for the Intense Cruise Bar, where the crowd dons its own interpretations of Tom of Finland combat gear, leather, and uniforms. Depending on the crowd, this can be intense, amusing, or both. 26B Dublin St. ℭ **0131/538-7775.**

Planet Out   This place hosts a mixed crowd, but attracts more women than most gay bars. It describes itself as a friendly and unpretentious neighborhood bar where you're likely to run into your favorite gay uncle or aunt and share a bit of family gossip, and then meet either the love of your life or a decent building contractor. There's an occasional drag night. Open Monday through Friday from 4pm to 1am and Saturday and Sunday from 12:30pm to 1am. 6 Baxters Place. ℭ **0131/524-0061.**

10 Side Trips from Edinburgh: The Best of the Lothian Region

Armed with a good map, you can explore the major attractions of the countryside south of the Firth of Forth enveloping Edinburgh in just a day. Most attractions are no more than an hour's drive from the city. The highlights are **Hopetoun House** of Robert Adam fame and the impressive ruins of **Linlithgow Palace,** birthplace of Mary Queen of Scots in 1542.

One of the best day trips from the Scottish capital is to the ancient town of **Dunfermline,** north of Edinburgh. It can easily be visited in a day, which will give you time to see its famous abbey and palace as well as the Andrew Carnegie Birthplace Museum. See chapter 8, "Fife & the Central Highlands," for details.

LINLITHGOW & ITS PALACE

In 1542, Mary Queen of Scots was born in the royal burgh of Linlithgow in West Lothian, 29km (18 miles) west of Edinburgh. You can visit the site of her birth, Linlithgow Palace. Buses and trains depart daily from Edinburgh for the 20- to 25-minute ride, which costs £6 ($9) round-trip. If you're driving from central Edinburgh, follow A8 toward Glasgow and then merge with M9, following the signs to Linlithgow.

Linlithgow Palace ✶ Birthplace of Mary Queen of Scots, this was once a favorite residence of Scottish kings and is now one of the country's most poignant ruins. Although the palace is roofless, its pink-ocher walls climb five floors and are supported on the lower edge by flying buttresses. It's most dramatic and evocative when floodlit at night. Many of the former royal rooms are still remarkably preserved, so you can get a clear idea of how grand it used to be. In one of the many tragic events associated with Scottish sovereignty, the palace burned to the ground in 1746, along with many of the hopes and dreams of Scottish independence. You can still visit the impressive shell. A small display in the first floor Great Hall shows some of the more interesting architectural relics.

On A706, on the south shore of Linlithgow Loch, 1km (½ mile) from Linlithgow Station. ✆ **01506/842-896.** Admission £3 ($4.80) adults, £2.30 ($3.70) seniors, £1 ($1.60) children. Apr–Oct daily 9:30am–6:30pm; Nov–Mar (last admission 3:30pm).

St. Michael's Parish Church South of the palace stands the medieval kirk of St. Michael the Archangel, site of worship of many a Scottish monarch since its consecration in 1242. Despite being ravaged by the disciples of John Knox (who then chided his followers for their "excesses") and transformed into a stable by Cromwell, this is one of Scotland's best examples of a parish church.

Adjacent to Linlithgow Palace. ✆ **01506/842-188.** Free admission. May–Sept daily 10am–4pm; Oct–Apr Mon–Fri 10:30am–3pm.

Hopetoun House ✶ Amid beautifully landscaped grounds laid out along the lines of those at Versailles, Hopetoun is Scotland's greatest Robert Adam mansion and a fine example of 18th-century architecture (note its resemblance to Buckingham Palace). Seven bays extend across the slightly recessed center, and the classical style includes a complicated tympanum, with hood molds, quoins, and straight-headed windows. A rooftop balustrade with urns completes the ensemble. You can wander through splendid reception rooms filled with 18th-century furniture, paintings, statuary, and other artworks and check out the panoramic view of the Firth of Forth from the roof. After touring the house, you can take the nature trail, explore the deer parks, see the Stables Museum, or stroll through the formal gardens. Refreshments are available near the Ballroom Suite.

3km (2 miles) from the Forth Road Bridge near South Queensferry, 16km (10 miles) from Edinburgh off A904. ✆ **0131/331-2451.** Admission £6 ($9.60) adults, £5 ($8) seniors, £3 ($4.80) children, £16 ($26) families of up to 6. Mar 30–Sept 20 daily 10am–5:30pm (last admission 4:30pm). Closed Sept 21–Mar 29.

WHERE TO DINE

Champany Inn ✶✶ SCOTTISH You'll find the best steaks in Britain in this converted farmhouse. Owner Clive Davidson is an expert on beef and insists his steaks be 3cm (1¼ in.) thick; his meat is hung for at least 4 weeks, adding greatly to its flavor. He also prepares an assortment of oysters, salmon, and lobsters kept in a pool on the premises. Next door to the main dining room is a chophouse that has less expensive cuts; you can choose your own cut and watch it being grilled. The wine list has won an award for excellence from *Wine Spectator*.

The inn also rents 16 handsomely furnished guest rooms, each with TV, minibar, hair dryer, and phone. The rate of £125 ($200) for a double includes a full breakfast.

Champany Corner, Linlithgow. ✆ **01506/834-532.** Fax 01506/834302. www.champany.com. Reservations required. Main courses £21.50–£45.50 ($34–$73); fixed-price lunch £16.75 ($27). AE, DC, MC, V. Mon–Fri noon–2pm and 6:30–10pm. Closed Jan 1–2 and Dec 25. Take M9 until junction 3, then A904 until you reach the restaurant.

Side Trips from Edinburgh

SCOTLAND

Edinburgh

ENGLAND

Area of detail

0   20 mi

0   20 km

5 mi

5 km

9 North Berwick

8 Dirleton

7 Gullane

A198

Haddington

A1

A6093

A6137 Humbie

Pencaitland

Pathead

A68

Gorebridge

A7

North Middleton

A6094

Firth of Forth

Cockenzie and Port Seton

Tranent

Musselburgh

Dalkeith

Bonnyrigg

Loanhead

Penicuik

A701

A702

A703

A68

A7

A198

6 Leith

Edinburgh

A702

A720

Balerno

A7

A71

Wilkieston

A70

Burntisland

A987

Inverkeithing

North Queensferry

3 South Queensferry

A90

Dalmeny

A8

Broxburn

M8

Livingston

A921

Hopetown

4 Newton

A904

M9

Winchburgh

A89

A92

A985

Dunfermline

2 1

A994

5 Linlithgow

Andrew Carnegie Birthplace Museum **2**

Britannia **6**

Deep Sea World **3**

Dirleton Castle **8**

Dunfermline Abbey & Palace **1**

Hopetoun House **4**

Linlithgow Palace **5**

Muirfield Golf Course **7**

St. Michael's Parish Church **5**

Tantallon Castle **9**

121

Livingston's ✦ MODERN SCOTTISH/FRENCH   Chef Julian Wright reigns supreme in this cottagelike restaurant of converted stables with sandstone walls and Black Watch tartan carpets. A conservatory overlooks a neat little garden, and candlelight makes the atmosphere warm and romantic. The chef is inventive and uses quality ingredients imaginatively. The saddle of venison is the most requested dish, and rightly so. It comes in a cassis sauce with glazed shallots and a cassoulet of butter beans. Pigeon pie and brambles often appear on the menu, as does a risotto of wild mushrooms and truffles made all the more delectable by a shaving of Parmesan. Elegant dessert selections may include a chilled soup of strawberries and champagne accompanied by a chocolate mousse. There is an ample wine list, including bottles from California.

52 High St. (opposite the post office), Linlithgow. ℂ **01506/846-565.** Reservations recommended. Fixed-price 2-course lunch £13.50 ($22); 3-course lunch £16.50 ($26); fixed-price dinner £27 ($43) for 2 courses, £32.50 ($52) for 3 courses. MC, V. Tues–Sat noon–2pm and 6–9pm. Closed first 2 weeks in Jan.

NORTH BERWICK

This royal burgh dating from the 14th century is an upmarket holiday resort, drawing visitors to its golf courses, beaches, and harbor life on the Firth of Forth. In East Lothian, 39km (24 miles) east of Edinburgh, the town is on a direct rail line from Edinburgh; the trip takes 30 minutes. There's also bus service from Edinburgh, taking 1¼ hours. Both cost £2.75 ($4.40) one-way. If you're driving, take A1 in the direction marked THE SOUTH and DUNBAR; then turn onto A198, following the signs to North Berwick.

At the **tourist office,** Quality Street (ℂ **01620/892-197**), you can get information on how to take boat trips to the offshore islands, including **Bass Rock,** a breeding ground inhabited by about 10,000 gannets. The gannets return from Africa in the spring, usually around April, to nest here until fall. It's possible to see the rock from the harbor, but the viewing is even better at **Berwick Law,** a volcanic lookout point.

Some 3km (2 miles) east of North Berwick and 40km (25 miles) east of Edinburgh on A198 stand the ruins of the 14th-century diked and rose-colored **Tantallon Castle** (ℂ **01620/892-727**). This was the ancient stronghold of the Douglases from its construction in the 14th century until its defeat by Cromwell's forces in 1650. Overlooking the Firth of Forth, the ruins are still formidable, with a square five-story central tower and a dovecote, plus the shell of its east tower. It's open April to September, daily from 9:30am to 6:30pm; and October to March, Monday through Wednesday and Saturday from 9:30am to 4pm, Thursday from 9:30am to 4:30pm, and Sunday from 2 to 4:30pm. Admission is £3 ($4.80) for adults, £2.30 ($3.70) for seniors, and £1 ($1.60) for children.

WHERE TO STAY & DINE

The Glebe House   This dignified 1780 home belongs to Gwen and Jake Scott, who have worked hard to preserve its original character as the residence of the pastor for the nearby Presbyterian Church. Glebe House is near many golf courses and is just a minute's walk south of the town's main street, near the edge of the sea. Each cozy guest room boasts part of Mrs. Scott's collection of hand-painted porcelain, artfully arranged on tabletops, in wall niches, and on hanging shelves. (She'll point out the various manufacturers, which include Quimper, Rouen, and Staffordshire.) Views include 1.6 hectares (4 acres) of field, garden, and horse paddock. The breakfasts are served in a formal, high-ceilinged dining room.

4 Law Rd., North Berwick, East Lothian EH39 4PL. ℂ and fax **01620/892-608.** www.aboutscotland.com/glebe/house.html. 4 units, 3 with private bathroom. £60–£80 ($96–$128) double. Rates include breakfast. No credit cards. *In room:* TV, coffeemaker, hair dryer.

The Marine   This turreted Victorian commands panoramic views across the West Links Course, some of whose putting greens come close to the hotel's foundations. It's a home for Nicklaus, Trevino, Player, and most of the U.S. Ryder Cup Team during the Open and is nearby to nearly 20 golf courses. The hotel feels like an elegant country house. Although its guest rooms vary in size, all are clean and comfortable. The bar is lined with antique golf photos. The dining room is open to nonguests and serves the best food in town: international cuisine, with many Scottish specialties.

18 Cromwell Rd., North Berwick, East Lothian EH39 4LZ. ℂ **800/225-5843** in the U.S., or 0870/400-8129. Fax 01620/894-480. www.macdonaldhotels.co.uk. 83 units. £90–£120 ($144–$192) double; £150–£270 ($240–$432) suite. AE, DC, MC, V. **Amenities:** Restaurant; bar; outdoor heated pool; tennis court; sauna; 24-hr. room service; laundry service. *In room:* TV, coffeemaker, hair dryer, iron/ironing board.

GULLANE & THE MUIRFIELD GOLF COURSE

Lying 31km (19 miles) east of Edinburgh in East Lothian, Gullane, with a population of around 2,000, is an upscale resort with a fine sandy beach and one of Scotland's great country hotels. There's no rail service into Gullane. Buses, including nos. 124 and 125, depart from the St. Andrews Square station in Edinburgh (ℂ **0800/23-23-23** for information). They take 20 to 25 minutes and cost £3 ($4.80) each way. If you're driving, take A1 in the direction marked THE SOUTH and DUNBAR; then turn onto A198, following the signs to Gullane.

On the western edge of the village, **Gullace Hill** is a nature reserve and bird sanctuary, where some 200 species of birds have been spotted. You cross a small wood footbridge from the car park to enter the reserve.

What really puts Gullane on the tourist map, other than its fine dining and accommodations, is the 1891 **Muirfield Golf Course** (ℂ **01620/842-123**), ranked 6th among the world's 100 greatest golf courses by the editors of *GolfWeb.* Developed from a boggy piece of low-lying links, Muirfield has hosted 10 open championships and is a par-70, 6,601-yard (6,007m), 18-hole course. A round costs £100 ($160).

WHERE TO STAY & DINE

Greywalls Hotel ✪✪   This is an elegant, exclusive retreat. The Edwardian country house was designed in 1901 as a private home by the most renowned architect of his day, Sir Edwin Lutyens. It was visited from time to time by Edward VII, who admired the views across the Firth of Forth and south to the Lammermuir Hills. The gardens were laid out by one of England's most respected landscape architects, Gertrude Jekyll. In the paneled library, guests relax on comfortable sofas before a blazing log fire. The guest rooms vary in size; some smaller ones are simply decorated, while the more spacious units are furnished with period pieces. Each comes with a beautifully kept bathroom. The light French-style dishes served in the elegant dining room are almost as appealing to the eye as to the palate; specialties include fresh seafood.

Muirfield, Duncur Rd., Gullane, East Lothian EH31 2EG. ℂ **01620/842-144.** Fax 01620/842-241. www.greywalls.co.uk. 23 units. £190–£240 ($304–$384) double. Rates include Scottish breakfast. AE, DC, MC, V. Closed Oct 15–Apr 15. Follow the signs from A198 about 8km (5 miles) from North Berwick. **Amenities:** Restaurant; bar; putting green; 2 tennis courts; room service (7am–10pm); babysitting; laundry service. *In room:* TV, hair dryer.

DIRLETON 🌟: THE PRETTIEST VILLAGE IN SCOTLAND

Midway between North Berwick and Gullane is the lovely little town of Dirleton, which is generally cited as the prettiest village in Scotland. The town was drafted in the early 16th-century, and remains little changed today. It's picture postcard perfect, not like a real town at all, but one that appears to have been created for a movie set. Since the main A198 bypasses the village, there is little traffic. The village green is the center of local life. In the center is a ghostly castle abandoned by its residents in 1663. Even the rail station is closed, the last train running through in 1954. Every private cottage looks like it's waiting to be photographed and home maintenance is high. The biggest news occurred in the 1940s when President Roosevelt and Sir Winston Churchill met in Dirleton to plan D-Day landings.

It's on the Edinburgh–North Berwick road (A198); North Berwick is 8km (5 miles) east and Edinburgh 31km (19 miles) west. There's no train service. Buses, including nos. 124 and 125, depart from the St. Andrews Square station in Edinburgh (📞 **0800/23-23-23** for information). They take 25 minutes and cost £2 ($3.20) one-way. If you're driving, take A1 in the direction marked THE SOUTH and DUNBAR; then turn onto A198, following the signs to Dirleton.

Dirleton Castle 🌟 A rose-tinted 13th-century castle with surrounding gardens, Dirleton Castle looks like a fairy tale fortification, with towers, arched entries, and an oak ramp similar to the drawbridge that used to protect it. Reputed to have been fully sacked by Cromwell in 1650, the building was in fact only partially destroyed by him and was further torn down by the Nesbitt family, who, after building nearby Archiefield House, desired a romantic ruin on their land. You can see the ruins of the Great Hall and kitchen, as well as what's left of the lord's chamber: windows and window seats, a wall with a toilet and drains, and other household features. The 16th-century main gate has a hole through which boiling tar or water could be poured to discourage unwanted visitors. The castle's country garden and a bowling green are still in use.

Dirleton, East Lothian. 📞 **01620/850-330.** Admission £3 ($4.80) adults, £2.30 ($3.70) seniors, £1 ($1.60) children. Apr–Sept daily 9:30am–6pm; Oct–Mar Mon–Sat 9:30am–4pm, Sun 2–4pm.

WHERE TO STAY & DINE

Castle Inn Opposite the village green and the castle and unspoiled by modernization, this is a most satisfactory village inn, with 10 dormer windows and a pair of entrances. The small guest rooms are pleasant and comfortably furnished. The most desirable units are in the main house, with smaller and more modestly furnished rooms in an adjoining modern annex (all with shower-only bathrooms). Guests are welcome in a lounge with rugged stone walls and a freestanding stone fireplace where, during the day, light snacks are served.

Off A198, Dirleton, East Lothian EH39 5EP. 📞 **01620/850-221.** infocastleinn@aol.com. 8 units. £60 ($96) double. MC, V. **Amenities:** Restaurant; 2 bars. *In room:* Coffeemaker, hair dryer.

Open Arms The Open Arms will receive you with you know what. This old stone hostelry, off A198 overlooking the castle ruins, has been transformed into a handsome hotel that serves the finest food in the area. The average-size guest rooms come with small, shower and tub bathrooms. Log fires crackle and blaze, and golfers will find 20 courses within a 32km (20 mile) radius. The owners have built a local reputation for serving Scottish dishes using regional venison, beef, lamb, and freshly caught salmon. The whiskies used in the sauces are of the region, too.

Main St. Dirleton, East Lothian EH39 5EG. ⓒ **01620/850-241.** Fax 01620/850-570. www.openarmshotel.com. 10 units. £80–£130 ($128–$208) double. Rates include Scottish breakfast. MC, V. Free parking. **Amenities:** 2 restaurants; bar; room service (8am–11pm); laundry service. *In room:* TV, coffeemaker, hair dryer.

INTO THE DEEP AT DEEP SEA WORLD

Although it's in the Fife region, another popular day trip from Edinburgh is to Deep Sea World. From central Edinburgh, drive 19km (12 miles) west, following the signs to Inverkeithing and the Forth Road Bridge. By train, go to either the Waverley or the Haymarket stations in Edinburgh and take any train stopping at North Queensferry (departing at 35-min. intervals); from the North Queensferry station, follow the signs to Deep Sea World, about a 10-minute walk. Round-trip fare is £9 to £11 ($14–$18).

Deep Sea World *Kids*   In the early 1990s, a group of entrepreneurs sealed the edges of an abandoned rock quarry with a sheathing of concrete and positioned a 109m (364-ft.) cement-and-acrylic tunnel on the quarry's bottom. They then flooded the quarry with a million gallons of seawater, stocked it with a menagerie of watery creatures, and opened it as Scotland's most comprehensive aquarium. You can either stand on a moving mechanical sideway or walk on a carpeted surface along the tunnel's length. En route, you pass through underwater microclimates featuring views of a kelp forest; sandy flats that shelter bottom-dwelling schools of stingray, turbot, and sole; murky caves favored by conger eels and small sharks; and a scary trench whose sponge-encrusted bottom careens abruptly away from view. Schools of shark and battalions of as many as 5,000 fish stare back at you. On the premises are a cafe, a gift shop, and an audiovisual show. Allow at least 90 minutes for your visit, and try to avoid the weekend crowds.

North Queensferry, in Fife. ⓒ **01383/411-880.** Admission £7.50 ($12) adults, £6 ($9.60) students, £5.50 ($8.80) children 3–15, £23 ($37) per family. Apr–June and Sept–Oct daily 10am–6pm; July–Aug daily 10am–6:30pm; Nov–Mar Mon–Fri 10am–5pm, Sat–Sun 10am–6pm.

5

The Borders & Galloway Regions

The romantic castle ruins and skeletons of Gothic abbeys in the **Borders** region stand as mute reminders of the battles that once raged between England and Scotland. For a long time, the "Border Country" was a no-man's land of plunder and destruction, lying south of the line of the Moorfoot, Pentland, and Lammermuir hill ranges and east of the Annandale Valley and the upper valley of the River Tweed.

The Borders is the land of Sir Walter Scott, master of romantic adventure, who topped the bestseller list in the early 19th century. The remains of the four great mid-12th-century abbeys are here: Dryburgh (where Scott is buried), Melrose, Jedburgh, and Kelso. And because of its abundant sheep-grazing land, the Borders is the home of the cashmere sweater and the tweed suit. Ask at the tourist office for a *Borders Woollen Trail* brochure, detailing where you can visit woolen mills, shops, and museums and follow the weaving process from start to finish.

Southwest of the Borders is the often-overlooked **Galloway** region (aka Dumfries and Galloway), a land of unspoiled countryside, fishing harbors, and romantic ruins. Major centers to visit are the ancient city of Dumfries, perhaps the best base for touring Galloway, and the artists' colony of Kirkcudbright, an ancient burgh filled with color-washed houses. In the far west, Stranraer is a major terminal for those making the 56km (35-mile) ferry crossing into Northern Ireland. Among the major sights are Sweetheart Abbey, outside Dumfries, and the Burns Mausoleum at Dumfries. If you have the time, explore Threave Garden, outside Castle Douglas.

Edinburgh Airport is about 64km (40 miles) northwest of Selkirk in the Borders and **Glasgow Airport** about 121km (75 miles) north of Dumfries in the Galloway region. Trains from Glasgow run south along the coast, toward Stranraer, intersecting with the rail stations at Ayr and Girvan en route. Another rail line from Glasgow extends south to Dumfries, depositing and picking up passengers before crossing the border en route to the English city of Carlisle. In direct contrast, southbound trains from Edinburgh almost always bypass most of the Borders towns en route, making direct, usually nonstop, transits for Berwick, in England. Consequently, to reach most of the Borders towns covered here, you'll probably rely on a rental car or on bus service from Edinburgh or Berwick to reach Peebles, Selkirk, Melrose, and Kelso. For train information and schedules, call **National Rail Enquiries** (© **08457/484-950**).

From England, trains from London's King's Cross Station to Edinburgh's Waverley Station enter Scotland at Berwick-upon-Tweed in 6 hours. From Berwick, a network of buses runs among the villages and towns. Three rail lines pass through the region from London's Euston Station en route to Glasgow. Dumfries or Stranraer is the best center if you're traveling by rail in the Uplands. Bus travel isn't recommended for reaching the region, but once you get here, you'll find it a reliable means of public transportation.

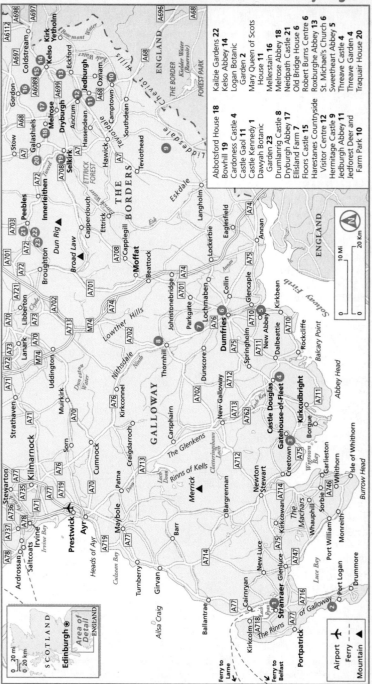

The Borders & Galloway Regions

Kalzie Gardens 22
Kelso Abbey 14
Logan Botanic Garden 2
Mary Queen of Scots House 11
Mellerstain 16
Melrose Abbey 18
Neidpath Castle 21
Old Bridge House 6
Robert Burns Centre 6
Roxburghe Abbey 13
St. Michael's Church 6
Sweetheart Abbey 5
Threave Castle 4
Threave Garden 4
Traquair House 20

Abbotsford House 18
Bowhill 19
Cardoness Castle 4
Castle Gaol 11
Castle Kennedy 1
Dawyah Botanic Garden 23
Drumlanrig Castle 8
Dryburgh Abbey 17
Ellisland Farm 7
Floors Castle 15
Harestanes Countryside Visitor Centre 12
Hermitage Castle 9
Jedburgh Abbey 11
Jedforest Deer and Farm Park 10

127

1 Jedburgh: Gateway to the Borders (★

77km (48 miles) SE of Edinburgh, 92km (57 miles) N of Newcastle-upon-Tyne, 21km (13 miles) S of Melrose

The little town of Jedburgh, divided by the River Jed, developed around Jedburgh Abbey on a Roman road called Dere Street. Today the market town gives little hint of the turbulence of its early history as home for royalty in the beleaguered Borders area.

If you have limited time to spend in the region, note that Jedburgh is a typical Borders town and makes a good base: It not only boasts some of the most impressive and evocative abbey ruins around, but is also the home of a fortified town house once inhabited by Mary Queen of Scots. In its environs you can enjoy some of the area's loveliest walks and excursions.

ESSENTIALS

GETTING THERE   There's no direct rail link to Jedburgh. The nearest **rail station** is at Berwick-upon-Tweed (© **08457/484-950** for information and tickets), from which you must take two buses (see below). Depending on the day's schedule, it's sometimes more practical to take a train to Newcastle-upon-Tyne (England), and from there take a bus to Jedburgh (see below).

There are daily **buses** from Edinburgh; a 9:15am bus arrives in Jedburgh at 10:55am and costs £6.75 ($11) one-way or £10.75 ($17) round-trip. Call © **08705/808-080** for schedules. From England, take the train to Berwick and then the bus (a 75-min. trip) from Berwick to Kelso. In Kelso, transfer to another bus (six to eight per day) that continues to Jedburgh, a 25-minute ride. One-way fares are £3.25 ($5.20). For information, call the Jedburgh tourist office (which has all the schedules) or the Kelso bus station (© **01573/224-141**). Two buses a day run from Newcastle-upon-Tyne to Jedburgh, taking 90 minutes and charging £9 to £11 ($14–$18) one-way.

If you're **driving,** at Corbridge (England), continue north into Scotland along A68, using Jedburgh as your gateway into the Borders. From Edinburgh, take A7 and then A68, following the signs to Jedburgh. From the center of Edinburgh, expect a driving time of around 75 minutes.

VISITOR INFORMATION   The **Jedburgh Visitor Centre** (© **01835/863-435**) is at Murray's Green, near the police station, adjacent to the spot where buses pull in, behind the Town Hall, and very close to the famous abbey. It's open in April and May, Monday through Saturday from 9:30am to 5pm, Sunday 10am to 5pm; June, Monday through Saturday from 9:30am to 6pm, Sunday 10am to 5pm; July and August, daily from 9am to 7pm, Sunday 10am to 6pm; September, Monday through Saturday from 9am to 6pm, Sunday 10am to 5pm; and October through March, Monday through Saturday from 9:30am to 4:30pm.

SEEING THE SIGHTS

Castle Gaol   This museum stands on the site of Jedburgh Castle, a 12th-century royal residence and the scene of many a hunting party because the ancient Jed Forest once surrounded the area. The castle was torn down in the 15th century to keep it from falling under English control. In the 1820s, a Georgian prison was built in its place and became the most modern in the country; its cells even had central heating, a far cry from the typical dungeon prisons of the day.

Castlegate. © **01835/863-254.** Admission £2 ($3.20) adults, £1.50 ($2.40) seniors and students free admission for children. Easter–Oct Mon–Sat 10am–4pm, Sun 1–4pm. Closed Nov to Easter.

Jedburgh Abbey ✸✸   This famous ruined abbey, founded by David I in 1138, is one of Scotland's finest. Under the Augustinian canons from Beauvais, France, it achieved abbey status in 1152 (when enough of its infrastructure was complete to allow a formal endorsement by the Augustinian hierarchies in Rome), and went on to witness much royal pageantry, like the coronation of the founder's grandson, Malcolm IV (1153–65), and the marriage of Alexander III (1249–86) to his second wife, Yolande de Dreux.

The abbey was sacked in 1544 and 1545 by the English during the frequent wars that ravaged the villages along the Scottish and English borders. Its roof was burned, allowing rains to penetrate and further destroy much of the interior detailing. After 1560, the ascendancy of the straitlaced Church of Scotland acted as a disincentive for rebuilding any grand-scale "papist monuments," so no efforts were made to repair the abbey.

For about 300 years, a small section of it was the town's parish church, but in 1875 other premises were found for day-to-day worship. Then teams of architects set to work restoring the place to its original medieval design. The abbey is still roofless but otherwise fairly complete, with most of its exterior stonework still in place. You can view the late-12th-century west front; three pedimented gables remain at the doorway, and the solid buttresses and rounded arches in the Norman style are relatively intact. You can also walk through the nave and the ruins of the former cloister. In a century-old outbuilding is the **Jedburgh Abbey Visitor Centre,** Abbey Place (✆ **01835/863-925**), open the same hours as the abbey.

Abbey Place. ✆ **01835/863-925.** Admission £3.50 ($5.60) adults, £2.50 ($4) seniors, £1.20 ($1.90) children under 16. Apr–Sept daily 9:30am–6:30pm; Oct–Mar Mon–Sat 9:30am–4:30pm, Sun 2–4:30pm. Last entrance 30 min. prior to closing.

Mary Queen of Scots House ✸   Here, in 1566, Mary Stuart spent 6 weeks and almost died of a mysterious ailment after a tiring 64km (40-mile) return ride from a visit to her wounded beloved, the earl of Bothwell, at Hermitage Castle (see "Exploring the Countryside," below). In a later lament, commenting on the emotional agonies of the last 20 years of her life, she wrote, "Would that I had died at Jedburgh." The house, in the center of High Street, contains articles dealing with Mary's life, paintings, and engravings. Ancient pear trees still stand on the grounds, a reminder of the days when Jedburgh was famous for its fruit. "Jethard pears" were once hawked in the streets of London.

Queen St. ✆ **01835/863-331.** Admission £3 ($4.80) adults, £2 ($3.20) seniors and children. Mar–Nov Mon–Sat 10am–4:30pm, Sun 11–4:30pm. Closed Dec–Feb.

EXPLORING THE COUNTRYSIDE

You can rent a bike in the nearby town of Hawick, at the **Hawick Cycle Centre,** 45 N. Bridge St. (✆ **01450/373-352**), where you'll pay £10 ($16) per day or £50 ($80) per week, plus a £50 ($80) deposit. It's open Monday through Saturday from 9am to 5pm.

Harestanes Countryside Visitor Centre   For another experience with nature, head north of Jedburgh (it's signposted) to this visitor center. You can follow marked trails or take guided walks through one of the most beautiful spots in the Borders. The center houses a Discovery Room with wildlife displays, a gift shop that sells local crafts, and a tearoom.

At the junction of A68 and B6400, Monteviot. ✆ **01835/830-306.** Free admission. Apr–Oct daily 10am–5pm. Closed Nov–Mar.

Hermitage Castle If you want to follow in the footsteps of Mary Queen of Scots, you can drive from Jedburgh to Hermitage Castle. It was to Hermitage that Mary was headed when she made her famous 64km (40-mile) ride from Jedburgh to rush to the bedside of her wounded lover, the earl of Bothwell (1535–78), the victim of a raid into Scottish territory by English troops. Still mired in the misty gloom of the Middle Ages, this 1300s castle was restored in the early 1800s. Its original owner, Lord Soulis, was accused of devil worship and boiled alive by the angry townspeople.

On an unclassified road (the castle is signposted) between A7 and B6399, 16 km (10 miles) south of Hawick in Liddesdale. ✆ **01316/688-800**. Admission £2 ($3.20) adults, £1.50 ($2.40) seniors, 70p ($1.10) children. Apr–Sept daily 9:30am–6pm. Closed Oct–Mar.

Jedforest Deer and Farm Park *Finds* You'll find the area's most interesting walks and nature experiences at this deer and farm park. Approximately 32 hectares (80 acres) of this 405-hectare (1,000-acre) farm are open to the public and dotted with unusual species of pigs, chickens, and especially deer. Owner Marion Armitage prides herself on her herds of red fallow and Asian Sitka deer (bred for food), which either nuzzle or flee from visitors. You can buy a bag of special deer food for 30p (50¢) and follow one of the two trails along the softly undulating, partially forested terrain. The trail marked with brown signposts requires 30 minutes; the trail marked with green signposts takes an hour. Each is peppered with signs explaining the flora and fauna you'll see en route.

An unusual side attraction in the park is Diana Durman-Walters and her **Birds of Prey Experience.** The staff members exercise the owls, buzzards, eagles, hawks, and falcons at periodic intervals every day, feeding them raw rabbit meat or chicken—but not so much that they lose their incentive to catch rats, rabbits, and field mice during their exercise regimes. If the art of falconry interests you, you can participate in a half-day Hawk Walk for £50 ($80) or a full-day Hawk Walk for £75 ($120). Participation requires an advance reservation (call the number below) and is limited to no more than six people. Wear sturdy walking shoes and sensible clothing that won't wilt in a rain shower. If you're willing, you can handle one of these temperamental birds and experience the way it returns to the glove after spotting, catching, and killing a rodent or rabbit.

Camptown, 8 km (5 miles) south of Jedburgh along A68. ✆ **01835/840-364**. Admission £4 ($6.40) adults, £2.50 ($4) children 3–16, £13 ($21) per family. May–Oct daily 10am–5:30pm; Sept–Oct daily 11am–4pm. Closed Nov–Apr.

WHERE TO STAY

Ancrum Craig Most of this place dates from the 1830s, when a simple 1722 farmhouse was massively expanded into a red-sandstone Victorian home. Surrounded by landscaped gardens, with views stretching out over the valley of the Teviot, Ancrum Craig is a fine example of baronial, somewhat chilly, Scottish living. It's called "the perfect first stop in Scotland." The guest rooms are cozy, one with bath and the other two with a shower-only bathroom. The largest is the Gold Room, with a bay window boasting a sweeping view. The smallest is the Heather Room, which overlooks the original medieval core, long ago made into an outbuilding. The breakfasts are generous.

Ancrum, Jedburgh, Rosburghshire TD8 6UN. ✆ **01835/830-280**. Fax 01835/830-259. www.ancrumcraig. co.uk. 3 units. £40–£54 ($64–$86) double. Rates include breakfast. MC, V. Free parking. Call for directions. Dogs welcome. *In room:* TV, coffeemaker, hair dryer.

Ferniehirst Mill Lodge   Built in 1980, this chalet-inspired modern guesthouse is in a quiet neighborhood away from the town center and attracts those (including hunters and anglers) seeking quiet and rural charm. On 10 hectares (25 acres) of private land, a haven for wild fowl, it stands in a secluded valley beside the fast-moving Jed Water. Its pine-paneled guest rooms are functional but comfortable, each with a private, shower-only bathroom. Horseback riding (for experienced riders only) costs about £15 ($24) per hour (minimum of 2 hr.), and riders must supply their own riding habits.

Hwy. A68, Jedburgh, Roxburghshire TD8 6PQ. (C) and fax **01835/863-279.** www.ferniehirstmill.co.uk. 9 units. £23 ($37) per person. Rates include breakfast; dinner £14 ($22) extra. Riding packages available for those willing to stay 1 week. MC, V. Free parking. Take A68 4km (2½ miles) south of Jedburgh. **Amenities:** Bar. *In room:* Coffeemaker.

Glenfriar's Hotel   This small private hotel is in a Georgian house on a quiet corner next to St. John's Church. It features antique wooden furnishings, including four-poster beds in two rooms, and well-maintained bathrooms with showers.

The Friars, Jedburgh, The Borders TD8 6BN. (C) and fax **01835/862-112.** 6 units. £50 ($80) double. Rates include breakfast. AE, MC, V. *In room:* TV, coffeemaker, hair dryer.

The Spinney Guest House and Lodges (*Finds*   Run by Mr. and Mrs. Fry, this B&B complex includes a main house, a modernized cottage with three doubles, and three pinewood chalets with bathrooms, sitting rooms, and kitchens. Leather and wood furnishings are found throughout the well-maintained guest rooms. The Scottish Tourist Board recently bestowed the guesthouse with a deluxe rating.

Langlee, Jedburgh, The Borders TD8 6PB. (C) **01835/863-525.** Fax 01835/864-883. www.thespinney-jedburgh.co.uk. 3 units, 3 chalets. £23–£40 ($37–$64) per person. Rates for regular double rooms include breakfast. MC, V. Free parking. Main house B&B closed Dec–Feb; chalets open year-round. Take A68 3km (2 miles) south of Jedburgh. Pets welcome in chalets by prior arrangement. *In room:* TV, coffeemaker, hair dryer.

WHERE TO DINE

Carter's Rest SCOTTISH/CONTINENTAL   This pub, with a downstairs dining room built of old abbey stones, is the favorite gathering place for locals. Mr. Jonentz, the owner, serves wholesome and hearty food and drink. The simple but tasty menu includes dishes like steaks, scampi, chicken Cordon Bleu, pork or lamb chops, and fresh vegetables in season. The pub also has eight regional beers on tap.

Abbey Place. (C) **01835/863-414.** Main courses £5–£12 ($8–$19); bar lunches £4.50–£8 ($7.20–$13). MC, V. Restaurant daily noon–2:30pm and 6–9pm; pub Mon–Sat 11am–11pm, Sun 11am–10:30pm.

Simply Scottish SCOTTISH   In the heart of town, amid the stripped pinewood floors and heavy pine furniture of what was built around 1900 as a department store, this decent, well-scrubbed restaurant serves savory lunches and dinners, plus countless pots of tea for all the locals who drop by. Menu items, made entirely from Scottish ingredients, are likely to include a salad of smoked chicken and avocado, haggis with white onion sauce, grilled Borders lamb steak with Arran mustard, and roasted salmon with herb-flavored butter sauce. A preferred dessert is summer fruit pudding with fruit compote and honey-flavored ice cream.

6-8 High St. (C) **01835/864-696.** Reservations recommended for dinner. Lunch main courses £4–£8 ($6.40–$13); pot of tea with scones and jam £2.50 ($4); fixed-price dinner £11.95 ($19); dinner main courses £6.95–£11.50 ($11–$18). MC, V. Daily 10am–8:30pm, Saturday closes at 9pm.

2 Kelso: Abbey Ruins & Adam Architecture ⚐★

71 km (44 miles) SE of Edinburgh, 19km (12 miles) NE of Jedburgh, 110km (68 miles) NW of Newcastle-upon-Tyne, 19km (12 miles) E of Melrose, 39km (23 miles) W of Berwick-upon-Tweed

A typical historic border town like Jedburgh, Kelso lies at the point where the River Teviot meets the River Tweed. Sir Walter Scott called it "the most beautiful, if not the most romantic, village in Scotland." The settlement that grew up here developed into a town around Kelso Abbey.

Kelso today is a flourishing market town, the center of an agricultural district boasting farming and raising livestock. But for visitors, the reasons to come are the ruined abbey and the palatial Floors Castle (by the great architect William Adam) and Mellerstain (begun by William but finished by his son Robert). The town is also one of the best centers for touring the Borders because it's near Jedburgh, Dryburgh Abbey, and Melrose.

ESSENTIALS

GETTING THERE   The nearest rail station connection is Berwick-upon-Tweed, from where you can take a bus to Kelso (see below). For information, call ⚐ **8457/484-950.**

From Edinburgh, board the bus to Saint Boswells, with connecting service to Kelso; the full trip lasts about 80 minutes and costs £6 ($9.60) one-way and £11 ($18) round-trip. Phone ⚐ **8705/808-080** for more information. From Berwick to Kelso, there are between six and eight buses a day, depending on the day of the week and the season. Transit costs £4 ($6.40) each way and takes an hour. Because three bus companies make the run, it's best to call the local tourist office at ⚐ **01573/223-464** for the schedules.

From Edinburgh, take A7 and follow the signs to Hawick; then change to A68, follow the signs to Jedburgh, and take A6089 to Kelso.

VISITOR INFORMATION   The **tourist office** is at Town House, The Square (⚐ **0870/608-0404**). April to June, it's open Monday to Saturday 10am to 5pm and Sunday 10am to 2pm; July and August, hours are Monday to Saturday 10:30am to 5:30pm and Sunday 10am to 2pm; September hours are Monday to Saturday 9:30am to 5pm and Sunday 10am to 2pm; and October hours are Monday to Saturday 10am to 4pm and Sunday 10am to 1pm.

SEEING THE SIGHTS

Floors Castle ⚐   On the banks of the Tweed, the home of the dukes of Roxburghe was designed in 1721 by William Adam and remodeled in the mid-19th century by William Playfair. Part of the castle contains superb French and English furniture, porcelain, tapestries, and paintings by Gainsborough, Reynolds, and Canaletto. You'll also find a licensed restaurant, a coffee shop, and a gift shop, as well as a walled garden and garden center. You might recognize Floors: It was a major location for the Tarzan film *Greystoke.*

Hwy. A697, 3km (2 miles) north of Kelso. ⚐ **01573/223-333.** Admission £5.75 ($9.20) adults, £4.75 ($7.60) seniors, £3.25 ($5.20) children age 3–15, free for children age 2 and under. Apr–Oct daily 11am–4:50pm (last admission 4pm). Closed Nov–Mar. Follow the signs north from Kelso center.

Kelso Abbey ⚐   Once a great ecclesiastical center, Kelso Abbey has lain in ruins since the late 16th century, when it suffered its last and most devastating attack by the English, who ripped off its roofs, burned it, and declared it officially defunct. The lands and remaining buildings were given to the earl of Roxburghe. The oldest (1128) and probably largest of the Border abbeys, it was once one of the richest, collecting revenues and rents from granges, fisheries, mills, and manor houses throughout the region. In 1919, the abbey was given to the nation.

Although the remains of this abbey may not be as impressive as those of Jedburgh (see "Jedburgh: Gateway to the Borders," earlier in this chapter), Kelso has had its moments in history, including the crowning of the infant James III. At the entrance is part of the south recessed doorway, where some of the sculpture on the arches is still fairly intact. The massive west transept tower still suggests its original massive construction, and a trio of building sections with round-headed openings remain. The west front and tower are visible, the whole flanked by buttresses crowned with rounded turrets. A partial cloister here dates from 1933, when it was built as the Roxburghe family vault. Sir Walter Scott knew Kelso Abbey well, as he spent time here studying at Waverley Cottage, which you can see from the abbey's parking area; it was once the Kelso Grammar School, where the famous author learned how to read and write.

Bridge St. Free admission. Apr–Dec Mon–Sat 10am–6:30pm, Sun 2–6:30pm; Jan–Mar by arrangement only.

Mellerstain ⋆⋆   Eleven kilometers (7 miles) northwest of Kelso stands Mellerstain, the seat of the earls of Haddington. This is one of the most famous of the mansions designed by Robert Adam and one of Scotland's greatest Georgian residences. William Adam built two wings on the house in 1725; the main building was designed by his more famous son, Robert, some 40 years later. (For more details on the Adam family of architectural geniuses, see "Robert Adam: Architect to the King," below.)

Mellerstain is associated with Lady Grisell Baillie (born Grisell Hume). In 1689, at 13 years of age, this Scottish heroine showed great courage by hiding her father in the village church's crypt, bringing him food and supplies in the dead of night, and facing down the English. Hounded by the English, she fled to Holland but returned in triumph with William of Orange (later William I of England) and later married into the Baillie family, scions of Mellerstain. You can see the interior, with its impressive library, paintings, and antique furniture. The garden terrace offers a panoramic view south to the lake, with the Cheviot Hills in the distance. Afternoon tea is served, and souvenir gifts are on sale.

Gordon. ☎ 01573/410-225. Admission £5.50 ($8.80) adults, £5 ($8) seniors, £3 ($4.80) children. May–Sept Sun–Fri 12:30–5pm; Oct–Apr by arrangement only. From Edinburgh, follow A68 to Earlston, then follow the signs to Mellerstain for another 8km (5 miles); from Kelso, head northwest along A6089 until you see the signposted turn to the left.

OUTDOOR PURSUITS

The 18-hole **Roxburghe Golf Course** (☎ 01573/450-331) is the only championship course in the region. This 7,111-yard (6,471m) course was designed by Dave Thomas, one of Britain's leading golf architects. Guests of the Roxburghe Hotel (see "Where to Stay & Dine," below) can most easily get tee times, but the course is open to nonmembers as well. Greens fees are £50 ($80) for 18 holes, or £70 ($112) for a full day's play.

Our favorite spot for drinking in the scenic countryside is the nearby village of **Kirk Yeetholm**, 11km (7 miles) southeast of Kelso on B6352. This is the northern terminus of the **Pennine Way**, a 403km (250-mile) hike that begins down in Yorkshire, England. Today Kirk Yeetholm is filled with tired hikers at the end of the trail, but it was once the Gypsy capital of Scotland—until 1883, a Gypsy queen was crowned here. You can see (at least from the outside) the "Gypsy palace," really a tiny cottage in the center of the village.

Robert Adam: Architect to the King

In the field of architecture, one Scottish name towers over all the rest: **Robert Adam** (1728–92), whose adaptations of the Italian Palladian style have been admired and duplicated in public and private buildings around the world. He has emerged as Britain's most prestigious neo-classical architect in a century that produced dozens of talented competitors. Today, owning an Adam building is an honor akin to being granted a knighthood by the queen, but (if you happen to be selling the building) infinitely more profitable.

Adam's genius derived from his synthesis of the decorative traditions of the French and Italian Renaissance with the ancient monuments of Greece and Rome. His designs are particularly notable for their lavish use of color, inspired by Grecian vase paintings and by what was being excavated from archaeological digs in places like Pompeii. Almost as important, Adam seemed to have a well-developed business sense and a knack for decorating the right house at the right time, and his moneyed clients helped propel him into the spotlight.

Throughout much of his career, he collaborated with his capable but less talented younger brother, **James** (1730–94), who handled many of the workaday details of the projects they executed together. And when an English or Scottish lord or lady hired the Adam brothers, they got more than an intensely detailed building—in most cases, the commission included every aspect of the interior decoration and most of the furnishings. The brothers' education in the visual arts began early: Their father, **William Adam** (1689–1748), was the leading Scottish architect of his day and designed dozens of manor houses in what has been called a crude but vigorous Palladian style.

Robert was born in Kirkcaldy, in Fife, but soon emigrated to the source of most of his large commissions, London. He laboriously studied the

Another place for walking and hiking is around **Smailholm Tower** (© 0131/ **668-8800**), on a ridge 13km (8 miles) west of Kelso and 3km (2 miles) south of Mellerstain (see listing, above), signposted off B6404. A so-called peel tower (fortified tower) from the 1500s, it has been restored and rises 18m (60 ft.) above a loch, providing some of the best views of the Borders. Open October to March Saturday 9:30am to 4:30pm and Sunday 2 to 4:30pm. April to September, it's open daily 9:30am to 6:30pm, charging £2.20 ($3.50) admission for adults, £1.60 ($2.55) for seniors and students, and 75p ($1.20) for children.

WHERE TO STAY & DINE

Abbey Bank   This sophisticated B&B started out as the home of a local doctor in 1815. Today, it's owned by Douglas McAdam and his wife, Diah, who have lived in Indonesia and Korea. The Georgian house is filled with a mix of British and Oriental furniture. Each sunny guest room has streamlined modern furniture, and most units come with a shower-only bathroom, others with tub baths. Because of Diah's familiarity with Indonesian cuisine, you'll be offered *nasi goreng*, the national rice-based dish, as well as a traditional Scottish breakfast of architecture of imperial Rome under the supervision of then-famous French antiquarian C. L. Clérisseau, with whom he toured widely in Italy and Dalmatia (later part of Yugoslavia). In 1764, he compiled the information he gathered during these tours in the widely acclaimed *The Ruins of the Palace of the Emperor Diocletian at Spalatro.* In 1761, Robert, along with architect William Chambers, was appointed architect of the king's works, at the time the most prestigious post in Britain. In 1773, an illustrated volume, *The Works of Robert and James Adam,* documented his and his brother's vision; they justifiably claimed credit for revolutionizing the principals of English aesthetics.

The Adam style, a richly detailed yet airy interpretation of neoclassicism, was a radical departure from the more ponderous and sometimes ecclesiastical forms that preceded it. Almost immediately, the Adam interpretation of ceiling decorations and mantelpieces was widely copied throughout Britain. And within less than a generation, this vision radically influenced furniture styles throughout Europe and North America, most notably France's Louis XVI style. Looser derivations are the Directoire, Sheraton, and Empire styles.

Adam buildings in Scotland include the **Old Quad** at Edinburgh University and **Mellerstain** in the Borders (described earlier in this chapter). Many more of his works remain in England, especially London, thanks to his careful cultivation of the wealthy English. Examples are **Kenwood House** (1767–69) in London, **Osterly Park** (1761–80) and **Syon House** (1762–69) in Middlesex, and **Luton Hoo** (1768–75) in Bedfordshire. Much more widespread than Adam buildings, however, are examples of their furniture and interior decor (especially chairs, sideboards, and mantelpieces), which are proudly displayed in museums and private homes across the United Kingdom and North America.

bacon, sausage, eggs, and haggis. A greenhouse contains peach vines and many of the seedlings Douglas nurtures during the coldest months. *Note:* Smoking is not permitted in the guest rooms.

The Knowes, Kelso, The Borders TD5 7BH. ℭ and fax **01573/226-550.** www.aboutscotland.com/kelso/abbey bank.html. 5 units. £60 ($96) double. Rates include breakfast. MC, V. *In room:* TV, coffeemaker, no phone.

The Cross Keys Hotel   Facing the cobbled main square of the town, the facade of this hotel is a stately Georgian style from 1769. Since then, guests have included Bonnie Prince Charlie and Beatrix Potter. The public areas are comfortable and busy, vaguely inspired by Scottish Art Nouveau master Charles Rennie Mackintosh. The midsize guest rooms are well appointed and have double-glazed windows; each has a shower-only bathroom. The superior rooms are larger and sport sofas; all are nonsmoking. The restaurant serves lunch and dinner daily, while the cozy Scottish-style bar, The 36, boasts an impressive collection of single-malt whiskies.

36 The Square, Kelso, The Borders TD5 7HL. ℭ **01573/223-303.** Fax 01573/225-792. www.cross-keys-hotel. co.uk. 28 units. £52–£104 ($83–$166) double. Rates include breakfast. AE, MC, V. **Amenities:** Restaurant; bar. *In room:* TV, coffeemaker, hair dryer (superior rooms only), iron/ironing board.

Edenwater House ✿✿ *Finds*   This former private manor house opening onto the Edenwater lies in the village of Ednam, 3.2km (2 miles) north of Kelso. It enjoys one of the most tranquil settings in the Borders, and is an exceedingly comfortable small private hotel known for its excellent cuisine and personal service. Guests meet each other in the formal and spacious drawing room where a log fire burns on chilly nights. In fair weather they can stroll through the garden and grounds. Bedrooms (all nonsmoking) are large and airy and beautifully furnished. Units contain a private bathroom, three with tub, one with shower. The food is among the best in the area, but the restaurant is open to nonresidents only for dinner on Friday and Saturday. A fixed-price menu costs £32.50 ($52).

Ednam (off the B6461), Kelso TD5 7QL. ✆ **01573/224-070.** Fax 01573/226-615. www.edenwaterhouse. co.uk. 4 units. £70–£90 ($112–$144) double. Rates include full breakfast. MC, V. Closed Jan 1–14. **Amenities:** Restaurant. *In room:* TV, coffeemaker, iron.

Ednam House Hotel ✿✿   The Ednam, on the fringe of Kelso, is a conversion of a 1761 Georgian house often referred to as "that lovely place beside the river." In the oldest section is an unusual collection of antiques. The so-called Principal Rooms—the original master bedrooms of the manor—lie on the third floor and offer a view of the river; less expensive and scenic are those on the first and second floors. The rooms vary in size, but all come with shower or bath and bathrobes.

The Georgian style Orangerie, a building where oranges were once grown, lies 9m (10 yd.) from the main house. Often rented to families or groups of friends, it houses two elegantly furnished and most comfortable upstairs bedrooms with a shared living room downstairs overlooking the river. These accommodations are very private and exclusive and feature loads of antiques.

Bridge St., Kelso, The Borders TD5 7HT. ✆ **01573/224-168.** Fax 01573/226-319. www.ednamhouse.com. 32 units. £89–£124 ($142–$198) double. Rates include breakfast. MC, V. **Amenities:** Restaurant; babysitting. *In room:* TV, coffeemaker, hair dryer, trouser press.

The Roxburghe Hotel and Golf Course ✿✿   This late-19th-century castle stands on 81 hectares (200 acres) of woodland, lawns, and gardens. It was built as the family home of the Roxburghes, who valued its location on the trout-filled Teviot. In 1982, it was converted into a country hotel: The old stable block contains 6 guest rooms; another 16 are in the main house. All are well appointed; suites and a few doubles have four-poster beds. Amid a subdued but elegant interior, the hotel has four log-burning fireplaces going, even in summer. The hotel also offers a number of leisure and sporting activities, from archery to biking to fishing.

Hwy. A698, Helton, Kelso, The Borders TD5 8JZ. ✆ **01573/450-331.** Fax 01573/450-611. www.roxburghe.net. 22 units. £125–£175 ($200–$280) double; £215 ($344) double with four-poster bed; £265 ($424) suite. Rates include breakfast. AE, DC, MC, V. Take A698 5km (3 miles) southwest of Kelso. **Amenities:** Restaurant; bar; golf course; tennis court; spa; room service (7:30am–9:30pm). *In room:* TV, hair dryer.

A SIDE TRIP TO DRYBURGH ABBEY

Sixteen kilometers (10 miles) west of Kelso and 6km (4 miles) southeast of Melrose (off A68), you'll find the town of **Dryburgh** and its ruined abbey. The adjoining town is **St. Boswells,** an old village on the Selkirk–Kelso road. Near Dryburgh is **Scott's View** ✿ (take B6356 north) over the Tweed to Sir Walter's beloved Eildon Hills; it's the most glorious vista in the region.

Dryburgh Abbey ✿✿   These Gothic ruins are surrounded by gnarled yew trees and cedars of Lebanon, said to have been planted by knights returning from the Crusades. It's still a lovely ruin, and its setting in a loop of the Tweed is memorable. The cloister buildings are relatively intact, but not much remains of the church itself, except a few foundation stones. You can see enough fragments to realize that the architectural style was transitional, between the Romanesque and the pointed Early English style. Sir Walter Scott is buried here in a pillared side chapel.

Hwy. A68, Dryburgh, Roxburghshire. © 01835/822-381. Admission £3 ($4.80) adults, £2.30 ($3.70) seniors, £1 ($1.60) children age 5–15, free for children age 4 and under. Apr–Sept daily 9:30am–6:30pm (July–Aug to 7:30pm); Oct–Mar Mon–Sat 9:30am–4:30pm, Sun 2–4:30pm. Drive south from Dryburgh along B6356 (it's signposted); from Edinburgh take A68 to St. Boswells and turn onto B6404 and then left onto B6356.

WHERE TO STAY & DINE

Clint Lodge Guest House Scotland ⭐ (Finds) This former lodge has been carefully converted into a small guesthouse of charm and grace. In the 18th century, the establishment was a sports lodge, and the setting is still tranquil, with panoramic views over the valley. The midsize bedrooms are comfortable and traditionally furnished, often with a treasure trove of family heirlooms. Each room has a private bathroom with shower; two rooms also have the original "deep fill" tubs. The menu features real "taste of Scotland" fare with such dishes as Border lamb with port and red currants, potato pancakes with smoked haddock, and a strawberry and Drambuie cream with homemade shortbread.

St. Boswells, Melrose TD6 0DZ. © 01835/822-027. Fax 01835/822-656. www.clintlodge.co.uk. 5 units. £70–£84 ($112–$134) double with breakfast; £120–£134 ($192–$214) double with breakfast and dinner. MC, V. At St. Boswells, take B6404, continue 3.2km (2 miles) across Mertoun Bridge, and turn left onto B6356 through Clint Mains village, veering left. This road leads to Clint Lodge, 1.6km (1 mile) away on the right. Pets accepted. In room: TV, coffeemaker.

Dryburgh Abbey Hotel ⭐⭐ Next to the abbey ruins, this hotel is the best in the area. It was built in 1845 as the home of Lady Grisell Baillie and remained in her family until 1929. It's said to be haunted by the "gray lady," who had an ill-fated affair with a monk that led to his execution and her suicide by drowning. After restoration, the deteriorated property was the first in the Borders to be awarded five crowns by the Scottish Tourist Board. The accommodations—named for fishing lures—include both deluxe rooms with half-tester or four-poster beds (some have small balconies) and standard abbey- or river-view rooms. The Tower Suites have separate sitting rooms, bathrobes, and abbey or river views.

Hwy. B6404, outside St. Boswells, The Borders TD6 0RQ. © 01835/822-261. Fax 01835/823945. www.dryburgh.co.uk. 37 units. £114–£164 ($182–$262) double; £194–£204 ($310–$326) suite for 2. Rates include full Scottish breakfast. AE, MC, V. **Amenities:** Restaurant; bar; heated indoor pool; 24-hr. room service; babysitting; laundry service. In room: TV, coffeemaker, hair dryer, iron/ironing board, trouser press.

3 Melrose ⭐

60km (37 miles) SE of Edinburgh, 113km (70 miles) NW of Newcastle-upon-Tyne, 65km (40 miles) W of Berwick-upon-Tweed

Rich in sights, Melrose is one of the highlights of the Borders: It offers one of the most beautiful ruined abbeys in the Borders as well as the region's most widely diversified shopping, and Abbotsford House, former home of Sir Walter Scott, is 3km (2 miles) west. And Melrose is close to the Southern Upland Way, which passes to the north of Melrose. Even if you can follow only part of this trail, take a day hike on the section along the River Tweed outside Melrose—it's one of the most delightful and scenic walks in Scotland.

ESSENTIALS

GETTING THERE The nearest rail station is in Berwick-upon-Tweed, where you can catch a bus to Melrose. From Berwick, about five buses per day travel to Melrose; travel time is about 90 minutes. Fares are about £4.55 ($7.30) one-way and £9 ($14) round-trip. Call the tourist office in Berwick-upon-Tweed at ✆ **01289/330-733** for bus schedules and ✆ **8457/484-950** for train schedules.

Many visitors prefer to take the bus into Melrose directly from Edinburgh. Travel time by bus from Edinburgh is 90 minutes, and buses depart every 1½ hours throughout the day. Phone ✆ **8705/808-080** for more information.

Driving from Edinburgh, you can reach Melrose by going southeast along A7 and following the signs to Galashiels. From Kelso, take A699 west to St. Boswells and at the junction with A6091 head northwest.

VISITOR INFORMATION The tourist office is at **Abbey House,** Abbey Street (✆ **0870/608-0404**). In April, May, and October, it's open Monday to Saturday 10am to 5pm and Sunday 10am to 1pm. June and September hours are Monday to Saturday 10am to 5:30pm and Sunday 10am to 2pm. July and August, hours are Monday to Saturday 9:30am to 6:30pm and Sunday 10am to 6pm.

SEEING THE SIGHTS

Abbotsford House ★★ This was the home Sir Walter Scott built and lived in from 1812 until he died. Designed in the Scots baronial style and considered, after his literary works, Scott's most enduring monument, it contains many relics, including artifacts, and mementos the famous author collected from the Waterloo battlefield. Other exhibits include his clothes and his death mask. Especially interesting is his study, with his writing desk and chair. In 1935, two secret drawers were found in the desk. One of them contained 57 letters, part of the correspondence between Sir Walter and his wife-to-be.

Scott purchased Cartley Hall farmhouse on the banks of the Tweed in 1812. In 1822, he had the old house demolished and replaced it with the building you see today. Scott was one of Britain's earliest souvenir hunters, scouring the land for artifacts associated with the historical characters he rendered into novel form. One of his proudest possessions was a sword given to the duke of Montrose by English king Charles I for his cooperation (some say collaboration) during the struggles between Scotland and England. The sword is proudly displayed near a gun, sword, dagger, and small knife owned by the sworn enemy of the duke, cattle herder Rob Roy, whose exploits were later crafted by Sir Walter Scott into one of his most enduring dramas. (You may remember the Liam Neeson film from a few years back.) You can see Scott's study, library (with 9,000 rare volumes), drawing room, entrance hall, and armories—even the dining room overlooking the Tweed where he died on September 21, 1832. There are also extensive gardens and grounds to visit, plus the private chapel, added after Scott's death.

Hwy. B6360, Melrose. ✆ **01896/752-043**. Admission £4.20 ($6.70) adults, £2.10 ($3.35) children. Mar–Oct Mon–Sat 9:30am–5pm, Sun 2–5pm; Nov–Feb Mon–Sat 9:30am–5pm. Head just off A7, south of the junction with A72, onto B6360, some 4km (2½ miles) southeast of Galashiels.

Melrose Abbey ★★ These lichen-covered ruins, among the most beautiful in Europe, are all that's left of the ecclesiastical community established by Cistercian monks in 1136. The complex's pure Gothic lines were made famous by Sir Walter Scott, who was instrumental in getting the decayed remains repaired and restored in the early 19th century. In *The Lay of the Last Minstrel,* Scott wrote, "If thou would'st view fair Melrose aright, go visit in the pale moonlight." You can still view its red-sandstone shell, built in the Perpendicular style and filled with elongated windows and carved capitals with delicate tracery. The heart of Robert the Bruce is supposed to be interred in the abbey, but the location is

A Walk Along the Borders

If you're feeling particularly saintly, you can walk in the footsteps of 7th-century St. Cuthbert along the Scotland-England border. The 101km (62-mile) path stretches from Melrose, 60km (37 miles) southwest of Edinburgh, across the border into northeast England to the Holy Island of Lindisfarne on the Northumberland coast. St. Cuthbert began his ministry in Melrose in about A.D. 650 and later was appointed prior at Lindisfarne. The walk passes many places linked to his legend, prehistoric relics, Roman ruins, and historic castles. The high point is Wideopen Hill, 434m (1,430 ft.) above sea level. Permission from landowners along the route has been obtained, and the walk is clearly marked. A leaflet suggests distances you can comfortably cover in a day and makes recommendations for overnight stops. Contact Roger Smith, Walking Development Officer, **Scottish Border Enterprise Center**, Bridge Street, Galashiels TB1 ISW (© **01896/758-991;** fax 01896/758-625), for information.

unknown. Look for the beautiful carvings and the tombs of other famous Scotsmen buried in the chancel.

Abbey St. © **01896/822-562.** Admission £3.50 ($5.60) adults, £2.50 ($4) seniors, £1.20 ($1.90) children. Apr–Sept daily 9:30am–6:30pm; Oct–Mar Mon–Sat 9:30am–4:30pm, Sun 2–4:30pm.

Thirlestane Castle ⭐ One of Scotland's most imposing country houses, Thirlestane has been owned by the Lauderdale family since 1218. A T-shaped building, the castle has a keep from around the end of the 16th century and was much altered after Queen Victoria took the throne. The interior is known for its ornamental plaster ceilings, the finest in the country from the Restoration period. In the old nurseries is the Historic Toy Collection, and Border Country Life exhibits depict life in the Borders from prehistoric times to the present.

16km (10 miles) north of Melrose, overlooking Leader Water, about 1km (½ mile) from Lauder. © **01578/722-430.** www.thirlestanecastle.co.uk. Admission £5.50 ($8.80) adults, £3 ($4.80) children, £15 ($24) families (2 adults and children). May 1–Oct 10 Sun–Fri 10:30am–4:30pm (last admission at 3:30pm). Closed late Oct–Mar. Take A68 to Lauder in Berwickshire, 16km (10 miles) north of Melrose and 45km (28 miles) south of Edinburgh on A68.

Traquair House ⭐⭐ Dating from the 10th century, this is perhaps Scotland's oldest and most romantic house, rich in associations with Mary Queen of Scots and the Jacobite uprisings. The great house is still lived in by the Stuarts of Traquair. One of the most poignant exhibits is an ornately carved oak cradle in the King's Room, in which Mary rocked her infant son, who later become James VI of Scotland and James I of England. Other treasures here are glass, embroideries, silver, manuscripts, and paintings. Of particular interest is a brew house equipped as it was 2 centuries ago and still used regularly. On the grounds are craft workshops as well as a maze and woodland walks.

Hwy. A72, 26km (16 miles) west of Melrose. © **01896/830-323.** www.traquair.co.uk. Admission £5.60 ($8.95) adults, £5.30 ($8.50) seniors, £3.10 ($4.95) students/children, £16.50 ($26) families of 5. Easter–May and Sept–Oct Mon–Sat 9:30am–5pm, Sun 2–5pm; June–Aug daily 9:30am–5pm. Closed Nov–Easter.

SHOPPING

Melrose is one of the best destinations for shopping in the Borders. Most shops are open Monday through Saturday from 9:30am to 5pm and Sunday from noon to around 4pm.

The Country Kitchen, Market Square (© **01896/822-586**), displays a comprehensive choice of English, French, and Scottish cheeses, along with pâtés and meat products. You can buy them prepackaged or order up gourmet sandwiches and picnic fixings. **Abbey Wines,** Abbey Street (© **01896/823-224**), stocks the town's largest wine selection, plus at least 150 malt whiskies, some from the most obscure distilleries in Scotland.

The town's most complete collection of books is for sale at **Talisman Books,** 9 Market Square (© **01896/822-196**), in an old-fashioned Edwardian shop. Gifts, especially impractical-but-charming items in porcelain and china, are available at **Butterfly,** High Street (© **01896/822-045**).

Feeling chilly in the Scottish fog? A meticulously crafted wool or cashmere sweater from **Anne Oliver Knitwear,** 1 Scott's Place (© **01896/822-975**), might provide the extra warmth you'll need. **Lochcarron of Scotland,** 5 Market Square (© **01896/823-823**), is larger, but stocks only its own goods. Designers like Calvin Klein, Ralph Lauren, and Jean-Paul Gaultier have ordered bulk amounts here for relabeling and distribution. For tartan and other fabrics, visit **The Fabric Shop,** High Street (© **01896/823-475**), which both high-class couturiers and homegrown dressmakers find appealing.

WHERE TO STAY

Burts Hotel *Value*   Nestled on the banks of the River Tweed and within walking distance of the abbey, this family-run inn dates from 1722. The traditional three-story town house offers a taste of small-town Scotland. The decor is modern, with an airy and restful feel. All guest rooms are well furnished, each equipped with a shower. In the attractive bar, which sports Windsor chairs and a coal-burning fireplace, tasty lunches and suppers are served (as well as 90 different single malt whiskeys).

Market Square, Melrose, The Borders TD6 9PN. © **01896/822-285.** Fax 01896/822-870. www.burtshotel. co.uk. 20 units. £92–£96 ($147–$154) double. Rates include Scottish breakfast. AE, DC, MC, V. Free parking. **Amenities:** Restaurant; bar; limited room service; laundry. *In room:* TV, coffeemaker, hair dryer.

King's Arms Hotel *Kids*   One of Melrose's oldest commercial buildings still in use, this 17th-century coaching inn has a three-story stone-and-brick facade that overlooks the pedestrian traffic of the main street. Inside is a series of cozy but slightly dowdy public rooms and half a dozen simple but comfortably furnished small guest rooms, each with a shower. One suite has a kitchen and is large enough for families, and a cottage is available in summer only. The nonsmoking restaurant serves an odd mix of international offerings, including Mexican tacos and enchiladas, Indian curries, British steak pies, and giant Yorkshire puddings.

High St., Melrose, The Borders TD6 9PB. © **01896/822-143.** Fax 01896/823-812. www.kingsarmsmelrose. co.uk. 7 units. £59.50 ($95) double. MC, V. **Amenities:** Restaurant; bar. *In room:* TV, coffeemaker, kitchen (in family suite only).

Millars of Melrose *Finds*   This well-maintained, family-owned hotel is in the heart of Melrose and easily recognizable by the colorful window boxes adorning its facade in summer. Most accommodations are medium in size and rather functionally but comfortably furnished. The most spacious unit comes with a traditional four-poster bed and a Jacuzzi; honeymooners sometimes stay here and are welcomed in style with a complimentary bottle of champagne, flowers, and chocolates. One room is set aside for use by families. Bathrooms are equipped either with tub or shower.

The split-level dining room offers tasty, reasonably priced meals. Meals are also served in the bar, which boasts a fine assortment of beers, wines, and whiskeys.

Market Square, Melrose TD6 9PQ. ℭ **01896/822-645.** Fax 01896/823-474. www.millarshotel.co.uk. 10 units. £85 ($136) double; £90 ($144) family room. Rates include breakfast. MC, V. Follow the A68 into Melrose to the center of town. **Amenities:** Restaurant; bar. *In room:* TV, hair dryer, coffeemaker, trouser press.

Traquair Arms Hotel ✰   This is the area's most tranquil retreat for those seeking a country-house atmosphere. The small hotel was built as a coaching inn around 1780 and has later Victorian additions. Open fires in the bar lounge and fresh flowers in the dining room create a pleasant ambience. The cozy guest rooms come with comfortable furnishings, well-maintained bathrooms, and views over the valley. The hotel is known for fine pub food; vegetarians and others with special dietary needs can be accommodated. All dishes are freshly prepared by chefs Hugh Anderson and Sara Currie. The hotel is within a 5-minute walk of the River Tweed and salmon and trout fishing can be arranged.

Traquair Rd., Innerleithen, The Borders EH44 6PD. ℭ **01896/830-229.** Fax 01896/830-260. traquair.arms@ scottishborders.com. 15 units. £72–£80 ($115–$128) double. Rates include breakfast; dinner £18 ($29). AE, MC, V. Take E69 from Melrose for 23km (14 miles). **Amenities:** Restaurant; bar. *In room:* TV, coffeemaker, hair dryer.

WHERE TO DINE

Don't miss the pastries at Melrose's best bakery, **Jackie Lunn, Ltd.,** High Street (ℭ **01896/822-888**).

Two of the town's most likable pubs are the one in the **King's Arms,** High Street (ℭ **01896/822-143**), where you'll generally find lots of rugby players lifting a pint or two, and the somewhat more sedate one in **Burts Hotel,** The Square (ℭ **01896/822-285**).

Marmion's Brasserie SCOTTISH   Across from the post office in a 150-year-old building, this tasteful restaurant is a cross between a brasserie and a coffee shop. The kitchen likes to use all-Scottish ingredients. The cheerful staff will offer menu items that frequently change, but might include dishes such as salmon in phyllo with ginger-and-lime sauce; breaded chicken with aged northern Italian Talleggio cheese; swordfish with butter beans, bacon, and sweet onions; exotic ostrich steak in red-wine sauce; and charcoal-grilled steaks done to perfection.

2 Buccleuch St. ℭ **01896/822-245.** Reservations recommended for dinner. Main courses £3–£11 ($4.80–$18) at lunch; £6–£16 ($9.60–$26) at dinner. MC, V. Mon–Sat 9am–10pm.

4 Selkirk: At the Heart of Scott Country

65km (40 miles) SE of Edinburgh, 118 km (73 miles) SE of Glasgow, 11km (7 miles) S of Galashiels

In the heart of Sir Walter Scott country, Selkirk is a great base if you want to explore many of the region's historic homes, including Bowhill (see below) and Traquair House (see "Melrose," above). Jedburgh and Melrose offer more to see and do, but this ancient royal burgh can easily occupy a morning of your time.

Selkirk was the hometown of the African explorer Mungo Park (1771–1806), whose exploits could have made a great Harrison Ford movie. Park was a doctor, but won fame for exploring the River Niger; he drowned while escaping in a canoe from hostile natives. A statue of him is at the east end of High Street in Mungo Park.

Sir Walter Scott: Master of Romance

Today it's hard to imagine the fame this poet/novelist enjoyed as the best-selling author of his time. His works are no longer so widely read, but in his day, Sir Walter Scott (1771–1832) was considered a master storyteller. He invented a new genre, the romantic adventure in a panoramic setting. He created lively characters and realistic pictures of Scottish life and customs in such works as *The Heart of Midlothian, Rob Roy,* and *Waverley.* He's now best known as the prolific father of the historical novel, a genre that began with *Ivanhoe* and its romantic Jewish heroine, Rebecca (played by Elizabeth Taylor in the popular film), followed by *Kenilworth, The Pirate,* and many others. He was also a popular poet.

Born into an older Border family at Edinburgh on August 14, 1771, Scott became permanently lame after an attack of fever in infancy. All his life he was troubled by ill health, and later by finances as well. He spent his latter years writing to clear his enormous debts. Scott made his country and its scenery fashionable with the English, and even persuaded George IV to wear that once-outlawed tartan during the king's visit to Scotland. Although Scott became the most prominent literary figure in Edinburgh, his heart lay in the Border Country. It 's where he chose to live and where he built his house in a style that became known as Scottish baronial, reflecting the nostalgia for medieval days his novels had popularized. Starting with a modest farmhouse, he enlarged Abbotsford into a mansion and fulfilled his ambition to become a *laird* (landlord or property owner). In the economic crash of 1826, he offered the estate to his creditors, who turned it down.

Still heavily in debt and suffering from the effect of several strokes, in 1831 Scott set out on a cruise through the Mediterranean but returned to Abbotsford the following year to die. He was buried at Dryburgh Abbey, sited in a loop of the Tweed 3km (2 miles) from the panoramic view of the river and the Eildon Hills he so admired. It's reported the horses pulling the author's hearse stopped at this spot out of habit, so accustomed were they to Scott's pausing to take in the vista.

Scott's name is also linked to the Trossachs, which he used as a setting for his poem "The Lady of the Lake" and his tale of Rob Roy MacGregor, the 18th-century outlaw. Edinburgh's Gothic-inspired Scott Monument is one of the most famous statues in Scotland.

ESSENTIALS

GETTING THERE   Berwick-upon-Tweed is the nearest rail station, where you can get a connecting bus to Selkirk, some of which require a connection in Kelso. The bus ride is just under 2 hours, costing £6 ($9.60) one-way or £12 ($19) round-trip. Call the tourist office in Selkirk at Ⓒ **0870/608-0404** for bus schedules or Ⓒ **8457/484950** for rail information.

Buses running between Newcastle-upon-Tyne and Edinburgh make stops at Selkirk. The trip takes about 2½ hours and costs £7 ($11) one-way or £12 ($19) round-trip.

Driving from Edinburgh, head southeast along A7 to Galashiels, then cut southwest along B6360. The trip takes about an hour. To get here from Melrose, take B6360 southwest to Selkirk; it's a 15-minute drive.

VISITOR INFORMATION A **tourist office** is located at Halliwell's House Museum (© **01750/720-054**). April, May, and June, it's open Monday to Saturday 10am to 5pm and Sunday 10am to noon; July and August, hours are Monday to Saturday 10am to 5:30pm and Sunday 10am to 1pm; September hours are Monday to Saturday 10am to 5pm and Sunday 10am to noon; October hours are Monday to Saturday 10am to 4pm and Sunday 10am to 2pm.

EXPLORING THE AREA

In Selkirk, the former royal hunting grounds and forests have given way to textile mills along its river banks, but there are many beautiful spots in the nearby countryside—notably **St. Mary's Loch,** 23km (14 miles) southwest. Sailors and fishermen love this bucolic body of water, as did literary greats like Thomas Carlyle and Robert Louis Stevenson. One of the most panoramic stretches of the Southern Upland Way, one of Scotland's great backpacking trails (see chapter 1), skirts the east shore of St. Mary's Loch. You can take a day hike on the 13km (8-mile) stretch from the loch to Traquair House (see "Melrose," earlier in this chapter).

Bowhill ✦✦ This 18th- and 19th-century Border home of the Scotts, the dukes of Buccleuch, contains a rare art collection, French furniture, porcelain, silverware, and mementos of Sir Walter Scott, Queen Victoria, and the duke of Monmouth. Its paintings include works by Canaletto, Claude, Gainsborough, and Reynolds. In the surrounding Country Park, you'll find an Adventure Woodland play area, a Victorian kitchen, an audiovisual presentation, a gift shop, and a tearoom/restaurant. Sotheby's "Works of Art" courses are offered at Bowhill.

Hwy. A708, 5km (3 miles) west of Selkirk. © **01750/222-04**. bht@buccleuch.com. Admission to house £6 ($9.60) adults, £4 ($6.40) seniors, £2 ($3.20) children; admission to Country Park £2 ($3.20). House: July daily 1–5pm. Country Park: Apr daily 11am–5pm; May weekends 11am–5pm; June & Aug Sat–Thurs 11am–5pm; July daily 11am–5pm. Closed other months.

WHERE TO STAY & DINE

Heatherlie House Hotel An imposing stone-and-slate Victorian mansion with steep gables and turrets, this hotel is set on .8 hectares (2 acres) of wooded lands and mature gardens, west from the center along the Green and a short walk from Selkirk. The guest rooms are spotlessly maintained and furnished with reproductions of older pieces. The lone single room has no bathroom of its own.

A coal-burning fireplace adds warmth to the lounge, where reasonably priced bar meals are available daily. The high-ceilinged dining room is open for dinner. Golf, fishing, and shooting packages can be arranged, and about half a dozen golf courses are within a reasonable drive.

Heatherlie Park, Selkirk, The Borders TD7 5AL. © **01750/721-200**. Fax 01750/720-005. www.heatherlie. freeserve.co.uk. 7 units, 6 with private bathroom. £70 ($112) double with bathroom. Rates include breakfast. MC, V. **Amenities:** Restaurant; bar. *In room:* TV, coffeemaker, hair dryer.

5 Peebles

37km (23 miles) S of Edinburgh, 85km (53 miles) SE of Glasgow, 32km (20 miles) W of Melrose

Peebles, a royal burgh and county town, is a market center in the Tweed Valley, noted for its large woolen mills and fine knitwear shopping. Scottish kings used to come here when they hunted in Ettrick Forest, 35km (22 miles) away. It's one of hundreds of forests scattered throughout the Borders and is very pretty, but no more so than forested patches closer to the town.

Peebles is known as a writer's town. It was home to Sir John Buchan (Baron Tweedsmuir, 1875–1940), a Scottish author who later was appointed governor-general of Canada. He's remembered chiefly for the adventure story *Prester John* and was the author of *The Thirty-Nine Steps,* the first of a highly successful series of secret-service thrillers and later a Hitchcock film. Robert Louis Stevenson lived for a time in Peebles and drew on the surrounding countryside in his novel *Kidnapped* (1886).

ESSENTIALS

GETTING THERE   The nearest rail station is in Berwick-upon-Tweed, but bus connections from there into Peebles are quite inconvenient. It's easier to get from Edinburgh to Peebles by a 50-minute bus ride. Bus fares from Edinburgh are around £4.15 ($6.65) one-way. Call ⓒ **8457/484-950** for rail and bus information.

If you're driving, take A703 south from Edinburgh. Continue west along A6091 from Melrose.

VISITOR INFORMATION   The **tourist office** is at the Chamber Institute, 23 High St. (ⓒ **0870/608-0404**). April 1 to June 1, it's open from Monday to Saturday 9am to 5pm and Sunday 11am to 4pm; June 2 to June 29, hours are Monday to Saturday 9am to 5:30pm and Sunday 10am to 4pm; June 30 to August 31 hours are Monday to Saturday 9am to 6pm and Sunday 10am to 4pm; September 1 to September 28, hours are Monday to Saturday 9am to 5:30pm and Sunday 10am to 4pm; September 29 to November 1, hours are Monday to Saturday 9am to 5pm and Sunday 11am to 4pm; November 2 to December, hours are Monday to Saturday 9:30am to 5pm and Sunday 11am to 3pm; January to March, hours are Monday to Saturday 9:30am to 4pm and closed on Sunday.

EXPLORING THE TOWN & THE COUNTRYSIDE

The tourist office (see above) provides pamphlets describing the best walking tours in the region. The £1 ($1.60) pamphlet **"Walks Around Peebles"** describes 20 walks, including one along the Tweed. The **Tweed Walk** begins in the center of Peebles, and—with the twists and turns described in the pamphlet—takes you downstream along the river, then upstream along the opposite bank for a return to Peebles. You can follow the path for segments of 4km (2½ miles), 7km (4½ miles), or 12km (7½ miles). Regardless of the length of your walk, you'll pass the stalwart walls of Neidpath Castle.

Glentress Bicycle Trekking Centre, Glentress, Peebles (ⓒ **01721/721-736**), is the place to rent a bike. You'll have to leave a refundable deposit of £50 ($80). Daily rates range from £12 ($19) for a half day and £16 ($26) for a full day, and rentals must be arranged in advance. It's open daily April to October 9am to 7pm (Sat and Sun it opens at 10am); November, Wednesday noon to 10pm and Saturday and Sunday 10am to 5pm.

Dawyck Botanic Garden   This botanical garden, run by the Royal Botanic Garden in Edinburgh, has a large variety of conifers, some exceeding 30m (100 ft.) in height, as well as many species of flowering shrubs. There's also a fine display of early-spring bulbs, plus wood walks rich in wildlife interest.

Hwy. B712, 13km (8 miles) southwest of Peebles. ⓒ **01721/760-254.** Admission £3 ($4.80) adults, £2.50 ($4) seniors/students, £1 ($1.60) children, £7 ($11) families. Mar daily 10am–5pm; Apr–Sept 10am–6pm; Oct 10am–5pm; Nov 10am–4pm. Local bus marked BIGGAR.

Kailzie Gardens   These 6.8 hectares (17 acres) of formal walled gardens, dating from 1812, include a rose garden, woodlands, and *burnside* (streamside) walks. Restored during the past 20 years, it provides a stunning array of plants from early spring to late autumn and has a collection of waterfowl and owls. There's also an art gallery, a shop, and a restaurant.

Kailzie on B7062, 4km (2½ miles) southeast of Peebles. © 01721/720-007. Admission £2.50 ($4) adults, 75p ($1.20) children; gardens only £1 ($1.60). Daily dawn–dusk.

Neidpath Castle   Once linked with two of the greatest families in Scotland (the Frasiers and the Hayes), Neidpath, a summer attraction, hasn't been occupied since 1958. Part of the interest here is the way the castle's medieval shell was transformed during the 1600s into a residence, using then-fashionable architectural conceits. Enormous galleries were divided into smaller, cozier spaces, with the exception of the Great Hall, whose statuesque proportions are still visible. The hall's medieval stonework is decorated with 11 batik panels crafted in the mid-1990s by noted artist Monica Hanisch; they depict the life and accomplishments of Mary Queen of Scots. Other parts of the museum are devoted to the role the castle has played in the filming of movies like *The Bruce* (an English film that had the bad luck to be released simultaneously with *Braveheart*), *Merlin, The Quest Begins,* and the courtyard scene in the recent TV miniseries "Joan of Arc," where the heroine was burnt at the stake. Recently filmed here were new British versions of *Hamlet* and *King Lear.*

Tweeddale, on A72, 1.6km (1 mile) west of Peebles. © 01721/720-333. Admission £3 ($4.80) adults, £2.50 ($4) seniors, £1 ($1.60) children, £7.50 ($12) families. June 30–Sept 15 and Apr 17–22 Mon-Sat 10:30am–5pm; Sun 12:30–5pm. Closed mid-Sept to June.

SHOPPING

Knitwear, crafted from yarn culled from local sheep, is the best buy in Peebles, and easily found as you stroll the High Street. General shopping hours are Monday through Saturday from 10am to 5:30pm. On Sundays, but only in July and August, some shops open from 10am to 5pm.

Woolgathering, 1 Bridge House Terrace (© **01721/720-388**), offers knitwear and all kinds of sweaters. Three sprawling branches of **Castle Warehouse,** at 1 Greenside (© **01721/723-636**), 7–13 Old Town (© **01721/720-348**), and 29–31 Northgate (© **01721/720-814**), sell gift items with a Scottish flavor as well as clothing, such as traditional Scottish garb and anything you might need for a fishing trip.

Caledonian Countrywear, Ltd., 74 High St. (© **01721/723-055**), and **Out & About,** 2 Elcho St. Brae (© **01721/723-590**), are sporting-goods stores with lots of durable clothing and hiking boots.

For Border handcrafts like pinewood furniture, stoneware, and porcelain, go to **Peebles Craft Centre,** 9 Newby Court (© **01721/722-875**), or the **Couchee Righ,** 26 Northgate (© **01721/721-890**).

Fewer than 10km (6 miles) from Walkerburn at Galashiels (head east along A72) is the **Peter Anderson Company,** Nether Mill (© **01896/752-091**). This factory outlet sells more than 750 types of tartan fabrics, all made on the premises on modernized looms. The shop is open Monday through Saturday from 9am to 5pm and from June to September Sunday from noon to 5pm. Dozens of other shops are in the nearby textile town of Galashiels.

WHERE TO STAY

Castle Venlaw Hotel ✦ *Kids*   Originally built in 1782 and enlarged in 1854, Castle Venlaw lies among 1.6 hectares (4 acres) of woodlands and offers lovely views of the surrounding countryside. The hotel's round tower and craw-stepped gables are an evocative example of the Scottish baronial style. In 1999, the hotel was completely redecorated, and the heating system and all bathrooms were modernized.

Castle Venlaw has 12 spacious and individually decorated rooms—each named for a different malt whisky—that all offer excellent views and a selection of books and magazines. A four-poster room has especially nice views, and the hotel's lone suite has a sitting room with a VCR in addition to the bedroom. In the tower at the top of the castle is a spacious family room with a children's den containing bunk beds, games, TV, and VCR.

Edinburgh Rd., Peebles EH45 8QG. ✆ **01721/720-384.** Fax 01721/724-066. www.venlaw.co.uk. 13 units. £120–£140 ($192–$224) double; £130–£150 ($208–$240) deluxe; £140–£160 ($224–$256) suite. Rates include breakfast. Children under age 12 staying in parent's room £15 ($24); children age 13–16 £20 ($32). MC, V. Free parking. Take A703 to Peebles. **Amenities:** Restaurant; bar; limited room service; laundry. *In room:* TV, coffeemaker.

Cringletie House Hotel ✶✶✶   This imposing 1861 red-sandstone Victorian mansion with towers and turrets is one of the most delightful country-house hotels in the Borders. Known for its charming setting and its luxurious rooms, the hotel stands on 11 hectares (28 acres) of well-manicured grounds, featuring a 17th-century walled garden that in itself is worth a visit. The tasteful house is immaculately maintained, with public rooms that range from an elegant cocktail lounge to an adjacent conservatory. There's even a small library, plus a large lounge where fellow guests from all over the world meet and chat, and thankfully, there's an elevator. Each of the spacious bedrooms is individually decorated; several units contain their own original fireplaces and a few have four-poster beds. All accommodations open onto views of the extensive grounds. The bathrooms are maintained in state-of-the-art condition and come with luxurious toiletries. All bedrooms are nonsmoking.

Eddleston, Peebles, The Borders EH45 8PL. ✆ **01721/730-233.** Fax 01721/730-244. www.cringletie.com. 13 units. £120–£140 ($192–$224) double. Rates include breakfast. AE, MC, V. Take A703 for 4km (2½ miles) north of Peebles. **Amenities:** Restaurant; bar; putting green; tennis court; babysitting. *In room:* TV, coffeemaker, hair dryer.

The Tontine ✶ *Finds*   The Tontine has been around since 1807, when it was built as a private club by a group of hunters who sold their friends shares in its ownership. French prisoners of war built it during the Napoleonic era; later enlargements were made by the Edwardians. Flower boxes adorn its stone lintels, and a stone lion guards the forecourt fountain. The modestly furnished guest rooms are in an angular modern wing built in back of the building's 19th-century core; they come with shower-only bathrooms. The most expensive rooms have river views. The Adam-style dining room is one of the town's architectural gems, with tall fan-topped windows and a minstrels' gallery. The Tweeddale Shoot Bar is cozily rustic. Perhaps you'll encounter the resident ghost, whom many visitors report lives and sleeps outside the hotel wine cellar.

39 High St., Peebles, The Borders EH45 8AJ. ✆ **01721/720-892.** Fax 01721/729-732. www.tontinehotel. com. 36 units. £70–£90 ($112–$144) double. Rates include breakfast. Children age 12 and under stay free in parent's room, but pay £5 ($8) for breakfast. AE, DC, MC, V. Free parking. **Amenities:** Restaurant; bar. *In room:* TV, coffeemaker, hair dryer, trouser press.

Whitestone House   On the eastern fringe of Peebles, this dignified dark stone house is from 1892. It used to house the pastor of a Presbyterian church that has been demolished and is now the genteel domain of Mrs. Margaret Muir.

Its windows overlook a pleasant garden and the glacial deposits of Whitestone Park. The high-ceilinged guest rooms are large and comfortable, evoking life in a quiet private home. Of the two shared bathrooms, one is large and has a shower and tub combination; the other only a shower. Mrs. Muir speaks French and German flawlessly, but presides over breakfast with a Scottish brogue.

Innerleithen Rd., Peebles, The Borders EH45 8BD. ℂ and fax **01721/720-337**. www.aboutscotland.com/peebles/whitestone.html. 5 units, none with private bathroom. £37–£38 ($59–$61) double. Rates include breakfast. No credit cards. Free parking. Closed Christmas and part of Jan. *In room:* TV, coffeemaker.

WHERE TO DINE

Horse Shoe Inn SCOTTISH   In the center of the nearby village of Eddleston, this country restaurant serves top-quality beef and steaks. Appetizers include everything from the chef's own pâté with oat cakes to smoked Shetland salmon with brown bread. House favorites are steak-and-stout pie, Meldon game pie, and vegetable moussaka. Food and drink are served in the bar most days, but the staff opens up a more formal dining room for dinner on Friday and Saturday nights and Sunday lunch.

The owners, Mr. and Mrs. Hathoway, bought the old school next door and converted it into a guesthouse with eight rooms at £23 to £45 ($37–$72) per person, depending on the season; the rates include breakfast.

Eddleston. ℂ **01721/730-225**. Reservations recommended Sat. Main courses £3.50–£16.95 ($5.60–$27). MC, V. Easter–Oct Mon–Thurs 11am–11pm, Fri–Sun 11am–midnight; Nov–Easter Mon–Thurs 11am–2:30pm and 5:30–11pm, Fri–Sat 11am–2:30pm and 5:30–midnight. Take A701 7km (4½ miles) north of Peebles.

PEEBLES AFTER DARK

Peebles has many options for drinking and dining, and some of the most appealing are in the hotels on the town's edge, even though they may seem rather staid at first glance. On Innerleithen Road, the **Park Hotel** (ℂ **01721/720-451**) and the nearby **Hotel Hydro** (ℂ **01721/720-602**) contain pubs and cocktail lounges.

For an earthier atmosphere, we highly recommend dropping into the town's oldest pub, at the **Cross Keys Hotel,** 24 Northgate (ℂ **01721/724-222**), where you'll find 300-year-old smoke-stained panels, a blazing fireplace, and an evocatively crooked bar. Ask the bartender about the resident ghost. Like the Loch Ness monster, she's taken on an almost mythical identity since her last sighting, but the rumor goes that she's the spirit of Sir Walter Scott's former landlady, Marian Ritchie. No one will be shy about telling you his or her theory, especially if you're buying.

6 Moffat

98 km (61 miles) S of Edinburgh, 35km (22 miles) NE of Dumfries, 97km (60 miles) SE of Glasgow

A small town at the head of the Annandale Valley, Moffat thrives as a center of a sheep-farming area, symbolized by a statue of a ram on the wide High Street. It's been a holiday resort since the mid–17th century because of the curative properties of its water, and it was here that Robert Burns composed the drinking song "O Willie Brewd a Peck o' Maut." Today, people visit this town on the banks of the Annan River for its great fishing and golf.

ESSENTIALS

GETTING THERE   The nearest rail station is in Lockerbie, 24km (15 miles) south of Moffat. Call ℂ **8457/484-950** for train information. Getting to Lockerbie sometimes requires a change of train in Dumfries, so passengers from

Edinburgh or Glasgow often transfer to a **National Express** bus at Dumfries for the 35-minute trip straight to Moffat's High Street, which costs £3 ($4.80) one-way. If you are coming from the Lockerbie rail station, though, you can get a National Express bus to Moffat; they run four times a day, and the fare is £4.05 ($6.50) each way. For more bus information, call © **8705/808-080.**

If you're driving from Dumfries, head northeast along A701. From Edinburgh, head south along A701; from Peebles, drive west, following the signs to Glasgow, then turn south on A702 and merge onto M74, following the signs to Moffat.

VISITOR INFORMATION   A tourist office is a 5-minute walk south of the town center, at Unit One, Ledyknowe, off Station Road (© **01683/220-620**). Hours are as follows: April 1 to June 29 Monday to Saturday 9:30am to 5pm, Sunday noon to 4pm; June 30 to September 14 Monday to Saturday 9:30am to 6pm, Sunday noon to 5pm; September 15 to October 19 Monday to Saturday 9:30am to 5pm, Sunday noon to 4pm; and October 20 to March 31 Monday to Friday 10am to 5pm, Saturday 9:30am to 4pm.

EXPLORING THE AREA

North of Moffat is lots of panoramic hill scenery. Eight kilometers (5 miles) northwest is a sheer-sided 152m-deep (500-ft.), 3km-wide (2 miles) hollow in the hills called the **Devil's Beef Tub,** where cattle thieves (reivers) once hid cattle lifted in their raids. This hollow is of interest to geologists because of the way it portrays Ice Age glacial action, and it makes for a good day hike in the quiet countryside. To reach it, walk north from Moffat along the **Annan Water Valley Road,** a rural route with virtually no vehicular traffic. In 6.5km (4 miles), the road will descend a steep slope whose contours form an unusual bowl shape. No signs mark the site, but you'll know it when you get there.

Northeast along Moffat Water, past 818m-high (2,696-ft.) White Coomb, is the **Grey Mare's Tail,** a 61m (200 ft.) hanging waterfall formed by the Tail Burn dropping from Loch Skene; it's part of the National Trust for Scotland.

GOLF

The region's most famous course is the **Moffat Golf Course,** Coates Hill (© **01683/220-020**), about 1.6km (1 mile) southwest of the town center. Nonmembers can play if they call in advance. From the first of April to October, a golf pass, valid for a week, allows 7 rounds of golf for £75 ($120) or 10 rounds for £95 ($152). The tourist office has a free brochure called *Golfing in Dumfries & Galloway.*

WHERE TO STAY

You can also find accommodations at **Well View Hotel** (see "Where to Dine," below).

Auchen Castle Hotel *✦*   About a 1.6km (1 mile) north of the village of Beattock, the area's most luxurious accommodations are at the Auchen, a Victorian mock-castle. It's really a country house built in 1849 on the site of Auchen Castle, with terraced gardens and a trout-filled loch. Most of the guest rooms are spacious. Ask for a unit in the main house (which is known as the castle); the others are in the Cedar Lodge, a less desirable annex built in the late 1970s.

Beattock, Dumfriesshire DG10 9SH. © **01683/300-407.** Fax 01683/300-667. www.auchen-castlehotel.co.uk. 25 units. £95 ($152) double in main house; £140 ($224) suite breakfast included; £55 ($88) double in Cedar Lodge, breakfast not included; £75 ($120) with breakfast. AE, DC, MC, V. Take A74 for 3km (2 miles) north of Moffat. **Amenities:** Restaurant; bar; limited room service (9am–10pm); laundry. *In room:* TV, coffeemaker, hair dryer.

Beechwood Country House Hotel *(Kids)* This is a charming country house hotel. The Beechwood was the 19th-century headquarters of Miss Thompson's Private Adventure Boarding Establishment and School for Young Ladies. You'll spot its facade of chiseled stone at the end of a narrow rural lane. A tea lawn, smooth as a putting green, is the site for outdoor refreshments on sunny days. The guest rooms have a certain amount of homespun charm; many have been recently renovated. Beds have Egyptian cotton linens and electric blankets to keep you warm on winter nights. Bathrooms were completely refurbished in 2002 and feature deep tubs and Penhaligon toiletries. The hotel has a room set aside for families and has a playpen and provides baby monitors to those traveling with young children. Golf, tennis, fishing, and riding can be arranged.

Harthope Place, Moffat, Dumfriesshire DG10 9HX. © **01683/220-210.** Fax 01683/220-889. www. beechwoodcountryhousehotel.co.uk. 7 units. £90 ($144) double with breakfast; £138 ($221) double with half-board. AE, MC, V. Free parking. **Amenities:** Restaurant. *In room:* TV, coffeemaker, hair dryer.

Moffat House Hotel The red- and black-stone Moffat House is one of the town's most architecturally noteworthy buildings; it was constructed in 1751 by John Adam. This Best Western affiliate's modernized guest rooms are comfortable and functional, each with a shower and tub bathroom. A few rooms have four-poster beds. Some rooms are equipped for families, others for travelers with disabilities.

Note: The hotel offers some of the best food in town, especially at night, when the chef prepares an international menu.

High St., Moffat, Galloway DG10 9HL. © **01683/220-039.** Fax 01683/221-288. www.moffathouse.co.uk. 21 units. £76–£94 ($122–$150) double. Rates include breakfast. AE, DC, MC, V. Free parking. **Amenities:** Restaurant; bar; limited room service. *In room:* TV, coffeemaker, hair dryer.

Star Hotel With a 17th-century brick facade, this place bears the quirky fame of being the narrowest free-standing hotel in the United Kingdom—it's only 6m (20 ft.) wide. The guest rooms, last refurbished in 1996, are small and unpretentious, with contemporary furnishings, and bathrooms with either a tub or a shower. The food here is popular; menu items are simple and straightforward but savory. The hotel also rents a 2-bedroom cottage (good for families) for £110 ($176) per night.

44 High St., Moffat, Galloway DG10 9EF. © **01683/220-156.** Fax 01683/221-524. www.famousstarhotel. com. 8 units. £56 ($84) double. AE, MC, V. **Amenities:** Restaurant; 2 bars; babysitting. *In room:* TV, coffeemaker, hair dryer.

WHERE TO DINE

Other dining options include the restaurants in the hotels listed above.

Well View *(★★)* BRITISH/CONTINENTAL Come to this hotel for some of the best food in the region. The setting is mid-Victorian, with Laura Ashley country-cottage charm and views of the kitchen garden. The set-price menus vary almost daily, depending on the season, and may include roasted breast of Perthshire pigeon with red-wine sauce, roasted saddle of venison with gin-and-juniper sauce, or filet of Aberdeen Angus beef with whole-grain mustard sauce.

Upstairs are five guest rooms and a junior suite, with modern furniture and reproduction antiques (including a four-poster bed), Laura Ashley fabrics, free sherry and fresh fruit, TVs, clock radios, tea/coffeemakers, and hair dryers. Depending on the season, doubles are £70 to £102 ($112–$163).

Ballplay Rd., Moffat DG10 9JU. © **01683/220-184.** Fax 01683/220-088. www.wellview.co.uk. Reservations recommended. Fixed-price 3-course lunch £15 ($24); fixed-price 6-course dinner £32 ($51). AE, MC, V. Sun–Fri 12:30–1:15pm; daily 7–8:30pm. Take A708 1.2km (¾ mile) east of Moffat.

7 Dumfries: An Ode to Burns

129km (80 miles) SW of Edinburgh, 127km (79 miles) SE of Glasgow, 55km (34 miles) NW of Carlisle

A county town and royal burgh, the Galloway center of Dumfries enjoys associations with national poet Robert Burns and *Peter Pan* author James Barrie. Burns lived in Dumfries from 1791 until his death in 1796 and wrote some of his best-known songs here, including "Auld Lang Syne" and "Ye Banks and Braes of Bonnie Doon." A statue of Burns stands on High Street; you can visit his house, his favorite pub, and his mausoleum. Barrie was a pupil at the Academy here and later wrote that he got the idea for *Peter Pan* from his games in the nearby garden.

The widest esplanade in Dumfries, **Whitesands,** flanks the edge of the River Nith. It was once the scene of horse and hiring fairs and is a fine place to park your car and explore this provincial town. The town center is reserved for pedestrians, and on the opposite bank of the Nith, the public Deer Park offers a small-scale manicured version of the wild majesty of Scotland. Allow a morning to visit the city's major sights, but there's even more to see in the surrounding countryside, including Sweetheart Abbey, Ellisland Farm, and Drumlanrig Castle at Thornhill, which is filled with art, including works by Rembrandt and Leonardo.

ESSENTIALS

GETTING THERE   Seven trains per day make the run from Glasgow's Central Station, taking 1¾ hours. Tickets cost £9.90 ($16) one-way but only £10 to £18.40 ($16–$29) round-trip, depending on time of departure. For 24-hour information, call ✆ **8457/484-950.**

Stagecoach buses depart from Glasgow (from Buchanan Street Station or Anderston Station); the trip is 2 hours and costs £6.50 ($10) one-way and £10 ($16) round-trip. Buses also run to Dumfries from Edinburgh's St. Andrew's Square. The prices are the same as from Glasgow, but the trip is 3 hours. For bus information, call ✆ **01387/253-496.**

If you're driving from Edinburgh, take A701 to Moffat, then continue southwest to Dumfries. From Glasgow, take M74, which becomes A74 before it approaches Moffat. At Moffat, continue southwest along A701.

VISITOR INFORMATION   The **tourist office** is at 64 Whitesands (✆ **01387/253-862**), a 2-minute walk from High Street and adjacent to the big parking lots. September to March, it's open Monday to Friday 10am to 5pm and Saturday 10am to 4pm; April to August, hours are Monday to Saturday 10am to 6pm (July and Aug also Sun noon–4pm).

EXPLORING THE TOWN

The 18th-century **St. Michael's Church,** on St. Michael's Street, is the original parish church of Dumfries. Its foundation is ancient—the site was sacred before the advent of Christianity, and a Christian church has stood here for more than 1,300 years. The earliest written records date from 1165 to 1214. The church and the churchyard are interesting to visit because of all their connections with Scottish history, continuing through World War II. You can still see the Burns family pew inside.

In St. Michael's Churchyard, a burial place for at least 900 years, stands the neo-Grecian **Burns Mausoleum.** Built of local sandstone and dripping with literary and patriotic nostalgia, the dome-capped mausoleum is one of the most important pilgrimage sites for Burns fans. The poet is buried here along with his wife, Jean Armour, and five of their children. Burns died in 1796, but his remains weren't moved to the tomb until 1815.

The **Mid Steeple** 🎵 on High Street was built in 1707 as municipal buildings, a courthouse, and a prison. The old Scots "ell" measure, the equivalent of almost 1m (37 in.), is carved on the front, and a table of distances includes the mileage to Huntingdon, England, which in the 18th century was the destination for Scottish cattle driven south for the London markets. Today it's used mostly as municipal archives, and its interior is used for government functions.

At Whitesands, the street paralleling the Nith's edge, **four bridges** span the river. The earliest was built by Devorgilla Balliol, widow of John Balliol. Their son, John, was made Scotland's "vassal king" by Edward I of England, the "Hammer of the Scots," who established himself as Scotland's overlord. The bridge (originally with nine arches but now with only six) is still in constant use as a footbridge.

The town's best **shopping** is along the High Street, which is lined with turn-of-the-century facades, and nearby Queensberry Street. **Alternatives,** 73–75 Queensberry St. (② **01387/257-467**), is an attractive new-age shop stocking herbal remedies, artful wind chimes, and gift items, especially jewelry inspired by Celtic designs. You'll find men's and women's kilts in dozens of tartan patterns, as well as sweaters, overcoats, hats, and socks, always at realistic prices, at the **Edinburgh Woolen Mill,** 8 Church Place (② **01387/267-351**).

If you want to explore the area on two wheels, the **Nithsdale Cycle Centre,** 46 Broon's Rd. (② **01387/254-870**), is the place to go. You'll have to leave a 25% deposit; rental rates are £5 ($8) for a half day, £10 ($16) daily or £35 ($56) weekly. It's open Monday to Saturday 10am to 5pm.

Burns House   In 1796, Scotland's national poet died in this unpretentious, terraced stone house off St. Michael's Street. Although he occupied the house during only the last 3 years of his life, it contains personal relics and mementos as well as much of the original furniture used by Burns during his creative years.

Burns St. ② **01387/255-297.** Free admission. Apr–Sept Mon–Sat 10am–5pm, Sun 2–5pm; Oct–Mar Tues–Sat 10am–1pm and 2–5pm.

Drumlanrig Castle 🎵 *Kids*   This pink castle, built between 1679 and 1689 in a parkland ringed by wild hills, is the seat of the dukes of Buccleuch and Queensberry. It's home to some outstanding paintings, including a famous Rembrandt, a Leonardo da Vinci, and a Holbein, plus relics related to Bonnie Prince Charlie. There's a playground with amusements for kids and a working crafts center in the old stable yard; the gardens are gradually being restored to their 1720 magnificence. Meals are served in the old kitchen, hung with gleaming copper.

Thornhill, 5km (3 miles) north of Thornhill off A76 and 16 miles (26km) southwest of A74 at Elvanfoot. ② **01848/330-248** or 01848/331-555. Admission £6 ($9.60) adults, £4 ($6.40) seniors, £2 ($3.20) children, £15 ($24) families. May–Aug Mon–Sat 11am–4pm, Sun noon–4pm. Closed Sept–Apr.

Dumfries Museum   Southwestern Scotland's largest museum occupies a converted 18th-century windmill atop Corbelly Hill. Visit it only if you have extra time and an interest in the region's early geology, history, and archaeology. The museum is rich in collections ranging from early Christian stones to artifacts of 18th-century country life. Some exhibits suggest the site's role as an astronomical observatory in 1836; note the 20-cm (8-in.) telescope used to observe Halley's Comet in July 1836. The camera obscura provides panoramic views of the town and surrounding countryside.

Church St. ℭ **01387/253-374**. www.dumfriesmuseum.demon.co.uk. Museum free; camera obscura £1.50 ($2.40) adults, 75p ($1.20) children/seniors. Museum, Apr–Sept Mon–Sat 10am–5pm, Sun 2–5pm; Oct–Mar Tues–Sat 10am–1pm and 2–5pm. Camera obscura, Apr–Sept Mon–Sat 10am–5pm, Sun 2–5pm. Cross the river at St. Michael's Bridge Rd. and turn right onto Church St.

Ellisland Farm *(Finds)*   From 1788 to 1791, Robert Burns made his last attempt at farming at Ellisland Farm; it was here that he wrote "Tam o' Shanter." After his marriage to Jean Armour, Burns leased the farm from Patrick Miller under the stipulation that he'd assist in erecting the building that's the centerpiece of the homestead. It's still a working farm for sheep and cattle, with many aspects devoted to a museum and shrine honoring Burns and his literary statements. On a circular 400-m (0.25-mile) trail ("the south trail") adjacent to the banks of the Nith, you can retrace the footsteps of Burns, who walked along it frequently during breaks from his writing.

10km (6 miles) north of Dumfries via A76 (follow the signs to Kilmarnock). ℭ **01387/740-426**. Admission £2.50 ($4) adults, £1 ($1.60) children/seniors. Apr–Sept Mon–Sat 10am–5pm, Sun 2–5pm; Oct–Mar Tues–Sat 10am–4pm.

Old Bridge House   Associated with the Burns House (see above), this building dates from 1660, when it replaced a structure that had been on the site since 1431. It was occupied as a private house until as late as 1957 and has been restored and furnished in a style typical of the period between 1850 and 1900, with tons of worthy Victoriana. Devorgilla Bridge itself was constructed in the 16th century.

Mill Rd. at the far end of Devorgillas Bridge. ℭ **01387/256-904**. Free admission. Apr–Sept Mon–Sat 10am–5pm, Sun 2–5pm. From Whitesands, cross the river at Devorgillas Bridge.

Robert Burns Centre   You'll find this converted 18th-century water mill on the banks of the River Nith. Facilities includes an exhibit on the poet, a restaurant, and an audiovisual theater showing films about Burns and the town of Dumfries.

Mill Rd. ℭ **01387/264-808**. Exhibition free; audiovisual theater £1.50 ($2.40) adults, 75p ($1.20) children/seniors/students. Apr–Sept Mon–Sat 10am–8pm, Sun 2–5pm; Oct–Mar Tues–Sat 10am–1pm and 2–5pm. From Whitesands, cross the river at Devorgillas Bridge.

Sweetheart Abbey *☆*   The village of New Abbey is dominated by Sweetheart Abbey's red-sandstone ruins. The walls are mostly extant, even though the roof is missing. Devorgilla Balliol founded the abbey in 1273. With the death of her husband, John Balliol the Elder, she became one of Europe's richest women—most of Galloway, as well as estates and castles in England and Normandy, belonged to her. Devorgilla founded Balliol College, Oxford, in her husband's memory. She kept his embalmed heart in a silver-and-ivory casket by her side for 21 years until her death in 1289 at age 80, when she and the casket were buried in front of the abbey altar. The abbey gained the name of "Dulce Cor," Latin for *sweet heart,* a term that has become a part of the English language.

On A710, New Abbey. ℭ **01387/770-244** (regional office of Historic Scotland). Admission £3 ($4.80) adults, £2.30 ($3.70) seniors, £1 ($1.60) children under age 16. Apr–Sept daily 9:30am–6:30pm; Oct–Mar Mon, Thurs, Sat 9:30am–4:30pm, Sun 2–4:30pm. Drive 11km (7 miles) southwest from Dumfries on A710 (follow the signs saying SOLWAY FIRTH HERITAGE).

WHERE TO STAY

Cairndale Hotel & Leisure Club *☆*   This is the finest hotel in Dumfries, easily outdistancing the Station and all other competition. A four-story stone-fronted building from around 1900, the Cairndale is a fine choice with handsome public rooms. It's owned and managed by the Wallace family. Its guest rooms have all been carefully modernized. Executive rooms and suites have queen-size beds, trouser presses, and whirlpool baths. The hotel's leisure facilities are noteworthy, and the restaurant hosts a popular dinner dance on Saturday nights.

132–136 English St., Dumfries, Galloway DG1 2DF. © **01387/254-111.** Fax 01387/250-555. www.cairndale hotel.co.uk. 91 units. £109–£125 ($174–$200) double; from £149 ($238) suite. Rates include breakfast. AE, DC, MC, V. Free parking. **Amenities:** Restaurant; bar; heated indoor pool; health club; Jacuzzi; 24-hr. room service; babysitting; laundry/dry cleaning service. *In room:* TV, minibar (in Executive rooms & suites), coffeemaker, hair dryer.

The Station   This is among the most traditional hotels in Dumfries, a few steps from the gingerbread-fringed train station. It was built in 1896 of hewn sandstone, in a design of heavy timbers, polished paneling, and soaring ceilings. The modernized but still somewhat dowdy guest rooms contain comfortable beds and shower-only bathrooms. The four-poster rooms and the suite feature Jacuzzi tubs. A new Garden Room lounge has recently been added, the creation of a Feng Shui consultant hoping to increase the *chi* or "good feeling" of guests.

49 Lovers Walk, Dumfries, Galloway DG1 1LT. © **01387/254-316.** Fax 01387/250-388. www.stationhotel. co.uk. 32 units. £80–£90 ($128–$144) double, £110 ($176) suite. Rates include breakfast. AE, DC, MC, V. Free parking. **Amenities:** 2 restaurants; 2 bars; limited room service; babysitting. *In room:* TV, dataport, minibar, coffeemaker, hair dryer, trouser press.

Trigony House Hotel   This pink-sandstone hotel was built around 1895 as the home of a local family. Its name *(trigony)* derives from the shape of the acreage, which is almost like a perfect isosceles triangle. Today, it contains a handful of comfortable but unpretentious high-ceilinged guest rooms, each opening onto countryside views. Adam (the chef of the hotel's restaurant) and Jan Moore are your hosts and will tell you all about the building's occupant during the 1930s: Frances Shakerley lived to be 107 within the walls of this house and thus became famous as the oldest woman in Scotland.

The hotel operates a busy pub and a dinner-only restaurant. Drop into the pub for affordable platters of simple food at lunch or dinner. Meals may include pâté of smoked trout, haggis with whisky-flavored cream sauce, salmon filets with lime-and-ginger glaze, and strips of beef with whisky-and-oatmeal sauce.

On the Dumfries–Ayr trunk road, Thornhill, Dumfries, Galloway DG3 5EZ. © **01848/331-211.** Fax 01848/ 331-303. www.trigonyhotel.co.uk. 8 units. £80–£90 ($128–$144) double. Rates include breakfast. MC, V. From Dumfries, drive 21km (13 miles) north along A76, following the signs to Thornhill. Trigony House is 1.6km (1 mile) south of Thornhill. Dogs accepted. **Amenities:** Restaurant; bar. *In room:* TV, coffeemaker, hair dryer.

WHERE TO DINE

Bruno's ITALIAN   It may seem ironic to recommend an Italian restaurant in the heart of Robert Burns territory, but Bruno's serves some of the best food in town. It's unassuming, but that's part of the charm. The chef's repertoire is familiar—first-rate minestrone, homemade pizza and pasta, veal with ham, and spicy chicken—but everything is done with a certain flair.

3 Balmoral Rd. © **01387/255-757.** Reservations required Sat–Sun. Main courses £6.50–£15.95 ($10–$26); fixed-price 3-course dinner £18.95 ($30); supper pasta menu £8.95 ($14). MC, V. Wed–Mon 5:30–10pm.

Globe Inn ✦ SCOTTISH   This is the traditional favorite. It was Burns's favorite haunt, in business since 1610, and he used an old Scottish expression, *howff* (meaning a small, cozy room), to describe his local pub. He was definitely a regular: He had a child with the barmaid, Anna Park. You reach the pub down a narrow flagstone passage off High Street, opposite the Marks & Spencer department store. You can go for a meal (perhaps kipper pâté, haggis, or Globe steak pie) or just to have a drink and play a game of dominoes. A little museum is devoted to Burns, and on window panes upstairs you can see verses he scratched with a diamond. Taps include Belhaven, Tennet's Lager, Galloway Ale, and Black Throne Cider.

56 High St. ✆ **01387/252-335.** Main courses £4.50–£5.50 ($7.20–$8.80). AE, MC, V. Mon–Thurs 10am–11pm; Fri–Sat 10am–midnight; Sun noon–midnight. Food served Mon–Sat 10–11:30am and noon–3pm.

Hullabaloo SCOTTISH This is the most unusual restaurant in Dumfries. It's in a renovated grain mill, which you reach by taking a lovely 10-minute stroll across the Nith from the commercial heart of town. Built around 1780 by a prominent engineer, Thomas Sneaton, the mill also shelters a small movie house and the Robert Burns Centre (see above). The offerings are prepared with Scottish ingredients and change with the seasons. A homemade soup of the day is always served along with freshly baked bread, or else you might opt for one of the imaginative salads, including a Thai prawn or else tabbouleh and bean salad. Instead of elaborate main courses, you get various baguettes with such enticements as smoked salmon and cream cheese, or else baked potatoes that are almost meals unto themselves. The aura is one of cafe dining with an emphasis on lighter fare than a major restaurant.

In the Robert Burns Centre, Mill Rd. ✆ **01387/259-679.** Reservations recommended. Main courses £6.95–£14.95 ($11–$24). MC, V. Easter–Sept Mon–Sat 11am–4pm, Tues–Sat 6–10pm, Sun 11am–3pm; Oct–Easter Tues–Sat 11am–4pm and 6–10pm.

DUMFRIES AFTER DARK

The town's most famous pub is the previously recommended **Globe Inn,** 56 High St. (✆ **01387/252-335**), where Robert Burns tipped many a dram. An equally historic pub loaded with local color is **The Hole in the Wall,** 156 High St. (✆ **01387/252-770**), where live music is usually provided by an accordionist. If you want to go dancing, head for either of the town's two discos, **Chancers Nightclub,** 25 Munches St. (✆ **01387/263-170**), or **The Junction,** 36 High St. (✆ **01387/267-262**). The crowd and music at these two clubs change often, depending on the theme for the night, so call ahead to make sure they'll suit you on any given evening.

8 Castle Douglas

26km (16 miles) SW of Dumfries, 158km (98 miles) SW of Edinburgh, 79km (49 miles) SE of Ayr

An old cattle- and sheep-market town, Castle Douglas, at the northern tip of Carlingwark Loch, is near such attractions as Threave Castle, Cardoness Castle, Kirkcudbright, and Sweetheart Abbey, and just southeast of the Galloway Forest Park. On one of the islets in the loch is an ancient lake dwelling known as a *crannog.*

ESSENTIALS

GETTING THERE The nearest rail station is in Dumfries (see "Dumfries: An Ode to Burns," above); from there, you can take a bus to Castle Douglas. Call ✆ **8457/484-950** for rail information.

The **Great Western Bus Co.** runs buses from Dumfries to Castle Douglas every hour throughout the day and early evening; travel time is about 30 minutes and costs £1.80 ($2.70) one-way. Call ✆ **8705/808-080** for bus information.

If you're driving from Dumfries, head southwest along A75.

VISITOR INFORMATION   A **tourist office** is at the Markethill Car Park
(© **01556/502-611**). April to October, it's open Monday to Friday 10am to
6pm, Saturday 10am to 5pm (July and Aug also Sun 10am–5pm).

SEEING THE SIGHTS

Threave Castle ⚷   This is the ruined 14th-century stronghold of the Black
Douglases. The seven-story tower was built between 1639 and 1690 by
Archibald the Grim, Lord of Galloway. In 1455, Threave was the last Douglas
stronghold to surrender to James II, who employed some of the most advanced
armaments of his day (including a cannon similar to Mons Meg, the massive
cannon now displayed in Edinburgh Castle) in its subjection. Over the doorway
projects the gallows knob from which the Douglases hanged their enemies. In
1640, the castle was captured by the Covenanters (the rebellious group of Scots
who questioned the king's right to make laws) and dismantled.

To reach the site, you must walk .8km (½ mile) through farmlands and then
take a small boat across the Dee. When you get to the river, ring a bell signaling
the custodian to come and ferry you across. The last sailing is at 6pm. For information, contact Historic Scotland, Longmore House, Salisbury Place, Edinburgh (© **01316/688-800;** www.historic-scotland.gov.uk).

2.5km (1½ miles) west of Castle Douglas on an islet in the River Dee. Admission (including ferry ride) £2.20
($3.50) adults, £1.60 ($2.55) seniors, 75p ($1.20) children under 16. Apr–Sept Mon–Sat 9:30am–6:30pm; Sun
2–6:30pm. Closed Oct–Mar.

Threave Garden ⚷⚷   About 1.6km (1 mile) southeast of Threave Castle,
these gardens are built around Threave House, a Scottish baronial mansion constructed during the Victorian era. It's run by the National Trust for Scotland,
which uses the complex as a school for gardening and a wildfowl refuge. The garden is at its best in April, when the daffodils bloom, and in June, when rhododendrons and the rock garden are in flower. On site are a visitor center and
restaurant.

Off A75 1km (½ mile) west of Castle Douglas. © **01556/502-575.** www.nts.org.uk. Admission £5 ($8)
adults, £3.75 ($6) children/seniors. Garden, daily 9:30am–5:30pm; visitor center, Mar and Nov–Dec daily
10am–4pm; Apr–Oct daily 9:30am–5:30pm.

WHERE TO STAY

Douglas Arms   Originally, a 17th-century coaching inn, this old favorite is
up to date and modernized even though it lies behind a rather stark two-story
facade. The public rooms are bright and cheerful, giving you a toasty feeling on
a cold night. The guest rooms were refurbished a few years ago and include
shower-only bathrooms.

King St., Castle Douglas, Galloway DG7 1DB. © **01556/502-231.** Fax 01556/504-000. doughot@aol.com.
24 units. £69.50 ($111) double. Rates include breakfast. AE, MC, V. **Amenities:** Restaurant; bar. *In room:*
TV, coffeemaker, hair dryer, trouser press.

King's Arms   This inn provides reasonably priced accommodations ranging
from single rooms to a family room. The guest rooms are touched up every year
and in good shape; nine come with shower-only bathrooms (guests in the tenth
room get a hallway bathroom with tub reserved solely for their use). The helpful staff will direct you to various activities in the area, including a nine-hole golf
course a 45-minute drive away. The sun patio is a great place for tea or coffee or
perhaps a sundowner of malt whisky. The cuisine is British with a Scottish
emphasis; the range is extensive, featuring local produce, Solway salmon, and
Galloway beef.

Finds **A Setting for a Sir Walter Scott Novel**

Unique in Scotland, **Orchardton Tower,** 9km (5½ miles) southeast of Castle Douglas off A711, is an example of a round tower house (they were usually built in Ireland). It was constructed around 1450 by John Cairns and later on was purchased by a member of the Maxwell family. The adventures of one family member, Sir Robert Maxwell of Orchardton, a fervent Jacobite captured in the Battle of Culloden, figured in Sir Walter Scott's novel *Guy Mannering.* If you ask the custodian who lives at the cottage next door, he'll let you see inside for free.

The **Mote of Urr,** 8km (5 miles) northeast of Castle Douglas off B794, is a circular mound enclosed by a deep trench. This is an example of the motte-and-bailey type of defense popular in Norman days.

St. Andrew's St., Castle Douglas, Galloway DG7 1EL. ℂ **01556/502-626.** Fax 01556/502-097. www.galloway-golf.co.uk. 10 units, 9 with private bathroom. £60 ($96) double with bathroom. Rates include breakfast. MC, V. Free parking. **Amenities:** Restaurant; bar. *In room:* TV, coffeemaker, hair dryer.

Longacre Manor This dignified building lies on about .6 hectare (1½ acres) of forest and garden and was constructed in 1927 as the home of a local grain trader. Under the gracious ownership of Elma and Charles Ball, it now offers plush and conservatively furnished large guest rooms, some with four-poster beds. The shower-only bathrooms feature bathrobes and Molton Brown toiletries. The lounge is cozy, and a three-course dinner can be prepared and served in the dining room. The bedrooms and the restaurant are strictly nonsmoking.

Ernespie Rd., Castle Douglas, Galloway DG7 1LE. ℂ **01556/503-576.** Fax 01556/503-886. www.about scotland.co.uk/south/longacre.html. 4 units. £70–£100 ($112–$160) double. Rates include breakfast. MC, V. From the center of Castle Douglas, drive 1km (½ mile) north, following the signs to Dumfries. No children under 10. **Amenities:** Restaurant; bar. *In room:* TV, coffeemaker, hair dryer, trouser press.

The Urr Valley Country House Hotel ⊛ *Finds* Reached by a long drive, this country hotel in the scenic Urr Valley is set in the midst of 5.6 hectares (14 acres) of lush woodlands and gardens, 1.6km (1 mile) east of the center of Castle Douglas. You're welcomed into a real Scottish macho atmosphere of stag heads and antique rods and reels, along with paneled walls and fireplaces with log fires. Most of the guest rooms are spacious; a few have four-poster beds and others are designed for families. Two rooms have been set aside for nonsmokers.

You can have a drink or enjoy a pub meal in the lounge and bar. In the main restaurant, both French and Scottish cuisine are served, with an emphasis on fresh seafood and local produce such as pheasant and Solway salmon. Dare you try the regional specialty, Scottish haggis?

Ernespie Road, Castle Douglas, Galloway DG7 3JG. ℂ **01556/502-188.** Fax 01556/504-055. www.scottish-inns.co.uk/urrvalley. 19 units. £50–£80 ($80–$128) double; £60–£90 ($96–$144) family room. Rates include breakfast. AE, MC, V. Free parking. Take A75 toward Castle Douglas. Dogs accepted by prior arrangement. **Amenities:** Restaurant; bar. *In room:* TV, coffeemaker, hair dryer, trouser press.

WHERE TO DINE

Plumed Horse Restaurant SCOTTISH/INTERNATIONAL Opened in July 1998, this restaurant combines high-quality cuisine with a relaxed, village atmosphere; it's set the rest of the local competition on its ear. The linen tablecloths, crystal, silver, and Villeroy & Boch tableware lend the Plumed Horse an air of elegance. Chef Tony Borthwick changes the menu regularly, but you might find roast Barbary duck breast, crisp filet of salmon, scallop ravioli, and roast monkfish among the choices. Desserts such as pistachio and praline parfait and banana brûlée in butterscotch sauce are favorites. Ingredients used in the meals are often luxurious, including wild mushrooms and foie gras. The restaurant also has an extensive wine and champagne list.

Main St., Crossmichael (5km/3 miles from Castle Douglas). © 01556/670-333. Reservations recommended. Main courses £17–£19 ($27–$30). MC, V. Tues–Sun 12:30–1:30pm and 7–9:30pm (closed on Sat at lunch). Take A713 toward Ayr.

9 Kirkcudbright: An Artists' Colony ★

174km (108 miles) SW of Edinburgh, 45km (28 miles) SW of Dumfries, 166km (103 miles) S of Glasgow, 81km (50 miles) E of Stranraer, 16km (10 miles) SW of Castle Douglas

The ancient burgh of Kirkcudbright (kir-*coo*-bree) is at the head of Kirkcudbright Bay on the Dee estuary. Many of this intriguing old town's color-washed houses belong to artists; a lively group of weavers, potters, and painters lives and works in the 18th-century streets and lanes. What makes Kirkcudbright so enchanting isn't really its sights (although it boasts several) but its artistic life and bohemian flavor. Various festivities take place in July and August; expect to find anything from marching bagpipe bands to exhibitions of Scottish country dancing to torchlight processions. And activities range from raft races to nearby walks, from a floodlit tattoo in front of MacLellan's Castle to a puppet festival. Check with the tourist office (see below) about what will be happening when you visit.

ESSENTIALS

GETTING THERE   Kirkcudbright is on the same bus route that serves Castle Douglas from Dumfries, with departures during the day about once per hour. The 40-minute ride from Dumfries is about £4 ($6.40) one-way, a day ticket is £5 ($8). For bus information, call © **8705/808-080** or the local tourist office.

If you're driving from Castle Douglas, continue along A75 southwest until you come to the junction with A711, which takes you into Kirkcudbright.

VISITOR INFORMATION   A **tourist office** is at Harbour Square (© **01557/ 330-494**). April 1 to June 29 and September 15 to October 26, it's open Monday to Saturday 10am to 5pm and Sunday 11am to 4:30pm; June 30 to September 14, hours are Monday to Saturday 9:30am to 6pm and Sunday 10am to 5pm.

SEEING THE SIGHTS

In the old town **graveyard** are memorials to Covenanters and to Billy Marshall, the tinker (Gypsy) king who died in 1792 at age 120, reportedly having fathered four children after age 100.

Broughton House   Regular exhibits are displayed at this 18th-century mansion that once belonged to artist Edward Atkinson Hornel (1864–1933). His portrait by Bessie McNicol is displayed in the former dining room. Although largely forgotten today, Hornel was a famous artist in his day, known for his scenes depicting life in his native Galloway. With his bold and colorful style, he became one of the major figures of the Glasgow School of Art. Broughton contains a large reference library with a Burns collection, along with pictures by Hornel and other artists. One of the most appealing aspects of this place is Hornel's small but charming Japanese-style garden, whose plantings sometimes appeared in his paintings.

12 High St. ✆ **01557/330-437**. Admission £3.50 ($5.60) adults, £2.60 ($4.15) seniors and children, £9.50 ($15) per family. Apr–June and Sept–Oct daily 1–5:30pm; July–Aug daily 11am–5:30pm. Closed Nov–Mar.

MacLellan's Castle   Dominating the center of town is this castellated castle built in 1582 for the town's provost, Sir Thomas MacLellan. It has been a ruin since 1752, but it's an impressive ruin and worth a visit. A large staircase goes from the cellars on the ground floor to the Banqueting Hall, where a massive fireplace comes with what was called a "lairds lug" (spy hole). From almost anywhere in town, the jagged fangs of the castle loom overhead.

Off High St. ✆ **0131/668-8800**. Admission £2 ($3.20) adults, £1.50 ($2.40) seniors, 75p ($1.20) children. Apr–Sept Mon–Sat 9:30am–6:30pm, Sun 2–6pm. Closed Oct–Mar.

Stewartry Museum   Built by the Victorians in 1892 as a showcase for the region's distinctive culture, this museum contains an unusual collection of antiquities, tools, and artworks depicting the history, culture, and sociology of this part of Galloway.

St. Mary St. ✆ **01557/331-643**. Free admission. July–Aug daily 10am–6pm; Sept–June Mon–Sat 11am–4pm.

Tolbooth Art Centre   The Tolbooth (1629) has functioned as a prison, town hall, and courthouse. In front of it is a 1610 Mercat Cross, while inside is a memorial to John Paul Jones (1747–92), the gardener's son from Kirkbean who became a slave trader, a privateer, and eventually the father of the American navy. For a time before his emigration, he was imprisoned for murder here. In 1993, Queen Elizabeth inaugurated the building as a gallery displaying paintings by famous local artists. You'll find works by Jessie M. King, Lena Alexander, Robert Sivell, and S. J. Peploe.

High St. ✆ **01557/331-556**. Admission £1.50 ($2.40) adults, 75p ($1.20) seniors/students/children. Apr–June and Aug–Oct Mon–Sat 11am–5pm, Sun 2–5pm; July daily 10am–6pm and Sun 2–5pm; Nov–Mar Mon–Sat 11am–4pm.

WHERE TO STAY

Selkirk Arms 🎔   This beloved old favorite—the finest inn in the area—is where Robert Burns stayed when he composed the celebrated "Selkirk Grace." It was built in the 1770s in a stone-fronted Georgian design with a slate roof. The guest rooms all have standard furniture and garden views. The restaurant/bistro offers a wide range of fresh local produce; bar lunches and suppers are also available. The lounge bar features an array of malt whiskies that would warm Burns's heart.

Old High St., Kirkcudbright, Galloway DG6 4JG. ✆ **01557/330-402**. Fax 01557/331-639. www.selkirkarms hotel.co.uk. 16 units. £95 ($152) double. Rates include breakfast. Children in parent's room pay only for breakfast. AE, DC, MC, V. Free parking. **Amenities:** Restaurant; bar. *In room:* TV, coffeemaker, hair dryer.

WHERE TO DINE

Auld Alliance Restaurant SCOTTISH/FRENCH   One of the most appealing restaurants in the region is this family-owned and -operated place in an interconnected pair of 1880s buildings constructed with stones from the ruins of Kirkcudbright Castle. The cooks are almost obsessed with the freshness of the fish they serve, and salmon (likely to have been caught several hours before preparation in the Kirkcudbright estuary and its tributary, the Dee) will be full of its legendary flavor. A house specialty is queenies (queen-size scallops from deeper waters than the great scallop).

5 Castle St. ✆ **01557/330-569**. Reservations recommended. Main courses £8.50–£15 ($14–$24). MC, V. Apr–Oct daily 6:30–9:30pm. Closed Halloween–Easter.

10 Portpatrick: Where the Southern Upland Way Begins

227km (141 miles) SW of Edinburgh, 13km (8 miles) SW of Stranraer, 156km (97 miles) SW of Glasgow, 129km (80 miles) W of Dumfries

Until 1849, steamers sailed the 34km (21 miles) from Donaghdee in Northern Ireland to Portpatrick, which became a "Gretna Green" for the Irish who wanted to marry quickly. Couples would land on Saturday, have the banns called on Sunday, and marry on Monday.

Today, you go to Portpatrick not because of its wealth of sights, although the Logan Botanic Gardens is worth the detour from Stranraer. You go instead because it's a major refueling stop for those driving along the Mull of Galloway. Portpatrick captures the flavor of an almost forgotten Scottish fishing port as few other towns do. It's a land of cliffs and rugged seascapes, with a lighthouse here and there and even a bird reserve.

Hikers come because Portpatrick is the beginning of one of the greatest long-distance footpaths in Scotland, the **Southern Upland Way** (see "The Best Hikes," in chapter 1). Starting here, the 341-km (212-mile) jaunt goes all the way to the Cockburnspath on the eastern coast of Scotland. Along the way, this path traverses the Galloway Forest Park and other scenic attractions of southern Scotland. Of course, very few will have the time or stamina to take the entire hike. But you can enjoy one of the least challenging stretches, going all the way from Portpatrick to Castle Kennedy, some 12km (7½ miles).

ESSENTIALS

GETTING THERE   Go to Stranraer by **train,** then take a bus to Portpatrick, 5 minutes away. For train information, call © **08457/484-950.** Bus no. 64 from Stranraer makes frequent runs throughout the day. The 5-minute ride costs around £1 ($1.60) one-way. For bus information, call © **08705/808-080.** If you're **driving** from Stranraer, take A77 southwest.

EXPLORING THE AREA

Commanding a clifftop 2.5km (1½ miles) south of the town center are the ruins of **Dunskey Castle,** a grim keep built in 1510. It's a dramatic site—the original stone walls and the chimney stacks, each rising abruptly from the top of the cliff, are all that remain. To walk or drive here from the town center, follow the clearly marked signs.

Some 16km (10 miles) south of Portpatrick is the little hamlet of Port Logan. In the vicinity is **Logan House** (not open to the public), the seat of the McDougall family, which claimed they could trace their ancestry so far back they were as old as the sun itself. This family laid out the gardens at Logan.

Approximately 23 km (14 miles) south of Stranraer off B7065, the **Logan Botanic Garden** (© **01776/860-231**), an annex of the Royal Botanic Garden in Edinburgh, contains a wide range of plants from the world's temperate regions. Cordylines, palms, tree ferns, and flowering shrubs grow well in the mild climate of southwestern Scotland. March through October, the garden is open daily from 10am to 6pm. Admission is £3 ($4.80) for adults, £2.50 ($4) for seniors, £1 ($1.60) for children, and £7 ($11) for families. At the entrance is a pleasant refreshment room.

Portpatrick has become something of a magnet for artisans who produce charming (and sometimes eccentric) handcrafts. You'll find examples of hand-crafted plant pots, slip-cast and glazed figurines, Spanish recycled glass, and Indian coffee tables at the port's largest gift shop, **Lighthouse Pottery,** South Pier

(© **01776/810-284**). The **Green Gillie Crafts Shop,** Main Street (© **01776/ 810-359**), specializes in woolen jerseys and mittens, throw rugs, and calfskins.

WHERE TO STAY

The **Crown Hotel** (see "Where to Dine," below) also rents rooms.

Fernhill Hotel   This gray-stone 1872 building stands above the village, looking down at the harbor a 5-minute walk from the first tee of the clifftop Dunskey Golf Course (which is scenic but not challenging). Renovated in 1990, the guest rooms are decorated with flair. Most desirable are the six executive rooms opening onto the sea; three have private balconies. Each unit comes with a small, shower-only bathroom. The cocktail bar and the Victorian conservatory have a panoramic view over the town and sea. The excellent cuisine, using Scottish produce whenever available, is one of the reasons for staying here. The house specialty is fresh lobster.

Heugh Rd., Portpatrick, Galloway DG9 8TD. © **01776/810-220**. Fax 01776/810-596. www.mcmillanhotels. com. 23 units. £100–£124 ($160–$198) double. Rates include breakfast. MC, V. Free parking. On the approach to Portpatrick, turn right at the War Memorial. **Amenities:** Restaurant; bar; access to nearby health club; limited room service; laundry service. *In room:* TV, coffeemaker, hair dryer.

Knockinaam Lodge ★★★   Built in 1869, this three-story Victorian hunting lodge is surrounded on three sides by towering cliffs. It's a country house of charm and grace in a picturesque coastal setting, boasting some of the finest cuisine served in the south of Scotland. Since it's west of town, it is far more tranquil than any other hotel in the area. You get a real feel for Scottish manorial living here, especially as you read your paper in the morning room overlooking the sea. The bedrooms are tastefully decorated and filled with thoughtful little extras, along with modernized bathrooms. This award-winning establishment also boasts luxurious lawns that lead down to a pristine, private beach. It was here on these 12 hectares (30 acres) of private woodland that Sir Winston Churchill met General Eisenhower and their chiefs of staff during the dark days of World War II.

Portpatrick Wigtownshire, Galloway DG9 9AD. © **01776/810-471**. Fax 01776/810-435. www.prideof britainhotels.com. 10 units. £195–£340 ($312–$544) double. Rates include breakfast and dinner. AE, DC, MC V. Free parking. From A77 or A75, follow signs to Portpatrick. It's 3km (2 miles) west of Lochans; watch for hotel sign on right. **Amenities:** Restaurant; bar; dry cleaning. *In room:* TV, hair dryer.

WHERE TO DINE

The **Knockinaam Lodge** serves the area's best food (see "Where to Stay," above).

Crown Hotel   SEAFOOD/INTERNATIONAL   One of the region's most popular restaurants occupies the ground floor of a century-old stone-sided hotel. You might enjoy a drink in the pub before heading into the dining room, which opens onto a wide-angled view of the ocean. Meat is available, but the biggest draw is seafood: scampi, monkfish, scallops in wine sauce, mullet, cod, and plaice, salmon, or sole filets. The Crown maintains 12 rooms upstairs, each with bathroom, TV, hair dryer, coffeemaker, and phone. Doubles rent for £72 ($115), which includes a hearty Scottish breakfast.

North Crescent, Portpatrick, Galloway DG9 8FX. © **01776/810-261**. Fax 01776/810-551. Reservations recommended. Main courses £10.65–£14.45 ($17–$23); fixed-price 3-course menu £14.95 ($24). MC, V. Daily noon–2:30pm and 6–10pm.

Glasgow & the Strathclyde Region

Glasgow ★★★ is only 65km (40 miles) west of Edinburgh, but there's an amazing contrast between the two cities. Scotland's economic powerhouse and its largest city (Britain's third largest), up-and-coming Glasgow is now the country's cultural capital and home to half the population. It has long been famous for ironworks and steelworks; the local shipbuilding industry produced the *Queen Mary,* the *Queen Elizabeth,* and other fabled ocean liners.

Once polluted and plagued with some of the worst slums in Europe, Glasgow has been transformed. Urban development and the decision to locate the Scottish Exhibition and Conference Centre here have brought great changes: Grime is being sandblasted away, overcrowding has been reduced, and more open space and less traffic congestion mean cleaner air. Glasgow also boasts a vibrant and even edgy arts scene; it has become one of the cultural capitals of Europe.

The splendor of the city has reemerged. John Betjeman and other critics have hailed Glasgow as "the greatest surviving example of a Victorian city." The planners of the 19th century thought on a grand scale when they designed the terraces and villas west and south of the center.

Glasgow's origins are ancient, making Edinburgh, for all its wealth of history, seem comparatively young. The village that grew up beside a fjord 32km (20 miles) from the mouth of

the River Clyde as a medieval ecclesiastical center began prospering commercially in the 17th century. As it grew, the city engulfed the smaller medieval towns of Ardrie, Renfrew, Rutherglen, and Paisley.

Glasgow is part of **Strathclyde,** a populous district whose origins go back to the Middle Ages. Irish chroniclers wrote of the kingdom of Stratha Cluatha some 1,500 years ago, and Strathclyde was known to the Romans, who called its people Damnonii. The old capital, Dumbarton, on its high rock, provided a natural fortress in the days when locals had to defend themselves against enemy tribes.

The fortunes of Strathclyde changed in the 18th century, when the Clyde estuary became the gateway to the New World. Glasgow merchants grew rich on tobacco and then on cotton. It was Britain's fastest-growing region during the Industrial Revolution, and Glasgow was known as the Second City of the Empire. Until 1996, Strathclyde functioned as a government entity that included Glasgow, but it's now broken down into several new divisions: the City of Glasgow; Inverclyde, which includes the important industrial center of Greenock; and several others.

Glasgow is a good gateway for exploring the heart of **Burns country, Culzean Castle,** and the **resorts along the Ayrshire coast,** an hour away by frequent train service (see "Side Trips from Glasgow: The Best of the Strath-clyde Region," later in this chapter). From Glasgow, you can also tour Loch Lomond, Loch Katrine, and the Trossachs (see chapter 8, "Fife & the Central Highlands," for more infor-mation). After a day or so in Glasgow, you can head to Burns country for perhaps another night. Also on Glas-gow's doorstep is the scenic estuary of the **Firth of Clyde,** which you can cruise on a paddle steamer. The Firth of Clyde, with its long sea lochs—Gareloch, Loch Long, Loch Goil, and Holy Loch—is one of the most scenic waterways in the world.

1 Essentials

ARRIVING

BY PLANE   The **Glasgow Airport** is at Abbotsinch (© **0141/887-1111**), 16km (10 miles) west of the city via M8. You can use the regular Glasgow CityLink bus service to get to the city center. From bus stop no. 2, take bus no. 900 or 901 to the Buchanan Street Bus Station in the center of town. The ride takes about 20 minutes and costs £4 ($6.40). A taxi to the city center costs about £15 ($24). You can reach Edinburgh by taking a bus from Glasgow Airport to Queens Station and then changing to a bus for Edinburgh. The entire journey, including the change, should take about 2 hours and costs £7 ($11) one-way or £12 ($19) round-trip.

Monday to Friday, British Airways (www.ba.com) runs almost hourly shuttle service from London's Heathrow Airport to Glasgow. The first flight departs London at 7:15am and the last at 8:25pm; service is reduced on weekends, depending on volume. For flight schedules and fares, call British Airways in London at © **0845/779-9977.**

From mid-May through October, **American Airlines** (© **800/433-7300;** www.aa.com) offers a daily nonstop flight to Glasgow from Chicago; the rest of the year, you'll make at least one transfer. **Northwest Airlines** (© **800/225-2525;** www.nwa.com) operates nonstop flights between Boston and Glasgow daily in summer, somewhat less frequently in winter.

British Midland (© **0870/607-0555;** www.flybmi.com) flies from Heathrow to Glasgow. **Aer Lingus** (© **800/223-6537** or 01/844-4711 in Ire-land; www.aerlingus.ie) flies daily from Dublin to Glasgow.

BY TRAIN   Headquarters for British Rail is at Glasgow's Central Station and Queen Street Station. For **National Rail Enquiries,** call © **08457/484-950.** The **Queen Street Station** serves the north and east of Scotland, with trains arriving from Edinburgh every 30 minutes during the day; the one-way trip between the two cities costs £8 ($13) and takes 50 minutes. You'll also be able to travel to such Highland destinations as Inverness and Fort William from here.

The **Central Station** serves southern Scotland, England, and Wales, with trains arriving from London's Euston and King's Cross Stations (call © **08457/484-950** in London for schedules) frequently throughout the day (trip time is about 5½ hr.). The trains leave Euston Monday to Saturday from 6:20am until 6:25pm, and then the night train departs at 11:40pm, getting into Glasgow at 7:16am. From Glasgow, trains leave for London every hour 6:15am to 5pm. The night train leaves at 11:55pm. Try to avoid Sunday travel—the frequency of trains is considerably reduced and the duration of the trip lengthened to at least 7 hours because of more stopovers en route.

BY BUS   The **Buchanan Street Bus Station** is 2 blocks north of the Queen Street Station on North Hanover Street (© **08706/082-608**). **National Express**

runs daily coaches from London's Victoria Coach Station to Buchanan frequently throughout the day. Buses from London take 8 hours and 40 minutes to reach Glasgow, depending on the number of stops en route. Scottish CityLink (② **08705/505-050**) also has frequent bus service to and from Edinburgh, with a one-way ticket costing £3 to £5 ($4.80–$8).

Contact National Express Enquiries at ② **0990/808-080** for more information.

BY CAR   Glasgow is 65km (40 miles) west of Edinburgh, 356km (221 miles) north of Manchester, and 625km (388 miles) north of London. From England in the south, Glasgow is reached by M74, a continuation of M8 that goes right into the city, making an S curve. Call your hotel and find out what exit you should take. M8, another express motorway, links Glasgow and Edinburgh.

Other major routes into the city are A77 northeast from Prestwick and Ayr and A8 from the west (this becomes M8 around the port of Glasgow). A82 comes in from the northwest (the Highlands) on the north bank of the Clyde, and A80 also goes into the city. (This route is the southwestern section of M80 and M9 from Stirling.)

VISITOR INFORMATION

The **Greater Glasgow and Clyde Valley Tourist Board,** 11 George Square (② **0141/204-4400;** Underground: Buchanan St.), is the country's most helpful office. October to May, it's open Monday to Saturday 9am to 6pm; June to September hours are daily 9am to 6pm; August daily 9am to 8pm.

CITY LAYOUT

The monumental heart of Glasgow—the Victorian City and the Merchant City, along with the Central Station—lies on the north bank of the **River Clyde.** The ancient center has as its core the great Cathedral of St. Kentigern, a perfect example of pre-Reformation Gothic architecture that dates in part to the 12th century. Behind it is the Necropolis, burial ground of many Victorians. Across the square is 1471 Provands Lordship, the city's oldest house. Down **High Street** you'll find the Tolbooth Steeple (1626) at Glasgow Cross, and nearer the River Clyde is **Glasgow Green,** Britain's first public park (1662).

From Ingram Street, South Frederick Street will take you to **George Square,** with its many statues, including one dedicated to Sir Walter Scott. This is the center of modern Glasgow.

The **Merchant City,** a compact area of imposing buildings, is the location of the National Trust for Scotland's shop and visitor center at Hutcheson's Hall. The broad pedestrian thoroughfares of **Buchanan, Argyle, and Sauchiehall streets** are the heart of the shopping district.

Glasgow's **West End** is Britain's finest example of a great Victorian city. The West End is just a short taxi journey from the city center, easily accessible from

---

(Value A First Day Bargain for Glasgow

For only £4 ($6.40), you can buy a FirstDay Tourist Ticket allowing you to hop on and off buses and to be granted discounts for such select attractions as the House for an Art Lover. A pocket-size city map is also provided. The ticket is valid daily from 9:30am to midnight. It's available at tourist information centers, underground or bus stations, and at certain attractions. For more information, check www.seeglasgow.com.

> **Tips   Finding an Address**
>
> Glasgow was built in various sections and districts over the years, and mas-sive sections have been torn down—some for slum clearance, others to make way for new highways. Following a consistent street plan can be tough, as squares or terraces can suddenly interrupt a route you're tracing.
>
> House numbers can run in odds or evens and clockwise or counter-clockwise, and sometimes Glaswegians don't even use numbers at all. So don't be surprised to see something like "Blackfriars Street," without a number, given as an address. Get a detailed map of Glasgow before set-ting out. Always find the nearest cross street, and then look for your loca-tion from there. If it's a hotel or restaurant, the sign for the establishment is likely to be more prominent than the number anyway.

any part of the city and close to M8 and the Clydeside Expressway. An exten-sive network of local bus routes serves the West End. The Glasgow Underground operates a circular service; by boarding at any station on the system, you can reach the four stations serving the district: Kelvinbridge, Hillhead (the most cen-tral), Kelvin Hall, and Partick. The terraces of the Park Conservation Area rise to afford excellent views. Across Kelvingrove Park is the **Art Gallery** and **Museum.** Nearby, the tower of Glasgow University dominates Gilmorehill. Beyond is the **Hunterian Art Gallery,** home to a famous collection of Whistlers. Just a few strides away is Byres Road, a street of bars, shops, and restaurants. To the north are the **Botanic Gardens.**

A little more than 5km (3 miles) southwest of the city center is the heavily wooded **Pollok Country Park,** which is home to the **Burrell Collection Gallery.** This museum is Scotland's top tourist attraction and the focal point of any visit to the South Side. Nearby is the 18th-century Pollok House. An exten-sive network of bus routes passes close by the area, which is also served by two suburban rail stations. An electric bus service is in operation from the Country Park gates on Pollokshaws Road to Pollok House and the Burrell Collection Gallery. Extensive parklands and greenery characterize the city's southern envi-rons. In addition to the Pollok Country Park, there are **Haggs Castle Golf Club,** home of the Glasgow Open, and **Bellahouston Park,** scene of the historic papal visit in 1983. En route to the Burrell Collection Gallery, you cross by the 59-hectare (148-acre) **Queens Park,** honoring Mary Queen of Scots. Near **Maxwell Park** is the Haggs Castle Museum, housed in a 400-year-old building.

THE NEIGHBORHOODS IN BRIEF

See the "Glasgow Attractions" map on p. 184 to see the locations of the following neighborhoods.

Medieval Glasgow Also referred to as Old Glasgow, this is where St. Mungo arrived in A.D. 543 and built his little church in what's now the northeastern part of the city. At the top of High Street stand the **Cathedral of St. Kentigern** and one of Britain's largest Victorian cemeteries. You enter the Necropolis by crossing over the Bridge of Sighs. It was patterned after the famous Bridge of Sighs in Venice over which the condemned prisoners walked into prison and perhaps death. Old Glasgow's major terminus is the High Street Station, near the former site of the University of Glasgow. **Glasgow Green,** opening onto the River Clyde, has been a public park since 1662. Today, vastly restored medieval Glasgow is the best place for strolls; however, it's not a popular place to stay because of limited accommodations.

Along the River Clyde It was once said that "The Clyde made Glasgow; Glasgow made the Clyde." Although the city is no longer so dependent on the river, you can still enjoy a stroll along the **Clyde Walkway** ⊛, which stretches from King Albert Bridge, at the western end of Glasgow Green, for 3km (2 miles) downstream to Stobcross, now the site of the **Scottish Exhibition and Conference Centre.** This is one of the city's grandest walks; on these waters, Glasgow shipped its manufactured goods around the world. However, if time is limited, you may want to concentrate on the major museums and historic Glasgow instead.

The Merchant City Glasgow spread west of High Street in the 18th century, largely because of profits made from sugar, cotton, and tobacco in trade with the Americas. The Merchant City extends from Trongate and Argyle Street in the south to George Street in the north. Its major terminus is the Queen Street Station; its major shopping venue, **Argyle Arcade.** It's also the site of City Hall and Strathclyde University and boasts some of Britain's most **elegant Georgian and Victorian buildings** as well as **Greek Revival churches.** Tobacco barons once occupied much of the area, but their buildings have been recycled for other uses.

Glasgow Center Continuing its western progression, the city center of Glasgow is now dominated by the Central Station on Hope Street. This is the major shopping district, including such venues as the **Princes Square Shopping Mall.** Also here are the Stock Exchange and the Anderston Bus Station (near the Central Station).

The West End Beyond Charing Cross in the west end are the University of Glasgow and several major galleries and museums, some of which are in **Kelvingrove Park.** The West End mixes culture, art, and parks, and is dominated by Glasgow University, with the university structures idyllically placed in various parks. The city itself has more green spaces per resident than any other in Europe; 16 hectares (40 acres) of the West End are taken up by the **Botanic Gardens.**

2 Getting Around

The best way to explore Glasgow is on foot. The center is laid out on a grid system, which makes map reading relatively easy. However, many of the major attractions, such as the Burrell Collection, are in the surrounding environs, and for those you'll need to rely on public transportation.

Remember: Cars drive on the left, so when you cross streets make certain to look both ways.

BY BUS

Glasgow is serviced by **First Glasgow Bus Company.** The buses come in a variety of colors, the lighter ones (blue and yellow) tending to serve the Kelvin Central and Strathclyde rural areas, with the darker ones covering the urban zones. Service is frequent throughout the day, but after 11pm service is greatly curtailed. The major bus station is the **Buchanan Street Bus Station,** Killermont

Street (call ℘ **0141/423-6600** for schedules), 2 blocks north of the Queen Station. Fares are £2.50 ($4), but you must have exact change. A special round-trip bus ticket for £2.10 ($3.35) operates after 9:30am.

BY UNDERGROUND

Called the "Clockwork Orange" (from the vivid orange of the trains) by Glaswegians, a 15-stop subway services the city. Most Underground trains operate from these stops every 5 minutes, with longer intervals between trains on Sunday and at night. The fare is 90p ($1.45). Service is Monday to Saturday 6:30am to 10pm and Sunday 11am to 6pm.

The **Travel Centre** at St. Enoch Square (℘ **0870/608-2608**), 2 blocks from the Central Station, is open Monday to Saturday 6:30am to 9:30pm and Sunday 7am to 9:30pm. Here you can buy a £8 ($13) **Underground pass,** valid for a week's access to all the tube lines of Glasgow, as well as access to all the trains serving routes between Central Station and the southern suburbs, or a £7.80 ($12) **daytripper card,** covering one adult and one child for a day. For details, call ℘ **0141/332-7133.**

BY TAXI

Taxis are the same excellent ones found in Edinburgh or London. You can hail them on the street or call **TOA Taxis** at ℘ **0141/429-7070.** Fares are displayed on a meter next to the driver. When a taxi is available on the street, a taxi sign on the roof is lit a bright yellow. Most taxi trips within the city cost £4 to £6 ($6.40–$9.60). The taxi meter starts at £1.80 ($2.90) and increases by 20p (30¢) every 61m (200 ft.), with an extra 10p (15¢) assessed for each additional passenger after the first two. An 80p ($1.30) surcharge is imposed midnight to 6am. Tip at least 10% of the fare shown on the meter.

BY CAR

Driving around Glasgow is a tricky business, even for locals. You're better off with public transportation. It's a warren of one-way streets, and parking is expensive and difficult to find. Metered parking is available, but you'll need 20p (30¢) coins, entitling you to only 20 minutes. You must watch out for zealous traffic wardens issuing tickets. Some zones are marked PERMIT HOLDERS ONLY—your vehicle will be towed if you have no permit. A yellow line along the curb indicates no parking. Multistory car parks (parking lots), open 24 hours a day, are found at Anderston Cross and Cambridge, George, Mitchell, Oswald, and Waterloo streets.

If you want to rent a car to explore the countryside, it's best to arrange the rental before leaving home (see chapter 2, "Planning Your Trip to Scotland"). But if you want to rent a car locally, most companies will accept your American or Canadian driver's license. All the major rental agencies are represented at the airport. In addition, **Avis Rent-a-Car** is at 70 Lancefield St. (℘ **0141/221-2827;** bus: 6 or 6A), **Budget Rent-a-Car** at Glasgow Airport (℘ **0141/221-9241;** bus: 38, 45, 48, or 57), and **Europcar** at 38 Anderson Quay (℘ **0141/248-8788;** bus: 38, 45, 48, or 57).

BY BICYCLE

Parts of Glasgow are fine for biking, or you might want to rent a bike and explore the surrounding countryside. For what the Scots call cycle hire, go to a well-recommended shop about a kilometer (½ mile) west of the town center, just off Great Western Road: **Western End Cycles,** 16–18 Chancellor St., in the Hillhead district (℘ **0141/357-1344;** Underground: Kelvin Bridge or Hillhead).

It rents 21-speed trail and mountain bikes that conform well to the hilly terrain of Glasgow and its surroundings. The cost of £12 ($19) per day must be accompanied by a cash deposit of £100 ($160) or the imprint of a valid credit card.

FAST FACTS: Glasgow

American Express The office is at 115 Hope St. (℗ 0141/226-3077; bus: 38, 45, 48, or 57), open Monday to Friday 8:30am to 5:30pm and Saturday 9am to noon (June and July to 4pm Sat).

Business Hours Most **offices** are open Monday to Friday 9am to 5 or 5:30pm. Most **banks** are open Monday to Wednesday and Friday 9:30am to 4pm, Thursday 9:30am to 5:30pm, and Saturday 10am to 7pm. Opening times can vary slightly from bank to bank. **Shops** are generally open Monday to Saturday 10am to 5:30 or 6pm. On Thursday, stores remain open until 7pm.

Currency Exchange The tourist office and the American Express office (see above) will exchange most major foreign currencies. City-center banks operate *bureaux de change,* and nearly all will cash traveler's checks if you have the proper ID.

Dentists If you have an emergency, go to the Accident and Emergency Department of **Glasgow Dental Hospital & School NHS Trust,** 378 Sauchiehall St. (℗ 0141/211-9600; bus: 57). Its hours are Monday to Friday 9:15am to 3:15pm and Sunday and public holidays 10:30am to noon.

Doctors The major hospital is the **Royal Infirmary,** 82–86 Castle St. (℗ 0141/211-4000; bus: 2 or 2A).

Embassies & Consulates See "Fast Facts" in chapter 2, "Planning Your Trip to Scotland."

Emergencies Call ℗ **999** in an emergency to summon the police, an ambulance, or firefighters.

Hospitals See "Doctors," above.

Hot lines Women in crisis may want to call **Women's Aid** at ℗ 0141/553-2022. Gays and lesbians can call the **Strathclyde Gay and Lesbian Switchboard** at ℗ 0141/847-0447 daily 7 to 10pm. The **Rape Crisis Centre** is at ℗ 0141/331-1990.

Internet Access You can send or read e-mail and surf the Net at **EasyEverything Internet Café,** 57–61 St. Vincent St. (℗ 0141/222-2365; Underground: Buchanan St.). This outlet offers 400 computers and good rates. Only £1 ($1.60) can buy 40 minutes or even 3 hours, depending on demand. Open daily 7am to 10:30pm.

Laundry/Dry Cleaning Try the **Park Laundrette,** 14 Park Rd. (℗ 0141/337-1285; Underground: Kelvin Bridge), open Monday to Friday 8:30am to 7:30pm and Saturday and Sunday 9am to 5pm.

Library The **Mitchell Library** is on North Street at Kent Road (℗ 0141/287-2999; bus: 57). One of the largest libraries in Europe, it's a massive 19th-century pile. Newspapers and books, as well as miles of microfilm, are available. It's open Monday to Thursday 9am to 8pm and Friday and Saturday 9am to 5pm.

Pharmacies The best is **Boots,** 200 Sauchiehall St. (© **0141/332-1925;** bus: 57), open Monday to Saturday 8:30am to 6pm, and Sunday 11am to 5pm.

Newspapers & Magazines Published since 1783, the *Herald* is the major newspaper with national, international, and financial news, sports, and cultural listings; the *Evening Times* offers local news.

Police In a real emergency, call © **999.** For other inquiries, contact police headquarters at © **0141/532-2000.**

Post Office The main branch is at 47 St. Vincent's St. (© **0141/204-3689;** Underground: Buchanan St.; bus: 6, 8, or 16). It's open Monday to Friday 8:30am to 5:45pm and Saturday 9am to 5:30pm.

Restrooms They can be found at rail stations, bus stations, air terminals, restaurants, hotels, pubs, and department stores. Glasgow also has a system of public toilets, often marked "wc." Don't hesitate to use them, but they're likely to be closed late in the evening.

Safety Glasgow is the most dangerous city in Scotland, but it's relatively safe when compared to cities of its size in the United States. Muggings do occur, and often they're related to Glasgow's rather large drug problem. The famed razor gangs of Calton, Bridgeton, and the Gorbals are no longer around to earn the city a reputation for violence, but you still should stay alert.

Weather Call the Glasgow Weather Centre at © **01891/248-7272.**

3 Where to Stay

It's important to reserve your room well in advance (say, 2 months beforehand), especially in late July and August. Glasgow's rates are generally higher than those in Edinburgh, but many business hotels offer bargains on weekends. The airport and the downtown branches of Glasgow's tourist office offer an **Advance Reservations Service**—with 2 weeks' notice, you can book your hotel by calling © **0141/221-0049.** The cost for this service is £3 ($4.50).

MERCHANT CITY
VERY EXPENSIVE

Millennium Hotel Glasgow 🌟🌟🌟   Following a $5 million upgrade, this striking landmark, the original Copthorne from 1810, is now better than ever. It stands near Queen Street Station where trains depart for the north of Scotland. When its high-ceilinged public rooms were renovated, designers searched out antiques and glistening marble panels to give it the aura of the Victorian era. Even though the building is old, it has been completely modernized with all the amenities and services you'd expect of such a highly rated hotel.

The decor is lighter and more comfortable than ever before. Guest rooms are among the finest in Glasgow, with new furnishings and first-class bathrooms. The best accommodations are at the front of the building facing St. George Square; less desirable are those in the rear, which have no view.

The Millennium's new managers have installed some of the best and most elegant drinking and dining facilities in Glasgow, including the classic Brasserie on George Square.

Glasgow Accommodations & Dining

ACCOMMODATIONS ■

Albion Hotel **1**
Ambassador Hotel **2**
Argyll Hotel **11**
The ArtHouse **22**
Babbity Bowster **32**
Brunswick Hotel **30**
The Corus Hotel **27**

Hilton Glasgow Hotel **18**
Kelvin Park Lorne Hotel **10**
Kirkland House **13**
Kirklee Hotel **5**
Langs **23**
Malmaison **20**
Manor Park Hotel **6**
Millennium Hotel Glasgow **24**

Number Thirty-six **14**
One Devonshire Gardens **5**
Quality Hotel Glasgow **26**
Theatre Hotel **19**
Town House **6**
Wickets Hotel **7**

DINING ◆

Air Organic **12**
Amaryllis **5**
ArtHouse Grill **22**
Ashoka West End **9**
The Belfry **17**
Brasserie Malmaison **20**
The Buttery **17**

Café Cossachok **35**
Café Gandolfi **34**
Cameron's **18**
City Merchant **33**
Corinthian **31**
Ho Wong Restaurant **28**
Koh-i-Noor **16**
La Parmigiana **5**

Mitchell's Charing Cross **15**
October **29**
Rogano **25**
Stravaigin **3**
Two Fat Ladies **8**
Ubiquitous Chip **5**
Windows Restaurant **21**

George Square, Glasgow G2 1DS. ℰ **0141/332-6711.** Fax 0141/332-4264. www.millenniumhotels.com. 117 units. £198—£350 ($317–$560) double, £258–£410 ($413–$656) suite. AE, DC, MC, V. Parking: £5 ($8) underground: Buchanan St. **Amenities:** Restaurant; 2 bars; concierge; car rental; business center; 24-hr. room service; babysitting; same-day laundry/dry cleaning service. *In room:* A/C, TV, dataport, minibar, coffeemaker, hair dryer, iron/ironing board, safe, trouser press.

MODERATE

Babbity Bowster *Value* In Merchant City, this small but delightful Robert Adam–designed hotel doubles as an art gallery. The guest rooms vary in size but are all attractive, with Victorian reproductions and white-lace bedding (some with shower only). The hotel attracts students and faculty from Strathclyde University and displays the work of Glaswegian artists (most are for sale). In summer, there's an outdoor barbecue area.

16–18 Blackfriars St., Glasgow G1 1PE. ℰ **0141/552-5055.** Fax 0141/552-7774. 5 units. £70 ($112) double. Rates include Scottish breakfast. AE, MC, V. Free parking. Underground: Buchanan St. **Amenities:** Restaurant; bar; limited room service. *In room:* TV, coffeemaker, hair dryer, no phone.

Brunswick Hotel ✯ *Finds* In the Merchant City area, this new structure stands in dramatic contrast between two old warehouses, each 5 centuries old. A trendy minimalist design prevails, from the leather-walled restaurant to the bedrooms with their sleek look. The rooms are soothing and inviting with neutral tones, exceedingly comfortable mattresses, and tiny but adequate bathrooms (most with both tub and shower).

106–108 Brunswick St., Glasgow G1 1TF. ℰ **0141/552-0001.** Fax 0141/552-1551. www.brunswickhotel. co.uk. 18 units. £55–£95 ($88–$152) double. Rates include buffet breakfast. AE, DC, MC, V. Underground: Buchanan St. **Amenities:** Restaurant; bar; 24-hr. room service; laundry/dry cleaning service. *In room:* TV, dataport (in most rooms), coffeemaker, hair dryer.

GLASGOW CENTER
VERY EXPENSIVE

Hilton Glasgow Hotel ✯✯✯ *Kids* Glasgow's only government-rated five-star hotel occupies Scotland's tallest building (20 floors). Dignified and modern, it rises in the heart of the city's business district, near the northern end of Argyle Street and exit 18 (Charing Cross) of M8. The good-size guest rooms—plush and conservative, popular with both vacationers and business travelers—offer fine views as far as the Clyde dockyards. The executive floors enjoy the enhanced facilities of a semiprivate club. The youthful staff is alert and helpful.

1 William St., Glasgow G3 8HT. ℰ **800/445-8667** in the U.S. and Canada, or 0141/204-5555. Fax 0141/ 204-5004. www.Glasgow.hilton.com. 331 units. £94–£190 ($150–$304) double; £134–£230 ($214–$368) suite. Weekend discounts often available. AE, DC, MC, V. Parking £5 ($8). Bus: 62. **Amenities:** 2 restaurants; bar; indoor heated pool; exercise room; sauna; concierge; business center; salon; 24-hr. room service; massage; babysitting; laundry/dry cleaning service. *In room:* A/C, TV, minibar, coffeemaker, hair dryer, iron/ironing board, safe, trouser press.

EXPENSIVE

Langs ✯ *Finds* If you're looking for Victorian Glasgow, head elsewhere. But if you gravitate to a minimalist Japanese style, check in here in this trendy and exceedingly contemporary hotel close to the Buchanan Galleries Shopping Mall and the Glasgow Royal Concert Hall. A diverse medley of bedrooms in various shapes, sizes, and configurations await you, but each has a certain flair. Nothing is overly adorned here, yet comfort and style, along with different colors and textures, make every unit a winner. The smallest are the studios, but you can also rent a duplex, a theme suite, or a very large suite. The beautifully-kept bathrooms contain such extras as power showers with body jets. Nothing is evocative of Glasgow in any way. To emphasize the Asian theme all the more, Japanese body treatments are offered in the on-site Oshi Spa.

You can feast on both a Mediterranean cuisine as well as an array of light fusion foods, including teriyaki and sushi, in the hotel's two restaurants

2 Port Dundas Place, Glasgow G2 3LD. © **0141/333-1500.** Fax 0141/333-5700. www.langshotels.com. 100 units. £110–£140 ($176–$224) double; £160–£210 ($256–$336) suite. AE, DC, MC, V. Underground: Queen Street Station. **Amenities:** 2 restaurants; bar; exercise room; spa; sauna; 24-hour room service; massage; laundry/dry cleaning service. *In room:* TV, minibar, hair dryer, coffeemaker, iron/ironing board.

Malmaison ★★ *Finds*   This place beats out all competitors in having the best contemporary interior. The hip hotel opened in 1994 in a historically important building constructed in the 1830s as a Greek Orthodox church. Inside, few of the original details remain—the decor is sleek and ultramodern. In 1997, an annex—designed to preserve the architectural character of the church's exterior—was added to provide additional guest rooms. Bedrooms vary in size from smallish to average, but are chic and appointed with extras like CD players, specially commissioned art, and top-of-the-line toiletries.

278 W. George St., Glasgow G2 4LL. © **0141/572-1000.** Fax 0141/572-1002. www.malmaison.com. 72 units. £125 ($200) double; from £145 ($232) suite. AE, DC, MC, V. Parking nearby £7 ($11). Bus: 11. **Amenities:** Restaurant; 2 bars; exercise room; 24-hr. room service; babysitting; laundry/dry cleaning service. *In room:* A/C, TV, dataport, minibar, coffeemaker, hair dryer, iron/ironing board, safe.

MODERATE

The ArtHouse ★★ *Finds*   Acclaimed for its contemporary interior, this 1911 Edwardian building, 6 blocks northwest of Central Station, originally housed school board offices. Today, it's one of the most striking hotels in Glasgow, with dramatic colors and textures blending in perfectly with the older structure. Commissioned art and period pieces evoke some of the original Edwardian splendor, although everything has been given a modern overlay with rich, bold tones. Sleek furniture and state-of-the-art bathrooms are grace notes. The restaurant is one of the city's finest (see "Where to Dine," later in this chapter).

(Kids Family-Friendly Hotels

One Devonshire Gardens (p. 174)   Although this elegant hotel is full of antiques, it's happy to cater to kids with toys, cots, and highchairs. There's an interconnecting bedroom that's perfect for families to book. Children are offered appropriate videos, and there are special facilities for heating food and sterilizing bottles. The restaurant is fully prepared to cook meals that kids adore, like pizza or fish fingers.

Hilton Glasgow Hotel (p. 172)   Children arriving on the weekend are presented with fun packs, containing drawings, games, bubble bath, and comics. Kids will enjoy the pool. Cots and highchairs are available. Minsky's offers kids' meals, and room service is more than happy to provide the likes of sausages or chicken nuggets.

Kirklee Hotel (p. 176)   This small hotel lies in a safe area near the university and the Botanic Gardens where guests often go for a stroll or a picnic every night. Some of its comfortably and attractively furnished bedrooms are big enough to house small families.

129 Bath St., Glasgow G2 2SY. ℂ **0141/221-6789.** Fax 0141/221-6777. www.arthousehotel.com. 65 units. £110–£150 ($176–$240) double. AE, DC, MC, V. Underground: St. Enoch. **Amenities:** 2 restaurants; 2 bars; salon; 24-hr. room service; laundry/dry cleaning service. *In room:* TV, dataport, minibar, hair dryer.

Quality Hotel Glasgow   When it opened in 1883 by the rail station, this was the grandest hotel Glasgow had seen, the landmark of the city's most famous street. Now restored to at least a glimmer of its former glory, the place may be too old-fashioned for some, but traditionalists like it. The baronial wooden staircase has been stripped and refinished, and sandblasting the facade revealed elaborate Victorian cornices and pilasters. The guest rooms, with an uninspired decor, are priced according to size and plumbing.

99 Gordon St., Glasgow G1 3SF. ℂ **0141/221-9680.** Fax 0141/226-3948. www.quality-hotels-glasgow.com 222 units. £90–£105 ($144–$168) double; £140 ($224) suite. AE, DC, DISC, MC, V. Parking £9.20 ($15) overnight. Underground: Central Station. **Amenities:** Restaurant; 2 bars; indoor pool; exercise room; Jacuzzi; sauna; 24-hr. room service; laundry/dry cleaning service. *In room:* TV, dataport (on request), coffeemaker, hair dryer, iron/ironing board, trouser press.

INEXPENSIVE

The Corus Hotel *Value*   Two blocks west of the central rail depot, this contemporary seven-story hotel is surrounded by dreary commercial buildings, but is a viable budget option in the center of Glasgow. You check into a rather cramped area, but once upstairs, the rooms are more inviting—although they, too, are small. Location, location, location is what sells this property.

377 Argyle St. (opposite Cadogan Sq.), Glasgow G2 8LL. ℂ **0141/248-2355.** Fax 0141/221-1014. 121 units. £70–£95 ($112–$152) double. AE, DC, MC, V. Underground: St. Enoch. **Amenities:** Restaurant; bar; 24-hr. room service; laundry/dry cleaning service. *In room:* TV, hair dryer.

Kirkland House   On a quiet street about a 10-minute walk from the Glasgow Art Gallery and Museum, the university, and the Scottish Exhibition Centre, the Kirkland is an impeccably maintained 1832 Victorian crescent house. A mix of antiques and reproductions is used in the large guest rooms, each equipped with a shower-only bathroom. You get a warm welcome from owners Carole and Ewing Divers and their daughter Sally. Ewing is a keen admirer of American swing music and displays a collection of 78-rpm gramophone records, old photographs, and pictures. You're welcome to listen to recordings of Harry James, Benny Goodman, and many others.

42 St. Vincent Crescent, Glasgow G3 8NG. ℂ **0141/248-3458.** Fax 0141/221-5174. www.kirkland.net43. co.uk. 5 units. £65 ($104) double. Rates include continental breakfast. No credit cards. Free parking. Underground: Exhibition Centre. *In room:* TV, coffeemaker, no phone.

THE WEST END
VERY EXPENSIVE

One Devonshire Gardens ★★★ *Kids*   This hotel tops even perfection, beating out the Hilton Glasgow and all others as the most glamorous, most elegant, and most tranquil hotel in Scotland. Its Amaryllis restaurant also serves a finer cuisine than any of the major Glasgow restaurants (see "Where to Dine," later in this chapter). In the Hyndland district just west of the center, the house at no. 1 was built in 1880 and is now even more elegant than it was in its heyday. At the ring of the doorbell, a pair of Edwardian chambermaids with frilly aprons and dust bonnets appear to welcome you. Each of the eight guest rooms in this building is furnished in period style, with lots of luxurious accessories. The success of no. 1 led to the acquisition of nos. 2 and 3. The newer rooms have the same elegant touches and high price tags.

1 Devonshire Gardens, Glasgow G12 0UX. ℭ **0141/339-2001**. Fax 0141/337-1663. www.onedevonshire
gardens.com. 38 units. £125–£185 ($200–$296) double; £345–£475 ($552–$760) suite. AE, DC, MC, V. Free
parking. Underground: Hillhead. **Amenities:** 2 restaurants; bar; 24-hr. room service; laundry/dry cleaning
service. *In room:* TV, minibar, hair dryer, iron/ironing board, safe.

MODERATE

Kelvin Park Lorne Hotel ⭐ *Finds*   This discreet hotel is located in the heart
of the residential West End. The hotel consists of an early-19th-century building (four floors) and a later five-story structure. The public rooms—including
the bar—are in the style of early-1900s Scottish designer Charles Rennie Mackintosh. The guest rooms were renovated in 1995, resulting in a kind of neutral
contemporary comfort; they vary in size, the older ones being noticeably larger.
Most of the bathrooms are equipped with combination tub and shower.

923 Sauchiehall St., Glasgow G3 7TE. ℭ **0141/314-9955**. Fax 0141/337-1659. www.regalhotels.co.uk
100 units. £75 ($120) double; £120 ($192) suite. AE, DC, MC, V. Free parking. Underground: Kelvin Hall.
Amenities: Restaurant; bar; 24-hr. room service; laundry/dry cleaning service. *In room:* TV, coffeemaker, hair
dryer, trouser press.

Manor Park Hotel   This impressive West End town house was a private
home when it was built in 1895 in the closing years of Victoria's reign. In 1947
it was converted into a hotel, and it has been much improved and upgraded
since that time. Owners Angus and Catherine MacDonald—true Scots to the
core, both of whom speak Gaelic—offer grand Scottish hospitality. Naturally,
with such a Scottish background, they freely use the tartan when decorating.
Their home is a blend of modern and traditional furnishings, including beechwood pieces set against a background floral wallpaper. Each guest room comes
with a neat little bathroom with either tub or shower.

28 Balshagray Dr., Glasgow G11 7DD. ℭ **0141/339-2143**. Fax 0141/339-5842. www.manorparkhotel.com.
9 units. £67–£75 ($107–$120) double. Rates include full breakfast. AE, MC, V. Free parking. Underground:
Partick Station. *In room:* TV, hair dryer, coffeemaker, trouser press.

Theatre Hotel ⭐ *Finds*   This late 19th-century theater and dance has been
handsomely and cozily converted into a charming hotel. The guest rooms are
tastefully and comfortably furnished, and all the modern in-room amenities
have been installed in spite of all the traditional architectural details such as
wood paneling and stained glass. Rooms range from small to spacious; the larger
units are more contemporary in styling. In lieu of a dining room, breakfast is
served in your bedroom.

25-27 Elmbank St., just off Sauchiehall St. Glasgow G2 4PB. ℭ **0141/227-2712**. Fax 0141/227-2774.
www.theatrehotel.activehotels.com/FIL. 58 units. £60–£80 ($96–$128) double; £90 ($144) triple. Rates
include breakfast. MC, V. Parking nearby £7.50 ($12). Underground: Cowcaddens. **Amenities:** Room service
7–9am; business center; laundry/dry cleaning service. *In room:* TV, dataport, fridge, coffeemaker, hair dryer,
trouser press.

Town House ⭐⭐ *Value*   This is one of the most upmarket and charming of
the B&Bs of Glasgow. The stone-built Victorian terraced house has been successfully converted to receive guests to its tranquil little cul-de-sac tucked away
in the West End, with a tennis club in the back and a rugby club to the front.
The place justifiably wins praise from its many repeat visitors. The hospitality,
the comfort level, and the atmosphere are first rate. Guests may gather in the living room with its many books and coal-burning fireplace. The large bedrooms
have been faithfully restored and have first-rate private bathrooms with showers.
The high quality furnishings, including many traditional wooden pieces, are set
against a decor of blue or yellow.

4 Hughenden Terrace, Glasgow G12 9XR. ℂ **0141/357-0862.** Fax 0141/339-9605. www.thetownhouse glasgow.com. 10 units. £72–£84 ($115–$134) double. Rates include Scottish breakfast. MC, V. Free parking. Underground: Hillhead. **Amenities:** Bar; limited room service; laundry. *In room:* TV, dataport, coffeemaker, hair dryer, iron/ironing board.

The Wickets Hotel   Better known for its restaurant and bar than for its comfortable guest rooms, this hotel from the 1890s is an undiscovered West End gem, opposite one of the city's largest cricket grounds (the West of Scotland Cricket Club). The bedrooms are pleasantly spacious, each with a cheerful decor.

The **Conservatory Restaurant** is a glamour spot, serving up moderately priced regional and Continental fare amidst a setting of old photos of local cricket teams. Adjacent is one of the few open-air beer gardens in Glasgow, where meals can be eaten alfresco. Randall's Wine Bar sells wine by the glass in an Art Deco setting.

52–54 Fortrose St., Glasgow G11 5LP. ℂ and fax **0141/334-9334.** www.wicketshotel.co.uk. 11 units. £70 ($112) double; £88 ($141) family room. Rates include Scottish breakfast. AE, MC, V. Free parking. Underground: Partick. **Amenities:** Restaurant; 2 bars; 24-hr. room service; laundry/dry cleaning service. *In room:* TV coffeemaker.

INEXPENSIVE

Albion Hotel   This unpretentious hotel was formed by connecting two nearly identical beige-sandstone row houses. In the heart of Glasgow's West End, it offers high-ceilinged guest rooms with modern furniture and small refrigerators. All the units contain a shower-only bathroom. If your hotel needs are simple, you'll likely be happy here.

405–407 N. Woodside Rd., Glasgow G20 6NN. ℂ **0141/339-8620.** Fax 0141/334-8159. www.glasgow hotelsandapartments.co.uk. 16 units. £49–£60 ($78–$96) double. Rates include breakfast. AE, DC, MC, V. Free parking. Underground: Kelvin Bridge. **Amenities:** Bar; laundry. *In room:* TV, dataport, fridge, coffeemaker, hair dryer, iron/ironing board, safe, trouser press.

Ambassador Hotel ⭐ *Value*   Across from the BBC Studios and the Botanic Gardens, and overlooking the Kelvin River, this small hotel in a circa-1900 Edwardian town house is one of the better B&Bs in Glasgow. After a refurbishment in 2002, the hotel is looking quite stylish. Each of the individually decorated and attractively furnished bedrooms has a well-maintained bathroom with tub or shower. The hotel is well situated for exploring the West End, with several art galleries nearby and many good restaurants or brasseries close at hand.

7 Kelvin Dr., Glasgow G20 8QJ. ℂ **01419/461018.** Fax 01419/455377. www.glasgowhotelsandapartments. co.uk. 16 units. £58 ($93) double without breakfast; £66 ($106) double with breakfast.. AE, DC, MC, V. Free parking. Underground: Hillhead. **Amenities:** Bar; laundry. *In room:* TV (w/VCR and DVD players available upon request), coffeemaker, hair dryer, iron/ironing board, safe, trouser press.

Argyll Hotel   This hotel is small but special, a Georgian building near Glasgow University, the Art Gallery and Museum, the Kelvin Hall International Sports Arena, and the Scottish Exhibition Centre. Although completely modernized and comfortable, it shows a healthy respect for tradition.

969–973 Sauchiehall St., Glasgow G3 7TQ. ℂ **0141/337-3313.** Fax 0141/337-3283. www.argyllhotel glasgow.co.uk. 38 units. £72 ($115) double. Rates include Scottish breakfast. AE, MC, V. Parking on nearby streets. Underground: Kelvin Hall. Bus: 9, 16, 42, 57, 62, or 64. **Amenities:** Restaurant; bar; limited room service; laundry/dry cleaning service. *In room:* TV, coffeemaker, hair dryer, iron/ironing board.

Kirklee Hotel *Kids*   This red-sandstone Edwardian terraced house is near the university, the Botanic Gardens, and the major art galleries. It is graced with a rose garden that has won several awards. Guests arriving at the ornate stained-glass front door will be welcomed by owners Rosemary and Douglas Rosen. Most of the high-ceilinged guest rooms are of average size but some are large enough to accommodate families. For guests who request it, breakfast is served in their room.

11 Kensington Gate, Glasgow G12 9LG. ☎ **0141/334-5555**. Fax 0141/339-3828. www.kirkleehotel.co.uk. 9 units. £68 ($109) double; £75–£95 ($120–$152) family room. Rates include Scottish breakfast. MC, V. Parking nearby. Underground: Hillhead. **Amenities:** Bar. *In room:* TV, coffeemaker, hair dryer, trouser press.

Number Thirty-Six   In the heart of the West End, this hotel occupies the two lower floors of a four-story sandstone building that was conceived as an apartment house in 1848. Hardworking entrepreneur John MacKay maintains the high-ceilinged pastel guest rooms in fine working order. Each is equipped with a tidy, shower-only bathroom.

36 St. Vincent Crescent, Glasgow G3 8NG. ☎ **0141/248-2086**. Fax 0141/221-1477. www.no36.co.uk. 5 units. £50–£60 ($80–$96) double. No credit cards. Bus: 42, 63, or 64. **Amenities:** Room service (7:30–9am).

4 Where to Dine

The days are long gone when a meal out in Glasgow meant mutton pie and chips. Some of the best Scottish food is served here (especially lamb from the Highlands, salmon, trout, Aberdeen Angus steaks, and exotic delights like moor grouse), and there's an ever-increasing number of ethnic restaurants. This still being Britain, however, you'll find the usual fish-and-chip joints, burger outlets, fried-chicken eateries, and endless pubs. Many restaurants close on Sunday, and most are shut by 2:30pm, reopening again for dinner around 6pm.

Note: For the locations of the restaurants below, see the "Glasgow Accommodations & Dining" map, on p. 170.

MERCHANT CITY
EXPENSIVE
Rogano ✿✿ SEAFOOD   Rogano boasts a perfectly preserved Art Deco interior from 1935, when Messrs. Rogers and Anderson combined their talents and names to create a restaurant that has hosted virtually every star of the British film industry. You can enjoy dinner amid lapis-lazuli clocks, etched mirrors, ceiling fans, semicircular banquettes, and potted palms. The menu always emphasizes seafood, such as halibut in champagne-and-oyster sauce and lobster grilled or Thermidor.

A less expensive menu is offered down in the **Cafe Rogano,** where main courses begin at £9.50 ($15).

11 Exchange Place. ☎ **0141/248-4055**. Reservations recommended. Main courses £17.50–£33.50 ($28–$54); fixed-price lunch £16.50 ($26). AE, DC, MC, V. Restaurant daily noon–2:30pm and 6:30–10:30pm; cafe Mon–Thurs noon–11pm, Fri–Sat noon–midnight, Sun noon–11pm. Underground: Buchanan St.

MODERATE
Café Cossachok ✿ *Finds* RUSSIAN   Before the opening of this restaurant near the Tron Theatre, Glasgow was about the last place you'd look for Russian cuisine. A favorite with a lot of actors appearing at the theater nearby, this is an inviting oasis with its beautiful and authentic Russian decor, including plenty of mahogany pieces and ample use of the color of red.

The chefs concentrate mainly on Russian fare but are also adept at turning out a selection of Armenian, Georgian, and Ukrainian dishes. Come here to feat on all the famous Russian dishes such as borscht and savory blinis. The beef Stroganoff, served with fried straw potatoes, is the finest we've had in Scotland.

Chicken Vladimir, a breaded breast of chicken with a mushroom sauce resting under a cheese topping, is another excellent offering. Cossachok's moussaka successfully blends eggplant, tomatoes, mushrooms, soy beans, garlic, and coriander spicing, and Zakuski Tzar is a tasty version of home-baked pork flavored with garlic and served with a dip inspired by the kitchens of Georgia.

10 King St., Merchant City. ✆ **0141/553-0733.** Reservations recommended. Main courses £7–£13 ($11–$21); pre-theater 2-course dinner (5–7pm) £9.95 ($16). MC, V. Tues-Sun 11am–3pm and 6–11pm; Sun 3–11pm. Underground: St. Enoch.

October ⭐ INTERNATIONAL   At the top of the Princes Square shopping district, this bar and restaurant offers a widely diverse cuisine. Of the several vegetarian dishes, one of the best is a type of potato sandwich filled with roasted vegetables. There's a wide array of choices—everything from club sandwiches to mussels with white wine to bites like potato wedges and nachos. For dessert, try the raspberry tart.

The Rooftop, Princes Square, Buchanan St. ✆ **0141/221-0303.** Reservations recommended. Main courses £5.95–£8.50 ($9.50–$14). AE, MC, V. Mon–Fri noon–9pm; Sat 12:30–4:30pm. Underground: St. Enoch.

INEXPENSIVE

Cafe Gandolfi SCOTTISH/FRENCH *(Kids)*   Many students and young professionals will tell you this popular place in Merchant City is their favorite "caff"—you may sometimes have to wait for a table. A remake of a Victorian pub, it boasts rustic wooden floors, benches, and stools. If you don't fill up on soups and salads, try smoked venison with *gratin dauphinois* or smoked pheasant with an onion tartlet in winter. Vegetarians will find solace here.

64 Albion St. ✆ **0141/552-6813.** Reservations recommended on weekends. Main courses £7.50–£16 ($12–$26). MC, V. Mon–Sat 9am–11pm; Sun noon–11pm. Underground: St. Enoch/Cannon St.

Corinthian INTERNATIONAL   This restaurant in Lanarkshire House opened in 2000 with a 7.5m (25-ft.) illuminated glass dome as its stunning centerpiece. Crystal chandeliers and rococo friezes make for a luxurious atmosphere. The menu is based on the freshest products available. You might feast on tender lamb brochettes from Highland sheep or an enticing grilled tuna. In the two bars, you can relax on Italian leather sofas while listening to music spun by the local DJ.

191 Ingram St. ✆ **0141/552-1101.** Reservations recommended. Main courses £12–£15.95 ($19–$26); fixed-price pre-theater dinner (daily 5:30–7pm) £9.75 ($16) for 2 courses, £12.50 ($20) for 3 courses. AE, MC, V. Mon–Sat 11am–3am; Sun noon–3am. Underground: St. Enoch.

GLASGOW CENTER
VERY EXPENSIVE

Cameron's ⭐⭐ MODERN SCOTTISH   Outfitted like a baronial hunting lodge in the wilds of the Highlands, Cameron's is most glamorous restaurant in Glasgow's best hotel. The chef's conservative menu holds few surprises, but is a celebration of market-fresh ingredients deftly prepared. Small slip-ups sometimes mar the effect of a dish or two, but we have always come away pleased. Your best bet is to stay Scottish when ordering. Go with whisky-cured Isle of Arran salmon, confit of Highland duck, or Firth of Lorne sea scallops—and those are only the appetizers. For a main course, we recommend the rack of Scottish lamb with a crust of whisky-steeped oatmeal and Arran mustard.

In the Hilton Glasgow Hotel, 1 William St. ✆ **0141/204-5555.** Reservations recommended. Set-price menu £28 ($45) for 2 courses, £33 ($53) for 3 courses. AE, DC, MC, V. Mon–Fri noon–1:45pm and 7–9:45pm; Sat 7–9:45pm. Bus: 6A, 16, or 62.

⬭Kids Family-Friendly Restaurants

Brasserie Malmaison (p. 180)   Dining here is like taking your kid to church—well, not really. The former Greek Orthodox church has given way to a Scottish and Continental cuisine. The chefs serve some of the city's best fries, salmon cakes, and grilled chicken dishes. Adjacent to the brasserie is a cafe with fresh salads, sandwiches, and pizzas.

Cafe Gandolfi (p. 178)   Children always find something to order here, and the staff offers half portions of all main courses. The chef also cooks up constantly changing plates for kids. Of course, the main course has to be followed by one of Cafe Gandolfi's homemade ice creams, the best in the city.

Willow Tea Room (p. 181)   Thousands of locals fondly remember coming here as children to enjoy delectable pastries and ice cream dishes—and it's still a big treat for any kid.

EXPENSIVE

The Buttery ⭐ SCOTTISH/FRENCH   This is the perfect hunter's restaurant, with oak panels and an air of baronial splendor. The anteroom bar used to be the pulpit of a church, and the waitresses wear high-necked costumes of which Queen Victoria would have approved. Menu items include smoked trout, rare roast beef, terrine of Scottish seafood, venison, and tuna steak with tarragon and tomato-butter sauce.

Adjacent is the Oyster Bar, outfitted in church-inspired Victoriana; its menu is shorter and a bit less expensive. The Belfry, which is less formal, is in the cellar (see below).

652 Argyle St. ☏ 0141/221-8188. Reservations recommended. Set-price menu £32 ($51) for 2 courses, £36 ($58) for 3 courses; Oyster Bar lunch main courses £12–£15 ($19–$24). AE, DC, MC, V. Mon–Fri noon–2:30pm; Mon–Sat 6–10:30pm. Underground: St. Enoch.

MODERATE

ArtHouse Grill ⭐ *Finds* CONTINENTAL   This sophisticated, modern enclave inhabits one of Glasgow's most unusual hotels. A Japanese teppanyaki grill serves as a stage for the theatrical experience of a meal here. Dig into the sage-flavored pork chop served with caramelized apples or the tender lamb shank braised to perfection and served with a mint-flavored couscous. For a snack and refreshment, there's an oyster bar and cocktail lounge.

In the ArtHouse Hotel, 129 Bath St. ☏ 0141/221-6789. Reservations required. Main courses £12–£35 ($19–$56). AE, DC, MC, V. Mon–Sat noon–3pm and 6–10pm. Underground: Buchanan St.

The Belfry ⭐ SCOTTISH/FRENCH   The pews, pulpits, and stained glass that adorn this place are from a church in northern England. It's the only pub in Glasgow where you can contemplate Christ in Majesty while you enjoy a pint of ale. The kitchen produces daily specials like steak pie with roast potatoes; roast rack of lamb with rosemary, thyme, and caramelized shallots; and the Belfry mussel bowl with shallots. The cook is well known for making clever use of fresh Scottish produce.

In the basement of the Buttery (see above), 652 Argyle St. ☏ 0141/221-0630. Reservations recommended. Main courses £9–£13 ($14–$21). AE, MC, V. Fri–Sat 6:30–9:30pm. Underground: St. Enoch.

Brasserie Malmaison (Kids) SCOTTISH/CONTINENTAL In a hip hotel converted from a Greek Orthodox church (see "Where to Stay," earlier in this chapter), this restaurant in the crypt, beneath the original vaults, serves imaginative food in a dark, masculine setting, with a large bar and wooden banquettes. Menu items arrive in generous portions and include French-style rumpsteak with garlic butter and pommes frites, salmon fish cakes with spinach, and grilled chicken with roasted red-pepper salsa.

In contrast, the greenhouse-inspired **Champagne Bar,** adjacent to the brasserie, has a menu of salads, sandwiches, pizzas, light platters, and—you guessed it—champagne.

In the Malmaison Hotel, 278 W. George St. ℂ **0141/572-1000.** Reservations recommended for dinner Thurs–Sun. Brasserie main courses £10.50–£16.50 ($17–$26). AE, DC, MC, V. Brasserie daily noon–2:30pm and 5:30–10:30pm; Champagne Bar daily 10am–midnight. Bus: 11.

City Merchant SCOTTISH/INTERNATIONAL This cozy restaurant in the heart of the city offers friendly service, an extensive menu, and service throughout the day. The cuisine is more reliable than stunning, but it delivers quite an array of well-prepared fresh food at a good price. Try the roast breast of duck, rack of lamb, or escalope of venison. Also tempting are the fast-seared scallops and classic smoked haddock. Some of the desserts evoke old-time Scotland, such as the clootie dumpling, made with flour, spices, and fried fruit and served with home-churned butter.

97–99 Candlebiggs. ℂ **0141/553-1577.** Reservations recommended. Main courses £7.95–£24.95 ($13–$40); fixed-price lunch £9.50–£12 ($15–$19). AE, DC, MC, V. Mon–Sat noon–10:30pm. Underground: St. Enoch.

Ho Wong Restaurant ⚜ CANTONESE One of the city's finest Chinese restaurants, Jimmy Ho and David Wong opened this remote outpost of their Hong Kong establishment 2 blocks from the Central Station. There are at least eight duck dishes on the menu, along with four types of fresh lobster and some sizzling platters.

82 York St. ℂ **0141/221-3550.** Reservations required. Main courses £15–£20 ($24–$32); fixed-price 2-course lunch £8.90 ($14); fixed-price banquet £27 ($43) (5-courses). AE, DC, MC, V. Mon–Sat noon–2pm and 6pm–midnight; Sun 6pm–midnight. Underground: Central Station.

Mitchell's Charing Cross MODERN SCOTTISH Named for its location near Glasgow's largest library (the Mitchell), this upscale bistro offers Scottish cuisine moderne in a large room lined with plants and paintings. Options may include red snapper, grouper, and salmon netted off the Hebridean coast; duck; and haggis with fresh tatties (potatoes), neeps (turnips), and chive mayonnaise. Consider dropping in for a pint in the basement bar.

157 North St., Charing Cross. ℂ **0141/204-4312.** Reservations recommended. Main courses £4–£8 ($6.40–$13) at lunch, £8–£18 ($13–$29) at dinner; fixed-price pre-theater supper (5–7pm) £9.95–£11.95 ($16–$19). AE, DC, MC, V. Tues–Fri noon–2:30pm; Tues–Sat 5pm–midnight. Bus: 23 or 57.

Two Fat Ladies ⚜ MODERN BRITISH/SEAFOOD This ranks high on the list of everybody's favorite restaurants, especially for irreverent diners who appreciate the unexpected. The "Two Fat Ladies" are its street number—a nickname for the number 88 in Scotland's church-sponsored bingo games (there's no connection to the "Two Fat Ladies" of TV Food Network fame). The custard-colored decor is minimalist and "post-punk." The restaurant packs in crowds for specialties like pan-fried squid salad with coriander-flavored yogurt sauce, grilled chicken salad with apple chutney, and charcoal-grilled king scallops with tomato-basil sauce. The best dessert is the Pavlova (a chewy meringue) with summer berries and Drambuie sauce.

88 Dumbarton Rd. ✆ **0141/339-1944.** Reservations recommended. Fixed-price lunch £10.95–£12.95 ($18–$21); fixed-price pre-theater supper (6–7pm) £10.95–£12.95 ($18–$21); main courses £14–£16.95 ($22–$27). MC, V. Mon–Sat noon–3pm and daily 6–10pm. Bus: 16, 42, or 57.

Windows Restaurant ✸ SCOTTISH   On the 7th floor of the Carlton George Hotel, this restaurant is aptly named, as it opens onto panoramic views of Glasgow. It doesn't stop there, however, as its chefs feature an innovative menu prepared with a high standard of ingredients. Diners get a true "Taste of Scotland" with such dishes as seared West Coast scallops or the grilled filet of Scottish beef with chanterelle mushrooms. You might also try such other Scottish delights as a tomato and mozzarella stuffed in a pastry or a grilled tuna steak with herb noodles and soy dressing. For dessert, opt for the freshly baked lemon tart or the fresh raspberries flavored with lime.

In the Carlton George Hotel, 44 West George St. ✆ **0141/353-6373.** Reservations recommended. Main courses £12.95–£15.95 ($21–$26); 2-course lunch £10.95 ($18), 3-course lunch £14.95 ($24); 2-course dinner £11.95 ($19), 3-course dinner £15.95 ($26). AE, MC, V. Daily noon–2:30pm and 5–9:30pm. Underground: Buchanan Street.

THE WEST END
EXPENSIVE

Amaryllis ✸✸✸ SCOTTISH/FRENCH   One Devonshire Gardens is not only one of our favorite hotels in all of Scotland, but its on-site restaurant has blossomed into the finest in Glasgow. The venue recreates the aura—and the service—of the Edwardian Age. Drinks are served in the elegant drawing room, and you can dine amid Victoriana.

The restaurant has been taken over by Gordon Ramsey, England's most acclaimed chef. Of course, this *enfant terrible* of British cookery is hardly on site every night, but he's the consultant and supervisor. The actual chef is the talented David Dempsy, who uses only the finest of high-quality ingredients, which he fashions into a fabulous temptation for your palate.

Among his heavenly dishes are a pot-roasted rump of lamb with a truffle and potato purée along with braised shallots, a garlic confit, and thyme *jus.* Every dish we've sampled here has been superb, including a creamy risotto flavored with spring onions and fresh herbs and served with Parmesan shavings. The

---

Moments   **Tea for Two**

For tea, a light lunch, or a snack, try the famed **Willow Tea Room,** 217 Sauchiehall St. (✆ **0141/332-0521;** Underground: Cowcaddens). When it opened in 1904, the Willow became a sensation because of its Charles Rennie Mackintosh design, and it has been restored to its original condition. Thousands of locals fondly remember coming here as children to enjoy delectable pastries and ice-cream dishes—and it's still a big treat for any kid.

On the ground floor is a well-known jeweler, M. M. Henderson Ltd. The "room de luxe" is in the heart of the building, and it's fashionable to drop in for tea at any time of day. Reservations are recommended, and afternoon tea with pastry is £8.95 ($14). It's open Monday to Saturday 9am to 4:30pm and Sunday noon to 3:30pm.

---

pan-fried filet of sea bream comes with one of the kitchen's sauces that always seem to approach perfection.

In One Devonshire Gardens Hotel, 1 Devonshire Gardens, Glasgow G12 0UX. ✆ **0141/337-3434.** Reservations required. Main courses £9–£14 ($14–$22); table d'hôte menu £35 ($56). AE, MC, V. Daily 7–9:30pm. Underground: Hillhead.

Ubiquitous Chip ✿ SCOTTISH This restaurant is inside the rough-textured stone walls of a former stable; its glass-covered courtyard boasts masses of climbing vines. Upstairs is a pub where simple platters are served with pints of lager and drams of whisky; these may include chicken, leek, and white-wine casserole or finnan haddie with bacon (but no fish-and-chips, as you might think from the name). The downstairs bistro-style restaurant might feature free-range chicken, shellfish with crispy seaweed snaps, or wild rabbit. Vegetarians are catered to at both places.

12 Ashton Lane, off Byres Rd. ✆ **0141/334-5007.** Reservations recommended. Restaurant fixed-price lunch £21.50 ($34) for 2 courses, £26.50 ($42) for 3 courses; fixed-price dinner £32.50 ($52) for 2 courses, £37.50 ($60) for 3 courses; bar meals £5–£8 ($8–$13) at lunch, £10–£15 ($16–$24) at dinner. AE, DC, MC, V. Restaurant Mon–Sat noon–2:30pm, daily 5:30–11pm; bar Sun 1–11pm. Underground: Hillhead.

MODERATE

Air Organic ✿ *Finds* ORGANIC FUSION Space-age Air Organic is designed like an airport lounge, with white walls and sky-blue tables. The menu, designed to look like a plane ticket, features both organic and non-organic foods. The Thai seafood broth with coconut, lime, and coriander is exceptional, as is the Thai pumpkin curry. The restaurant also specializes in Japanese cooking, offering a variety of bento boxes. We were especially taken with the char-siu roast pork with sticky mustard apples. For dessert, there's nothing better than the steamed banana and ginger pudding. The friendly service, wide range of choices, and unique design make this a place worth visiting.

36 Kelvingrove St. ✆ **0141/564-5200.** Reservations recommended. Main courses £8–£17 ($13–$27); fixed-price 2-course dinner (daily 5–7pm) £11.95 ($19); bento boxes £12–£16.50 ($19–$26). AE, DC, MC, V. Sun–Thurs noon–10pm; Fri–Sat noon–10:30pm. Underground: Hillhead.

Ashoka West End ✿ INDIAN/PUNJABI This is a culinary landmark in Glasgow, serving the finest cuisine of the Sub-Continent. Novice chapatti chompers and vindaloo veterans alike discover this restaurant with each new generation. Many Glaswegians learned to "eat Indian" at this very restaurant. The decor is a bit eclectic, involving rugs, brass objects, murals, and greenery.

The dishes are full of flavor with a fragrant and most pleasing aroma when served. You might launch your repast with Pakora, which is deep fried chicken, mushrooms, or fish. From here you can go on to order Jalandhri, a potent fusion of ginger, garlic, onions, peppers, coconut cream, and fresh herbs which can be served with a choice of chicken, lamb, or mixed vegetables. Sing Sing Chandni is a sweet and spicy Cantonese-style dish with crispy peppers, spring onions, and cashew nuts served most often with chicken. Those preferring something less robust will find Chasni, a light and smooth creamy sauce served with chicken, lamb, or mixed vegetables.

1284 Argyle St. ✆ **0800/454-817.** Reservations required. Main courses £6–£13 ($9.60–$21). AE, DC, MC, V. Sun–Thurs 4pm–12:30am; Fri noon–1am; Sat 5pm–1am; Wed–Thurs noon–2pm. Underground: Kelvin Hall.

INEXPENSIVE

Koh-i-Noor PUNJABI INDIAN This is one of the city's top Indian restaurants. The family that runs this spacious place comes from the Punjab in Pakistan, and naturally Punjabi specialties like *paratha* and *bhuna* lamb are recommended. The Sunday Indian buffet is one of the great food values of the city; the Indian buffet held on weekdays is another treat. You can also order a three- or four-course business lunch.

235 North St., Charing Cross. ✆ 0141/221-1555. Reservations recommended. Main courses £9–£15 ($14–$24); fixed-price business lunch £4.95 ($7.90) for 3 courses, £6.95 ($11) for 4 courses; Sun–Thurs buffet £10.95 ($18); Fri–Sat buffet £12.95 ($21). AE, DC, MC, V. Sun–Thurs noon–midnight; Fri–Sat noon–1am. Underground: St. Georges.

La Parmigiana *Value* ITALIAN   This seems to be everyone's favorite trattoria, providing a cosmopolitan Continental atmosphere and a good change of pace from the typical Glasgow dining scene. Even Italians living in Glasgow swear by the food here. A long-established family dining room, it offers the usual array of pasta dishes, some especially delectable, like the lobster-stuffed ravioli in basil cream sauce. Try also the chargrilled scallops cooked quickly in olive oil and served with fresh lemon juice.

447 Great Western Rd. ✆ 0141/334-0686. Reservations required. Main courses £15–£20 ($24–$32); fixed-price lunch £9.80 ($16); fixed-price dinner £10.30–£12.50 ($16–$20). AE, DC, MC, V. Underground: Kelvinbridge.

Stravaigin ★★ GLOBAL   We've never seen any restaurant like this in Glasgow. The chef and owner truly roams the globe for inspiration. Although some of his ideas might come from as far away as China or the Caribbean, he also knows how to use the finest of the regional bounty of Scotland. Expect concoctions such as Vietnamese-inspired marinated quail served on a candy smoked eggplant concasse. Rabbit is perfectly cooked and served with lentils from the Pyrenees, while mullet comes on a bed of Thai noodles with bits of mussels and mushrooms. Many locals finish with a selection of Scottish cheeses with quince jelly and bannocks.

28 Gibson St., Hillhead. ✆ 0141/334-2665. Reservations required. Fixed-price menus (lunch or dinner) £22.95–£28.95 ($37–$46). AE, DC, MC, V. Fri–Sat noon–2:30pm; Tues–Sun 5–11:30pm. Underground: Kelvinbridge.

5 Seeing the Sights

THE TOP ATTRACTIONS

The center of Glasgow is **George Square,** dominated by the **City Chambers** that Queen Victoria opened in 1888. Of the statues in the square, the most imposing is that of Sir Walter Scott, atop a 25m (80-ft.) column. Naturally, you'll find Victoria along with her beloved Albert, plus Robert Burns. The **Banqueting Hall,** lavishly decorated, is open to the public on most weekdays.

The Burrell Collection ★★★   This museum houses the mind-boggling treasures left to Glasgow by Sir William Burrell, a wealthy ship owner who had a lifelong passion for art. Burrell started collecting art when he was 14, his passion continuing until 1958 when he died at the age of 96. His tastes were eclectic: Chinese ceramics, French paintings from the 1800s, tapestries, stained-glass windows from churches, even stone doorways from the Middle Ages. It is said that the collector "liked about everything," including one of the very few original bronze casts of Rodin's *Thinker.* He did find some art to his distaste, including avant garde works ("Monet was just too impressionistic"). You can see a vast aggregation of furniture, textiles, ceramics, stained glass, silver, art objects, and pictures in the dining room, hall, and drawing room reconstructed from Sir

Glasgow Attractions

The Burrell Collection **1**

Cathedral of St. Kentigern **11**

Glasgow Necropolis **12**

Glasgow School of Art **7**

Glasgow Science Centre **2**

House for an Art Lover **1**

Hunterian Art Gallery **5**

Hunterian Museum **4**

The Lighthouse **9**

McLellan Galleries **8**

SCOTLAND

Edinburgh
Glasgow

0   20 mi
0   20 km   ENGLAND

St. Georges Rd.
Garscube Rd.
Craighall Rd.
N. Canalbank St.
Fountainwell Rd.
Pinkston Rd.
Pinkston Dr.

New City Rd.

Dobbie's Rd.
COWCADDENS
West Graham St.
Milton St.
Buccleuch St.
Scott St.
Hill St.
Renfrew St.
Sauchiehall St.
Cambridge St.
Port Dundas Rd.
Cowcaddens Rd.
Dobbie's Loan
Kyle St.
Baird St.
Kennedy St.

6
7
8

Bath St.
GLASGOW CENTER
West Regent St.
West George St.
Royal Highland Fusiliers Museum
North Hanover St.
St. Mungo Ave.
St. James Rd.
Stirling Rd.
Castle St.
Cathedral of St. Kentigern

10
11
12

Pitt St.
Douglas St.
Blythswood St.
West Campbell St.
Renfield St.
West Nile St.
BUCHANAN ST.
Queen Street Station
Cathedral St.
St. Vincent St.
Bothwell St.
Waterloo St.
George Square
Montrose St.
George St.
Rotten Row
MEDIEVAL GLASGOW

Argyle St.
York St.
Wellington St.
Hope St.
Union St.
Gordon St.
MERCHANT CITY
Buchanan St.
Queen St.
Cochrane St.
Ingram St.
Glassford St.
Candleriggs
High St.
Bell St.
High Street Station
Duke St.

9

Central Station
Oswald St.
Jamaica St.
Argyle St.
Trongate
Osborne St.
King St.
Gallowgate

Broomielaw
ST. ENOCH
Howard St.
Stockwell St.
Bridgegate
Saltmarket
Greendyke St.
Charlotte St.
London Rd.

Clyde Pl.
King George V Bridge
Glasgow Bridge
Bridge St.
Clyde St.
Victoria Bridge

Kingston St.
Nelson St.
Commerce St.
Oxford St.
Carlton Pl.
Adelphi St.
GLASGOW GREEN

13

West St.
Centre St.
Cook St.
Ellington St.
Norfolk St.
Sheriff Court
BRIDGE ST.
Ballater St.
Gorbals St.
Laurieston Rd.
Bedford St.

Museum of Transport **3**

Nelson's Monument **13**

St. Mungo Museum of
  Religious Life and Art **10**

Theatre Royal **6**

0   1/5 mi
0   0.2 km

N

☦ Church
— Railway
Ⓤ Underground

185

William's home, Hutton Castle at Berwick-upon-Tweed. Ancient artifacts, Asian art, and European decorative arts and paintings are featured. There is a restaurant on site, and you can roam through the surrounding park, 5km (3 miles) south of Glasgow Bridge.

Pollok Country Park, 2060 Pollokshaws Rd. ℂ **0141/287-2550.** www.glasgowmuseums.com. Free admission. Mon–Thurs and Sat 10am–5pm; Fri and Sun 11am–5pm. Closed Jan 1 and Dec 25. Bus: 45, 48, or 57.

Glasgow Science Centre ★★★ (Kids)   This is Britain's most successful millennium project. On the banks of the River Clyde, it lies in the heart of the city, opposite the Scottish Exhibition and Conference Centre. Opened in 2001, the center is the focal point of Glasgow's drive to become one of Europe's major high-tech locations. In three landmark buildings, the center features the first titanium-clad structures in the United Kingdom, including Scotland's only Space Theatre. The complex also contains the only 360-degree rotating tower in the world. Other features include innovative laboratories, multimedia and science theaters, and interactive exhibits. The overall theme is that of documenting the challenges facing Scotland in the 21st century. The center is also a showcase depicting Glasgow's contribution to science and technology in the past, present, and future.

Children will love the hands-on activities: They'll be able to make their own soundtrack and animation, do a 3-D head scan and rearrange their own features, or star in their own digital video. At special shows and workshops, you'll see a glass smashed by sound, "catch" shadows, experience a million volts of indoor lighting, see liquid nitrogen, view bacteria that lurk on you, and build a lie detector.

The IMAX Theatre, a first for Glasgow and Scotland, uses a film with a frame size 10 times larger than the standard 35mm film. It projects a picture that's the size of a five-story tenement building onto the screen. There are some 150 films currently available that take viewers into all kinds of experiences—perhaps to explore the hidden secrets of natural wonders like the Grand Canyon or even the inside of an atom, and certainly the magic of space. The theater charges separate admission: £5.95 ($9.50) for adults or £4.45 ($7.10) for students and children, with a family ticket £17.95 ($29) for two adults and two children. It's open from 11am to 6pm Sunday to Wednesday and 11am to 8pm Thursday and Saturday.

50 Pacific Quay. ℂ **0141/420-5010.** www.gsc.org.uk. Admission £6.95 ($11) adults, £4.95 ($7.90) students and seniors, £18.95 ($30) family pass (2 adults and 2 children). Daily 10am–6pm. Underground: Buchan Street Station to Cessnock, from which there's a 10-min. walk.

Hunterian Art Gallery ★★   This gallery owns the artistic estate of James McNeill Whistler, with some 60 of his paintings bestowed by his sister-in-law. It also boasts a Charles Rennie Mackintosh collection, including the architect's home (with his own furniture) on three levels, decorated in the original style. The main gallery exhibits 17th- and 18th-century paintings (Rembrandt to Rubens) and 19th- and 20th-century Scottish works. Temporary exhibits, selected from Scotland's largest collection of prints, are presented in the print gallery, which also houses a permanent display of print-making techniques.

University of Glasgow, 22 Hillhead St. ℂ **0141/330-5431.** www.hunterian.gla.ac.uk. Free admission. Mon–Sat 9:30am–5pm (Mackintosh House closed 12:30–1:30pm). Closed Jan 1, Jul 21, Sept 29, Dec 25. Underground: Hillhead.

Hunterian Museum   Opened in 1807, this is Glasgow's oldest museum, in the main Glasgow University buildings 3km (2 miles) west of the heart of the city. It's named after William Hunter, its early benefactor, who donated his private collections to get the museum going. The collection is wide-ranging, from dinosaur fossils to coins to relics of the Roman occupation and plunder by the Vikings. The story of Captain Cook's voyages is pieced together in ethnographic material from the South Seas. The museum has a bookstall and an 18th-century-style coffeehouse.

University of Glasgow, Main/Gilbert-Scott Building. (✆ **0141/330-4221**, ext. 4221. Free admission. Mon–Sat 9:30am–5pm, additional hours for special exhibits vary. Closed Jan 1, July 21, Sept 29, Dec 25. Underground: Hillhead.

The Lighthouse (Scotland's Centre for Architecture, Design and the City) *Kids*   The Lighthouse, which opened in July 1999, is based in Charles Rennie Mackintosh's first public commission, which housed the *Glasgow Herald* from 1895. Unoccupied for 15 years, the building is now the site of a seven-story, state-of-the-art exhibition center with a unique blue neon-tracked escalator that leads to four galleries, lecture facilities, education suites, and a cafe.

The **Mackintosh Interpretation Centre** is the first facility to provide an overview of Mackintosh's art, design, and architecture. The impressive glass timeline wall illustrates his achievements. There are also interactive stations with models, drawings, and computer and video displays. Visitors can ride the lift up to the Mackintosh Tower and see a panorama of the city. The education program offers tours, lectures, films, and workshops for people of all ages. The Wee People's City is an interactive play area for children under 9. The IT Hotspot features Macintosh computers with printing facilities, video conferencing, and a large selection of software for research, training, and hands-on activities.

11 Mitchell Lane. (✆ **0141/221-6362**. www.thelighthouse.co.uk. Admission to Lighthouse and Mackintosh Interpretation Center £3 ($4.80) adult, £1.50 ($2.40) seniors, and 80p ($1.30) children 5 and over, free for children under 5. Mon and Wed–Sat 10:30am–5pm; Tues 11am–5pm; Sun noon–5pm. Underground: Buchanan Station.

McLellan Galleries *Finds*   This used to be an unimportant and little visited gallery. Today that's all changed. Even though it hardly rivals The Burrell Collection, McLellan came into prominence in 2003 with the closing down of the Kelvingrove Art Gallery and Museum for a major restoration slated to be completed in 2006. Since the Kelvingrove Art Gallery was the repository of some of the city's greatest art, a decision was made to transfer some of its most important pieces, including oil paintings and sculpture, to the heretofore unimportant McLellan.

The McLellan was already the repository of an impressive collection of Italian works from the 16th and 17th centuries, and it is also a showcase for modern, pop art. Many of its exhibits on loan from the Kelvingrove Art Gallery include a superb collection of Dutch and Italian Old Masters, featuring Giorgione and Rembrandt. Such international artists as Botticelli are also represented. Perhaps you'll get to see Whistler's *Arrangement in Grey and Black no 2: Portrait of Thomas Carlyle,* the first Whistler work to be hung in a British gallery. Expect a rotating series of art.

270 Sauchiehall St. (✆ **0141/565-4100**. Free admission. Mon–Thurs and Sat 10am–5pm; Fri–Sun 11am–5pm. Underground: Queen St. Station.

Museum of Transport *★★*   This museum contains a fascinating collection of all forms of transportation and related technology. Displays include a simulated 1938 Glasgow street with period shopfronts, era-appropriate vehicles, and a

A Man Ahead of His Time: Charles Rennie Mackintosh

Although legendary today, tragic genius Charles Rennie Mackintosh (1868–1928) was largely forgotten in Scotland at the time of his death. This brilliant architect, designer, and decorator is a perfect example of the old saw that the prophet is accorded little honor in his own country. His approach, poised between Art Nouveau and Bauhaus, influenced everyone from Frank Lloyd Wright in Chicago to Josef Hoffmann in Vienna. Mackintosh's ideas, however, were too revolutionary in Glasgow's Victorian age, with its pompous eclecticism and overstuffed fussiness.

Born on June 7, 1868, Mackintosh began his career in 1889 as a draftsman for the architectural firm of Honeyman & Keppie. By the 1880s, Glasgow had become the British Empire's second city, and hundreds of new homes, public buildings, rail stations, and factories were needed. The situation seemed the perfect opportunity for a rising young architect. In 1896, Mackintosh's design for a new headquarters of the Glasgow School of Art won a prestigious competition. (Actually, he won because his design was the cheapest to build.) He had drunk deeply from the creative cauldron of artistic development that swept Europe during the final days of the Belle Epoque, and his theories insisted not that decoration should be constructed but that construction should be decorated. The forms of nature, especially plants, were used in his interiors, which had a simplicity and harmony that were utterly new. Instant applause came from the Vienna secessionists and the Arts and Crafts movement in such faraway places as England and America, but Glasgow wasn't so pleased. Today, Mackintosh's design for the headquarters of the **Glasgow School of Art,** 167 Renfrew St. (© **0141/0353-4526**), near Charing Cross, is recognized as one of the city's greatest architectural treasures.

Alas, Mackintosh was neither tactful nor diplomatic, and he developed a reputation as a meticulous planner of rigid ideas who refused to compromise with builders or their crews. Later failures to win either commissions or architectural awards led to local ridicule of his avant-garde ideas, a break with his partners, and an eventual move out of Glasgow. He declared Glasgow a Philistine city. Recent research has shown he was actually exiled from his native Scotland in 1914 because of his Austrian/German artistic connections. In London, he continued to have difficulties, and his career there never got off the ground. By 1923, Mackintosh and his wife, English architect Margaret MacDonald, gave up the struggle and moved to the south of France. There he devoted himself to watercolor paintings of botanical specimens and landscapes. The Mackintoshes returned to London in 1927, where the architect died a year later.

Most of the acclaim that made Mackintosh the most famous designer ever to emerge from Scotland came from Europe, England, and the United States. In 1902, Hermann Muthesius, a leading German architect and critic, wrote, "In any enumeration of the creative geniuses of modern architecture, Charles Rennie Mackintosh must be counted among the first."

reconstruction of one of the Glasgow Underground stations. The superb and varied ship models in the Clyde Room reflect the significance of Glasgow and the River Clyde as one of the world's foremost areas of shipbuilding and engineering.

1 Bunhouse Rd., Kelvin Hall. © 0141/287-2720. www.glasgowmuseums.com Free admission. Mon–Thur and Sat 10am–5pm; Sun and Fri 11am–5pm. Closed Jan 1 and Dec 25. Underground: Kelvin Hall.

ADDITIONAL ATTRACTIONS

Cathedral of St. Kentigern 🛦🛦🛦   Also known as St. Mungo's, this cathedral was consecrated in 1136, burned down in 1192, and rebuilt soon after. The Laigh Kirk (lower church), whose vaulted crypt is said to be the finest in Europe, remains to this day and holds St. Mungo's tomb, where a light always burns. The edifice is mainland Scotland's only complete medieval cathedral from the 12th and 13th centuries. It was once a place of pilgrimage, but 16th-century zeal purged it of all monuments of idolatry.

Highlights of the interior include the 1400s nave, with a stone screen (unique in Scotland) showing the seven deadly sins. Both the choir and the lower church are in the mid-1200s First Pointed style. The church, though a bit austere, is filled with intricate details left by long-ago craftspeople—note the tinctured bosses of the ambulatory vaulting in the back of the main altar. The lower church, reached via a set of steps north of the pulpit, is where Gothic reigns supreme, with an array of pointed arches and piers.

For the best view of the cathedral, cross the Bridge of Sighs into the **Glasgow Necropolis** (© **0141/287-3961;** bus: 2 or 27), the graveyard containing almost every type of architecture in the world. Built on a rocky hill and dominated by a statue of John Knox, this fascinating graveyard was opened in 1832. Typical of the mixing of all groups in this tolerant cosmopolitan city, the first person to be buried here was a Jew, Joseph Levi.

Cathedral Square, Castle St. © 0141/552-6891. Free admission. Apr–Sept Mon–Sat 9:30am–6pm, Sun 1–5pm; Oct–Mar Mon–Sat 9:30am–4pm, Sun 1–4pm. Sun services at 11am and 6:30pm. Underground: Queen St. Station.

House for an Art Lover   This house, which opened in 1996, is based on an unrealized and incomplete 1901 competition entry of Charles Rennie Mackintosh. The impressive building, with its elegant interiors, was brought to life by contemporary artists and craftspeople. The tour begins in the main hall and leads through the dining room, with its lovely gesso panels, and on to the music room, which shows Mackintosh designs at their most inspirational. Also here are an art cafe and design shop (© **0141/353-4779**), and a striking parkland setting adjacent to Victorian walled gardens.

Bellahouston Park, 10 Dumbreck Rd. © 0141/353-4770. www.houseforanartlover.co.uk. Admission £3.50 ($5.60) adults, £2.50 ($4) for children, students and seniors. Apr 1–Sept 30 Sun–Thurs 10am–4pm, Sat 10am–3pm; Oct 1–Mar 31 Sat–Sun 10am–4pm, call for weekday times. Cafe and shop daily 10am–5pm. Underground: Ibrox. Bus: 9A, 39, 54, 59, or 36.

St. Mungo Museum of Religious Life and Art 🛦 *Finds*   Opened in 1993, this is an eclectic and often controversial museum lying close to the Glasgow Cathedral. It embraces a collection that spans the centuries and highlights various religious groups that have lived in Glasgow and the surrounding area over the years. The museum is hailed as unique in the world in that Buddha, Ganesha, Shiva, and all the "gang" are represented. The most controversial exhibit is the infamous painting of *Christ of St. John the Cross,* a work of the surrealistic Salvador Dalí (1904–1989). Also on display is the Chinese robe worn in the film, *The Last Emperor,* by Bernardo Bertolucci. In back of the museum is the U.K.'s only Japanese Zen garden.

2 Castle St. ℂ 141/552-2557. Free admission Mon–Thurs and Sat 10am–5pm; Fri and Sun 11am–5pm. Bus: 11, 36, 37, 38, 42, 89, or 138.

MARITIME GLASGOW

Scottish Maritime Museum   Irvine Harbour outside Glasgow was once a major trading port, and its maritime history lives on at this restoration. Tours take you through a shipyard worker's tenement flat and you can also see a collection of vessels moored at the harbor. These include the SV *Carrick,* the world's oldest existing colonial clipper, which made 22 return passages to Adelaide, Australia. You can also see the SY *Carola,* built on the Clyde in 1898 as a private family yacht, and the oldest seagoing steam yacht in Great Britain.

Harbourside, Irvine. ℂ 01294/278-283. www.scottishmaritimemuseum.org. Admission £3.50 ($5.60) adults, £1.75 ($2.80) seniors, students, and children, £8 ($13) family ticket. Daily 10am-5pm. Braehead bus from Central Station.

The Tall Ship at Glasgow Harbour   Here's a rare chance to explore one of the last remaining Clyde-built tall ships, the SV *Glenlee* built in 1896, a vessel that circumnavigated Cape Horn 15 times. Restored in 1999, *Glenlee* is one of only 5 Clyde-built sailing ships that remain afloat. You can explore the ship and while onboard take in an exhibition detailing the vessel's cargo-trading history. On the dock, the Victorian Pumphouse Centre contains a restaurant and a nautical gift shop along with exhibition galleries.

100 Stobcross Rd. ℂ 0141/222-2513. www.glenlee.co.uk. Admission £4.50 ($7.20) adults, £3.25 ($5.20) seniors, students, and children. Mar–Nov daily 10am–5pm, Dec–Feb daily 11am–4pm. Take the low-level train from Glasgow Central to Finnieston/SECC.

GARDENS & PARKS

Glasgow's **Botanic Gardens,** Great Western Road (ℂ **0141/334-2422;** Underground: Hillhead), covers 16 hectares (40 acres); it's an extensive collection of tropical plants and herb gardens. The garden is acclaimed especially for its

---

Frommer's Favorite Glasgow Experiences

Touring The Burrell Collection   The pièce de résistance of Glasgow (some say of Scotland), this gallery is the city's major attraction. See what good taste and an unlimited budget can acquire in a lifetime.

Following Walkways & Cycle Paths   Greater Glasgow has an array of trails and bike paths cutting through areas of historic interest and scenic beauty, including the Paisley/Irvine Cycle and Walkway, 27km (17 miles) of unused railway line converted to a trail.

Riding the World's Last Seagoing Paddle Steamer   From spring to early fall, the *Waverley* (ℂ **0141/221-8152**) makes day trips to scenic spots on the Firth of Clyde, past docks that once supplied more than half the tonnage of oceangoing ships.

Shopping Paddy's Market   This daily market by the railway arches on Shipbank Lane gives you the real flavor of the almost-vanished Glaswegian style of street vending.

spectacular orchids and begonias. It's open daily from 7am to dusk. The green-houses are open March to October 10am to 4:45pm and November to February 10am to 4:15pm. Admission is free.

   Linn Park, on Clarkston Road (bus: 24 or 36), is 86 hectares (212 acres) of pine and woodland, with many scenic walks along the river. Here you'll find a nature trail, pony rides for children, an old snuff mill, and a children's zoo. The park is open daily from 8am to dusk. **Gleniffer Braes Country Park** (© **0141/ 884-3794**), Glenfield Road, in Paisley, covers 526 hectares (1,300 acres) of woodland and moorland and has picnic areas and an adventure playground. It's open daily from dawn to dusk.

ORGANIZED TOURS

The *Waverley* is the world's last seagoing paddle steamer, and from the last week of June to the end of August (depending on weather conditions), the Paddle Steamer Preservation Society conducts 1-day trips from Anderston Quay in Glasgow to historic and scenic places beyond the Firth of Clyde. As you sail along, you can take in what were once vast shipyards, turning out more than half the earth's tonnage of oceangoing liners. You're welcome to bring your own sandwiches for a picnic aboard, or you can enjoy lunch in the Waverley Restaurant. Boat tours cost £7.95 to £29 ($13–$46). For details, contact **Waverley Excursions,** Waverley Terminal, Anderston Quay, Broomielaw (© **0141/221-8152**).

   There's also regular ferry service run by **Caledonian MacBrayne** (© **01475/ 650-100**) in Gourock on the banks of the Clyde. The ferry stands close to the station in Gourock, connected to Glasgow Central Station by trains that leave every hour and take 30 to 45 minutes. The ferry service, which can take cars, runs every hour to the attractive seaside resort of Dunoon at the mouth of the Clyde. The journey takes about 20 minutes, and ferries run every hour from 6:20am to 8:20pm, April to October 16; in winter the service is less frequent and visitors are advised to check beforehand as it's liable to change. The round-trip costs £4.25 ($6.80) adults and £2.50 ($4) seniors/children.

   The best Glasgow tours are run by **Scotguide Tourist Services (City Sighting Glasgow)**, operated from 153 Queen Street at George Square, opposite the City Chambers (© **0141/204-0444;** Underground: Buchanan St.). April 1 to October 31, departures are every 15 minutes 9:30am to 4pm. The price is £8 ($13) adults, £6 ($9.60) students/seniors, and £3 ($4.80) children under age 7.

   If you prefer to stay on terra firma, **Mercat Walks** (© **0141/586-5378**) focus on a ghostly, ghoulish Glasgow. Historians re-create macabre Glasgow—a parade of goons like hangmen, ghosts, murderers, and body snatchers. Tours leave from the tourist information center on George Square at 7 and 8pm daily, costing £7.50 ($12) for adults, £5.50 ($8.80) for seniors, students and children, with a family ticket going for £20 ($32). The tours take 1 ½ hours.

6 Special Events

The **Royal Bank Glasgow Jazz Festival** (www.jazzfest.co.uk) usually opens in the last days of June and runs through the first week of July. This festival has attracted some big names in the past, including the late Miles Davis and Dizzy Gillespie. Tickets are available from the Ticket Centre, Candleriggs (© **0141/ 240-1111**), but some free events are always announced.

   On June 10, the **Bearsden** and **Milngavie Highland Games** are held at Burnbray in the small town of Milngavie (pronounced *mill*-guy), 10km

(6 miles) from Glasgow. The games include tug-of-war, wrestling, caber tossing, piping, and Highland dancing, and offer a fun day out of the city. In case you were wondering, a caber is a young tree trunk used for tossing—the aim of the competition is to toss a 5.7m (19-ft.) -long pine tree into the air and have it land on a straight line. Call Cameron Wallace at ✆ **0141/942-5177** for details.

The **Glasgow Fair** (held during most of the month of July) is likely to have carnivals, tea dances, European circuses, Victorian rides, and even a country-and-western stampede. For information, call ✆ **0141/287-2000.**

OUTDOOR PURSUITS

BIKING   The tourist office provides maps with detailed bike paths. Rentals are available from **West End Cycles,** 16–18 Chancellor St. (✆ **0141/357-1344;** Underground: Kelvin Hall), charging £12 ($19) per day and requiring a deposit of £100 ($160) or two pieces of ID.

GOLF   Several courses are near Glasgow, but there's a limited number actually in the city itself. Two nine-hole courses are **Alexander Park,** Alexandra Parade (✆ **0141/556-1294**), and **Knightswood,** Lincoln Avenue (✆ **0141/959-6358**). Neither offers caddy service or rentals of clubs and carts. Both Alexander, a 2,281-yard (2,076m), par-31 course, and Knightswood, a 2,793-yard (2,542m), par-34 course, charge greens fees of £3.90 ($6.25) per round. Open daily from 10am to 5pm in winter; daily from 7am to 8pm in summer.

SPORTS COMPLEXES   The **Kelvin Hall International Sports Arena** is on Argyle Street (✆ **0141/357-2525;** Underground: Kelvin Hall), near the River Kelvin. It offers volleyball and basketball courts, as well as an indoor track. Daily from 9am to 10:30pm, you can use the weight room for £2.90 ($4.65) or the fully equipped gym for £4.20 ($6.70). This is also the country's major venue for national and international sports competitions; check with the tourist office for any events scheduled for the time of your visit.

The outdoor **Crownpoint Sports Complex,** 183 Crownpoint Rd. (✆ **0141/554-8274;** bus 62 or 64), also hosts national and international tournaments. It has two artificial-turf parks, an athletics park, and a track. Nonmembers can use the complex Monday through Friday from 3 to 9:30pm and Saturday and Sunday from 10am to 5pm. Use of the track costs £2 ($3.20); the weight room costs £3 ($4.80).

Scotstoun Leisure Centre, James Drive, Scotstoun (✆ **0141/959-4000;** bus: 9, 44, 62, or 64), is about 3km (2 miles) from the center of Glasgow. It's open Monday through Wednesday and Friday from 9am to 10pm, Thursday from 10am to 10pm, and Saturday and Sunday from 9am to 6pm. There's an obligatory induction of £6.80 ($11) for anyone wanting to use the gym; entry thereafter is £4.20 ($6.70).

WATERSPORTS & ICE-SKATING   The **Lagoon Leisure Centre,** Mill Street, Paisley (✆ **0141/889-4000**), offers indoor facilities including a freeform pool with a wave machine, fountains, and flume. You'll also find sauna suites with sunbeds, Jacuzzis, and a Finnish steam room. The ice rink boasts an international ice pad with six curling lanes and is home to the Paisley Pirates hockey team. There are also bar and catering facilities.

The center is open for swimming Monday through Friday from 10am to 10pm and Saturday and Sunday from 9:30am to 5pm. Monday from 9 to 10pm, it's adults only, and Wednesday from 9 to 10pm, it's women only. The sauna facilities are open Monday through Friday from 10am to 10pm, Saturday from 9am to 10pm, and Sunday from 9:30am to 5pm. Most days are segregated by gender, so call beforehand to check. Ice-skating is available Monday through Friday from 9:30am to noon and Monday, Wednesday, and Thursday from 1:30 to 4pm; Tuesday from 12:30 to 3pm and 7:30 to 9:30pm; Friday from 2:45 to 5pm and 7:30 to 10pm; and Saturday and Sunday from 10:45am to 12:45pm and 2:30 to 4:30pm. Admission to the rink is £3.40 ($5.45) for adults and £2.60 ($4.15) for children. You can go swimming for £2.80 ($4.50) for adults and £1.60 ($2.55) for children. A combined ticket for the pool and skating rink is £4.70 ($7.50) for adults and £3.40 ($5.45) for children. Use of the sauna is £3.60 to £5 ($5.75–$8). There are frequent trains throughout the day from Glasgow Central Station to Paisley.

7 Shopping

One of the major hunting grounds is **Sauchiehall Street,** Glasgow's fashion center, where many shops and department stores frequently offer good bargains, particularly in woolen goods. About 3 blocks long, this street has been made into a pedestrian mall. **Argyle Street,** which runs by the Central Station, is another major shopping artery.

All dedicated world shoppers know of **Buchanan Street,** a premier pedestrian thoroughfare. This is the location of the famed Fraser's Department Store (see below). From Buchanan Street you can also enter **Princes Square,** an excellent shopping complex with many specialty stores, restaurants, and cafes.

In the heart of Glasgow is the city's latest and most innovative shopping complex, the **St. Enoch Shopping Centre** (Underground: St. Enoch; bus: 16, 41, or 44), whose merchandise is less expensive but a lot less posh than what you'd find at the Princes Square shopping center. You can shop under the biggest glass roof in Europe. The center is to the east of Central Station on St. Enoch Square.

The **Argyll Arcade** is at 30 Buchanan St. (Underground: Buchanan St.). Even if the year of its construction (1827) wasn't set in mosaic tiles above the entrance, you'd still know that this is collection of shops beneath a curved glass ceiling has been here for a while. The arcade contains what's possibly the largest single concentration of retail **jewelers,** both antique and modern, in Europe, surpassing even Amsterdam. It's considered lucky to purchase a wedding ring here.

Dedicated fashion mavens should take a trip to the **Italian Shopping Centre** (Underground: Buchanan St.), a small complex in the Courtyard, off Ingram Street, where most of the units sell clothes, including Versace, Prada, Gucci, and Armani.

The latest contribution to mall shopping has come in the form of the **Buchanan Galleries** (Underground: Buchanan St.), which connects Sauchiehall, Buchanan, and Argyll streets and was completed in 1999. This plush development includes an enormous **John Lewis department store** and the biggest **Habitat** in Europe—a nirvana for anyone wanting reasonably priced contemporary furniture or accessories.

The Barras, held Saturday and Sunday 9am to 5pm, takes place about .5km (¼ mile) east of Glasgow Cross. This century-old market has some 800 traders selling their wares in stalls and shops. Not only can you browse for that special treasure, you can also become a part of Glasgow life and be amused by the *buskers* (colorfully and amusingly garbed street entertainers). **Paddy's Market,** by the rail arches on Shipbank Lane, operates daily if you'd like to see an old-fashioned slice of Glaswegian street vending.

Tips　Bring That Passport!

Take along your passport when you go shopping in case you make a purchase that entitles you to a **VAT (value-added tax) refund**.

General **shopping hours** are Monday to Saturday 9am to 5:30 or 6pm, depending on the merchant. On Thursdays, shops stay open to 8pm.

ANTIQUES

Victorian Village　This warren of tiny shops stands in a slightly claustrophobic cluster. Much of the merchandise isn't particularly noteworthy, but there are many exceptional pieces if you're willing to go hunting. Several of the owners stock reasonably priced 19th-century articles; others sell old jewelry and clothing, a helter-skelter of artifacts. 93 W. Regent St. ☎ **0141/332-0808**. Bus: 23, 38, 45, 48, or 57.

ART

Compass Gallery　This gallery offers refreshingly affordable pieces; you could find something special for as little as £25 ($40), depending on the exhibition. The curators tend to concentrate on local artists, often university students. 178 W. Regent St. ☎ **0141/221-6370**. Bus: 23, 38, 45, 48, or 57.

Cyril Gerber Fine Art　One of Glasgow's most respected art galleries veers away from the avant-garde, specializing in British paintings, sculptures, and ceramics crafted between around 1880 and today and Scottish landscapes and cityscapes. Cyril Gerber is a respected art authority with lots of contacts in art circles throughout Britain. Objects begin at around £200 ($320). 48 W. Regent St. ☎ **0141/221-3095**. Bus: 23, 38, 45, 48, or 57.

BOOKS

Borders　An impressive bookseller, with premises overlooking Royal Exchange Square, in the heart of Glasgow, this organizations sells books, videos, and music CDs, with a gratifying emphasis on the cultural phenomenon (travel, architecture, history, and botany) of Scotland. In some ways, it's a de facto social club as well, hosting contemporary book and film discussion groups, author's readings and signings, and piano concerts from emerging musical celebrities. There are even once-a-month discussion groups focusing on new works in Italian, Spanish, and German. 98 Buchanan St. ☎ **0141/222-7700**. Underground: Buchanan St.

CLOTHING

James Pringle Weavers　In business since 1780, this shop is owned by the Edinburgh Woollen Mill, known for their high quality clothing that includes well-crafted sweaters from the Island of Arran, and a tasteful selection of ties, kilts, and tartans. Some of the merchandise is unique to this stop. Ever slept in a tartan nightshirt? 130 Buchanan St. ☎ **0141/221-3434**.

CRAFTS

Scottish Craft Centre　The work of some of the finest craftspeople in Scotland is highlighted at this showcase. Most of the items are exquisitely crafted in porcelain, metal, glass, and wood. You can select from such items as metal candle holders, hand-carved wooden boxes, exquisite glasses and china, porcelain vases, and other choice items. Princes Square Mall, 48 Buchanan St. ☎ **0141/248-2885**. Underground: St. Enoch. Bus 9, 12, 44, 66, and 75.

A DEPARTMENT STORE

Fraser's Department Store   Fraser's is Glasgow's version of Harrods. A soaring Victorian-era glass arcade rises four stories, and inside you'll find everything from clothing to Oriental rugs, from crystal to handmade local artifacts of all kinds. Buchanan St. © 0141/221-3880. Underground: Buchanan St.

GIFTS & DESIGN

Catherine Shaw   Named after the long-deceased matriarch of the family that runs the place today, Catherine Shaw is a somewhat cramped gift shop that has cups, mugs, postcards, and gift items based on the designs of Charles Rennie Mackintosh. There are also some highly evocative Celtic mugs called *quaichs* (welcoming cups or whisky measures, depending on whom you talk to) and tankards in both pewter and silver. It's a great place for easy-to-pack and somewhat offbeat gifts. Look for another branch at 31 Argyll Arcade (© **0141/221-9038**); entrances to the arcade are on both Argyll and Buchanan streets. 24 Gordon St. © 0141/204-4762. Underground: Buchanan St.

Mackintosh Shop 🤍🤍🤍   This tiny shop prides itself on its stock of books, cards, stationery, coffee and beer mugs, glassware, and sterling-and-enamel jewelry created from the original designs of Mackintosh. Although the shop doesn't sell furniture, the staff will refer you to a craftsman whose work they recommend: **Bruce Hamilton, Furnituremaker,** 4 Woodcroft Ave., Broomhill (© **01505/322-550;** bus: 6, 16, or 44), has been involved in the restoration of many Mackintosh interiors and has produced a worthy group of chairs, sideboards, and wardrobes authentic to Mackintosh's designs. Expect to pay around £250 ($400), not including upholstery fabric, for a copy of the designer's best-known chair (the Mackintosh-Ingram chair); there'll be a delay of at least a month before your furniture is shipped to your home. In the foyer of the Glasgow School of Art, 4 Napier St. © 0141/353-4526. Underground: Queen St.

National Trust for Scotland Shop 🤍   Drop in here for maps, calendars, postcards, pictures, dish towels, bath accessories, and kitchenware. Some of the crockery is in Mackintosh-design styles. The neoclassical building, constructed as a charity and hospice in 1806, is on the site of a larger hospice built in 1641. Hutcheson's Hall, 158 Ingram St. © 0141/552-8391. Underground: Buchanan St.

KILTS & TARTANS

Hector Russell 🤍🤍🤍   Founded in 1881, Hector Russell is Scotland's oldest kiltmaker. This elegant store might be the most prestigious in Scotland. The welcome of the experienced sales staff is genuinely warm-hearted. Crystal and gift items are sold on street level, but the real heart and soul of the place is on the lower level, where you'll find impeccably crafted and reasonably priced tweed jackets, tartan-patterned accessories, waistcoats, and sweaters of top-quality wool for men and women. Men's, women's, and children's hand-stitched kilts are available. 110 Buchanan St. © 0141/221-0217. Underground: Buchanan St.

MUSIC

Fopp   In our view, this is Glasgow's finest and coolest record outlet, even better than the Virgin Megastore on Union Street. They offer one of the best selections of CDs and DVD videos on Glasgow, ranging from the classics to today's hottest hits. For some real values, search out their "bargain bin." Their range of traditional Scottish music is a special highlight. 358 Byrnes Rd. © 0141/357-0774. Underground: Hillhead.

PORCELAIN & CRYSTAL

Stockwell Bazaar   This is Glasgow's largest purveyor of porcelain, its four floors bulging with Royal Doulton, Wedgwood, Noritake, and Royal Worcester, plus crystal stemware by many manufacturers. Anything you buy can be insured and shipped to whatever address you specify. 67–77 Glassford St. (C) 0141/552-5781. Underground: St. Enoch.

8 Glasgow After Dark

Glasgow, not Edinburgh, is the cultural center of Scotland, and the city is alive with performances. Before you leave home, check *Time Out* (www.timeout.co.uk) for the latest round-up of who's playing in the clubs and concert halls. After you've arrived, pick up a copy of the free monthlies *Culture City* or *What's On* at the tourist office or your hotel. In addition, at most newsstands you can get a free copy of *The List,* published every other week. It details arts and other events for Edinburgh as well as Glasgow.

THE PERFORMING ARTS

OPERA & CLASSICAL MUSIC   The **Theatre Royal,** Hope Street and Cowcaddens Road ((C) **0141/332-9000;** Underground: Cowcaddens; bus: 23, 48, or 57), is the home of the **Scottish Opera** as well as of the **Scottish Ballet.** The theater also hosts visiting companies from around the world. Called "the most beautiful opera theatre in the kingdom" by the *Daily Telegraph,* it offers splendid Victorian Italian Renaissance plasterwork, glittering chandeliers, and 1,547 comfortable seats, plus spacious bars and buffets on all four levels. However, it's not the decor but the ambitious repertoire that attracts opera-goers. Ballet tickets run £3.50 to £30 ($5.60–$48) and opera tickets cost £3.50 to £55 ($5.60–$88). On performance days, the box office is open Monday to Saturday 10am to 8pm; on nonperformance days, hours are Monday to Saturday 10am to 6pm. In winter, the **Royal Scottish National Orchestra** offers Saturday-evening concerts at the **Glasgow Royal Concert Hall,** 2 Sauchiehall St. ((C) **0141/332-6633;** Underground: Buchanan St.). The **BBC Scottish Symphony Orchestra** presents Friday-evening concerts at the **BBC Broadcasting House,** Queen Margaret Drive (Underground: St. Enoch), or at **City Halls,** Albion Street (Underground: St. Enoch). In summer, the Scottish National Orchestra has a short Promenade season (dates and venues are announced in the papers). Tickets can only be purchased at individual venues.

THEATER   Although hardly competition for London, Glasgow's theater scene is certainly the equal of Edinburgh's. Young Scottish playwrights often make their debuts here, and you're likely to see anything from Steinbeck's *The Grapes of Wrath* to Wilde's *Salome* to *Romeo and Juliet* done in Edwardian dress.

The prime symbol of Glasgow's verve remains the **Citizens Theatre,** Gorbals and Ballater streets ((C) **0141/429-0022;** bus: 12 or 66), founded after World War II by James Bridie, a famous Glaswegian whose plays are still produced on occasion there. It's home to a repertory company, with tickets at £5 to £15 ($8–$24). The box office hours Mon–Sat 9:30–6:30pm. The company is usually closed June to the first week in August.

The **Glasgow Arts Centre,** 12 Washington St. ((C) **0141/221-4526;** bus: 2, 4, or 21), always seems to be doing something interesting, including children's productions and other theatrical performances. It's open Monday to Friday 9:30am to 5pm and 6:30 to 10pm; in summer, it's closed in the evening. The center is funded by the Glasgow Council and performances are free. The **King's Theatre,** 297 Bath St. (✆ **0141/240-111;** bus: 57), offers a wide range of productions, including straight plays, musicals, and comedies. During winter it's noted for its pantomime presentations. Tickets are £6 to £26 ($9.60–$42), and the box office is open Monday to Saturday 10am to 6pm.

The **Mitchell Theatre,** 6 Granville St. (✆ **0141/287-5511;** bus: 57), has earned a reputation for staging small-scale entertainment, ranging from dark drama to dance, as well as conferences and seminars. A small modern theater, it adjoins the well-known Mitchell Library. The theater box office is open when there are performances from 4pm until the show. Ticket prices vary with each production. The **Pavilion Theatre,** 121 Renfield St. (✆ **0141/332-1846;** bus: 21, 23, or 38), specializes in modern versions of vaudeville (which, as they'll assure you around here, isn't dead). The Pavilion sells its own tickets for £10 to £25 ($16–$40); they're not available at City Centre. The box office is open Monday to Saturday 10am to 8pm.

The **Tron Theatre,** 63 Trongate (✆ **0141/552-4267;** Underground: St. Enoch), occupies one of the three oldest buildings in Glasgow, the former Tron Church. The church, with its famous Adam dome and checkered history, has been transformed into a small theater presenting the best of contemporary drama, dance, and music events. The Tron also has a beautifully restored Victorian cafe/bar serving traditional home-cooked meals, including vegetarian dishes and a fine selection of beer and wine. The box office is open Monday to Saturday 10am to 6pm, over the counter and until 9pm by phone. Tickets are £2 to £15 ($3.20–$24) adults and £1 to £7 ($1.60–$11) children.

THE CLUB & MUSIC SCENE

Barrowland   This hall seats 2,000 and is open only on nights shows are booked. July and August are the quiet months, as most shows are geared toward a student audience. The cover runs highest when the hall hosts popular bands like The Proclaimers or the Black Rebel Motorcycle Club. Gallowgate. ✆ **0141/552-4601.** Cover £10–£22 ($16–$35). Underground: St. Enoch. Bus: 61 or 62.

Fury Murry's   Most of the crowd here is made up of students looking for nothing more complicated than a good, sometimes rowdy, time listening to disco music that's upbeat but not ultra-trendy. It's in a cellar, a 2-minute walk from the very central St. Enoch Shopping Centre. There's a very busy bar, a dance floor, and ample opportunities to meet the best and brightest in Scotland's university system. Jeans and T-shirts are the right garb. It's open Thursday to Sunday 10:30pm to 3:30am. Thursday and Friday feature live bands, and other nights are strictly for dancing or can be reserved for private parties. 96 Maxwell St. ✆ **0802/538-550.** Cover £2–£6 ($3.20–$9.60). Underground: St. Enoch.

The Garage   A big student crowd tests the limits of the 1,478-person capacity here on weekends. In the downstairs area, surrounded by rough stone walls, you get the impression you're in a castle with a Brit pop and indie soundtrack. Most regulars, however, gravitate to the huge main dance floor, where lots of shiny metal fixtures stand out in contrast to the stone walls. There are three bars downstairs and two upstairs. Open daily 11pm to 3am. 490 Sauchiehall St. ✆ **0141/332-1120.** Cover £2–£7 ($3.20–$11). Underground: Buchanan St.

Grand Ole Opry   In a sprawling sandstone building 2.5km (1½ miles) south of Glasgow's center, the Grand Ole Opry is the largest club in Europe devoted to country-western music. There's a bar and dancing arena on both levels and a chuck-wagon eatery serving affordable steaks and other such fare on the upper level. Live music is always performed from a large stage at the front. Performers are usually from the United Kingdom, but a handful of artists from the States turn up. Open Friday to Sunday and occasionally Thursday (if demand warrants it) from 6:30pm to 12:30am. 2–4 Govan Rd., Paisley Toll Rd. ℂ 0141/429-5396. Cover £3–£10 ($4.80–$16). Bus: 23 or 23A.

King Tut's Wah-Wah Hut   This sweaty, crowded rock bar has been in business for nearly a decade. It's a good place to check out the Glasgow music and arts crowd, as well as local bands and the occasional international act. Successful Scottish acts My Bloody Valentine and Teenage Fan Club got their starts here. Open Monday to Saturday noon to midnight and Sunday 6pm to midnight. 272 St. Vincent St. ℂ 0141/221-5279. Cover £4–£10 ($6.40–$16). Bus: 6, 8, 9, or 16.

Nice 'n' Sleazy   This club books live acts Thursday to Sunday. The cover is quite reasonable, but it can get more expensive if you catch a band like the Cranberries, Alice Donut, or Helmet. Holding some 200 patrons, it provides a rare opportunity to catch internationally popular bands in an intimate setting. Upstairs on Sunday and Monday nights, DJs spin an eclectic mix of music for dancing, but most people come for the bands. Open daily 11:30am to 11:45pm. 421 Sauchiehall St. ℂ 0141/333-9637. Cover usually £3.50 ($5.60); higher if a big name is playing. Bus: 23 or 48.

The 13th Note   This club has moved away from jazz in the past couple of years and now books mainly heavy rock bands on Tuesday, Wednesday, and Thursday nights; country on Monday. On Friday, Saturday, and Sunday, the night is dedicated to ambient and alternative music. Open daily noon to midnight. 50–60 King St. ℂ 0141/553-1638. Bus: 21, 23, or 38.

Renfrew Ferry   This old car ferry once provided service on the River Clyde. Musical acts are booked infrequently during the year. 42 Clyde Place. ℂ 0169/826-5511. Cover £6–£20 ($9.60–$32). Bus: 21, 23 38 45, 48, or 57.

Victoria's Nightclub   Victoria's prides itself on being the only club in Scotland with cabaret performances. The building is on two floors of high-tech design in the heart of town, with a first-floor dance club and a second-floor cabaret bar/restaurant where singers, comedians, and other artistes amuse and titillate 7:30pm to 3am on Friday and Saturday. Dress is smart casual, and the crowd tends to be people over age 25, with a bit of money and sophistication. The dance club is open Thursday to Sunday 10:30pm to 3am and the cabaret on Friday and Saturday 7:30pm to 3am. 98 Sauchiehall St. ℂ 0141/332-1444. Cover £3–£8 ($4.80–$13) for dance club only, £13.95–£14.95 ($22–$24) for dance club, cabaret, and buffet dinner. Underground: Buchanan St.

FAVORITE PUBS

Bon Accord   This amiably battered pub is a longtime favorite. There's an array of hand-pumps—a dozen devoted to real British ales, the rest to beers and stouts from the Czech Republic, Belgium, Germany, Ireland, and Holland. The pub is likely to satisfy your taste in malt whisky as well, and offers affordable bar snacks. Open Monday to Saturday noon to midnight, Sunday noon to 11pm. 153 North St. ℂ 0141/248-4427. Bus: 6, 8, or 16.

Cask and Still   Here's the best place for sampling malt whisky. You can taste from a selection of more than 350 single malts, at a variety of strengths (perhaps not on the same night) and maturities (that is, years spent in casks). Many prefer the malt whisky that has been aged in a sherry cask. There's good bar food at lunch, including cold meat salads and sandwiches. Open Monday to Thursday noon to 11pm, Friday and Saturday noon to midnight. 154 Hope St. ✆ 0141/333-0980. Bus: 21, 23, or 38.

Corn Exchange ✪   Opposite the Central Station, this place was really the Corn Exchange in the mid–19th century but now is one of Glasgow's most popular pubs. Amid dark paneling and high ceilings, you can enjoy a pint of lager until 11pm Sunday to Wednesday and until midnight Thursday to Saturday. Affordable pub grub is served daily noon to 9pm. 88 Gordon St. ✆ 0141/248-5380. Bus: 21, 23, or 38.

L'Attaché   One of several traditional Scottish pubs in its neighborhood, L'Attaché is outfitted with stone floors and rows of decorative barrels. At the self-service food counter you can order cheap steak pie, lasagna, and salads; at the bar you can order from an impressive array of single malts. There's a live jazz band on Saturday afternoons. Open Monday to Saturday noon to midnight. 27 Waterloo St. ✆ 0141/221-3210. Bus: 21, 23, or 48.

THE GAY SCENE
There's no strongly visible lesbian bar or nightclub scene in Glasgow. Many lesbians who attend bars frequent those that cater mainly to males.

Bennet's, 90 Glassford St. (✆ **0141/552-5761**) is one of the major gay/lesbian nightclubs in town. On certain nights (especially Tuesday) it's the most fun and crowded gay disco in Scotland. The crowd includes men and women age 17 to 60, and the music plays on and on, interrupted only by the occasional drag show. **C. D. Frost,** 8–10 W. George St. (✆ **0141/332-8005**), is a busy bar catering primarily to a trendy young mixed crowd. It's minimalist chic, with low lighting. Drag acts are occasionally featured, but it's better known for the Wednesday-night quiz, kept in check by resident entertainer, "George." The **Court Bar,** 69 Hutcheson St. (✆ **0141/552-2463**), is a small, cozy pub that's a popular meeting place for a gay/lesbian crowd to gather for drinks and talk. The pub gets decidedly more male after 7pm and is a good starting point for a gay evening on the town. Attracting a slightly older crowd, **Waterloo Bar,** 306 Argyle St. (✆ **0141/221-7359**), gets most packed during happy hour (9pm–midnight), when you can make your drink a double for just £2.50 ($4).

9 Side Trips from Glasgow: The Best of the Strathclyde Region

Just as Sir Walter Scott dominates the Borders, the presence of **Robert Burns** is felt in the Strathclyde region around Ayr. A string of famous seaside resorts stretches from Girvan to Largs. Some of Britain's greatest golf courses, including **Turnberry,** are here. Glasgow makes a good gateway to Burns country, as it has excellent bus and rail connections to Ayr, which is your best bet for exploring the area. If you're driving, take A77 southwest from Glasgow to Ayr.

AYR: A POPULAR WEST COAST RESORT
The royal burgh of Ayr is the most popular resort on Scotland's west coast. Facing the Isle of Arran and the Firth of Clyde, it's 130km (81 miles) southwest of Edinburgh, and 56km (35 miles) southwest of Glasgow. A busy market town, it offers 4km (2½ miles) of beach (alas, spoiled by pollution), steamer cruises, fishing, and golf, and is a manufacturing center for fabrics and carpets. Ayr also boasts the top racecourse in Scotland.

Backpacking the West Highland Way

One of Scotland's most legendary long-distance footpaths is the **West Highland Way** (see "The Best Hikes," in chapter 1), set aside by the government in 1967 to preserve its beauty. It begins north of Glasgow in the town of Milngavie and winds its way for 153km (95 miles) north along Loch Lomond with its bonnie, bonnie banks. The trail continues through Glencoe, site of a famous passage, and goes on to Fort William and eventually to Ben Nevis, Scotland's highest mountain. The most dramatic part of this walk is from the Bridge of Orchy to Glencoe.

Trains run frequently throughout the day from the Queen's Street railway station in central Glasgow to Milngavie, starting point of the walk. The 15-minute trip costs £2.50 ($4) one-way. For information and a map of this footpath, contact the **Scottish Tourist Board,** 23 Ravelston Terrace, Edinburgh EH4 3EU (© **0131/332-243;** www.visitscotland.com; Underground: Buchanan St.).

Trains from Glasgow's Central Station (© **08457/484-950**) will whisk you to Ayr in 50 minutes; the fare is £5.30 ($8.50). Stagecoach Express (© **01292/613-500**) buses from Glasgow arrive in Ayr in 1 hour, costing £4 ($6.40) one-way.

The **tourist office** is at 22 Sandgate, Ayr (© **01292/678-100**). It's open from Easter to August, Monday through Saturday from 9am to 6pm (July and Aug, also Sun 10am–5pm); and September to Easter, Monday through Saturday from 9:15am to 5pm.

SEEING THE SIGHTS

Ayr is full of Burns associations. The 13th-century **Auld Brig o' Ayr,** the poet's "poor narrow footpath of a street where two wheelbarrows tremble when they meet" was renovated in 1910.

On Blackfriar's Walk on the banks of the River Ayr, the **Auld Kirk of Ayr** dates from 1653 to 1655, when it replaced the 12th-century Church of St. John, which had been seized by Cromwell and dismantled. Its greatest curiosity is a grim series of "mort safes" dating from 1655—they were used to cover freshly filled graves to discourage body-snatchers. Robert Burns was baptized in the kirk. The church is open Monday through Saturday from 8:30am to 7pm and Sunday from noon to 7pm.

The **Wallace Tower,** on High Street, rises some 34m (112 ft.). Constructed in 1828, it has a statue of William Wallace (remember *Braveheart?*) by local sculptor James Thom. Tradition holds that Wallace was imprisoned here and made a daring escape.

Another architectural curiosity is **Loudoun Hall** (© **01292/286-385**), Boat Vennal, at the junction of Hope and High streets, off Cross Street, in the heart of town. A wealthy merchant had this town house constructed in the late 1400s, and it's one of the oldest examples of burgh architecture left in the country. From mid-July to the end of August, it's open Monday through Saturday from 11am to 6pm.

About 2.5km (1½ miles) south of Ayr off the road to the Burns Cottage at Alloway (see below), the **Maclaurin Gallery and Rozelle House,** on Monument Road in Rozelle Park (© **01292/443-708**), are installed in what were once stables and servants' quarters. A Henry Moore bronze sculpture and a major collection of contemporary art are on display. A nature trail winds through the

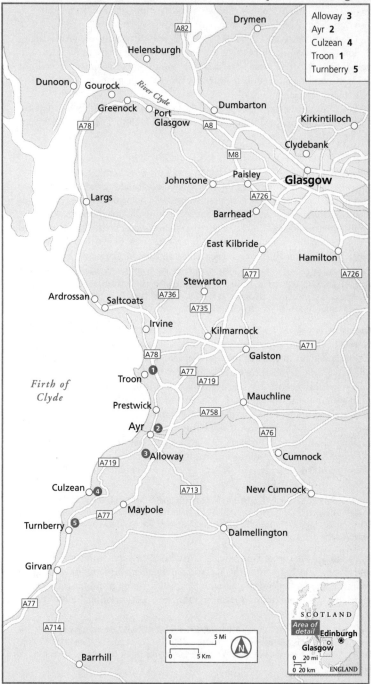

Side Trips from Glasgow

Alloway **3**
Ayr **2**
Culzean **4**
Troon **1**
Turnberry **5**

Drymen

Helensburgh

A82

Dunoon Gourock
Greenock Port
Glasgow

A78

River Clyde

Dumbarton

A8

Kirkintilloch

Clydebank

M8

Johnstone Paisley **Glasgow**

A726

Largs

Barrhead

East Kilbride

Hamilton

A77 A726

Stewarton

Ardrossan Saltcoats

A736

A735

Irvine

Kilmarnock

A78

A71

Galston

A77

A719

Troon **1**

Prestwick

Mauchline

A758

Ayr **2**

A76

3 Alloway

Cumnock

A719

New Cumnock

Culzean **4**

A713

Maybole

Turnberry **5**

A77

Dalmellington

Girvan

A77

A714

*Firth of
Clyde*

0   5 Mi
0   5 Km

N

Barrhill

SCOTLAND
*Area of
detail* **Edinburgh**
Glasgow
0   20 mi
0 20 km   ENGLAND

201

woodland. It's open Monday through Saturday from 10am to 5pm (Apr–Oct, also Sun 2–5pm). Admission is free.

The **Ayr Racecourse** (© **01292/264-179;** www.ayr-racecourse.co.uk), about 2.5km (1½ miles) north of the town center (follow the signs on A77), is open year-round. Races are usually held Friday, Saturday, and Monday, generally at 2:15pm. Peak racing season is May to October, with jumping events held in November, January, and April.

There are three nearby golf courses; the best is the municipal **Belle Isle Golf Course,** Doonfoot Road, Alloway (© **01292/441-258**). There are some three dozen courses in the greater area.

WHERE TO STAY

Fairfield House ⭐   On the seafront near Low Green, this 1912 Edwardian town house has been restored to its original elegance and converted into Ayr's best hotel. The staff is especially attentive and will help you arrange tee times at nearby golf courses. Lady Henrietta Spencer-Churchill, noted designer of classic British interiors, decorated the rooms in a country-house style. The guest rooms are large and luxurious, many done in chintz; most of the bathrooms have bidets. The food at Fairfield has been called an oasis in a culinary desert.

12 Fairfield Rd., Ayr, Ayrshire KA7 2AR. © 01292/267-461. Fax 01292/261-456. www.fairfieldhotel.co.uk. 44 units. £125 ($200) double; £165 ($264) suite. Rates include Scottish breakfast. AE, DC, MC, V. Free parking. **Amenities:** 2 restaurants; bar; indoor pool; health club; spa; sauna; 24-hr. room service; laundry/dry cleaning service. *In room:* A/C, TV, dataport available, coffeemaker, hair dryer, trouser press.

Glenapp Castle ⭐⭐⭐   This beautifully decorated castle offers spectacular, baronial living and was recently opened by Graham and Fay Cowan. All other accommodations in the area pale in comparison. The castle was constructed in 1870 by David Bryce, a celebrated architect of his day. This vast Victorian mansion stands high above a village overlooking the Irish Sea. Elegant lounges and dining rooms await you, as do 17 spacious and individually furnished bedrooms and suites. Antiques, oil paintings, and elegant Victorian touches are seen at every turn. Tall Victorian windows let in the Scottish sun making the rooms bright and sunny on many days. Dining is a gourmet experience with some of the finest wine cellars in the area. The castle stands on 12 hectares (30 acres) of lovely, secluded grounds, with many rare plants. The kitchen uses fresh herbs and fruit from the garden.

Ballantrae, Ayrshire KA26 0NZ. © 01465/831-212. Fax 01465/831-000. www.glenappcastle.com. 17 units. £440 ($704) double; £480 ($768) suite; £550 ($880) master room. Rates include all meals. AE, MC, V. Lies 30km (20 miles) south of Ayr. Free parking. **Amenities:** Restaurant; bar; tennis court; room service (8am–midnight); laundry. *In room:* TV.

Ramada Jarvis Ayr   This hotel is a few hundred yards from Ayr's seashore and 455m (500 yd.) from the rail station. It offers large, refurbished guest rooms, many with views and all with neat, shower-only bathrooms. Bart's Bar and Grill is a lively place to meet and eat, with a selection of freshly roasted joints on the captain's table.

Dalblair Rd., Ayr, Ayrshire KA7 1UG. © 01292/269-331. Fax 01292/610-722. www.ramadajarvis.co.uk. 118 units. £85–£115 ($136–$184) double; £140 ($224) suite. AE, DC, MC, V. Free parking. **Amenities:** Restaurant; bar; health club; 24-hr. room service; laundry/dry cleaning service. *In room:* TV, coffeemaker, hair dryer, trouser press.

Quality Hotel Station   The Station, an Ayr landmark since 1885, is still going strong. Connected to the town's rail station, it sits behind a red-sandstone Victorian exterior, and although it isn't the most modern hotel in town, many visitors consider its high ceilings, elaborate detailing, and old-world charm more than enough reason to check in. Many of the guest rooms are quite spacious but routinely furnished. All come with small shower-only bathrooms.

Burns Statue Sq., Ayr, Ayrshire KA7 3AT. (℃) **01292/263-268.** Fax 01292/262-293. www.choicehotels europe.com. 75 units. £83 ($133) double; £96 ($154) suite. Children under 14 stay free in parent's room. AE, DC, MC, V. Free parking. Pets accepted. **Amenities:** Restaurant; bar; 24-hr. room service; laundry service. *In room:* TV, coffeemaker, hair dryer, iron/ironing board.

Savoy Park Hotel ☆   For more than 30 years, the Henderson family has welcomed guests to their classic country hotel, which was designed in the Victorian and Scottish baronial style. The atmosphere is traditional, with paneled walls and ornate ceilings, but modern conveniences have been discreetly added. The pricier bedrooms are larger and more charming. All units include shower-only bathrooms. Evoking a Highland hunting lodge, the Oak Room serves time-tested dishes such as baked lemon sole. The Savoy Park is a short drive from 30 first-rate golf courses, and fishing is also possible nearby.

16 Racecourse Rd., Ayr, Ayrshire KA7 2UT. (℃) **01292/266-112.** Fax 01292/611-488. www.savoypark.com. 15 units. £85–£105 ($136–$168) double. Rates include breakfast. AE, MC, V. Free parking. Follow A70 for 3km (2 miles), go through Parkhouse St., turn left into Beresford Terrace, and make first right onto Bellevue Rd. **Amenities:** Restaurant; bar. *In room:* TV, dataport, coffeemaker, hair dryer, iron/ironing board.

WHERE TO DINE

Fouter's Bistro MODERN SCOTTISH   In the historic heart of Ayr, this restaurant occupies the cellar of an 18th-century bank, retaining the original sandstone floor and a vaulted ceiling covered in terra-cotta tiles. The restaurant's name derives from Scottish argot: *foutering about* is a charming way of saying "bumbling about" (although this place is anything but bumbling). The seamless service focuses on modern Scottish cuisine with a nod to Thailand. You can sample the likes of venison with rowanberry sauce, local Gresshingham duck with black-cherry sauce, and seafood served with saffron cream sauce. In spring, one of the most delicious items is the organically reared lamb from the neighboring Carrick Hills.

2A Academy St. (℃) **01292/261-391.** Reservations recommended. Main courses £7–£8.50 ($11–$14) at lunch, £10–£12 ($16–$19) at dinner; fixed-price lobster lunch (in season only) £16 ($26). AE, DC, MC, V. Tues–Sat noon–2pm and 6:30–10:30pm.

Tudor Restaurant SCOTTISH/INTERNATIONAL   This busy family-oriented restaurant is imbued with a real Tudor look with dark half-timbering. Most popular here are the fixed-price lunch and the high tea served from 3:15pm to closing. The food includes such rib-sticking specialties as a version of chicken Maryland (breaded and fried breast of chicken with bacon, tomatoes, peaches, and pineapple fritters).

8 Beresford Terrace, on Burns Statue Sq. (℃) **01292/261-404.** Main courses from £6 ($9.60); fixed-price meal £7.95 ($13) for 2 courses, £8.95 ($14) for 3 courses; high tea £6–£8.50 ($9.60–$14). AE, DC, MC, V. Mon–Sat 9am–9pm; Sun noon–8pm.

AYR AFTER DARK

The famous **Rabbie's Bar** ☆, Burns Statue Square (℃ **01292/262-112**), mixes Scottish poetry with electronic music. The stone walls are highlighted with the pithy verses of Robert Burns, who used to drop in for a pint of ale and conversation. A portrait of Rabbie is painted directly onto the wall. However, don't come here expecting poetry readings in a quiet corner. The crowd, while not particularly literary, is talkative and fun and enjoys live music several nights a week. There's a busy bar, crowded banquettes and copper-topped tables, and a

Robert Burns: National Poet & Penniless Genius

And, wow! Tam saw an unco sight!
Warlocks and witches in a dance:
Nae Cotillion, brent new frae France,
But hornpipes, jigs, strathspeys, and reels,
Put life and mettle in their heels.

—Robert Burns, *Tam o' Shanter*

Scotland's national poet, Robert Burns (1759–96), or Rabbie, carried the Scottish vernacular to its highest point in his satiric, earthly, and bawdy romantic poems and songs. Born in Alloway in Ayrshire on a wind-tossed night, Burns was the son of an impoverished gardener who encouraged him to read and seek an education. Burns became an unsuccessful farmer and later a taxman, but the world knows him as the "heaven-taught ploughman," author of the narrative masterpiece *Tam o' Shanter* and the humanitarian *A Man's a Man for A' That.*

Rabbie was a great womanizer ("Once heartily in love, never out of it") who fathered at least 15 children, 9 of whom were legitimate. In his short time on earth, he wrote about 370 poems and songs, only to die at age 37, wracked with rheumatic fever and harassed by his debtors for the sum of £5 ($7.50). His pregnant wife, Jean, had to beg a shilling from the poet's brother to feed her children on the day of his funeral.

Every year on his birthday, January 25, the poet is honored all over the world—from Edinburgh to San Francisco, from Bombay to Tokyo—at male-dominated Bachelors' Clubs like the one founded by Burns and his friends. Even Shakespeare doesn't get this kind of attention. At these Burns suppers, guests who are entitled get to wear kilts; non-Scottish admirers of the poet dress formally. After a dram of whisky is drunk as a welcome, the first course, or *Het Hail,* is carried in; it's invariably cock-a-leekie soup, made with chicken and leeks. Next comes *Caller Fish Frae Loch and Sea,* usually fresh salmon. But for the main course, there can be no deviation in the menu: It must be the Great Chieftain o' the Puddin' Race, the dreaded haggis. The chef comes in bearing the haggis on a large platter, preceded by a kilted piper playing "Scotland the Brave." Of course, everyone drinks a whisky to the health of the haggis—after all, a small nip is known as *uisge beatha* ("water of life").

The chairman of the club—again, after a quaff of whisky—takes out a Scottish dirk and recites Burns's "Address to a Haggis" before plunging the blade into the beast. Out gushes the meat, entrails, or whatever the chef decided to stuff into the sheep's stomach. All the "bachelors" enjoy this seasoned mix of meat, oatmeal, and onions.

The sad truth is that although haggis is consumed at all birthday celebrations for Burns, the poor poet missed out on it himself. He considered haggis "one of the most delicious meals on earth" but could rarely afford it, settling instead for *tatties* (mashed potatoes) or *neeps* (turnips).

large TV showing videos. It's open Monday through Saturday from 11am to 12:30am and Sunday from noon to midnight.

ALLOWAY ✿: BIRTHPLACE OF RABBIE BURNS

Some 3km (2 miles) south of Ayr, Alloway is where Scotland's national poet was born on January 25, 1759, in the gardener's cottage—the "auld clay biggin"—that his father, William Burns, built in 1757.

SEEING THE SIGHTS

Auld Brig Over the Ayr, mentioned in *Tam o' Shanter,* still spans the river, and **Alloway Auld Kirk,** also mentioned in the poem, stands roofless and haunted not far away. The poet's father is buried in the graveyard of the kirk.

Burns Cottage and Museum ✿   The cottage still contains some of its original furniture, including the bed in which the poet was born. Chairs displayed here were said to have been used by Tam o' Shanter and Souter Johnnie. Beside the poet's cottage is a museum.

Alloway. ✆ **01292/441-215.** Admission £3 ($4.80) adults, £1.50 ($2.40) children and seniors, £9.50 ($15) per family. Apr–Oct daily 9:30am–5:30pm; Nov–Mar Mon–Sat 10am–5pm Drive 3km (2 miles) south of Ayr on B7024.

Burns Monument and Gardens   About 1km (½ mile) from the Burns Cottage, this monument is a Grecian-style building erected in 1823, containing relics, books, and manuscripts associated with Robert Burns. The gardens overlooking the River Doon contain shrubs; some were brought back from the Himalayas and are relatively rare. Everything is small-scale but choice.

Alloway. ✆ **01292/441-215.** Admission £1 ($1.60). Apr–Oct daily 9:30am–5pm; Nov–Mar Mon–Sat 10am–4pm, Sun noon–4pm. Drive 3km (2 miles) south of Ayr on B7024.

Tam o' Shanter Experience   Here, adjacent to the gardens of the Burns Monument, you can watch a film on Burns's life, his friends, and his poetry. There's a well-stocked gift shop plus a tearoom. The Russians are particularly fond of Burns and his poetry, and many visit annually to pore over his original manuscripts; the museum has been presented with a translation of the poem *Tam o' Shanter* by Russian enthusiasts.

Murdoch's Lane. ✆ **01292/443-700.** Admission £1.50 ($2.40) adults, 75p ($1.20) children and seniors. Daily 9:30am–5:30pm. Drive 3km (2 miles) south of Ayr on B7024.

WHERE TO STAY & DINE

Belleisle House Hotel *Kids*   Beside A719, this imposing 1755 country house stands in a public park noted for its two golf courses. It has a stone exterior and interior paneling with ornate carvings depicting some scenes from Burns's *Tam o' Shanter,* with blazing fireplaces adding to the ambience. The guest rooms range from midsize to spacious; each has traditional furnishings and a small, shower-only bathroom. The place extends a special welcome to children and has a play area set aside for them. The Scottish cooking is excellent.

Belleisle Park, Doonfoot Rd., Alloway, Ayr, Ayrshire KA7 4DU. ✆ **01292/442-331.** Fax 01292/445-325. 14 units. £75 ($120) double; £90 ($144) bridal suite. Rates include Scottish breakfast. AE, MC, V. Free parking. Drive 3km (2 miles) south of Ayr on A719. Pets accepted. **Amenities:** Restaurant; bar; 2 golf courses; room service (7am–9pm); laundry/dry cleaning service. *In room:* TV, coffeemaker, hair dryer.

Brig o' Doon Hotel ✿   One of Scotland's most famous footbridges, the Brig o' Doon, is a few steps from this new-style hotel, on the river's east bank. With gardens so lovely that they often host weddings, this is the choice place to stay.

Everything from the plumbing—mainly with both tub and shower—to the stylish guest rooms is state of the art. Reserve early, especially in summer.

Alloway, Ayr, Ayrshire KA7 4PQ. ℂ **01292/442-466.** Fax 01292/441-999. www.costley-hotels.co.uk. 5 units. £100 ($160) double. Rates include Scottish breakfast. AE, MC, V. Free parking. Drive 3km (2 miles) south of Alloway on B7024. **Amenities:** 2 restaurants; bar; laundry service. *In room:* TV, coffeemaker, hair dryer.

CULZEAN

Some 19km (12 miles) south-southwest of Ayr and 6.5km (4 miles) west of Maybole on A719 is Culzean Castle. Maidens Bus (no. 60) from the Sandgate Bus Station in Ayr runs to Culzean six times per day; a 1-day round-trip ticket is £4.20 ($6.70) for adults and £2 ($3.20) for children.

Culzean Castle ★★   Built by famous Scottish architect Robert Adam in the late 18th century, this clifftop creation is a fine example of his castellated style, with a view to the south of Alisa Craig, a 334m (1,100-ft.) -high rounded rock 16km (10 miles) offshore that's a nesting ground and sanctuary for seabirds. Culzean (pronounced cul-*lane*) replaced an earlier Scots tower house as the family seat of the powerful Kennedy clan. In 1945, the castle and grounds were given to the National Trust for Scotland. It's well worth a visit and is of special interest to Americans because of General Eisenhower's connection—in 1946, the National Guest Flat was given to the general for his lifetime in gratitude for his services as supreme commander of Allied Forces in World War II. An exhibit of Eisenhower memorabilia, including his North African campaign desk, is sponsored by Scottish Heritage U.S.A., Inc. Culzean stands near the famous golf courses of Turnberry and Troon, a fact that particularly pleased the golf-loving Eisenhower. The tour also includes the celebrated round drawing room, delicately painted ceilings, and outstanding Adam oval staircase.

Overlooking the Firth of Clyde ℂ **01655/884-455.** www.culzeancastle.net. Admission (including entrance to the Country Park below) £9 ($14) adults, £6.50 ($10) seniors/children, £23 ($37) families (2 adults and 2 children). Apr–Oct daily 10:30am–5pm (last admission ½-hour before closing). Closed Nov–Mar.

Culzean Country Park ★ *(Kids)*   Part of the land surrounding the castle includes what in 1969 became the first country park in Scotland. The 228 hectare (565 acre) grounds contain a walled garden, an aviary, a swan pond, a camellia house, an orangery, an adventure playground, and a newly restored 19th-century pagoda, as well as a deer park, kilometers of woodland paths, and beaches. It has gained an international reputation for its visitor center (Adam's home farm) and related visitor and educational services.

On the land surrounding Culzean Castle. ℂ **01655/884-400.** Admission included in admission to Culzean Castle. Daily 9am–dusk.

TURNBERRY: WORLD-CLASS GOLF ★

On the Firth of Clyde, the little town of Turnberry, south of the castle, was part of the Culzean Estate, owned by the marquess of Ailsa. It began to flourish early in this century, when the Glasgow and South Western Railway developed rail service, golfing facilities, a recognized golfing center, and a first-class hotel.

From the original two 13-hole golf courses, the complex has developed into the two 18-hole courses, Ailsa and Arran, known worldwide as the **Turnberry Hotel Golf Courses.** The Ailsa, one of the most exacting courses yet devised, has been the scene of numerous championship tournaments and PGA events. Come here for the prestige, but prepare yourself for the kind of weather a lobster fisherman in Maine might find daunting. (Its par is 70, its SSS 72, and its yardage 6,976 [6,348m].) Newer, and usually shunted into the role of also-ran, is the Arran Course. Call © **01655/334-032** for details. Guests of the hotel get priority on the Ailsa course. The greens fee of £90 to £105 ($144–$168) for guests, and £130 ($208) (Mon–Friy) or £175 ($280) (weekends) for nonguests includes 18 holes on the Ailsa course and an 18-hole round on the Arran course. Clubs rent for £40 ($64) per round or £55 ($88) per day; caddy service costs £30 ($48) plus tip. If you're not staying here, give them a call in the morning to check on any unclaimed tee times—but it's a long shot.

A short drive east of Turnberry takes you to **Souter Johnnie's Cottage,** Main Road, in Kirkoswald (© **01655/760-603**), 6.5km (4 miles) west of Maybole on A77. This was the 18th-century home of the village cobbler, John Davidson (Souter Johnnie), who, with his friend Douglas Graham of Shanter Farm, was immortalized by Burns in *Tam o' Shanter.* The cottage contains Burnsiana and contemporary cobbler's tools, and in the churchyard are the graves of Tam o' Shanter and Souter Johnnie. From Good Friday to September, the cottage is open daily from 11:30am to 5pm; in October, hours are Saturday and Sunday from 11:30am to 5pm. Off-season admittance is sometimes available by appointment. Admission is £3.50 ($5.60) for adults and £1.60 ($2.55) for seniors, students, and children.

A final sight is **Carleton Castle,** along A77 some 23km (14 miles) south of Culzean Castle and 5km (3 miles) south, following the coast, from the little seaside town of Girvan. In its heyday it was a watchtower, built to guard the coastline against invaders. A famous ballad grew out of a legend surrounding the castle: It was said to be the headquarters of a baron who married eight times. When this Bluebeard got tired of a wife, he pushed her over the cliff and found himself another. However, he proved no match for his eighth wife, May Cullean. "The Ballad of May Colvin" relates how she's supposed to have tricked and outlived him.

WHERE TO STAY

Best Western Malin Court Hotel   On one of the most scenic strips of the Ayrshire coast, this well-run hotel fronts the Firth of Clyde and the Turnberry golf courses. It is not a great country house, but rather a serviceable, welcoming retreat offering a blend of informality and comfort. Bedrooms are mostly medium in size. The staff can arrange hunting, fishing, riding, sailing, and golf.

Turnberry, Ayrshire KA26 9PB. © **01655/331-457.** Fax 01655/331-072. www.malincourt.co.uk. 18 units. £104–£124 ($166–$198) double. Rates include breakfast. AE, DC, MC, V. Free parking. Take A74 to Ayr exit, then A719 to Turnberry and Maidens. **Amenities:** Restaurant; bar; 24-hr. room service; laundry/dry cleaning service. *In room:* TV, dataport, coffeemaker, hair dryer, iron/ironing board.

Westin Turnberry Resort ⭐⭐⭐   The 1908 Turnberry, 81km (50 miles) south of Glasgow on A77, is a remarkable and opulent Edwardian property. From afar, you can see the hotel's white facade, red-tile roof, and dozens of gables. The public rooms contain Waterford crystal chandeliers, Ionic columns, molded ceilings, and oak paneling. Each guest room is furnished in unique early-1900s style and has a marble-sheathed bathroom. The rooms, which vary in size, open onto views of the lawns, forests, and (in some cases) Scottish coastline.

Maidens Rd., Turnberry, Ayrshire KA26 9LT. © **01655/331-000.** Fax 01655/331-706. www.turnberry.co.uk. 221 units. £375–£415 ($600–$665) double; £495 ($792) suite. Off-season rates lower. Rates include Scottish breakfast. AE, DC, MC, V. Free parking. **Amenities:** 3 restaurants; 3 bars; indoor pool; tennis courts; exercise room; spa; Jacuzzi; sauna; car-rental desk; salon; 24-hr. room service; babysitting; massage; laundry/dry cleaning service. *In room:* TV, dataport, minibar, coffeemaker, hair dryer, trouser press.

WHERE TO DINE

Cotters Restaurant SCOTTISH   Exemplary service, a scenic location, and the finest local ingredients make a winning combination. The modern, tasteful decor creates a casual, relaxed atmosphere. The lunch menu offers everything from melon slices to deep-fried haddock in beer batter. For dinner, you might start with melon and peaches glazed with an orange sabayon, or salmon and asparagus terrine with chive butter. For a main course, try the baked Ayrshire lamb and chicken mousseline wrapped in phyllo pastry. The tempting desserts include a chocolate and hazelnut tart, warm bread and plum pudding awash in a sea of vanilla sauce, and a fine selection of cheeses.

In the Malin Court Hotel, Turnberry. ℂ **01655/331-457**. Reservations recommended. Main courses £5–£13 ($8–$21); table d'hôte £25 ($40). AE, DC, MC, V. Daily 12:30–2pm and 7:30–9pm.

TROON & THE ROYAL TROON GOLF CLUB ✿

The resort town of **Troon,** 11km (7 miles) north of Ayr, 50km (31 miles) south-west of Glasgow, and 124km (77 miles) southwest of Edinburgh, looks out across the Firth of Clyde to the Isle of Arran. It's a 20th-century town, its earlier history having gone unrecorded. Troon takes its name from the curiously shaped promontory jutting out into the Clyde estuary on which the old town and the harbor stand. The promontory was called Trwyn, the Cymric word for "nose," and later this became Trone and then Troon. A massive statue of *Britannia* stands on the seafront as a memorial to the dead of the two world wars.

Troon offers several golf links, including the **Royal Troon Golf Club,** Craigends Road, Troon, Ayrshire KA10 6EP (ℂ **01292/311-555**). This is a 7,097-yard (6,458m) course (one of the longest in Scotland) with an SSS of 74 and a par of 71. Dignified Georgian and Victorian buildings and the faraway Isle of Arran are visible from fairways, which seem deliberately designed to steer your golf balls into the sea or the dozens of sand traps flanking your shot. The **Old Course** is the more famous, reserved for men. Nonmembers may play only on certain days. A newer addition, the 6,289-yard (5,723m), par 71 Portland, is open to both men and women and is, by some estimates, even more challenging than the Old Course. The British Open has been played here off and on since 1923. The greens fee—£170 ($272) for a day—includes a buffet lunch and two 18-hole sets. For one round of play, a trolley rents for £3 ($4.80) and a caddy £30 ($48); club rental is £25 ($40) per round or £40 ($64) per day.

In summer, visitors find plenty of room on Troon's 3km (2 miles) of **sandy beaches** stretching along both sides of its harbor; the broad sands and shallow waters make it a safe haven. From here you can take steamer trips to Arran and the Kyles of Bute.

Trains from Glasgow's Central Station arrive at the Troon station several times daily (trip time: 40 min.). Call ℂ **08457/484-950** for 24-hour information. Trains also connect Ayr with Troon, a 10-minute ride. Buses and trains from Glasgow cost £5.30 ($8.50) each way. From the Ayr bus station, you can reach Troon and other parts of the area by bus, costing £1.90 ($3.05) each way. Call ℂ **08706/082-608** for details. From Prestwick, motorists head north along B749.

WHERE TO STAY

You also might want to consider **Highgrove House** (see "Where to Dine," below).

Lochgreen House Hotel ✿✿   Adjacent to the fairways of the Royal Troon Golf Course, one of Scotland's loveliest country-house hotels is set on 12 lush hectares (30 acres) of forest and landscaped gardens. The property opens onto views of the Firth of Clyde and Ailsa Craig. The interior evokes a more elegant bygone time, with detailed cornices, antique furnishings, and elegant oak and cherry paneling. Guests meet and mingle in two luxurious sitting rooms with log fires, or take long walks on the well-landscaped grounds. The spacious bedrooms have the finest mattresses.

Monktonhill Rd. Southwood, Troon, Ayrshire KA10 7EN. ℂ 01292/313-343. Fax 011292/317-661. www.costley-hotels.co.uk. 40 units. £130–£160 ($208–$256) double. Rates include breakfast. AE, MC, V. Free parking. Take B749 to Troon. **Amenities:** 2 restaurants; 2 bars; tennis court; 24-hr. room service; laundry/dry cleaning service. *In room:* TV, coffeemaker, hair dryer, trouser press.

Piersland House Hotel   This hotel was built more than a century ago by Sir Alexander Walker of the Johnnie Walker whisky family. The importation of 17,000 tons of topsoil transformed its marshy surface into a lush 1.6-hectare (4-acre) garden. The moderately sized guest rooms have traditional country-house styling.

15 Craigend Rd., Troon, Ayrshire KA10 6HD. ℂ 01292/314-747. Fax 01292/315-613. www.piersland.co.uk. 30 units. £124 ($198) double; £140–£170 ($224–$272) suite. Rates include Scottish breakfast. AE, DC, MC, V. Free parking. Drive 3 minutes south of the town center on B749. **Amenities:** Restaurant; bar; 24-hr. room service; laundry/dry cleaning service. *In room:* TV, minibar, coffeemaker, hair dryer, trouser press.

WHERE TO DINE

The dining room at the **Piersland House Hotel** (see "Where to Stay," above) is also recommended.

Fairways Restaurant SCOTTISH/INTERNATIONAL   This landmark 1890s hotel stands on the Ayrshire coast overlooking the Royal Troon Golf Course. The restaurant can satisfy your hunger pangs with some degree of style. Traditional Scottish and French dishes include pillows of smoked Scottish salmon, followed by turbot with langoustines or shrimp.

In the Marine Highland Hotel, 8 Crosbie Rd. ℂ 01292/314-444. Reservations required. Set-price lunch £9.50–£11.50 ($15–$18); main courses £11–£19 ($18–$30). AE, DC, MC, V. Daily 12:30–2pm and 7–9:30pm.

Highgrove House TRADITIONAL SCOTTISH   This charming white-painted, red-roofed brick building is isolated on a hillside known for its scenic view over the sea and the Isle of Arran. The bustling restaurant moves big crowds in and out quickly. Menu items include several varieties of steamed salmon and Scottish venison with rowanberry sauce.

Upstairs are nine simple but comfortable guest rooms with TVs, phones, and hair dryers; breakfast included, they rent for £100 ($160).

Old Loan's Rd., Troon, Ayrshire KA10 7HL. ℂ 01292/312-511. Reservations recommended. Main courses £8–£16 ($13–$26) lunch; £13–£17 ($21–$27) dinner. AE, MC, V. Daily noon–2:30pm and 6–9:30pm. Drive 3km (2 miles) north of Troon on A78.

Lochgreen House Hotel Restaurant ✦ SCOTTISH/FRENCH   This is one of the region's most agreeable culinary stopovers, where you'll be tempted by the finest seafood, game, and Scottish beef. The elegant dining room, with its views of woodland and garden, somehow makes the food taste even better. The service is just as flawless. For a main course, sample the poached halibut on a mussel and fennel stew with saffron potatoes and chives. The wine list roams the world for inspiration, and the desserts often feature the fresh fruit of the season.

Monktonhill Rd., Southwood ℂ 01292/313-343. Reservations required. Set-price menu £16 ($26) for a 3-course lunch; £32.50 ($52) for a 4-course dinner. AE, MC, V. Daily noon–2pm and 7–9pm. Take B749 to Troon.

7

Argyll & the Southern Hebrides

The old county of Argyll (in Gaelic, *Earraghaidheal,* "coastland of the Gael") on and off the coast of western Scotland is a rewarding journey. Summers along the coast are usually cool and damp and winters relatively mild but wet, with little snow.

The major center of Gaelic culture for the district is **Oban** ("small bay"), a great port for the Western Isles and the gateway to the Inner Hebrides (see chapter 11).

There are several island destinations off the Argyll coast meriting your time. The long **peninsula of Kintyre** separates the islands of the Firth of Clyde from the islands of the Inner Hebrides.

From the Isle of Islay to the Mull of Kintyre, the climate is mild. The land is rich and lush, especially on Arran. The peat deposits on Islay lend flavor to the making of such fine malt whiskies as Lagavulin, Bruichladdick, and Laphroaig. There's a diversity of scenic beauty: hills and glens, fast-rushing streams, and little roads that eventually lead to coastal villages displaying B&B signs in summer. The unspoiled and remote island of Jura is easily reached from Islay.

And the best news for last: These islands, as well as the Kintyre peninsula, are among the best travel bargains in the British Isles.

1 The Isle of Arran: Scotland in Miniature ★★

Brodick: 119km (74 miles) W of Edinburgh, 47km (29 miles) W of Glasgow

At the mouth of the Firth of Clyde, the Isle of Arran is often described as "Scotland in miniature" because of its wild and varied scenery—the glens, moors, lochs, sandy bays, and rocky coasts that have made the country famous. Once you're on Arran, buses will take you to various villages, each with its own character. A coast road, 97km (60 miles) long, runs around the length of the island.

Arran boasts some splendid mountain scenery, notably the conical peak of **Goatfell** in the north (called the "mountain of the winds"), reaching a height of 869m (2,866 ft.). Arran is also filled with beautiful glens, especially **Glen Sannox,** in the northeast, and **Glen Rosa,** north of Brodick. Students of geology flock to Arran to study igneous rocks of the Tertiary period. Cairns and standing stones at Tormore intrigue archaeologists as well. The island is only 40km (25 miles) long and 16km (10 miles) wide and can be seen in a single day.

ESSENTIALS

GETTING THERE High-speed electric trains operate from Glasgow Central direct to Ardrossan Harbour, taking 1 hour and costing £4.70 ($7.50) one-way. For 24-hour rail inquiries, call © **8475/484-950.** (If you're driving from Glasgow, head southwest along A737 until you reach Ardrossan.) At Ardrossan, you must make a 30-minute ferry crossing to Arran, arriving in Brodick, Arran's main town, on its east coast.

In summer, a small ferry runs between Lochranza in the north of Arran across to Claonaig in Argyll, providing a gateway to the Highlands and a visit to

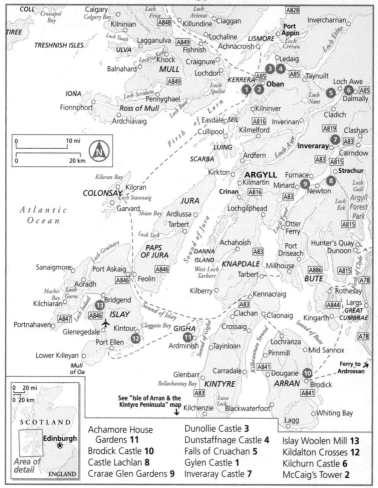

Achamore House Gardens **11**
Brodick Castle **10**
Castle Lachlan **8**
Crarae Glen Gardens **9**
Dunollie Castle **3**
Dunstaffnage Castle **4**
Falls of Cruachan **5**
Gylen Castle **1**
Inveraray Castle **7**
Islay Woolen Mill **13**
Kildalton Crosses **12**
Kilchurn Castle **6**
McCaig's Tower **2**

Kintyre. There are six boats daily, and the fare is £47.50 ($76) for a vehicle, plus £8 ($13) per passenger for a return journey. For information about ferry departures (which change seasonally), check with **Caledonian MacBrayne** (© **01457/ 650-100**) at the ferry terminal in Gourock.

VISITOR INFORMATION The **tourist office** is at The Pier, Brodick (© **01770/302-140;** www.ayrshire-arran.com). June to August, it's open Monday to Saturday 9am to 7:30pm and Sunday 10am to 5pm; September to May, hours are Monday to Saturday 9am to 5pm.

EXPLORING THE ISLAND

After the ferry docks at Brodick, you may want to head for Arran's major sights, **Brodick Castle** and the **Isle of Arran Heritage Museum** (see below).

The most intriguing walks on the island are signposted. But if you're really serious about hiking, buy one of two detailed guides at the tourist office— **Seventy Walks in Arran** for £2.50 ($4) and **My Walks in Arran** for £2.25

($3.60). While at the office, ask about any guided walks the Forestry Commission might be conducting. They are scheduled frequently in summer and range from 2 to 5 hours, costing £4 to £7 ($6.40–$11).

If you'd prefer to do your exploring on two wheels, stop by **Mr. Bilsland,** The Gift Shop, Brodick (© **01770/302-272**). You'll have to show an ID as deposit; rental rates include a helmet and are £5 to £10 ($8–$16) daily £16 to £33 ($26–$53) weekly. It's open daily 9:30am to 6pm. **Brodick Cycles,** Brodick (© **01770/302-460**), requires a £5 to £25 ($8–$40) deposit, depending on the type of bike. Daily rentals range from £7.50 to £10 ($12–$16), with £17 to £34 ($27–$54) for a full week. It's open in summer Monday to Saturday 9am to 6pm and Sunday 10am to 6pm.

South from Brodick is the village/resort of **Lamlash,** opening onto Lamlash Bay. From here, a ferry takes you over to Holy Island with its 303m (1,000-ft.) peak. A disciple of St. Columba founded a church on this island. In the north, **Lochranza** is a village with unique appeal. It opens onto a bay of pebbles and sand, and in the background lie the ruins of a castle that was reputedly the hunting seat of Robert the Bruce.

Brodick Castle ⭐⭐   The historic home of the dukes of Hamilton, this red-sandstone castle dates from the 13th century and contains superb silver, antiques, portraits, and objets d'art. Some castle or other has stood on this site since about the 5th century, when the Dalriada Irish, a Celtic tribe, came here and founded their kingdom. The castle is now the property of the National Trust for Scotland and boasts award-winning gardens. Laid out in the 1920s by the duchess of Montrose, they're filled with shrubs, trees, perennials, and herbs from Tasmania, New Zealand, Chile, the Himalayas, and northern Britain. Especially noteworthy are the rhododendrons, which are one of the focal points of the Country Park (a semi-domesticated forest) bordering the more formal gardens.

2.5km (1½ miles) north of the Brodick pierhead. © **01770/302-202.** www.nts.org.uk. Admission to both castle and gardens £7 ($11) adults, £5.30 ($8.50) seniors/students, children age 5 and under free. Castle Apr–Oct daily 9am–4:30pm (to 5pm July–Aug); gardens and Country Park daily 11am–sunset. Bus: Any labeled "Brodick Castle."

Isle of Arran Heritage Museum   A compound of antique structures once used as outbuildings for the nearby castle, this museum provides the best overview of life on Arran from prehistoric times to the present. The most prominent of the buildings is a stone-sided cottage filled with 19th-century memorabilia, costumes, and artifacts, including a working kitchen. Also on site are a blacksmith's shop and forge, geological artifacts, and an archive room housing historic records associated with Arran. Access to the archive room is reserved for scholars pursuing academic research.

⌒**Moments   Down a Lovely Glen with a Picnic in Hand**

The best way to discover the island's beauty is to stroll around. Right beyond the Isle of Arran Heritage Museum, at the point where String Road divides the island, you can follow the signs to a beauty spot called **Glen Rosa.** This is the island's loveliest glen, and you might want to pick up the makings of a picnic lunch before setting out. Another great walk is to the village of **Corriegills,** which is signposted along A841 south of Brodick. As you stroll, you'll be treated with the finest views of Brodick Bay.

The Isle of Arran & the Kintyre Peninsula

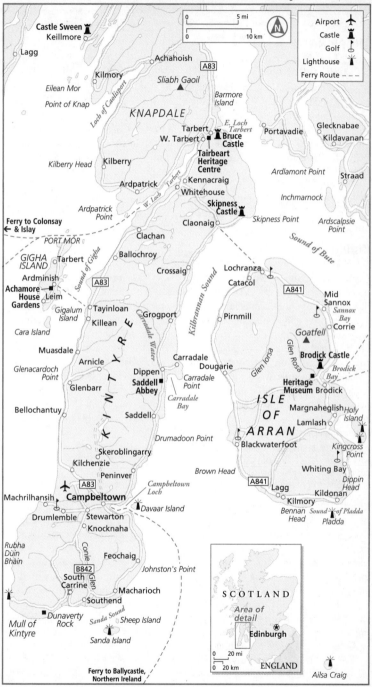

Castle Sween
Keillmore
Lagg
Achahoish
A83
Kilmory
Sliabh Gaoil
Eilean Mor
Point of Knap
Barmore Island
KNAPDALE
Loch of Caolisport
Tarbert
W. Tarbert
Bruce Castle
E. Loch Tarbert
Portavadie
Glecknabae
Kildavanan
Tairbeart Heritage Centre
Kilberry Head
Kilberry
Ardpatrick
Kennacraig
Whitehouse
Ardlamont Point
Straad
Inchmarnock
Ardpatrick Point
Skipness Castle
Skipness Point
Ardscalpsie Point
Ferry to Colonsay
← & Islay
Claonaig
PORT MOR
Clachan
Sound of Bute
GIGHA ISLAND
Tarbert
Ballochroy
Crossaig
Lochranza
Catacol
A841
Mid Sannox
Ardminish
A83
Achamore House Gardens
Leim
Gigalum Island
Tayinloan
Grogport
Pirnmill
Goatfell
Sannox Bay
Corrie
Killean
Cara Island
Kilbrannan Sound
Glen Rosa
Brodick Castle
Muasdale
Arnicle
Carradale
Dougarie
Brodick Bay
Glenacardoch Point
Dippen
Saddell Abbey
Carradale Point
Glen Iorsa
Heritage Museum
Brodick
Glenbarr
Carradale Bay
Bellochantuy
Saddell
ISLE OF ARRAN
Margnaheglish
Lamlash
Holy Island
Skeroblingarry
Drumadoon Point
Blackwaterfoot
Kingcross Point
Kilchenzie
Peninver
Brown Head
Whiting Bay
Machrilhansih
A83
Campbeltown
Campbeltown Loch
A841
Lagg
Kildonan
Dippin Head
Drumlemble
Stewarton
Davaar Island
Kilmory
Bennan Head
Sound of Pladda
Knocknaha
Pladda
Rubha Dùin Bhàin
Conie Glen
Feochaig
Johnston's Point
South Carrine
B842
Macharioch
Southend
Mull of Kintyre
Dunaverty Rock
Sanda Sound
Sheep Island
Sanda Island
Ferry to Ballycastle, Northern Ireland

SCOTLAND
Area of detail
Edinburgh
ENGLAND

Ailsa Craig

Airport
Castle
Golf
Lighthouse
Ferry Route

0   5 mi
0   10 km

Rosaburn, 2.5km (1½ miles) north of the Brodick ferry piers. © **01770/302-636.** www.arranmuseum.co.uk. Admission £2.50 ($4). Apr–Oct Mon–Sat 10am–5pm; Sun 11am–4pm. Bus: Any labeled "Brodick Castle."

SHOPPING

Divided into three businesses, the **Duchess Court Shops,** Home Farm, Brodick (© **01770/302-831**), is made up of the Home Farm Kitchen, selling locally produced chutneys, jams, and marmalades; the Nature Shop, dealing in books, jewelry, wood carvings, T-shirts, and other assorted goods; and Something Special, featuring natural grooming products.

About 10km (6 miles) north of Brodick in Corrie, **Corriecraft & Antiques,** Hotel Square (© **01770/810-661**), sells small Arran antiques and pottery. In Lamlash, **Patterson Arran Ltd.,** The Old Mill (© **01770/600-606**), offers chutneys, mustards, preserves, and other locally produced condiments.

The **Old Byre Showroom,** Auchencar Farm (© **01770/840-227**), 8km (5 miles) north of Blackwaterfoot along the coastal road in Machrie, sells sheepskin, leather, and tweeds, but its biggest draw is the large selection of locally produced wool sweaters.

WHERE TO STAY

IN BRODICK

Auchrannie Country House Hotel 🌟🌟 *(Kids)*   Acclaimed as the island's finest hotel and restaurant, this Victorian mansion (once the home of the dowager duchess of Hamilton) stands in pristine glory on 2.4 hectares (6 acres) of landscaped gardens and woods, about 1.6km (1 mile) from the Brodick ferry terminal. Guest rooms in the new wing are the most comfortable, but all the rooms are furnished with taste, using select fabrics and decorative accessories. Family suites (two bedrooms) and four-poster rooms are available.

The property's noteworthy leisure center features an indoor pool, a kids' pool, a playroom, a spa, games room, and sauna. You can enjoy drinks in the cocktail bar or sun lounge before heading for the Garden Restaurant, which offers fixed-price dinners—pricey, but the finest on Arran. The chef is really in his element when preparing West Coast seafood. Nonguests should reserve ahead.

Auchrannie Rd., Brodick, Isle of Arran KA27 8BZ. © **01770/302-234.** Fax 01770/302-812. www.auchrannie. co.uk. 28 units. £72–£126 ($115–$202) double with breakfast; £116–£168 ($186–$269) double with half board. AE, MC, V. **Amenities:** 2 restaurants; bar; room service; heated indoor pool; exercise room; spa; sauna; limited room service; babysitting; laundry. *In room:* TV, minibar, coffeemaker, hair dryer.

Kilmichael Country House Hotel 🌟🌟   It was voted Country House Hotel of the Year in a "Taste of Scotland" contest in 1998, and if anything, it's better than ever. The island's most scenically located house, it's said to be the oldest house on Arran, perhaps once a stamping ground for Robert the Bruce, complete with some reports of a resident ghost. A combination of the tasteful new and antique is used throughout. The guest rooms—all nonsmoking—are beautiful, as are the bathrooms, which offer luxury toiletries. Some rooms have four-poster beds and Jacuzzi tubs. The aura of gentility is reflected in the log fires and the fresh flowers from the garden. A suite and two other rooms, all with private entrances, are located in a converted 18th-century stable a few yards from the main building. The staff is helpful and welcoming.

The food is also noteworthy, using local produce whenever possible. International dishes are featured, and fine wines and an attention to detail go into the expensive fixed-price menus.

Brodick, Isle of Arran KA27 8BY. © **01770/302-219.** Fax 01770/302-068. www.kilmichael.com. 9 units. £150 ($240) double; £190 ($304) suite. Rates include Scottish breakfast. No children under 12. Small dogs accepted by prior arrangement. **Amenities:** Restaurant; bar; limited room service. *In room:* TV, coffeemaker, hair dryer, iron/ironing board (in some).

IN LAMLASH

Glenisle Hotel *(Finds*   Across the road from the waterfront, Glenisle could be one of the oldest buildings in the village, but no one knows its age or even the century of its construction. The well-kept gardens of this white-sided B&B, with a view across the bay to the Holy Isle, have flowerbeds and tall old trees. The reception lounge, water-view dining room, and lounge where drinks are available are cheerfully decorated. Each relatively simple but comfortable guest room has flowered curtains, good mattresses, a small but tidy bathroom, and a tasteful decor.

Shore Rd., Lamlash, Isle of Arran KA27 8LY. ℰ **01770/600-559.** Fax 01770/600-966. www.glenislehotel. com. 13 units. £42 ($67) per person with Scottish breakfast; £108 ($173) double with half board. MC, V. Take the Whiting bus from Brodick. **Amenities:** Restaurant; bar; laundry service. *In room:* TV, coffeemaker, hair dryer.

IN WHITING BAY

Grange House Hotel *(Kids*   Opening onto views across the Firth of Clyde, this country-house hotel is operated by Janet and Clive Hughes, who take a personal interest in their guests. A gabled stone house standing on landscaped grounds, the Grange offers tastefully furnished, traditional guest rooms. Some units can be arranged to accommodate a family, and one room is suitable for travelers with disabilities. Eight rooms open onto views of the Holy Isle and the Ayrshire coast. Some of the bathrooms are equipped with a tub, others with a shower only. The hosts no longer serve an evening meal, but are happy to make dinner reservations for you in the village.

Whiting Bay, Isle of Arran KA27 8QH. ℰ and fax **01770/700-263.** 9 units, 7 with private bathroom. £56–£69 ($90–$110) double without bathroom; £59–£72 ($94–$115) double with bathroom. Rates include Scottish breakfast. MC, V. Take the Whiting Bay bus from Brodick. **Amenities:** Bar; small exercise room; sauna; room service (8–10am). *In room:* TV, coffeemaker, no phone.

Royal Hotel   This granite house, located in the center of the village beside the coastal road, was one of the first hotels ever built on Arran, going back to 1895. True to its original function as a temperance hotel, it serves no alcohol, but guests can bring their own wine or beer into the dining room, which serves moderately priced dinners nightly at one sitting. Some of the bedrooms enjoy a vista over the bay and its tidal flats. One room contains a four-poster bed and lots of chintz, while another has a small sitting room. Each comes with a neat little shower-only bathroom.

Whiting Bay, Isle of Arran KA27 8PZ. ℰ and fax **01770/700-286.** 5 units. £52 ($83) double or suite. Rates include Scottish breakfast. No credit cards. Closed Nov–Mar. Take the Whiting Bay bus from Brodick. **Amenities:** Dining room. *In room:* TV, coffeemaker, hair dryer.

IN KILDONAN

Kildonan Hotel   Built as an inn in 1760, with a section added in 1928, the hotel rises a few steps from the island's best beach. It's in Scottish farmhouse style, with a slate roof, white-painted stone walls, and ample views of seabirds and gray seals basking on the rocks of Pladda Island opposite. The rooms were upgraded in early 2003 and range from small to midsize. They are traditionally furnished with comfortable beds, and all have private bathrooms with either a tub or shower. Some of the rooms are wheelchair accessible, and there is also a family suite, which rents for £100 ($160) a night.

Moments Seeing the Argyll on Horseback

There's no better way to experience the majestic beauty of the moors, Highlands, and headlands in the Argyll area than on horseback. To arrange an outing, contact the **Ardfern Riding Centre,** Croabh Haven, Loch Gilphead, Argyll ℂ **01852/500-632**). A 1-hour ride costs £15 ($24), a 2-hour ride £27 ($43), and a 4-hour ride (with lunch) £39 ($62). In addition to maintaining around 16 horses and a working cattle-and-sheep farm between Oban and Loch Gilphead, the center has a cottage that groups of up to 8 equestrians can rent for £250 to £300 ($400–$480) per week. The center is open all year, but the best times to go are from May to early June and from September to October.

The spacious dining room features moderately priced dinners; less formal lunches and dinners are served in the bar. A specialty available in either setting is crab or lobster salad made from fresh shellfish. A crowd of locals is likely to compete in a friendly fashion over the dartboard and billiards tables in the pub.

Kildonan, Isle of Arran, KA27 8SE. ℂ 01770/820-207. Fax 01770/820-320. www.kildonanhotel.com. 22 units. £75 ($120) double. Rates include Scottish breakfast. No credit cards. **Amenities:** Restaurant; bar; limited room service. In room: Hair dryer, no phone.

Kinloch Hotel This hotel, made from two joined cream-colored Victorian buildings, appears deceptively small from the road. It's actually the largest building in the village of Blackwaterfoot, with a contemporary wing jutting out along the coast. The midsize guest rooms are modestly comfortable and conservative, each with an excellent mattress, and a small bathroom. Most of the double rooms have sea views, but the singles tend to look out over the back gardens. A few have four-poster beds. The hotel also offers 7 self-contained suites with kitchen facilities, plus five 2-bedroom suites with a lounge and a small kitchenette. *Note:* The hotel's website claims the suites on the second floor are new, but they are actually 10 years old.

Blackwaterfoot, Isle of Arran KA27 8ET. ℂ 01770/860444. Fax 01770/860-447. www.kinloch-arran.com. 44 units. £68 ($109) per person with half board (Scottish breakfast and dinner); £140 ($224) suite. AE, DC, MC, V. Take the Blackwaterfoot bus from Brodick. **Amenities:** Restaurant; 2 bars; indoor heated pool; exercise room; sauna; limited room service; babysitting; laundry. In room: TV, coffeemaker, hair dryer.

WHERE TO DINE
IN BRODICK
The hotels reviewed above also have fine restaurants.

Creelers Seafood Restaurant SCOTTISH This dining choice lies in a mini-compound of gift shops and bistros created from a 1920s-era farm associated with Brodick Castle and is about 1.6km (1 mile) north of the center of Brodick Village. The most appealing of the places here is Creelers, a family-run enterprise specializing in seafood. It includes a "smokery" where salmon, scallops, and duck breast are carefully smoked and served almost immediately. You won't go wrong ordering any of the versions of smoked salmon, presented with capers and horseradish or with mushroom-studded risotto. In a cheerful yellow-and-green dining room, you'll find some of the freshest seafood in Scotland, much of it pulled in from local fishing boats that day. Especially appealing are seared Arran scallops with monkfish and pesto, and Scottish lobster with herb-flavored butter sauce.

The Home Farm, Brodick. ✆ **01770/30-810.** Reservations recommended. Set-price lunch £9.50–£10.50 ($15–$17); main courses £8–£14 ($13–$22) at lunch, £12–£20 ($19–$32) at dinner. MC, V. Tues–Sun noon–2:30pm and 6:30–10pm.

IN LAMLASH

Carraig Mhor ⭐ CONTINENTAL   Carraig Mhor, in a modernized peb-bledash (a mortar containing a mixture of pebbles) 1700s cottage in the village center overlooking the water, serves imaginative and beautifully presented din-ners. The chef makes extensive use of local products, especially seafood and game. All bread and ice creams, among other offerings, are made on the prem-ises. The menu changes seasonally, and there are separate dining rooms for smokers and nonsmokers.

Lamlash. ✆ **01770/600-453.** Reservations recommended. Fixed-price menus £19.50 ($31) for 2 courses, £25 ($40) for 3 courses. MC, V. Mon–Sat 7–9pm. Closed 2 weeks in Jan and first 2 weeks in Feb. Take the Whiting bus from Brodick.

ARRAN AFTER DARK

Regulars gather in Brodick's pubs to talk, argue, and drink. The **Brodick Bar,** in the center but without a street address (✆ **01770/302-169**), is an old wooden pub open Monday to Saturday 11am to midnight. Drop in for some real Scot-tish ale and a bar meal of local seafood (meals are served Mon–Saturday noon–2:30pm and 5:30–10pm). Featuring wood-and-leather chairs and walls hung with old photographs and riding gear, **Duncan's Bar,** also in the center but with no street address (✆ **01770/302-531**), keeps the same hours and serves real cask ales and lagers. Meals, available daily noon to 2pm and 5:30 to 8pm, always include a roast and seafood items.

2 The Kintyre Peninsula

The longest peninsula in Scotland, Kintyre stretches more than 97km (60 miles), with scenery galore, sleepy villages, and miles of sandy beaches. It's one of the country's most unspoiled areas, owing perhaps to its isolation. Kintyre was ancient Dalriada, the first kingdom of the Scots.

If you drive all the way to the tip of Kintyre, you'll be only 19km (12 miles) from Ireland. Kintyre is joined to the mainland of Scotland by a narrow neck of land near the old port of Tarbert. The largest town on the peninsula is the port of Campbeltown, on the southeastern coast.

AREA ESSENTIALS

GETTING THERE   Loganair (✆ **0141/889-1111**) makes two scheduled 45-minute flights a day from the Glasgow Airport to Campbeltown, the chief town of Kintyre.

From Glasgow, you can take buses to the peninsula (schedules vary season-ally). The trip takes 4 hours one-way and costs £10.50 ($17) each way. Inquire at the **Scottish City Link,** Buchanan Street Bus Station, Glasgow (✆ **0990/ 505-050**).

Kintyre is virtually an island unto itself, and the most efficient way to travel is by car. From Glasgow, take A82 up to the Loch Lomond side and cut across to Arrochar and go over the "Rest and Be Thankful" route to Inveraray (A83). Then cut down along Loch Fyne to Lochgilphead and continue on A83 south to Tarbert (see below), which can be your gateway to Kintyre. You can take A83 along the western coast or cut east at the junction of B8001 and follow it across the peninsula to B842. If your target is Campbeltown, you can reach it by either the western shore (much faster and a better road) or the eastern shore.

TARBERT

A sheltered harbor protects the fishing port and yachting center of Tarbert, on a narrow neck of land at the northern tip of the Kintyre. It's between West Loch Tarbert and the head of herring-filled Loch Fyne and has been called the "world's prettiest fishing port."

Tarbert means "drawboat" in Norse and referred to a place where Vikings dragged their boats across land on rollers from one sea to another. In 1093, King Malcolm of Scotland and King Magnus Barelegs of Norway agreed the Western Isles were to belong to Norway and the mainland to Scotland. An island was defined as anything a Viking ship could sail around, so Magnus proclaimed Kintyre an island by having his dragon ship dragged across the 1.6km (1 mile) of dry land from West Loch Tarbert on the Atlantic to East Loch Tarbert on Loch Fyne. After the Vikings gave way, Kintyre came under the control of the MacDonald lordship of the Isles.

EXPLORING THE AREA

The castle at Tarbert dates from the 13th century and was later extended by Robert the Bruce. The castle ruins, **Bruce Castle,** are on a hillock above the village on the south side of the bay. The oldest part still standing is a keep from the 13th century.

One of the major attractions of the peninsula is the remains of **Skipness Castle and Chapel,** at Skipness along B8001, 16km (10 miles) south of Tarbert, opening onto Loch Fyne. The hamlet was once a Norse village. The ruins of the ancient chapel and castle look out onto the Sounds of Kilbrannan and Bute. In its heyday, it could control shipping along Loch Fyne. A five-story tower remains.

Before striking out to visit the peninsula, consider stopping at the **Tarbert Heritage Centre** (© **01880/820-190**), immediately south of the village. Through various artifacts and exhibits, it traces life on the peninsula that's now largely vanished. Costing £3 ($4.80) it's open daily 10am to 5pm.

WHERE TO STAY

Stonefield Castle Hotel ⭐⭐   The best hotel choice in the area occupies a commanding position on 24 hectares (60 acres) of wooded grounds and luxurious gardens 3km (2 miles) outside Tarbert. The Stonefield, with turrets and a steeply pitched roof, was built in the 19th century by the Campbells. The well-appointed guest rooms come in a variety of sizes; smoking is not permitted in any of them. Some family suites are available as well as some four-poster rooms. The hotel's renowned gardens feature plants from all over the world and are one of the world's best repositories for more than 20 species of tree-size Himalayan rhododendrons, which in April are a riot of color. Book well in advance, as Stonefield has a large repeat crowd.

The kitchen staff does its own baking, and meals feature produce from the hotel's garden.

Tarbert PA29 6YJ. © **01880/820-836.** Fax 01880/820-929. www.stonefieldcastle.co.uk. 33 units. Sun–Thurs £160–£220 ($256–$352) double; Fri–Sat £190–£220 ($304–$352) double. Rates include half board. AE, MC, V. **Amenities:** Restaurant; bar; limited room service. *In room:* TV, coffeemaker, hair dryer.

West Loch Hotel   This 18th-century stone inn stands in a rural setting beside A83, 1.6km (1 mile) southwest of town in low-lying flatlands midway between the forest and the loch. Painted white with black trim, it contains two bars and a handful of open fireplaces and wood-burning stoves. The small guest rooms are modestly furnished but comfortable, many with views of the estuary. Each has a small bathroom with either tub or shower. The hotel contains a pub and a restaurant specializing in local seafood and game, using only the best local ingredients.

Tarbert PA29 6YF. (©) **01880/820-283**. Fax 01880/820-930. 8 units. £60 ($96) double. Rates include Scottish breakfast. MC, V. **Amenities:** Restaurant; 2 bars; limited room service. *In room:* TV, coffeemaker, hair dryer.

WHERE TO DINE

Anchorage Restaurant ★ *Finds* SCOTTISH/SEAFOOD   The Anchorage remains unpretentious despite its many culinary awards. Housed in a stone harborfront building that was once a customs house, it's run by Clare Johnson. Her daily menu includes such perfectly crafted seafood dishes as king scallops sautéed with lemon-lime butter and brochette of monkfish with saffron rice. A selection of European wines is available to accompany your fish.

Harbour St., Quayside. (©) **01880/820-881**. Reservations recommended. Main courses £12–£18 ($19–$29). MC, V. Daily 7–10pm. Closed Jan.

CAMPBELTOWN

Campbeltown is a fishing port and resort at the southern tip of the Kintyre Peninsula, 283km (176 miles) northwest of Edinburgh and 217km (135 miles) northwest of Glasgow. Popularly known as the "wee toon," Campbeltown has long been linked with fishing and has a **shingle beach.** For one of the greatest walks on the peninsula, see the box titled "Escape to the Isle That Time Forgot" below.

The **tourist office** is at MacKinnon House, The Pier (© **01586/552-056;** www.scotlandheartland.org). It's open from late June to mid-September, Monday through Saturday from 9am to 6:30pm and Sunday from 11am to 5pm; mid-September to late October, Monday through Friday from 10am to 5pm and Sunday from 10am to 4pm; late October to March, Monday through Friday from 10am to 4pm; April, Monday through Saturday from 10am to 5pm; and May to late June, Monday through Saturday from 10am to 5pm and Sunday from noon to 5pm.

EXPLORING THE AREA

On the quayside in the heart of town is the 14th-century **Campbeltown Cross.** This Celtic cross is the finest piece of carving from the Middle Ages left in Kintyre.

One of the area's most famous golf courses, the **Machrilhansih Golf Club,** lies nearby (© **01586/810-213**). It's a 6,228-yard (5,667m), par-70 course. Monday through Friday and Sunday, the greens fees are £30 ($48) per round or £50 ($80) per day; on Saturday, the fees are £40 ($64) per round or £60 ($96) per day. No club rentals are available; trolleys cost £4 ($6.40).

Moments **Escape to the Isle That Time Forgot**

Davaar Island, in Campbeltown Loch, is accessible at low tide by those willing to cross the Dhorlin, a 1km (½-mile) run of shingle-paved causeway; boat trips are also possible (ask at the tourist office). Once on the island, you can visit a **crucifixion cave painting,** the work of local Archibald MacKinnon, painted in 1887. It takes about 1½ hours to walk around this tidal island, with its natural rock gardens.

Oystercatcher Crafts & Gallery, 10 Hall St. (© 01586/553-070), sells Campbeltown pottery, wood carvings, and paintings by local artists. If you'd like to take a scenic drive and go shopping at the same time, head for Ronachan Silks, Ronachan Farmhouse at Clachan (© 01880/740-242), 40km (25 miles) north of Campbeltown on Route 83. In this unusual location, you can buy fashionable clothing and accessories, including kimonos, caftans, women's scarves, men's ties, and cushions. Call ahead to confirm opening times.

WHERE TO STAY & DINE

The Argyll Arms *Kids*   The Duke of Argyll no longer calls this his home, although he still maintains a suite on the second floor of this imposing stone building. The public rooms of this converted hotel still possess an aura of Victorian opulence, but the guest rooms are modernized and fairly modest. The rooms come in a variety of sizes, each traditionally furnished and outfitted with a small bathroom. Family rooms are also available. The restaurant specializes in moderately priced fish fresh from the quay.

Main St., Campbeltown PA28 6AB. © 01586/553-431. Fax 01586/553-594. 25 units. £60 ($96) double. Rates include Scottish breakfast. AE, MC, V. **Amenities:** Restaurant; 2 bars. *In room:* TV, coffeemaker, hair dryer, iron/ironing board.

Craigard House   This 1882 inn is in a neck-and-neck race with Argyll Arms as the best place to stay in the area. The dignified, monastic-looking pile with a bell tower is perched on the northern edge of the loch, about 1.6 km (1 mile) from the town center. The guest rooms come with contemporary-looking furniture and some vestiges of the original plasterwork, while the public areas are more traditional and Victorian. Most rooms open onto panoramic views of Campbeltown Loch, and each room comes with a small bathroom, some with tub, some with shower only.

The restaurant's weekly menu may include savory fish crepes, pan-fried duck breast with brandy and pepper-cream sauce, and chicken cacciatore.

Low Askomil, Campbeltown PA28 6EP. © 01586/554-242. Fax 01586/551-137. 8 units. www.craigard-house.co.uk. £65–£110 ($104–$176) double. Rates include breakfast. AE, MC, V. **Amenities:** Restaurant; bar; room service (10am–9:30pm); laundry. *In room:* TV, coffeemaker, hair dryer.

CAMPBELTOWN AFTER DARK

Pubs, not surprisingly, are the nightlife here, including two that host live music. They're in the center of the village, next door to each other. The **Feathers Cross Street** (© 01586/554-604), with stone walls, wooden floors, and hanging lamps, hosts bands playing a range of musical styles on Thursday nights. Open daily from 11am to 12:30am. The **Commercial Cross Street** (© 01586/553-703) has a variety of live music on Fridays and alternate Saturdays. A specialty here is real ale. Open Monday through Saturday from 11am to 1am and Sunday from 12:30pm to 1am. You'll find a quieter evening at the **Burnside Bar,** Burnside Street (© 01586/552-306), open daily from 11am to 1am. Conversation and local single malts are the preferred distractions here.

SOUTHEND & THE MULL OF KINTYRE

Some 16km (10 miles) south of Campbeltown, the village of Southend stands across from the Mull of Kintyre, and Monday through Saturday three buses a day run here from Campbeltown. It has sandy beaches, a golf course, and views across the sea to the Island of Sanda and to Ireland. Legend has it that footprints on a rock near the ruin of an old chapel mark the spot where St. Columba first

---

Finds **A Journey to Blood Rock**

Dunaverty Rock is a jagged hill marking the extreme southern tip of the Kintyre Peninsula. Located 15km (9 miles) south of Campbeltown and called "Blood Rock" by the locals, it was once the site of a MacDonald stronghold known as Dunaverty Castle, although nothing remains of it today. In 1647, it was the scene of a great massacre, in which some 300 citizens lost their lives. You can reach it by a local bus (marked SOUTH END) traveling from Campbeltown south about six times a day. Nearby, you'll find a series of isolated, unsupervised beaches and the 18-hole **Dunaverty Golf Course** (© 01586/830-677).

---

set foot on Scottish soil. Other historians suggest the footprints mark the spot where ancient kings were crowned.

About 18km (11 miles) from Campbeltown is the Mull of Kintyre. From Southend, you can take a narrow road until you reach the "gap," from where you can walk down to the lighthouse, a distance of 2.5km (1½ miles) before you reach the final point. Expect westerly gales as you go along. This is one of the wildest and most remote parts of the peninsula, and it's this desolation that appeals to visitors. The Mull of Kintyre is only 21km (13 miles) from Ireland. When local resident Paul McCartney made it the subject of a song, hundreds of fans flocked to the area.

3 The Isle of Gigha & Scotland's Finest Gardens

5km (3 miles) W of Kintyre's western coast

The 10km (6-mile) long Isle of Gigha boasts Scotland's finest gardens. Often called sacred and legendary, little has changed on the southern Hebridean isle over the centuries.

ESSENTIALS

GETTING THERE   Take a **ferry** to Gigha from Tayinloan, halfway up the west coast of Kintyre. Sailings are daily and take about 20 minutes, depositing you at **Ardminish,** the main hamlet on Gigha. The round-trip fare is £18.85 ($30) for an auto plus £5 ($8) per passenger. For ferry schedules, call © **08705/ 650-000** in Kennacraig.

VISITOR INFORMATION   There's no local tourist office, so ask at Campbeltown on the Kintyre Peninsula (see "The Kintyre Peninsula," earlier in this chapter).

GETTING AROUND   Because most likely you'll arrive without a car and there's no local bus service, you can either walk or call **Oliver's Taxi** at © **01583/505-251.**

EXPLORING THE ISLAND

Gigha is visited mainly by those wanting to explore its famous gardens. Be prepared to spend your entire day walking. The **Achamore House Gardens** ✦✦✦, 1.6km (1 mile) from the ferry dock at Ardminish, overflow with roses, hydrangeas, camellias, rhododendrons, and azaleas. On a 20-hectare (50-acre) site, they were the creation of the late Sir James Horlick, one of the world's great gardeners. The house isn't open to the public, but the gardens are open year-round, daily from dawn to dusk. Admission is £2 ($3.20). For information about the gardens, call the Gigha Hotel (see below).

The island has a rich Viking past (the Vikings stored their loot here after plundering the west coast of Scotland), and cairns and ruins still remain. **Creag Bhan,** the highest hill, rises more than 100m (330 ft.). From the top you can look out onto the islands of Islay and Jura as well as Kintyre; on a clear day, you can also see Ireland. The **Ogham Stone** is one of only two standing stones in the Hebrides that bears an Ogham inscription, a form of script used in the Scottish kingdom of Dalriada. High on a ridge overlooking the village of Ardminish are the ruins of the **Church of Kilchattan,** dating back to the 13th century.

WHERE TO STAY & DINE

Gigha Hotel ✶   Standing in a lonely, windswept location, this hotel lies a 5-minute walk from the island's ferry landing. Built in the 1700s as a farmhouse, it contains Gigha's only pub, one of its two restaurants, and its only accommodations except for some cottages. Each small but cozy room contains a shower-only bathroom. Rather expensive fixed-price dinners are served daily to both guests and nonguests; bar lunches are more affordable.

Ardminish, Isle of Gigha PA41 7AA. (✆ **01583/505-254.** Fax 01583/505-244. www.isle-of-gigha.co.uk/hotel. 13 units, 11 with private bathroom. £79 ($126) double with shared facilities; £130 ($195) with private bathroom. Rates include half-board. MC, V. Closed Dec 24–26. Dogs accepted. **Amenities:** Restaurant; bar. *In room:* TV, coffeemaker, hair dryer.

4 The Isle of Islay: Queen of the Hebrides ✶✶

26km (16 miles) W of the Kintyre Peninsula, 1km (¾ mile) SW of Jura

Islay (pronounced *eye*-lay) is the southernmost island of the Inner Hebrides, separated only by a narrow sound from Jura. At its maximum, Islay is only 32km (20 miles) wide and 40km (25 miles) long. Called the "Queen of the Hebrides," it's a peaceful and unspoiled island of moors, salmon-filled lochs, sandy bays, and wild rocky cliffs—an island of great beauty, ideal for long walks.

ESSENTIALS

GETTING THERE   MacBrayne **steamers** provide daily service to Islay. You leave West Tarbert on the Kintyre Peninsula, arriving in Port Askaig on Islay in about 2 hours. There's also service to Port Ellen. For information about ferry departures, check with Caledonian MacBrayne (✆ **01880/730-253**) at the ferry terminal in Gourock.

VISITOR INFORMATION   The **tourist office** is at Bowmore, The Square (✆ **01496/810-254**). May to September, it's open Monday to Saturday 9:30am to 5pm and Sunday 2 to 5pm; October to April, hours are Monday to Friday noon to 4pm.

EXPLORING THE ISLAND

Near **Port Charlotte** are the graves of the U.S. seamen and army troops who lost their lives in 1918 when their carriers, the *Tuscania* and the *Otranto,* were torpedoed off the shores of Islay. There's a memorial tower on the **Mull of Oa,** 13km (8 miles) from Port Ellen. For the greatest **walk** on the island, go along Mull of Oa Road heading toward the signposted solar-powered Carraig Fhada lighthouse, some 2.5km (1½ miles) away. The Oa peninsula was once the haunt of illicit whisky distillers and smugglers; the area is filled with sheer cliffs riddled with caves.

The island's capital is **Bowmore,** on the coast across from Port Askaig. Here you can see a fascinating Round Church (no corners for the devil to hide in). But the most important town is **Port Ellen** on the south coast, a holiday and golfing resort and Islay's principal port. The 18-hole **Machrie golf course** (© **01496/302-310**) is 5km (3 miles) from Port Ellen.

You can see the ancient seat of the lords of the Isles, the ruins of two castles, and several Celtic crosses. The ancient **Kildalton Crosses** are in the Kildalton churchyard, about 12km (7½ miles) northeast of Port Ellen—they're two of the finest Celtic crosses in Scotland. The ruins of the 14th-century fortress, **Dunyvaig Castle,** are just south of Kildalton.

In the southwestern part of Islay in Port Charlotte, the **Museum of Islay Life** (© **01496/850-358**), has a wide collection of island artifacts, ranging from unrecorded times to the present. Easter to October, the museum is open Monday to Saturday 10am to 4pm. Admission is £2.60 ($4.15) adults, £1.40 ($2.25) seniors, and £1.20 ($1.90) children. The Portnahaven bus from Bowmore stops here.

TOURING THE DISTILLERIES

The island is noted for its distilleries, which still produce single-malt Highland whiskies by the antiquated pot-still method. Of these, **Laphroaig Distillery,** about 1.6km (1 mile) along the road from Ardbeg to Port Ellen (© **01496/302-418**), offers a guided tour Monday to Friday in the morning at 10:15am and in the afternoon at 2:15pm. Admission is free and includes a sample dram. Call for an appointment. **Lagavulin,** Port Ellen (© **01496/302-400**), offers tours Monday to Friday at 10 and 11:30am, and 2:30pm. Admission is £3 ($4.80) per person and comes with a £3 ($4.80) voucher off the price of a bottle of whisky. A sample is included in the tour. A distillery gift shop is open Monday to Friday 8:30am to noon and 1 to 4:30pm.

Bowmore Distillery, School Street, Bowmore (© **01496/810-671**), conducts tours Monday to Friday at 10:30am and 2pm. In summer, there are additional tours during the week at 10am, 11:30am, and 2pm, and Saturday at 10:30am. The admission is £2 ($3.20), which includes a voucher worth £2 ($3.20) off the price of a bottle. Samples are included in the tour. Purchases can be made without taking the tour by stopping at the on-premises gift shop, open Monday to Friday 9am to 4:30pm and Saturday 10am to 12:30pm.

Moments **For Birdies and Ramblers**

Loch Gruinart cuts into the northern part of Islay, 11km (7 miles) northeast of Port Charlotte and 13km (8 miles) north of Bowmore. As the winter home for wild geese, it has attracted bird-watchers for decades. In 1984, the 1,215 hectares (3,000 acres) of moors and farmland around the loch were turned into the **Loch Gruinart Nature Reserve.**

This is another place for great walks. Beaches rise out of the falling tides, but they're too cold and rocky for serious swimming. This is a lonely and bleak coastline, but because of that it has a certain kind of beauty, especially as you make your way north along its eastern shoreline. On a clear day, you can see the Hebridean islands of Oronsay and Colonsay in the distance.

Port Askaig is home to two distilleries, **Bunnahabhain** (© **01496/840-646**), which offers tours at no charge by appointment and runs a gift shop on Monday to Friday 9am to 4pm, and **Coal Ila** (© **01496/840-207**), which runs no tours from October to Easter, but thereafter offers four tours (two morning, two afternoon) a day on Monday, Tuesday, Thursday, and Friday, and two morning tours on Wednesday. Admission is £3 ($4.80). Its gift shop is open to visitors at the end of each tour.

SHOPPING

The **Islay Woolen Mill,** Bridgend (© **01496/810-563**), has been making a wide range of country tweeds and accessories for more than a century. It made all the tweeds used in Mel Gibson's *Braveheart.* The mill shop, open Monday through Saturday from 10am to 5pm, sells items made with the *Braveheart* tweeds as well as tasteful Shetland wool ties, mufflers, Jacob mufflers and ties, flat caps, travel rugs, and scarves.

Another good place to find souvenirs is **Port Ellen Pottery,** Port Ellen (© **01496/302-345**), which sells brightly colored goblets, jugs, mugs, and other functional wares daily from 10am to 5pm. Note that the shop is very small and doesn't handle shipping on larger purchases.

WHERE TO STAY

Bridgend Hotel 🖈   Victorian spires cap the slate-covered roofs, while roses creep up the walls of this hotel, part of a complex including a roadside barn and one of the most beautiful flower and vegetable gardens on Islay. This is one of the oldest hotels on the island, with somber charm and country pleasures. Guests enjoy drinks beside the open fireplaces in the Victorian cocktail lounge and the rustic pub, where locals gather at the end of the day. The midsize bedrooms are comfortably and conservatively furnished, each with a small bathroom with either a tub or a shower.

The hotel serves up lots of local produce and many nonguests opt for a moderately priced dinner in the high-ceilinged dining room.

Bridgend, Isle of Islay PA44 7PJ. © **01496/810-212.** Fax 01496/810-960. www.bridgend-hotel.com. 11 units. £45.50 ($73) per person; £64 ($102) per person with dinner. Rates include Scottish breakfast. MC, V. **Amenities:** Restaurant; 2 bars; limited room service; laundry. *In room:* TV, coffeemaker, hair dryer.

Harbour Inn   Although this establishment is better known for its seafood restaurant (see below), it also offers delightful little bedrooms adjacent to Bowmore Harbour. Family run, the place exudes Hebridean hospitality. Each room is individually decorated in bright colors such as lime or cherry, and the furnishings are mainly wood pieces offset with graceful accessories. Each unit is equipped with a tidy little bathroom with tub or shower. Every room has a theme for its decor, ranging from a Victorian garden aura to a "captain's cabin" in mahogany. Two accommodations are suitable for families. The building dates from the 19th century but it was completely modernized in 2001. The coffee lounge adjacent to the ground-floor dining room feature both specialty coffees and fine views of northern Islay and the Paps of Jura.

The Square, Bowmore, Isle of Islay, Argyll PA43 7JR. © **01496/810-330.** Fax 01496/810-990. www.harbour-inn.com. 8 units. £95–£105 ($152–$168) double. Rates include full breakfast. AE, MC, V. **Amenities:** Restaurant; bar; exercise room; sauna; babysitting; laundry. In room: TV, coffeemaker, hair dryer, iron/ironing board.

Port Askaig Hotel   On the Sound of Islay overlooking the pier, this inn dates from the 18th century but was built on the site of an even older inn. It offers island hospitality and Scottish fare and is a favorite of anglers; the bar is popular with local fisherfolk. Bar meals are available for lunch and dinner. The guest rooms are a bit small, but each is furnished in a comfortable though not stylish way, with a little bathroom, some of which contain a tub and shower combination, the others a shower only.

Hwy. A846 at the ferry crossing to Jura, Port Askaig, Isle of Islay PA46 7RD. ⓒ 01496/840-245. Fax 01496/840-295. www.portaskaig.co.uk. 8 units. £76–£82 ($122–$131) double. Rates include Scottish breakfast. AE, MC, V. Dogs accepted. **Amenities:** Restaurant; 2 bars; limited room service. *In room:* TV, coffeemaker, hair dryer.

Port Charlotte Hotel   This 1829 hotel—actually a trio of cottages joined together—stands next to the small sandy beaches of Port Charlotte with views over Loch Indaal. It has been refurbished and immediately won a four-crown rating from the Scottish Tourist Board. The guest rooms are beautiful, most with antiques and oriental rugs. A small bathroom has been installed in each bedroom. The hotel is wheelchair accessible. Features include a large conservatory, a comfortable lounge, and a public bar.

The hotel is also the best place to dine in the area, with main courses costing £18 to £22 ($29–$35). Typical dishes include sirloin of Islay steak, freshly caught Islay lobster, and grilled filet of Scottish turbot.

Main St., Port Charlotte, Isle of Islay PA48 7TU. ⓒ 01496/850-360. Fax 01496/850-361. www.portcharlotte hotel.co.uk. 10 units. £59 ($94) single, £100 ($160) double. Rates include Scottish breakfast. MC, V. **Amenities:** Restaurant; bar; bike rentals; limited room service; laundry. *In room:* TV, coffeemaker, hair dryer.

WHERE TO DINE

You can also dine at any of the hotels listed above.

The Croft Kitchen BRITISH   On the main highway running through town, this is a low-slung, homey, and utterly unpretentious diner/bistro with a friendly staff. Holding no more than 40 customers at a time, it serves wine, beer, and whisky distilled on Islay, along with generous portions of down-home food. You'll find lots of fresh fish and shellfish, as well as soups, fried scallops, roasted Islay venison with rowanberry jelly, and steamed mussels with garlic mayonnaise.

Port Charlotte, Isle of Islay. ⓒ 01496/850-230. Sandwiches £3 ($4.80); main courses £9–£12 ($14–$19) at lunch, £10–£16 ($16–$26) at dinner. MC, V. Daily 10am–8:30pm (last order). Closed mid-Oct to mid-Mar.

Harbour Inn Restaurant. ☆ SEAFOOD/MODERN BRITISH   Back in 2000 this restaurant won the Automobile Association's seafood restaurant of the year award, and the fish is as fresh and as good as ever. High-quality ingredients are used to produce the Scottish bounty served here that includes not only the best of the catch of the day but some outstanding Scottish lamb and beef dishes as well. We've enjoyed some of the best crab, prawns and lobster in the Hebrides here. Each dish is prepared to order so be prepared to enjoy the wait. You can begin with a selection of smoked Islay seafood with a savory lemon and garlic mayonnaise, or else a terrine of roe deer with a melon and ginger chutney. For a main course opt for such delights as stir-fried Lagavulin scallops with fresh lime and sprigs of curry plant, or else a bubbling kettle of Islay seafood stew flavored with fennel and served on a bed of linguini with "eggplant spaghetti." The restaurant also offers a selection of locally distilled single malt whisky from Islay itself.

The Square, Bowmore, Isle of Islay, Argyll PA43 7JR. ⓒ 01496/810-330. Reservations recommended on weekends. Lunch main courses £6–£10 ($9.60–$16); dinner main courses £12–£20 ($19–$32). AE, MC, V. Daily noon–2:30pm and 6–9pm.

ISLAY AFTER DARK

After work, distillery employees gather at the pub at the **Harbour Inn,** Main Street in Bowmore (℅ **01496/810-330**), an old pub with stone walls, a fireplace, and wooden floors and furnishings. It's open Monday through Saturday from 11am to 1am and Sunday from noon to 1am. Local seafood is served at lunch and dinner. In summer, reservations are recommended.

5 The Isle of Jura: Deer Island ⭐

1km (¾ mile) E of Islay

Jura is the fourth largest of the Inner Hebrides, 43km (27 miles) long and varying from 3km to 13km (2–8 miles) in breadth. It takes its name from the Norse *jura,* meaning "deer island." The red deer on Jura—at 1.2m (4 ft.) high, the largest wild animals roaming Scotland—outnumber the people by about 20 to 1. The hearty islanders number only about 250, and most of them live along the east coast. Jura is relatively unknown, and its mountains, soaring cliffs, snug coves, and moors make it an inviting place.

ESSENTIALS

GETTING THERE   From Kennacraig (West Loch, Tarbert) you can go to Port Askaig on Islay (see above) taking one of the **Caledonian MacBrayne ferries** (℅ **01880/730-253**). The cost is £59 ($94) for a car and £10.50 ($17) per passenger each way (4-day return tickets are more economical). From Port Askaig, you can take a second ferry to Feolin on Jura; call **Western Ferries** at ℅ **01496/840-681.** Car spaces must be booked in advance. The cost for a vehicle is £8 ($13), plus £1.20 ($1.90) for a passenger one-way.

VISITOR INFORMATION   The Isle of Islay (see, "The Isle of Islay: Queen of the Hebrides," earlier in this chapter) has the nearest tourist information office.

EXPLORING THE ISLAND

Since most of the island is accessible only by foot, wear sturdy walking shoes and bring raingear. The best place for walks is the **Jura House Garden and Grounds** at the southern tip. These grounds were laid out by the Victorians to take advantage of the natural beauty of the region, and you can visit the gardens with their sheltered walks and panoramic views daily 9am to 5pm. Admission is £3 ($4.80). June to August, it's also the best place on the island to have tea, but only Saturday and Sunday. Call ℅ **01496/820-315** for details.

The capital, **Craighouse,** is hardly more than a hamlet. From Islay, you can take a 5-minute ferry ride to Jura from Port Askaig, docking at the Feolin Ferry berth.

The island's landscape is dominated by the **Paps of Jura,** which reach a peak of 780m (2,571 ft.) at Beinn-an-Oir. An arm of the sea, **Loch Tarbert** nearly divides the island, cutting into it for nearly 10km (6 miles).

⌐**Fun Fact** **The Gloom & Doom of Orwell's *1984***

George Orwell was quite ill when he lived on Jura in the bitter postwar winters of 1946 and 1947 while working on *1984.* After a close call when he and his adopted son ventured too close to the whirlpool in the Gulf of Corryvreckan—they were saved by local fishermen—he went on to publish his masterpiece in 1949, only to die in London of tuberculosis in 1950.

The square tower of **Claig Castle,** now in ruins, was the stronghold of the MacDonalds until they were subdued by the Campbells in the 17th century.

WHERE TO STAY & DINE

Jura Hotel ★ (Finds)   The island's only hotel is a sprawling gray-walled building near the center of the hamlet. (Craighouse lies east of Feolin along the coast). Sections date from the 1600s, but what you see today was built in 1956. The midsize guest rooms are of high quality, with comfortable mattresses and, in most cases, small bathrooms with a tub and shower combination. In this remote outpost, you'll get a tranquil night's sleep. Kenya-born Fiona Walton and her husband, Steve, are the managing directors. Affordable meals are served daily at lunch and dinner; the dining room's specialty is Jura-bred venison.

Craighouse, Isle of Jura PA60 7XU. (© 01496/820-243. Fax 01496/820-249. www.jurahotel.co.uk. 18 units, 12 with private bathroom. £80 ($128) double without bathroom; £100 ($160) double with bathroom; £100 ($160) suite. Rates include Scottish breakfast. AE, DC, MC, V. Closed 2 weeks at Dec–Jan. Dogs accepted. **Amenities:** Restaurant; bar; limited room service. *In room:* Coffeemaker, no phone.

6 Inveraray ★★

159km (99 miles) NW of Edinburgh, 92km (57 miles) NW of Glasgow, 61km (38 miles) SE of Oban

The small resort and royal burgh of Inveraray occupies a splendid setting on the upper shores of Loch Fyne. It's particularly attractive when you approach from the east on A83. Across a little inlet, you can see the town lying peacefully on a bit of land fronting on the loch.

ESSENTIALS

GETTING THERE   The nearest **rail station** is at Dumbarton, 72km (45 miles) southeast, where you can make bus connections to Inveraray. For rail schedules, call © **08457/484-950.**

The City Link-926 Service operates **buses** out of Glasgow, heading for Dumbarton, before continuing to Inveraray. Transit time is about 2 hours. Monday through Saturday, three buses make this run (only two on Sunday). The fare is £6.10 ($9.75) one-way, £12.20 ($20) round-trip. For bus schedules, call © **08705/505-050.**

If you're **driving** from Oban, head east along A85 until you reach the junction with A819, at which point you continue south.

VISITOR INFORMATION   The **tourist office** is on Front Street (© **01499/ 302-063**). It's open from June to mid-September, daily from 9am to 6pm; mid-September to October, April, and May, Monday through Saturday from 10am to 3pm and Sunday from noon to 5pm; and November to March, daily from noon to 4pm.

EXPLORING THE ISLAND

At one end of the main street of the town is a **Celtic burial cross** from Iona. The parish church is divided by a wall that enables mass to be held simultaneously in Gaelic and English.

Because so many of its attractions and those in its environs involve walking, hope for a sunny day. A local beauty spot is the **Ardkinglas Woodland Garden** (© **01499/600-263**), 6.5km (4 miles) east of Inveraray at the head of Loch Fyne. People drive from all over Britain to see Scotland's greatest collection of conifers and its masses of rhododendrons bursting into bloom in June. Admission is £3 ($4.80); it's open daily from 9am to 5pm.

Hiking in Argyll Forest Park

Argyll Forest Park, in the southern Highlands, stretches almost to Loch Fyne and is made up of Benmore, Ardgartan, and Glenbranter. The park covers an area of 24,000 hectares (60,000 acres), contains some of Scotland's most panoramic scenery, and takes in a wide variety of habitats, from lush forests and waterside to bleaker grassy moorlands and mountains. The Clyde sea lochs cut deep into the forested areas, somewhat in the way fjord "fingers" cut into the Norwegian coast; in the northern part are the Arrochar Alps (so called), where **Ben Arthur** reaches a height of 877m (2,891 ft.).

The park attracts those interested in natural history and wildlife as well as rock climbers, hikers, and hill walkers. There are many recreational activities and dozens of forest walks for trail blazers with all degrees of skill. Trails leading through forests to the loftier peaks are strenuous and meant for skilled hikers; others are easier, including paths from the **Younger Botanic Garden** by Loch Eck leading to Puck's Glen.

There's abundant wildlife in the sea lochs: shark, sea otters, gray seals, sea scorpions, crabs, shrimp, sea lemons, sea anemones, and sea slugs, among other inhabitants. Boats and canoes are available for rent. One of the park's biggest thrills is exploring the underwater caves of Loch Long.

In the early spring and summer, the park trails are at their most beautiful—woodland birds create choruses of song, and the forest is filled with violets, wood anemones, primroses, and bluebells. Sometimes the wildflowers are so thick they're like carpets. In the rainy climate of the southern Highlands, ferns and mosses also grow in abundance.

To reach the park, take A83 to B828 heading for Loch Goil or follow A815 to Loch Eck and Loch Long. Both Arrochar and Tarbet, stops on the Glasgow–Fort William rail line, are on the periphery of the park's northeast frontier.

The best place for lodging is **Dunoon,** to the south on the Cowal Peninsula, an easy gateway to the park. Dunoon has been a holiday resort since 1790, created for the "merchant princes" of Glasgow. Recreational facilities abound, including an indoor pool, tennis courts, and an 18-hole golf course. To pick up information about the park and a trail map, go to the **Dunoon Tourist Center,** 7 Alexandra Parade (© **01369/703-785**). It's open April to late June, September, and October, Monday through Friday from 9am to 5:30pm and Saturday and Sunday from 10am to 5pm; late June to August, Monday through Saturday from 9am to 6pm and Sunday from 10am to 5pm; November to March, Monday through Thursday from 9am to 5:30pm and Friday from 9am to 5pm.

If you have a car, you can explore this scenic part of Scotland from Cairndow. Head east along A83 until you reach the junction with A815, at which point proceed south along the western shore of Loch Fyne until you come to the famous inn at Creggans (see below), directly north of **Strachur.** About 8km

(5 miles) south from the Creggans Inn along the loch will take you to the old **Castle Lachlan** at Strathiachian, the 13th-century castle of the MacLachlan clan. Now in romantic ruins, it was besieged by the English in 1745. The MacLachlans were fervent Jacobites and played a major role in the uprising.

Crarae Glen Gardens ✦   Lying along Loch Fyne, these are among Scotland's most beautiful gardens, some 20 hectares (50 acres) of rich plantings along with waterfalls and panoramic vistas of the loch. You can enjoy the beauty while hiking one of the many paths.

13km (8 miles) southwest of Inveraray along A83, near the hamlet of Minard. © **01546/886-614.** Admission £3.50 ($5.60) adults, £2.60 ($4.15) children, £9.50 ($15) per family. Daily 10am–5pm.

Inveraray Castle ✦✦   The hereditary seat of the dukes of Argyll, Inveraray Castle has been headquarters of the Clan Campbell since the early 15th century. The gray-green stone castle is among the earliest examples of Gothic Revival in Britain and offers a fine collection of pictures and 18th-century French furniture, old porcelain, and an Armoury Hall, which alone contains 1,300 pieces. On the grounds is a **Combined Operations Museum,** the only one of its kind in the United Kingdom. It displays the role No. 1 Combined Training Centre played at Inveraray in World War II. On exhibit are scale models, newspaper reports, campaign maps, photographs, wartime posters and cartoons, training scenes, and other mementos. A shop sells souvenirs, and a tearoom serves homemade cakes and scones.

1km (¾ mile) northeast of Inveraray on Loch Fyne. © **01499/302-203.** www.inveraray-castle.com. Admission £5.50 ($8.80) adults, £4.50 ($7.20) seniors, £3.50 ($5.60) children, £14 ($22) per family. Apr–May and Oct 10am–1pm and 2–5:45pm, Sun 1–5:45pm; Jun–Aug and Sept Mon–Sat 10am–5:45pm, Sun 1–5:45pm.

WHERE TO STAY & DINE

Argyll Hotel   This 1755 waterfront inn boasts views of Loch Fyne and Loch Shira. The comfortable, midsize guest rooms feature decors ranging from flowered chintz to modern, no-nonsense functionality and most open onto panoramic views of Loch Fyne. Four so-called executive rooms have either four poster or Queen Anne beds. Most rooms come with small, shower-only bathrooms, although some contain bathtubs. In general accommodations open onto panoramic views of Loch Fyne. On site are a wood-and-gilt public bar, a guests-only cocktail lounge, and a dignified restaurant serving five-course dinners. Even if you're not a guest, consider having a meal here, as the chefs feature the best of local produce, especially fish and shellfish from Loch Fyne.

Front St., Inveraray PA32 8XB. © **01499/302-466.** Fax 01499/302-389. www.the-argyll-hotel.co.uk. 37 units. £70–£158 ($115–$253) double. Rates include Scottish breakfast. AE, DC, MC, V. **Amenities:** Restaurant; 2 bars; room service (7:30am–11:30pm); laundry service. *In room:* TV, coffeemaker, hair dryer.

The Creggans Inn ✦   This inn commemorates the spot where Mary Queen of Scots is said to have disembarked from her ship in 1563 on her way through the Highlands. Painted white and flanked by gardens, the inn rises across A815 from the sea and is owned by Sir Charles MacLean and his mother, Lady MacLean, author of several best-selling cookbooks, most of which are for sale here. The guest rooms are elegant and understated, all traditionally furnished and well-maintained, and each is equipped with a private bathroom. Guests may use the upstairs sitting room and the garden-style lounge. The restaurant has a charcoal grill that produces succulent versions of Aberdeen Angus steaks and lamb kebabs, but you can also enjoy fresh seafood and venison. Reservations are a must. The bar features pub lunches beside an open fire.

Strachur PA27 8BX. ⓒ **01369/860-279.** Fax 01369/860-637. www.creggans-inn.co.uk. 14 units. £105–£114 ($168–$182) double; £134 ($214) suite. Rates include Scottish breakfast. AE, DC, MC, V. **Amenities:** Restaurant; bar; room service (8am–11pm); laundry service. *In room:* TV, coffeemaker, hair dryer.

The George Hotel ⭐   One of the most charming hotels in town lies behind a facade built around 1775. Part of the charm derives from the old-fashioned bar, where the Guinness simply seems to taste better than in less evocative settings. The public areas are marked with flagstone floors, beamed ceilings, and blazing fireplaces. The guest rooms are cozy, done in an old-fashioned Scottish style. Some have king-size beds (unusual for Scotland) and claw-foot tubs or else full-length Victorian roll-top bathtubs or Jacuzzis. The restaurant is among the most popular in town with locals, serving moderately priced lunches and dinners daily. Your choices include steaks prepared with pepper or mushroom sauce, grilled halibut, and grilled Loch Fyne salmon with white wine, prawns, and scallops.

Main St. E, Inveraray PA32 8TT. ⓒ **01499/302-111.** Fax 01499/302-098. www.thegeorgehotel.co.uk. 12 units. £60–£120 ($96–$192) double. Rates include breakfast. AE, DC, MC, V. **Amenities:** Restaurant; 2 bars. *In room:* TV, coffeemaker.

7 Loch Awe: Scotland's Longest Loch ⭐⭐

159km (99 miles) NW of Edinburgh, 39km (24 miles) E of Oban, 109km (68 miles) NW of Glasgow

Only 1.6km (1 mile) wide in most places and 36km (22 miles) long, Loch Awe is the longest loch in Scotland and acted as a natural freshwater moat protecting the Campbells of Inveraray from their enemies to the north. Along its banks are many reminders of its fortified past. The Forestry Commission has vast forests and signposted trails in this area, and a modern road makes it possible to travel around Loch Awe, so more than ever it's a popular center for angling and walking.

ESSENTIALS

GETTING THERE   The nearest train station is in Oban, where you'd have to take a connecting bus. **Scottish CityLink,** 1 Queens Park Place in Oban (call ⓒ **01631/562-856** for schedules), has service to Glasgow with stopovers at Loch Awe.

If you're driving from Oban, head east along A85.

VISITOR INFORMATION   Consult the **tourist office** in Oban (see, "Oban: Gateway to Mull & the Inner Hebrides," below).

EXPLORING THE AREA

To the east of the top of Loch Awe, **Dalmally** is small, but because of its strategic position it has witnessed a lot of Scottish history. Its 18th-century church is built in an octagonal shape.

A convenient way to reach it is by taking any of about five boats a day (March to November) departing from the piers in the village of Loch Awe. The ferries are maintained by the **Loch Awe Steam Packet Company,** Loch Awe Piers (ⓒ **01838/200-440**). Per-person transit across the loch (a 20-min. ride each way) costs £5 ($8) and includes entrance to the ruins of Kilchurn Castle (see the box titled "Castle of the Once Mighty Campbells" below). This steamship company and the **Hotel Ardanaiseig** (see below) are the only sources of info about the castle, which doesn't maintain an on-site staff.

For reminders of the days when the Campbells of Inveraray held supreme power in the Loch Awe region, there's another ruined **castle** at Fincharn, at the

Moments **Castle of the Once Mighty Campbells**

The ruins of **Kilchurn Castle** are at the northern tip of Loch Awe, west of Dalmally, and across from the south bank village of Loch Awe. A stronghold of the Campbells of Glen Orchy in 1440, it's a spectacular ruin with much of the original structure still intact. The ruins have been completely reinforced and balconied so you can now explore them when the weather permits. Access to the ruins is from an unmarked graveled lot. A path leads to the castle's remains, but you may need a pair of boots if the weather is bad.

Once you reach the castle, don't expect a guided tour, as the site is likely to be abandoned except for a patrol of goats and sheep, and there's no guardian to enforce strict opening hours. Although it's presently owned by a consortium of five local businessmen, its grass is cut and its masonry maintained by Historic Scotland. You can wander at will through the ruins following a self-guided tour marked by signs.

---

southern end of the loch, and another on the island of Fraoch Eilean. The Isle of Inishail has an ancient **chapel and burial ground.**

The bulk of **Ben Cruachan,** rising to 1,119m (3,689 ft.), dominates Loch Awe at its northern end and attracts climbers and hikers. On the Ben is the world's second-largest hydroelectric power station, which pumps water from Loch Awe to a reservoir high up on the mountain.

Below the mountain are the **Falls of Cruachan** and the wild **Pass of Brander,** where Robert the Bruce routed the Clan MacDougall in 1308. The Pass of Brander was the scene of many a fierce battle in bygone times, and something of that bloody past seems to brood over the narrow defile. Through it the waters of the Awe flow on their way to Loch Etive. This winding sea loch is 31km (19 miles) long, stretching from Dun Dunstaffnage Bay at Oban to Glen Etive, reaching into the Moor of Rannoch at the foot of the 910m (3,000-ft.) **Buachaille Etive** (the Shepherd of Etive), into which Glencoe also reaches.

WHERE TO STAY & DINE

Hotel Ardanaiseig *★★*   Although this gray-stone manorial seat was built in 1834 by a Campbell patriarch, it's designed along 18th-century lines. Its builder also planted some of the rarest trees in Britain, many of them exotic conifers. Today, clusters of fruit trees stand in a walled garden, and the rhododendrons and azaleas are a joy in May and June. Until recently a private home, the hotel has formal sitting rooms graced with big chintzy chairs, fresh flowers, and polished tables. The guest rooms are named for various local mountains and lochs, and are uniquely and traditionally furnished with antiques; some have four-poster beds. The price of a room depends on its size, ranging from a small room to a master bedroom with a loch view. The beautifully maintained bathrooms come with either a tub and shower combination or a shower only.

Kilchrenan by Taynuilt PA35 1HE. ⓒ **800/548-7790** in the U.S., 800/463-7595 in Canada, or 01866/833-333. Fax 01866/833-222. www.ardanaiseig-hotel.com. 16 units. £82–£186 ($131–$298) double. AE, DC, MC, V. Closed Jan to mid-Feb. Drive 34km (21 miles) south of Oban by following the signs to Taynuilt, then turning onto B845 toward Kilchrenan. Turn left at the Kilchrenan Pub and continue on for 6km (3¾ miles), following signs into Ardanaiseig. **Amenities:** Restaurant; tennis court. *In room:* TV, coffeemaker, hair dryer.

8 Oban: Gateway to Mull & the Inner Hebrides ⭐

137km (85 miles) NW of Glasgow, 81km (50 miles) SW of Fort William

One of Scotland's leading coastal resorts, the bustling port of Oban is in a sheltered bay almost landlocked by the island of Kerrera. A busy fishing port in the 18th century, Oban is now heavily dependent on tourism. Since it lacks major attractions of its own, it's often used as a major refueling stop for those exploring the greater west coast of Scotland.

Oban is the gateway to **Mull,** largest of the Inner Hebrides, and to the island of **Iona.** See chapter 11 for information about these destinations, including ferry service from Oban.

ESSENTIALS

GETTING THERE   From Glasgow, the West Highland lines run directly to Oban, with departures from Glasgow's Queen Street Station (call ℭ **08457/ 484-950** for 24-hr. info). Three trains per day (only two on Sun) make the 3-hour run to Oban, a one-way fare costing £15 ($24).

Frequent coaches depart from Buchanan Station in Glasgow, taking about the same time as the train, although a one-way fare is only £11.80 ($19). Call **Scottish CityLink** at ℭ **08705/505-050** in Glasgow or ℭ **01631/563-059** in Oban.

If you're driving from Glasgow, head northwest along A82 until reaching Tyndrum, then go west along A85 until you come to Oban.

VISITOR INFORMATION   The **tourist office** is on Argyll Square (ℭ **01631/ 563-122**). April to mid-June and mid-September to October, it's open Monday to Friday 9:30am to 5pm and Saturday and Sunday 10 to 4pm; mid-June to mid-September, hours are Monday to Saturday 9am to 8pm and Sunday 9am to 7pm; and November to March, it's open Monday to Saturday 9:30am to 5pm and Sunday noon to 4pm.

SPECIAL EVENTS   The **Oban Highland Games** are held in August, with massed pipe bands marching through the streets. Ask at the tourist office for details. The **Oban Pipe Band** regularly parades on the main street throughout summer.

EXPLORING THE AREA

To appreciate the coastal scenery of Oban to its fullest, consider renting a bike and cycling around. They're available at **Oban Cycles,** 9 Craigard Rd. (ℭ **01631/ 562-444**).

Fun Fact Folly? Or Source of Pride?

Overlooking the town of Oban is an unfinished replica of the Colosseum of Rome, **McCaig's Tower,** built by a banker, John Stuart McCaig, from 1897 to 1900 as a memorial to his family and to create a local work opportunity during an employment slump. Its walls are 61cm (2 ft.) thick and 11m to 12m (37 ft.–40 ft.) high. Set atop **Pulpit Hill,** the tower offers a fine view across the Firth of Lorn and the Sound of Mull. The courtyard within is landscaped, and the tower is floodlit at night. Outsiders have been heard to refer to the tower as "McCaig's Folly," but Obanites are proud of the structure and deplore this term.

Near the little granite **Cathedral of the Isles,** 1.6km (1 mile) north of the end of the bay, is the ruin of the 13th-century **Dunollie Castle,** seat of the lords of Lorn, who once owned a third of Scotland.

On the island of Kerrera stands **Gylen Castle,** home of the MacDougalls, dating back to 1587.

You can visit **Dunstaffnage Castle** ✦ (© **01631/562-465**), 5.5km (3½ miles) north, believed to have been the royal seat of the Dalriadic monarchy in the 8th century. It was probably the site of the Scots court until Kenneth MacAlpin's unification of Scotland and the transfer of the seat of government to Scone in the 10th century. The present castle was built around 1263. The castle is open April to October from 9am to 6:30pm (until 8pm July and Aug), and from November to March from 9:30am to 4:30pm. Admission is £2 ($3.20) adults, £1.40 ($2.25) seniors, and £.80 ($1.30) children. You can take a bus from the Oban rail station to Dunbeg, but it's still a 2.5km (1½-mile) walk to the castle.

SHOPPING

Cathness Glass Oban, Railway Pier (© **01631/563-386**), is the best place for shopping, but you'll find plenty of gift and souvenir shops around town. At this center, locally produced glass items range from functional dinner- and glassware to purely artistic curios. This firm has one of the most prestigious reputations in Scotland.

Many of the crafts items produced in local crofts and private homes eventually end up at gift shops in Oban, where they're proudly displayed as among the finest of their kind in the West Country. One of the best outlets is **McCaig's Warehouse,** Argyll Square (© **01631/566-335**), where the tartan patterns of virtually every clan in Scotland are for sale, either by the meter or in the form of kilts, jackets, traditional Highland garb, or more modern interpretation of traditional fashions.

Celtic-patterned jewelry, made from gold, silver, or platinum, and sometimes studded with semiprecious gems, is featured at **The Gem Box,** Esplanade (© **01631/562-180**).

If all other shopping options fail, consider the gift items displayed at the **Oban Tourist Information Office,** Argyll Square (© **01631/563-122**). Inventories include tartans, jewelry, woodwork, and glassware, usually crafted into Celtic designs, and books covering the myriad aspects of what to see and do in Scotland.

If you absolutely, positively must have a kilt, a cape, or a full outfit based on your favorite Highland regiment, head for one of the town's two best tailors: **Hector Russell, Kiltmaker,** Argyll Square (© **01631/570-240**), and **Geoffrey Tailors,** Argyll Square (© **01631/570-557**).

WHERE TO STAY

You may also want to check out the rooms offered at the **Balmoral Hotel** or the **Knipoch Hotel Restaurant** (see "Where to Dine," below).

VERY EXPENSIVE

Isle of Eriska Hotel ✦✦✦   The grandest place to stay in the Greater Oban area is this Victorian House that welcomes you at the end of a winding drive. In the Middle Ages, this 121-hectare (300-acre) forested island was a church-protected sanctuary. No more. In the 19th century an industrialist purchased it and planted hundreds of beech trees, building a bridge to the mainland. Today you can savor the splendors of country life in an elegant setting. From the estate you'll enjoy a panorama of the surrounding waterways and views of a local colony of deer. The surrounding forest is a private park.

A magnificent front door leads to the entrance hall where a log burns on chilly nights. A formal sitting room and a library/bar lie on the ground floor. A wide staircase leads to the baronial bedrooms. Each of the accommodations is individually furnished, offering both style and comfort with fully tiled and well-lit bathrooms.

Families might consider renting the beautifully and tastefully furnished cottage. Called Lilac Cottage, it lies 100m (328 ft.) from the main building and it comes with its own private garden, sitting rooms, and 2 bedrooms with private bathrooms.

The hotel is known for its refined Scottish cuisine crafted largely from local produce. Adjoining is the Stables Spa with its large heated pool.

Ledaig, by Oban, Argyll PA37 1SD. © 01631/720-371. Fax 01631/720-531. www.eriska-hotel.co.uk. 17 units. £240 ($384) double; £290 ($464) suite; cottage £465 ($744). Winter rates significantly lower. Rates include breakfast, morning coffee, and afternoon tea. Lies 6km (10 miles) N of Oban. **Amenities:** Restaurant; bar; indoor heated pool; 6-hole golf course; tennis court; health club; spa; sauna; 24-hr. room service; babysitting; laundry; steam room. *In room:* TV, coffeemaker, hair dryer, iron, trouser press.

EXPENSIVE

Manor House Hotel ✹   This is your best bet for an overnight in Oban. On the outskirts of Oban, opening onto panoramic views of Oban Bay, this 1780 stone house was once owned by the duke of Argyll. Many antiques grace the public rooms. The good-sized guest rooms are filled with tasteful reproductions, and coordinated curtains and bedcovers create a pleasing effect, often in sun-splashed golds and yellows. All have midsize private bathrooms, some with both tub and shower. *Note:* Children under 12 are not welcome as guests.

The restaurant is one of the most satisfying in the area; for more on dining here, see "Where to Dine" below.

Gallanach Rd., Oban PA34 4LS. © **01631/562-087.** Fax 01631/563-053. www.manorhouseoban.com. 11 units. £128–£170 ($205–$272) double. Rates include half board. AE, MC, V. From the south side of Oban, follow the signs for the car ferry but continue past the ferry entrance for about 1km (½ mile). No children under age 12. **Amenities:** Restaurant; bar; room service; laundry. *In room:* TV, coffeemaker, hair dryer.

MODERATE

Alexandra Hotel   On the promenade 1.6km (1 mile) from the train station, the late-1860s stone Alexandra boasts gables and turreted towers and a Regency front veranda. From its public room you can look out onto Oban Bay, and two sun lounges overlook the seafront. The midsize guest rooms are modestly furnished but pleasing, with small bathrooms. Some rooms are specially equipped for those with limited mobility. Most units are rented at the lower rate (see below), except for two spacious bedrooms opening onto dramatic sea views. The restaurant, serving good food, also opens onto the panorama.

Corran Esplanade, Oban PA34 5AA. © **01631/562-381.** Fax 01631/564-497. 77 units, 2 suites. £95–£114 ($152–$182) double. Rates include Scottish breakfast. AE, MC, V. **Amenities:** Restaurant; bar; indoor pool; small exercise room; limited room service; laundry; steam room. *In room:* TV, coffeemaker, hair dryer, iron/ironing board (in some).

Columba Hotel   This is one of the most impressive Victorian buildings in Oban. The Columba was built in 1870 by the same McCaig who constructed the hilltop extravaganza known as McCaig's Tower. The location is among the best in town, and the modernized big-windowed dining room offers views of the port. The small guest rooms are unremarkable but well maintained, each with a small bathroom with a tub and shower combination, or just a shower. The restaurant, offers a mix of seafood and local produce. Live folk music is sometimes presented in the informal Harbour Inn Bar.

The Esplanade, North Pier, Oban PA34 5QD. © **01631/562-183**. Fax 01631/564-683. 50 units. £75–£95 ($120–$152) double. Rates include breakfast. AE, MC, V. Free parking. The Scottish Midland Bus Company's Ganavan bus passes by. **Amenities:** Restaurant; bar; limited room service. *In room:* TV, coffeemaker, hair dryer.

Dungallan House Hotel ⚡   One of the more upscale inns around Oban, this circa-1870 home built for the Campbells. It was used as a hospital during World War I and as a naval office during World War II, but today is the artfully furnished domain of George and Janice Stewart, who maintain the high-ceilinged proportions and antique furniture with devotion. The guest rooms have been refurbished, each with firm mattresses and quality furnishings. All but two single rooms have small bathrooms, some of which contain a tub and shower combination. Breakfasts are served in grand style in the formal dining room; dinners can be arranged, and though priority is granted to guests, nonguests can usually arrange a meal if they phone ahead. Two hectares (5 acres) of forest and gardens surround the house, and views stretch out over the Bay of Oban and its islands.

Gallanach Rd., Oban PA34 4PD. © **01631/563-799**. Fax 01631/566-711. www.dungallanhotel-oban.co.uk. 13 units, 11 with private bathroom. £82.50 ($132) double without bathroom; £120 ($192) double with bathroom. MC, V. Closed Nov–Mar. From Oban's center, drive 1km (½ mile), following the signs to Gallanach. *In room:* TV, no phone.

Dungrianach ⚡ *(Finds)*   It has only a handful of rooms, but if you can get a reservation, this is a little B & B charmer. In Gaelic, the name of the place means "the sunny house on the hill," and the description is apt. It sits in the midst of a wooded area, overlooking Oban Bay and some of the islands of the Inner Hebrides. The location is tranquil and seemingly remote, yet it's only a few minutes' walk from the ferry terminal. The house is impressively furnished with both antiques and reproductions. The owners rent a double and a twin-bedded accommodation, each with a little private bath with shower. Guests meet fellow guests in the living room, which has a collection of books on Scotland and travel literature in general.

Pulpit Hill, Oban, Argyll PA34 4LU. © and fax **01631/562-840**. www.dungrianach.com. 2 units. £50 ($80). No credit cards. Free parking. *In room:* TV, coffeemaker, no phone.

The Oban Caledonian Hotel   This choice, a favorite of coach tours, makes good on its promise of giving you a "taste of the Highlands." A fine example of Scottish 19th-century architecture, it occupies a landmark position, with a view opening onto the harbor and Oban Bay. This convenient location puts you close to the rail, bus, and ferry terminals from which you can book passage to the Isles. The guest rooms have up-to-date amenities and small bathrooms with combination tub/showers. The front rooms are the most desirable. Good, reasonably priced Scottish fare is served in the dining room.

Station Sq., Oban PA34 5RT. © **01631/563-133**. Fax 01631/562-998. 59 units. £140–£180 ($224–$288) double; £280 ($448) suite. Rates include Scottish breakfast and dinner. MC, V. Free parking. **Amenities:** 2 restaurants; bar; 24-hr. room service; babysitting; laundry. *In room:* TV, coffeemaker, hair dryer.

INEXPENSIVE

Foxholes ⚡ *(Finds)*   Far from a foxhole, this is actually a spacious country house set in a tranquil glen to the south of Oban. Operated by Barry and Shirley Dowson-Park, it's for those seeking seclusion. The cozy, tasteful, and comfortable bedrooms are painted in soft pastels and furnished traditionally. All rooms open onto panoramic views of the countryside and the hotel's well-maintained gardens. All the bathrooms are in excellent condition, some with a combination tub and shower. In the restaurant, Mrs. Dowson-Park provides traditional, moderately priced Scottish meals. The property is entirely nonsmoking.

Cologin, Lerags, Oban. PA34 4SE. ✆ **01631/564-982.** www.hoteloban.com. 7 units. £60–£70 ($96–$112) double. Rates include full Scottish breakfast. MC, V. Closed Dec–Mar. Free parking. Take A816 1.8km (3 miles) south of Oban. **Amenities:** Restaurant; bar. *In room:* TV, coffeemaker, hair dryer, no phone.

Glenburnie Hotel   One of Oban's genuinely grand houses is on the seafront esplanade a 5-minute walk west of the town center. Built in 1897 of granite blocks, with elegant ecclesiastical-looking bay windows, it was designed as the surgical hospital and home of a prominent doctor. Today, it's a guesthouse operated by Graeme and Allyson Strachan, who have outfitted the rooms with comfy furniture, much of it antique. Bathrooms are small but tidy, and most have a tub and shower combination. The entire hotel is nonsmoking.

The Esplanade, Oban PA34 5AQ. ✆ and fax **01631/562-089.** www.glenburnie.co.uk. 14 units. £56–£78 ($90–$125) double. MC, V. Closed Nov–Easter. *In room:* TV, coffeemaker.

Lancaster   Along the seafront on the crescent of the bay, the Lancaster is distinguished by its attractive pseudo-Tudor facade. Its public rooms command views of the islands of Lismore and Kerrera and even the more distant peaks of Mull. The guest rooms are modestly furnished in a somewhat 1960s style, some with complete bathrooms with tub and shower combinations (three singles have no private bathroom). There are three rooms set aside for families. This is only one of the two hotels in Oban featuring a heated indoor pool, a sauna, a Jacuzzi, and a solarium. Its fully licensed dining room offers moderately priced dinners. *Note:* There is no elevator.

Corran Esplanade, Oban PA34 5AD. ✆ and fax **01631/562-587.** www.lancasteroban.com. 27 units, 24 with private bathroom. £66 ($106) double with bathroom. Rates include Scottish breakfast. MC, V. **Amenities:** Bar; heated indoor pool; sauna; Jacuzzi. *In room:* TV, coffeemaker, hair dryer, no phone.

WHERE TO DINE
EXPENSIVE

Knipoch Hotel Restaurant 👍👍 SCOTTISH   Oban offers a truly fine restaurant 10km (6 miles) south of town on the shores of Loch Feochan. Jenny and Colin Craig, a mother-and-son team, welcome you to their whitewashed Georgian house (the oldest part dates from 1592) and offer a choice of three dining rooms as well as a daily changing menu of five delectable courses. Salmon and halibut are smoked on the premises, and the menu relies heavily on Scottish produce, including fresh fish. Try the cock-a-leekie soup, followed by Sound of Luing scallops. The wine cellar is excellent, especially in its Bordeaux.

The hotel rents 21 well-furnished rooms, charging £130 to £150 ($208–$240) per night in a double, with a suite costing £13 ($21) per person extra. A full Scottish breakfast is included in the rate.

Hwy. A816, Kilninver, Knipoch, by Oban PA34 4QT. ✆ **01852/316-251.** Fax 01852/316-249. www.knipoch hotel.co.uk. Reservations required. Table d'hôte dinner £33.50 ($54) for 3 courses, £42.50 ($68) for 5 courses. AE, DC, MC, V. Daily 7:30–9pm. Closed mid-Dec to mid-Feb. Drive 10km (6 miles) south of Oban on A816.

The Manor House 👍 SCOTTISH   Located in the 1780 house built by the duke of Argyll, this formal but not stuffy restaurant overlooks Oban Bay and is one of the finest dining choices along the coast. A traditional Scottish cuisine is served—truly fresh and creative cooking—and the chef uses ingredients of the highest quality. Against a backdrop of Georgian paneling, you can peruse the constantly changing menu. Many visitors to the Highlands opt for venison, and it comes with accompaniments such as black pudding, caramelized root vegetables, and rowanberry glaze. Or try the delicious fresh scallops wrapped in smoked bacon. There are also some selections for vegetarians. You can order such old-fashioned British desserts as sticky toffee pudding with butterscotch sauce, but for something really Scottish, try marinated brambles with whisky custard.

In the Manor House Hotel, Gallanach Rd. (c) **01631/562-087**. Reservations recommended. Main courses £22 ($35); set-price 5-course meal £35 ($56). AE, MC, V. Tues 6:45–9pm; Wed–Sat noon–2pm and 6:45–9pm.

MODERATE

Balmoral Hotel BRITISH   At the top of a granite staircase whose corkscrew shape is an architectural marvel, this is one of the most popular restaurants in town. Filled with 19th-century charm, it contains Windsor chairs and reproduction Georgian tables. Specialties include sliced chateaubriand with mushrooms, smoked Tobermory trout, haggis with cream and whisky, venison casserole, and roast pheasant. Less expensive platters are served in the adjacent bar.

The hotel stands on the eastern extension of the town's main commercial street (George Street), a 4-minute walk from the center. It rents 12 well-furnished rooms, with TVs, costing £55 to £70 ($88–$112) double, Scottish breakfast included.

Craigard Rd., Oban PA34 5AQ. (c) **01631/562-731**. Reservations recommended in midsummer. Main courses £7.20–£17.20 ($12–$28); bar meals £3.25–£8 ($5.20–$13). AE, DC, MC, V. May to mid-Oct daily noon–2pm and 6–10pm; Mar–Apr and mid-Oct to Dec daily noon–2pm and 6–8pm.

The Gathering BRITISH   Opened in 1882, this imposing building, ringed with verandas, is no longer a private hunting and social club. Today, its ground floor functions as an Irish pub (open Mon–Sat 11am–1am and Sun noon–11pm) and its wood-sheathed upper floor as a well-managed restaurant. Dishes are straightforward but tasty. Menu items include lots of local produce, fish, and game dishes, like pheasant, lobster, and lamb. Especially noteworthy are the Highland venison filets with port jelly sauce, loin of saddle of venison with herb-and-port sauce, and local crayfish lightly grilled in garlic butter.

Breadalbane St. (c) **01631/565-421**. Reservations recommended. Bar platters £5.50–£13.50 ($8.80–$22); set-price dinners in restaurant £12–£18 ($19–$29). AE, MC, V. June–Sept daily noon–2pm; year-round dinner daily 5–10pm.

MacTavish's Kitchen SCOTTISH   Like its cousin in Fort William, this place is overrun with visitors and it's the most popular—not the best—restaurant in town. Downstairs is a self-service restaurant offering breakfast, lunch, dinner, and tea with shortbread and scones. Upstairs is the Lairds Bar, and on the ground floor is MacTavish's Bar, where bar meals are available all day. The licensed second-floor restaurant has a more ambitious Scottish and Continental menu with higher prices. Offerings include haggis, Loch Fyne kippers (oak-smoked herring), prime Scottish steaks, smoked salmon, venison, and local mussels. If you don't expect too much in the way of cuisine here, you won't be disappointed.

34 George St. (c) **01631/563-064**. Main courses £8–£15.50 ($13–$25); budget 2-course lunch £5 ($8); fixed-price 3-course dinners £7.50–£17 ($12–$27). MC, V. Self-service restaurant daily 9am–9pm; licensed restaurant daily noon–2pm and 6–10:30pm.

OBAN AFTER DARK

Mid-May to the end of September, entertainment is provided at **MacTavish's Kitchen** (see above), with Scottish music and Highland dancing by local artists nightly 8:30 to 10:30pm. Admission is £4 ($6.40) adults and £2 ($3.20) children. Reduced admission for diners is £2 ($3.20) adults and £1.50 ($2.40) children.

You can while away the evening with the locals at the **Oban Inn,** Stafford Street and the Esplanade (© **01631/562-484**), a popular pub with exposed beams and a flag-covered ceiling. Pints include McEwan's Export, Ale, and Gillespie's Stout. The pub is open daily 11 to 1am.

Another popular hangout is the town's Irish pub, **O'Donnells,** Breadalbane Street (© **01631/566-159**), where you can always expect a warm reception. They serve the ever-popular Guinness and a variety of Irish and Scottish malt whisky. Thursday to Saturday, entertainment is either a live band or a DJ. Over the busy summer, something is scheduled almost every night. Hours are daily 3pm to 1am.

Fife & the Central Highlands

North of the Firth of Forth from Edinburgh, the County of Fife still likes to call itself a kingdom. Even today, its name suggests the romantic episodes and pageantry during the reign of the early Stuart kings, and some 14 of Scotland's 66 royal burghs lie in this shire. You can visit many of the former royal palaces and castles, either restored or in colorful ruins.

Legendary **Loch Lomond** is the largest and most beautiful of the Scottish lakes. At Balloch in the south, it's a Lowland landscape of gentle hills and islands. But as it moves north, the loch narrows and takes on a stark, dramatic Highland character, with moody cloud formations and rugged steep hillsides.

The **Trossachs** is the collective name given to that wild Highland area east and northeast of Loch Lomond. Here and along Loch Lomond you find Scotland's finest scenery in moor, mountain, and loch. The area has been famed in history and romance ever since Sir Walter Scott's vivid descriptive passages in "The Lady of the Lake" and *Rob Roy*.

Many sections of the area lie on the doorsteps of Glasgow and Edinburgh; either city can be your gateway to the central Highlands. You can easily reach **Dunfermline** and **St. Andrews** by rail from Edinburgh. (St. Andrews also has good bus connections with Edinburgh.) By car, the main motorway is M9, the express highway that starts on the western outskirts of Edinburgh and is linked to M80 from Glasgow. M9 passes close to Stirling. M90, reached by crossing the Forth Road Bridge, will take you north into the Fife region. **Stirling** is the region's major rail center, with stops at such places as **Dunblane,** and much of Loch Lomond has rail connections. The towns and some villages have bus service, but you'll probably find the connections too limited or infrequent. For bus connections, Stirling is the central point.

However, your best bet for discovering the hidden villages and scenic lochside roads of the Trossachs or the fishing villages of East Neuk is by renting a car and driving at your own pace.

1 Dunfermline ⊀ & Its Great Abbey

23km (14 miles) NW of Edinburgh, 63km (39 miles) NE of Glasgow, 84km (52 miles) SW of Dundee

The ancient town of Dunfermline was once the capital of Scotland and is easily reached by the Forth Road Bridge, opened by Elizabeth II in 1964. Scots called their former capital the "auld grey town," and it looms large in their history books. The city is still known for its **Dunfermline Abbey** and former royal palace (now largely gone). When Scotland reunited with England in 1603, the royal court departed to London, leaving Dunfermline to wither with only its memories. In time, however, the town revived as the center of Scottish linen making, specializing in damask. But by World War I, the market had largely disappeared.

Some of the most interesting sights in Fife are within easy reach of Dunfermline, including one of Scotland's most beautiful villages, **Culross.** Dunfermline also makes the best base for exploring **Loch Leven** and **Loch Leven Castle.**

ESSENTIALS

GETTING THERE   Dunfermline is a stop along the main rail route from London via Edinburgh to Dundee, which means it has frequent connections to the Scottish capital. For rail schedules and fares, call ✆ **0870/608-2608.**

From its station at St. Andrews Square in Edinburgh, Scottish **CityLink** (✆ **0990/505-050**) operates frequent service to Dunfermline.

If you're driving from Edinburgh, take A90 west, cross the Forth Road Bridge, and follow the signs north to the center of Dunfermline.

VISITOR INFORMATION   A **tourist booth** is at 1 High Street (✆ **01383/720-999**). It's open Monday to Saturday 9:30am to 5pm.

EXPLORING THE AREA

Andrew Carnegie Birthplace Museum   In 1835, American industrialist and philanthropist Andrew Carnegie was born at a site about 182m (600 ft.) down the hill from the abbey. The museum comprises the 18th-century weaver's cottage in which he was born and a memorial hall provided by his wife. Displays tell the story of the weaver's son who emigrated to the United States to become one of the richest men in the world. From the fortune he made in steel, Carnegie gave away more than £244 million ($390 million) before his death in 1919. Dunfermline received the first of the 2,811 free libraries he provided throughout Britain and the States and also received public baths and Pittencrieff Park and Glen, rich in history and natural charm. A statue in the park honors Carnegie, who once worked as a bobbin boy in a cotton factory.

Moodie St. ✆ **01383/724-302.** Admission £2 ($3.20) adults, £1 ($1.60) seniors, free for children age 15 and under. Apr–Oct Mon–Sat 11am–5pm, Sun 2–5pm. Closed Nov–Mar. In the City Centre, at the corner of Moodie Street and Priory Lane (10-min. walk from train statioon).

Dunfermline Abbey and Palace ✿   The abbey is on the site of two earlier structures, a Celtic church and an 11th-century house of worship dedicated to the Holy Trinity, under the auspices of Queen Margaret (later St. Margaret). Culdee Church, from the 5th and 6th centuries, was rebuilt in 1072. Traces of both buildings are visible beneath gratings in the floor of the old nave. In 1150, the church was replaced with a large abbey, the nave of which remains, an example of Norman architecture. Later, St. Margaret's shrine, the northwest baptismal porch, the spire on the northwest tower, and the flying buttresses were added. While Dunfermline was the capital of Scotland, 22 royal personages were buried in the abbey. However, the only visible memorial or burial places known are those of Queen Margaret and King Robert the Bruce, whose tomb lies beneath the pulpit.

The once-royal palace of Dunfermline stands adjacent to the abbey. The palace witnessed the birth of Charles I and James I. The last king to reside here was Charles II, in 1651. Today, only the southwest wall remains of this once-gargantuan edifice.

St. Margaret's St. (10-min. walk from train station.) ✆ **01383/739-026.** Admission £2.20 ($3.50) adults, £1.60 ($2.55) seniors, £.75 ($1.20) children. Apr–Sept daily 9:30am–6pm; Oct–Mar Mon–Wed and Sat 9:30am–4pm, Thurs 9:30am–noon, Sun 2–4pm.

The Kingdom of Fife

SCOTLAND
Area of detail
Edinburgh
ENGLAND

0   20 mi
0   20 km

St. Andrews

Castle of St. Andrews
St. Andrews Cathedral

EAST NEUK

Secret Bunker
Scottish Fisheries Museum

Fife Ness →
Crail
Anstruther
Pittenweem

Elie

Earlsferry

Isle of May

Castle
Church
Golf

Dundee ↗

Firth of Tay

Rathillet
Newburgh
Cupar

Leven
Methil
Buckhaven

Firth of Forth

Glencarse

Auchtermuchty

Falkland Palace
Falkland

Glenrothes

Kirkcaldy

Lochgelly

5 mi

5 km

Perth

Ochil Hills

Loch Leven Castle
Loch Leven
St. Serf's Is.

Kinross

Kelty

Cowdenbeath

Andrew Carnegie Birthplace Museum

Dunfermline Abbey
Dunfermline

Inverkeithing

Dunning

Powmill

Gleneagles

Auchterarder

Dollar

Culross Abbey
Culross

Bo'ness

Grangemouth

Muthill

Braco

Dunblane

Alloa

Larbert

Cumbernauld

← Stirling

WHERE TO STAY

Best Western Keavil House Hotel ⚘   This tranquil country hotel, only a 30-minute drive from Edinburgh, is set on 4.8 hectares (12 acres) of forested land and gardens and offers lots of leisure facilities. The bedrooms are generous in size and well appointed, each with such amenities as a writing desk and mid-size bathrooms (some with tubs). Master bedrooms contain four-poster beds. The hotel offers fine, formal dining in its Conservatory Restaurant (see "Where to Dine," below) and less formal food in its Armoury Alehouse & Grill.

Main St., Crossford, Dunfermline, Fife KY12 8QW. ℂ **800/528-1234** or 01383/736258. Fax 01383/621-600. www.keavilhouse.co.uk. 47 units. £120–£140 ($192–$224) double; £135–£195 ($216–$312) family suite. AE, DC, MC, V. Closed Dec 31–Jan 1. Free parking. Take A994, 3.2km (2 miles) west of Dunfermline; the hotel is off the main street at the west end of village. **Amenities:** 2 restaurants; bar; the finest leisure/health club in the area; indoor heated pool; Jacuzzi, sauna; limited room service; babysitting; laundry; steam room. *In room:* TV, dataport, coffeemaker, hair dryer, ironing board, trouser press.

Davaar House Hotel and Restaurant   This large Georgian-style house, in a residential neighborhood a 5-minute walk west of the town center, was built late in the 19th century and boasts distinctive architectural features like a sweeping oak staircase, elaborate moldings, and marble mantelpieces. The largest guest rooms, with the loftiest ceilings, are one floor above street level; slightly less grand rooms are two floors above street level. Each is uniquely decorated in traditional Scottish style. Some of the bathrooms contain a shower only.

The restaurant here is recommended; it's open for dinner Monday through Saturday. Look for moderate prices and home-style cooking from a talented team, with dishes like Scottish salmon with mustard-dill sauce and suprême of chicken and broccoli in phyllo pastry and white-wine sauce.

126 Grieve St., Dunfermline, Fife KY12 8DW. ℂ **01383/721-886.** Fax 01383/623-633. 10 units. £110–£190 ($176–$304) double. Rate includes breakfast. MC, V. Closed Dec 23–Jan 13. Free parking. **Amenities:** Restaurant; bar; limited room service; laundry service. *In room:* TV/VCR, coffeemaker, hair dryer (in some).

King Malcolm Thistle Hotel   The best in-town choice for either a meal or a bed is this stylish, modern, pastel-colored hotel on a roundabout 1.6km (1 mile) south of Dunfermline on A823. Named after the medieval king of Fife (and later of Scotland), Malcolm Canmore, it was built in 1972 but has been thoroughly revamped since then. The guest rooms are well furnished though rather standardized.

Richmond's, a glass-sided bar and restaurant, offers Scottish and Continental cuisine at dinner daily.

Queensferry Rd., Dunfermline, Fife KY11 5DS. ℂ **01383/722-611.** Fax 01383/730-865. www.peelhotel.com. 48 units. £120–£160 ($192–$256) double. Children age 13 and under stay free in parent's room. AE, DC, MC, V. Free parking. Bus: D3 or D4. **Amenities:** Restaurant; 2 bars; limited room service; laundry/dry cleaning service. *In room:* TV, coffeemaker, hair dryer, trouser press.

WHERE TO DINE

Conservatory Restaurant MODERN SCOTTISH   Some of the best local produce is used deftly here to create true "taste of Scotland" specialties—and that means the best of Scottish beef, locally caught game, and fish from local rivers. Old-time recipes are given a modern twist by the chef. The imaginative dishes are served with flair and originality, appealing to both traditionalists and those with more adventurous tastes. Try the smoked salmon and prawns with salad and Arran mustard dressing, for example, or a real local specialty, a chanterelle and "tattie" scone pocket with a malt vinegar demi-glaze. You can follow with dessert of caramelized heather honey and apple parfait. There's an extensive and well-chosen wine list.

In the Keavil House Hotel, Main St., Crossford. (C) **01383/736-258**. Reservations recommended. Fixed-price 3-course menu £25 ($40), 2-course £20 ($32). AE, DC, MC, V. Daily noon–2pm and 7–9pm. Closed Dec 31–Jan 1.

New Victoria SCOTTISH   To reach Dunfermline's oldest restaurant, established in 1923, you must walk up 2 flights of stairs off High Street, in a pedestrian zone in the center overlooking the abbey. The cozy dining room serves generous portions of good old-fashioned cooking using healthy ingredients. You might begin with a robust soup, then follow with steak-and-kidney pie, grilled fish, roast beef, or any of an array of grilled Aberdeen Angus steaks. It's also a good choice if you're in the neighborhood seeking a high tea.

2 Bruce St. (C) **01383/724-175**. Main courses £5–£16.50 ($8–$26); Scottish high tea £6–£13.60 ($9.60–$22). MC, V. Mon–Thurs 11am–8pm; Fri–Sat 11am–9pm; Sun noon–7pm.

SIDE TRIPS FROM DUNFERMLINE: CULROSS & LOCH LEVEN

The old royal burgh of **Culross** ★★★, 10km (6 miles) west of Dunfermline, has been renovated by the Scottish National Trust and is one of the country's most beautiful. As you walk its cobblestone streets, admiring the whitewashed houses with their crow-stepped gables and red pantiled roofs, you'll feel as if you're taking a stroll back into the 17th century.

Set in tranquil walled gardens in the village center, **Culross Palace** ★★ ((C) **01383/880-359**) was built between 1597 and 1611 for prosperous merchant George Bruce. It contains a most beautiful series of paintings on its wooden walls and ceilings portraying moral scenes with passages in Latin and Scottish, illustrating principles like "Honor your parents" and "The spoken word cannot be retracted." A National Trust restoration from 1991 to 1994 involved replacing all the wooden paneling that had rotted with Russian pine, taking care to match the salvaged panels. During the restoration, archaeologists uncovered the remains of a foundation of a long-forgotten building on the east end of the courtyard and the original doorway; there are plans to restore it for use as the public entrance. From Easter to September, the palace is open daily from 12:30 to 4:40pm; in October, only the town house and study are open, Saturday and Sunday from 12:30 to 4:30pm; from November to Easter, visits are by appointment only. Admission is £5 ($8) for adults, £4 ($6.40) for seniors and students, free for those under 19, and £14.50 ($23) per family.

The other important attraction is 10km (6 miles) southwest of Dunfermline (take A994, following the signs to Culross): **Culross Abbey,** a Cistercian monastery founded by Malcolm, earl of Fife, in 1217. Parts of the nave are still intact, and the choir serves as the Culross parish church. There's also a central tower. From Easter Saturday to the last Saturday in August, the abbey is open daily from 9am to 7pm; at other times, you can visit by prior arrangement with the Church of Scotland ((C) **01383/880-231**).

Loch Leven ★, 19km (12 miles) north of Dunfermline and 16km (10 miles) south of Falkland via A911, contains seven islands. On **St. Serf's,** the largest of the islands, are the ruins of the Priory of Loch Leven, built on the site of one of the oldest Culdee establishments in Scotland. If you're interested in seeing the ruins, contact the Kinross tourist office at (C) **01577/863-680** and you'll be put in touch with one of the fishermen who make boat trips to the island.

In **Kinross,** 40km (25 miles) north of Edinburgh, you can take the ferry over to Castle Island to see the ruins of **Loch Leven Castle** ((C) **0777/804-0483**).

"Those never got luck who came to Loch Leven," and this saying sums up the history of this Douglas fortress dating from the late 14th century. Among its ill-fated prisoners, none was more notable than Mary Queen of Scots; inside its forbidding walls, she signed her abdication on July 24, 1567, but she escaped from Loch Leven on May 2, 1568. Thomas Percy, seventh earl of Northumberland, supported her cause and "lodged" in the castle for 3 years until he was handed over to the English, who beheaded him at York. Today, you can see a 14th-century tower house and a 16th-century curtain wall, all that remains of a castle that loomed large in Scottish history. The castle is open from April to September, daily from 9:30am to 6:30pm; and October to March, Monday through Saturday from 9:30am to 4:30pm and Sunday from 2 to 4:30pm. Admission is £3.50 ($5.60) for adults, £2.50 ($4) for seniors, and £1.20 ($1.90) for children. The admission includes the cost of a round-trip ferry from Kinross to Castle Island.

WHERE TO STAY & DINE

Dunclutha Guest House   A 3-minute walk northeast of the town center is this dignified stone house, which was built around 1890 for the priest at the adjacent Episcopal church. Today, it's the domain of Mrs. Pam McDonald, who infuses lots of personalized hominess into her hotel. The non-smoking spacious guest rooms are clean, well maintained, and (in most cases) sunny, thanks to big windows with garden views. Breakfast is served in the sunny breakfast room, which adjoins a lounge containing games and a piano.

16 Victoria Rd., Leven, Fife KY8 4EX. © **01333/425-515.** Fax 01333/422-311. pam.leven@dunclutha-accomm.demon.co.uk. 5 units. £50 ($80) double. Rate includes breakfast. AE, MC, V. Free parking. *In room:* TV, coffeemaker, hair dryer (on request), no phone.

2 East Neuk's Scenic Fishing Villages ⋆⋆

Within half an hour's drive south of St. Andrews, on the eastward-facing peninsula incorporating St. Andrews and Anstruther, is the district of East Neuk, dotted with some of eastern Scotland's most scenic and unspoiled fishing villages. You can't reach these villages by rail; the nearest stations are Ladybank, Cupar, and Leuchars, on the main London-Edinburgh-Dundee-Aberdeen line serving northeast Fife. Buses from St. Andrews connect the villages, but you'll really want to have your own car here.

If the weather's right, you can cycle among the villages along some of the most delightful back roads in Fife. Rent a bike at **East Neuk Outdoors,** Cellardyke Park in Anstruther (© **01333/311-929**). This same outfitter can also fix you up for a canoe trip.

PITTENWEEM

If you're at Pittenweem Monday through Saturday morning, try to get caught up in the action at the **fish auction** held under a large shed. The actual time depends on the tides. Afterward, go for a walk through the village and admire the sturdy stone homes, some of which have been preserved by Scotland's National Trust.

The *weem* in the name of the town means "cave," a reference to **St. Fillan's Cave** (© **01333/311-495**), at Cove Wynd in the vicinity of the harbor. This cave is said to contain the shrine of St. Fillan, a hermit who lived in the 6th century. Hours are daily 10am to 5pm, costing £1 ($1.60) admission, free for children under 15 years old.

The best way to reach **Anstruther** (see below) is to hike the 2.5km (1½ miles) over to it, because the road isn't paved. If the day is clear, this is one of the loveliest walks in eastern Scotland. From Pittenweem, follow a signpost directing you to

Anstruther; you'll cross Scottish meadows and can say hello to a few lambs. You can also take the walk in reverse, as most visitors do. In Anstruther, the path begins at the bottom of West Braes, a small cul-de-sac off the main road in the village.

WHERE TO STAY

The Pittenweem Harbour Guest House   Set directly on the harbor, this charming stone building was erected around 1910 as a private home. The guest rooms contain pinewood furniture and comfortable twin beds, each a cozy, no-frills refuge from the chilly winds and crashing seas. Each unit contains a small, shower-only bathroom. Because it's run by a local company and not by a family, Harbour is a bit more businesslike than a conventional B&B; in fact, it feels like a fishing lodge—the staff will direct you to local entrepreneurs who can take you out for a half-day's fishing or point out spots on the nearby piers and boardwalks where a rod and reel might attract fish.

14 Mid Shore, Pittenweem, Fife KY10 2NL. ℭ **01333/311-273.** Fax 01333/310-014. www.pittenweem.com. 4 units. £42–£60 ($67–$96) double. Rates include breakfast. Discounts of £8 ($13) per person off nightly rate Nov–Mar. AE, DC, MC, V. *In room:* TV, coffeemaker, hair dryer.

ANSTRUTHER

Once an important herring-fishing port, Anstruther is now a summer resort, 74km (46 miles) northeast of Edinburgh, 55km (34 miles) east of Dunfermline, 6.5km (4 miles) southwest of Crail, and 37km (23 miles) south of Dundee. The **tourist office** is on High Street (ℭ **01333/311-073**); it's open April through September, Monday through Saturday from 10am to 5pm and Sunday from noon to 5pm. (Tues–Thurs, it closes from 1–2pm.)

You'll enjoy taking a brisk stroll along the beaches here; it's too chilly for swimming, but it's invigorating and scenic nonetheless. The best nearby is **Billow Ness Beach,** a 10-minute walk east of the center.

The **Scottish Fisheries Museum,** St. Ayles, Harbourhead (ℭ **01333/310-628;** bus: 95), is down by the harbor. It was expanded in 1999 to include a neighboring building that was an 18th-century tavern and several re-creations of restored fishing boats. Here you can follow the fisherfolk through every aspect of their industry—from the days of sail to modern times. Associated with the museum but afloat in the harbor is an old herring drifter, *The Reaper,* which you can board to look around. April to October, the museum is open Monday to Saturday from 10am to 5:30pm and Sunday from 11am to 5pm; November to March, hours are Monday to Saturday from 10am to 4:30pm and Sunday from 2 to 4:30pm. Admission is £3.50 ($5.60) adults, £2.50 ($4) seniors/children, and £10 ($16) families. Last admission one hour before closing time.

From the museum, you can walk to the tiny hamlet of **Cellardyke,** adjoining Anstruther. You'll find many charming stone houses and an ancient harbor where in the year Victoria took the throne (1837), 140 vessels used to put out to sea. You can rent a bike from **East Neuk Outdoors,** Cellardyke Park (ℭ **01333/311-929**), where rental rates are £12 ($19) daily and £30 to £50 ($48–$80) weekly, plus a deposit. It's open daily April to September from 9am to 5pm. Open by appointment only in winter.

The **Isle of May** ⟨❀⟩, a nature reserve in the Firth of Forth, is accessible by boat from Anstruther. It's a bird observatory and a field station and contains the ruins of a 12th-century chapel as well as an early 19th-century lighthouse.

The **May Princess** (ℭ **01333/310103;** www.isleofmayferry.com) is a 100-passenger boat that departs for the Isle of May from the Lifeboat Station at

Anstruther Harbour every day, weather permitting, between mid-April and late September. Tickets for the trip go on sale one hour before departure from a kiosk beside Anstruther Harbour. The five-hour trip, door-to-door, costs £13 ($21) for adults, £11 ($18) for seniors and students and £6 ($9.60) for children 3 to 14. Departure times vary with the season, the day of the week, and the vagaries of the weather, so call in advance before planning for the five-hour trip. Between May and July, expect to see hundreds, even thousands, of puffins, which mate on the Isle of May at that time.

WHERE TO STAY

Craw's Nest Hotel   This black-and-white step-gabled Scottish manse is a popular hotel, with views over the Firth of Forth and May Island. The midsize guest rooms are handsomely appointed, each with a combination tub and shower. Some of the rooms contain four-posters, and two accommodations are set aside for those with disabilities. The public areas, including a lounge bar as well as a bustling public bar, are simply decorated and cozy. The food in the dining room and the wine reasonably priced.

Bankwell Rd., Anstruther, Fife KY10 3DA. ℭ **01333/310-691.** Fax 01333/312-216. www.crawsnesthotel. co.uk. 50 units. £70–£210 ($112–$336) double. Rates include Scottish breakfast. AE, DC, MC, V. Bus: 915. **Amenities:** Restaurant; 2 bars; limited room service; laundry/dry cleaning service. *In room:* TV, coffeemaker, hair dryer, trouser press.

Smuggler's Inn   This warmly inviting inn evokes memories of smuggling days, with low ceilings, uneven floors, and winding stairs. An inn has stood on this spot since 1300, and in Queen Anne's day it was a well-known tavern. The guest rooms are comfortably furnished; some bathrooms contain a shower only. The restaurant serves moderately priced regional cuisine at dinner nightly. Affordable bar lunches are also available.

High St., East Anstruther, Fife KY10 3DQ. ℭ **01333/310-506.** Fax 01333/312-706. 9 units. £50–£60 ($80–$96) double. Rates include Scottish breakfast. MC, V. Bus: 95. **Amenities:** Restaurant; bar; laundry. *In room:* TV, coffeemaker, hair dryer.

WHERE TO DINE

The Cellar SEAFOOD   Within the solid stone walls of a cellar that dates from 1875 (but possibly from the 16th century), this seafood restaurant is the best in town. It's lit by candlelight and, in winter, by twin fireplaces at opposite ends of the room. The menu offers fresh fish hauled in from nearby waters and prepared with light sauces. The best examples are grilled halibut suprême dredged in breadcrumbs and citrus juices and served with hollandaise sauce; lobster, monkfish, and scallops roasted with herb-and-garlic butter and served on sweet pepper risotto; and a limited array of meat dishes.

24 East Green, Anstruther. ℭ **01333/310-378.** Reservations recommended. Fixed-price dinner 2-courses £24.50 ($39), 3-courses £29.50 ($47), 4-courses £32.20 ($52); fixed price lunch 2-courses £15.50 ($25), 3-courses £18.50 ($30). AE, DC, MC, V. Wed–Sun 12:30–1:30pm; Tues–Sat 7–9:30pm. Bus: 95.

Haven SCOTTISH   Set within a pair of interconnected 300-year-old fisherman's cottages, this is the only restaurant with a position directly on the harbor of Anstruther. Defining itself as a restaurant with a cocktail lounge (not a pub), it serves simple, wholesome food that's flavorful and utterly unpretentious: panfried breaded prawns, halibut filets, Angus steaks, local crabmeat salad, and homemade soups and stews. The upper floor contains one of the town's most popular bars, where the same menu is served. The street level, more formal and sedate, is the site of high teas and evening meals.

1 Shore Rd., Cellardyke, Anstruther. (Ⓒ 01333/310-574. Reservations recommended. Main courses £7.95–£13.95 ($13–$22); high teas (tea, toast, and a meal-size platter of food) £7.95–£8.35 ($13–$13). MC, V. Mon–Thurs 11am–9pm; Fri–Sun 11am–11pm. Bus: 95; a James Anderson & Co. bus runs every hour from St. Andrews, 13km (8 miles) south, to the door of the restaurant.

AFTER DARK

Dreel Tavern ⋇, 16 High St. (Ⓒ **01333/310-727**), was a 16th-century coaching inn and is now a wood-and-stone pub where locals gather to unwind in the evening. Caledonian 80 Shilling and Orkney Dark Island are available on hand pump, along with two guest beers that change weekly. It's open Monday through Saturday from 11am to 11pm and Sunday from noon to 11pm.

ELIE ⟨⋇

With its step-gabled houses and little harbor, Elie, 18km (11 miles) south of Anstruther, is many visitors' favorite village along the coast. Only a 25-minute car ride from Edinburgh, Elie and its close neighbor, Earlsferry, overlook a crescent of gold-sand beach, with more swimming possibilities to be found among sheltered coves. The name Elie is believed to be derived from the *ailie* (island) of Ardross, which now forms part of the harbor and is joined to the mainland by a road. A large stone building, a former granary, at the harbor is a reminder of the days when Elie was a busy trading port. Of all the villages of East Neuk, this one seems best suited for walks and hikes in all directions.

Earlsferry, to the west, got its name from an ancient ferry crossing, which Macduff, the thane of Fife, is supposed to have used in his escape from Macbeth.

East of the harbor stands a stone structure known as the **Lady's Tower,** used by Lady Janet Anstruther, a noted 18th-century beauty, as a bathing cabana. Another member of the Anstruther family, Sir John, added the interesting **bell tower** to the parish church that stands in the center of the village.

Beyond the lighthouse, on a point of land to the east of the harbor, lies **Ruby Bay,** so named because you can find garnets here. Farther along the coast is **Fossil Bay,** where you can find a variety of fossils.

WHERE TO STAY

The Elms Guest House ⟨Value ⟨Kids   Run by Mr. and Mrs. Terras, this 1880 building is on the wide main street behind a conservative stone facade, with a crescent-shaped rose garden in front. The comfortably furnished but small guest rooms contain good beds, washbasins, and showers. There's also a self-catering cottage available for rent that can sleep six comfortably. Home cooking is a specialty of the place, and dishes include Scottish lamb, Pittenweem haddock, haggis, and Arbroath kippers. A simple dinner is available to nonguests. In the walled flower garden behind the house is a large conservatory for guests' use.

14 Park Place, Elie, Fife KY9 1DH. (Ⓒ and fax **01333/330-404**. www.elms-elie.co.uk. 8 units. £52 ($83) double; cottage £110 ($176). Rates include Scottish breakfast. MC, V. Closed Nov–Mar. *In room:* TV, hair dryer, coffeemaker.

Rockview Guest House ⟨Kids   Next to the Ship Inn (see below), the Rockview overlooks fine sandy beaches around Elie Bay. The small guest rooms are nicely furnished, each with a good bed and shower-only bathroom. Maintenance is of a high level, and the welcome is warm. A twin-bedded room has a bunk bed for younger children to share with their parents. Of course, food and drink are available at the Ship Inn.

The Toft, Elie, Fife KY9 1DT. (Ⓒ **01333/330-246**. Fax 01333/330-864. www.ship-elie.com. 6 units. £50 ($80) double. Rates include breakfast. MC, V. *In room:* TV, coffeemaker.

WHERE TO DINE

Ship Inn ★ SCOTTISH   Even if you're not stopping over in Elie, we suggest you drop in at the Ship (from the center, follow the signs marked HARBOUR) and enjoy a pint of lager or real ale or a whisky from the large selection. The building occupied by this pub dates from 1778, and a bar has been in business here since 1830. In summer, you can sit outdoors and look over the water; in colder months, a fireplace burns brightly. On weekends in July and August, a barbecue operates outside. The set menu with daily specials features such items as steak pie, Angus beefsteaks, lasagna, and an abundance of fresh seafood.

The Toft. © 01333/330-246. Main courses £7–£16 ($11–$26). MC, V. Mon–Sat noon–midnight; Sun 12:30–11pm; open to 1am Fri-Sat.

CRAIL ★★

The pearl of the East Neuk of Fife, Crail is 81km (50 miles) northeast of Edinburgh, 37km (23 miles) south of Dundee, and 15km (9 miles) south of St. Andrews. It's an artists' colony, and many painters live in cottages around the little harbor. Natural bathing facilities are at Roome Bay, and many **beaches** are nearby. The **Balcomie Golf Course** is one of the oldest in the world and is still in good condition.

The old town grew up along the harbor, and you can still see a lot of fishing cottages clustered here. Crab and lobster boats continue to set out hoping for a big catch. **Upper Crail** overlooks the harbor and also merits exploration. The **tollbooth** dates from 1598 and is crowned by a belfry. **Marketgate** is lined with trees and flanked by small two- and three-floor houses. Follow the walkway to **Castle Walk,** which offers the most panoramic view of Crail.

To understand the villages of East Neuk better, call at the **Crail Museum & Heritage Centre,** 62 Marketgate (© 01333/450-869), which contains artifacts related to fishing and the former trading links of these tiny villages. Admission is free. June to September the center is open Monday to Saturday from 10am to 1pm and 2 to 5pm and Sunday from 2 to 5pm; and April to May hours are Saturday to Sunday from 2 to 5pm.

WHERE TO STAY & DINE

Croma Hotel   This family run hotels offers small, very simply furnished but comfortable rooms, all of which are non-smoking. Four rooms have private bathrooms with tubs or showers; two rooms share bathroom facilities and can be rented as a suite. One notable feature is the fully licensed Chart Room bar, open from 5pm to midnight, where you can drop in for drinks. In the traditional dining room, dinner is served on weekends, using fresh local produce, especially freshly caught seafood.

33–35 Nethergate, Crail, Fife KY10 3TU. © 01333/450-239. Fax 01333/451-4333. www.cromahotel.co.uk. 6 units, 4 with private bathroom. £47 ($75) double without bathroom; £54 ($86) double with bathroom. Rates include Scottish breakfast. MC, V. Free parking. Closed Dec–Jan. **Amenities:** Bar; laundry. *In room:* TV, coffeemaker, hair dryer.

Denburn House *(Kids)*   Near the town center, in a historic neighborhood known as Marketgate, this guesthouse occupies a 200-year-old, stone-sided building that retains many of its interior architectural features, including the paneling in the lounge and an elaborate staircase. In 1998, most of the interior was tastefully renovated; all the guest rooms were redecorated in a conservative but very pleasing style, each with a shower-only bathroom. A self-catering apartment out back comes complete with 3 spacious bedrooms, (2 twins and a king-size) plus a shower-only bathroom, kitchen, and a combined dining room and lounge. The rear garden offers a scattering of lawn furniture and access to the great Scottish outdoors. Everything is very low-key and unpretentious.

1 Marketgate North, Crail, Fife KY10 3TQ. © **01333/450-253**. www.s-h-systems.co.uk/hotels/denburnh. html. 6 units. £46–£52 ($74–$83) double; apartment June–Sept £75 ($120), Oct–May £60 ($96). Rates include breakfast. AE, MC, V. Free parking. **Amenities:** Laundry service. *In room:* TV, coffeemaker, hair dryer.

3 St. Andrews: The Birthplace of Golf /★/★

23km (14 miles) SE of Dundee, 82km (51 miles) NE of Edinburgh

The medieval royal burgh of St. Andrews was once filled with monasteries and ancient houses that didn't survive the pillages of Henry VIII; regrettably, only a few ruins rising in ghostly dignity remain. Most of the town as you'll see it today was built of local stone during the 18th, 19th, and early 20th centuries. This historic sea town in northeast Fife is also known as the seat where the rules of golf in Britain and the world are codified and arbitrated. Golf was played for the first time in the 1400s, probably on the site of St. Andrews's Old Course, and was enjoyed by Mary Queen of Scots here in 1567. Golfers consider this town to be hallowed ground.

ESSENTIALS
GETTING THERE   BritRail stops 13km (8 miles) away at the town of Leuchars (rhymes with "euchres") on its London–Edinburgh–Dundee–Aberdeen run to the northeast. About 28 trains per day make the trip. Trip time from Edinburgh to Leuchars is about an hour, and a one-way fare is £8.50 ($14). For information, call © **08457/484-950.**

Once at Leuchars, you can take a bus the rest of the way to St. Andrews. Bus no. 99 departs about every 20 minutes. Fife Scottish bus no. X24 travels from Glasgow to Glenrothes daily, and from there to St. Andrews. Buses operate daily 7am to midnight, the trip taking between 2½ and 3 hours. Buses arrive at the St. Andrews Bus Station, Station Road, just off City Road (call © **01334/474-238** for schedules).

By car from Edinburgh, head northwest along A90 and cross the Forth Road Bridge north. Take A921 to the junction with A915 and continue northeast until you reach St. Andrews.

A Princely Attraction

The arrival of Prince William to attend classes at the **University of St. Andrews** has created a new type of tourist to the golfing capital of Scotland. Golfers still flock here, but lately more and more young girls from America, England, and the continent are coming here to catch a glimpse of Prince Charming. The second in line to the British throne can sometimes be spotted about town, usually in a dark sweater and faded jeans. His appearances are greeted with shrieks and screams, as if he were a 1940s movie star. Today's movie stars don't get such adulation. In spite of the objections of Prince Charles, this small town is not treating William like an ordinary student, not with paparazzi and star-gazers lurking behind every thistle.

VISITOR INFORMATION   The **tourist office** is on 70 Market St. (© 01334/ 472-021; www.standrews.com). January to March, November, and December, it's open Monday to Saturday from 9:30am to 5pm; April hours are Monday to Saturday from 9:30am to 5pm and Sunday from 11am to 4pm; May, June, September, and October, hours are Monday to Saturday from 9:30am to 6pm and Sunday from 11am to 4pm; and July and August, hours are Monday to Saturday from 9:30am to 7pm and Sunday from 10am to 6pm.

HITTING THE LINKS

All six of the St. Andrews courses are fully owned by the municipality and open to the public on a more or less democratic basis—ballots are polled 1 day in advance. This balloting system might be circumvented for players who reserve with the appropriate starters several days or weeks in advance. To play the hallowed Old Course, you must present a current handicap certificate and/or letter of introduction from a bona-fide golf club.

The misty and verdant golf courses are the very symbol of St. Andrews: the famous **Old Course;** the 6,604-yard (6,010m), par-72 **New Course** (opened in 1896); the 6,805-yard (6,192.5m), par-71 **Jubilee Course** (opened in 1897 in honor of Queen Victoria); the 6,112-yard (5,562m), par-70 **Eden** (opened in 1914); the **Balgove** (a nine-hole course for children's golf training, opened in 1972), and the 5,094-yard (4,635.5m), par-67 **Strathtyrum** (the newest and most far-flung, an eight-hole course opened in 1993). Encircled by all of them is the world's most prestigious golf club, the **Royal and Ancient Golf Club** (© 01334/472-112), founded in St. Andrews in 1754—it remains more or less rigidly closed as a private-membership men's club. The Royal and Ancient traditionally opens its doors to the public only on St. Andrews Day so that nonmembers may view the legendary trophy room. This usually, but not always, falls around November 30.

The **Old Course,** Pilmour Cottage (© 01334/466-666), is the world's most legendary temple of golf, one whose difficulty is shaped by nature and the long-ago paths of grazing sheep. Over the centuries, stately buildings have been erected near its start and finish. Aristocrats from virtually everywhere have lent their names and reputations to enhance its glamour, and its nuances have been debated, usually in reverent tones, by golfers in bars and on fairways throughout the world. This fabled par-72 course hosted the 2000 British Open, when golf fans from around the world watched in awe as Tiger Woods became the youngest golfer in history to complete a grand slam (and only the fifth golfer ever to perform the feat). Greens fees are £105 ($168), a caddy costs £38 ($61) plus tip, and clubs rent for £20–£30 ($32–$48) per round. There are no electric carts allowed, and you can rent a trolley on afternoons only between May and September for £3 ($4.80).

Facilities for golfers in St. Andrews are legion—virtually every hotel in town maintains some kind of facility to assist golfers. The most interesting clubhouse in town is **The Links Clubhouse,** West Sand Road (© 01334/466-666). Owned and operated by the St. Andrews Links Trust, and located within 400 yards (365m) of the Old Course's 18th hole, it offers, without charge, lockers, showers, and changing facilities. You can lock up your gear for a day without charge, since lockers are operated with £1 ($1.60) coins, which are refunded when you surrender your key at the end of the day. On site, there's also a bar and restaurant.

Two Californians, Mark Parsinen and Art Dunkley, have invaded the capital of golf and opened a new championship-ready links, **Kingsbarns Golf Links**

(© **01334/460-860**). The land and adjoining North Sea beachfront were utilized as a rehearsal ground during the build-up for the D-Day invasion of Normandy in June of 1944. During some of the uprooting of the earth, a 3,000-year-old mummy was discovered. The course is challenging and beautiful, with sometimes blustery winds of the North Sea as a backdrop. "Tighten your kilts, laddies," a woman caddy, Emily Thompson, sometimes tells players facing the course, which plays to a yardage of 7,126.

For more details on golf associations and golf tours, see "Teeing Off: Golfing in Scotland," in chapter 3.

EXPLORING THE AREA

Founded in 1411, the **University of St. Andrews** is the oldest in Scotland and the third oldest in Britain and has been called the "Oxbridge" of Scotland. At term time, you can see packs of students in their characteristic red gowns. The university grounds stretch west of the St. Andrews Castle between North Street and the Scores.

The university's most interesting buildings are the tower and church of St. Salvator's College and the courtyard of St. Mary's College, from 1538. An ancient thorn tree, said to have been planted by Mary Queen of Scots, stands near the college's chapel. St. Leonard's College church is also from medieval days. In 1645, the Scottish Parliament met in what was once the University Library and is now a students' reading room. A modern University Library, containing many rare ancient volumes, was opened in 1976.

Castle of St. Andrews ✦   This ruined 13th-century castle eerily poised at the edge of the sea boasts a bottle dungeon and secret passages. Founded in the early part of the 13th century, it was reconstructed several times and was once a bishop's palace and later a prison for reformers. The bottle dungeon is carved 7m (24 ft.) down into the rock, and both prisoners and food were dropped through it. There's said to be no nastier dungeon in all Scotland.

Much of the eeriness here concerns the 1546 arrest of religious reformer George Wishart and the show trial that followed. Convicted by a group of Catholic prelates spearheaded by Cardinal Beaton, Wishart was burned at the stake, reputedly while Beaton and his entourage watched from an upper-floor window. Vowing revenge, a group of reformers waited 3 months before gaining access to the castle while disguised as stonemasons. They overpowered the guards (some they killed, some they threw into the castle's moat) and murdered Beaton—and, rather bizarrely, preserved his corpse in salt so they could eventually give it a proper burial. The reformers retained control of the castle for several months, until the Catholic forces of the earl of Arran laid siege. As part of their efforts, the attackers almost completed a tunnel (they called it "a mine"), dug virtually through rock, beneath the castle walls. The (Protestant) defenders, in response, dug a tunnel ("a countermine") of their own, which intersected the first tunnel at a higher elevation, allowing the defenders to drop rocks, boiling oil, or whatever else on the attackers' heads. The resulting underground battle took on epic proportions during the virtually implacable year-long siege. As part of the tour, you can stumble down the narrow countermine to the place where besieged and besiegers met in this clash.

The Scores (273m/900 ft. northwest of the cathedral). © **01334/477-196**. Admission £3 ($4.80) adults, £2.50 ($4) seniors, £1 ($1.60) children. Combined tickets (castle and cathedral) £4 ($6.40) adults, £3 ($4.80) seniors, £1.25 ($2) children. Apr–Sept daily 9:30am–6:30pm; Oct–Mar daily 9:30am–4:30pm. Last admission 30 minutes before closing time.

Holy Trinity Church   Called the Town Kirk, this restored medieval church once stood on the grounds of the now-ruined cathedral (see below). The church was moved to its present site in 1410, considerably altered after the Reformation of 1560, and restored in the early 20th century. You'll find much fine stained glass and carvings inside.

Opposite St. Mary's College, off South St. ℂ **01334/474-494.** Free admission, but call in advance to make sure someone is in attendance. Sat 10am–noon.

St. Andrews Cathedral and Priory 𝕒   Near the Celtic settlement of St. Mary of the Rock, by the sea at the east end of town, is the semi-ruin of St. Andrews Cathedral and Priory. It was founded in 1160 and begun in the Romanesque style; however, the cathedral's construction suffered many setbacks. By the time of its consecration in 1318 in the presence of King Robert the Bruce, it had a Gothic overlay. At the time the largest church in Scotland, the cathedral established St. Andrews as the ecclesiastical capital of the country, but today the ruins can only suggest its former beauty and importance. There's a collection of early Christian and medieval monuments, as well as artifacts discovered on the cathedral site.

Off Pends Rd. ℂ **01334/472-563.** Admission £2 ($3.20) adults, £1.50 ($2.40) seniors, £.75 ($1.20) children age 5–15 years. Apr–Sept daily 9:30am–5pm; Oct–Mar Mon–Sat 9:30am–4pm, Sun 2–4pm.

Secret Bunker 𝕒   Scotland's best-kept secret for 40 years of cold war, this amazing labyrinth, built 30m (100 ft.) below ground and encased in 4.5m (15 ft.) of reinforced concrete, is where central government and military commanders would have run the country from if the United Kingdom had been attacked and nuclear war broken out. Built (in great secrecy) in 1951 to withstand aerial attack, it has a guardhouse entrance designed to look like a traditional Scottish farmhouse. You can visit the BBC studio where emergency broadcasts to Scotland would have been made and the switchboard room set up to handle 2,800 outside lines. The bunker could allow 300 people to live, work, and sleep in safety while coordinating war efforts, like aboveground retaliation. It also contains two cinemas showing authentic cold war films, an audiovisual theater, a cafe, and a gift shop.

You can wander at will through the underground labyrinth, but 30-minute guided tours depart daily at 11am, 1pm, and 3pm. For some amazing reason, the chapel here has been the site of several local weddings since decommissioning in 1993.

Underground Nuclear Command Centre, Crown Buildings (near St. Andrews), Fife. ℂ **01333/310-301.** Admission £7.20 ($12) adults, £5.95 ($9.50) seniors, £4.50 ($7.20) children age 5–16, £22 ($35) families, free for children age 4 and under. Apr–Oct daily 10am–5pm. From St. Andrews, follow the signs to Anstruther, driving 12km (7½ miles) south. At that point, signs show the way to the bunker.

SHOPPING

Specializing in Scottish art, **St. Andrews Fine Arts,** 84A Market St. (ℂ **01334/474-080**), also sells prints, drawings, and watercolors. All paintings were produced within the national boundaries of Scotland sometime between 1800 and the present. **Renton Oriental Rugs,** 72 South St. (ℂ **01334/476-334**), is one of Scotland's leading dealers of Oriental carpets, whether you're seeking antique rugs or reasonably priced reproductions. Rugs come in many sizes, prices, and styles. At **St. Andrews Pottery Shop,** 4 Church Sq. (ℂ **01334/477-744**), an array of decorative stoneware, ceramics, and enameled jewelry—most of it produced locally—is for sale. **Bonkers,** 80 Market St. (ℂ **01334/473-919**), is a typical tourist shop, hawking T-shirts, regional pottery, and other souvenirs, along with cards and stationery.

WHERE TO STAY
EXPENSIVE

St. Andrews Bay Golf Resort & Spa ★★★   At last Eastern Scotland has a premier, government-rated five-star hotel. It lies perched on a cliff overlooking the North Sea and the River Tay. The hotel and its 2 championship golf courses sit on 210 hectares (520 acres). The sprawling resort complex, opened by Donald and Nancy Panoz, who run the Château Élan resort and winery in north Georgia, also offers a magnificent spa and a fitness club that numbers Prince William among its members.

Bedrooms are the finest in the area, each spacious and equipped with such extras as DVD players and high-speed Internet links. Style and functionality in the bedrooms combine for grand comfort, ranging from the luxurious bathtubs with separate showers to the soft duvet covers. The most luxurious accommodations are the so-called Manor homes next to the 4th fairway of the Torrance Course, each with four large bedrooms and five bathrooms plus a farmhouse-style kitchen. Some of the finest chefs in the U.K. were hired to create an award-winning cuisine whose scope ranges from Mongolian barbecues to Scottish products such as salmon, Ayrshire pork, and Perthshire lamb.

Golf is still the main attraction, however, including the 7,049 yard (6,446m), par-71 Devlin, designed by Australian pro Bruce Devlin, and the 7,037 yard (6,435m), par-72 Torrance designed by Rider Cup captain Sam Torrance. With its treacherous Cliffside green, the most thrilling hole is the 14th.

St. Andrews Bay, St. Andrews, KY16 8PN. ☎ **01334/837-000.** www.standrewsbay.com. 211 units. £145–£230 ($232–$368) double; £195–£280 ($312–$448) suite; £900 ($1440) Manor Home. AE, MC, V. Free valet parking. Lies 5.6km (3½ miles) south of St. Andrews. **Amenities:** 4 restaurants; 3 bars; heated indoor pool; 2 golf courses; health club; spa; Jacuzzi; sauna; children's program on weekends; business center; 24-hr. room service; massage; babysitting; laundry/dry cleaning service; steam room. *In room:* TV, dataport, minibar, coffeemaker, hair dryer, iron, safe, trouser press.

Peat Inn ★★   About 11km (7 miles) from St. Andrews, in the village of Cupar, the Peat is in an inn/post office built in 1760, where beautifully furnished guest rooms and spacious suites are offered, and David Wilson prepares exceptional cuisine in the restaurant. All units are suites that have separate bedrooms and living areas. Most rooms come with shower; some also have a tub. The high-priced restaurant offers local ingredients—even the pigeons come from a St. Andrews farm—and serves lunch and dinner Tuesday through Saturday.

Cupar, Fife KY15 5LH. ☎ **01334/840-206.** Fax 01334/840-530. www.thepeatinn.co.uk/ourhome.htm. 8 units. £145–£155 ($232–$248) suite for 2. Rates include continental breakfast. AE, MC, V. From St. Andrews, drive 11km (7 miles) southwest along A915, then branch onto B940. Free parking. **Amenities:** Restaurant; bar; limited room service. *In room:* TV, hair dryer (in some).

Rufflets Country House Hotel ★   The garden-and-golf crowd loves this cozy 1924 country house in a 4.1-hectare (10-acre) garden. Each good-size guest room is furnished in a homelike way (often in Queen Anne style), some with canopied or four-poster beds and all with combination tub and showers. The most modern rooms are in two separate lodges, but traditionalists request space in the handsome main building. Accommodations specially designed for families and for wheelchair-bound guests are available. Special extras in all the rooms include bathrobes, upscale toiletries, and teddy bears on the beds. Reserve well in advance—Rufflets is very popular with British vacationers.

Even if you aren't staying here, you may want to reserve a table at the garden-style Rufflets Hotel Restaurant, overlooking the award-winning garden. Excellent fresh ingredients are used in the Continental and Scottish dishes.

Strathkinness Low Rd., St. Andrews, Fife KY16 9TX. ℂ **01334/472-594.** Fax 01334/478-703. www.rufflets. co.uk. 24 units. £90–£210 ($144–$589) double; £230–£240 ($368–$384) suite. Rates include Scottish breakfast. AE, DC, MC, V. Take B939 2.5km (1½ miles) from St. Andrews. **Amenities:** Restaurant; bar; limited room service; babysitting; laundry/dry cleaning service. *In room:* TV, dataport, coffeemaker, hair dryer, trouser press.

Rusacks Hotel St. Andrews

A grand Victorian pile built in 1887 by Josef Rusack, a German from Silesia who recognized St. Andrews's potential as a golf capital, Rusacks sits at the edge of the famous 18th hole of Pilmour Links of the Old Course. The hotel's stone walls are capped with neoclassical gables and slate roofs. Inside, chintz picks up the tones from the bouquets of flowers sent in fresh twice a week. Between the panels and Ionic columns of the public rooms, racks of lendable books re-create the atmosphere of a private country-house library. Upstairs, the spacious guest rooms are themed around some of the world's most famous golfers, tournaments, and course hazards (such as the Valley of Sin room). All contain some carved antiques and modern conveniences, but are nothing to equal the St. Andrews Old Course Hotel (see below). Each unit comes with a beautifully maintained private bathroom.

The basement Golf Club has golf-related photos, trompe-l'oeil racks of books, Chesterfield sofas, and vested waiters. Light meals and snacks are served here. The Old Course restaurant, overlooking the 18th hole, offers daily specials along with local game, meat, and fish, accompanied by a wine list from a well-stocked cellar.

Pilmour Links, St. Andrews, Fife KY16 9JQ. ℂ **800/225-5843** in the U.S., or 01334/474-321. Fax 01334/477-896. www.macdonaldhotels.co.uk. 68 units. £110–£189 ($176–$302) double; from £220 ($352) suite. AE, DC, MC, V. **Amenities:** Restaurant; bar; sauna; 24-hr. room service; laundry service. *In room:* TV, coffeemaker, hair dryer, safe (in some), trouser press.

St. Andrews Golf Hotel

A combination of greenery, sea mists, and tradition makes this late-Victorian property extremely popular with golfers, despite the fact that many of them confuse it at first glance with the larger and more prestigious St. Andrews Old Course Hotel (see below). About 200 yards (182m) from the first tee-off of the famous golf course, it was built as two stately Victorian homes and later expanded and transformed into a hotel run by Brian and Maureen Hughes. The comfortable but unstylish midsize guest rooms are individually decorated; some have four-poster beds and others boast sea views. The rooms in the front get the view but also the noise.

Bar lunches are served Monday to Saturday, and table d'hôte dinners are presented nightly in an oak-paneled restaurant with a fireplace.

40 The Scores, St. Andrews, Fife KY16 9SP. ℂ **01334/472-611.** Fax 01334/472-188. www.standrews-golf.co.uk. 22 units. £160–£200 ($256–$320) double; from £200–£600 ($320–$960) suite. Rates include Scottish breakfast. AE, DC, MC, V. Free parking. **Amenities:** Restaurant; 2 bars; 24-hr. room service; laundry/dry cleaning service. *In room:* TV, coffeemaker, hair dryer, safe (in some), trouser press.

St. Andrews Old Course Hotel

Many dedicated golfers choose the five-story St. Andrews Old Course Hotel, close to A91 on the outskirts of town, where it overlooks the 17th fairway, the Road Hole of the Old Course. (Don't let the name mislead you: The hotel isn't related to the links of the same name, and guests here find access to the course just as difficult as it is elsewhere.) Fortified by finnan haddie (smoked haddock) and porridge, a real old-fashioned Scottish breakfast, you can face that diabolical stretch of greenery where the Scots have been whacking away since the early 15th century. Some £16 million

($26 million) has been spent to transform the place into a world-class hotel (with price tags to match), and the facade was altered to keep it in line with St. Andrews's more traditional buildings; its balconies afford top-view seats at all golf tournaments. The guest rooms and suites have been remodeled and refurbished, offering traditional wooden furniture and state-of-the-art marble bathrooms.

Well-prepared and high-priced international cuisine is served in the Road Hole Grill. In summer, light meals and afternoon tea are offered in a casual dining room known as Sands.

Old Station Rd., St. Andrews, Fife KY16 9SP. © **01334/474-371.** Fax 01334/477-668. www.oldcoursehotel. co.uk. 146 units. £225–£375 ($360–$600) double; from £295–£445 ($472–$712) junior suite. Rates include Scottish breakfast. Children under 12 stay free in parents' room. AE, DC, MC, V. **Amenities:** 3 restaurants; 4 bars; indoor pool; health club; spa; Jacuzzi; salon; 24-hour room service; massage; babysitting; laundry service; steam rooms. *In room:* TV, minibar, coffeemaker, hair dryer, safe (in some).

MODERATE

Inn at Lathones ⚐   Once a coaching inn, this 200-year-old manor has been thoughtfully restored and provides a reasonable alternative for golfers who can't afford the grand hotels. All of its midsize guest rooms are nicely furnished, with individually controlled heating and bathrooms with power showers in the bathtubs. Two units have log-burning stoves and Jacuzzis with separate showers. The public rooms reflect Scottish tradition, with open fires and beamed ceilings.

The restaurant is under the guidance of chef Marc Guibert, who has created a French-inspired Continental cuisine using fresh Scottish produce.

By Largoward, St. Andrews, Fife KY9 1JE. © **01334/840-494.** Fax 01334/840-694. www.theinn.co.uk. 14 units. £90–£160 ($144–$256) double. Rates include Scottish breakfast. MC, V. Take A915, 8km (5 miles) southwest of the center of St. Andrews. **Amenities:** Restaurant; bar; laundry service; limited room service. *In room:* TV, dataport, coffeemaker, hair dryer.

Russell Hotel   Once a 19th-century private home, the Russell enjoys an ideal location overlooking St. Andrews Bay, a 2-minute walk from the Old Course's first tee. It's well run by Gordon and Fiona de Vries and offers fully equipped though standard guest rooms with tub-only bathrooms (showers in some). Some of the rooms offer sea views. The cozy Victorian pub serves drinks and bar suppers to a loyal local crowd, while the rather unremarkable restaurant offers moderately priced fixed-price dinners nightly.

26 The Scores, St. Andrews, Fife KY16 9AS. © **01334/473-447.** Fax 01334/478-279. www.russellhotel standrews.co.uk. 10 units. £80–£110 ($128–$176) double. Rates include Scottish breakfast. AE, MC, V. Closed Dec 24–Jan 12. **Amenities:** Restaurant; bar; laundry. *In room:* TV, coffeemaker, hair dryer.

INEXPENSIVE

Ashleigh House Hotel   This B&B near the town center was built in 1883 as a fever hospital to quarantine patients afflicted with scarlet fever, diphtheria, and other plagues of the day. After World War I, it was transformed into an orphanage; in the late 1980s, it was finally converted to a B&B. The trio of thick-walled stone cottages are connected by means of covered passageways. The guest rooms are outfitted with good beds and flowered upholstery, and almost all provide tub or shower bathrooms. One bedroom has to use the corridor bathroom, which is a well-maintained and has a tub and shower combination. The bar offers a wide assortment of single malts and a rough-and-ready kind of charm.

37 St. Mary St., St. Andrews, Fife KY16 8AZ. © **01334/475-429.** Fax 01334/474-383. www22.brinkster.com/ ashleighhouse. 10 units, 9 with private bathroom. £50–£70 ($80–$112) double without bathroom; £60–£110 ($96–$176) double with bathroom. Rates include breakfast. MC, V. **Amenities:** Restaurant; bar; sauna. *In room:* TV, coffeemaker, hair dryer.

Bell Craig Guest House   Occupying a century-old–stone-fronted house, this B&B is in a historic neighborhood, a 3-minute walk from the Old Course. This guesthouse has had long practice at housing the parents of students at the nearby university. Sheila Black, the hardworking owner, runs the place with decency and pride and makes a point to spruce up each room in a different style at regular intervals. (Our favorite is the room done in tartan.) Each unit is high-ceilinged, cozy, completely unpretentious, and well scrubbed. Most units contain a shower and tub; two are fitted with a tub only.

8 Murray Park, St. Andrews, Fife KY16 9AW. ℂ **01334/472-962.** www.bellcraig.co.uk. 6 units. £40–£60 ($64–$96) double. Rates include breakfast. MC, V. *In room:* TV, coffeemaker, hair dryer.

WHERE TO DINE

Balaka BANGLADESHI/EUROPEAN/INTERNATIONAL   In the heart of St. Andrews, this Indian and International restaurant has won a number of local culinary awards for its savory cuisine, which has done much to wake up the tastebuds of the local populace. This restaurant is a celeb favorite, drawing such luminaries as Sean Connery (Scotland's favorite son), Arnold Palmer, and even the King and Queen of Malaysia. Behind a facade of gray Scottish stone, the restaurant lies in a .4-hectare (1-acre) garden that is planted with vegetables, flowers, and herbs, each used by the kitchen staff. The flowers being used for decoration, of course. The Rouf family is exceptionally hospitable and will explain menu items to you as you sit at crisp white tablecloths, smelling the perfumed roses on your table. Homegrown coriander, fresh spinach, spring onions, and mint, among other ingredients, figure into many of the recipes. Start, perhaps, with a *samosa,* a spicy ground beef or vegetable pastry, and follow with such delights as green herb chicken with spring onions, garlic, and freshly chopped coriander with tomato. *Mafbangla* is another justifiably local favorite— Scottish filet of salmon marinated in lime juice and flavored with turmeric, green chile, and other palette-pleasing spices.

Alexandra Place. ℂ **013334/474-825.** Reservations recommended. 2-course lunch £6.95 ($11); main courses £7.65–£9.55 ($12–$15). AE, MC, V. Mon–Sat noon–3pm and 5pm–1am.

Grange Inn SCOTTISH/SEAFOOD   An old-fashioned hospitality prevails in this country cottage with its garden, offering a good choice of dishes made from fresh produce. Local beef and lamb always appear on the menu, as do fish and shellfish from the fishing villages of East Neuk. Fruits and herbs come from Cupar. Typical of the offerings are beef filet with port sauce complemented by wild mushrooms, or chicken suprême stuffed with julienne of vegetables and coated with almonds. A classic opener and an old favorite is a stew of mussels and onions.

Grange Rd., at Grange (on B959). ℂ **01334/472-670.** Reservations recommended. Fixed-price dinner £23.95 ($38). DC, MC, V. Daily 12:30–2pm and 7–8:45pm. Drive about 2.5km (1½ miles) from St. Andrews on B959.

Ostlers Close ✿ BRITISH/INTERNATIONAL   Sophisticated and intensely concerned with the quality of its cuisine, this charming restaurant occupies a 17th-century building that functioned in the early 20th century as a temperance hotel. Today, in the heart of the hamlet of Cupar, 11km (7 miles) from St. Andrews, it contains a kitchen in what used to be the hotel's stables, with a severely elegant set of dining rooms in the hotel's former public areas. Menu items are prepared with seasonal Scottish produce and are likely to include roasted saddle of roe venison with wild-mushroom sauce; pan-fried scallops with fresh asparagus and butter sauce; a fresh medley of seafood with champagne-flavored butter sauce; and filet of Scottish lamb stuffed with *skirlie,* an old-fashioned but flavorful combination of bacon-flavored oatmeal and herbs. Whenever it's available, opt for the confit of duckling with salted pork and lentils.

25 Bonnygate, in the nearby town of Cupar. ℂ 01334/655-574. Reservations recommended. Main courses £9.50–£14 ($15–$22) at lunch, £16–£19 ($26–$30) at dinner. AE, MC, V. Tues–Sat 7–9:30pm; Sat 12:15-1:30pm. Closed 2 weeks April. From St. Andrews, go along A91 for 11km (7 miles) to the southwest until you reach the village of Cupar.

ST. ANDREWS AFTER DARK

The cultural center of St. Andrews is the **Byre Theatre,** Abbey Street (ℂ **01334/ 476-288**), which features drama ranging from Shakespeare plays to musical comedies. Tickets cost £6 to £14 ($9.60–$22) adults, £5 to £9 ($8–$14) children. Pick up a weekly version of *What's on in Fife* from the local tourist office to find out what's featured.

Victoria, 1A St. Mary's Place (ℂ **01334/476-964**), is the place to catch a live band in St. Andrews. This student-filled pub features folk, rock, and blues acts occasionally, as well as karaoke every Friday. Because of the absence of students over the summer, there's no live music. John Smiths, Beamish Stout, McEwans Lager, 78 Shilling, and 80 Shilling are available on tap. Open Tuesday to Saturday from 10 to 1am; Sunday 11am to midnight; and Monday 10am to midnight.

A pub since 1904, the **Central Bar,** at the corner of Market and College Street (ℂ **01334/478-296**), is an antiquated room with a jukebox, and it may become rowdy during a football or tennis match. The best brews here are Old Peculiar, Theakstons XB, and McEwans Lager. Open Monday to Saturday from 11:30 to 1am.

Chariots, The Scores (ℂ **01334/472-451**), in the Scores Hotel, attracts mainly a local crowd, ranging from 30 to 60 years, who gather in the evening for conversation over a pint. Despite a strong regional tradition of beer brewing, two outsiders, Guinness and Millers, are featured on tap. Open daily from 5pm to midnight.

4 Stirling ⋆⋆

56km (37 miles) NW of Edinburgh, 45km (28 miles) NE of Glasgow

Stirling is dominated by its impressive castle, perched on a 76m (250-ft.) basalt rock formed by the Rivers Forth and Clyde and the relatively small parcel of land between them. The ancient town of Stirling, on the main east–west route across Scotland, grew up around the castle. It lies in the heart of an area so turbulent in Scottish history it was called the "cockpit of Scotland." (Here "cockpit" refers to the pit where male chickens would be forced to engage in cockfights.) One memorable battle fought here was the Battle of Bannockburn in 1314, when Robert I (the Bruce) defeated the army of Edward II of England and gained Scotland its independence. Another was the Battle of Stirling Bridge in 1297 (see "The True Story of *Braveheart,*" below).

Ever since the release of Mel Gibson's *Braveheart,* world attention has focused on the Scottish national hero William Wallace, a freedom fighter who became known as the "hammer and scourge" of the English. However, *Braveheart* was filmed mostly in Ireland, and the Battle of Stirling Bridge in the movie was played out on a plain with not a bridge in sight.

Stirling is the central crossroads of Scotland, giving easy access by rail and road to all its major towns and cities. If you use it as a base, you'll be only a short distance from many attractions, including Loch Lomond, the Trossachs, and the Highlands.

ESSENTIALS

GETTING THERE Frequent trains run between Glasgow and Stirling (a 45-min. trip) and between Edinburgh and Stirling (a 60-min. trip). A 1-day round-trip ticket from Edinburgh is £9 ($14) and from Glasgow is £8 ($13). For schedules, call **National Express Enquiries** at © **0345/484-950.**

Frequent buses run to Stirling from Glasgow (a 40-minute trip). A 1-day round-trip ticket from Glasgow costs £5.30 ($8.50). Check with **Scottish CityLink** (© **8705/505-050**) for details.

If you're driving from Glasgow, head northeast along A80 to M80, at which point continue north. From Edinburgh, head northwest along M9.

VISITOR INFORMATION The **tourist office** is at 41 Dumbarton Rd. (© **01786/475-019;** www.visitscotland.com). April to May, it's open Monday to Saturday from 9am to 5pm; June to August, hours are Monday to Saturday from 9am to 7:30pm and Sunday from 9:30am to 6:30pm; September hours are Monday to Saturday from 9am to 6pm and Sunday from 10am to 5pm; October hours are Monday to Saturday from 9:30am to 5pm; and November to March, it's open Monday to Friday from 10am to 5pm and Saturday from 10am to 4pm.

SEEING THE SIGHTS

To get a real feel for Stirling, stroll the **Back Walk,** beginning near Rob Roy's statue, near the Guildhall in the town center. Following this trail along the outside of the town's once-fortified walls, you'll find good views, see an old watchtower (and a place where prisoners were hanged), and eventually reach Stirling Castle.

Church of the Holy Rude ⭐
From the early 15th century, the Church of the Holy Rude is said to be the only church in the country still in use that has witnessed a coronation. It was 1567 when the 13-month-old James VI—Mary Queen of Scots' son who was to become James I of England—was crowned here. John Knox preached the sermon. Constructed with the simplest of building tools more than 600 years ago and built as a reminder of the cross (rude) on which Christ was supposedly crucified, the church is memorable for its rough but evocative stonework and its elaborate 19th-century stained glass—particularly on the south side of the choir. Recent restorations have been done in the most tasteful and unobtrusive of styles.

St. John St. © **01786/475-275.** Free admission. Mid-Apr to Sept daily 10am–5pm. Closed Oct to mid-Apr.

Stirling Castle ⭐⭐
There are traces of a 7th-century royal habitation of the Stirling area, and on the right bank of the Forth, Stirling Castle dates from the Middle Ages, when its location on a dividing line between the Lowlands and the Highlands made it the key to the Highlands. The castle became an important seat of two kings, James IV and James V, both of whom added to it, the latter following classic Renaissance style, then relatively unknown in Britain. Mary Queen of Scots lived here as an infant monarch for the first 4 years of her life. After its final defeat in 1746, Bonnie Prince Charlie's army stopped here. Later, the castle became an army barracks and headquarters of the Argyll and Sutherland Highlanders, one of Britain's most celebrated regiments. An audiovisual presentation explains what you're about to see.

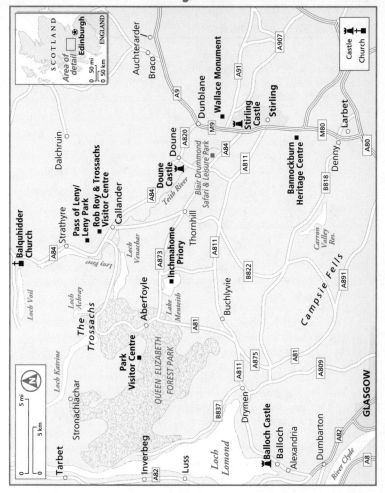

In the castle is the **Museum of the Argyll and Sutherland Highlanders** (© **01786/475-165**), presenting an excellent exhibit of colors, pipe banners, and regimental silver, along with medals (some of which go back to the Battle of Waterloo) won by Scottish soldiers for valor. Run by Britain's Ministry of Defense, it functions as a showcase for a military unit.

Upper Castle Hill. © **01786/450-000**. Admission to castle £7.50 ($12) adults, £5.50 ($8.80) seniors, £2 ($3.20) children age 6–15 years, free for children age 5 and under; free admission to museum. Castle Apr–Sept daily 9:30am–6pm; Oct–Mar daily 9:30am–5pm; last entry to castle 45 min. before closing time. Museum Mar–Sept Mon–Sat 10am–5:45pm, Sun 11am–4:45pm; Oct–Feb daily 10am–4:15pm.

EXPLORING NEARBY BANNOCKBURN

You can take an interesting detour to Bannockburn, a name that looms large in Scottish history. It was there that Robert the Bruce, his army of 6,000 outnumbered three to one, defeated the forces of Edward II in 1314. Before nightfall on that day, Robert the Bruce had won back the throne of Scotland. The battlefield,

The True Story of *Braveheart*

Sir Robert the Bruce at Bannockburn
Beat the English in every wheel and turn,
And made them fly in great dismay
From off the field without delay . . .
                                        —William McGonagall, "The Battle of Bannockburn"

Robert the Bruce (1274–1329) was the first of three kings of Scotland named Robert. Although neither Mel Gibson nor Liam Neeson selected this daring man as the subject for a movie, they might well have done so, for Robert the Bruce led a life filled with all the excitement and thrills of a 1930s Errol Flynn adventure flick.

In 1292, Edward I of England gave the Scottish crown to John de Balliol, known as the "vassal king," demanding that Scotland pay homage to the English throne. But instead, the Scots formed what was to become known as the Auld Alliance with France in October 1295. Edward viewed this as a declaration of war, and the "Hammer of Scotland" stormed into Scotland, devastating the countryside and capturing and taking home the Stone of Destiny from Scone (the coronation stone of Scottish kings).

William Wallace (1274–1305) defeated the English at the 1297 Battle of Stirling Bridge and was made "Guardian of the Realm." Edward, in turn, defeated Wallace at the Battle of Falkirk the following year. Outlawed for his activities, Wallace hid for 7 years until his capture, at which time he was paraded through the streets of London and hanged and drawn and quartered, with his entrails burned before his eyes as he died. This horrific English method of execution reputedly was devised by Edward especially for Wallace.

Robert the Bruce replaced Wallace as "Guardian of Scotland." In March 1306, Bruce had himself crowned king of Scotland. Edward rushed north and defeated Bruce's forces at Methven and Dalry. Like Wallace, Bruce became an outlaw, forced into hiding, probably on the island of Rathlin off the Irish coast. There he was said to have learned patience, courage, and hope by watching a spider persevere in spinning a web, swinging from one rafter to another on a fragile thread.

In 1307, he returned to Scotland, where he captured Perth in 1313 and Edinburgh in 1314. At Bannockburn, also in 1314, he defeated the forces of Edward's son, Edward II. The pope excommunicated Bruce, and his sovereignty was not recognized by the royal houses of Europe.

Upon Edward III's coronation in 1327, the Scots launched a raid into England. The following year, Edward was almost captured when he led a retaliatory army into Scotland. But in 1328 a peace treaty was signed, acknowledging Scotland's independence. David, Bruce's 4-year-old son, was "married" to Joan, Edward III's 7-year-old sister. The Bruce ruled Scotland wisely until his death at Cardross Castle on the Clyde.

which makes for a peaceful walk today, lies off M80, 3km (2 miles) south of Stirling.

At the **Bannockburn Heritage Centre,** Glasgow Road (© **01786/812-664**), an audiovisual presentation tells the story of these events, while *The Kingdom of the Scots* exhibit traces the history of Scotland from William Wallace to the Union of Crowns. The site is open all year, while the Heritage Centre and shop are open April through October, daily from 10am to 5:30pm, and in March, November, and December, daily from 10:30am to 4pm. The last audiovisual showing is at 5:30pm. Admission is £3.50 ($5.60) for adults, £2.60 ($4.15) for seniors and children, and £9.50 ($15) per family.

From the **Borestone,** where Robert the Bruce commanded his forces at the start of his battle for Stirling, you can see Stirling Castle and the Forth Valley. He planted his standards (flags) as inspiration for his troops, and today a flagpole capped with the standards of Scotland still flies proudly from atop this low hill. It's located off M80/M9 at Junction 9.

SHOPPING

Stirling's town center has some interesting shopping. One good hunting ground is the **Thistle Centre** indoor shopping plaza, home of about 65 shops at the junction of Port Street and Murray Place.

The book dealer **McCutcheon's,** 51 Baker St. (© **01786/461-771**), specializes in antiquarian volumes and carries a startlingly vast range of books.

The best woolen goods are at **R. R. Henderson,** 6–8 Friar St. (© **01786/ 473-681**), a Highland outfitter selling not only sweaters and scarves but also made-to-order kilts and tartans.

Some of the best shopping is not in Stirling itself but in the outlying area. Take A9 to Larbert and at the roundabout follow A18 west until you see the sign for **Barbara Davidson's Pottery Studio,** Muirhall Farm, Larbert (© **01324/ 554-430**), 14km (9 miles) south of Stirling. At this 18th-century farmstead, one of Scotland's best-known potters operates her studio and workshop. A large selection of functional wares is exhibited and sold here.

East of Stirling, three towns form the **Mill Trail Country:** Alva, Alloa, and Tillicoultry. Many quality textile mills have factory outlets here, offering bargain prices on cotton, woolens, and even cashmere goods. The best selection of sweaters is available at **Inverallen Handknitters Ltd.,** Alva Industrial Estate, Alva (© **01259/762-292**). The hand-knitted traditional sweaters here are particularly appealing. A good selection of clothing for children and infants supplements the selections for men and women at **Glen Alva Ltd.,** Hallpark, Whine Road, Alloa (© **01259/723-024**). If you're inspired to knit your own creation, head to **Patons & Baldwins,** Kilcraigo Mill, Alloa (© **01325/394- 394**), which manufactures quality yarns.

For more complete details, including any directional information, seasonal closings, or whatever, call or visit the **Mill Trail Visitor Centre,** West Stirling Street at Alva (© **01259/769-696**), 14km (9 miles) east of the center of Stirling. January to June and September to December, it's open daily 10am to 5pm; July to August, it's open daily 9am to 5pm.

WHERE TO STAY
EXPENSIVE
The Stirling Highland Hotel ★★   One of Stirling's finer hotels occupies a former high school dating from the early Victorian era. In the center, it lies

within an easy stroll of the castle. The historic atmosphere was treated with respect, and many of the architectural features were kept. Florals, tartans, and solid wood furnishings dominate the public rooms and the guest rooms; the guest rooms, fairly routine, are in a three-story annex. Each unit comes with a shower, and a few are also equipped with tubs. From its position close to Stirling Castle, the hotel enjoys views over the town and surrounding region.

Rather high-priced Scottish cuisine is featured in Scholars Restaurant, and Rizzio's Restaurant serves Italian cuisine.

Spittal St., Stirling, Stirlingshire FK8 1DU. © **01786/272-727.** Fax 01786/272-829. www.paramount-hotels. co.uk. 96 units. £150–£160 ($240–$256) double. AE, DC, MC, V. Free parking. **Amenities:** Restaurant; indoor pool; health club; Jacuzzi; secretarial services; salon; 24-hour room service; babysitting; laundry/dry cleaning service; squash courts; steam room. *In room:* TV, coffeemaker, hair dryer, trouser press.

MODERATE

Golden Lion Flagship Hotel About a block downhill from Holyrood Church, the Golden Lion dates from 1786, when it was a coaching inn; but, its sandstone shell was greatly enlarged with the addition of modern wings in 1962. It's now one of the oldest and largest hotels in town and has recently improved and modernized most of its guest rooms. The rooms are simple and easy on the eye, and bathrooms are equipped with either tub or shower.

8–10 King St., Stirling, Stirlingshire FK8 2ND. © **01786/475-351.** Fax 01786/472-755. 67 units. £80–£110 ($128–$176) double. Rates include Scottish breakfast. AE, DC, MC, V. **Amenities:** Restaurant; bar; limited room service; laundry/dry cleaning service. *In room:* TV, coffeemaker, hair dryer, trouser press (in some).

The Park Lodge Hotel ⭐ This stylish hotel occupies a 19th-century Italianate mansion, across from a city park in a residential neighborhood. Built of stone blocks and slate, it has a Doric portico, Tudor-style chimney pots, a Georgian-era core from 1825, and century-old climbing roses and wisteria. Anne and Georges Marquetty house guests in 10 upstairs rooms and suggest that they dine at their elegant restaurant, The Heritage (see below), a 10-minute walk away. Each room contains antique furnishings (no. 6 has a four-poster bed) as well as tub and shower combination. You might enjoy tea in the walled garden, with its widely spaced iron benches and terra-cotta statues.

32 Park Terrace, Stirling, Stirlingshire FK8 2JS. © **01786/474-862.** Fax 01786/449-748. www.parklodge.net. 9 units. £85–£105 ($136–$168) double. Rates include Scottish breakfast. AE, MC, V. **Amenities:** Restaurant; bar. *In room:* TV, coffeemaker, hair dryer, trouser press (in some).

Terraces Hotel *(Value)* Built originally as a fine Georgian house of sandstone, this hotel stands on a raised terrace in a quiet residential neighborhood and is now one of the best values in town. Each midsize guest room is furnished in a country-house motif of flowered curtains and solidly traditional furniture, with a shower bathroom (some with tubs) (some bathrooms contain showers only). One room has a lovely carved four-poster bed. The half-paneled cocktail bar and velvet-upholstered restaurant are popular settings for local parties and wedding receptions. Melville's Restaurant offers a moderately priced Scottish and Continental menu.

4 Melville Terrace, Stirling, Stirlingshire FK8 2ND. © **01786/472-268.** Fax 01786/450-314. www.s-h-systems. co.uk/hotels/terraces.html. 17 units. £90 ($144) double. Rates include Scottish breakfast. AE, DC, MC, V. Free parking. **Amenities:** Restaurant; bar; limited room service; business facilities; laundry service. *In room:* TV, coffeemaker, hair dryer, trouser press (in some).

INEXPENSIVE

Allan's Guest House *(Kids)* Private and personal, this rambling 1840s stone house is the domain of Mrs. Allan, who rents two of her five bedrooms to guests.

The cozy rooms are painted and decorated in shades of pale pink. Mrs. Allan welcomes families with small children.

15 Albert Place (a 10-minute walk north of the town center), Stirling FK8 2RE. © **01786/475-175.** 2 units, none with private bathroom. £45 ($72) double. Rates include breakfast. No credit cards. Closed Nov–Feb. *In room:* Coffeemaker, no phone.

West Plean House ☆ *Value*   This working farm is a delight. It not only has a lovely walled garden but also is a great base for taking walks into the surrounding woodland. Your hosts are welcoming and helpful, and they offer extremely good value. Their guest rooms are spacious and well furnished, with an eye to comfort and conveniences, and each is equipped with a shower-only bathroom. Their home-cooked breakfast makes this place a winner.

Denny Rd. (6km / 3½ miles from Stirling on A872), Stirling FK7 8HA. © **01786/812-208.** Fax 01786/480-550. http://freespace.virgin.net/west.plean. 3 units. £50–£55 ($80–$88) double. Rates include breakfast. No credit cards. Closed 2 weeks in late Dec. *In room:* TV, coffeemaker, no phone.

WHERE TO DINE

The Heritage ☆ FRENCH/SCOTTISH   Culinary sophistication and beautiful decor rank this as one of the best restaurants in the district. It's in the stylish Park Lodge Hotel (see above), on a quiet residential street near the center of town, a 5-minute walk east of the rail station. You can enjoy a drink in the gentleman's parlor, with somber walls and enviable antiques, before descending to the low-ceilinged basement. Amid a French-inspired decor, you'll taste some of the best cuisine in Stirling, prepared with finesse by Georges Marquetty. In his youth, he worked as an executive chef in Paris and later spent 12 years in Cincinnati (where he was voted one of the leading chefs of America). His specialties include scallops, scampi, and prawns in Pernod sauce; filet of wild venison with port and black-currant sauce; scallops with smoked ham in lemon sauce; and foie gras with truffles.

At The Park Lodge Hotel. 32 Park Terrace, Stirling, Stirlingshire FK8 2QC. © **01786/473-660.** Fax 01786/449-748. Reservations recommended. Main courses £10–£16 ($16–$26); fixed-price 2-course lunch £10 ($16); fixed-price 3-course dinner £22.50 ($36). MC, V. Daily noon–2pm and 6:30–9:30pm. Closed Sun in winter.

Hermann's Brasserie AUSTRIAN/SCOTTISH   This reliable favorite is housed in an old and traditional town house with high beamed ceilings and features pine tables and chairs and tartan carpeting. Part of the restaurant opens onto a conservatory. You get not only tried-and-true platters of Scottish food here, but a touch of Vienna as well, especially in the golden-brown Wiener Schnitzel, served with a salad and sautéed potatoes. Scottish Highland venison is a regular feature; the plate here is attractively adorned with a whisky cream sauce. You might start your meal with the most typical of Scottish soups: *Cullen skink,* made with smoked fish and potatoes. Our forever favorite is the fast seared filet of salmon served with a savory sauce laced with pink peppercorns.

58 Broad St. © **01786/450-632.** Reservations recommended. Main courses £12–£17 ($19–$27). AE, MC, V. Daily noon–2:30pm and 6–9:30pm.

STIRLING AFTER DARK

On the campus of Stirling University, the **Macrobert Arts Centre** (© **01786/466-666**) features plays, music, films, and art exhibits. The 497-seat main theater often presents dramas and symphony concerts, and the 140-seat studio theater is used mainly for films. Cinema tickets cost £4 ($6.40) adults and £3 ($4.80) seniors/children, and theater tickets generally run £7 to £10 ($11–$16). Admission to most concerts is £10 to £13 ($16–$21). Call for current listings.

All that Jazz, 9 Upper Craigs (© **01786/451-130**), is a lively bar popular with students. Music is usually provided via the stereo, but bands also appear infrequently. The bar serves a good range of single malts and pints of Kronenberg, Beamish Red, and McEwans. The adjoining restaurant serves a mix of Cajun and traditional Scottish fare, including haggis, between 5 and 10pm every evening. The same menu is available throughout the day in the bar, which is open from 11am to midnight; Friday and Saturday 11am to 1am.

O'Neill's, 11 Maxwell Place (© **01786/459-901**), is a traditional Irish pub popular with Scottish students, who come to hear the Irish and Scottish folk bands play. To find out who's playing, check the flyers posted in the pub. There's never a cover. Open Sunday to Thursday noon to midnight and Friday and Saturday 11am to 1am.

5 Dunblane & Its Grand Cathedral

11km (7 miles) N of Stirling, 68km (42 miles) NW of Edinburgh, 47km (29 miles) SW of Perth, 53km (33 miles) NE of Glasgow

A small cathedral city on the banks of the Allan Water, Dunblane takes its name from the Celtic church of St. Blane, which once stood on the site now occupied by the fine 13th-century Gothic cathedral. The cathedral is the main reason to visit; if that doesn't interest you, you'll find more romantic and lovelier places from which to explore the nearby Trossachs and Loch Lomond (say, Callander or Aberfoyle).

ESSENTIALS

GETTING THERE Trains run between Glasgow and Dunblane with a stopover at Stirling, a one-way fare costing £5.40 to £6.70 ($8.65–$11). Rail connections are also possible through Edinburgh via Stirling for £5.60 to £7.30 ($8.95–$12) one-way. For 24-hour information, call © **08457/484-950.**

Buses travel from the Goosecroft Bus Station in Stirling to Dunblane, costing £1.80 ($2.90) each way. Call © **01786/446-474** in Stirling for schedules, or contact **First Edinburgh Busline** at © **01324/613-777.**

If you're driving from Stirling, continue north along M9 to Dunblane.

VISITOR INFORMATION A year-round **tourist office** is on Stirling Road (© **01786/824-428**). April 1 to June 1, it's open Monday to Saturday 9am to 5pm; June 2 to June 29 Monday to Saturday from 9am to 6pm, Sundays 10am to 4pm; June 30 to August 31 Monday to Saturday 9am to 7:30pm, Sundays 9:30am to 6:30pm; September 1 to September 7 Monday to Saturday 9am to 7pm and Sundays 10am to 5pm; September 8 to September 21 Monday to Saturday 9am to 6pm, Sunday 10am to 4pm; September 22 to October 19 Monday to Saturday 9:30am to 5pm; October 20 to March 31 Monday to Friday 10am to 5pm, Saturday 10am to 4pm.

SEEING THE SIGHTS

After you visit the cathedral, you can wander and discover the streets around it. They're narrow and twisting and flanked by mellow old town houses, many from the 18th century.

Cathedral Museum In the 1624 Dean's House, the Cathedral Museum contains articles and papers displaying the story of Dunblane and its ancient cathedral; you can also visit an enclosed garden with a very old (restored) well. A 1687 structure on the grounds contains the library of Bishop Robert Leighton, an outstanding 17th-century churchman; if you're a serious scholar, you'll find a great deal of material on the effects of the troubled times in Scotland, most from before the Industrial Revolution. It's open the same hours as the Cathedral Museum.

On Cathedral Square in the Dean's House. © **01786/823-440.** Free admission. May–Sept Mon–Sat 10:30am–4:30pm.

Dunblane Cathedral ⭐⭐ An excellent example of 13th-century Gothic ecclesiastic architecture, this cathedral was spared the ravages of attackers who destroyed other Scottish worship centers. Altered in the 15th century and restored several times in the 19th and 20th centuries, it may have suffered most from neglect subsequent to the Reformation. A Jesse Tree window is in the west end of the building; and of interest are the stalls, the misericords, the pulpit with carved figures of early ecclesiastical figures, and the wooden barrel-vaulted roof with colorful armorials. A Celtic stone from about A.D. 900 is in the north aisle.

Cathedral Close. © **01786/823-388.** www.dunblanecathedral.org.uk. Free admission. Apr–Sept Mon–Sat 9:30am–6pm, Sun 1:30–6pm; Oct–Mar Mon–Sat 9:30am–4pm, Sun 2–4pm.

WHERE TO STAY

Cromlix House ⭐⭐⭐ This manor house, built in 1880 as the seat of a fam- ily that has owned the surrounding 1,215 hectares (3,000 acres) for the past 500 years, is now the area's most elegant hotel. The owners still live on the estate and derive part of their income from organizing hunting and fishing expeditions in the surrounding moors and forests and on the River Allan. Fishing in three pri- vate lakes and hunting is available, as is tennis, and you can walk through the surrounding forests and farmland. It's also a popular spot for weddings.

The manor has an elegant drawing room with big bow windows, and antiques are scattered about both the public and guest rooms. Bouquets of fresh flowers and open fires in cool weather add to the overall charm and comfort of the place. The individually decorated guest rooms (including eight suites with sitting rooms) are carpeted, and most have Queen Anne furnishings.

Kinbuck, Dunblane FK15 9JT. © **01786/822-125.** Fax 01786/825-450. www.cromlixhouse.com. 14 units. £225–£260 ($360–$416) double; £285–£320 ($456–$512) suite. AE, DC, MC, V. Closed Jan. Take A9 to B8033; the hotel is 5km (3¼ miles) north of Dunblane just beyond the village of Kinbuck. **Amenities:** Restaurant; bar; laundry; limited room service. *In room:* TV, coffeemaker, hair dryer, trouser press (in some).

Kippenross ⭐ *Finds* This country manor boasts a richer and more unusual history than many of the region's B&Bs. It was built in 1750 according to the Palladian-neoclassical lines of William Adam, father of Britain's most celebrated neoclassical architect, Robert Adam. Surrounded by 81 hectares (200 acres) of parks, lawns, and gardens and artfully landscaped with exotic plantings, it's a perfect example of Scottish country-house living, supervised by the Stirling-Aird family. Two of the guest rooms overlook the sprawling front lawns; the other overlooks the forests at the back. Each unit comes with a tub or shower. Guests are welcomed into the family's drawing room and to formal breakfasts in the dining room. If any guest wants to stay for dinner and reserves in advance, Susan Stirling-Aird prepares elegant dinners. The Stirling-Airds invite guests to bring their own liquor or wine, because the place doesn't have a liquor license; smok- ing is forbidden on the premises. *Note:* Susan's husband, Patrick, is a devoted ornithologist and bird-watcher.

Dunblane FK15 0LQ. © **01786/824-048.** Fax 01786/823-124. www.aboutscotland.com/stirling/kippenross. html. 3 units. £76 ($122) double. MC, V. From Stirling, drive 8km (5 miles) north, taking A9 toward Perth, then exiting onto B8033 and following the signs to Dunblane. *In room:* Hair dryer (at front desk), no phone.

6 Callander & a Trio of Lochs ⟨★⟩

26km (16 miles) NW of Stirling, 69km (43 miles) N of Glasgow, 84km (52 miles) NW of Edinburgh, 68km (42 miles) W of Perth

In Gaelic, the Trossachs means the "bristled country," an allusion to its luxuriant vegetation. The thickly wooded valley contains three lochs: Venachar, Achray, and Katrine. In summer, the steamer on Loch Katrine offers a fine view of the splendid wooded scenery.

For many, the small town of Callander makes the best base for exploring the Trossachs and Loch Katrine, Loch Achray, and Loch Venachar. (The town of Aberfoyle, discussed later in this chapter, is another excellent choice.) For years, motorists—and before them, passengers traveling by bumpy coach—stopped here to rest up on the once-difficult journey between Edinburgh and Oban.

Callander stands at the entrance to the Pass of Leny in the shadow of the Callander Crags. The Rivers Teith and Leny meet to the west of the town.

ESSENTIALS

GETTING THERE   Stirling (see "Stirling," earlier in this chapter) is the nearest rail link. Once at Stirling, continue the rest of the way to Callander on a First Edinburgh Bus from the Stirling station on Goosecroft Road. Contact the bus station at ⟨ℂ⟩ **01786/446-474** or **First Edinburgh Buses** at ⟨ℂ⟩ **01324/613-777.** A one-way fare is £2.90 ($4.65).

Driving from Stirling, head north along M9, cutting northwest at the junction of A84 to Callander, bypassing Doune.

VISITOR INFORMATION   The **Rob Roy & Trossachs Visitor Centre** is at Ancaster Square (⟨ℂ⟩ **01877/330-342**). It distributes a map pinpointing all the sights. April 1 to May 31, it's open daily 10am to 5pm; June 1 to June 30 daily from 9:30 am to 6pm; July 1 to August 31 daily 9am to 6pm; September 1 to September 30 daily 10am to 6pm; October 1 to December 31 daily 10am to 5pm; January 1 to March 31 daily 11am to 3pm. The second floor is home to a permanent **Rob Roy exhibit,** complete with a video presentation about his life and times. Entrance is £3.25 ($5.20) adults, £2.25 ($3.60) seniors and students, £2 ($3.20) children.

EXPLORING THE AREA

In the scenic Leny Hills to the west of Callander beyond the Pass of Leny lie **Leny Park** and **Leny Falls.** At one time all the lands in Leny Park were part of the Leny estate, home of the Buchanan clan for more than 1,000 years. In the wild Leny Glen, a naturalist's paradise, you can see deer grazing. Leny Falls is an impressive sight, near the confluence of the River Leny and the River Teith. In this area you'll see the remains of an abandoned railway; it's a wonderful footpath or cycling path for exploring this scenic area. Rent a bike at **Wheels/ Trossachs Backpackers,** on Invertrossachs Road in Callander (⟨ℂ⟩ **01877/331-100;** www.scotland-info.co.uk; open daily 10am to 6pm), which charges £12.50 ($20) for a full day, £7.50 to £10 ($12–$16) for a half day, and from £35 ($56) for a week. It also provides bikers with sleeping rooms for £12.50 ($20) per night, including continental breakfast, conducts organized walks, and can arrange canoe trips. You must make reservations in advance.

About 6.5km (4 miles) beyond the Pass of Leny lies **Loch Lubnaig** (crooked lake), divided into two reaches by a rock and considered fine fishing waters. Nearby is **Little Leny,** the ancestral burial ground of the Buchanans.

You'll find more falls at **Bracklinn,** 2.5km (1½ miles) northeast of Callander. In a gorge above the town, Bracklinn is one of the most scenic of the local beauty spots.

One of the most interesting sites around Callander is **Balquhidder Church** ⚜, 21km (13 miles) northwest off A84. This is the burial place of Rob Roy Mac-Gregor. The church also has the St. Angus Stone from the 8th century, a 17th-century bell, and some Gaelic Bibles.

A good selection of woolens is at **Callander Woollen Mill,** 12–18 Main St. (© **01877/330-273**)—everything from scarves, skirts, and jackets to kilts, trousers, and knitwear. Another outlet for woolen goods, tartans, and woven rugs is the **Trossachs Woollen Mill** (© **01877/330-178**), 1.6km (1 mile) north of Callander on A84 in the hamlet of Kilmahog.

The town has an excellent golf course, the wooded and scenic **Callander Golf Course,** Aveland Road (© **01877/330-090**). At this 5,125-yard (4,664m) par-66 course, greens fees are £9 to £18 ($14–$29) per round or £26 ($42) per day on weekdays, £13 to £26 ($21–$42) per round or £31 ($50) per day on Saturdays and Sundays. The trolley charge is included in club rental, which runs £10 to £15 ($16–$24) for 18 holes. No caddy service is available. The hilly fairways offer fine views, and the tricky moorland layout demands accurate tee shots.

WHERE TO STAY

Rooms are also available at **Dalgair House Hotel** (see "Where to Dine," below).

Arden House ⚜   This stone-sided Victorian B&B is instantly recognizable to several generations of British TV viewers because of its 1970s role as the setting for a BBC series, *Dr. Finlay's Casebook.* (Its plot involved two bachelor doctors and their interactions with their attractive housekeeper and the fictional town of Tannochbrae, which was modeled after Callander.) Built in 1870 as a vacation home for Lady Willoughby and still maintained by two attractive bachelors, William Jackson and Ian Mitchell, it offers a soothing rest amid gardens at the base of a rocky outcropping known as the Callander Crags. The well-known Bracklinn Falls are within a 5-minute walk. The public areas boast Victorian antiques, while the high-ceilinged guest rooms are tasteful and comfortable (the most appealing is the plush Tannochbrae Suite). Each guest room comes with a shower; only the suite has a tub bath. Children under 14 are not accepted as guests and smoking is forbidden on premises.

Bracklinn Rd., Callander FK17 8EQ. © **01877/330-235.** Fax 01877/330-235. www.ardenhouse.org.uk. 5 units. £55–£60 ($88–$96) double; £65–£70 ($104–$112) suite. Rates include breakfast. MC, V. From Callander, walk for 5 minutes north, following the signs to Bracklinn Falls. No children under age 14. *In room:* TV, coffeemaker. No phone.

Highland House Hotel   Owned and managed by Robert and Lorna Leckie, who took over in 1998, this Georgian stone building stands on a quiet, tree-lined street a few yards from the Teith and a short walk from the visitor center. All of the guest rooms are charming come with shower-equipped bathrooms (a few with tub). Scottish-style meals are served nightly 6 to 9pm in the dining room or in simpler versions at the bar. Game casserole, with choice pieces of game in a rich red wine and port gravy, is a house specialty. The lounge offers 20 to 25 brands of malt whiskies, some relatively obscure.

S. Church St. (just off A84, near Ancaster Square), Callander FK17 8BN. © **01877/330-269.** Fax 01877/339-004. www.smoothhound.co.uk/hotels/highl.html. 9 units. £42–£52 ($67–$83) double. Rates include Scottish breakfast. MC, V. Free parking. Pets welcome by arrangement. **Amenities:** Bar; limited room service. *In room:* TV, coffeemaker, trouser press.

Finds **A Side Trip to Loch Voil**

This was an area known to Rob Roy MacGregor, who died in 1734 but lives on in legend as the Robin Hood of Scotland and in the Liam Neeson film. If you visit Rob Roy's grave at Balquhidder, you may find this remote part of Scotland so enchanting you'll want to continue to drive west and explore the **Braes o' Balquhidder** and the banks of **Loch Voil,** where you can enjoy some of the loveliest countryside walks in the Trossachs. You can go through the churchyard where the Scottish hero is buried up to Kirkton Glen, continuing along through grasslands to a little lake. This signposted footpath leads to the next valley, called Glen Dochart, before it links up once again with A84, on which Callander lies.

Roman Camp Country House Hotel ★★★   This is the leading hotel in town. Once a 17th-century hunting lodge with pink walls and small gray-roofed towers, it was built on the site of a Roman camp. Today you drive up a 182m (200-yd.) driveway, with shaggy Highland cattle and sheep grazing on either side. Inside, owners Eric & Marion Brown welcome you into a gracious country house. The dining room was converted in the 1930s from the old kitchen. The ceiling design is based on Scottish painted ceilings of the 16th and 17th centuries. The library, with its ornate plasterwork and richly grained paneling, is an elegant holdover from yesteryear.

Seven of the comfortable guest rooms are on the ground floor, and one is adapted for travelers with limited mobility; all have shower-equipped bathrooms (two with tub). Some rooms are furnished with bedhead crowns, gilt-framed mirrors, and stenciled furnishings; a few have four-posters, and others are contemporary with blond-wood pieces. Suites have separate sitting areas.

Main St., Callander FK17 8BG. ℂ **01877/330-003.** Fax 01877/331-533. www.roman-camp-hotel.co.uk. 14 units. £110–£165 ($176–$264) double; from £180 ($288) suite. Rates include Scottish breakfast. AE, DC, MC, V. As you approach Callander on A84, the entrance to the hotel is signposted between 2 pink cottages on Callander's Main St. **Amenities:** Restaurant; bar; limited room service. *In room:* TV, coffeemaker, hair dryer, trouser press.

WHERE TO DINE

Dalgair House Hotel SCOTTISH   This place is best known for its food and wine cellar. The bar, lined in gray bricks, boasts rustic accessories and flickering candles. Australian, German, and Austrian wines, sold by the glass, give the place the aura of a wine bar. The menu choices include halibut and Dover or lemon sole, steaks, and game casseroles. More formal meals are served after dark in the restaurant, where menu items might include sliced pork on cucumber noodles with oregano and ginger sauce, chicken filet in champagne-butter sauce, and preparations of salmon and Angus steaks.

The hotel's eight rooms contain hair dryers, TVs, and tub and shower combos. Rooms rent for £55 to £75 ($88–$120) double, Scottish breakfast included.

113–115 Main St., Callander FK17 8BQ. ℂ **01877/330-283.** Fax 01877/331-114. www.dalgair-house-hotel. co.uk Reservations recommended in restaurant, not necessary in bar. Main courses £8–£14 ($13–$22) in restaurant, £3.50–£6 ($5.60–$9.60) in bar. AE, DC, MC, V. Restaurant daily noon–8:30pm; bar food service daily 11am–8:30pm.

Lade Inn INTERNATIONAL/SCOTTISH   Surrounded by fields and within earshot of the Leny River, the Lade was built as a teahouse, then converted after

World War II to a pub and restaurant. The local favorite attracts residents from the surrounding farmlands as well as visitors from afar to enjoy the Highland scenery (which includes Ben Ledi, one of the region's most prominent peaks) and sample the wide range of cask-conditioned ales and cider. If you're hungry, new owners Alan and Frank Roebuck prepare meals of such Scottish standards as rack of lamb, pigeon, venison, steaks, salmon, and trout.

Trossachs Rd. at Kilmahog, Callander FK17 8HD. © 01877/330-152. Main courses £9.65–£17.75 ($15–$28). MC, V. Mon–Sat noon–2:30pm and 5:30–9pm; Sun 12:30–9pm. Lies 1.6km (1 mile) north of Callander on A84.

CALLANDER AFTER DARK

The **Bridgend Hotel Pub,** Bridgend (© **01877/330-130**), is an old watering hole that has been done up in matching dusky red wood paneling and carpeting. Tennant brews are available on tap. On Friday and Saturday they have karaoke, and Sunday nights enjoy some live Scottish music. Open Monday to Wednesday 11:30am to 2:30pm and 5:30pm to midnight; Thursday and Sunday 11:30 am to midnight; and Friday and Saturday 11:30am to 12:45am.

Another old-fashioned bar that's a local favorite is the **Crown Hotel Pub,** 13 Main St. (© **01877/330-040**); it sometimes features live folk music. Otherwise it's a mellow old place for a pint of lager. Open Sunday to Thursday from 11am to 11pm and Friday and Saturday 11 to 1am.

7 Aberfoyle: Gateway to the Trossachs (★)

90km (56 miles) NW of Edinburgh, 44km (27 miles) N of Glasgow

Looking like an alpine village in the heart of Rob Roy country, the small resort of Aberfoyle, near Loch Ard, is the gateway to the Trossachs, one of the most beautiful and bucolic regions of Scotland. As one poet wrote: "So wondrous and wild, the whole might seem the scenery of a fair dream."

This was the land of Rob Roy (1671–1734), the outlaw and leader of the Mac-Gregors. Sir Walter Scott recounted the outlaw's exploits in *Rob Roy,* first published in 1818. Scott's romantic poem "The Lady of the Lake" greatly increased tourism to the area, eventually attracting Queen Victoria, who was enchanted by its beauty. Wordsworth and Coleridge were eventually lured here away from England's Lake District. Wordsworth was so inspired, he wrote "To a Highland Girl."

ESSENTIALS

GETTING THERE It's tough to get here by public transportation; you'll really need to drive. From Stirling, take A84 west until you reach the junction of A873 and continue west to Aberfoyle.

VISITOR INFORMATION The **Trossachs Discovery Centre** is on Main Street (© **01877/382-352**). It's open April through June, daily from 10am to 5pm; July and August, daily from 9:30am to 7pm; September and October, daily from 9:30am to 5pm; and November through March, Monday through Friday from 10am to 5pm and Saturday from 10am to 4pm.

EXPLORING THE AREA

About 6.5km (4 miles) east of Aberfoyle on A81, **Inchmahome Priory** stands on an island in Lake Menteith. From the Port of Menteith, you can take a ferry to the island if the weather's right. The fare is £3.50 ($5.60) for adults, £2.30 ($3.70) for seniors and students, and £1.30 ($2.10) for children. Once here, you'll find the ruins of a 13th-century Augustinian house where Mary Queen of Scots was sent as a baby in 1547. For information, call © **01877/385-294.**

A nature lover's delight, the **Queen Elizabeth Forest Park** 🐾 lies between the eastern shore of Loch Lomond and the Trossachs. Some 18,225 hectares (45,000 acres) of moor, woodland, and mountain have been set aside as a preserve for walking and exploring. From mid-March to mid-September, it's open daily from 10am to 6pm. Admission is free. From the lodge, you'll enjoy views of Ben Lomond, the Menteith Hills, and the Campsie Fells. For walking maps and information, stop at the **Queen Elizabeth Forest Park Visitor Centre** (© **01877/ 382-258**), in the David Marshall Lodge, off A821, 1.6km (1 mile) north of Aberfoyle.

Another great walk in the area is the **Highland Boundary Fault Walk,** which follows the Highland boundary fault edge. Here you can see the most panoramic views of the Highlands to the north and the Lowlands to the south. It begins 10km (6 miles) south of the Trossachs on A821. Detailed information is provided by the Forestry Commission in Aberfoyle (© **01877/382-383**).

North of Aberfoyle, **Dukes Pass** (A821) climbs through Achray Forest past the Queen Elizabeth Forest Park Visitor Centre (see above), where you can stop for snacks and a panoramic view of the Forth Valley. Information on numerous walks, cycling routes, the Achray scenic forest drive, picnic sites, parking areas, and many other activities is available at the center. The road runs to the Trossachs between Lochs Achray and Katrine.

Loch Katrine 🐾🐾, where Rob Roy MacGregor was born, owes its fame to Sir Walter Scott's poem "The Lady of the Lake." The loch is the principal reservoir of the city of Glasgow. A small steamer, the **SS** *Sir Walter Scott,* plies the waters of the loch, which has submerged the romantic poet's Silver Strand. Sailings are twice a day from Easter to late October, between Trossachs Pier and Stronachlachar, at a round-trip fare of about £6.80 ($11) for adults and £4.80 ($7.70) for children and seniors, or £14.70 ($24) per family. Prices vary depending on time of day. (Morning sailings are more expensive.) Complete information on sailing schedules is available from the **Trossachs' Discovery Center** (© **0141/355-5333**). Light refreshments are available at Trossachs Pier.

If you'd like to explore the countryside on two wheels, head for **Trossachs' Cycle Hire,** Trossachs Holiday Park, Aberfoyle (© **01877/382-614**). The rental rates are £12 ($19) per day and £35 ($56) per week. Open daily from 8:30am to 6pm.

Shoppers will want to check out the **Scottish Wool Centre,** Main Street (© **01877/382-850**), which sells a big selection of knitwear and woolens from surrounding mills, including jackets, hats, rugs, sweaters, and cashmere items. It also houses an amphitheater that holds a textile display area, along with live specimens of different breeds of Scottish sheep (but no clones yet). Spinning and weaving demonstrations are presented, and baby lambs fill a children's petting zoo. Admission to the shop is free, but the exhibition costs £4 ($6.40) for adults or £9 ($14) per family. The whole complex is open daily from 10am to 6pm, with exhibitions taking place at 11am, noon, 2pm, and 3pm.

WHERE TO STAY

Creag-Ard House 🐾 This stone-sided Victorian villa is one of the most stately houses in the region. It's steep rooflines and stone-ringed bay windows give it an appealingly quirky, even Gothic-looking allure. Built in 1885 on 1.2 hectares (3 acres) of forested parkland with spectacular stands of azaleas and rhododendrons (blooming in late May), it's a stone throw from the shores of Loch Ard, the inn's private lake. Guests are welcome to fish from the water's edge or may rent a row boat should they wish to drop a line farther from shore or just while away an afternoon admiring the surrounding mountains. The inn offers cozy, well-upholstered rooms with attractive furniture, lots of sun, and private bathrooms. Smoking is prohibited on the premises.

Milton, Aberfoyle FK8 3TQ. *C* and fax **01877/382-297**. www.creag-ard.co.uk. 6 units. £60–£80 ($96–$102) double. Rates include breakfast. Open Easter–Oct. MC, V. From Aberfoyle, drive 1.6km (1 mile) west, following B829 toward Kinlochard. Free parking. Dogs are welcome by prior arrangement. **Amenities:** Bar; boat rental. *In room:* Coffeemaker, no phone.

Inchre Castle The Covenanters Inn

Overlooking the waters of the River Forth, this pleasing inn was built in the 1800s as a private home with architecture inspired by Scottish castles. It was enlarged in the 1960s and 1980s and transformed into a hotel. Part of its name comes from the famous convention held here in 1949, when a group of Scots church and political leaders issued a then-famous Second Covenant promoting the separation of Scotland from England. On Christmas Eve of 1952, the hotel again became famous (or notorious) after the theft from Westminster Abbey of the Stone of Scone. Following appeals from Buckingham Palace, the Stone was recovered after having spent a night here, it's claimed. (A controversy continues as to the authenticity of the recovered artifact.)

Cozy public areas have oak-beamed ceilings and stone fireplaces. The dignified yet comfortable guest rooms are furnished in Scottish country-house style, and many offer splendid views of the Trossachs.

The bar serves drinks from a wide selection of single-malt whiskies, as well as affordable meals. The more formal restaurant offers moderately priced dinners.

Duchray Rd. (about 1km/½ mile southwest of Aberfoyle), Aberfoyle FK8 3XD. *C* **01877/382-347.** Fax 01877/382-785. www.covenantersinn.co.uk 45 units. £90–£110 ($144–$176) double. Rates include half-board. AE, DC, MC, V. Free parking. From Aberfoyle take A81 south. Turn right on Duchray Rd. **Amenities:** Restaurant; bar; access to indoor swimming pool and health club (a 20 min. drive away). *In room:* TV, coffeemaker, hair dryer.

WHERE TO DINE

Braeval Restaurant ★ SCOTTISH

Overlooking a golf course, this restaurant is housed in a former stone mill, and owners Andrew and Pauline Carter have kept an antique waterwheel to remind diners of the building's former function. The chefs here display inventiveness and solid technique. We especially like how the kitchen takes full advantage of the region's riches, including game in season. The repertoire embraces both traditional and modern British dishes on a changing fixed-price menu. You might begin with game terrine with pear chutney; for main dishes, sample such delights as seared bass bream with salad Niçoise, a lasagna of chicken livers flavored with lemon and thyme, or filet of salmon with mussel-and-basil butter sauce.

Callander Rd. (A81). *C* **01877/382-711.** Reservations required. Main courses £10–£14 ($16–$22); Sat night fixed-price menu £24.50–£33 ($39–$53). MC, V. Tues–Sun 10am–5pm; Sat 7:30–9pm by reservation only. Closed 1 week in Feb, 1 week in June, and 2 weeks in Oct. Drive 1.6km (1 mile) east of Aberfoyle on A81 (Callander Rd.).

8 On the Bonnie, Bonnie Banks of Loch Lomond ★★★

The largest of Scotland's lochs, **Loch Lomond** ★★ was the center of the ancient district of Lennox, in the possession of the branch of the Stewart (Stuart) family to which Lord Darnley (second husband of Mary Queen of Scots) belonged. The ruins of **Lennox Castle** are on Inchmurrin, one of the 30 islands of the loch; Inchmurrin has ecclesiastical ruins and is noted for its yew trees, planted

---

(*Moments* **You Take the High Road, and I'll Take the Low Road**

One of the great marked footpaths of Scotland, the **West Highland Way** goes along the complete eastern sector of lovely Loch Lomond. The footpath actually began at Milngavie outside Glasgow. Serious backpackers often do the entire 153km (95-mile) trail, but you can tackle just sections of it for marvelous day hikes that will allow you to enjoy the scenery.

---

by King Robert the Bruce to ensure a suitable supply of wood for the bows of his archers. The loch is fed by at least 10 rivers from west, east, and north and is about 39km (24 miles) long; it stretches 8km (5 miles) at its widest point. On the eastern side is Ben Lomond, which rises to a height of 968m (3,192 ft.).

The song "Loch Lomond" is supposed to have been composed by one of Bonnie Prince Charlie's captured followers on the eve of his execution in Carlisle Jail. The "low road" of the song is the path through the underworld that his spirit will follow to his native land after death, more quickly than his friends can travel to Scotland by the ordinary high road.

The easiest way to see the famous loch is not by car but by one of the local ships owned by **Sweeney's Cruisers Ltd.,** and based at Sweeney's Shipyard, 26 Balloch Rd., Balloch G83 8LQ (© **01389/752-376**). Cruises on various boats last for about an hour and in summer depart every hour 10:30am to 7:30pm (departures in other months are based on demand). At £5.20 ($8.30) per person round-trip, cruises sail from Balloch toward a wooded island, Inchmurrin, year-round home to five families, several vacation chalets, and a summer-only nudist colony. The ship doesn't dock at the island, however.

BALLOCH

At the southern end of Loch Lomond, Balloch is the most touristy of the towns and villages around the lake. It grew up on the River Leven, where the water leaves Loch Lomond and flows south to the Clyde. Today, Balloch is visited chiefly by those wanting to take boat trips on Loch Lomond; these sail in season from Balloch Pier.

EXPLORING THE AREA

The best place to go for information on the area is **Loch Lomond Shores,** standing side-by-side with the **National Park Gateway Centre,** Ben Lomond Way (© **01389/722-199**). Staffed by park rangers, the center contains information about Scotland's first National Park—comprised of both Loch Lomond and the Trossachs—local wildlife and flora, organized talks, or ways to explore this vast scenic attraction. There's a rooftop viewing gallery for panoramic vistas of both the loch and the new National Park. The center also features a 40-minute film, *Legend of Loch Lomond.* On site are restaurants, cafes, and shops. Hours are daily: 10am to 6pm in June, 10am to 8pm in July and August, 10am to 7pm in September, and 10am to 6pm in October. Entrance is free.

The 81-hectare (200-acre) **Balloch Castle Country Park** is on the bonnie banks of Loch Lomond, 1.2km (¾ mile) north of Balloch Station. The present **Balloch Castle** (© **01389/722-199**), replacing one that dated from 1238, was constructed in 1808 for John Buchanan of Ardoch in the castle-Gothic style. Its visitor center explains the history of the property. The site has a walled garden, and the trees and shrubs, especially the rhododendrons and azaleas, reach the zenith of their beauty in late May and early June. You can also visit a Fairy Glen. The park is open all year, daily 8am to dusk, with no admission. Easter to the end of October, the visitor center is open daily 10am to 6pm.

Dumbarton District's Countryside Ranger Service is based at Balloch Castle and conducts **guided walks** at various locations around Loch Lomond throughout the summer.

WHERE TO STAY & DINE

Balloch Hotel   Called Balloch's grande dame hotel, this was the first hotel to be built in the town. In 1860, it welcomed the Empress Eugénie, wife of Napoleon III, when she toured Scotland. (She slept in the Inchmoan Room.) It stands beside the river in the center of the village, offering basic, functionally furnished rooms, each with a shower (some with a tub as well).

Balloch Rd., Balloch G83 8LQ. ℂ **01389/752-579.** Fax 01389/755-604. 10 units. £57 ($91) double. Rates include Scottish breakfast. AE, DC, MC, V. **Amenities:** Restaurant; bar; limited room service. *In room:* TV, coffeemaker, hair dryer, trouser press.

Cameron House ⭐⭐⭐ *Kids*   This is one of the great country houses of Scotland, the family home of the Smollets. Its most distinguished son was Tobias Smollet, the 18th-century novelist whose humorous works have been read around the world. Over the years the house has been visited by such illustrious guests as the Emperor of Brazil, Sir Winston Churchill, Princess Margaret, and Earl Mountbatten. Literary celebrities have also shown up at the doorstep, none more famous than Dr. Samuel Johnson and his indefatigable biographer, James Boswell. Dr. Johnson later wrote, "We have had more solid talk in this house than in any other place where we have been."

Today this house has been converted into a top-rated accommodation with one of the best spas in this part of Scotland. The resort also contains some of the finest indoor leisure facilities in the area. The smallest rooms are called "house rooms," with standard rooms being slightly larger and better. Best of all are the spacious suites, furnished with four-poster beds. Much of the furnishings are in the traditional Georgian style, with dark mahogany pieces set against floral bathrooms. Bathrooms are wide ranging: some with tubs, some with showers, and others with a combo. All rooms are non-smoking.

Children are warmly welcomed and the hotel has a supervised playroom where parents can leave kids for a couple of hours while they relax in the gorgeous lagoon pool or the spa. The Scottish and French cuisine served in the Georgian Room is among the most refined in this part of Scotland. You can also dine informally in two more restaurants. Many sporting adventures ranging from golf to fishing to private yacht parties can be arranged.

Alexandria, Loch Lomond, G83 8QZ. ℂ **01389/755-565.** Fax 01389/759-522. www.cameronhouse.co.uk. 96 units. £242–£282 ($387–$451) double; £380–£480 ($608–$768) suite. Rates include full breakfast. AE, DC, MC, V. Take M8 to A82 to Loch Lomond; follow signs to hotel. **Amenities:** 3 restaurants; bar; indoor heated pool; golf course; health club; spa; watersports equipment/rentals; children's center; 24-hr. room service; babysitting; laundry/dry cleaning service; steam room; Turkish bath. *In room:* TV, dataport, minibar, coffeemaker, hair dryer.

LUSS

The village of Luss, 14km (9 miles) north of Balloch on A82 on the western side of Loch Lomond, is the traditional home of the Colquhouns. Among its stone cottages, on the water's edge, is a branch of the Highland Arts Studios of Seil. Cruises on the loch and boat rentals may be arranged at a nearby jetty.

If your travels in Scotland inspire you to put on a kilt and blow your own set of bagpipes, stop by **Thistle Bagpipe Works** (② **01436/860-250**), in the center of Luss. Here, not only can you order custom-made bagpipes but you can also purchase a clan kilt to go with the instrument. Your neighbors back home will be thrilled.

WHERE TO STAY & DINE

The Lodge on Loch Lomond Hotel   Surrounded by mountain, loch, and woodland, you can live in Scottish country-house style and take in panoramic views of legendary Loch Lomond. The hotel, in fact, was designed to take in the views. But that's not the only reason to stay here. This lodging, much improved in recent years, offers tasteful bedrooms and numerous comforts. The executive rooms are set up for wheelchair access, and each contains a two-person sauna. The hotel will also arrange local activities, including salmon fishing and private charter cruises along with horseback riding.

The hotel is launched upon a major new development to add 20 luxuriously furnished bedrooms by early 2004 along with an indoor heated pool, a sauna, and a first rate gym.

The fine restaurant is yet another excellent reason to stay here, or at least to drop in for an evening. Using only the finest and freshest local ingredients, this restaurant serves individually prepared meals that are the best in the area. The accommodating staff makes this a relaxed, comfortable place. Although the menu changes, main courses might include pan-fried venison loin with haggis skirlie, or speared tiger prawns with chile and garlic nut-brown butter. There is a wide selection of Aberdeen Angus beef priced according to weight, and lobster is served in a multitude of ways. For something really Scottish, try roast pheasant with bacon-braised barley and a whisky cream sauce. Those who want a lighter meal can opt for a burger, fish-and-chips, pasta, or pizza. The quality of the food is excellent, matched by panoramic views of the loch. Reservations are recommended and can be made by calling ② **01436/860-201.** Main courses are £9.50 to £21 ($15–$34). American Express, MasterCard, and Visa are accepted. The restaurant is open daily noon to 2:30pm and 6 to 9:30pm

Luss, Argyll G83 8PA. ② **01436/860-201.** Fax 01436/860-203. www.loch-lomond.co.uk. 28 units. £112–£179 ($179–$286); £224 ($358) suite. Rates include full Scottish breakfast. AE, MC, V. Free parking. Take A82 from Glasgow. **Amenities:** Restaurant; bar; room service (7am–10pm); laundry. *In room:* TV, dataport, coffeemaker, hair dryer, computer.

9

Aberdeen & the Tayside & Grampian Regions

The two historic regions of Tayside and Grampian offer a vast array of sightseeing, even though they're relatively small. Tayside, for example, is about 137km (85 miles) east to west and 97km (60 miles) south to north. The regions share the North Sea coast between the Firth of Tay in the south and the Firth of Moray farther north, and the so-called Highland Line separating the Lowlands in the south from the Highlands in the north crosses both. The Grampians, Scotland's highest mountain range, are to the west of this line.

Carved out of the old counties of Perth and Angus, **Tayside** is named for its major river, the 192km-long (119-mile) Tay. The region is easy to explore, and its waters offer some of Europe's best salmon and trout fishing. Tayside abounds with heather-clad Highland hills, long blue lochs under forested banks, and miles of walking trails.

Perth and Dundee are among Scotland's largest cities. Tayside provided the backdrop for many novels by Sir Walter Scott, including *The Fair Maid of Perth, Waverley,* and *The Abbot.* And its golf courses are world famous, ranging from the trio of 18-hole courses at Gleneagles to the open championships links at Carnoustie.

Grampian boasts Aberdeen, Scotland's third-largest city, and Braemar, site of the most famous of the Highland Gatherings. The queen herself comes here for holidays, to stay at Balmoral Castle, her private residence, a tradition dating back to the days of Queen Victoria and her consort, Prince Albert. As you journey on the scenic roads of Scotland's northeast, you'll pass moorland and peaty lochs, wood glens and rushing rivers, granite-stone villages and ancient castles, and fishing harbors as well as North Sea beach resorts.

1 Aberdeen: The Castle Country ★★

209km (130 miles) NE of Edinburgh, 108km (67 miles) N of Dundee

Bordered by fine sandy beaches (delightful if you're a polar bear), Scotland's third city, Aberdeen, is often called the "Granite City" because its buildings are constructed largely of pink or gray granite, hewn from the Rubislaw quarries. The harbor is one of the country's largest fishing ports, filled with kipper and deep-sea trawlers, and Aberdeen lies on the banks of the salmon- and trout-filled Don and Dee rivers. Spanning the Don is the **Brig o' Balgownie,** a steep Gothic arch begun in 1285.

Although it hardly compares with Glasgow and Edinburgh, Aberdeen is the center of a vibrant university; it boasts a few marvelous museums and galleries; and it's known for great nightlife and shopping, the best in the northeast. Old Aberdeen is the seat of one of Scotland's major cathedrals, St. Machars. It's also a good base for exploring the greatest castles of Grampian and the towns and villages along the splendid salmon river, Deeside.

ESSENTIALS

GETTING THERE Aberdeen is served by a number of airlines, including British Airways, British Midland, Easy Jet, and KLM. For flight information, phone the Aberdeen Airport at ℂ **01224/722-331.** The airport is about 11km (7 miles) away from the heart of town and is connected to it by a bus service costing £1.45 ($2.30) one-way. Taxis cost about £12 ($19).

Aberdeen has direct rail links to the major cities of Britain. SuperSaver fares, available by avoiding travel on Friday and Saturday, make the price difference between a one-way fare and a round-trip ticket negligible. Another efficient way of saving on fares by another £10 ($16) is reserving through the booking agency, Apex. For fares in Scotland, call ℂ **0845/755-0033** with at least 48 hours' notice. For fares from London, call ℂ **0845/722-5225** with a minimum of 1 week's notice. The prices here are for tickets bought on the day of departure, excluding Friday, when prices are higher. Nineteen trains per normal weekday arrive from Edinburgh; a regular one-way ticket costs £16.50 to £19.80 ($26–$32). Trip time is about 3½ hours. Another 19 trains per day arrive from Glasgow, costing £31.60 ($51) one-way or £46.50 ($74) round-trip. Some 12 trains per day arrive from London as well, with a one-way fare of £70 ($112) and a round-trip fare of only £95.50 ($153). For rail schedules, call ℂ **0345/ 484-950.**

Several bus companies have express routes serving Aberdeen, and many offer special round-trip fares to passengers avoiding travel on Friday or Saturday. Frequent buses arrive from both Glasgow, costing £21.50 to £25 ($34–$40) round-trip, and from Edinburgh, costing £20 to £25 ($32–$40) round-trip. There are also frequent arrivals from Inverness, a round-trip costing £10.50 to £12.50 ($17–$20). For bus schedules in Aberdeen, call ℂ **01224/212-266.**

It's also easy to drive to the northeast. From the south, drive via Edinburgh over the Forth and Tay Road bridges and take the coastal road. From the north and west, approach the area from the much-improved A9, which links Perth, Inverness, and Wick.

VISITOR INFORMATION The **Aberdeen Tourist Information Centre** is in St. Nicholas House, Broad Street, Aberdeen, Aberdeenshire AB10 1DE (ℂ **01224/632-727**). July and August, it's open Monday to Friday from 9am to 7pm, Saturday from 9am to 5pm, and Sunday from 10am to 4pm; April to June and September, hours are Monday to Friday from 9am to 5pm and Saturday from 10am to 2pm; October to March, it's open Monday to Friday from 9am to 5pm and Saturday from 10am to 2pm.

EXPLORING ABERDEEN

In old Aberdeen is **Aberdeen University,** a fusion of two colleges. Reached along University Road, **King's College** (ℂ **01224/272-137;** bus: 6 or 20) is Great Britain's oldest school of medicine. The college is known for its circa-1500 chapel with pre-Reformation carved woodwork, the finest of its kind in Scotland; it's open daily 9am to 4:30pm, charging no admission. On Broad Street is **Marischal College** (ℂ **01224/273-131**), founded in 1593 by Earl Marischal— it's the world's second biggest granite structure (El Escorial outside Madrid is much larger). The main structure is no longer in use, but on site is the Marischal Museum displaying exhibits and photos of the university and the Scottish

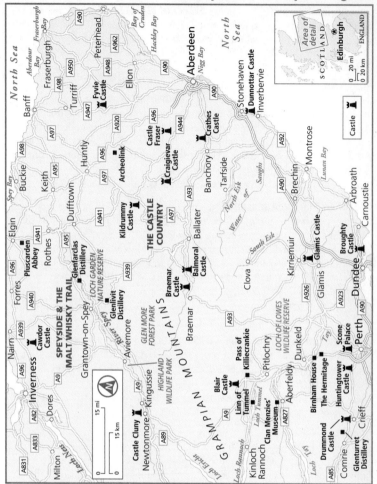

culture of the northeast in general; admission is free, and the museum is open Monday to Saturday from 10am to 5pm and Sunday from 2 to 5pm. In 1860, the colleges joined together to form the nucleus of the University of Aberdeen.

Also at the University of Aberdeen, the **Cruickshank Botanic Garden,** St. Machar Drive (© **01224/272-704;** bus: 6 or 20), displays alpines, shrubs, and many herbaceous plants, along with rock and water gardens. It's open Monday to Friday from 9am to 5pm; in summer, it's also open Saturday and Sunday from 2 to 5pm. Admission is free.

The **Cathedral of St. Machar,** Chanonry (© **01224/485-988** in the morning or 01224/317-424 in the afternoon; bus: 1, 2, 3, 4, 5, 6, 7, or 26), was founded in 1131, but the present structure dates from the 15th century. Its splendid heraldic ceiling contains three rows of shields. Be sure to note the magnificent modern stained-glass windows by Douglas Strachan and the pre-Reformation woodwork. The cathedral is open daily 9am to 5pm.

At **Alpine Bikes,** 66–70 Holburn St. (✆ **01224/211-455**), you can rent a bike so that you can go exploring on two wheels. Rates are £12 ($19) daily or £24 ($38) for weekends, with weekly rates at £60 ($96). It's open Sunday from 11am to 5pm, Monday to Wednesday and Friday from 9am to 6pm, and Thursday from 9am to 8pm.

Aberdeen Art Gallery 🗽 Built in 1884 in a neoclassical design by A. Marshall MacKenzie, this building houses one of the most important art collections in Great Britain. It contains 18th-century portraits by Raeburn, Hogarth, Ramsay, and Reynolds and acclaimed 20th-century works by Paul Nash, Ben Nicholson, and Francis Bacon. The exhibits also include excellent pieces by Monet, Pissarro, Sisley, and Bonnard as well as a collection of Scottish domestic silver. Special exhibits and events are frequently offered.

Schoolhill. ✆ **01224/523-700**. www.aagm.co.uk. Free admission. Mon–Sat 10am–5pm; Sun 2–5pm. Bus: 20.

Aberdeen Maritime Museum   Using a unique collection of ship models, paintings, artifacts, computer interaction, and exhibits, this museum tells the story of the city's long and fascinating relationship with the sea. A major display on the offshore oil industry features a model of the Murchison oil platform. The complex is on four floors, incorporating the 1593 Provost Ross House linked by a modern glass structure to the granite Trinity Church. Windows open onto panoramic views of the harbor.

Shiprow. ✆ **01224/337-700**. www.aagm.co.uk. Free admission. Mon–Sat 10am–5pm; Sun noon–3pm. Bus: 20.

Provost Skene's House   This attraction is named for a rich merchant who was Lord Provost of Aberdeen from 1676 to 1685. Off Broad Street, it's a museum with period rooms and artifacts of domestic life. Provost Skene's kitchen has been converted into a cafe.

5 Guestrow, off Broad St. ✆ **01224/641-086**. Free admission. Mon–Fri 10am–5pm; Sat 10am–4pm; Sun 1–3pm. Bus: 20.

Dunnottar Castle   The well-preserved ruins of Dunnottar are on a rocky promontory towering 49m (160 ft.) above the surging sea, and the best way to get here is by a dramatic 30-minute walk from Stonehaven along the cliffs. The ruins include a great square tower and a chapel built in 1392. William Wallace stormed it in 1297, but failed to take it. In 1991, it was the setting for Zeffirelli's film of *Hamlet,* starring Mel Gibson. You can reach Stonehaven from Aberdeen by taking Bluebird Northern bus no. 107, costing £5.40 ($8.65) round-trip, and then walking for 5 minutes. Trains run about every ½-hour from Aberdeen to Stonehaven, costing £5 to £7 ($8–$11) round-trip. Departures are every 30 minutes during the day; the trip takes 30 minutes.

3km (2 miles) south of Stonehaven off A92. ✆ **01569/762-173**. Admission £3.50 ($5.60) adults, £2 ($3.20) seniors and students, £1 ($1.60) children. Easter–Oct Mon–Sat 9am–6pm; Sun 2–5pm; Nov–Easter Mon–Fri 9am–3:30pm.

SHOPPING

The main shopping districts center on specialty shops on **Chapel** and **Thistle streets** and the well-known chains on **George** and **Union streets.** Of interest to collectors, **Colin Wood,** 25 Rose St. (✆ **01224/643-019**), stocks furniture, wall clocks, and grandfather clocks from the 17th to the early 20th centuries. Its specialty, however, is maps from the Elizabethan through the Victorian eras. The shop also sells 17th- to early-20th-century prints of northern Scotland. You may

Aberdeen

0   1/10 mi
0   0.2 km

Tillydrone Rd.

Don St.

SEATON PARK **1**

Chanonry

2

Tillydrone Ave.

King St.

Aberdeen
SCOTLAND

Edinburgh ⊛

0   20 mi
0   20 km   ENGLAND

St. Machar Dr.

Bedford Ave.

**OLD
ABERDEEN**

High St.

Leslie Rd.

Great Northern Rd.

Regent Walk

Clifton Rd.

Bedford Rd.

Meston Walk

College Bounds

3

University Rd.

King St.

Linksfield Rd.

Sunnybank Rd.

Orchard St.

Spital

Pittodrie St.

Froghall
Terrace

Merkland Rd.

King's Crescent

Seaforth Rd.

Canal Rd.

Causewayend

Nelson St.

Urquhart Rd.

Park Rd.

Hutcheon St.

West North St.

Westburn Rd.

Skene Square

Spring Garden

Jasmine
Terrace

Mount St.

Maberly St.

George St.

Gallowgate

Park St.

Watson St.

Rosemount Pl.

Baker St.

John St.

St. Andrews St.

Little John St.

**North Church
of St. Andrew** †

Beach
Blvd.

Leadside
Rd.

4

Schoolhill

5

Broad St.

Justice St.

Whitehall Pl.

Viaduct

**St. Nicholas
Kirk** †

7

St. Nicholas St.

Queen St.

Castle
St.

Virginia St.

Albert St.

Skene St.

Rose St.

Summer St.

Huntley St.

Union Terrace

Belmont St.

Union St.

6

Shiprow

Market St.

Trinity Quay

Regent Qua

**Victoria
Dock**

Waverly Pl.

Thistle St.

Bridge St.

**Bus
Station**

**Upper
Dock**

Albyn Pl.

Union St.

Justicemill Ln.

Langstane Pl.

Bon-Accord St.

Crown St.

Guild St.

**Train
Station**

**Goods
Depot**

College St.

Commercial Quay

*Albert
Basin*

Railway ———

Victoria Bridge →

Aberdeen Art Gallery **4**

Aberdeen Maritime Museum/
Provost Ross House **6**

Cathedral of St. Machar **1**

Cruickshank Botanic Garden **2**

King's College **3**

Marischal College **5**

Provost Skene's House **7**

also want to browse through the eclectic mix of bric-a-brac antiques at **Elizabeth Watts Studio,** 69 Thistle St. (© **01224/647-232**), where items include glass, brass, antique jewelry, china, silver, and a few small furniture pieces. The shop is actually best known for its china and glass restoration studio. For one-stop gift shopping, drop in at **Nova,** 20 Chapel St. (© **01224/641-270**), which stocks china, silver jewelry, rugs, clothing, toys, cards, and gift paper.

To trace your Scottish ancestry, go to the **Aberdeen Family History Shop,** 164 King St. (© **01224/646-323**), where membership to the Aberdeen and North East Family History Society costs £15 ($24) cash, check, or credit card. Once you join, you can go through a vast range of publications kept on hand to help members trace their family histories.

Other interesting shops are **Grandad's Attic,** 12 Marischal St. (© **01224/ 213-699**), which specializes in Art Deco ceramics and antique pine furniture; **Just Scottish,** 4 Upperkirkgate (© **01224/621-755**), retailers of quality items—all made in Scotland, including ceramics, knitwear, textiles, silver, and jewelry; and **Alex Scott & Co.,** 43 Schoolhill (© **01224/643-924**), the town's finest kiltmakers.

HITTING THE LINKS

Aberdeen has a good range of golf courses in and around the city, with several other notable courses within an easy drive. As always, reservations are essential at any course. If the two below don't suit you, ask the tourist office for details on other options.

Among the top courses is **Balgownie, the Royal Aberdeen Golf Club** (© **01224/702-221**), created in 1780 in classic links style. Its uneven layout, sea breezes, and grassy sand dunes add to the challenge of this 6,204-yard (5,646m), par-70 course. Greens fees are £65 to £75 ($104–$120) per round, or £90 ($144) per day, but only Monday through Friday.

About 11km (7 miles) west of Aberdeen, the par-69 **West Hills Golf Course,** West Hill Heights, West Hill Skene (© and fax **01224/740-159**), features 5,921 yards (5,388m) of playing area. Greens fees are £24 ($38) for nonguests and £14 ($22) for guests Monday through Friday, or £27 ($43) for nonguests and £20 ($32) for guests Saturday and Sunday.

WHERE TO STAY

Because of increasing numbers of tourists and business travelers to the Granite City—Europe's offshore oil capital—hotels are likely to be heavily booked any time of year. If you haven't reserved ahead, stop by the **Aberdeen Tourist Information Centre,** St. Nicholas House on Broad Street (© **01224/632-727**), where the staff can usually find just the right lodging for you—whether a family-run B&B, guesthouse, or hotel. A £2.50 ($4) service fee is charged.

Rooms are also available at **Ferryhill House** (see "Where to Dine," below).

EXPENSIVE

Hilton Aberdeen Treetops ☞ *Kids* A 10-minute drive west of the center of Aberdeen off A93, this comfortable hotel built in the 1960s and renovated in 1991 offers a sweeping white facade of traditional design. The windows of it contemporary guest rooms look over landscaped grounds; some units have balconies with lake views, half are set aside for nonsmokers, and all have well-maintained bathrooms with combination tub and shower. Some 30 accommodations are large enough to house families, and a playground is available for children.

161 Springfield Rd., Aberdeen AB15 7AQ. ✆ **01224/313-377.** Fax 01224/312-028. www.aberdeen.hilton. com. 120 units. £68–£118 ($109–$189) double; £98–£148 ($157–$237) suite. AE, DC, MC, V. Free parking. Bus: 11. **Amenities:** Restaurant; bar; health club; children's programs; business center; 24-hr. room service; babysitting; laundry/dry cleaning service. *In room:* TV, coffeemaker, hair dryer, trouser press.

Marcliffe at Pitfodels ★★★

On the city's western edge less than ½-hour from the airport, this deluxe hotel is superior to the other hotels in the area. The traditional three-story manor house was constructed around a courtyard and stands on 3.2 hectares (8 acres) of landscaped grounds. The Oriental rugs, placed on stone floors, and the tartan sofas set the decor note in the public rooms; a scattering of antiques add a graceful note. The rather spacious guest rooms are furnished in Chippendale and reproduction pieces, with armchairs and desks, plus a host of extras such as fresh milk in the minibar.

At breakfast you can sample Aberdeen *rowies,* a local specialty made with butter like a croissant that's been flattened. The conservatory restaurant offers regional dishes like Highland lamb and fresh Scottish salmon, and the more expensive Invery Room is favored by businesspeople entertaining out-of-town guests. In the library lounge, you can choose from more than 130 scotches, 500 wines, and 70 cognacs.

N. Deeside Rd., Aberdeen AB1 9YA. ✆ **01224/861-000.** Fax 01224/868-860. www.marcliffe.com. 42 units. £175–£295 ($280–$472) double. Rates include breakfast. AE, DC, MC, V. Free parking. Lies on the Deeside Rd. out of Aberdeen (well signposted). **Amenities:** 2 restaurants; bar; 24-hr. room service; laundry/dry cleaning service. *In room:* TV, minibar, coffeemaker, hair dryer, iron/ironing board.

Simpson's Hotel ★

This hotel, which opened in 1998, enjoys great popularity. Two traditional granite town houses were joined to offer comfortable accommodations. Rooms are decorated with furniture from Spain and painted in rich, bold colors that create a cool, Mediterranean ambience. Amenities include complimentary use of the health spa.

The hotel bar and brasserie offers a range of moderately priced Scottish and international dishes prepared with the finest of local ingredients.

59 Queens Rd., Aberdeen AB15 4YP. ✆ **01224/327-777.** Fax 01224/327-700. www.simpsonshotel.co.uk. 50 units. Sun–Thurs £130–£140 ($208–$224) double, suites from £150 ($240); Fri–Sat £85–£95 ($136–$152) double, suites from £115 ($184). Rates include breakfast. AE, MC, V. Follow signs for A96 North, and turn right at Queens Rd. Roundabout. **Amenities:** Restaurant; bar; spa; 24-hr. room service; laundry/dry cleaning service; babysitting. *In room:* A/C, TV, minibar, coffeemaker, hair dryer, iron/ironing board, trouser press.

Thistle Aberdeen Caledonian ★

The Thistle occupies a grand stone-fronted Victorian in the center of Aberdeen, lying a 2-minute walk form the rail station. Recent restorations have added a veneer of Georgian gloss to one of the most elegant series of public rooms in town. The guest rooms are at the top of a 19th-century stairwell, with Corinthian columns and a freestanding atrium. They vary a good deal in size, but all contain double-glazed windows and bathrooms with tub and shower combinations. Each accommodation is comfortably furnished with taste.

10–14 Union Terrace (off Union St.), Aberdeen AB10 1WE. ✆ **01224/640-233.** Fax 01224/641-627. www. thistlehotels.com/aberdeencaledonian. 80 units. £98–£118 ($157–$189) double; from £220 ($352) suite. Children age 11 and under stay free in parent's room. AE, DC, MC, V. Limited free parking. Bus: 17. Pets allowed. **Amenities:** 2 restaurants; bar; secretarial services; 24-hr. room service; laundry/dry cleaning service. *In room:* TV, dataport, minibar, coffeemaker, hair dryer, iron/ironing board.

MODERATE

Craiglynn Hotel

This hotel was created from a granite-block Victorian built in 1901 as a home for a successful fish merchant. The high-ceilinged double bedrooms are monochromatic, with traditional furniture and small bathrooms. All guest rooms are non-smoking. If advance notice is given, a moderately priced dinner can be prepared, featuring dishes like fricassee of lamb and a house version of sticky toffee pudding with Drambuie-flavored ice cream. Two lounges (one nonsmoking) with fireplaces provide a perfect setting for an after dinner cocktail.

36 Fonthill Rd., Aberdeen AB11 6UJ. ℂ **01224/584-050.** Fax 01224/212-225. www.craiglynn.co.uk. 8 units. £65–£90 ($104–$144) double with bathroom. Rates include breakfast. AE, V. Free parking. Closed Dec 25–26. Bus: 17. Lies a 10-min. walk south of the train station. *In room:* TV, coffeemaker.

The Jays Guest House *Value* This is one of the nicest guesthouses in Aberdeen, located near the university and the Offshore Survival Centre. Alice and George Jennings are most welcoming hosts, and many repeat visitors consider Alice their candidate for "landlady of the year." Everything runs smoothly, and the guest rooms—all nonsmoking—are bright and airy, each newly renovated.

422 King St., Aberdeen AB24 3BR. ℂ and fax **01224/638-295.** www.jaysguesthouse.co.uk. 10 units. £60–£80 ($96–$128) double. Rates include Scottish breakfast. MC, V. Free parking. Lies 3 blocks north of the Civic Centre. Bus: 1, 2, 3, 4, or 7. *In room:* TV, coffeemaker, no phone

Mannofield Hotel Built of silver granite around 1880, this hotel is a Victorian fantasy of step gables, turrets, spires, bay windows, and a sweeping mahogany-and-teakwood staircase. Owners Bruce and Dorothy Cryle offer a warm Scottish welcome. The guest rooms, refurbished in 1998 with paisley curtains and quilts, are equipped with well-maintained, shower-only bathrooms.

447 Great Western Rd., Aberdeen AB10 6NL. ℂ **01224/315-888.** Fax 01224/208-971. 9 units. £64 ($102) double. Rates include Scottish breakfast. AE, DC, MC, V. Free parking. Bus: 18 or 19. Dogs welcome by arrangement. **Amenities:** Restaurant; limited room service; babysitting; laundry/dry cleaning service. *In room:* TV, coffeemaker, hair dryer.

The Palm Court Hotel Aberdeen Set a bit apart from the exact center and a bit more tranquil, this is a highly praised, well-run hotel that Aberdeen citizens recommend to friends who will be visiting. The hotel is known for its good value and fine bedrooms. They're not huge but are comfortably furnished and well decorated in bright pastels. Each comes with a small but tidily kept bathroom with tub or shower. If you don't want to wander the streets of Aberdeen at night, seeking a restaurant, you'll find a good dining room on site at Hickory's Restaurant, specializing in fine Scottish food such as salmon.

81 Seafield Rd., Aberdeen AB15 7YX. ℂ **01224/310-351.** Fax 01224/312-707. 24 units. £60–£99 ($96–$158). AE, MC, V. Rates include full breakfast. Free parking. Bus: 11. **Amenities:** Restaurant; bar; business services; limited room service; laundry service. *In room:* TV, coffeemaker, hair dryer, trouser press.

LUXURY ACCOMMODATIONS ON THE OUTSKIRTS OF ABERDEEN

Ardoe House Hotel *Finds* This turreted baronial 1878 mansion sits in the midst of lush gardens and manicured grounds, offering panoramic views of the River Dee. Though it's close to Aberdeen, it's a world apart. Its old-fashioned interior, with wood paneling, carved fireplaces, and stained-glass windows, reflects the best in traditional Victorian style. The mansion was recently expanded, but even so, each room is individually decorated and well appointed with many extras, including immaculate bathrooms. In the formal dining room, you can order a blend of traditional and modern Scottish cuisine, using fresh local ingredients that are prepared with French flair.

S. Deeside Rd. (3km/5 miles south of Aberdeen on B9077), Blairs, Aberdeen AB12 5YP. © 01224/867-355. Fax 01224/860-644. www.macdonaldhotels.co.uk. £160–£200 ($256–$320) double. MC, V. **Amenities:** Restaurant; bar; indoor pool; health club; spa; Jacuzzi; sauna; 24-hr. room service; laundry/dry cleaning service; steam room. *In room:* TV, dataport, coffeemaker, hair dryer, iron/ironing board.

Kildrummy Castle Hotel ★★   This 19th-century gray-stone mansion, on acres of landscaped gardens, overlooks the ruined castle of Kildrummy. Its guest rooms, many furnished with antiques, vary in size; some of the master rooms feature four poster beds and fireplaces. The dignified public rooms have oak-paneled walls and ceilings, mullioned windows, and window seats. The drawing room and bar open onto a flagstone terrace.

Traditional Scottish food, including *Cullen skink* (smoked haddock soup) and filet of sole stuffed with smoked Scottish salmon, is served in the dining room.

Kildrummy by Alford AB33 8RA. © 01975/571-288. Fax 01975/571-345. www.kildrummycastlehotel.co.uk. 16 units. £139–£185 ($222–$296) double. Rates include Scottish breakfast. AE, MC, V. Closed Jan. From Aberdeen, take A944 and follow signs to Alford; then take A97, following signs to Kildrummy. Dogs welcome. **Amenities:** Restaurant; bar; room service (8am–9pm); babysitting; laundry service. *In room:* TV, coffeemaker, hair dryer, trouser press.

Pittodrie House ★★   Dating from 1490, the castle here was burned down and then rebuilt in 1675 as a family home—and that in turn became a country-house hotel when Royal Deeside became prominent through Queen Victoria's adoption of Balmoral as her holiday retreat. The guest rooms are divided between those in the old house (with good views and antique furniture) and the smaller rooms in the recent extension (decorated in keeping with the style of the house but with less atmosphere). Most of the bathrooms have combination tub and shower. The public rooms boast antiques, oil paintings, and open fires. The elegant restaurant serves venison, grouse, partridge, pheasant, and fresh fish.

Chapel of Garioch, Pitcaple AB5 5HS. © 888/892-0038 or 01467/681-444. Fax 01467/681-648. www. pittodrie-house.co.uk. 27 units. £140 ($224) double. Rates include Scottish breakfast. AE, DC, MC, V. From Aberdeen, take A96, following signs to Inverness; remain on A96, bypassing Inverurie, then follow signs to Chapel of Garioch. **Amenities:** Restaurant; bar; room service (10am–11pm); laundry service. *In room:* TV, coffeemaker, hair dryer, iron/ironing board.

Thainstone House Hotel ★★★   One of northeast Scotland's most elegant country hotels, set on 16 hectares (40 acres), the four-star Thainstone House is a Palladian-style mansion whose adornments give it the air of a country club. It can serve as both a retreat and a center for exploring this historic part of Scotland, including the Malt Whisky Trail. (See "Speyside & the Malt Whisky Trail" later in this chapter.) Guests enter the mansion, which was designed by Archibald Simpson (the famed architect of many of Aberdeen's public buildings), through a grand portal up an elegant stairway. The high ceilings, columns, neoclassical plaster reliefs, and cornices evoke Simpson's trip to Italy. A new section of the house skillfully blends the old with the new. The elegantly furnished guest rooms vary in size and offer extra touches such as sherry and shortbread.

The chef at Simpson's Restaurant turns out a Continental and Scottish menu with a light, inventive touch.

Inverurie AB51 5NT. © 01467/621-643. Fax 01467/625-084. www.macdonaldhotels.co.uk. 48 units. £85–£200 ($136–$320) double; £250 ($400) suite. Rates include Scottish breakfast. AE, DC, MC, V. From Aberdeen, take A96, following signs to Inverness; just before Inverurie, turn left and follow signs to the hotel. **Amenities:** Restaurant; bar; indoor pool; health club; spa; Jacuzzi; 24-hr. room service; massage; babysitting; laundry service; steam room. *In room:* TV, coffeemaker, hair dryer, iron/ironing board, trouser press.

WHERE TO DINE

Elrond's Cafe Bar INTERNATIONAL   White marble floors, a long oak-capped bar, candlelight, and a garden-inspired decor create the ambience here. No one will mind if you show up for just a drink, a pot of tea, a midday salad or snack, or a full-blown feast. Specialties are burgers, steaks, pastas, fresh fish, chicken Kiev, and vegetarian dishes. This isn't the world's greatest food, but it's popular nevertheless. Though it's in one of Aberdeen's well-known hotels, the restaurant has a separate entrance onto Union Terrace.

In the Caledonian Thistle Hotel, 10–14 Union Terrace. ℭ **01224/640-233.** Main courses £7–£15 ($11–$24); pot of tea with pastry £4 ($6.40). AE, DC, MC, V. Mon–Sat 10am–midnight; Sun 10am–11pm. Bus: 16 or 17.

Ferryhill House INTERNATIONAL   In its own park and garden on the city's southern outskirts, Ferryhill House dates back 250 years. It has Georgian detailing, but recent refurbishment has removed many of the original panels and all the ceiling beams. The restaurant boasts one of the region's largest collections of single-malt whiskies—more than 140 brands. There's a fireplace for chilly afternoons and a beer garden for midsummer, as well as a conservatory. The food is not exceptional but is prepared with market-fresh ingredients. It's more whole-some, hearty, and filling than gourmet. Menu items include steak or vegetable tempura, chicken dishes like chicken fajita, fried haddock filet, pastas, and chili.

Ferryhill House also rents nine standard guest rooms, with TVs, phones, and hair dryers. Breakfast included, the double rate is £79 ($126) Sunday to Thursday and £52 ($83) Friday and Saturday.

Bon Accord St., Aberdeen AB11 6UA. ℭ. **01224/590-867.** Fax 01224/586-947. Reservations recommended Sat–Sun. Main courses £9.50–£14.50 ($15–$23). AE, DC, MC, V. Free parking. Bus: 16.

Howies Aberdeen ★ SCOTTISH/INTERNATIONAL   This is the latest—and even better—reincarnation of the locally famous Gerard's, which stood here for many years. Modern Scottish cookery with international influences is presented exceedingly well. The medallions of Aberdeen Angus filet are always reliable, as are the fresh fish and chicken dishes, each prepared with a certain flair. The bar stocks a wide range of single malts and ports in addition to some wines unavailable elsewhere in the region.

50 Chapel St. ℭ **01224/639-500.** Reservations recommended. Fixed-price lunch £7.95–£9.95 ($13–$16); fixed-price dinner £15.50–£17.95 ($25–$29). AE, MC, V. Daily noon–2:30pm and 6–10:30pm. Lies a 15-min. walk southwest of train station.

Martha's Vineyard Bistro/The Courtyard Restaurant SCOTTISH/CON-TINENTAL   One of the most appealing restaurant complexes in Aberdeen occupies two floors of what was built around 1900 as an extension of the local hospital. Today, a robust and rustic-looking bistro (Martha's Vineyard) is on the street level, with a more formal restaurant (The Courtyard) upstairs. The bistro menu ranges from smoked salmon and asparagus salad to gigot of lamb with a compote of leeks in mustard sauce. Upstairs, you'll find dishes like local brie wrapped in smoked salmon or rosemary-flavored loin of Highland venison with wild mushrooms. Dessert in either place might be warm orange pudding with Grand Marnier sauce served with vanilla-ginger ice cream.

Alford Lane. ℭ **01224/213-795.** Reservations recommended in The Courtyard, not necessary in Martha's Vineyard. Main courses £5–£12 ($8–$19) bistro; £11.50–£18 ($18–$29) in restaurant. Mon–Sat noon–2:15pm; Tues–Sat 6–10pm. AE, DC, MC, V. Bus: 1, 2, 3, or 4.

Silver Darling ★★ FRENCH/SEAFOOD   Silver Darling (a local nickname for herring) is a definite asset to the dining scene in Aberdeen. Occupying a former Customs House at the mouth of the harbor, it spins a culinary fantasy around the freshest catch of the day. You might begin with a savory fish soup, almost Mediterranean in flavor, then go on to one of the barbecued fish dishes. Salmon is the invariable favorite of the more discriminating diners.

Pocra Quay, Footdee. ☎ **01224/576-229.** Reservations recommended. Main courses £14–£24 ($22–$38); 2-course fixed-price lunch £21.50 ($34); 3-course fixed-price lunch £26 ($42). AE, DC, MC, V. Mon–Fri noon–2pm and 7–9:30pm; Sat 7–9:30pm; Sun 6–9pm summer only. Closed Dec 23–Jan 8. Bus: 14 or 15.

ABERDEEN AFTER DARK

Tickets to events at most venues are available by calling the **Aberdeen Box Office** at ☎ **01224/641-122.** Open Monday to Saturday 9am to 6:30pm.

THE PERFORMING ARTS The **Aberdeen Arts Centre,** King Street (☎ **01224/635-208**), has a 350-seat theater that is rented to professional and amateur groups hosting everything from poetry readings and plays to musical concerts in various styles. Ticket prices and performance times vary; call for information. Also on the premises is a 60-seat video projection theater that screens world cinema offerings, and ticket prices vary depending on what is showing but start at £8 ($13). A large gallery room holds month-long exhibitions of visual art in many different styles and mediums. A cafe/bar, offering light meals and drinks, is open during performance times.

Near Tarves, about 32km (20 miles) from Aberdeen, you'll find **Haddo House** (☎ **01651/851-440**), which hosts operas, ballets, and plays from Easter to October. An early-20th-century hall built of pitch pine, Haddo House is based on the Canadian town halls that Lord Aberdeen saw in his travels abroad. The hall was built for the people of the surrounding area on Aberdeen family land, and the present Lady Aberdeen still lives in a house on this property. Follow B9005, 29km (18 miles) north to Tarves, then follow the National Trust and Haddo House signs 3km (2 miles) east to arrive here. Ticket prices range from £7 to £19 ($11–$30). Admittance to the house is £7 ($11) for adults and £5.25 ($8.40) for seniors and children. The house is open daily from 11am to 4:30pm, the shop from 11am to 4:30pm, and the gardens from 9:30am to 4pm. A stylish cafe offers light meals, tea, and other beverages daily, Easter to October, from 11am to 6pm.

The 19th-century **Music Hall,** Union Street (☎ **01224/641-122**), is an ornately gilded 1,282-seat theater that stages concerts by the Scottish National Orchestra, the Scottish Chamber Orchestra, visiting international orchestras, and pop bands, as well as hosting ceilidhs, crafts fairs, and book sales. Tickets for year-round musical performances average £10 to £30 ($16–$48). The **Aberdeen International Youth Festival** is held annually in this hall in August, and features youth orchestras, choirs, and dance and theater ensembles. Daytime and evening performances are held, and tickets range from £10 to £14 ($16–$22). Contact the Music Hall or the Aberdeen Box Office (above) for more information.

His Majesty's Theatre, Rosemount Viaduct (☎ **01224/641-122**), was designed by Frank Matcham in 1906 and is the only theater in the world build entirely of granite. The interior is late Victorian, and the 1,445-seat theater stages operas, dance performances, dramas, classical concerts, musicals, and comedy shows year-round. Tickets range from £10 to £25 ($16–$40).

A mixed venue is the **Lemon Tree,** 5 W. North St. (☎ **01224/642-230**). Its 150-seat theater stages dance recitals, theatrical productions, and stand-up comedy, with tickets generally priced between £7 to £22 ($11–$35). On Saturday, there's often a matinee at 2 or 3pm, and evening performances are at 7pm.

Downstairs, the 500-seat cafe/theater hosts folk, rock, blues, jazz, and comedy acts, with shows starting between 8 and 10pm. On Wednesday the Folk Club is onstage, and other nights have varied offerings. On Sunday afternoon there's free live jazz.

DANCE CLUBS   **DeNiro's,** 120 Union St. (© **01224/640-641**), has dancing to house music from 10pm until 2am on Friday and Saturday only. The cover charge is £7 ($11), but may vary depending on the guest DJ.

The **Pelican,** housed in the Hotel Metro, 17 Market St. (© **01224/583-275**), offers dancing Thursday to Saturday 10pm to 2am. The cover charge on Thursday is £4 ($6.40) and Friday and Saturday £6 ($9.60). There's a live band every second Thursday.

The ever-popular **Ministry,** 16 Dee St. (© **01224/211-661**), is a sophisticated dance club that features different theme nights throughout the week. On Monday, Moist is a popular student night. On Fridays, guest DJs from England and America take over the sound system, so you might catch New York's hottest DJ of the moment. Cover charges range from £2 to £12 ($3.20–$19) throughout the week, depending the DJ is or the band.

A PUB   The **Prince of Wales** ⚐, 7 St. Nicholas Lane (© **01224/640-597**), in the heart of the shopping district, is the best place in the old city center to go for a pint. Furnished with pews in screened booths, it boasts Aberdeen's longest bar counter. At lunch, it's bustling with regulars who devour chicken in cider sauce or Guinness pie. On tap are such beers as Buchan Gold and Courage Directors. Orkney Dark Island is also sold here.

SIDE TRIPS FROM ABERDEEN: CASTLE COUNTRY

Aberdeen is the center of "castle country"—40 inhabited castles lie within a 65km (40-mile) radius. Here is a selection of the best of them.

Castle Fraser ⚐   One of the most impressive of the fortress-like castles of Mar, Castle Fraser stands on 10 hectares (25 acres) of parkland. The sixth laird, Michael Fraser, began the structure in 1575, and his son finished it in 1636. Visitors can tour the spectacular Great Hall and wander around the grounds, which include an 18th-century walled garden.

Sauchen, Inverurie. © **01330/833-463.** Admission £5.50 ($8.80) adults, £4 ($6.40) seniors, £1.75 ($2.80) children, free for children age 4 and under. Easter weekend and Oct Sat–Sun 2–4:45pm; May–June daily 1:30–5pm; July–Aug daily 11am–4:45pm; Sept daily 1:30–5:30pm. Closed Nov–Mar. Head 5km (3 miles) south of Kemnay, 26km (16 miles) west of Aberdeen, off A944.

Craigievar Castle ⚐   Structurally unchanged since its completion in 1626, Craigievar Castle is an exceptional tower house where Scottish baronial architecture reached its pinnacle of achievement. It has contemporary plaster ceilings in nearly all its rooms. The castle was continuously lived in by the descendants of the builder, William Forbes, until it came under the care of the National Trust for Scotland in 1963. The family collection of furnishings is complete.

Some 6km (4 miles) south of the castle, clearly signposted on a small road leading off A980, near Lumphanan, is **Macbeth's Cairn,** where the historical Macbeth is supposed to have fought his last battle. Built of timber in a rounded format known by historians as "motte and bailey," it's now nothing more than a steep-sided rounded hillock marked with a sign and a flag.

Hwy. A980, 10km (6 miles) south of Alford. © **01339/883-635.** Admission £7 ($11) adults, £4.50 ($7.20) seniors/children. Castle May–Sept daily 1:30–4:45pm; grounds year-round daily 9:30am–sunset. Head west on A96 to Alford, then south on A980.

Scotland's Castle Trail

Scotland's Castle Trail takes visitors on a tour of fairy tale castles, imposing stately homes, magnificent ruins, and splendid gardens open to the public. The only signposted route of its kind in Scotland, it guides motorists around rural Aberdeenshire. The accompanying leaflet highlights 11 of the finest properties, from the ruins of the 13th-century Kildrummy Castle and the elegant five-towered Fyvie Castle to two grand examples of the work of the 18th-century architect William Adam—Duff House and Haddo House.

The leaflet also details other places that can be visited, including Balmoral Castle, a royal home since Queen Victoria's day; and Pitmedden Garden, where the centerpiece Great Garden was laid out in 1675. The leaflet, *Scotland's Castle Trail,* is available at local tourist offices or by calling ✆ **0845/225-5121.** Information can also be found on the Aberdeen and Grampian Tourist Board website (**www.agtb.org**).

Crathes Castle & Gardens ★★   This castle, 3km (2 miles) east of Banchory, has royal historical associations from 1323, when the lands of Leys were granted to the Burnett family by King Robert the Bruce. The castle's features include remarkable late-16th-century painted ceilings and a garden that's a composite of eight separate gardens, giving a display all year. The great yew hedges date from 1702. The grounds are ideal for nature study, and there are five trails, including a long-distance layout with ranger service. The complex includes a licensed restaurant, a visitor center, a souvenir shop, a plant sales area, a wayfaring course, and picnic areas.

Banchory. ✆ **01330/844-525.** Admission £9 ($14) adults, £6.50 ($10) children and seniors, £23 ($37) per family. Grounds, adventure area, and park daily 9:30am–sunset; visitor center, shop, and restaurant Good Friday–Oct daily 10:30am–5:30pm; castle Good Friday–Oct daily 11am–4:45pm. From Aberdeen, take A93 24km (15 miles) west.

Fyvie Castle ★   The National Trust for Scotland opened this castle to the public in 1986. The oldest part, dating from the 13th century, has been called the grandest existing example of Scottish baronial architecture. There are five towers, named after the families who lived here over 5 centuries. Originally built in a royal hunting forest, Fyvie means "deer hill" in Gaelic. The interior, created by the first Lord Leith of Fyvie, reflects the opulence of the Edwardian era. His collections contain arms and armor, 16th-century tapestries, and important artworks by Raeburn, Gainsborough, and Romney. The castle is rich in ghosts, curses, and legends.

Turriff, on the Aberdeen-Banff road. ✆ **01651/891-266.** Admission £7 ($11) adults, £5.60 ($8.95) seniors and children. Easter–June and Sept daily noon–5pm; July–Aug daily 11am–5pm; Oct Sat–Sun noon–5pm. Closed Nov–Mar. Take A947 for 37km (23 miles) northwest of Aberdeen.

2 Perth ★: Gateway to the Highlands & Scone Palace

71km (44 miles) N of Edinburgh, 35km (22 miles) SW of Dundee, 103km (64 miles) NE of Glasgow

From its majestic position on the Tay, the ancient city of Perth was the capital of Scotland until the mid-15th century. It's here that the Highlands meet the Lowlands. Perth makes a good stop if you're heading north to the Highlands. Perth itself has few historic buildings, but it does offer some good shopping. The main attraction, Scone Palace, lies on the outskirts, and the surrounding countryside is wonderful for strolling and hiking.

ESSENTIALS

GETTING THERE   By Train   ScotRail provides service between Edinburgh and Perth (trip time: 90 min.), with continuing service to Dundee. The trip to Perth costs £9.40 ($15) from Edinburgh; phone ✆ **8457/484-950** for 24-hour information.

By Bus   Edinburgh and Perth are connected by frequent bus service (trip time: 1½ hours). The fare is £6.50 ($10). For more information and schedules, check with CityLink (✆ **0990/505-050**).

By Car   To reach Perth from Edinburgh, take A90 northwest and go across the Forth Road Bridge, continuing north along M90 (trip time: 1½ hr.).

VISITOR INFORMATION   The **tourist information center** is at Lower City Mills, West Mill St. (✆ **01738/450-600**), and is open April to June daily 9am to 6pm, July to September daily from 9am to 7pm, October daily from 9am to 6pm, and November to March, Monday to Saturday from 10am to 5pm.

EXPLORING THE AREA

For the best view of this scenic part of Scotland, take Bowerswell Road 1.6km (1 mile) to the east of Perth center to visit **Kinnoull Hill,** rising 240m (792 ft.). After an easy climb, you can get a bird's-eye view of the geological Highland Line dividing the Highlands from the Lowlands. A marked nature trail beginning at the Braes Road car park leads, after a 25-minute walk, to the panoramic view from the top. Here you can see a folly, the **Kinnoull Watch Tower,** and its counterpart, 1.6km (1 mile) to the east, **Binn Hill.** Both structures are imitations of castles along the Rhine.

⟨Tips⟩ Calling All Artists

In May, the 10-day **Perth Festival of the Arts** attracts international orchestras and chamber music societies. There are some dance recitals as well, and a recent trend is a celebration of some aspects of pop culture. Concerts are held in churches, auditoriums, even Scone Palace.

Balhousie Castle   In the 16th century, this was the home of the earls of Kinnoull, but today it houses the Black Watch Regimental Museum, with hundreds of weapons, medals, and documents of the Black Watch Regiment from the 18th century on. The regiment was recruited in 1739 by Gen. George Wade to help the government pacify rebellious Highlanders and became famous all over the United Kingdom for its black tartans in contrast to the red of government troops.

After visiting the castle, you can explore **North Inch,** a 41-hectare (100-acre) parkland extending north along the west bank of the Tay. This is the best place for a long walk in the Perth area. The grounds are given over mainly to sports facilities, particularly the domed Bells Sports Centre. North Inch, as depicted in Scott's *The Fair Maid of Perth,* was the site of the great 1396 Clan Combat between 30 champions from the clans Kay and Chattan, attended by Robert III and his queen.

Hay St., right beyond Rose Terrace on the west side of North Inch. ✆ 0131/310-8530. Free admission. May–Sept Mon–Sat 10am–4:30pm; Oct–Apr Mon–Fri 10am–3:30pm.

Branklyn Garden ✿   Once the finest private garden in Scotland, the Branklyn now belongs to the National Trust for Scotland. It has a superb collection of rhododendrons, alpines, and herbaceous and peat-garden plants from all over the world.

116 Dundee Rd. (A85), in Branklyn. ℰ **01738/625-535**. Admission £4.25 ($6.80) adults, £2 ($3.20) children, students, and seniors, family ticket £7.50 ($12). Mar–Oct daily 9:30am–sunset. Closed in winter.

Kirk of St. John the Baptist   This is the main sightseeing attraction of "the fair city." It's believed that the original foundation is from Pictish times. The present choir dates from 1440 and the nave from 1490. In 1559, John Knox preached his famous sermon attacking idolatry, which caused a turbulent wave of iconoclasm to sweep across the land. In its wake, religious artifacts, stained glass, and organs were destroyed all over Scotland. The church was restored as a World War I memorial in the mid-1920s.

31 St. John Place. ℰ **01738/622-241**. Free admission. Mon–Fri 10am–noon and 2–4pm.

Perth Art Gallery and Museum   This museum displays paintings illustrating the town's history along with archaeological artifacts. The growth of the whisky industry and its major role in the area's economy is particularly emphasized. You'll find everything from grandfather clocks to Georgian silver to even an effigy of a 29kg (65-lb.) salmon caught by some proud fisherman back in 1922. The most notable artworks are large Scottish landscapes by John Millais (1829–96). Horatio McCulloch (1805–67) was known as a specialist of Highland scenes, and his *Loch Katrine* (1866) is one of his finest works.

George St., at the intersection of Tay St. and Perth Bridge. ℰ **01738/632-488**. Free admission. Mon–Sat 10am–5pm.

Round House and Fergusson Gallery   If you're interested in Scottish art, head for the Fergusson Gallery, which displays some 6,000 works of Scottish artist J. D. Fergusson (1874–1961). Fergusson is acclaimed as one of the best watercolorists in the country, and his Scottish scenes are widely produced on postcards and calendars. In the paintings *Princess Street Gardens* and *The White Dress,* you can view the muted colors of his early portraits and landscapes. Later, as he was more inspired by Fauvism, his work became more vibrant and luminous, as evoked by *Cassis from the West* and *Sails at Royan.* His female nudes, however, always generate the most excitement, especially *Danu Mother of the Gods, The Parasol,* and *Bathers in Green. The Red Dress* (1950) is very evocative of Glasgow scenes.

Marshall Place. ℰ **01738/441-944**. Free admission. Mon–Sat 10am–5pm.

SHOPPING

Cairncross Ltd., 18 St. John's St. (ℰ **01738/624-367**), sells jewelry, both custom-made and from other manufacturers. The specialty is Scottish freshwater pearls. **Timothy Hardie,** 25 St. John's St. (ℰ **01738/633-127**), deals in antique jewelry and has a large selection of Victorian pieces. It also sells antique silver tea services. **Whispers of the Past,** 15 George St. (ℰ **01738/635-472**), offers an odd mix of items: jewelry, both new and antique, ranging from costume baubles to quality gold and silver pieces; china; pine furniture; and some linens.

C & C Proudfoot, Unit 104, 104 South St. (ℰ **01738/632-483**), is an eclectic shop whose merchandise includes leather jackets, hand-knitted Arran sweaters, Barbour waxed-cotton jackets, sheepskin jackets and rugs, and wool rugs, as well as a range of handbags, briefcases, scarves, and gloves.

Watson of Perth, 163–167 High St. (© **01738/639-861**), has been in business since 1900. It specializes in bone china produced by Royal Doulton, Wedgwood, and others; it also offers cut crystal from Edinburgh, Stuart, and Waterford.

Caithness Glass, Inveralmond Industrial Estate, on A9 (© **01738/637-373**), is a glass factory on the edge of Perth. Follow A9, going through the roundabout marked A9 NORTH to Inverness; the factory is in the industrial complex a short way past the roundabout. Its outlet sells paperweights, vases, and bowls, balanced with a range of Royal Doulton items. While here, you can watch the glassblowers at work.

Perthshire Shop, Lower City Mills, Mill Street (© **01738/627-958**), sells jams, mustards, and oatmeal along with items produced in the neighboring mills. On the shelves are wooden bowls, *spirtles* (wooden stirrers often used in making porridge), and Perthshire tartan scarves and ties, along with a large selection of cookbooks.

HITTING THE LINKS NEARBY

North of Perth is one of Scotland's acclaimed golf links, the 18-hole **Blairgowrie,** Golf Course Road, Rosemont, Blairgowrie (© **01250/872-622**), which includes 6,229 yards (5,668m) of playing area with a par of 72. This is a challenging course, with a rolling, wild layout of pine, birch, and fir; you might even spot a deer or two grazing on the course. The greens fees are £45 to £50 ($72–$80) for one round, £75 ($120) for the day, with even higher rates on weekends. There's a pro shop where you can rent clubs and trolleys; caddy service is £24 ($38), plus tip.

WHERE TO STAY

Dupplin Castle ★★ Only a 1-hour drive from Edinburgh, this modern, severely dignified mansion was built in 1968 by well-known architect Schomber Scott to replace the last of the three castles that had once risen proudly from the site. Surrounded by 12 hectares (30 acres) of forest and spectacular gardens (some of its specimens are 250 years old), the site is one of the most beautiful near Perth. Rooms are rented in a spirit of elegance and good manners, and the views from many of them overlook the valley of the River Earn. Meals are served at one large table, dinner-party style, but you must book 24 hours in advance. *Note:* Children under 12 can stay here only if you book the entire castle. Smoking is prohibited in guest rooms and in dining room.

Near Aberdalgie, Perth PH2 0PY. © **01738/623-224.** Fax 01738/444-140. www.dupplin.co.uk. 7 units. £120–£140 ($192–$224) double. Rates include breakfast. MC, V. From Perth, follow the main highway to Glasgow, turning left onto B9112 toward Aberdalgie and Forteviot. Pets welcome by prior arrangement. **Amenities:** Dining room; clay shooting. *In room:* coffeemaker, hair dryer.

Huntingtower Hotel ★ This late-Victorian country house is set on 1.4 hectares (3½ acres) of well-manicured gardens, with a modern wing of rooms added in 1998. Taste and concern went into the interior decoration. Rooms, which vary wildly in size, each have their specific charm. Seven offer spa baths. The cottage suites are in a renovated bungalow; each has twin beds and a sitting room.

The fine Scottish and Continental cuisine is reason enough to stay here. The elegant main restaurant serves nightly table d'hôte dinners.

Crieff Rd., Perth PH1 3JT. © **01738/583-771.** Fax 01738/583-777. www.huntingtowerhotel.co.uk 34 units. £94–£156 ($150–$250); from £105 ($168) cottage suite. Rates include Scottish breakfast. AE, DC, MC, V.

Drive 6km (3½ miles) west on A85. Free parking. Pets allowed. **Amenities:** Restaurant; bar; 24-hr. room service; laundry/dry cleaning service. *In room:* TV, minibar, coffeemaker, hair dryer.

Kinfauns Castle ★★★   When James Smith, the Scot who ran all of Asia's Hiltons, was told in the 1990s to ship out from his base in Hong Kong, he returned home with some of the Hilton's best furnishings. He installed them in this venerable 1822 castle, making for an unusual decorative wedding of Scotland and the Far East. Guests here stay in the lap of luxury on 11 hectares (26 acres) of forested lands and gardens close to the Highlands. The grandeur of the entrance hall sets the tone, holding the six tartans of the families who have inhabited the castle. The gallery continues the baronial theme, with a ceiling decorated with gold-leaf rosettes and an ornately carved fireplace. Of special interest is the Lady Gray lounge, which is unchanged since the castle was constructed; it contains the original marble fireplace and William Morris machine-printed wallpaper from 1910. The luxurious bedrooms are individually decorated in great style, with modern amenities such as marble bathrooms with phones. Many units have real log fireplaces and four-poster beds.

The Library Restaurant (see below) serves the finest food in the area. *Note:* Gentlemen are required to wear a jacket and tie in the lounge and dining room after 6pm; no jeans, denims, or T-shirts permitted.

Kinfauns (5km/3 miles east of Perth on A90), Perth PH2 7JZ. ℭ **01738/620-777.** Fax 01738/620-778. www.kinfaunscastle.co.uk. 16 units. £200 ($320) double; £280 ($448) junior suite; £320 ($512)) suite. Rates include Scottish breakfast. AE, DC, MC, V. Closed 3 weeks in Jan. No children under age 12 accepted in the hotel. Dogs accepted at the discretion of management, by prior arrangement only. **Amenities:** Restaurant; bar; concierge; room service (noon–9pm); laundry service. *In room:* TV, coffeemaker, minibar, hair dryer safe.

Parklands Hotel ★   This hotel near the rail station opened in 1991 and immediately became the most fashionable lodging within Perth itself. The classic Georgian town house was the former home of Perth's Lord Provost from 1867 to 1873. The spacious and beautifully decorated guest rooms, filled with wood paneling and cornices, overlook the South Inch Park. The beautiful Victorian conservatory is ideal for afternoon tea.

2 St. Leonard's Bank, Perth PH2 8EB. ℭ **01738/622-451.** Fax 01738/622-046. www.s-h-systems.co.uk/hotels/parkland.html. 14 units. £79–£115 ($126–$184) double. Rates include breakfast. AE, DC, MC, V. From the M90 (Edinburgh or Dundee) take junction 10. Take the right-hand fork signed for Perth. At the end of the road turn left at the traffic lights and follow the edge of South Inch Park. Parklands is the first building on the left-hand side. **Amenities:** Restaurant; bar; room service (9am–9pm); laundry/dry cleaning service. *In room:* TV, coffeemaker, hair dryer.

WHERE TO DINE

Keracher's Restaurant and Oyster Bar ★ SCOTTISH/SEAFOOD   For five generations, the Kerachers have been serving some of the finest seafood in Perth. Chef Andrew Keracher carries on the family tradition by using the freshest ingredients, which are cooked to order. Food is prepared with imagination and panache, but also with a healthy respect for the natural tastes and textures of the produce. Among the main courses on the extensive menu is a filet of Scottish salmon glazed with honey-mustard and served with a leek and vermouth cream sauce. For dessert, try the steamed ginger pudding with vanilla ice cream and lime anglais. The Oyster Bar has a retail counter where you can grab a quick, tasty range of Keracher products.

168 South St. (45 minutes from Edinburgh on the A90) ℭ **01738/449-777.** Reservations recommended. Main courses £8.90–£15.90 ($14–$25) ; set menus £9.90 ($16) for 2 courses, £12.90 ($21) for 3 courses. MC, V. Tues–Sat noon–2:30pm and 6–10pm. Closed 2 weeks in Jan.

Let's Eat ✰ BRITISH/INTERNATIONAL   The most visually striking, and most appealing, restaurant in Perth occupies an 1822 theater and intersperses its tables amid soaring white columns. There's a particularly cozy lounge, site of a log-burning stove and comfy sofas, where you might want a drink before your meal. Menu items, which change frequently, are among the most thoughtful and sophisticated in town. They might include a gratin of goat cheese studded with roasted peppers and served with rocket salad, new potatoes, and chutney; grilled brochettes of monkfish with king prawns, rice, and salad; handmade black puddings served with "smash" (mashed potatoes), applesauce, and onion gravy; and risotto studded with wild mushrooms. Be careful not to confuse this restaurant with its less grand, less expensive sibling, Let's Eat Again.

77–79 Kinnoull St. (3 blocks north of High St.). (✆ **01738/643-377**. Reservations recommended. Lunch main courses £8.95–£10.50 ($14–$17); dinner main courses £9.75–£16.50 ($16–$26). AE, MC, V. Tues–Sat noon–2pm and 6:30–9:45pm.

The Library Restaurant ✰✰ SCOTTISH   If you're in the mood to dine in a grand castle with equally grand food and service, head here. Using the costliest of Scottish ingredients, all deftly handled, chef Jeremy Brazelle has established a reputation for excellence. The best of venison, Angus beef, and salmon are offered along with one of the finest wine lists in the area. A sample meal might include pumpkin-and-leek soup followed by filet of halibut with buttered noodles, stir-fried vegetables, and chili and soy dressing. You might also try roast rump of black-faced lamb with fresh vegetables cooked in the Provençal style with virgin olive oil and garlic.

In Kinfauns Castle (see "Where to Stay" above). (✆ **01738/620-777**. Reservations required. Jacket and tie required for men. Fixed-price 3-course lunch £20.75–£22.50 ($33–$36); fixed-price dinner £34 ($54) for 3 courses, £37.50 ($60) for 5 courses. AE, MC, V. Daily noon–1:30pm and 7–8:30pm. Closed 3 weeks in Jan.

PERTH AFTER DARK

The Victorian **Perth Repertory Theatre,** 185 High St. (✆ **01738/621-031**), hosts performances of plays and musicals between mid-September and May. From the end of May to early June, it's also a venue for some of the events of the Perth Festival of the Arts. The box office is open Monday through Saturday from 10am to 7:30pm. Tickets cost £6.50 to £25 ($10–$40).

Perth City Hall, King Edward Street (✆ **01738/475-200**), is a year-round venue for musical performances and dances; many local organizations (including the Freemasons, the Royal Geographical Society, churches, and various amateur societies) book events here year after year. Entertainment is usually along the lines of a classical concert or a Highland ball.

A SIDE TRIP TO SCONE

Old Scone, 3km (2 miles) from Perth on the River Tay, was the ancient capital of the Picts. The early Scottish monarchs were enthroned here on a lump of sandstone called the "Stone of Destiny." In 1296, Edward I, the "Hammer of the Scots," moved the stone to Westminster Abbey, and for hundreds of years it rested under the chair on which British monarchs were crowned. The Scots have always bitterly resented this theft, and at last, it has been returned to Scotland, to find a permanent home in Edinburgh Castle, where it can be viewed by the public.

The seat of the earls of Mansfield and birthplace of David Douglas (of fir-tree fame), **Scone Palace** ✰✰, along A93 (✆ **01738/552-300**), was largely rebuilt in 1802, incorporating the old palace of 1580. Inside is an impressive collection of French furniture, china, ivories, and 16th-century needlework, including bed hangings executed by Mary Queen of Scots. A fine collection of rare conifers is found on the grounds in the Pinetum. Rhododendrons and azaleas grow profusely in the gardens and woodlands around the palace. To reach the palace, head northeast of Perth on A93. The site is open April 1 to October 31 only, daily from 9:30am to 5pm. Admission is £6.35 ($10) for adults, £5.50 ($8.80) seniors, £3.75 ($6) for children age 16 years old and under, including entrance to both house and grounds. Admission to the grounds only is £3.25 ($5.20) for adults and £1.80 ($2.90) for children.

WHERE TO STAY & DINE

Murrayshall House Hotel & Golf Courses ★★★   This elegant country-house hotel, set on 122 hectares (300 acres) of parkland, was completely refurbished in 1987 and reopened as one of the showpieces of Perthshire. Golfers and their families flock here for the excellent, challenging courses. The hotel's public rooms and guest rooms are all traditionally styled, but bedrooms vary in size and comfort. The superior accommodations are the suites and executive rooms, which have the best amenities and views. The less desired standard rooms are also comfortable but lack the character of the others. *Note:* On a windy night in Scotland there is no better place to be than the well-stocked bar with its log fire.

New Scone, Perthshire PH2 7PH. © **01738/551-171.** Fax 01738/552-595. www.murrayshall.com. 41 units. £150–£170 ($240–$272) double; from £180–£200 ($288–$320) suite; lodge £150 ($240). Rates include Scottish breakfast. AE, DC, MC, V. Take A94 2.5km (1½ miles) east of New Scone. **Amenities:** Restaurant; 2 bars; 2 golf courses; tennis courts; exercise room; Jacuzzi; room service (6:30am–10:30pm); babysitting; laundry/dry cleaning service; steam room. *In room:* TV, dataport, hair dryer.

3 Gleneagles: Hitting the Links

90km (56 miles) NE of the Glasgow Airport, 81km (50 miles) NW of the Edinburgh Airport

This famous golfing center and sports complex is on a moor between Strathearn and Strath Allan. Gleneagles has four **18-hole golf courses:** King's Course, the longest one; Queen's Course, next in length; Prince's Course, shortest of all; and Glendevon, the newest of the quartet, built in 1980. They're among the best in Scotland, and the sports complex is one of the best-equipped in Europe.

The center gets its name from the Gaelic *Gleann-an-Eaglias,* meaning "glen of the church."

ESSENTIALS

GETTING THERE   By Train   The 15-minute ride from Perth costs £4 ($6.40). The trip takes 1 hour and 25 minutes from Edinburgh and costs £8.90 ($14). For information, call © **08457/484-950.**

By Bus   The only service departs from Glasgow. The trip takes slightly more than an hour and costs £6 ($9.60). For information and schedules, call © **01738/ 26847.**

By Car   Gleneagles is on A9, about halfway between Perth and Stirling, a short distance from the village of Auchterarder. It lies 88km (55 miles) from Edinburgh and 72km (45 miles) from Glasgow.

VISITOR INFORMATION   The year-round tourist center is at 90 High St., Auchterarder (© **01764/663-450**). It's open November to March Monday to Friday from 10am to 2pm, Saturday from 11am to 3pm; April to June Monday to Saturday from 9:30am to 5:30pm, Sunday from 11am to 4pm; July and

August Monday to Saturday from 9am to 7pm, Sunday from 11am to 6pm, and September and October Monday to Saturday from 9:30am to 5:30pm, Sunday from 11am to 4pm.

WHERE TO STAY & DINE

The Gleneagles Hotel ✦✦✦   Britain's greatest golf hotel stands on its own 336-hectare (830-acre) estate. When it was built in isolated grandeur in 1924, it was Scotland's only government-rated five-star hotel. It is a true resort and kept up with the times by offering spa treatments as well as many other activities. Public rooms are classical, with pilasters and pillars. The guest rooms vary greatly in size. The best and most spacious choices are in the 60 to 90 block series; they have recently been refurbished. The less desirable rooms are called courtyard units; these are a bit small and equipped with shower-only bathrooms. Linked to the rest of the hotel through a glass walkway, Braid House, which opened in the autumn of 2002, added another 59 deluxe rooms to the existing property. Braid House guests have separate check-in facilities and private access.

In yet another development, Gleneagles has lured Andrew Fairlie, Michelin-star winning chef of Glasgow's One Devonshire Gardens, to open a new restaurant on the grounds. Just one of his signature dishes is reason enough to go here—smoked lobster delicately infused from lobster shells slow-smoked over oak chips taken from malt whisky barrels.

Auchterarder PH3 1NF. ✆ **01764/662-231.** Fax 01764/662-134. www.gleneagles.com. 270 units. £320–£445 ($512–$712) double; from £740 ($1,184) suite. Rates include Scottish breakfast. AE, DC, MC, V. Free parking. Take A9 2.5km (1½ miles) southwest of Auchterarder. **Amenities:** 4 restaurants; 4 bars; indoor heated pool; outdoor hot pool; lap pool; 3 golf courses; tennis court; health club; spa; Jacuzzi; sauna; complimentary bike use; concierge; salon; 24-hr. room service; massage; babysitting; laundry/dry cleaning service; equestrian center; falconry school; hunting and fishing excursions; squash court; Turkish bath. *In room:* TV/w Internet access (some w/VCR and/or DVD player), dataport, minibar, coffeemaker, hair dryer, iron/ironing board, safe, trouser press.

4 Crieff ✦ & Drummond Castle Gardens ✦

29km (18 miles) W of Perth, 97km (60 miles) NW of Edinburgh, 81km (50 miles) NE of Glasgow

From Perth, head west on A85 for 29km (18 miles) to Crieff. At the edge of the Perthshire Highlands, with good fishing and golf, Crieff makes a pleasant stopover. This small burgh was the seat of the court of the earls of Strathearn until 1747, and the gallows in its marketplace were once used to execute Highland cattle rustlers.

You can take a "day trail" into **Strathearn,** the valley of the River Earn, the very center of Scotland. Here highland mountains meet gentle Lowland slopes, and moorland mingles with rich green pastures. North of Crieff, the road to Aberfeldy passes through the narrow pass of the **Sma' Glen,** a famous spot of beauty, with hills rising on either side to 600m (2,000 ft.).

ESSENTIALS

GETTING THERE   By Train   There's no direct service. The nearest rail stations are at Gleneagles, 14km (9 miles) away, and at Perth, 29km (18 miles) away. Call ✆ **08457/484-950** for information and schedules.

By Bus   Once you arrive in Perth, you'll find regular connecting bus service hourly during the day. For information and schedules, call **Stagecoach** at ✆ **01738/629-339.** The bus service from Gleneagles is too poor to recommend.

By Taxi   A taxi from Gleneagles will cost from £12 to £15 ($19–$24).

VISITOR INFORMATION   The year-round **tourist information office** is in the Town Hall on High Street (© **01764/652-578**). It's open November to March, Monday to Friday from 9:30am to 5pm, Saturday from 10am to 2pm; April to June, Monday to Saturday from 9:30am to 5:30pm, Sunday from 11am to 4pm; July and August, Monday to Saturday from 9am to 7pm, Sunday from 11am to 6pm, and September and October, Monday to Saturday from 9:30am to 5:30pm, Sunday from 11am to 4pm.

EXPLORING THE AREA

Drummond Castle Gardens 🎯   The gardens of Drummond Castle, first laid out in the early-17th century by John Drummond, second earl of Perth, are among the finest formal gardens in Europe. There's a panoramic view from the upper terrace, overlooking an example of an early Victorian parterre in the form of St. Andrew's Cross. The multifaceted sundial by John Mylne, master mason to Charles I, has been the centerpiece since 1630.

Grimsthorpe, Crieff. © **01764/681-257.** Admission £3.50 ($5.60) adults, £2.50 ($4) seniors, £1.50 ($2.40) children. May–Oct daily 2–6pm; Easter weekend 2–6pm. Closed Nov–Apr. Take A822 for 5km (3 miles) south of Crieff.

The Glenturret Distillery Ltd.   Scotland's oldest distillery, Glenturret was established in 1775 on the banks of the River Turret. Visitors can see the milling of malt, mashing, fermentation, distillation, and cask filling, followed by a free "wee dram" dispensed at the end of the tour. Guided tours take about 25 minutes and leave at frequent intervals—sometimes as often as every 10 minutes when there's a demand for it. This can be followed or preceded by a 20-minute video, *The Water of Life,* that's presented adjacent to a small museum devoted to the implements of the whisky trade.

The Hosh, Hwy. A85, Glenturret. © **01764/656-565.** Guided tours £6 ($9.60), £5 ($8) seniors, £3 ($4.80) children age 12–17, free for children age 11 and under. May–June daily 9am–6pm; July–Aug daily 9am–6:30pm; Sept–Dec daily 9am–6pm. Closed Jan–Apr. Take A85 toward Comrie; 1.2km (³/₄ mile) from Crieff, turn right at the crossroads; the distillery is .5km (¹/₄ mile) up the road.

WHERE TO STAY

Murraypark Hotel   This 19th-century stone-fronted house lies in a residential neighborhood about a 10-minute walk from Crieff's center and close to a golf course. In 1993, a new wing was opened, enlarging the public areas and the number of well-furnished rooms. The property was purchased by new owners in 1999 and has been considerably upgraded, especially its mattresses and the neatly maintained bathrooms. Bedrooms in this former sea captain's house vary in size and shape, but most open onto views. Although rooms in the new wing are more comfortable, they are hardly as evocative; we still prefer the older wing's traditional Victorian aura.

The hotel's excellent restaurant serves traditional Scottish cuisine in a candle-lit dining room.

Connaught Terrace, Crieff PH7 3DJ. © **01764/653-731.** Fax 01764/655-311. www.murraypark.com 19 units. £65–£80 ($104–$128) double or suite. Rates include Scottish breakfast. AE, DC, MC, V. Free parking. Dogs welcome by arrangement. A 10-min. walk from the center of Crieff; the hotel lies northwest of Perth Street. **Amenities:** Restaurant; bar; babysitting. *In room:* TV, coffeemaker, hair dryer, trouser press.

WHERE TO DINE

The Bank MODERN SCOTTISH   This dignified red-sandstone building was constructed in 1901 as a branch of the British Linen Bank, now part of the Bank of Scotland. Today, it contains one of the most appealing restaurants in town, thanks to the superb cuisine, a hardworking staff, and a decor of mostly original paneling, an ornate plaster ceiling, and a huge arched window. Menu items may include wild mushroom risotto with truffle oil and cheddar cheese from the Isle of Mull; prime rib of Scottish beef with potatoes and red-wine sauce; and charcoal-grilled salmon with crayfish, asparagus, and shellfish-studded saffron sauce.

32 High St. (lies right on the main street in the exact center of town). © **01764/656-575.** Reservations recommended. Main courses £13.50–£15.50 ($22–$25). AE, DC, MC, V. Tues–Sun noon–2:30pm; Tues–Sat 7–10pm (Aug, also Sun 7–10pm).

5 Dunkeld ⭑

93km (58 miles) N of Edinburgh, 23km (14 miles) N of Perth, 158km (98 miles) SW of Aberdeen

Dunkeld lies in a thickly wooded valley of the Tay River at the edge of the Perthshire Highlands. Once a major ecclesiastical center, it's one of the seats of ancient Scottish history and was an important center of the Celtic church. It's an attractively restored town that invites exploration on foot.

The surrounding countryside is beautiful, and you can take great walks and day hikes that stretch out on both sides of the River Tay going from Dunkeld to Birnam. In all, there are 58km (36 miles) of paths that have been joined to create a network of circular routes. Pick up maps and detailed descriptions from the tourist office and set out on a day's adventure, armed with the makings of a picnic, of course.

ESSENTIALS

GETTING THERE **By Train** Trains from Perth arrive every 2 hours and cost £6.20 ($9.90). Travel time by train is 1½ hours. Call © **0345/484-950** for information and schedules.

By Bus Pitlochry-bound buses leaving from Perth make a stopover in Dunkeld, letting you off at the Dunkeld Car Park, which is at the train station (trip time: 50 minutes). The cost is £3.75 ($6). Contact **Stagecoach** at © **01738/629-339.**

By Car From Aberfeldy, take A827 east until you reach the junction of A9 heading south to Dunkeld.

VISITOR INFORMATION A **tourist information office** is at The Cross (© **01350/727-688**). It's open April to June, Monday to Saturday from 9:30am to 5:30pm and Sunday from 11am to 4pm; July 1 to September 8, Monday to Saturday from 9:30am to 6:30pm and Sunday from 11am to 5pm; September 9 to October 27, Monday to Saturday from 9:30am to 5:30pm and Sunday from 11am to 4pm; October 28 to December, Monday to Saturday from 9:30am to 5:30pm (closed Jan–Mar).

EXPLORING THE AREA

Founded in A.D. 815, **Dunkeld Cathedral** ⭑ was converted from a church to a cathedral in 1127 by David I. It stands on Cathedral Street in a scenic setting along the River Tay. The cathedral was first restored in 1815, and traces of the 12th-century structure remain today. Admission is free, and the cathedral is open May to September Monday to Saturday from 9:30am to 6:30pm, Sunday from 2 to 6:30pm; October to April, Monday to Saturday from 9:30am to 4pm.

The National Trust for Scotland has restored many of the old houses and shops around the marketplace and cathedral. The trust owns 20 houses on **High**

Street and Cathedral Street as well. Many of them were constructed in the late 17th century after the rebuilding of the town following the Battle of Dunkeld. The Trust runs the Ell Shop, The Cross (© 01350/727-460), which specializes in Scottish handicrafts. Easter weekend to December 24, it's open Monday through Saturday from 10am to 5:30pm.

Shakespeare fans may want to seek out the oak and sycamore in front of the destroyed Birnam House, 1.6km (1 mile) south. This was believed to be a remnant of the Birnam Wood in *Macbeth;* you may recall, "Macbeth shall never vanquished be until great Birnam Wood to high Dunsinane Hill shall come against him."

The Hermitage, off A9 about 3km (2 miles) west of Dunkeld, was called a folly when it was built in 1758 above the wooded gorge of the River Braan. Today, it makes for one of the most scenic woodland walks in the area.

Our favorite spot in the area is the Loch of Lowes Wildlife Reserve 𝒜 (© 01350/727-337), 3km (2 miles) from the center of town, along A923 heading northeast. It can be accessed from the south shore, where there's an observation lookout and a visitor center. Filled with rich flora and fauna, the 99-hectare (245-acre) reserve takes in the freshwater lake that's home to rare ospreys. Although common in the United States, these large brown-and-white sea eagles are on the endangered-species list in Britain, and bird-watchers from all over the country come here to observe them.

PLAYING GOLF

Dunkeld & Birnam, at Dunkeld (© 01350/727-524), is touted as the best in the area, and offers sweeping views of the surrounding environs. Greens fees: Monday through Friday £20 ($32) for 18 holes; Saturday and Sunday £25 ($40) for 18 holes. There are no electric carts; pull carts are available for £4 ($6.40) per round. Hours are daily 7am to 11pm April to September. October to March, greens fees are reduced and hours are daily from 8am to 4pm. There's no official dress code, although if the starter feels you are not dressed "appropriately" you will be asked to "smarten up" the next time you play the course. Jeans are not acceptable.

WHERE TO STAY & DINE

Birnam House Hotel This mock-medieval building was erected in 1863 in the baronial style as a vacation home for a wealthy industrialist. In the 1980s and 1990s, many updates were made, stripping the interior of at least some of its ornate detail. What you'll find today is a cozy set of high-ceilinged guest rooms, each uniquely decorated. A bar serves affordable lunches, while formal dinners are served nightly in the restaurant. A 5-minute walk away is the last tree remaining from Birnam Wood, so feared by Macbeth.

Perth Rd., Birnam, Dunkeld PH8 0BQ. © 01350/727-462. Fax 01350/728-979. www.countryhotels.net/birnam. 30 units. £84–£120 ($134–$192) double. Rates include breakfast. AE, DC, MC, V. From Dunkeld, drive south across the Dunkeld Bridge; you'll then see Perth Rd. and the hotel. Amenities: Restaurant; bar. *In room:* TV, coffeemaker.

Hilton Dunkeld House Hotel 𝒜𝒜 This hotel offers the quiet dignity of a Scottish country house and is ranked as one of the leading leisure and sports hotels in the area. On the banks of the Tay, the surrounding grounds—113 hectares (280 acres) in all—make for a parklike setting. The house is beautifully kept, and rooms come in a wide range of sizes, styles, and furnishings. In 1999, an annex was converted into an extra wing offering another nine rooms. Salmon and trout fishing are possible right on the grounds, as are an array of other outdoor activities.

Dunkeld PH8 0HX. © **01350/727-771.** Fax 01350/728-924. www.hiltondunkeldhouse.co.uk. 96 units. £199–£234 ($318–$374) double; £249–£269 ($398–$430) suite. Rates include Scottish breakfast. AE, DC, MC, V. Free Parking. Pets in kennels accepted. Follow Atholl Street out of town; the hotel is signposted. **Amenities:** Restaurant; bar; indoor heated pool; putting green; tennis courts; health club; sauna; business center; salon; 24-hr. room service; massage; babysitting; laundry/dry cleaning service; fishing; skeet/trap-shooting; steam room. *In room:* TV, dataport, minibar, hair dryer, trouser press.

Kinnaird Estate ★★★ This small hotel of great charm and comfort is the best hotel in Scotland. All the pursuits that intrigued the Edwardian gentleman, including Edward VII, can be pursued on this mansion's 3,600-hectare (9,000-acre) estate, including salmon and trout fishing on the River Tay, shooting clays, and walks through gorse-riddled moors. This place is so special that you'll find a bedside decanter of "Highland Heater," a wonderful elixir of whisky (of course), fresh herbs, and spices. There's a house party feeling here, and indeed Kinnaird looks and feels like a perfectly restored private mansion. Built in 1770 as a hunting lodge, the house has been restored to its previous grandeur. All the beautifully furnished rooms have king-size beds, full private bathrooms, and views. Some overlook the valley of the River Tay; others open onto gardens and woodlands. There are eight cottages on the estate, two of which sleep eight and the others four.

Kinnaird, Kinnaird Estate, Dunkeld PH8 0LB. © **01796/482-440.** Fax 01796/482-289. www.kinnairdestate. com. 9 units and 8 estate cottages. £375–£400 ($600–$640) double; £525 ($840) suite; £335–£630 ($536–$1,008) estate cottages. Double and suite rates include dinner and Scottish breakfast; meals are not included in the cottage rates. AE, MC, V. Free parking. No children under age 12 accepted in the hotel, but they may stay in the cottages. Heated kennels are available on the grounds for pets. From Perth take the A9 north (signposted Inverness) and travel for 15 miles (24 km) to Dunkeld. Do not exit Dunkeld, continue on for another 2 miles (3.2km). Turn left on to the B898 which is signposted for Dalguise, Kinnaird, and Balnagard. Follow this road for 4.5 miles and the main gates of Kinnaird will be on your right hand side. **Amenities:** Restaurant; bar; tennis court; salon; limited room service; laundry/dry cleaning service. *In room:* TV, dataport, hair dryer.

6 Pitlochry ★

114km (71 miles) NW of Edinburgh, 44km (27 miles) NW of Perth, 24km (15 miles) N of Dunkeld

A popular resort, Pitlochry is a good base for touring the Valley of the Tummel. Ever since Queen Victoria declared it one of the finest resorts in Europe, it has drawn the hordes. It's also home to the renowned **Pitlochry Festival Theatre,** Scotland's theater in the hills.

Pitlochry doesn't exist just to entertain visitors, although it would appear that way in summer—it also produces scotch whisky. And it's a good overnight stop between Edinburgh and Inverness, 137km (85 miles) north. You can spend a very busy day in town, visiting its famous distilleries, seeing its dam and fish ladder, and budgeting some time for the beauty spots in the environs, especially **Loch Rannoch** and the **Pass of Killiecrankie,** both ideal for walks. At Blair Atholl stands one of the most highly visited and intriguing castles in the country, **Blair Castle.**

ESSENTIALS

GETTING THERE Five **trains** (© **08457/484-950**) per day arrive from Edinburgh, and an additional three from Glasgow (trip time from each: 2 hours). A one-way fare is £21 ($34) from either city. **Buses** arrive hourly from Perth. The one-way fare is £4 ($6.40). Contact **Stagecoach** (© **01738/629-339**) for schedules. If you're **driving** from Perth, continue northwest along A9.

VISITOR INFORMATION The **tourist office** is at 22 Atholl Rd. (© **01796/472-215**). From June to September, it's open daily from 9am to 8pm; May and October, hours are daily from 9am to 6pm; and November to April, hours are Monday through Friday from 9am to 5pm and Saturday from 10am to 3pm.

EXPLORING THE AREA

Pitlochry Dam was created because a power station was needed, but in effect the engineers created a new loch. The famous **salmon ladder** was built to help the struggling salmon upstream. An underwater portion of the ladder has been enclosed in glass to give sightseers a fascinating look. An exhibition (© **01796/473-152**) is open from Easter to the last Sunday in October, daily from 10am to 5:30pm; it costs £2 ($3.20) for adults, £1.20 ($1.90) for seniors, and £1 ($1.60) for children.

There are terrific scenic hikes along the **Linn of Tummel,** with several signposted trails going along the river and into the forest directly to the north of the center. Just north of here you come to the stunning **Pass of Killiecrankie** ❀. If you're driving, follow A9 north. The national trust has established the **Killiecrankie Visitor Centre** (© **01796/473-233**) here, open April to October daily from 10am to 5:30pm. You can learn about a famous battle that occurred here during the 1689 Jacobite rebellion. John Graham of Cleverhouse (1649–89) rallied the mainly Highlander Jacobite army to meet government troops. Graham was killed, and the cause of Scottish independence soon fizzled.

B8019 leads to **Loch Rannoch,** almost 16km (10 miles) long and 1.2km (¾ mile) wide. Many consider this to be the most beautiful lake in the Highlands. The setting so impressed Robert Louis Stevenson, he wrote about it in *Kidnapped* (1886): "Much of it was red with heather, much of the rest broken up with bogs and hags and peaty pools." To see this desolate but awesomely beautiful spot, follow B8019 to the Linn of Tummel north of Pitlochry, venturing onto B846 at the Bridge of Tummel.

Blair Castle ❀ Home of the dukes of Atholl, this is one of the great historic castles of Scotland. Dating from 1269, it has seen many alterations before it was finally turned into a Georgian mansion. Plan to spend about 2 hours viewing the palace's antiques, 18th-century interiors, and paintings, along with an outstanding arms, armor, and porcelain collection. After viewing the castle, you can stroll through the Victorian walled garden and take a long walk in the parklands.

Blair Atholl. © **01796/481-207.** Admission £6.70 ($11) adults, £5.70 ($9.10) seniors, £4.20 ($6.70) children. Apr to late Oct daily 9:30am–4:30pm. Closed Nov–Mar. From the town center, follow A9 to Blair Atholl, where you'll see signs.

⌒ *Fun Fact* **The Wee-est of Wee Drams**

Stop in at **Edradour Distillery,** Scotland's smallest distillery, for a complimentary "wee dram" and a tour of this picturesque facility. The gift shop sells Edradour single malts, as well as various blends that contain the whisky. March through October tours are available 9:30am to 5pm Monday to Saturday and noon to 5pm Sunday; November to mid-December tours are available Monday to Saturday 10am to 4pm. The distillery is closed for two weeks over Christmas and New Year. Take A924 3km (2 miles) east toward Braemar.

WHERE TO STAY

East Haugh House (see "Where to Dine," below) also rents rooms.

Acarsaid Hotel   This graceful but solid-looking stone house dates from 1880, when it was the home of the countess of Kilbride. Greatly expanded, the hotel contains cozy guest rooms, with contemporary furnishings and immaculately kept, shower-only bathrooms. The bar serves snacks at lunch (for guests only), while the more elaborate restaurant offers fixed-price dinners. Menu items focus on fresh ingredients, most of them Scottish.

8 Atholl Rd., Pitlochry PH16 5BX. (✆) **01796/472-389.** Fax 01796/473-952. www.acarsaidhotel.com. 20 units. £68–£74 ($109–$118) double. Rates include breakfast. MC, V. Free parking. Small dogs accepted by prior arrangement. **Amenities:** Restaurant; bar; access to nearby health club; business services; laundry service. *In room:* TV, coffeemaker, hair dryer.

Balrobin   This traditional Scottish country house opens onto views of the Perthshire Hills and the Tummel Valley. Originally an 1889 "holiday cottage" used for fishing and shooting holidays, it's now a government-rated two-star hotel with average-size guest rooms furnished in simple provincial style (with shower-only bathrooms). Added to the "auld hoose" were a west and east wing in keeping with the stone construction. Affordable dinners are served nightly, and there's a guests-only bar and country lounge. Smoking is prohibited throughout the premises.

Higher Oakfield, Pitlochry PH16 5HT. (✆) **01796/472-901.** Fax 01796/474-200. www.balrobin.co.uk. 14 units. £67–£81 ($107–$130) double. Rates include Scottish breakfast. MC, V. Closed Mid-Oct to Apr 1. **Amenities:** Restaurant; bar. *In room:* TV, coffeemaker, hair dryer, no phone.

The Green Park Hotel   The white-painted mansion with carved eaves is set against a backdrop of woodland about 1km (½ mile) from the center. Guest rooms vary in style and size; the half dozen or so rooms in the garden wing enjoy a view of nearby Loch Faskally. Some rooms contain showers only.

Drinks are available in a lounge overlooking the water. Popular during festival season, the dining room serves dinner nightly, with many traditional Scottish dishes. *Note:* Smoking is prohibited throughout the premises.

Clunie Bridge Rd., Pitlochry PH16 5JY. (✆) **01796/473-248.** Fax 01796/473-520. www.thegreenpark.co.uk. 39 units. £92–£142 ($147–$227) double. Rates include half-board. MC, V. Pets are welcome by prior arrangement. Signposted from A9 north of Pitlochry. **Amenities:** Restaurant; bar. *In room:* TV, coffeemaker, hair dryer, trouser press.

Killiecrankie Hotel 🖈   This typically Scottish country house, built in 1840 for the local church minister, is surrounded by lawns and woodlands, including a herbaceous border garden. The guest rooms are individually decorated in subtle tones, and most of the bathrooms contain combination shower and tub. The walls are a foot thick, so light sleepers can rest in peace. The restaurant serves high-priced dinners that feature fresh produce and seasonal meat, fish, and game.

A924, Killiecrankie PH16 5LG. (✆) **01796/473-220.** Fax 01796/472-451. www.killiecrankiehotel.co.uk. 10 units. £158–£218 ($253–$349) double. Rates include half-board. MC, V. Free parking. Signposted from A9 north of Pitlochry. Dogs welcome. **Amenities:** Restaurant; bar; room service (8:30am–9:30pm). *In room:* TV coffeemaker, hair dryer.

Knockendarroch House 🖈 *Finds*   Built in 1880, this award-winning Victorian mansion opens onto panoramic views of the Tummel Valley set amidst lovely gardens. The bedrooms, which vary in size and style, are attractively decorated in cool colors. The cozy attic units have balconies overlooking the rooftops of Pitlochry. Guests are offered a free glass of sherry before dinner, which might be wild venison chops in red wine and juniper berry jus, or mushroom and nut roast on the chiffonade of cabbage in rich tomato and sherry sauce. The food is of the finest quality, and prices are more moderate than might be expected. Overall, the warmth of the staff and the evocative atmosphere of the mansion make it a place worth visiting. *Note:* This is a nonsmoking hotel.

Higher Oakfield, Pitlochry PH16 5HT. ℰ **01796/473-473.** Fax 01796/474-068. www.knockendarroch.co.uk. 12 units. £128 ($205) double. Rates include breakfast and dinner. MC, V. Closed Nov–Mar. Turn off A9 going north at Pıtlochry sign. After rail bridge, take 1st right, then 2nd left. **Amenities:** Restaurant; bar; laundry service. *In room:* TV, coffeemaker, hair dryer.

Pine Trees Hotel ⭐   This 19th century country house is a 15-minute walk from the town center and 5 minutes from the golf course that serves as home of the Highland Open Championships. The family-run Pine Trees has spacious public rooms, an atmosphere of warmth, and a reputation for good food and wine. The guest rooms are in either the main house or a 1970s annex designed to blend into the period of the central structure. Bar lunches and full lunch and dinner menus are offered, with fresh and smoked salmon always featured. trout and salmon fishing can usually be arranged.

Strathview Terrace, Pitlochry PH16 5QR. ℰ **01796/472-121.** Fax 01796/472-460. www.pinetreeshotel.co.uk. 20 units. £104–£148 ($166–$237) double. Rates include Scottish breakfast. AE, MC, V. Turn right up Larchwood Rd., below the golf course on the north side of Pitlochry. **Amenities:** Restaurant; bar; dry cleaning. *In room:* TV, coffeemaker, hair dryer.

WHERE TO DINE

East Haugh House ⭐ MODERN BRITISH   Although it contains 13 comfortable guest rooms, East Haugh House is best known for its well-prepared cuisine. In a Teutonic-looking granite house commissioned in the 1600s by the duke of Atholl for one of his tenant farmers, it offers a menu that relies exclusively on fresh Scottish ingredients. Meals in the cozy bar may include mixed grills, steaks, and haggis. The cuisine in the elegant restaurant is more adventurous, featuring such dishes as zucchini flowers stuffed with wild-mushroom duxelles, terrine of local pigeon with orange salad and *mange tout* (a kind of bean), and many variations of salmon.

The spacious guest rooms will make you think you're staying in a country mansion. Including a Scottish breakfast, doubles run £90 to £168 ($144–$269).

Old Perth Rd., East Haugh, Pitlochry PH16 5JS. ℰ **01796/473-121.** Fax 01796/472-473. www.easthaugh. co.uk. Reservations recommended. Table d'hôte dinner £27.95 ($45); bar platters £1.75–£15 ($2.80–$24). MC, V. Restaurant daily 7–9pm; bar daily noon–2:30pm and 6–9pm. Drive 1.6km (1 mile) south of Pitlochry on A9 toward Inverness; it's across the road from the Tummel River.

PITLOCHRY AFTER DARK

The town is famous for its **Pitlochry Festival Theatre** (ℰ **01796/484-626**). Founded in 1951, it draws people from all over the world to its repertory of plays, concerts, and varying art exhibits, presented from April 30 to October 9. The theater complex opened in 1981 on the banks of the River Tummel near the dam and fish ladder, with a parking area; a restaurant serving coffee, lunch, and dinner; and other facilities for visitors. Tickets for plays and concerts are £16 to £20 ($26–$32).

For the area's best pub, head to the peaceful grounds of the **Killiecrankie Hotel,** signposted from A9 north of Pitlochry (ℰ **01796/473-220**). It serves 20 malt whiskies as well as reasonably priced great food. Upholstered chairs, wildlife paintings, and plants and flowers make for an inviting atmosphere.

7 Dundee & Glamis Castle

102km (63 miles) N of Edinburgh, 108km (67 miles) SW of Aberdeen, 36km (22 miles) NE of Perth, 134km (83 miles) NE of Glasgow

The old seaport of Dundee on the north shore of the Firth of Tay, the fourth-largest city in Scotland, is now an industrial city. When steamers took over the whaling industry from sailing vessels, Dundee took the lead as home port for the ships from the 1860s until World War I. Long known for its jute and flax operations, Dundee is linked with the production of rich Dundee fruitcakes and Dundee marmalades and jams.

Spanning the Firth of Tay is the **Tay Railway Bridge,** opened in 1888. Constructed over the tidal estuary, the bridge is 3km (2 miles) long, one of the longest in Europe. There's also a road bridge 2km (1¼ miles) long, with four traffic lanes and a walkway in the center.

Dundee has only minor attractions itself, but it's a base for exploring Glamis Castle (one of the most famous in Scotland) and the little town of Kirriemuir, which Sir James M. Barrie, author of *Peter Pan,* disguised in fiction as the Thrums. Dundee also makes a good base for those who want to play at one of Scotland's most famous golf courses, Carnoustie.

ESSENTIALS

GETTING THERE   **By Train**   ScotRail offers frequent service between Perth, Dundee, and Aberdeen. One-way fare from Perth to Dundee is £5 ($8); from Aberdeen, £19.50 ($31). Phone ℂ **08457/484-950** for schedules and departure times.

By Bus   CityLink buses offer frequent bus service from Edinburgh and Glasgow. Call ℂ **0990/505-050** for information.

By Car   The fastest way to reach Dundee is to cut south back to Perth along A9 and link up with A972 going east.

VISITOR INFORMATION   The **tourist information office** is at 21 Castle St. (ℂ **01382/527-527**). Hours are April to September, Monday to Saturday from 9am to 6pm, Sunday from 10am to 4pm; October to March, Monday to Saturday from 9am to 5pm.

EXPLORING THE AREA

For a panoramic view of Dundee, the Tay Bridge across to Fife, and the mountains to the north, go to **Dundee Law,** a 174m (572-ft.) hill 1.6km (1 mile) north of the city. The hill is an ancient volcanic plug.

Broughty Castle   This 15th-century estuary fort is 6.5km (4 miles) east of the city center at Broughty Ferry, a fishing village that was the terminus for ferries crossing the Firth of Tay until the bridges were built. Besieged by the English in the 16th century and attacked by Cromwell's army under General Monk in the 17th, it was restored in 1861 as part of Britain's coastal defenses. The museum has displays on local history, arms and armor, seashore life, and Dundee's whaling story. The observation area at the top of the castle provides fine views of the Tay estuary and northeast Fife.

Castle Green, Broughty Ferry. ℂ **01382/436-916.** Free admission. July–Sept Mon 11am–5pm, Tues–Thurs 10am–4pm, Sun 2–4pm; Oct–June Mon 10am–5pm, Tues–Thurs 10am–5pm. Bus: 75 or 76.

HMS *Unicorn* ✿   This 46-gun ship of war commissioned in 1824 by the Royal Navy, now the oldest British-built ship afloat, has been restored and visitors can explore all four decks: the quarter-deck with its 32-pound (14.5kg) carronades, the gundeck with its battery of 18-pound (8kg) cannons and captain's quarters, the berth deck with its officers' cabins and crew's hammocks, and the orlop deck and hold. Various displays portraying life in the sailing navy and the history of the *Unicorn* make this a rewarding visit.

Victoria Dock. ✆ **01382/200-900.** Admission £3.50 ($5.60) adults, £2.50 ($4) seniors and children, £7.50–£9.50 ($12–$15) family ticket. Easter–Oct daily 10am–5pm; Nov–Easter Wed–Sun 10am–4pm. Bus: 6, 23, or 78.

Verdant Works   This refurbished ex-mill, known as the Jute House, is dedicated to the history of an industry that sustained Dundee throughout most of the 19th and 20th centuries. The first floor shows how raw jute from Bangladesh was processed and includes a display on a weaver's loom. On the second floor is a section on the socio-historical aspect of the city and how the different social classes lived in 19th-century Dundee. In the courtyard are 18th- and 19th-century street games, such as stilts and whips and tops.

West Henderson's Wind. ✆ **01382/225-282.** Admission £6.2 ($9.90) adults, £4.70 ($7.50) seniors, £3.75 ($6) children. Apr–Oct Mon–Sat 10am–5pm, Sun 11am–5pm; Nov–Mar Mon–Sat 10am–4pm, Sun 11am–4pm. Lies a 15-min. walk north of train station (it's well signposted).

WHERE TO STAY

Craigtay Hotel   Although this hotel was constructed around the core of an 18th-century farm building, few if any hints of its age are visible. In the 1960s, it was Dundee's first disco, before a local entrepreneur transformed it into a tea-room. Much enlarged and modernized, it's now a small hotel lying 1.6km (1 mile) from the center with functional guest rooms and small, shower-only bathrooms. The pub and restaurant serve moderately priced dinners nightly.

101 Broughty Ferry Rd, Tayside, Dundee DD4 6JE. ✆ **01382/451-142.** Fax 01382/452-940. www.craigtay. co.uk. 18 units. £55 ($88) double. Rates include breakfast. AE, MC, V. From Dundee, drive 1.6km (1 mile) east of town, following signs to Broughty Ferry. Free parking. **Amenities:** Restaurant; bar; laundry facility. *In room:* TV, dataport, coffeemaker, hair dryer (on request), iron, trouser press.

Hilton Dundee ★   This chain hotel helps to rejuvenate the once-seedy waterfront of Dundee. Although built in a severe modern style, the five-story block contains well-furnished guest rooms, some of which overlook the Firth, the river, or the Tay Bridge. Both business and leisure travelers will find solace here in rooms with bright floral upholstery and draperies, blond wood furnishings, and small bathrooms.

Earl Grey Place, Dundee DD1 4DE. ✆ **01382/229-271.** Fax 01382/200-072. www.dundee.hilton.com 130 units. £128–£148 ($205–$237) double; from £208 ($333) suite. AE, DC, MC, V. Free parking. Bus: 1A, 1B, or 20. From the south, the hotel is on the left hand side as you come over the Tay Road Bridge into town. **Amenities:** Restaurant; bar; indoor pool; health club; sauna; concierge; business center; 24-hr. room service; laundry/dry cleaning service; steam room. *In room:* TV, coffeemaker, hair dryer, trouser press.

Invercarse Hotel   In landscaped gardens overlooking the River Tay, this Best Western hotel lies 5km (3 miles) west of the heart of Dundee. Many prefer it for its fresh air, tranquil location, and Victorian country-house aura. Well-maintained rooms come in a variety of sizes and open onto views across the Tay to the hills of the kingdom of Fife.

371 Perth Rd., Dundee DD2 1PG. ✆ **800/528-1234** in the U.S. or 01382/669-231. Fax 01382/644-112. www. redwoodleisure.co.uk/invercarse. 44 units. £90 ($144) double; £100 ($160) suite. Rates include Scottish breakfast. AE, DC, MC, V. Free parking. Pets accepted. Drive 5km (3 miles) west of Dundee on the Perth Road. The hotel is clearly signposted. **Amenities:** Restaurant; bar; limited room service; access to nearby health club; business center; laundry/dry cleaning service. *In room:* TV, coffeemaker, hair dryer; iron/ironing board, trouser press.

Queen's Hotel ⚐ For the past century and a quarter, this hotel has been a venue for that special occasion in town, be it a wedding or a school reunion. This historical hotel has stayed abreast of the times in terms of services and amenities, but it has retained much of its Victorian charm. Bedrooms come in a variety of sizes but most of them are quite large, each with a well-kept bathroom. Rooms are decorated in rich colors, such as classic shades of amber gold or red-wine burgundy. One room is suitable for guests with limited mobility. A local favorite, Nosey Parkers, is a bistro and restaurant, with a Scottish and continental menu supplemented by blackboard specials.

160 Nethergate, Dundee DD1 4DU. ℂ **01382/322-515.** Fax 01382/202-668. www.queenshotel-dundee. com. 52 units. Mon–Thurs £92 ($147) double, Fri–Sun £62 ($99) double; Mon–Thurs £100 ($160) suite, Fri–Sun £82 ($131) suite. Rates include breakfast. AE, DC, MC, V. Free parking. Lies a 4-min. walk west of the Dundee Train Station. **Amenities:** Restaurant; bar; limited room service; laundry/dry cleaning service. *In room:* TV, coffeemaker, hair dryer, iron/ironing board.

Swallow Hotel ⚐ *Kids* This restored Victorian mansion sits on 2.2 hectares (5 acres) of well-landscaped gardens on the outskirts of Dundee. It comes complete with a nature trail and an adventure playground for the kids. It's also one of the best-equipped hotels in the area, with a leisure club, an outdoor heated pool, and a spa. Bedrooms are well laid out, tastefully furnished, and most comfortable, each with a carefully maintained bathroom. The so-called executive rooms are more modern than the standard and more traditional doubles. Most of the rooms are tartan-themed, though others are aflame in floral colors.

Kingsway West, Invergowrie, DD2 5JT. ℂ **01382/631-200.** Fax 01382/631-201. www.swallowhotels.com/ dundee. 104 units. £100–£120 ($160–$192) double, £140 ($224) suite. AE, MC, V. Free parking. Signposted on the Dundee Kingsway, on the western outskirts of Dundee. **Amenities:** Restaurant; bar; outdoor heated pool; health club; spa; 24-hr. room service; babysitting; laundry/dry cleaning service; steam room. *In room:* TV, hair dryer, coffeemaker, iron/ironing board.

WHERE TO DINE
Other dining options include the restaurants in the hotels listed above.

Het Theatercafe INTERNATIONAL In the Dundee Repertory Theatre, this is both a cafe-bar upstairs, with an excellent restaurant on the ground floor. It's become one of the most fashionable places in Dundee to dine. Naturally, it's ideal for pre-theater meals. Freshly prepared and good-tasting food is highlighted here, and that combined with reasonable prices makes it a success. The most popular item on the menu is steak frites—an 8-ounce ribeye steak resting with chips. You can also order tasty fish cakes with deep-fried potatoes and an herb-laced salad, or else hot and spicy blackened chicken breast. If you like your chicken even more exotic, opt for the marinated grilled chicken served with a spicy peanut sauce. Another good choice is penne pasta with a chili pesto.

Tay Square. ℂ **01382/206-699.** Reservations recommended. Main courses £6.50–£9.90 ($10–$16). MC, V. Mon–Sat noon–3pm and 5–9pm.

Howies Dundee ⚐ SCOTTISH The cuisine here is called "Scottish with a twist." The restaurant stands opposite the Rep Theatre (see "Dundee After Dark" below), which is quickly becoming the city's cultural quarter. Owner David Howie Scott operates what he terms "a restaurant with rooms." The restaurant is on two floors. Below street level is a chic bar, The Basement. For starters, opt for Scottish salmon with a wholegrain mustard and dill dressing or the spinach, lemon, and lentil soup. For a main course, offerings include such well-prepared and tasty choices as pan-seared chicken supreme with roasted cherry tomatoes or a casserole of Scottish beef with wild mushrooms and shallots. You can finish with a selection of Scottish farmhouse cheeses or a sticky toffee pudding with butterscotch sauce.

The restaurant also rents four handsomely furnished bedrooms with private bathroom for £50 to £60 ($80–$96) per night, complete with minibar, coffeemaker, and hair dryer.

25 Tay St. ⓒ 01382/200-399. Reservations recommended. 2-course lunch £7.95 ($13), 3-course lunch £9.95 ($16); 2-course dinner £15.50 ($25), 3-course dinner £17.95 ($29); pre-theatre menu (Sun–Thurs 5:30–7:30pm) £11.95 ($19) for 2 courses. MC, V. Daily noon–2.30 and 5:30–10pm.

Jahangir Tandoori INDIAN   Built around an indoor fish pond in a dining room draped with the soft folds of an embroidered tent, this is the best Indian restaurant in Dundee and one of the most exotic in the region. Meals are prepared with fresh ingredients and cover the gamut of recipes from both north and south India. The food is sometimes slow-cooked in clay pots (tandoori) and is seasoned to the degree of spiciness you prefer. Both meat and vegetarian dishes are available.

1 Sessions St. (at the corner of Hawk Hill). ⓒ 01382/202-022. Reservations recommended. Main courses £10–£15 ($16–$24). AE, MC, V. Daily 5pm–midnight.

DUNDEE AFTER DARK

The **Dundee Rep Theatre,** Tay Square (ⓒ 01382/223-530), is likely to stage any and everything from *Peter Pan* to an opera, from plays to Scottish ballet or even flamenco. You can purchase tickets Monday through Saturday from 10am to 7:30pm (to 6pm on performance days). Tickets generally cost £7 ($11) to £19 ($30). On site is the **Het Theatercafe** (see above).

A SIDE TRIP TO GLAMIS CASTLE

The little village of Glamis (pronounced without the "i") grew up around **Glamis Castle** ⚜⚜, Castle Office, Glamis (ⓒ 01307/840-393). Next to Balmoral Castle, visitors to Scotland most want to see Glamis Castle for its link with the crown. For 6 centuries, this castle has been connected to members of the British royal family: The Queen Mother was brought up here; and Princess Margaret was born here, making her the first royal princess born in Scotland in 3 centuries. The present owner is the queen's great-nephew. The castle contains Duncan's Hall—the Victorians claimed this was where Macbeth murdered King Duncan, but in the play, the murder takes place at Macbeth's castle (Cawdor) near Inverness. In fact, Shakespeare was erroneous, as well—he had Macbeth named Thane of Glamis, but Glamis wasn't made a thaneship (a sphere of influence in medieval Scotland) until years after the play takes place.

The present Glamis Castle dates from the early 15th century, but there are records of a hunting lodge having been here in the 11th century. The Lyon family has owned Glamis Castle since 1372, and it contains some fine plaster ceilings, furniture, and paintings.

A self-service restaurant has been installed in the old kitchens, with a chalkboard featuring daily specials and excellent home-cooked and baked dishes.

The castle is open to the public, with access to the Royal Apartments and many other rooms, as well as the fine gardens, the end of March to the end of October only, daily from 10:30am to 5:30pm. Admission to the castle and gardens is £6.70 ($11) adults, £3.50 ($5.60) children, family ticket £18 ($29). If you wish to visit the grounds only, the charge is £3.50 ($5.60) adults, £2.50 ($4) children. Buses run between Dundee and Glamis. The 35-minute ride costs £4

In Search of Peter Pan

The little town of **Kirriemuir** is reached by heading north of Glamis Castle for 6.5km (4 miles) or by traveling 26km (16 miles) north of Dundee via A929 and A928. Thousands of visitors per year come here to pay their respects to Sir James M. Barrie (1860–1937), author of *Peter Pan.*

The little town of red-sandstone houses and narrow crooked streets, in the heart of Scotland's raspberry country, saw the birth of Barrie in 1860. His father was employed as a hand-loom weaver of linen. **Barrie's birthplace** still stands at 9 Brechin Rd. (© 01575/572-646), now a property of the National Trust for Scotland. The small house contains manuscripts and mementos of the writer. From May to September, the house is open Monday through Saturday from noon to 5pm and Sunday from 1:30 to 5pm; October, hours are Saturday from noon to 5pm and Sunday from 1:30 to 5pm. Admission is £5 ($8) for adults, £4 ($6.40) for seniors, students, and children.

Barrie first became known for his sometimes-cynical tales of Kirriemuir, disguised as Thrums, in such works as *Auld Licht Idylls* (1888) and *A Window in Thrums* (1889). Barrie then turned to the theater and in time became known for bringing supernatural and sentimental ideas to the stage. It's said that talking to a group of children while walking his dog gave him the idea for the stories about Peter Pan, which were first presented to the public in 1904. It wasn't until 1957 that *When Wendy Grew Up: An Afterthought* was published.

He went on to write more dramas, including *Alice Sit-by-the-Fire* (1905), *What Every Woman Knows* (1908), *The Will* (1913), and *Mary Rose* (1920), the latter a very popular play in its day. But who remembers these works today except a Barrie scholar? On the other hand, Peter Pan has become a legendary figure, known by almost every child in the Western world through films, plays, musicals, and the original book.

Although he spent most of his working life in London, Barrie is buried in Kirriemuir Cemetery. To reach **Barrie's grave,** turn left off Brechin Road and follow the cemetery road upward. The path is clearly marked, taking you to the grave pavilion. A camera obscura in the **Barrie Pavilion** on Kirriemuir Hill gives views over Strathmore to Dundee and north to the Highlands.

($6.40) one-way. *Note:* Buses don't run on Sunday, and they don't stop in front of the castle, which lies 1km (1½ mile) from the bus stop.

WHERE TO STAY

Castleton House ✦ *Finds*   This country-house hotel is run with love and care by owners, David Webster and Verity Nicholson, who acquired it in 2000. In cool weather you're greeted by welcoming coal fires in the public lounge; the youthful staff is the most considerate we've encountered in the area. Rooms of various sizes are furnished with reproductions of antiques; the suite features a genuine Regency four-poster bed. Chef Andrew Wilkie presides over the award-winning restaurant, where most of the fruits and vegetables served are grown on the hotel's grounds.

Eassie by Glamis, Forfar, Tayside DD8 1SJ. ℂ **01307/840-340.** Fax 01307/840-506. www.castletonglamis. co.uk. 6 units. £120 ($192) double. Rates include Scottish breakfast. AE, MC, V. Drive 5km (3 miles) west of Glamis on A94. **Amenities:** 2 restaurants; bar; 9-hole putting green; limited room service; laundry/dry cleaning service. *In room:* TV, coffeemaker, hair dryer.

WHERE TO DINE

Strathmore Arms CONTINENTAL/SCOTTISH   Try this place near the castle for one of the best lunches in the area. You might begin with the freshly made soup of the day or the fresh prawns. Some of the dishes regularly featured might include steak pie or venison. For something a little more exotic, go for the Indian chicken breast marinated in yogurt and spices; for vegetarians phyllo parcels stuffed with asparagus and cauliflower.

The Square Glamis. ℂ **01307/840-248.** Reservations recommended. Main courses £7.50–£18.50 ($12–$30). AE, MC, V. Daily noon–2pm and 6:30–9pm.

8 Ballater & Balmoral Castle ⟨★⟩

179km (111 miles) N of Edinburgh, 66km (41 miles) W of Aberdeen, 108km (67 miles) NE of Perth, 113km (70 miles) SE of Inverness

On the Dee River, with the Grampian Mountains in the background, Ballater is a resort center, but most visitors come here with only one goal in mind—to walk the grounds of Balmoral Castle, the far northern home of the Windsors. The town still centers on its Station Square, where the royal family used to be photographed as they arrived to spend holidays. (The railway is now closed.) From Ballater, you can drive west to view the scenery of Glen Muick and Lochnagar, where you'll see herds of deer. Incidentally, the drive between Ballater and Braemar (see "Braemar," below) is very scenic.

ESSENTIALS

GETTING THERE By Train   Go to Aberdeen and continue the rest of the way by connecting bus. For rail schedules and information, call ℂ **08457/ 484-950.**

By Bus   Buses run hourly from Aberdeen to Ballater. The bus and train stations in Aberdeen are next to each other on Guild Street (ℂ **01224/212-266** for information). Bus 201 from Braemar runs to Ballater (trip time: 1¼ hr.). The fare is £4 ($6.40).

By Car   From Braemar, go east along A93.

VISITOR INFORMATION   The **tourist information office** is at Station Square (ℂ **01339/755-306**). Hours are July and August, daily from 10am to 1pm and from 2 to 6pm; September and October and May and June, Monday to Saturday from 10am to 1pm and from 2 to 5pm, Sunday from 1 to 5pm. Closed November through April.

THE CASTLE

Balmoral Castle ⟨★⟩   "This dear paradise" is how Queen Victoria described Balmoral Castle, rebuilt in the Scottish baronial style by her beloved Albert. And Balmoral was the setting for the story of Victoria and her faithful servant, John Brown, as shown in the film *Mrs. Brown.* Today, Balmoral is still a private residence of the British sovereign. Albert, Victoria's prince consort, leased the property in 1848 and bought it in 1852. As the original castle of the Farquhar-sons proved too small, the present edifice was built, completed in 1855. Its principal feature is a 30m (100-ft.) tower. Of the actual castle, only the ballroom is open to the public; it houses an exhibit of pictures, porcelain, and works of art. On the grounds are many memorials to the royal family, along with gardens, country walks, souvenir shops, a refreshment room, and pony trekking for £20 ($30) for a 2-hour ride (available to adults and children over 12 from 10am–noon or 2–4pm).

Balmoral, Ballater. © 01339/742-534. Admission £4.50 ($7.20) adults, £3.50 ($5.60) seniors, £1 ($1.60) for children age 5–16, free for children age 4 and under. Apr 10–May 3 Mon–Sat 10am–5pm; June 1–Aug 2, daily 10am–5pm. Closed Aug 3–Apr 9. Crathie bus from Aberdeen to the Crathie station; Balmoral Castle is sign-posted from there (a short walk).

WHERE TO STAY

You can also stay at the **Green Inn** (see "Where to Dine," below).

Balgonie Country House ✦ *Finds*　In the heart of Royal Deeside, to the west of town, this Edwardian country house is set amid 1.6 hectares (4 acres) of gardens, overlooking the Ballater Golf Course and providing panoramic views of the hills of Glen Muick. It offers a peaceful haven of beautifully furnished rooms (some with shower only) and fine Scottish food. The owners can advise on golfing, salmon fishing, and hiking in the area.

Braemar Place, Ballater AB35 5NQ. © 01339/755-482. www.royaldeesidehotels.com. 9 units. £123 ($197) double. Rates include breakfast. AE, MC, V. Closed Jan. Free parking. Signposted off A93, Ballater-Perth, on the western outskirts. **Amenities:** Restaurant; bar. *In room:* TV, hair dryer.

Darroch Learg Hotel ✦ *Finds*　Built in 1888 as an elegant country home, this pink-granite hotel stands in 2 hectares (5 acres) of lush woodlands opening onto views of the Dee Valley toward the Grampian Mountains. Constructed at the peak of the golden age of Victorian Royal Deeside, the hotel is imbued with a relaxing charm. The individually decorated bedrooms are divided between the main house and Oakhall, a baronial mansion on the same grounds. Some units have four-poster beds and private terraces; some are equipped for guests with disabilities; and all have well-maintained bathrooms with showers. The hotel's main attraction is its Conservatory Restaurant, which is open to nonguests (see "Where to Dine" below). The chef will accommodate special diets by arrangement.

Darroch Learg, Braemar Rd. (on A93 at the west end of Ballater), Ballater AB35 5UX. © 01339/755-443. Fax 01339/755-252. 17 units. £128–£158 ($205–$253) double in main house; £82 ($131) double in Oakhall. Rates include breakfast. AE, DC, MC, V. Closed Christmas and last 3 weeks in Jan. Free parking. Pets accepted. **Amenities:** Restaurant; room service (7am-10pm); laundry service. *In room:* TV, coffeemaker, hair dryer, trouser press.

Deeside Hotel　This well-managed guesthouse occupies an 1890 pink-granite house surrounded by late-Victorian gardens and is a 3-minute walk west of the town center. The small guest rooms are simple, with white walls, wood furniture, and bathrooms with showers. Upscale dinners are prepared nightly. Recent offerings included grilled oatmeal-dredged herring with Dijon mustard sauce and venison filet with hawthorn jelly.

45 Braemar Rd., Ballater AB35 5RQ. © 01339/755-420. Fax 01339/755-357. www.deesidehotel.co.uk. 9 units. £50–£56 ($80–$90) double. Rates include breakfast. MC, V. Closed Jan. **Amenities:** Restaurant; bar. *In room:* TV, coffeemaker, no phone.

Hilton Craigendarroch Hotel ★ *Kids*　This hotel, built in the Scottish baronial style, is set amid old trees on an 11-hectares (28-acre) estate. Modern comforts have been added, but a 19th-century aura remains. Public areas are luxurious, especially the study with oak paneling, a log fire, and book-lined shelves. The fair-size guest rooms, opening onto views of Ballater and the River Dee. Each is furnished in individual style, with shower-only bathroom. For longer stays, you can inquire about renting one of the 1-, 2-, or 3-bedroom villas, each with a private terrace.

Braemar Rd., Ballater AB35 5XA. ℂ **01339/755-858.** Fax 01339/755-447. www.hilton.com. 45 units. £115–£135 ($184–$216) double; £190 ($304) suite. Rates include Scottish breakfast. AE, DC, MC, V. Free parking. Signposted directly west of town on the road to Braemar. **Amenities:** 3 restaurants; 2 bars; indoor pool; tennis court; health club; Jacuzzi; sauna; children's playground; business center; salon; 24-hour room service; babysitting; laundry/dry cleaning service; squash court; steam room; summer ski slope. *In room:* TV, dataport, hair dryer, trouser press.

Monaltrie Hotel *(Kids* This 1835 hotel is the first in the region and its Arbeen granite finish speaks of its old days as a health spa. Today its clientele come for the live music in its pub and for the savory food served, the most unusual of which is a Thai cuisine. Each of the fair-sized guest rooms sports an unobtrusive monochromatic decor and comfortable beds along with a tiled shower-only bathroom. The hotel lies a 3-minute walk east of the center of town.

5 Bridge Sq., Ballater AB35 5QJ. ℂ **01339/755-417.** Fax 01339/755-180. www.monaltriehotel.co.uk. 24 units. £60–£70 ($96–$112) double. Rates include continental breakfast. AE, DC, MC, V. Free parking. **Amenities:** 2 restaurants; bar; children's play area. *In room:* TV, coffeemaker.

WHERE TO DINE

Other dining options include the restaurants in the hotels listed above.

Balgonie Country House Restaurant SCOTTISH/FRENCH   For Scottish salmon, local game, or Aberdeen Angus beef, this restaurant is among the finest in the Royal Deeside. John and Priscilla Finnie welcome hotel guests and nonguests to their dining room, where the kitchen makes a major effort to secure some of the finest Scottish products. The menu changes daily, but you're likely to find tender filet of beef flambéed in cognac and topped with black peppercorn sauce, or loin of lamb with a red currant jus. While enjoying views of the Glenmuick Hills, you can delight in any number of French-inspired dishes, such as halibut with asparagus and a tomato confit.

In the Balgonie Country House (see "Where to Stay," above), Braemar Place. ℂ **01339/755-482.** Reservations recommended. Fixed-price 4-course menu £32.50 ($52). AE, MC, V. Daily 12:30–2pm and 7–9pm. Closed Jan.

The Conservatory Restaurant ✦ SCOTTISH   Head here for innovative, imaginative cuisine. This award-winning dining room affords views over the River Dee. The chef uses only the freshest ingredients, like lamb, venison, and Aberdeen Angus beef. Seafood options include filet of halibut with basil and olive oil crust combined with fried squid and avocado salsa.

In the Darroch Learg Hotel (see "Where to Stay," above), Darroch Learg, Braemar Rd. ℂ **01339/755-443.** Reservations required. Fixed-price 3-course menu £37.50 ($60). AE, DC, MC, V. Daily 12:30–2pm and 7–9pm. Closed Christmas and last 3 weeks in Jan.

Green Inn SCOTTISH   In the heart of town, once a former temperance hotel, this is now one of the finest dining rooms in town, especially for traditional Scottish dishes. The chef places emphasis on local produce, including homegrown vegetables when available. In season, loin of venison is served with a bramble sauce, and you can always count on fresh salmon and the best of Angus beef.

Three simply furnished double rooms, with shower-only bathroom, TV, and half-board, go for £55 ($82.50) per person.

9 Victoria Rd., Ballater AB35 5QQ. (C) and fax **01339/755-701**. Reservations required. Fixed-price menu £27.50 ($44) for 2 courses, £32.50 ($52) for 3 courses. AE, DC, MC, V. Mar–Oct daily 7–9pm; Nov–Feb Tues–Sat 7–9pm.

La Mangia Toia ITALIAN   In a converted early-18th-century stable beside the River Dee in the heart of Ballater, this is one of the most architecturally unusual restaurants in the region. Amid a deliberately rustic decor that includes artfully positioned bales of hay, lots of horsey accessories, and a high wooden ceiling, you can order from a widely varied menu that includes a savory array of barbecue dishes. Choices include chicken, salmon, pastas, meal-size salads, baguette sandwiches, steaks, and fresh fish, usually prepared as simply as possible as a means of allowing the basic freshness and flavor to come through. Everybody's favorite dessert seems to be sticky toffee pudding.

Bridge Sq. (C) **01339/755-999**. Main courses £4.75–£9.50 ($7.60–$15) lunch; £8.95–£14.50 ($14–$23) dinner. MC, V. Mon–Fri 5–10pm; Sat–Sun noon–10pm.

Oaks Restaurant ✦ BRITISH   The most glamorous restaurant in the region, the Oaks is in a century-old mansion that was originally built by the marmalade kings of Britain, the Keiller family. This is the most upscale of the restaurants in a resort complex that includes hotel rooms, time-share villas, and access to a nearby golf course. To start, try the venison and duck terrine flavored with orange and brandy and served with a warm black conch vinaigrette. Main courses include roast rack of lamb, breast of Grampian chicken, and loin of venison.

In the Hilton Craigendarroch Hotel (see "Where to Stay" above), Braemar Rd. (C) **01339/755-858**. Reservations strongly recommended. Fixed-price 4-course dinner £32.50 ($52). AE, DC, MC, V. Daily 7–10:30pm.

9 Braemar

137km (85 miles) N of Edinburgh, 93km (58 miles) W of Aberdeen, 82km (51 miles) N of Perth

In the heart of some of Grampian's most beautiful scenery, Braemar is known for its romantic castle. It's also a good center for exploring the area that includes Balmoral Castle (see above) and is home to the most famous of the Highland Gatherings. The village is set against a massive backdrop of hills, covered with heather in summer, where Clunie Water joins the River Dee. The massive **Cairn Toul** towers over Braemar, reaching a height of 1,287m (4,241 ft.).

ESSENTIALS

GETTING THERE   By Train   Take the train to Aberdeen, then continue the rest of the way by bus. For information and schedules, call (C) **08457/ 484-950**.

By Bus   Buses run daily from Aberdeen to Braemar 6 times a day (trip time: 2 hours). One-way fare is £7.20 ($12). The bus and train stations in Aberdeen are next to each other on Guild Street ((C) **01224/212-266** for information about schedules).

By Car   To reach Braemar from Dundee, return west toward Perth, then head north along A93, following the signs into Braemar. The 113km (70-mile) drive will take 70 to 90 minutes.

VISITOR INFORMATION   The year-round **Braemar Tourist Office** is in The Mews, Mar Road ((C) **01339/742-208**). In June, hours are daily from 10am to 6pm; July and August daily from 9am to 7pm, and in September daily from 10am to 1pm and from 2 to 6pm. In off-season hours are Monday to Saturday from 10am to 1pm and from 2 to 5pm, Sunday from noon to 5pm.

SPECIAL EVENTS   The spectacular **Royal Highland Gathering** takes place annually in late August or early September in the Princess Royal and Duke of Fife Memorial Park. The queen herself often attends the gathering. These ancient games are thought to have been originated by King Malcolm Canmore, a chieftain who ruled much of Scotland at the time of the Norman conquest of England. He selected his hardiest warriors from all the clans for a "keen and fair contest."

Call the tourist office (see "Visitor Information," above) for more information. Braemar is overrun with visitors during the gathering—anyone thinking of attending would be wise to reserve accommodations anywhere within a 32km (20-mile) radius of Braemar no later than early April.

EXPLORING THE AREA

If you're a royal family–watcher, you might be able to spot members of the family, even the queen, at **Crathie Church,** 14km (9 miles) east of Braemar on A93 (© **01339/742-208**), where they attend Sunday services when in residence. Services are at 11:30am; otherwise the church is open to view April to October, Monday to Saturday from 9:30am to 5:30pm and on Sunday from 2 to 5:30pm.

Nature lovers may want to drive to the **Linn of Dee,** 10km (6 miles) west of Braemar, a narrow chasm on the River Dee, which is a local beauty spot. Other beauty spots include Glen Muick, Loch Muick, and Lochnagar. A **Scottish Wildlife Trust Visitor Centre,** reached by a minor road, is located in this Highland glen, off the South Deeside road. An access road joins B976 at a point 26km (16 miles) east of Braemar. The tourist office (see above) will give you a map pinpointing these beauty spots.

Braemar Castle &   This romantic 17th-century castle is a fully furnished private residence with architectural grace, scenic charm, and historical interest. The castle has barrel-vaulted ceilings and an underground prison and is known for its remarkable star-shaped defensive curtain wall.

On the Aberdeen-Ballater-Perth Rd. (A93). © **01339/741-219.** Admission £4 ($6.40) adults, £3 ($4.80) seniors and students, £1.50 ($2.40) children age 5–15, free for children age 4 and under. Mon after Easter to Oct Sat–Thurs 10am–6pm. Closed Nov–Easter. Take A93 .8km (½ mile) northeast of Braemar.

PLAYING GOLF

Braemar Golf Course, at Braemar (© **01339/741-618**), is the highest golf course in the country. The second hole green is 380m (1,250 ft.) above sea level—this is the trickiest hole on the course. Pro golf commentator Peter Alliss has deemed it "the hardest par 4 in all of Scotland." Set on a plateau, the hole is bordered on the right by the River Clunie and lined on the left by rough. Greens fees are as follows: Monday to Friday £20 ($32) for 18 holes and £19.50 ($31) for a day ticket; Saturday and Sunday £17.50 ($28) for 18 holes and £23 ($37) for a day ticket. Pull carts can be rented for £4 ($6.40) per day, and sets of clubs can be borrowed for £7 ($11) per day. The only dress code is "be reasonable." The course is open only April to October daily (call in advance as hours can vary).

WHERE TO STAY & DINE

Braemar Lodge Hotel   This hotel, popular with skiers who frequent the nearby Glenshee slopes, is set on extensive grounds at the head of Glen Clunie. Bedrooms vary in shape and size, but each is comfortable and well equipped,

containing well-maintained bathrooms. Rooms are bright and airy, with soothing color schemes. Two rooms are large enough for families. On cool evenings,
guests are greeted with log fires. The hotel is on the road to the Glenshee ski
slopes near the cottage where Robert Louis Stevenson wrote *Treasure Island.*
Three log cabins have been built recently on the grounds. Fully equipped with
all modern conveniences, they sleep up to six persons.

6 Glenshee Rd., Braemar AB35 5YQ. ✆ and fax **01339/741-627.** www.braemarlodge.co.uk. 7 units. £75
($120) double; £220–£470 ($352–$752) log cabin. Rates include Scottish breakfast. MC, V. Free parking.
Closed Nov. Lies a 2-min. walk south from the bus station. **Amenities:** Restaurant; bar; laundry/dry cleaning
service. *In room:* TV, hair dryer.

Callater Lodge Hotel *(Finds*   Full of rural charm, this 1861 granite house
stands about .5km (¼ mile) south of the center of Braemar, off the side of A93
in a spacious garden. Built around 1865, with a small-scale enlargement completed during the 1970s, it bristles with bay and dormer windows and offers a
different decor in each of its cozy guest rooms. Each room has a bathroom with
shower; two rooms have bathtubs as well. The owners will prepare picnics and
offer advice on great scenic places to hike. Evening meals can be arranged.

9 Glenshee Rd., Braemar AB35 5YQ. ✆ **01339/741-275.** Fax 01339/741-345. www.hotel-braemar.co.uk. 6
units. £48–£56 ($77–$90) double. Rates include breakfast. MC, V. Closed Dec. Free parking. From the center
of Braemar, drive south on Glenshee Rd. *In room:* TV, coffeemaker, hair dryer, no phone.

Invercauld Arms Thistle Hotel *(R*   This is the town's leading inn, with more
amenities and greater comfort than Braemar Lodge. The oldest part of this old
granite building dates from the 18th century. In cool weather there's a roaring
log fire on the hearth. You can go hill walking and see deer, golden eagles, and
other wildlife. Fishing and, in winter, skiing are other pursuits in the nearby
area. Rooms are comfortably furnished. Although they lack any style or glamour, they serve their purpose well and come in a wide range of sizes. In the pub
close by, you'll meet the "ghillies" and "stalkers" (hunting and fishing guides),
then return to the hotel for its Scottish and international fare.

Invercauld Rd., Braemar AB35 5YR. ✆ **01339/741-605.** Fax 01339/741-428. 68 units. £111 ($178) double.
Rates include Scottish breakfast. AE, DC, MC, V. Free parking. Bus: 201. **Amenities:** Restaurant; bar; laun-
dry/dry cleaning service. *In room:* TV, coffeemaker, hair dryer.

10 Speyside *(★* & the Malt Whisky Trail *(★*

Much of the Speyside region covered in this section is in the Moray district, on
the southern shore of the Moray Firth, a great inlet cutting into the northeastern coast of Scotland. The district stretches in a triangular shape south from the
coast to the wild heart of the Cairngorm Mountains near Aviemore. It's a land
steeped in history, as its many castles, battle sites, and ancient monuments testify. It's also a good place to fish and, of course, play golf. Golfers can purchase
a 5-day ticket from tourist information centers that will allow them to play at
more than 11 courses in the area.

One of the best of these courses is **Boat of Garten,** Speyside (✆ **01479/831-
282**). Relatively difficult, the almost 6,000-yard (5,500m) course is dotted with
many bunkers and wooded areas. April to October greens fees are £25 ($40)
Monday to Friday and hours are from 7:30am to 11pm. Saturday greens fees are
£32 ($51) , and hours are from 10am to 4pm. In winter, call to see if the course
is open. Greens fees are then reduced to £15 ($24). Pull-carts can be rented for
£4 ($6.40), and electric carts are available for £7 ($11). Dress reasonably; blue
jeans are not acceptable.

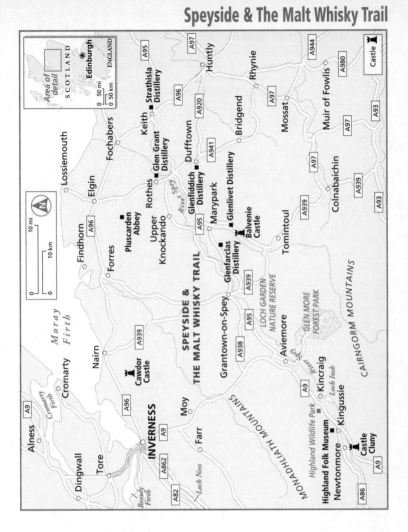

The valley of the second-largest river in Scotland, the Spey, is north and south of Aviemore and a land of great natural beauty. The Spey is born in the Highlands above Loch Laggan, which lies 65km (40 miles) south of Inverness. Little more than a creek at its inception, it gains in force, fed by the many "burns" that drain water from the surrounding hills. It's one of Scotland's great rivers for salmon fishing, and it runs between the towering Cairngorms on the east and the Monadhliath Mountains on the west. Its major center is Grantown-on-Spey.

The major tourist attraction in the area is the **Malt Whisky Trail,** 113km (70 miles) long, running through the glens of Speyside. Here distilleries, many of which can be visited, are known for their production of *uisge beatha* or "water of life." "Whisky" is its more familiar name.

Half the malt distilleries in the country lie along the River Spey and its tributaries. Here peat smoke and Highland water are used to turn out single-malt (unblended) whisky. There're five malt distilleries in the area: **Glenlivet,**

Glenfiddich, Glenfarclas, Strathisla, and **Tamdhu.** Allow about an hour each to visit them.

The best way to reach Speyside from Aberdeen is to take A96 northwest, signposted Elgin. If you're traveling north on the A9 road from Perth and Pitlochry, your first stop might be at Dalwhinnie, which has the highest whisky distillery in the world at 575m (1,888 ft.). It's not in the Spey Valley but is at the northeastern end of Loch Ericht, with views of lochs and forests.

KEITH

Keith, 18km (11 miles) northwest of Huntly, grew up because of its strategic location, where the main road and rail routes between Inverness and Aberdeen cross the River Isla. It has an ancient history, but owes its present look to the town planning of the late 18th and early 19th centuries. Today it's a major stopover along the Malt Whisky Trail.

The oldest operating distillery in the Scottish Highlands, the **Strathisla Distillery,** on Seafield Avenue (*©* **01542/783-044**), was established in 1786. Hours are February to mid-March, Monday to Friday from 9:30am to 4pm; mid-March to November 30, Monday to Saturday from 9:30am to 4pm, Sunday from 12:30 to 4pm; closed December and January. Admission is £5.50 ($8.80) for adults, free for children age 8 to 18, children age 7 and under are not admitted. The admission fee includes a £3 ($4.80) voucher redeemable in the distillery shop against a 70cl bottle of whisky. Be warned that tours of this distillery are self-guided.

WHERE TO STAY

Grange House *(★ (Finds*   This dignified-looking stone house dates from 1815, when it was the manse (home of a minister) for the nearby Church of Scotland, which is still the most prominent building in this tiny hamlet. Doreen Blanche and her husband, Bill, rent two well-decorated and comfortable rooms within their private home. The venue is upscale, charming, and comfortable, with a calm and quiet that's enhanced by the 3.2 hectares (8 acres) of parks and gardens that surrounds this isolated place. Ask the owners to point out the late Victorian addition, completed in 1898, that greatly enlarged the size of the original house. No smoking indoors.

Grange, near Keith AB55 6RY. *©* and fax **01542/870-206.** www.aboutscotland.com/banff/grangehouse.html. 2 units. £60 ($96) double. Rates include breakfast. No credit cards. From Keith, drive 5km (3 miles) east of town, following the signs to Banff, into the hamlet of Grange. Free parking. Dogs welcome (outdoors only) by prior arrangement. **Amenities:** Laundry; babysitting. *In room:* Coffeemaker, hair dryer.

DUFFTOWN

James Duff, the fourth earl of Fife, founded Dufftown in 1817. The four main streets of town converge at the battlemented **clock tower,** which is also the **tourist office** (*©* **01340/820-501**). April to June, September, and October, the office is open Monday through Saturday from 10am to 1pm and 2 to 5:30pm and Sunday from 1 to 5pm; July and August hours are Monday through Saturday from 10am to 7pm and Sunday from 1 to 7pm.

A center of the whisky-distilling industry, Dufftown is surrounded by seven malt distilleries. The family-owned **Glenfiddich Distillery** is on A941, 1km (½ mile) north (*©* **01340/820-373**). It's open Monday through Friday from 9:30am to 4:30pm (Easter to mid-October, also Sat from 9:30am–4:30pm and Sun from noon–4:30pm). Guides in kilts show you around the plant and explain the process of distilling. A film of the history of distilling is also shown.

At the finish of the tour, you're given a dram of malt whisky to sample. The tour is free, but there's a souvenir shop where the owners hope you'll spend a few pounds.

Other sights include **Balvenie Castle,** along A941 (© **01340/820-121**), the ruins of a moated 14th-century stronghold that lie on the south side of the Glenfiddich Distillery. During her northern campaign against the earl of Huntly, Mary Queen of Scots spent 2 nights here. April to September, it's open daily from 9:30am to 6:30pm. Admission is £1.80 ($2.90) for adults, £1.30 ($2.10) for seniors, and 50p ($.80) for children.

DINING

Taste of Speyside ⚔ SCOTTISH   True to its name, this restaurant in the town center, just off the main square, avidly promotes Speyside cuisine as well as the product of Speyside's 46 distilleries. A platter including a slice of smoked salmon, smoked venison, smoked trout, pate flavored with malt whisky, locally made cheese (cow or goat), salads, and homemade oat cakes is offered at noon and at night. Nourishing soup is made fresh daily and is served with homemade bread. There's also a choice of meat pies, including rabbit or venison with red wine and herbs. For dessert, try Scotch Mist, which contains fresh cream, malt whisky, and crumbled meringue.

10 Balvenie St. © **01340/820-860.** Reservations recommended for dinner. Main courses £12–£14 ($19–$22); Speyside platter £11.95 ($19) lunch, £15 ($24) dinner. MC, V. Mon–Sat noon–9pm. Closed Nov–Feb.

GRANTOWN-ON-SPEY

This vacation resort, with its gray-granite buildings, is 55km (34 miles) southeast of Inverness in a wooded valley with views of the Cairngorm Mountains. It's a key center of winter sports in Scotland. Fishers are also attracted to this setting, because the Spey is renowned for its salmon. One of Scotland's many 18th-century planned towns, it was founded on a heather-covered moor in 1765 by Sir James Grant of Grant and became the seat of that ancient family. The town was famous in the 19th century as a Highland tourist center.

From a base here, you can explore the valleys of the Don and Dee, the Cairngorms, and Culloden Moor, scene of the historic battle in 1746, when Bonnie Prince Charlie and his army were defeated.

A year-round **tourist information office** is on High Street (© **01479/872-773**). Hours April to October are daily from 9am to 5pm, Sunday from 10am to 4pm; November to March, Monday to Friday from 9am to 4pm, Saturday from 10am to 4pm.

WHERE TO STAY

Garth Hotel   The elegant, comfortable Garth stands on 1.6 hectares (4 acres) beside the town square. Guests enjoy the use of a spacious lounge, whose high ceilings, wood-burning stove, and vine-covered veranda make it an attractive place for morning coffee or afternoon tea. The handsomely furnished guest rooms have all the necessary amenities, including well-maintained bathrooms with shower units. The extensive and selective meals with a French slant here favor Scottish dishes, with an emphasis on fresh local produce.

The Square, Castle Rd., Grantown-on-Spey, Morayshire PH26 3HN. © **01479/872-836.** Fax 01479/872-116. www.garthhotel.com. 18 units. £62 ($99) double. Rates include Scottish breakfast. MC, V. Free parking. **Amenities:** Restaurant; bar; limited room service. *In room:* TV, coffeemaker, hair dryer.

Skye of Curr Hotel ⚔ *Finds*   A splendid country home set amidst private grounds and woods, this is a welcoming place for an extended stay. Built in 1902 as a Victorian hunting lodge for the Lipton tea family, the hotel overlooks the Cairngorm Mountains and retains many of its original Victorian features, including open fireplaces and wood paneling. Bedrooms are well appointed, with immaculate, shower-only bathrooms.

4.8km (3 miles) south of Grantown-on-Spey by A95 on A938, Dulnain Bridge, PH26 3PA. © **01479/851-345.** Fax 01479/821-173. www.skyeofcurr.com. 9 units. £80 ($128) double with breakfast; £120 ($192) double with breakfast and dinner. MC, V. **Amenities:** Restaurant; 2 bars; lounge. *In room:* TV, hair dryer, coffeemaker, no phone.

Tulchan Lodge ★★   Its fans seem about equally divided into two distinctly different camps. There are those who retreat into its baronial granite walls for a taste of manorial country living, coming out only for tours of the region and walks in the nearby hills. Others opt to take advantage of the salmon and sea-trout fishing within the river Spey, 12.8km (8 miles) of which (both banks) meander through the 10,000 hectares (25,000 acres) that surround it on all sides. Regardless, this place offers elegant accommodations and vivid insights into the grandeur of country living during the height of the British Imperial Age. It was originally built in 1906 by the founder of the McCorquodale publishing empire, who conceived it as a symbol of the power of the British press. If you opt to stay within the main house, expect relatively formal evenings, a daytime emphasis on the sporting life, an immersion into the rituals of breakfast, lunch, and dinner at a communal dining table, chitchatting with other guests, and an insight into the stately home aesthetic that has been the subject of endless PBS programs. Scattered in isolated positions across the undulating terrain outside, you'll find 7 houses (the staff refers to them as "cottages" even though some contain up to five separate bedrooms), suitable for between 4 and 9 occupants. Cottages each have fully equipped kitchens, and a decor that reflects the elegance of the main house. Favored mostly by fishing enthusiasts, they do not include meal service, and are rented exclusively by the week.

Advie, near Grantown-on-Spey PH26 3PW. © **01807/510-200.** Fax 01807/510-234. www.tulchan.com. 13 bedrooms in the main house, 7 outlying cottages. £367–£525 ($588–$840) double. Rates include full board. Cottages £650–£1,350 ($1,040–$2,150) for 4–9 occupants, without meals. MC, V. Closed Feb–Mar. Drive 14km (8½ miles) northeast of Grantown on B9102, following the signs to Elgin. **Amenities:** 2 dining areas; bar; tennis court; limited room service; laundry/dry cleaning service; babysitting. *In room:* TV, hair dryer.

WHERE TO DINE

Craggan Mill BRITISH/ITALIAN   This licensed restaurant and lounge bar, a 10-minute walk south of the town center, is housed in a restored granite mill whose waterwheel is still visible. The owners offer British or Italian cuisine at attractive prices. Your appetizer might be smoked trout in deference to Scotland, or ravioli inspired by sunny Italy. Main courses might be breast of chicken with cream or chicken cacciatore, followed by a dessert of rum-raisin ice cream or peach Melba. You've probably had better versions of all the dishes offered here, but what you get isn't bad. A good selection of Italian wines is also offered.

Hwy. A95 1.2km (¾ mile) south of Grantown-on-Spey. © **01479/872-288.** Reservations recommended. Main courses £3.95–£16.99 ($6.30–$27). MC, V. May–Sept daily noon–2pm and 6–11pm; Oct–Apr Tues–Sun 7–10pm. Closed the first 2 weeks in Nov.

GLENLIVET

As you leave Grantown-on-Spey and head east along A95, drive to the junction with B9008; go south and you won't miss the **Glenlivet Distillery.** The location of the **Glenlivet Reception Centre** (© **01542/783-220**) is 16km (10 miles) north of the nearest town, Tomintoul. Near the River Livet, a Spey tributary, this distillery is one of the most famous in Scotland. It's open mid-April to October Monday to Saturday from 10am to 4pm, and Sunday from 12:30 to 4pm. July and August, Monday to Saturday from 10am to 4pm and Sunday from 12:30pm to 4pm. Admission is free.

Back on A95, you can visit the **Glenfarclas Distillery** at Ballindalloch (© **01807/500-245**), one of the few malt whisky distilleries that's still independent of the giants. Founded in 1836, Glenfarclas is managed by the fifth generation of the Grant family. There's a small craft shop, and each visitor is offered a dram of Glenfarclas Malt Whisky. The admission of £3.50 ($5.60) is for visitors over age 18, and there's a discount of £1 ($1.60) on any purchase of £10 ($16) or more. It's open all year, Monday to Friday from 10am to 5pm; June to September, it's also open Saturday from 10am to 5pm and Sunday from 10am to 4pm.

WHERE TO STAY

Minmore House Hotel ✦   This impressive country house stands on 2 hectares (5 acres) of private grounds adjacent to the Glenlivet Distillery. It was the home of the distillery owners before becoming a hotel. The hotel operators have elegantly furnished their drawing room, which opens onto views of the plush Ladder Hills. The well-furnished bedrooms, some with four-poster beds, have all the vital amenities, and the oak-paneled lounge bar has an open log fire on chilly nights.

Glenlivet, Ballindalloch AB37 9DB. © **01807/590-378.** Fax 01807/590-472. www.minmorehousehotel.com. 10 units. £190 ($304) double. Rates include breakfast, afternoon tea, and 4-course dinner. AE, MC, V. Closed Feb. **Amenities:** Restaurant; bar; outdoor pool; tennis court; hunting and fishing outings. *In room:* Coffeemaker, hair dryer.

KINCRAIG

Kincraig enjoys a scenic spot at the northern end of Loch Insh, overlooking the Spey Valley to the west and the Cairngorm Mountains to the east. Near Kincraig, the most notable sight is the **Highland Wildlife Park** ✦ (© **01540/651-270**), a natural area of parkland with a collection of wildlife, some of which is extinct elsewhere in Scotland. Herds of European bison, red deer, shaggy Highland cattle, wild horses, St. Kilda Soay sheep, and roe deer range the park. In enclosures are wolves, polecats, wildcats, beavers, badgers, and pine martens. You can observe protected birds, such as golden eagles and several species of grouse—of special interest is the capercaillie ("horse of the woods"), a large Eurasian grouse native to Scotland's pine forests. There's a visitor center with a gift shop, cafe, and exhibition areas. Ample parking and a picnic site are also available.

You need a car to go through the park; walkers are discouraged and are picked up by park rangers. The park is open every day at 10am. April and October, the last entrance is at 4pm, except during July and August, when the last entrance is at 5pm. November to March, the last entrance is at 2pm. All people and vehicles are expected to vacate the park within 2 hours of the day's last admission. Admission to the park is £6.50 ($10) for adults, £5.40 ($8.65) for seniors, and £4.35 ($6.95) for children. A family ticket costs £21.70 ($35).

KINGUSSIE

Your next stop along the Spey might be at the little summer vacation resort and winter ski center of Kingussie (it's pronounced king-*you*-see), just off A9, the capital of Badenoch, a district known as "the drowned land" because the Spey can flood the valley when the snows of a severe winter melt in the spring.

Kingussie, 188km (117 miles) northwest of Edinburgh, 66km (41 miles) south of Inverness, and 18km (11 miles) southwest of Aviemore, practically adjoins Newtonmore (see below), directly northeast along A86.

The **Highland Folk Museum** ⚐, Duke St. (⟨ **01540/661-307**), was the first folk museum established in Scotland (1934), and its collections are based on the life of the Highlanders. You'll see domestic, agricultural, and industrial items. Open-air exhibits are a turf kailyard (kitchen garden), a Lewis "black house," and old vehicles and carts. Traditional events, such as spinning, music making, and handcraft fairs, are held throughout the summer. Admission is £2 ($3.20) for adults, £1 ($1.60) for children and seniors, £15 ($24) for a family ticket. Hours are April to October Monday to Saturday from 10:30am to 4pm.

A summer-only **tourist center** is on King Street (⟨ **01540/661-297**). It's open only April to October, Monday to Saturday from 10am to 1pm and from 2 to 6pm, and on Sunday from 10am to 1pm and from 2 to 5pm.

WHERE TO STAY

Homewood Lodge ⚐ *Kids*   One of the best B&Bs in the area, this small Highland house in a garden and woodland setting offers large, simply furnished rooms, each with a shower-only bathroom. The sitting room has an open fireplace. Good traditional fare is served in the evening (reservations recommended). Summer barbecues are also offered, and children are welcome.

Newtonmore Rd., Kingussie PH21 1HD. ⟨ 01540/661-507. www.homewood-lodge-kingussie.co.uk. 4 units. £40–£50 ($64–$81) double. Rates include Scottish breakfast. No credit cards. Free parking. **Amenities:** Restaurant; laundry/dry cleaning service. *In room:* TV, coffeemaker, hair dryer.

Osprey Hotel   This 1895 Victorian structure, 275m (300 yd.) from the rail station, is a convenient place to stay, with comfortable though plain bedrooms, all with shower-only bathrooms, electric blankets, and electric fires. The place is known for its fresh, homemade food. Prime Scottish meats are served; in summer, salmon and trout from local rivers are offered either fresh or peat-smoked.

Ruthven Rd. (at High St.), Kingussie PH21 1EN. ⟨ and fax 01540/661-510. www.ospreyhotel.co.uk. 8 units. £98–£112 ($157–$179) double. Rates include half-board. MC, V. Free parking. **Amenities:** Restaurant; bar; babysitting. *In room:* TV, coffeemaker, hair dryer, no phone.

WHERE TO DINE

The Cross ⚐⚐ SCOTTISH   This chic restaurant comes as a surprise: In an out-of-the-way setting in a remote Highland village, it serves superlative meals that involve theater as much as fine food. The restaurant stands on 1.6 hectares (4 acres), with the Gynack Burn running through the grounds. The main building is an old tweed mill. It has an open-beam ceiling and French doors leading out onto a terrace over the water's edge where al fresco dinners are served. Specialties depend on the availability of produce in the local markets and might include venison Francatelli, wild pigeon with grapes, or Highland lamb with sorrel.

Nine rooms are rented in a new building. Each room is different in size and style—for example, two rooms have canopied beds, and another has a balcony overlooking the mill pond. Doubles, including half board, cost from £197 ($315). Rooms have direct dial telephones but no televisions. Personal service and attention to detail go into the running of this place, operated by Ruth and Tony Hadley, and Ruth's cooking has put it on the gastronomic map of Scotland.

Tweed Mill Brae, off the Ardbroilach road, Kingussie PH21 1TC. ⟨ 01540/661-166. Fax 01540/661-080. www.thecross.co.uk. Reservations recommended. Fixed-price 5-course dinner £40.50 ($65). MC, V. Wed–Mon 7–9pm. Closed Dec–Feb.

ROTHES

A Speyside town with five distilleries, Rothes is just to the south of the Glen of Rothes, 79km (49 miles) east of Inverness and 100km (62 miles) northwest of Aberdeen. Founded in 1766, the town is between Ben Aigan and Conerock Hill. A little settlement, the basis of the town today, grew up around **Rothes Castle,** ancient stronghold of the Leslie family, who lived here until 1622. Only a single massive wall of the castle remains.

The region's best distillery tours are offered by the **Glen Grant Distillery** (© 01542/783-318). Opened in 1840 by a hardworking and hard-drinking pair of brothers, James and John Grant, and now administered by the Chivas & Glenlivet Group (a division of Seagram's), it's 1km (½ mile) north of Rothes, beside the Elgin-Perth (A941) highway. It's open April to October, Monday through Saturday from 10am to 4pm and Sunday from 12:30 to 4pm. Admission is £4 ($6.40) for adults and free for children 8 to 18; children under 8 aren't allowed. Visits include the opportunity to buy the brand's whisky at a discount.

ELGIN ⚘

The center of local government in the Moray district and an ancient royal burgh, the cathedral city of Elgin is on the Lossie River, 61km (38 miles) east of Inverness and 110km (68 miles) northwest of Aberdeen. The city's medieval plan has been retained, with "wynds" and "pends" connecting the main artery with other streets. The castle, as was customary in medieval town layouts, stood at one end of the main thoroughfare, with the cathedral—now a magnificent ruin—at the other. Nothing remains of the castle, but the site is a great place for a scenic walk. Samuel Johnson and James Boswell came this way on their Highland tour and reported a "vile dinner" at the Red Lion Inn in 1773.

Lady Hill stands on High Street, opposite the post office. This is the hilltop location of what was once the royal castle of Elgin. **Birnie Kirk,** at Birnie, 5km (3 miles) south of Elgin and west of A941 to Rothes, was for a time the seat of a bishopric. It dates from about 1140, when it was constructed on the site of a much earlier church founded by St. Brendan. One of the few Norman churches in Scotland still in regular use, it's open daily from 10am to 4pm.

On King Street are the ruins of the **Elgin Cathedral** ⚘ (© 01343/547-171), off North College Street near A96. It was founded in 1224 but destroyed in 1390 by the "wolf of Badenoch," the natural son of Robert II. After its destruction, the citizens of Elgin rebuilt their beloved cathedral and turned it into one of the most attractive and graceful buildings in Scotland. However, when the central tower collapsed in 1711, the cathedral was allowed to fall into decay. It's open April to September, daily from 9:30am to 6:30pm; and October to March, Monday through Wednesday and Saturday from 9:30am to 4:30pm, Thursday from 9:30am to 12:30pm, and Sunday from 2 to 4:30pm. Admission is £3 ($4.80) for adults, £2.10 ($3.35) for seniors, and £1.20 ($1.90) for children.

After exploring Elgin, you can drive 10km (6 miles) southwest to **Pluscarden Abbey,** off B9010. This is one of the most beautiful drives in the area, through the bucolic Black Burn Valley where a priory was founded in 1230 by Alexander II. After long centuries of decline, a new order of Benedictines arrived in 1974 and re-established monastic life. You can visit restored transepts, monastic buildings, and the church choir. The admission is free to this active religious community, which is open daily from 5am to 8:30pm.

If you're a fan of Scottish ruins, head for **Spynie Palace** (© 01343/546-358), reached along A941. The former 15th-century headquarters of the bishops of

Moray was used until 1573, when it was allowed to fall into ruins—for safety reasons, you can view them only from the outside. This is another great place for country walks, and from the top of a tower are magnificent vistas over the Laigh of Moray. It's open April to September, daily from 9:30am to 6:30pm; and October to March, Saturday from 9:30am to 4pm and Sunday from 2 to 4:30pm. Admission is £3.50 ($5.60).

WHERE TO STAY

Mansion House Hotel ⋆⋆   This elegantly appointed hotel, with the baronial proportions of the original design intact, is at the edge of the River Lossie, about .5km (¼ mile) from the center of Elgin. The guest rooms are standard; most have four-poster beds.

The Haugh, Elgin IV30 1AW. *℃* **01343/548-811.** Fax 01343/547-916. www.mansionhousehotel.co.uk. 23 units. £135–£165 ($216–$264) double. Rates include Scottish breakfast. AE, DC, MC, V. Follow A96 onto Alexandra Rd. to the turnoff onto Haugh Rd. Free parking. **Amenities:** Restaurant; bar; heated indoor pool; health club; Jacuzzi; sauna; salon; room service (6am–9pm); massage; babysitting; laundry service. *In room:* TV, coffeemaker, hair dryer.

WHERE TO DINE

Abbey Court Restaurant SCOTTISH/ITALIAN   Abbey Court, in the center of town behind the county building, is an excellent restaurant decorated with stone- and earth-colored quarry tile, along with an artificial pergola, a separate bistro corner, and a more formal dining area in the rear. The fresh pasta is homemade and fresh fish delivered daily. The cooking is straightforward and unpretentious.

15 Greyfriars St. *℃* **01343/542-849.** Reservations recommended. Main courses £9–£17.50 ($14–$28). AE, DC, MC, V. Mon–Sat noon–2pm; Mon–Thurs 6:30–9:30pm; Fri–Sat 6:30–10pm.

10

Inverness & the West Highlands

The romantic glens and rugged mountain landscapes of the West Highlands are timeless and pristine. You can see deer grazing only yards from the highway and stop by your own secluded loch to enjoy a picnic or to fish for trout and salmon. The shadow of Macbeth still stalks the land. (Locals will tell you this 11th-century king was much maligned by Shakespeare.) The area's most famous resident, however, is said to live in mysterious Loch Ness: First sighted by St. Columba in the 6th century, "Nessie" has cleverly evaded searchers ever since.

Centuries of invasions, rebellions, and clan feuds are distant memories now. The Highlands aren't as remote as they once were, when many Londoners seriously believed the men of the Highlands had tails.

Fort William is a major center for the West Highlands, surrounded by wildly beautiful **Lochaber,** the "land of bens, glens, and heroes." Dominating the area is **Ben Nevis,** Britain's highest mountain. This district is the western end of what is known as the **Glen Mor**—the Great Glen, geologically a fissure dividing the northwest of Scotland from the southeast and containing Loch Lochy, Loch Oich, and Loch Ness. The Caledonian Canal, opened in 1847, linked these lochs, the River Ness, and Moray Firth, providing sailing boats a safe alternative to the stormy route around the north of Scotland. Larger steamships made the canal out of date commercially, but fishing boats and pleasure steamers still

use it. Good roads run the length of the Great Glen, partly following the line of Gen. George Wade's military road. The English general became famous for his road and bridge building in Scotland, which did much to open the Highlands to greater access from the south. From Fort William, you can take steamer trips to Staffa and Iona (see chapter 11, "The Hebridean Islands," for more information).

Aviemore and the villages and towns of the Spey Valley offer many activities for the visitor. In the Spey Valley you're at the doorway to the Malt Whisky Trail (see chapter 9, "Aberdeen & the Tayside & Grampian Regions," for more information). Aviemore is the **winter-sports capital of Britain,** and Aviemore Centre offers a multitude of outdoor pursuits: golfing, angling, skiing, and ice-skating.

Inverness and legendary **Loch Ness** are the most popular attractions of the West Highlands and overcrowded in summer, but they're surrounded by villages and towns that also make good centers, especially if you're driving. If you're dependent on public transportation, make Inverness your base, as it has good rail and bus connections to the rest of Scotland and also to England.

Finally, if you have the time to spare, you can extend your stay by visiting the loneliest part of Scotland, the far north. This section of the Highlands, **Sutherland** and **Caithness,** isn't for everyone. Crumbling watchtowers no longer stand guard over anything except the sheep-cropped wilderness. Moss-green glens give way to inland lochs and sea fords. Summer, of course, is the best time to view these deep-blue lochs, towering cliffs, and gentle glens. Many relics of Scotland's turbulent past dot the landscape, with castles left in ruins. Today, visitors come to get away from it all and enjoy outdoor activities in a wild, pristine setting. Potteries and craft centers have also sprung up, with artisans taking inspiration from their surroundings and putting it to work in silversmithing, stone polishing, glassmaking, and most definitely weaving.

1 Around Loch Linnhe & Loch Leven

South of Fort William is one of the most historic sections of Scotland, a group of settlements around Loch Linnhe and Loch Leven (not the also-famous Loch Leven near Dunfermline). The best-known village is **Glencoe,** site of the famous 1692 massacre when the Campbells slaughtered the MacDonalds. Glencoe is the most dramatic glen in Scotland, austere in its beauty. Around both lochs are impressive landscapes and moorland, with flora and fauna unique to the West Highlands. Robert Louis Stevenson captured much of the essence of this moorland and wilderness in his novel *Kidnapped.*

The best all-round outfitter for all kinds of sports in the region near Fort William is **Alfresco Adventure,** Onich (② **01855/821-248**). Nick and Angie Scott will rent motorboats, canoes, sailboats, fishing tackle, and more; they're a great source of advice for enjoying the great Highland outdoors. They also offer guided hill walks at £20 ($32) per person for half a day; and guided canoe trips at £40 ($64) per person for a full day.

ONICH

On the shores of Loch Linnhe, the charming little village of Onich lies to the north of Ballachulish Bridge, 14km (9 miles) southwest of Fort William. It's a good center if you're taking the western route to Inverness or going to Skye and Fort William.

WHERE TO STAY & DINE

Allt-nan-Ros Hotel ⟨⟩   This inn lies across the highway from the edge of the loch and boasts dozens of elaborate gables and interesting architectural touches. Allt-nan-Ros was built around 1885 as a hunting lodge and weekend getaway for an industrialist. Today, this much-enlarged place with relatively recent additions offers comfortable guest rooms and a well-managed dining room open to the public. The rooms have dark mahogany furniture and floral-patterned upholsteries in an Edwardian country-house style, and most offer views of the loch or the stream running through the garden. Some bathrooms contain showers only. In "The Stables" are found two spacious country cottage-like bedrooms, with four-poster beds.

Onich, Fort William PH33 6RY. ② **01855/821-210.** Fax 01855/821-462. www.allt-nan-ros.co.uk. 20 units. £99–£120 ($158–$192) double. Rates include breakfast. AE, DC, MC, V. From Fort William, drive 18km (11 miles) south along A82. Pets. **Amenities:** Restaurant; bar. *In room:* TV, coffeemaker, hair dryer.

The Lodge on the Loch Hotel ⟨⟩   Between the edge of the loch and a semi-forested rocky ridge, this granite hotel dates from the 19th century. Only a handful of the high-ceilinged guest rooms are in the mansion's core; most are in a bulky-looking 1960s extension but are just as comfortable, with a mix of conservative and traditional furnishings. Some units even have an Eastern influence or even Art Deco. The most expensive units have plush extras like CD players,

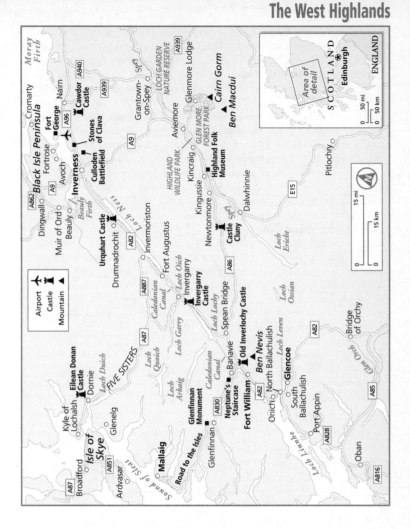

bathrobes, and Jacuzzi baths. If the hotel is full, there are two other choices (under the same management) within a short drive.

The restaurant is one of the big draws, serving an expensive fixed-price dinner that features Scottish produce and many preparations of salmon, trout, and pheasant. There's also a cocktail bar with a log fire and a fine selection of whiskies.

Onich, near Fort William PH33 6RY. ℂ **0871/222-3462.** Fax 0871/222-3463. www.freedomglen.co.uk. 16 units. £70–£130 ($112–$208) double. Rates include breakfast and dinner. MC, V. Closed Nov–Mar. From Fort William, drive 16km (10 miles) south of town, following A82 and the signs to Glasgow. Children under 16 discouraged. Pets. **Amenities:** Restaurant; bar; access to nearby health club; limited room service; massage. *In room:* TV, coffeemaker, hair dryer, iron/ironing board.

GLENCOE: SCENERY & SORROW ★★

Near the spot where Loch Leven joins Loch Linnhe, **Ballachulish Bridge** links the villages of North and South Ballachulish at the entrance to Glencoe. The bridge saves a long drive to the head of the loch if you're coming from the north, but the scenic drive to Kinlochleven lets you come on the celebrated wild Glencoe from the east. Glencoe runs from Rannoch Moor to Loch Leven between majestic mountains, including 1,147m (3,766-ft.) **Bidean nam Bian.** This is an area of massive splendor, with towering peaks and mysterious glens where you can well imagine the fierce battle among the kilted Highlanders to the skirl of the pipes and the beat of the drums.

Known as the "Glen of Weeping," Glencoe is the place where, on February 11, 1692, the Campbells massacred the MacDonalds—men, women, and children— who'd been their hosts for 12 days. Although mass killings weren't uncommon in those times, this one shocked even the Highlanders because it was a breach of hospitality. The **Monument to the Massacre of Glencoe,** at Carnoch, was erected by the chief of the MacDonald clan. After the incident, the crime of "murder under trust" was introduced into Scottish law as an aggravated form of murder that carried the same penalty as treason.

The **Glencoe Visitor Centre** at Glencoe (© **01855/811-307**), is built on the site of the massacre of the Clan Maclains. The center tells the story of the massacre and offers a fine exhibition on mountaineering. Visitors can also see an audiovisual presentation. It is open Easter to October daily, charging £3.50 ($5.60) for admission.

Glen Orchy, to the south, is well worth a visit for its wild river and photogenic mountain scenery. It was the birthplace of Gaelic bard Duncan Ban MacIntyre, whose masterpiece is the song "In Praise of Ben Doran."

This is great country for hiking and bike rides. In Glencoe village, go to the **Mountain Bike Hire** at the Clachaig Inn (© **01855/811-644**), where you can not only rent a bike but also get advice about scenic routes that suit your available time and your ability. The cost is £8 to £10 ($13–$16) per ½-day or £12 to £15 ($19–$24) per day.

WHERE TO STAY & DINE

You can also base yourself in Fort William (see "Fort William: Gateway to Ben Nevis," below) and explore the Glencoe area on day trips.

Ballachulish House ★★   This charming country inn's lime-washed stone form dates back to the 1640, though it was tastefully expanded in 1997. The owners spent enormous sums renovating the place, and since then have hosted the occasional celebrity. The guest rooms have flowered wallpaper and a mix of old and new furniture; each has a view of the loch or forest. The more luxurious units have bathrooms with both tub and shower. There's ample opportunity for long walks beside the loch. (Sometimes one of the owners' dogs will join you.) Dinner is a treat, making use of fresh ingredients and careful preparation.

Ballachulish, near Fort William PA39 4JX. © 0871/222-3460. Fax 0871/222-3461. www.freedomglen.co.uk. 54 units. £140–£246 ($224–$394) double. Rates include dinner and breakfast. MC, V. Closed Jan. Drive west of Ballachulish for 4km (2½ miles), following A82 until it intersects with A828. Follow the signs to Ballachulish House. Pets accepted. **Amenities:** Restaurant; bar; access to nearby health club. *In room:* TV, coffeemaker.

The Clachaig Inn   After the bleakness of Glencoe, the trees ringing this place make it seem like an oasis. It's the only hotel in the glen, on the site where the massacre took place. The Daynes family offers Highland hospitality, good food, and an excellent selection of British ales. They rent some contemporary chalets in the back garden, plus several small to midsize guest rooms in the main house. The furnishings are basic, each of the double rooms comes with a small, shower-only bathroom Live folk music brings the place alive on Wednesday and Saturday nights.

Glencoe, Ballachulish PH49 4HX. ⓒ **01855/811-252.** Fax 01855/811-679. www.clachaig.com. 20 units, 18 with private bathroom. £60–£96 ($96–$154) double with bathroom. Rates include Scottish breakfast. MC, V. Take A82 south for 15km (9.3 miles) from Fort William; the inn is signposted. **Amenities:** Restaurant; 3 bars. *In room:* TV, coffeemaker, hair dryer.

King's House Hotel   The solid walls of this historic inn were built in the 1600s on a windswept plateau. It lies beside A82, 19km (12 miles) southeast of Glencoe village, at the strategic point where Glencoe joins the Glen Etive near a jagged mountain, Buachaille Etive Mor. Most of the modestly furnished guest rooms offer sweeping views; but are rather lacking in the amenities department; about half are equipped with small, tub-only bathrooms. Simple meals are served in the bar; the dining room boasts a selection of fine wines and freshly prepared meals. The hotel is a 30-minute walk from a ski center with a chairlift.

Glencoe PA39 4HZ. ⓒ **01855/851-259.** Fax 01855/851-216. www.kingy.com. 22 units, 12 with private bathroom. £50 ($80) double without bathroom; £56 ($90) double with bathroom. MC, V. You can arrange to be met at the Bridge of Orchy rail station. **Amenities:** Restaurant; bar; laundry. *In room:* Coffeemaker, hair dryer.

2 Fort William ⓡ: Gateway to Ben Nevis ⓡⓡ

214km (133 miles) NW of Edinburgh, 109km (68 miles) S of Inverness, 167km (104 miles) N of Glasgow

Fort William, on the shores of Loch Linnhe, is the best place for an overnight stop between here and Inverness in the northeast. It's a good base for exploring **Ben Nevis,** Scotland's highest mountain, and also for a day trip to Glencoe (see above).

Fort William stands on the site of a fort built by General Monk in 1655 to help crush any rebellion Highlanders might have been plotting. After several reconstructions, it was finally torn down in 1864 to make way for the railroad. During the notorious Highland Clearances, many starving and evicted people were shipped from here to the United States. Today, Fort William is a bustling town, thriving on the summer tourist trade and filled with shops, hotels, and cafes.

ESSENTIALS

GETTING THERE   Fort William is a major stop on the West Highland rail line that begins at the Queen Street Station in Glasgow and ends at Mallaig on the west coast. Three trains a day run this route at a one-way cost of £21 ($34). For schedules, contact the tourist office (see below) or call ⓒ **01463/239-026** in Inverness.

Four buses run from Glasgow to Fort William per day, taking 3 hours and costing £12.40 ($20) one-way. Call the Citilink Bus Station at ⓒ **0870/550-5050** in Glasgow for schedules. If you're driving from Glasgow, head north along A82.

VISITOR INFORMATION   The **tourist office** is at Cameron Centre, Cameron Square (ⓒ **01397/703-781**). April and May, it's open Monday to Saturday from 9am to 5pm and Sunday from 10am to 4pm; June 1 to June 28, hours are Monday to Saturday from 9am to 5:30pm and Sunday from 10am to 4pm; June 29 to July 26, hours are Monday to Saturday from 9am to 7pm and Sunday from 10am to 6pm; July 27 to August 16, it's open Monday to Saturday from 9am to 8pm and Sunday from 10am to 6pm; and August 17 to August 30, hours are Monday to Saturday from 9am to 7pm and Sunday from 10am to 6pm. August 31 to September 20 hours are Monday to Saturday 9am to 6pm and Sunday 10am to 5pm; September 21 to November 1, hours are Monday to

Saturday 9am to 4pm and Sunday 10am to 3pm; and November 2 to March, Monday to Saturday 9am to 5:30pm and Sunday 10am to 4pm.

EXPLORING THE AREA

You can reach the ruins of **Old Inverlochy Castle,** scene of a famous battle, by driving 3km (2 miles) north of Fort William on A82. Built in the 13th century, the ruined castle still has round corner towers and a walled courtyard. One of the towers was the keep, the other a water gate. The castle looms in the pages of Scottish history—here in 1645 a small army of Scots defeated government forces, although 1,500 men were lost that day. The former castle was once the stronghold of a clan known as the Comyns, and Inverlochy was the scene of many battles.

Neptune's Staircase, 5km (3 miles) northwest of Fort William off A830 at Banavie, is a series of nine locks that were constructed at the same time as the Caledonian Canal, raising Telford's canal 19m (64 ft.). This "staircase" is one of Scotland's most prominent engineering triumphs of the mid–19th century, when the eastern seacoast at Inverness was connected, via the canal, to the western seacoast at Fort William. This greatly shortened the distance required for goods moving from the North Sea to the Atlantic Ocean and bypassed the treacherous storms that often rage around Scotland's northern tier.

Since much of Fort William is relatively flat, consider biking. The best rentals are at **Off Beat Bikes,** 117 High St. (© **01397/704-008**), costing £10 ($16) for a half-day, £15 ($24) for a full day. You need only your ID for the deposit. It's open Monday to Saturday from 9am to 5:30pm and Sunday from 9:30am to 5pm.

In the north end of town, the **Ben Nevis Woolen Mill,** Belford Road (© **01397/704-244**), is only a shop, not a functioning woolen mill. Here you'll find a large selection of clothing and accessories: wools, tweeds, tartans, and handknit Arran sweaters, and gifts and souvenir items. An on-premises restaurant features regional fare.

Shoppers might also want to check out the **Granite House,** High Street (© **01397/703-651**), a family-run business that has been around for a quarter of a century. The owners call themselves "giftmongers" and see their shop as a mini-department store. There's a large selection of Scottish jewelry, with silver pieces in both traditional and contemporary designs and numerous watches. Collectibles like Lilliput Lane china and crystal by Edinburgh, Wedgwood, and Border Fine Arts are found here, and the traditional music department offers more than 1,000 Irish and Scottish music CDs and an array of traditional instruments, including pennywhistles and the *bhodrain* (a large drum struck with a single stick using both ends). The store also carries traditional toys for all ages.

Scottish Crafts & Whisky Centre, 135–139 High St. (© **01397/704-406**), is another place with a good mix of the best of all things Scottish: regionally produced jewelry, garden fountains, rugs, and clothing. Whisky connoisseurs will find some limited-edition and very rare bottles stocked, including a 1958 Ben Nevis. Handmade chocolates by Fergusons are also available. **Treasures of the Earth,** Main Street, Corpach (© **01397/772-283**), 6.5km (4 miles) west of Fort William along A830, sells crystals, minerals, and polished stones from around the world. They are available loose or set in jewelry, watches, and clocks.

West Highland Museum   The collection in this museum sheds light on all aspects of local history, especially the 1745 Jacobite Rising; it also has sections on tartans and folk life. Among the Jacobite collections and Highland weaponry is a facsimile for the order of the Massacre of Glencoe (see above).

Climbing Britain's Tallest Mountain

In the Central Highlands, **Ben Nevis,** at 1,342m (4,406 ft.), is the tallest mountain in Britain. Although it's not exactly ready to challenge the towering Alps, Ben Nevis can still give hikers a good workout. The pony track to the top is often filled with walkers tackling the difficult 8-hour jaunt. The unpredictable Scottish weather adds to the challenge, requiring you to dress in layers and bring along at least a waterproof jacket. The mean monthly temperature of Ben Nevis falls below freezing; snow has been reported at all times of year, even during the hottest months of July and August. Howling winds are frequent.

Hikers head up for the view, but it's not guaranteed due to weather conditions. On a clear day, you can see the Irish foothills some 193km (120 miles) away, the Hebridean Isle of Rhum 148km (92 miles) away, and the Glencoe peaks (Ben Lawers, Torridon, and the Cairngorms). If you don't want to climb, a cable car can take to a height of 701m (2,300 ft.) for viewing.

The trail is much rougher but even more beautiful if approached from Glen Nevis, one of the country's most scenic glens. Clear rivers and cascading waterfalls add to the drama of the scenery; meadows and moors seem straight out of Austria.

Before going, discuss the climb with the staff at the tourist office in Fort William. They can give you advice as well as maps, and they'll pinpoint the best starting places. A signpost to the north of Nevis Bridge points to the path up Ben Nevis. Allow 8½ hours total for the under 16km (10-mile) trip. Take along a windbreaker, sturdy footwear, food, and water.

A word of warning: Sudden weather changes may pose a safety hazard. And that final 300m (1,000 ft.) is really steep terrain, but having gone this far, few can resist the challenge. Some Brits call Ben Nevis the "top of the world." It really isn't—it just feels that way when you finally reach the peak.

Cameron Sq. © **01397/702-169.** www.fort-william.net/museum. Admission £2 ($3.20) adults, £1.50 ($2.40) seniors, 50p ($.80) children. June–Sept Mon–Sat 10am–5pm (July–Aug also Sun 2–5pm); Oct–May Mon–Sat 10am–4pm.

Glenfinnan Monument   At Glenfinnan at the head of Loch Shiel, this monument marks the spot where Bonnie Prince Charlie unfurled his proud red-and-white silk banner on August 19, 1745, in his ill-fated attempt to restore the Stuarts to the British throne. The figure of a kilted Highlander tops the monument. At the visitor center, you can learn of the prince's campaign from Glenfinnan to Derby that ended in his defeat at Culloden.

About 23km (14 miles) west of Fort William, on A830 toward Mallaig. © **01397/722-250** for visitor center. Admission to visitor center £1.50 ($2.40). Visitor center mid-May to Aug daily 9:30am–6pm; Sept to early May daily 10am–5pm.

WHERE TO STAY

There's no shortage of B&Bs in Fort William; the tourist office can supply you with a list if the selections below are full.

VERY EXPENSIVE

Inverlochy Castle ★★★ Inverlochy Castle, against the scenic backdrop of Ben Nevis, hosted Queen Victoria in her day and remains the premier address in this entire part of Scotland. Back then, it was a newly built (1870) Scottish mansion; the monarch claimed in her diary, "I never saw a lovelier or more romantic spot." Now a Relais & Châteaux property, the Inverlochy has undergone a major refurbishment but has retained its charm. Luxurious appointments, antiques, artwork, and crystal, plus a profusion of flowers, create a mood of elegance and refinement. The prices certainly reflect this opulence.

The cuisine here is some of the finest in Scotland, with food cooked to order and served on silver platters. See "Where to Dine," below, for details. Nonguests can dine here if there's room, but reservations are mandatory.

Torlundy, Fort William PH33 6SN. ℂ 01397/702-177. Fax 01397/702-953. www.inverlochycastlehotel.com. 17 units. £395–£435 ($632–$696) double, £500–£550 ($800–$880) suite, high season. Rates lower off season. Rates include Scottish breakfast. AE, MC, V. Closed early Jan–late Feb. Free valet parking. Take A82 for 5km (3 miles) northeast of town. **Amenities:** Restaurant; tennis court; room service (7am–11pm); babysitting; laundry. *In room:* TV, hair dryer, iron/ironing board.

MODERATE

Alexandra Milton Hotel Across from the rail terminal, the Alexandra boasts the tall gables and formidable granite walls so common in this part of the Highlands. It has been completely modernized, offering pleasant and comfortably furnished guest rooms with shower-only bathrooms. The chef makes excellent use of fresh fish, and the wine cellar is amply endowed. Guests have free use of the facilities at the nearby Milton Hotel and Leisure Club.

The Parade, Fort William PH33 6AZ. ℂ **01397/702-241.** Fax 01397/705-554. www.miltonhotels.com. 97 units. £60–£135 ($96–$216) double. Rates include breakfast. AE, DC, MC, V. Free parking. From the north, take A82 into Fort William following signs for the town center. At the round-about, turn right and drive through the next round-about. The Alexandra is on the left-hand side. **Amenities:** 2 restaurants; bar; access to nearby health club; 24-hr. room service; laundry. *In room:* TV, coffeemaker.

The Moorings Hotel One of the most up-to-date hotels in the region, the Moorings was designed in a traditional style in the mid-1970s, with bay and dormer windows and a black-and-white facade. The interior is richly paneled in the Jacobean style. The guest rooms are attractive and modern, each with a shower-only bathroom. Bar lunches and suppers are offered in the Mariner Wine Bar, while more formal meals are served in the Moorings Restaurant, where an even greater selection of wine (more than 200 vintages) accompanies dishes like smoked venison, Scottish oysters, homemade terrines, and wild salmon in lemon-butter sauce.

Banavie, Fort William PH33 7LY. ℂ **01397/772-797.** Fax 01397/772-441. www.moorings-fortwilliam.co.uk. 28 units. £100–£110 ($160–$176) double. Rates include Scottish breakfast. AE, DC, MC, V. Drive 5km (3 miles) north of Fort William to the hamlet of Banavie, beside B8004. **Amenities:** Restaurant; bar; room service (noon–11pm). *In room:* TV, coffeemaker, hair dryer, iron/ironing board.

INEXPENSIVE

Croit Anna Hotel Overlooking Loch Linnhe, the Croit Anna Hotel opens onto fine views of the Ardgour Hills. It's owned and managed by the same family who built it on a traditional Highland croft that has been in their possession for more than 250 years. All the midsize guest rooms have tidily kept but small shower-only bathrooms. Entertainment is provided on most evenings in season.

Achintore Rd. Druimarbin, Fort William PH33 6RR. ℂ **01397/702-268.** Fax 01397/704-099. www.visit-fort william.coluk/croitanna. 80 units. £48–£54 ($77–$86) double with bathroom. Rates include Scottish breakfast.

MC, V. Take A82 4km (2½ miles) south of town. **Amenities:** Restaurant; 2 bars; laundry. *In room:* TV, coffeemaker, hair dryer, iron/ironing board.

The Lime Tree   This well-kept B&B in the center of town is housed in what is reputed to be the oldest fully surviving building in Fort William. It was built in the early 1800s in the town center as the manse (pastor's residence) for the nearby Church of Scotland. Today, it offers pastel guest rooms (with small, shower-only bathrooms) and exhibition space for local painters, including respected artist David Wilson.

The Old Manse, Achintore Rd., Fort William. ⓒ **01397/701-806.** www.limetreestudio.co.uk. 5 units, 3 with private bathroom. £40–£60 ($64–$96) double without bathroom; £30–£40 ($48–$64) double with bathroom. DC, MC, V. Free parking. Follow A82 into Fort William. *In room:* TV, coffeemaker, no phone.

Lochview Guest House *Value*   South from the center of Fort William and about a 15-minute walk uphill is this non-smoking guesthouse, designed around 1950. The guest rooms have been outfitted with comfortable furnishings by Denise and Alan Kirk, who maintain the .4 hectare (1 acre) of lawn surrounding their building and protect the view sweeping down over the loch and the rest of the town. Each unit comes with a small, shower-only bathroom. Other guesthouses in town might be more historic—but for the price, Lochview represents good value, and the Kirk family is unfailingly generous.

Heathercroft, Argyll Rd., Fort William PH33 6RE. ⓒ and fax **01397/703-149.** www.lochview.co.uk. 6 units. £44–£54 ($70–$86) double. Rates include breakfast. MC, V. Closed Oct–Easter. *In room:* TV, coffeemaker, no phone.

WHERE TO DINE

Crannog Seafood Restaurant SEAFOOD   Occupying a converted ticket office and bait store in a quayside setting overlooking Loch Linnhe, this restaurant serves seafood so fresh, locals claim "it fairly leaps at you." Much of the fish comes from the owners' own fishing vessels or from their smokehouse. Bouillabaisse is a specialty, as are Loch Linnhe prawns and langoustines. A vegetarian dish of the day is invariably featured.

Town Pier. ⓒ **01397/705-589.** Reservations recommended. Main courses £9–£16.95 ($14–$27). MC, V. Daily noon–2:30pm and 6–9:30pm. Closed Jan 1–2 and Dec 25–26.

Inverlochy Castle *✿✿✿* BRITISH   This is one of the grandest restaurants in Britain (as it should be, at these prices!). The cuisine here has been celebrated ever since Queen Victoria got a sudden attack of the munchies and stopped in "for a good tuck-in." The kitchen uses carefully selected local ingredients, including salmon from Spean, crayfish from Loch Linnhe, and produce from the hotel's own gardens. Partridge and grouse are offered in season, and roast filet of Aberdeen Angus beef is a classic. The chefs also do their own baking, and their specialty, an orange soufflé, may be the best we've ever tasted. Dinner is served in rooms decorated with period and elaborate furniture presented as gifts to Inverlochy Castle from the king of Norway. The formal service is the finest in the Highlands.

Torlundy, Fort William PH33 6SN. ⓒ **01397/702-177.** Reservations required. Fixed-price lunch £28.50 ($46) set-price dinner £52.50 ($84). AE, MC, V. Daily 12:30–1:30pm and 7–9pm. Closed Jan–Feb.

FORT WILLIAM AFTER DARK

Ben Nevis Bar, 103–109 High St. (ⓒ **01397/702-295**), offers free entertainment by rock, blues, jazz, and folk bands on Thursday and Friday. On tap are McEwan's, Foster's, and Kronenberg lagers, McEwan's 70 Shilling, and Guinness and Gillespie's stouts.

McTavish's Kitchen, High Street (© **01397/702-406**), presents a Scottish show just for tourists. It's fun but corny, featuring tartan-clad dancers, bagpipes, and other traditional instruments every night May to September from 8 to 10pm. You can see the show with or without dinner. A three-course "Taste of Scotland" meal costs £17.95 ($29). On tap is Tennant's Special and Lager, available for £2.65 ($4.25) per pint. Admission to the show is £4 ($6.40) adults and £2 ($3.20) children if you're eating; the show only is £2 ($3.20) adults and £1 ($1.60) children.

Grog & Gruel, 66 High St. (© **01397/705-078**), serves up regional cask-conditioned ales. There's an occasional live band, ranging from rock and pop to folk and Scottish music.

3 Invergarry

40km (25 miles) NE of Fort William, 254km(158 miles) NW of Edinburgh

A Highland center for fishing and for exploring Glen Mor and Loch Ness, Invergarry is noted for its fine scenery. At Invergarry, the road through the western Highland glens and mountains begins, forming one part of the famous "Road to the Isles" that terminates at Kyle of Lochalsh. If you're rushed for time, you can easily skip this place. Most people stop off here to stay at the Glengarry Castle Hotel, which looks haunted and even has the ruins of a long-abandoned castle on its grounds.

ESSENTIALS
GETTING THERE   The nearest **rail service** runs to Fort William, where you'll have to take a connecting bus to get to Invergarry, a half-hour ride away. **Highland Omnibuses** offer this service. The tourist office in Fort William can provide schedules. If you're **driving** from Fort William, proceed north on the Inverness road (A82) to Invergarry.

VISITOR INFORMATION   The nearest **tourist office** is in Fort William (see "Fort William: Gateway to Ben Nevis," earlier in this chapter).

SEEING THE SIGHTS
From Invergarry, drive 5.5km (3½ miles) south, following A82 toward Fort William if you want to visit the 1812 monument **Well of the Heads** (*Tobar nan Ceann* in Gaelic). The only sign indicating the well's position is a grocery store (Well of the Seven Heads Grocery & Convenience Mart). At the store, a staff member will direct you down a short forest path to the well itself. The well was erected by MacDonnell of Glengarry to commemorate the decapitation of seven brothers who had murdered the two sons of a 17th-century chief of Clan Keppoch, a branch of the MacDonnells, at Glengarry. An obelisk supports the bronzed heads of the seven victims. The legend of the well, alas, is more exciting than the actual site.

On the grounds of Glengarry Castle Hotel (see below), you can see the meager ruins of **Invergarry Castle,** the stronghold of the MacDonnells of Glengarry. A few grim walls remain. The site of the castle on Raven's Rock, overlooking Loch Oich in the Great Glen, was a strategic one in the days of clan feuds and Jacobite risings. Because the castle ruins aren't safe, you can view them only from outside. From Invergarry, drive 2.5km (1½ miles) south, following A82 toward Fort William, then turn off to follow the signs pointing to the hotel. The ruins lie beside the hotel's very long main driveway, surrounded by trees.

WHERE TO STAY & DINE

Glengarry Castle Hotel This 1866–69 mansion, with gables and chimneys, is an impressive sight. On its vast grounds are the ruins of Invergarry Castle (see above). The hotel makes a pleasant base for fishing, tennis, walking, and rowing. The midsize to spacious guest rooms are comfortably old-fashioned, reminiscent of the 1950s, and each comes with a small bathroom with tub. The dining room offers good, home-cooked, but rather basic meals. Nightly fixed-price dinners are rather high-priced. Affordable light lunches are served, but the special Sunday version is more elaborate and expensive.

Invergarry PH35 4HW. ✆ **01809/501-254.** Fax 01809/501-207. www.glengarry.net. 26 units. £82–£182 ($131–$291) double. Rates include Scottish breakfast. MC, V. Closed mid Nov–late Mar. From Invergarry, drive 2.5km (1½ miles) south, following A82 toward Fort William; turn off to follow signs pointing to the hotel. Pets. **Amenities:** Restaurant; lounge; tennis court. *In room:* TV, coffeemaker, hair dryer.

4 Aviemore ⭐

208km (129 miles) N of Edinburgh, 47km (29 miles) SE of Inverness, 137km (85 miles) N of Perth

A bit tacky for our tastes, Aviemore, a year-round resort on the Spey, was opened in 1966 in the heart of the Highlands, at the foot of the historic rock of **Craigellachie.** The center of Aviemore itself, with ugly concrete structures, has little of the flavor of Scotland. But visitors flock here for its accessibility to some of the most beautiful scenery in the Highlands, especially the Cairngorm Mountains, known for its skiing in winter and hiking in summer.

ESSENTIALS

GETTING THERE Aviemore, on the main Inverness–Edinburgh rail line, is the area's major transportation hub. For rail schedules in Aviemore, call ✆ **01479/810-221.** Some 8 trains a day from Inverness pass through (trip time: 30-45 min.), at £7.40 ($12) one-way. Twelve trains per day also arrive from Glasgow or Edinburgh. Trip time from each city is 3 hours, and a one-way ticket from either is £30 ($48).

Aviemore is on the main Inverness–Edinburgh bus line, with frequent service. The trip from Edinburgh takes about 3 hours (call ✆ **0990/808-080** in Edinburgh for schedules) and costs £5 ($8). Frequent buses throughout the day also arrive from Inverness (trip time: 40 min.).

If you're driving from Edinburgh, after crossing the Forth Bridge Road, take M90 to Perth, then continue the rest of the way along A9 into Aviemore.

VISITOR INFORMATION The **Highlands of Scotland Tourist Office** (Aviemore branch) is on Grampian Road (✆ **01479/810-363**). June to August, it's open Monday to Friday from 9am to 7pm, Saturday from 9am to 6pm, and Sunday from 10am to 5pm; September to May, hours are Monday to Friday from 9am to 5pm and Saturday and Sunday from 10am to 5pm.

EXPLORING THE AREA

North of Aviemore, the **Strathspey Railway,** Dalfaber Road (✆ **01479/810-725;** www.strathspeyrailway.co.uk), is your best bet in Scotland to learn first-hand what it was like to ride the rails in the 19th century. The railway follows the valley of the River Spey between Boat of Garten and Aviemore, a distance of 8km (5 miles). The train is drawn by a coal-burning steam locomotive. The newest locomotive used was made nearly 4 decades ago, the oldest being of 1899 vintage. The trip is meant to re-create the total experience of travel on a Scottish steam railway that once carried wealthy Victorians toward their hunting lodges in North Britain. The round-trip takes about an hour. The rail station at Boat of Garten, where you can board the train, has also been restored.

Round-trip passage costs £12 ($19) first class or £8.40 ($13) third class. Schedules change frequently, but from July to the end of August trains make four round-trips daily. From May to June and September, they run 3 times daily, and from March to April and October they run Sunday, Wednesday, and Thursday. There's no regular service in winter; however, special Christmas season trips are made with Santa Claus aboard. To complete the experience, you can wine and dine on board on Sunday and Friday in July and August, when a single-seating casual lunch is served; the cost for the fare and meal is £16 ($26). Reservations must be made for the meals. The dining car is a replica of a Pullman parlor car, the Amethyst. For reservations and hours of departure, call © **01479/831-692.**

Skiers are attracted to the area any time after October, when snow can be expected. You can rent ski equipment and clothing at the Day Lodge at the main Cairngorm parking area. Weather patterns can change quickly in the Cairngorm massif. Call the number above for a report on the latest weather conditions. To reach the area, take A951, branching off from A9 at Aviemore, then head for the parking area at the Day Lodge.

If you'd like to explore the countryside on two wheels, there are several places to rent bikes. **Speyside Sports,** Main Street (© **01479/810-656**), rents bikes at £8 ($13) for a ½-day, £12 ($19) for a full day, and £43 ($69) for 6 days. **Bothy Bikes,** 81 Grampian Rd. (© **01479/810-111**), charges £10 ($16) for a ½-day, £14 ($22) for a full day, £160 ($256) for 6 days. Discounts begin to apply when you rent for 2 days or more.

The tourist office will give you hiking maps and offer advice, especially about weather conditions. One of the best trails is reached by following B9760 to the signposted **Glenmore Forest Park,** in the vicinity of Loch Morlich.

For the grandest view of the Cairngorm peaks, you can take the **Cairngorm Mountain Railway** (© **01479/861-261**), to the top. The best views of the Valley of the Spey can be seen from the point where the funicular railway lets you off. At the peak is a visitor's center and restaurant. Wear warm gear as it gets mighty cold at the top, some 900m (3,000 ft.) above sea level. The railway is signposted off B9152. If weather permits, the train runs daily from 8:30am to 4:30pm, costing £7.50 ($12) for adults, £6.50 ($10) or seniors and students, and £5 ($8) for children.

WHERE TO STAY

Aviemore Highlands Hotel   This resort hotel caters to an outdoorsy clientele. It's a labyrinthine complex of wings, staircases, and long halls, which funnel into public rooms with big windows overlooking the countryside. In summer, doors open to reveal flagstone terraces ringed with viburnum and juniper. You can drink in the Illicit Still Bar, which has an antique whisky still and copper-top tables. The main restaurant is capped with a soaring ceiling, trussed with beams. The midsize guest rooms are well furnished, and some family rooms are also available. The bathrooms are tidily organized, some with shower only.

Aviemore Mountain Resort, Aviemore PH22 1PJ. © **01479/810-771.** Fax 01479/811-473. www.aviehighlands. demon.co.uk. 102 units. £90–£100 ($144–$160) double. Rates include Scottish breakfast. AE, DC, MC, V. Lies 2 blocks northwest of the train station. **Amenities:** Restaurant; 2 bars; 24-hr. room service; laundry; health club. *In room:* TV, coffeemaker, hair dryer.

Corrour House Hotel ✧ *Finds*   This isolated granite house is an oasis of personality in a sea of impersonal hotels. Built around 1880 on 1.6 hectares (4 acres) of forest and garden, it contains simple but comfortable rooms that are attractively decorated, each with a shower-only bathroom. Your hosts are the Catto family, who will prepare dinner if arranged in advance. Many of their dishes have a true "taste of Scotland" flavor, including Ballindalloch pheasant with a sauce made from red wine, oranges, red currants, and fresh herbs.

Rothiemurchus, by Aviemore PH22 1QH. ✆ **01479/810-220.** Fax 01479/811-500. www.corrourhouse hotel.co.uk. 8 units. £80–£100 ($128–$160) double. Rates include breakfast. AE, MC, V. Closed mid-Nov to Christmas. From Aviemore, drive 1km (½ mile) east on B970, following the signs to Glenmore. **Amenities:** Restaurant; bar. *In room:* TV, coffeemaker, hair dryer.

Hilton Aviemore ✧ *Kids*   This is the resort area's best hotel because of its extensive sports and leisure facilities, which are spread across 26 hectares (65 acres) of tree-studded grounds. The midsize guest rooms are spacious and well appointed, with comfortable furnishings and average-size bathrooms, some with both tub and shower. You have a choice of two dining rooms, although the food in both is fairly standard. There's often evening entertainment, particularly on weekends. In winter, downhill and cross-country ski equipment can be rented, and lessons are available. The sports and leisure hall's Fun House caters to children.

Center of Aviemore PH22 1PF. ✆ **01479/810-681.** Fax 01479/810-534. www.aviemore.hilton.com. 88 units. £115 ($184) double; £165 ($264) suite. AE, DC, MC, V. In Aviemore, turn into the junction immediately opposite the railway station at the south end of the village. Follow the round-about; the hotel is signposted. **Amenities:** Restaurant; bar; indoor heated pool; exercise room; sauna; business center; salon; 24-hr. room service; babysitting; laundry service. *In room:* TV, dataport, coffeemaker, hair dryer, iron/ironing board.

Lynwilg House ✧   The Victorian solidity of this house is particularly noteworthy in Aviemore, considering the relative modernity of the other resort hotels. It was built by the duke of Richmond in the 1880s. Today, it retains 1.6 hectares (4 acres) of its original park and gardens overlooking the mountains, with high-ceilinged guest rooms containing comfortable furnishings and shower-only bathrooms. In front of the house is a croquet lawn, and at the bottom of the well-tended garden is a stream where guests like to relax.

Lynwilg by Aviemore PH22 1PZ. ✆ and fax **01479/811-685.** www.lynwilg.co.uk. 4 units. £60–£70 ($90–$105) double. Rates include breakfast. MC, V. Follow A9 for 2.5km (1½ miles) south of Aviemore's center, following the signs to Perth. *In room:* TV, coffeemaker, hair dryer.

WHERE TO DINE

The Bar/The Restaurant SCOTTISH   Although the golf course, health club, and leisure facilities of this country club are open only to members, visitors are welcome in the cozy bar and restaurant, which is outfitted in tartan carpets and heavy brocade curtains. In the bar, where live entertainment is featured nightly, the fare includes venison cutlets, sandwiches, steak pies, and a variety of malt whiskies. The restaurant serves seafood, such as skewered tiger prawns soaked with butter, as well as grilled Angus steaks, main-course salads, and a limited number of vegetarian dishes. Several nights per week, the restaurant hosts theme nights with entertainment.

In the Dalfaber Golf and Country Club, about 1.5km (1 mile) north of the center of Aviemore. ✆ **01479/ 811-244.** Reservations required in the restaurant. Main courses £5.25–£6.95 ($8.40–$11); bar platters £3.50–£5.95 ($5.60–$9.50). MC, V. Restaurant daily 6–9:30pm. Bar daily 11am–11pm.

AVIEMORE AFTER DARK

Crofters, off Grampian Road at the Aviemore Mountain Resort (✆ **01479/ 810-771**), a 2-minute walk from the center of Aviemore, has dancing nightly from 10pm to 1am, with guest DJs bringing in their own music and setting the mood. No cover is charged.

5 Along Loch Ness ★★

Sir Peter Scott's *Nessitera rhombopteryx,* one of the world's great mysteries, continues to elude her pursuers. The Loch Ness monster, or "Nessie" as she's more familiarly known, has captured the imagination of the world, drawing thousands of visitors yearly to Loch Ness. Half a century ago, A82 was built alongside the banks of the loch's western shores, and since then many more sightings have been claimed.

All types of high-tech underwater contraptions have gone in after the Loch Ness monster, but no one can find her in spite of the photographs and film footage you might have seen in magazines or on TV. Dr. Robert Rines and his associates at the Academy of Applied Science in Massachusetts maintain an all-year watch with sonar-triggered cameras and strobe lights suspended from a raft in Urquhart Bay. However, some people in Inverness aren't keen on collaring the monster, and you can't blame them: An old prophecy predicts a violent end for Inverness if the monster is ever captured.

The loch is 39km (24 miles) long, 1.6km (1 mile) wide, and some 229m (755 ft.) deep. If you'd like to stay along the loch and monster-watch instead of basing yourself at Inverness, we've listed some choices below. Even if the monster doesn't put in an appearance, you'll enjoy the scenery. In summer, you can take boat cruises across Loch Ness from both Fort Augustus and Inverness.

If you're driving, take A82 between Fort Augustus and Inverness running along Loch Ness. Buses from either Fort Augustus or Inverness also traverse A82, taking you to Drumnadrochit.

DRUMNADROCHIT

The bucolic village of Drumnadrochit is about 1.6km (1 mile) from Loch Ness at the entrance to Glen Urquhart. It's the nearest village to the part of the loch in which sightings of the monster have been reported most frequently.

Although most visitors arrive at Drumnadrochit to see the Loch Ness monster exhibit (see "Seeing the Sights," below), you can also take an offbeat adventure in the great outdoors at the **Highland Riding Centre,** Borlum Farm, Drumnadrochit (© **01456/450-220**). This is a 343-hectare (850 acre) sheep farm on moorlands overlooking Loch Ness; follow A82 for about 23km (14 miles) west of Inverness and make a reservation in advance. In summer, the stable's 45 horses are booked throughout their working day. Tours depart almost every day, depending on demand; they leave between 9:30am and 4:30pm, last 60 to 120 minutes, and cost £14.50 to £24 ($23–$38).

Wilderness Cycles, The Cottage (© **01456/450-223**), will rent you a bike so you can go exploring on your own. Rentals costs £7 ($11) for a ½ day, £12 ($19) daily, and £35 to £50 ($56–$80) weekly. It's open daily 9am to 6pm.

Official Loch Ness Monster Exhibition   This is Drumnadrochit's big attraction, featuring a scale replica of Nessie. It opened in 1980 and has been packing 'em in ever since. Follow Nessie's story from A.D. 565 to the present in photographs, audio, and video, and then climb aboard the sonar research vessel *John Murray.* This is the most visited place in the Highlands of Scotland, with more than 200,000 visitors annually.

Spotting Nessie

She's affectionately known as Nessie, but her more formal name is *Nessitera rhombopteryx,* and she has the unflattering appellation of the Loch Ness monster. Is she the beast that never was, or the world's most famous living animal? You decide. Real or imagined, she's Scotland's virtual mascot, and even if she doesn't exist, she's one of the major attractions of the country. Who can drive along the dark waters of Loch Ness without staring at the murky depths and expecting a head or a couple of humps to appear above the water's surface at any minute?

Nessie's lineage is ancient. An appearance in A.D. 565 was recorded by respected 7th-century biographer St. Adamnan, not known as a spinner of tall tales. The claim is that St. Columba was en route along Loch Ness to convert Brude, king of the Picts, to Christianity. The saint ordered a monk to swim across the loch and retrieve a boat. However, as he was in midswim, Nessie attacked. The monk's life was saved only when Columba confronted the sea beast with a sign of the cross and a shouted invocation.

Columba's calming effect on Nessie must have lasted over the centuries, because no attacks have been reported since. Of course, there was that accident in the 1500s when a chronicle reported that "a terrible beast issuing out of the water early one morning about midsummer knocked down trees and killed three men with its tail." Again, in 1961, 30 hotel guests reported seeing two humps that rose out of the water just before their craft exploded and sank. Bertram Mill has offered £20,000 ($32,000) to have the monster delivered alive to his circus.

Because Scotland is the land not only of Nessie but also whisky, it might be assumed that some of these sightings were hallucinations brought on by the consumption of far too many "wee drams." However, sightings have come from people of impeccable credentials who were stone sober. Nessie seems to like to show herself to monks, perhaps a tradition dating from St. Columba. Several monks at the Fort Augustus Abbey claim to have seen her. A monk who's an organist at Westminster Cathedral reported a sighting in 1973.

Belief in Nessie's existence is so strong that midget yellow submarines and all types of high-tech underwater contraptions have been used in an attempt to track her down. Many photographs exist—most of them faked—usually from the site of the ruins of Urquhart Castle on the loch's shore. Other photographs haven't been so easily explained.

If Nessie does exist, exactly who is she? A sole survivor from prehistoric times? A gigantic sea snake? It has even been suggested she's a cosmic wanderer through time. Chances are you won't see her on your visit, but you can see a fantasy replica of the sea beast at the Official Loch Ness Monster Exhibition at Drumnadrochit.

Drumnadrochit. ℂ **01456/450-573.** Admission £5.95 ($9.50) adults, £4.50 ($7.20) students, £4.50 ($7.20) seniors, £3.50 ($5.60) children age 7–16, £14.95 ($24) families, free for children age 7 and under. Easter–May daily 9:30am–5pm; June and Sept daily 9am–6pm; July–Aug daily 9am–8pm; Oct daily 9:30am–5:30pm; Nov–Easter daily 10am–3:30pm. Follow the main A82 trunk road between Inverness and Fort William to the north shore of Loch Ness.

Urquhart Castle This ruined castle, one of Scotland's largest, is on a promontory overlooking Loch Ness. The chief of Clan Grant owned the castle in 1509, and most of the extensive ruins date from that period. In 1692, the castle was blown up by the Grants to prevent it from becoming a Jacobite stronghold. Rising from crumbling walls, the jagged keep still remains. It's at Urquhart Castle that sightings of the Loch Ness monster are most often reported.

Loch Ness along A82. ℂ **01456/450-551.** Admission £3.80 ($5.70) adults, £2.80 ($4.20) seniors, £1.20 ($1.80) children. Apr–Sept daily 9:30am–6:30pm (to 8:30pm July–Aug); Oct–Mar daily 9:30am–3:45pm. Drive 2.5km (1½ miles) southeast of Drumnadrochit on A82.

WHERE TO STAY & DINE

Polmaily House Hotel ✦ This is a snug haven in a sea of Loss Ness tourism and overcommercialization. The Edwardian inn, on a 7.3-hectare (18-acre) estate with mixed gardens and woodland, is believed to have been built in 1776 and now re-creates manorial country-house living. The spacious and elegant guest rooms contain tasteful antiques, high ceilings, leaded-glass windows, and flowered wallpaper. The restaurant attracts locals as well as hotel guests with dishes like Aberdeen beef and fresh salmon.

Drumnadrochit 1V63 6XT ℂ **01456/450-343.** Fax 01456/450-814. www.polmaily.co.uk. 14 units. £80–£124 ($128–$198) double. Rates include Scottish breakfast. MC, V. Drive 2 miles (3km) west of Drumnadrochit on A831. **Amenities:** Restaurant; bar; indoor heated pool; tennis court; room service (7am–10pm); babysitting; laundry service; croquet lawn; Internet cafe. *In room:* TV, coffeemaker, dataport, hair dryer.

FORT AUGUSTUS

Fort Augustus, 58km (36 miles) south of Inverness along A82 and 267km (166 miles) northwest of Edinburgh, stands at the head (the southernmost end) of Loch Ness. The town became fortified after the 1715 Jacobite rising. Gen. George Wade, of road- and bridge-building fame, headquartered here in 1724, and in 1729, the government constructed a fort along the banks of the loch, naming it Augustus after William Augustus, duke of Cumberland, son of George II. Jacobites seized the fort in 1745 and controlled it until the Scottish defeat at Culloden. Now gone, Wade's fort was turned into the Fort Augustus Abbey at the south end of Loch Ness. A Benedictine order was installed in 1867, and the monks today run a Catholic secondary school on the site.

Fort Augustus is mainly a refueling stop for those who want to stay on Loch Ness itself—perhaps in hopes of seeing the monster—instead of dropping anchor in a larger town like Fort William to the south or Inverness to the north. The only other reason to stop by is that it's the most panoramic place to see the locks of the Caledonian Canal in action.

Bisecting the actual village of Fort Augustus, the locks of the **Caledonian Canal** are a popular attraction when boats are passing through. Running across the loftiest sections of Scotland, the canal was constructed between 1803 and 1822. Almost in a straight line, it makes its way from Inverness in the north to Corpach in the vicinity of Fort William. The canal is 97km (60 miles) long: 35 man-made kilometers (22 miles), and the rest are natural lochs.

Caley Cruisers, Canal Road, Inverness (ℂ **01463/236-328;** fax 01463/714-879; www.caleycruisers.co.uk), maintains a fleet of 50 cruisers (with skippers) that groups of two to six people can rent from March to October—even if their marine experience is relatively limited. Rentals last for 1 week, long enough to negotiate the 97km (60 miles) of the Caledonian Canal in both directions between Inverness and Fort William. (There are about 15 locks en route; tolls are included in the rental fee). Depending on the craft's size and the season, a week's rental ranges from £415 to £1,523 ($664–$2,437); the cost of fuel and taxes for a week is £65 to £110 ($104–$176), plus another £20 to £30 ($32–$48) for a reasonably priced insurance policy. Except for the waters of Loch Ness, which can be rough, the canal is calm enough and doesn't pose the dangers of cruising on the open sea.

WHERE TO STAY & DINE

Inchnacardoch Lodge   Inchnacardoch Lodge is a family-run hotel in a panoramic setting overlooking Loch Ness, 1km (½ mile) north of the town center. In 1878 a country residence of the Fraser clan's chief, Lord Lovat, the hotel offers comfortable guest rooms along with efficiently organized bathrooms, most with combination tub and shower. The common areas have recently been refurbished, but the traditional ambience remains. You can relax in the bar while watching the waters for the mysterious monster; a wee dram of malt too much and you may just find her. If you can tear yourself away from the view of the water, the hotel restaurant offers moderately priced main courses. No smoking is permitted.

Hwy. A82, Fort Augustus PH32 4BL. © **01320/366-258.** Fax 10320/366-248. www.inchnacardoch.co.uk. 15 units. £60–£90 ($96–$144) double. Rates include Scottish breakfast. AE, MC, V. Parking. Drive 1km (½ mile) north of Fort Augustus on A82. **Amenities:** Restaurant; bar. *In room:* TV, coffeemaker.

6 Inverness ★: Capital of the Highlands

251km (156 miles) NW of Edinburgh, 216km (134 miles) NW of Dundee, 216km (134 miles) W of Aberdeen

The capital of the Highlands, Inverness is a royal burgh and seaport at the north end of Great Glen on both sides of the Ness River. For such a historic town, the sights are rather meager, but Inverness makes a good base for touring. If your time is limited, confine your visits to Culloden Battlefield, Cawdor Castle of *Macbeth* fame (see "Nairn & Cawdor Castle," later in this chapter), and Black Isle (see "The Black Isle Peninsula," later in this chapter), the most enchanting and scenic peninsula in Scotland.

ESSENTIALS

GETTING THERE   Domestic flights from various parts of Britain arrive at the Inverness Airport. Flight time from London's Gatwick to the Inverness/Dalcross Airport is 1¾ hours. Call © **01667/464-000** in Inverness for flight information.

Some five to seven trains per day arrive from Glasgow and Edinburgh (on Sun, two or three trains). The train takes 3½ hours from either city, and a one-way fare from either is £31.60 ($51). Trains pull into Station Square, off Academy Street in Inverness (© **08457/484-950** for schedules).

Scottish CityLink coaches provide service for the area (© **08705/505-050** for schedules). Frequent service through the day is possible from either Edinburgh or Glasgow (a 4-hr. trip each way), at a one-way fare of £14.70 ($24). The bus station is at Farraline Park, off Academy Street (© **01463/233-371**).

Driving from Edinburgh, take M9 north to Perth, then follow along the Great North Road (A9) until you reach Inverness.

VISITOR INFORMATION   The Inverness branch of the **Highlands of Scotland Tourist Board** is at Castle Wynd, off Bridge Street (© **01463/234-353**). October to mid-April, it's open Monday to Friday from 9am to 5pm and Saturday from 10am to 4pm; mid-April to May, hours are Monday to Friday from 9am to 5pm, Saturday from 9:30am to 5pm, and Sunday from 9:30am to 4pm; June hours are Monday to Friday from 9am to 6pm, Saturday from 9am to 5pm, and Sunday from 9:30am to 5pm; July and August, it's open Monday to Saturday from 9am to 6pm and Sunday from 9:30am to 5pm; September hours are Monday to Saturday from 9am to 6pm and Sunday from 9:30am to 5pm.

SPECIAL EVENTS   At the **Highland Games** in July, with its sporting competitions and festive balls, the season in Inverness reaches its social peak. For more information and exact dates, consult the tourist office (see above).

SEEING THE SIGHTS

Inverness is one of the oldest inhabited sites in Scotland. On **Craig Phadrig** are the remains of a vitrified fort, believed to date from the 4th century B.C. One of the most important prehistoric monuments in the north, the **Stones of Clava** are about 10km (6 miles) east of Inverness on the road to Nairn. These cairns and standing stones are from the Bronze Age.

The old castle of Inverness stood to the east of the present street Castlehill, and the site still retains the name "Auld Castlehill." David I built the first stone castle in Inverness around 1141, and the **Clock Tower** is all that remains of a fort erected by Cromwell's army between 1652 and 1657. The rebellious Scots blew up the old castle in 1746 to keep it from falling to government troops, and the present **castle** was constructed by the Victorians in the 19th century. Today, this landmark houses the law courts of Inverness and local government offices.

The 16th-century **Abertarff House,** Church Street, is now the headquarters of An Comunn Gaidhealach, the Highland association that preserves the Gaelic language and culture. Opposite the town hall is the **Old Mercat Cross,** with its Stone of the Tubs, said to be the stone on which women rested their washtubs as they ascended from the river. Known as "Clachnacudainn," the lozenge-shaped stone was the spot where local early kings were crowned.

St. Andrew's Cathedral (1866–69), Ardross Street, is the northernmost diocese of the Scottish Episcopal church and a fine example of Victorian architecture, both imposing and richly decorated. Be sure to check out the icons given to Bishop Eden by the tsar of Russia. The cathedral is open daily from 9:30am to 6pm. For information, get in touch with the Provost, 15 Ardross St. (© **01334/472-563**).

If you're interested in bus tours of the Highlands and cruises on Loch Ness, go to **Inverness Traction,** 6 Burnett Rd. (© **01463/239-292**). In summer, there are also cruises along the Caledonian Canal from Inverness into Loch Ness.

⌒ Moments   The Hill of the Fairies

West of the river rises the wooded hill of **Tomnahurich,** known as the "hill of the fairies." Now a cemetery, it's the best place to go for a country walk, with panoramic views. The boat-shaped hillock is immediately to the southwest of the center. In the Ness are wooded islands, linked to Inverness by suspension bridges, that have been turned into parks.

Shoppers might want to check out a family-owned shrine to Scottish kilt-making, **Duncan Chisholm & Sons,** 47–53 Castle St. (© **01463/234-599**). The tartans of at least 50 of Scotland's largest clans are available in the form of kilts and kilt jackets for men and women. If your heart is set on something more esoteric, the staff can acquire whatever fabric your ancestors would have worn to make up your garment. A section is devoted to Scottish gifts (ties, scarves, yard goods, kilt pins in thistle patterns) and memorabilia. You can visit the on-premises workshop. The town's best jewelry store, with an unusual collection of bangles and bracelets inspired by the decorative traditions of Celtic Scotland, is **D&H Norval,** 88 Church St. (© **01463/232-739**). At **Celtic Spirit,** 14 Church St. (© **01463/714-796**), the focus is on New Age books and an unusual collection of wind chimes.

Golfers can head about 64km (40 miles) north to hit the links at the renowned **Royal Dornoch Golf Club.** Closer at hand, the 4,960m (5,451-yard) **Torvean Golf Course,** Glen Q Road (© **01463/711-434**), offers an 18-hole, par-68 course with greens fees of £15.50 ($25) Monday to Friday, and £18.50 ($30) Saturday to Sunday.

Culloden Battlefield ✦ At Culloden Battlefield, Bonnie Prince Charlie and the Jacobite army were finally crushed on April 16, 1746. A path leads from the visitor center through the Field of the English, where 52 men of the duke of Cumberland's forces who died during the battle are said to be buried. Features of interest include the **Graves of the Clans,** communal burial places with simple stones bearing individual clan names; the great **memorial cairn,** erected in 1881; the **Well of the Dead;** and the huge **Cumberland Stone,** from which the victorious "Butcher" Cumberland is said to have reviewed the scene. The battle lasted only 40 minutes; the prince's army lost some 1,200 men out of 5,000, and the king's army 300 of 9,000. In the visitor center is an audiovisual presentation on the background and history of the famous battle. Also on the premises are a restaurant and bookshop.

Culloden Moor, 10km (6 miles) southeast of Inverness. ℂ **01463/790-607** for visitor center. Admission to visitor center £5 ($8) adults, £3.75 ($6) seniors/children, £13.50 ($22) families. Visitor center Apr–June and Sept–Oct daily 9am–6pm; July–Aug daily 9am–7pm; Nov–Dec and Feb-Mar 11am-4pm. Closed in Jan.

Fort George/Queen's Own Highlanders Regimental Museum   Fort George was called the "most considerable fortress and best situated in Great Britain" in 1748 by Lt. Col. James Wolfe, who went on to fame as Wolfe of Quebec. Built after the Battle of Culloden, the fort was occupied by the Hanoverian army of George II and is still an active army barracks. The rampart, almost 1.6km (1 mile) around, encloses some 17 hectares (42 acres). Dr. Samuel Johnson and James Boswell visited here in 1773 on their Highland trek. The fort contains the admission-free **Queen's Own Highlanders Regimental Museum,** with regimental exhibits from 1778 to today, representing a number of Highland regiments as well as its namesake. A new exhibit about the 1990s Gulf War has been recently added.

On Moray Firth by the village of Ardersier, 18km (11 miles) northeast of Inverness, 13km (8 miles) northwest of Cawdor along B9006. ℂ **0131/3108-701**. Admission £4.50 ($7.20) adults, £3 ($4.80) seniors, £2.50 ($4) children age 5–15; free for children age 4 and under. Apr–Sept daily 10am–6pm; Oct–Mar Mon–Fri 10am–4pm.

Inverness Museum and Art Gallery   This museum in the town center is a top attraction, its displays representing the social and natural history, archaeology, art, and culture of the Scottish Highlands, with special emphasis on the Inverness district. Don't miss the important collection of Highland silver and reconstructed silversmith's workshop, displays on the life of the clans, a reconstruction of a local taxidermist's workshop, and a reconstructed 1920s Inverness kitchen.

Castle Wynd, off Bridge St. ℂ **01463/237-114**. Free admission. Mon–Sat 9am–5pm.

WHERE TO STAY
EXPENSIVE

Bunchrew House Hotel and Restaurant ✦   This fine Scottish mansion on the shores of Beauly Firth is the ancestral home of both the Fraser and the McKenzie clans. The house dates to 1621 and is set on 8 hectares (20 acres) of landscaped gardens. You'll get a glimpse of a bygone era while relaxing in the paneled drawing room with roaring log fires. The guest rooms are individually decorated; the Lovat Suite, for example, has a canopied four-poster bed. Some bathrooms contain showers only. Guests can dine in the candlelit restaurant on prime Scottish beef, fresh lobster and crayfish, local game, and fresh vegetables.

Bunchrew, Inverness, Inverness-shire IV3 8TA. ℂ **01463/234-917**. Fax 01463/710-620. www.bunchrew-inverness.co.uk. 14 units. £150–£200 ($240–$320) suite for 2. Rates include Scottish breakfast. AE, MC, V. Drive 5km (3 miles) west of Inverness on A862. **Amenities:** Restaurant; bar; room service (7:30am–11pm); laundry service. In room: TV, fridge, coffeemaker, hair dryer.

Culloden House ✦✦   This is the most elegant country retreat in the area. Culloden House, a Georgian mansion with a much-photographed Adam facade, includes part of the Renaissance castle in which Bonnie Prince Charlie slept the night before Culloden, the last great battle on British soil. Superbly isolated, with extensive gardens and parkland, it's perfect for a relaxed Highland holiday. At the iron gates to the broad front lawn, a piper in full Highland garb often plays at sundown, the skirl of the bagpipe accompanied by the barking of house dogs. The prince of Wales and the crown prince of Japan have stayed here, perfectly at home among the exquisite furnishings and handsome plaster friezes. The cozy yet spacious guest rooms have sylvan views and a history-laden atmosphere.

Culloden, Inverness IV2 7BZ. © **01463/790-461.** Fax 01463/792-181. www.cullodenhouse.co.uk. 28 units. £199 ($318) double; £270 ($432) suite. Rates include Scottish breakfast. AE, DC, MC, V. Drive 5km (3 miles) east of Inverness on A96. **Amenities:** Restaurant; bar; tennis court; sauna; 24-hr. room service; laundry service; croquet lawn. *In room:* TV, hair dryer, trouser press.

Dunain Park Hotel 🍴🍴   The Dunain Park stands in 2.4 hectares (6 acres) of garden and woods between Loch Ness and Inverness. This 18th-century Georgian house is furnished with fine antiques, allowing it to retain its atmosphere of a private country house. Although Dunain Park has won its fame mainly as a restaurant (see "Where to Dine," below), it does offer guest rooms with a host of thoughtful details and pretty furnishings. Each unit has a shower or tub bathroom.

Dunain Park, Inverness IV3 8JN. © **01463/230-512.** Fax 01463/224-532. www.dunainparkhotel.co.uk. 11 units. £158 ($253) double; from £200 ($320) suite. Rates include Scottish breakfast. AE, MC, V. Drive 1.6km (1 mile) southwest of Inverness on A82. **Amenities:** Restaurant; bar; indoor pool; room service (8am–10pm); laundry service. *In room:* TV, fridge (in suite), coffeemaker, hair dryer, trouser press.

MODERATE

Glen Mhor Hotel   On the River Ness, this house of gables and bay windows is a hospitable family-run hotel. From many of the individually styled guest rooms you have views of the river, castle, and cathedral; some are suitable for families. Ten rooms are in an annex called the Cottage. Each unit has a well-maintained bathroom, all with shower, some with shower and tub combination. In the Riverview Restaurant overlooking the river and specializing in seafood and Scottish dishes, you can enjoy such fine food as salmon caught in the river outside. The wine list is one of the best in the country. There's also a European bistro bar called Nico's.

9–12 Ness Bank, Inverness IV2 4SG. © **01463/234-308.** Fax 01463/713-170. www.glen-mhor.com. 43 units. £88 ($141) double; from £120 ($192) junior suite. Rates include Scottish breakfast. AE, DC, MC, V. From Inverness, follow signs to Dores (B862); hotel is on the south bank. **Amenities:** 2 restaurants; bar; 24-hr. room service. *In room:* TV, dataport, coffeemaker, hair dryer.

Glenmoriston Town House Hotel 🍴 *Kids*   This hotel is on the River Ness, a short walk from the town center, and it's the finest town house hotel in town. Rooms have been stylishly refurbished, are well maintained and individually designed, and come with spacious private bathrooms. Some accommodations are suitable for use as family units. Each room is equipped with a fax machine and modem dataports. Guests can enjoy temporary membership at a nearby Squash and Tennis Club. Of the two hotel restaurants, La Terrazza is open daily for lunch, whereas La Riviera is more formal, specializing in a fine Italian cuisine, with many Tuscan dishes.

20 Ness Bank, Inverness IV2 4SF. © **01463/223-777.** Fax 01463/712-378. www.glenmoriston.com. 15 units. £115–£135 ($184–$216) double. Rates include full Scottish breakfast. AE, MC, V. Free parking. Lies a 5 minute walk south of the train station. **Amenities:** 2 restaurants; bar; access to nearby health club; room service (7am–10pm). *In room:* TV, fax, dataport, coffeemaker, hair dryer.

Inverness Marriott Hotel ⋆ Once a private mansion, this hotel is a charming 18th-century country house set amidst a woodland garden that's adjacent to an 18-hole golf course. Over the years it's attracted royals, high-ranking government officials, and film stars, even Robert Burns himself. The staff maintains the country-house atmosphere with an informal and hospitable style. The furnishings throughout are of a high quality, and all the guest rooms are attractively furnished, each with tub or shower bath.

The restaurant's fish dishes are exceptional at dinner. Bar lunches and snack meals offer a wide choice, including Scottish fare. A notice in the lobby tells you Robert Burns dined here in 1787, and the "Charles" who signed the guest register in 1982 was (you guessed it) the prince of Wales. His sister, Princess Anne, has also stayed here.

Culcabock Rd., Inverness IV2 3LP. ℂ **01463/237-166.** Fax 01463/225-208. www.marriott.com. 82 units. £88–£158 ($141–$253) double; £150–£170 ($240–$272) suite. Rates include Scottish breakfast. AE, DC, MC, V. Take Kingsmill Rd. 1.6km (1 mile) east of the center of Inverness. **Amenities:** Restaurant; bar; indoor pool; health club; sauna; salon; 24-hr. room service; laundry service; 3-hole mini-golf course. *In room:* TV, dataport, minibar, coffeemaker, hair dryer, iron/ironing board, trouser press.

The Royal Highland Hotel It's like Inverness of yesterday at this somber gray-stone hotel, built in 1859 across from the train station to celebrate the arrival of rail lines connecting the Highlands, through Inverness, to the rest of Britain. Today, it's an antiques-strewn, slightly faded hotel, despite the gradual modernizations and the contemporary decor in half of the guest rooms (the other half is charmingly dowdy). Each unit is equipped with a shower or tub bathroom. The massive lobby contains the showiest staircase in Inverness. The dining room retains its elaborate high ceiling and a sense of the Victorian age. Seafood and shellfish are house specialties.

18 Academy St., Inverness IV1 1LG. ℂ **01463/231-926.** Fax 01463/710-705. www.royalhighlandhotel.co.uk. 75 units. £120–£145 ($192–$232) double. Rates include breakfast. DC, MC, V. **Amenities:** Restaurant; 2 bars. *In room:* TV, dataport, coffeemaker, hair dryer, iron/ironing board, trouser press.

INEXPENSIVE

Ballifeary House Hotel ⋆ *Value* This well-maintained 1876 Victorian stone villa, with a pleasant garden, is one of the area's better B&Bs. Mr. and Mrs. Luscombe, the owners, offer their guests individual attention. The rooms, although a bit small, are comfortably furnished, with shower-only bathrooms. This nonsmoking hotel discourages families with small children.

10 Ballifeary Rd., Inverness IV3 5PJ. ℂ **01463/235-572.** Fax 01463/717-583. www.ballifearyhousehotel. co.uk. 8 units. £72–£78 ($115–$125) double. Rates include Scottish breakfast. MC, V. From Fort William on A82 as you're approaching Inverness, turn right on Ballifeary Rd. **Amenities:** Bar. *In room:* TV, coffeemaker, hair dryer, no phone.

Felstead Guest House Right on the River Ness, this Georgian guesthouse lies within walking distance of the heart of town. A comfortable structure of architectural interest, it was built in 1830 and has been extensively upgraded since then, though still retaining its original grace. The owners have decorated the rooms with taste and an eye toward comfort. The shower-only bathrooms are immaculately maintained. Thoughtful touches abound, such as freshly cut flowers and bubble baths. Scottish produce is featured at the morning breakfast.

18 Ness Bank. Inverness IV2 4SF. ℂ and fax **01463/231-634.** www.jafsoft.com/felstead/felstead.html. 8 units. £64–£72 ($102–$115) double. Rates include breakfast. AE, MC, V. On the right bank of River Ness, a 5–8 minute walk from center following Ness Bank Rd. *In room:* TV, coffeemaker, hair dryer, no phone.

Ivybank Guest House *(Value* This is one of the better B&Bs in town. Located off Castle Road about a 10-minute walk north of the town center, Ivybank was built in 1836 and retains its original fireplaces and an oak-paneled and beamed hall with a rosewood staircase. It features a walled garden and comfortably furnished guest rooms, each with hot and cold running water. Three units contain shower-only bathrooms. Mrs. Catherine Cameron is the gracious hostess, making guests feel at ease. Breakfast is the only meal served.

28 Old Edinburgh Rd., Inverness IV2 3HJ. *©* and fax **01463/232-796.** www.ivybankguesthouse.com. 6 units, 3 with private bathroom. £50 ($80) double without bathroom; £64 ($102) double with bathroom. Rates include Scottish breakfast. AE, MC, V. Pets accepted by prior arrangement. *In room:* TV, coffeemaker, hair dryer.

Trafford Bank   In a residential neighborhood about 1km (½ mile) west of Inverness center, this dignified sandstone house was built in 1873 as the manse for the Episcopal bishop. In 1994, when the bishop retired in a huff because of the ordination of women, the manse became available. Today, it is a B&B run by Lorraine Treel, who has improved the garden and plans other renovations.. The place has five comfortable guest rooms (with shower-only bathrooms) and a social life revolving around copious Scottish breakfasts.

96 Fairfield Rd., Inverness IV3 5LL. *©* **0143/241-414.** Fax 01463/241-421. www.traffordbankguesthouse. co.uk. 5 units. £60–£80 ($96–$128) double. Rates include breakfast. AE, MC, V. Bus: 19. From the town center, cross the Ness Bridge and turn right at the first traffic light. *In room:* TV, coffeemaker, hair dryer.

WHERE TO DINE

Café 1 INTERNATIONAL/SCOTTISH FUSION   One of the most pleasant restaurants in town is in a century-old stone-fronted building on a street dotted with shops. Inside, you'll find varnished paneling, wooden tables, potted plants, and a soothing New Age atmosphere. Dine on generous portions of venison steak with bean spouts, beetroot, and red caramelized port *jus;* brochette of king scallops wrapped in bacon, served with balsamic dressed rocket and parmesan salad; or prime angus scotch filet served on a bed of skirlie topped with red onion marmalade with a red wine *jus.* For dessert, try the dark-chocolate tart with white-chocolate shavings or a crepe filled with homemade Maltese ice cream with a butterscotch sauce.

75 Castle St. Inverness IV2 3EA. *©* **01463/716-363.** Reservations recommended. Main courses £6–£10 ($9.60–$16) lunch; £8–£16 ($13–$26) dinner. MC, V. Mon–Sat noon–2pm and 6–9:30pm.

Dickens International Restaurant INTERNATIONAL   On a downtown street next to the oldest house in Inverness, Aberton House, this restaurant boasts a decor that has been revamped and updated with furnishings in the style created by Charlie Rennie Mackintosh (1868–1928), Scotland's most famous designer. A wide selection of European, Chinese, and international dishes is offered, including seafood and vegetarian options, Dickens's own steak, aromatic duck, and chateaubriand. The wide choice of side dishes ranges from fried rice to bean sprouts to cauliflower with cheese.

77–79 Church St. *©* **01463/713-111.** Reservations required on weekends. Main courses £9–£12 ($14–$19). AE, DC, MC, V. Mon-Sat noon–2pm and 5:30–11pm.

Dunain Park Restaurant *⊛* SCOTTISH   Ann Nicoll presides over the kitchen here, offering Scottish fare with French flair, using fresh local ingredients. A game terrine of chicken and guinea fowl is layered with venison and pigeon, and meats are wrapped in bacon and served with a delicious onion confit. Other dishes that may appear on the changing menu are hare-and-pigeon casserole with roasted shallots and wild mushrooms and Shetland salmon baked in sea salt, served with a white port, lime, and ginger sauce. The restaurant also specializes in Aberdeen Angus steaks. Try one of the desserts from the buffet: crème brûlée, chocolate roulade, or marshmallow pudding.

In the Dunain Park Hotel, Dunain Park. ✆ **01463/230-512.** Reservations recommended. Main courses £15.95–£17.95 ($26–$29). AE, DC, MC, V. Daily 7–9pm.

Kong's Restaurant CHINESE/THAI Spicy and reasonably priced food awaits you here; especially noteworthy is the large variety of appetizers, including some dishes from Vietnam. Try the Thai chicken wings or the Szechuan squid before moving on to a wide array of seafood and poultry dishes, along with a selection of pork and beef. The Thai green and red curry dishes are especially flavorful, and the chef's specialties include Peking roast duck and steamed sole flavored with ginger and spring onions. Vegetarians are well catered to here.

64–66 Academy St. ✆ **01463/237-755.** Reservations recommended. Main courses £6–£9 ($9.60–$14) fixed-price menus £12–£21 ($19–$34) per person. AE, MC, V. Mon–Sat noon–2pm and daily 5:30–11pm.

Restaurant Riviera BRITISH/ITALIAN Often hosting local family celebrations, this rather staid restaurant occupies the ground floor of an early-20th-century stone-sided hotel on the riverbank near the center of Inverness. At least five chefs labor away in the kitchen. Meals here are part of an entire evening's entertainment, so plan on spending a leisurely evening here. Menu items include slices of warm breast of duckling scented with heather-flavored honey and dressed with walnut oil; Scottish beef filet with wild-mushroom polenta, shallots, and Parmesan crackling; and grilled king prawns with roasted tomatoes and pea purée.

In the Glenmoriston Hotel, 20 Ness Bank. ✆ **01463/223-777.** Reservations recommended. Main courses £15–£16.90 ($24–$27); 3-course fixed-price menu £25.95 ($42). AE, DC, MC, V. Daily noon–2pm and 6:30–9:30pm.

Riva ITALIAN/INTERNATIONAL One of Inverness's best restaurants occupies a site on the opposite *riva* (riverbank) from the rest of the town. Deliberately unpretentious, it has only 18 tables. At least a dozen kinds of pastas are offered as either starters or main courses. Entrees include tagliatelle with crumbly meatballs, monkfish in red-pepper sauce, and chicken with crispy Parma ham and risotto. Between mealtimes, the place functions as a simple cafe serving sandwiches.

4–6 Ness Walk. ✆ **01463/237-377.** Reservations required. Main courses £10–£16 ($16–$26) in restaurant. 2-course lunch £6.50 ($10); 3-course lunch £8.95 ($14). MC, V. Restaurant Mon–Sat noon–2pm and 6–9:30pm (last order), Sun 6–9:30pm; cafe Mon–Sat 10am–9:30pm, except during above-mentioned meal hours.

INVERNESS AFTER DARK

It may be the capital of the Highlands, but Inverness is a sprawling small town without much nightlife. You can spend an evening in the town's pubs sampling single-malt whiskies or beers on tap. Although the pubs here may not have the authentic charm of the isolated pubs in more rural areas, you'll still find a lot of Highlander flavor. Try the pub in the **Loch Ness House Hotel,** Glenurquhart Road (✆ **01463/231-248**), on the western periphery of town; **Gellions Pub,** 8–14 Bridge St. (✆ **01463/233-648**); **Gunsmith's Pub,** 30 Union St. (✆ **01463/ 710-519**). For punk rock and heavy metal, head for either of the town's discos: **Blue,** Rose Street (✆ **01463/222-712**), or **Gs,** 9–21 Castle St. (✆ **01463/ 233-322**).

SIDE TRIPS FROM INVERNESS
MUIR OF ORD

This small town, 16km (10 miles) west of Inverness, makes a good touring center for a history-rich part of Scotland. If you stay at the hotel recommended below, you can take day trips around Black Isle, which boasts beautiful scenery (see "The Black Isle Peninsula," later in this chapter). Outdoorsy types are drawn here for fishing, golf, and shooting.

Where To Stay & Dine

Dower House *(Finds Kids)*   This charming 18th-century guesthouse is a perfect base for exploring the area. The rooms are decorated in the fine tradition of a Scottish country house, with flowers cut from the garden. A small three-bedroom cottage is perfect for families. Be sure to make reservations for the Dower House well in advance; the comfortable atmosphere is very much in demand.

Even if you don't stay here, you might want to call for a dinner reservation. After a cocktail in the lounge, you proceed to the dining room for a four-course meal of modern British cuisine utilizing produce grown on the grounds; expensive fixed-price menus are served nightly.

Highfield, Muir of Ord IV6 7XN. © and fax **01463/870-090.** www.thedowerhouse.co.uk. 5 units. £90–£130 ($144–$208) double; £120–£150 ($192–$240) cottage. Rates include Scottish breakfast. MC, V. Drive 1.6km (1 mile) north of A862. Pets accepted by prior arrangement. **Amenities:** Restaurant; bar; 24-hr. room service; babysitting. *In room:* TV, coffeemaker, hair dryer, iron/ironing board.

BEAULY

The French monks who settled here in the 13th century named it literally "beautiful place"—and it still is. You'll see the **Highland Craftpoint** on your left as you come from Inverness. In summer, there's an interesting exhibit of Scottish handcrafts. Beauly is 19km (12 miles) west of Inverness on A862, and Inverness Traction, a local bus company, has hourly service from Inverness.

Dating from 1230, the **Beauly Priory** (© **01463/782-309**), now a roofless shell, is the only remaining one of three priories built for the Valliscaulian order, an austere body drawing its main components from the Cistercians and the Carthusians. Some notable windows and window arcading are still left among the ruins. Hugh Fraser of Lovat erected the Chapel of the Holy Cross on the nave's north side in the early 15th century. You can tour the priory at any time; if it's locked, ask for a key from the Priory Hotel across the way.

If you're interested in tweeds, don't miss **Campbells of Beauly,** Highland Tweed House (© **01463/782-239**), operated by the same family since 1858. An excellent selection of fine tweeds and tartans is offered, and you can have your material tailored. Blankets, travel rugs, tweed hats, and kilts are sold, as well as cashmere and lambswool sweaters. It's on the main street at the south end of the village square, next to the Royal Bank of Scotland.

Where To Stay & Dine

Priory Hotel   The Priory Hotel is on the historic main square of town, a short walk from the ruins of the priory. The hotel has recently expanded into an adjacent building, adding four rooms to its well-furnished offerings. A frequently changing dinner menu features a variety of fish and local game as well as a good selection of steaks; bar meals are similar dishes served in smaller portions. In addition, high tea is served daily.

The Square, Beauly IV4 7BX. © **01463/782-309.** Fax 01463/782-531. www.priory-hotel.com. 36 units. £90 ($144) double. Rates include Scottish breakfast. AE, DC, MC, V. **Amenities:** Restaurant; bar; 24-hr. room service; laundry/dry cleaning service. *In room:* TV, dataport, coffeemaker, hair dryer, iron/ironing board.

7 Nairn & Cawdor Castle ⟨★⟩

277km (172 miles) N of Edinburgh, 147km (91 miles) NW of Aberdeen, 26km (16 miles) E of Inverness

A favorite family seaside resort on the sheltered Moray Firth, Nairn (from the Gaelic for "Water of Alders") is a royal burgh at the mouth of the Nairn River. Its fishing harbor was constructed in 1820, and golf has been played here since 1672—as it still is today.

ESSENTIALS

GETTING THERE   Nairn can be reached by train from the south, with a change at either Aberdeen or Inverness. The service between Inverness and Nairn is frequent; this is the most popular route. For information, check with the Inverness train station at Station Square (© **08457/484-950**).

From Inverness, Inverness Traction runs daily buses to Nairn. Call © **0870/ 6082-608** for schedules.

If you're driving from Inverness, take A96 east to Nairn.

VISITOR INFORMATION   The **tourist office** is at 62 King St. (© **01667/ 452-753**). April to mid-May, it's open Monday to Saturday from 10am to 5pm; mid-May to June, hours are Monday to Saturday from 10am to 5pm and Sunday from 11am to 4pm; July and August, hours are Monday to Saturday from 9am to 6pm and Sunday from 10am to 5pm; and September and October, hours are Monday to Saturday from 10am to 5pm.

SEEING THE SIGHTS

Brodie Country, on A96, 5km (3 miles) east of Nairn in Brodie (© **01309/ 641-555**), is a family-owned shopping complex with shops carrying a variety of merchandise. Of greatest interest are the regionally produced knitwear, gift items, and foodstuff; the latter includes smoked meats, jams, mustards, and other condiments. Also on the premises is a fully licensed restaurant serving Scottish cuisine daily from 9:30am to 5pm (to 7pm Thurs), with main courses averaging about £6 ($9.60).

Nairn Antiques, St. Ninian Place (© **01667/453-303**), carries a broad range of antiques and a section of upscale crafts and reproductions. Of particular interest are the collections of Scottish pottery, silver, and fine porcelains, but there's also furniture and bric-a-brac from around the world. This is the only shop in the entire north country to stock high-quality Lalique crystal from France.

The Taste of Moray, on the Nairn-Inverness Road, 10km (6 miles) north of Nairn (© **01667/462-340;** www.tasteofmoray.co.uk), is all about the pleasures of preparing and consuming Scottish cuisine, with products ranging from quality cookware to regional domestic stoneware. The food hall offers an array of

---

⟨*Moments*⟩ **In the Footsteps of Macbeth**

A **large uncrowded beach** draws crowds in summer. Anglers also find the area is a good spot. Nairn is great walking country, and the tourist office will give you a map and details about the various possibilities, including hikes along the banks of the River Nairn. The best walks are five signposted nature trails, called the **Cawdor Castle Nature Trails.** They're signposted from Cawdor Castle of Macbeth fame, taking you along some of the loveliest and most varied forests and wooded areas in the Highlands.

Scottish condiments and smoked meats, and if shopping here makes you hungry, you can step into the adjacent restaurant, serving seafood dishes and steaks, with main courses averaging £5 to £25 ($8–$40). Food service is daily from 10am to 9pm.

The 18-hole **Nairn Dunbar Golf Club,** Loch Loy Road (© **01667/452-741**), consists of 6,700 yards (6,097m) of playing area with a par of 72. Greens fees are Sunday to Friday, £37 ($59) per round or £50 ($80) per day and Saturday £45 ($72) per round or £60 ($96) for the day.

Cawdor Castle 🅐   To the south of Nairn, you'll encounter 600 years of Highland history at Cawdor Castle, the home of the thanes of Cawdor since the early 14th century. Although the castle was constructed 2 centuries after his time, it has nevertheless been romantically linked to Shakespeare's *Macbeth,* once the thane of Cawdor. The castle has all the architectural ingredients you'd associate with the Middle Ages: a drawbridge, an ancient tower, and fortified walls. Its severity is softened by the handsome gardens and rolling lawns. On the grounds are five nature trails through beautiful woodland, a nine-hole golf course, a putting green, a snack bar, a picnic area, shops, and a licensed restaurant serving hot meals, teas, and coffees all day.

Between Inverness and Nairn on B9090 off A96, Cawdor. © **01667/404-615.** Admission £6.10 ($9.75) adults, £5.10 ($8.15) seniors, £3.30 ($5.30) children age 5–15, children under age 5 free. May–2nd Sun in Oct daily 10am–5pm.

WHERE TO STAY

Boath House 🅐🅐   This Georgian mansion is set amid 8 hectares (20 acres) of lush greenery. Built in 1825, the house has been restored to its original elegance. In spite of its classic look, the atmosphere is relaxed and informal. There are two lounges and a library where you can enjoy a dram of whisky. Bedrooms are splendidly decorated with antiques and period furniture. An on-site salon is open to both guests and nonguests, offering everything from aromatherapy to galvanic slimming treatments. The salon uses only products with natural ingredients from pure plant and flower essences. The hotel is also home to an award-winning restaurant (see "Where to Dine," below).

Auldearn, Nairn IV12 5TE. © **01667/454-896.** Fax 01667/455-469. www.boath-house.com. 6 units. £150–£200 ($240–$320) double. Rates include breakfast. AE, DC, MC, V. Free parking. 3.2km (2 miles) E of Nairn on A96. **Amenities:** Restaurant; exercise room; spa; salon. *In room:* TV, coffeemaker, hair dryer.

Clifton House 🅐🅐 *(Finds*   This intimate hotel reflects the dynamic personality of J. Gordon Macintyre, owner of the vine-covered, honey-sandstone Victorian mansion. His home for more than 60 years, it stands on the seafront, 3 minutes from the beach and equidistant to both golf links. Mr. Macintyre has spent a great deal of time and care in decorating and refurbishing the house. Most of the furniture is antique; the collection of paintings, engravings, and drawings is unusual and extensive. Each guest room is pleasantly appointed, with complete shower-and-tub bathroom. Mr. Macintyre organizes a series of concerts, plays, and recitals to entertain his guests.

Beginning in 2003, Mr. Macintyre closed down the on-site restaurant (which till then had been open to non-residents of his hotel), and began insisting that all overnight guests (and *only* his overnight guests) participate in the evening dinner ritual. This is conducted family-style, with a pre-determined (and pre-defined) dinner menu that's shared, by all parties, as part of the general house-party atmosphere. Mr. Macintyre, almost 80 years old, has adopted this as his new entertainment and lodging venue.

The hotel is a licensed theater, and performances are presented September through March.

1–3 Viewfield St., Nairn, Nairnshire IV4 4HW. ℭ **01667/453-119.** Fax 01667/452-836. www.clifton-hotel.co.uk. 8 units. £190 ($304) double. Rates include Scottish breakfast and dinner. AE, DC, MC, V. Turn east of the town roundabout on A96. *In room:* Coffeemaker, hair dryer, no phone.

Greenlawns *Value* This Victorian house within easy reach of the beaches and golf courses is a pleasant base for touring the Loch Ness region. The owners have completely refurbished the house while retaining its traditional charm. All of the good-size guest rooms come with showers or else large tubs. No smoking is permitted.

13 Seafield St., Nairn IV12 4HG. ℭ **01667/452-738.** Fax 01667/452-738. www.greenlawns.uk.com. 7 units. £40–£58 ($64–$93) double. Rates include Scottish breakfast. AE, MC, V. Turn down Albert St. from A96. **Amenities:** Restaurant; bar. *In room:* TV, coffeemaker, no phone.

WHERE TO DINE

The Boath House Restaurant ✿✿ SCOTTISH/CONTINENTAL Located in a Georgian mansion, this restaurant has won numerous awards. Traditional Scottish fare is given a Continental twist to create a well-balanced menu that changes daily. The atmosphere is romantic with antique decor, and in the evening, the room is bathed in candlelight. Menu items might include seared filet of sea bass on a citrus couscous, tapenade, and a basil-infused oil, or roasted gray-legged partridge with a ragout of red cabbage and onion. There is also a good selection of wines.

In the Boath House, Auldearn. ℭ **01667/454-896.** Reservations recommended. Fixed-price 5-course dinner £39.50 ($63); fixed-price lunch £29.50 ($47). AE, DC, MC, V. Daily noon–2pm and 7–8:30pm. Closed Mon–Tues to nonguests. On A96, 2 miles east of Nairn.

Cawdor Tavern MODERN SCOTTISH This atmospheric restaurant occupies what was built as a stone-sided carpenter shop for Cawdor Castle, fewer than 150m (500 ft.) away. Many visitors opt for just a drink, choosing any of the single-malt whiskies that adorn the bar. Others come for the food, served in generous portions with a focus on local produce and regional fish and meats. Examples include duck in white-wine sauce, crabmeat-and-salmon cakes with chive-cream sauce, and an unusual preparation of chicken stuffed with haggis (nationalistically labeled "chicken Culloden").

The Lane, Cawdor. ℭ **01667/404-777.** Reservations recommended for dinner. Main courses £5.95–£9.50 ($9.50–$15) lunch; £8.95–£16 ($14–$26) dinner. AE, DC, MC, V. Daily noon–2:30pm and 5:30–9pm.

The Longhouse SCOTTISH Opened in 1997, the domain of the Rennie family is a cream-colored stone house in the center of town, named after the early-1900s building's long and narrow design. Cozy and candlelit, it seats only 33 diners at a time. The menu is less ambitious at lunch, when platters are likely to include lasagna, fried fish, and roasted pork with wine sauce. High tea is favored by locals inclined to retire early. At dinner, the cuisine shines. Its tradition is strongly Scottish—expect sauces laced with whisky and dishes like black pudding with whisky-mustard sauce; rack of lamb with wine-rosemary sauce and mint-infused poached pears; and mussels in white wine, onion, and dill sauce. Desserts usually include a slice of shortbread with fresh cream and fresh raspberries. The restaurant is licensed only for alcohol served with meals.

8 Harbour St. ℭ **01667/455-532.** Reservations recommended. Main courses £2.50–£8.55 ($4–$14) lunch; £6.95–£16 ($11–$26) dinner; high tea £6.95 ($11). AE, MC, V. Daily lunch 9am–4:30pm; high tea 5–6:30pm; dinner 5–9pm. Closed Wed from Oct–Mar and 2 weeks in Oct.

NAIRN AFTER DARK

Locals gather to drink and talk at the **Claymore House Hotel Bar,** Seabank Road (© **01667/453-731**). During cold weather, an open fireplace takes the chill out of the air, as does the selection of malt whiskies. The **Millford Hotel Pub,** Mill Road (© **01667/453-854**), features free live music on Saturday, mainly middle-of-the-road country, pop, blues, or folk bands. Once a month, there's a country-western night with dancing.

   Clifton House, 1–3 Viewfield St. (© **01667/453-119**), offers classical concerts by solo artists and small ensembles about once every 3 weeks between September and May.

8 The Black Isle Peninsula ⊕

Cromarty: 37km (23 miles) NW of Inverness (via Kessock Bridge)

The Black Isle is one of Scotland's most enchanting peninsulas, a land rich in history, beauty, and mystery. Part of Ross and Cromarty County, it's northwest of Inverness, a 20-minute drive or bus ride away. A car tour would be about 60km (37 miles), but allow plenty of time for stops and country walks along the way.

   There's much confusion about the name of the peninsula, because it's neither black nor an island. In summer, the land is green and fertile, with tropical plants flourishing. It has forests, fields of broom and whin, and scattered coastal villages. The peninsula has been inhabited for 7,000 years, as 60-odd prehistoric sites testify. Pictish kings, whose thrones passed down through the female line, once ruled this land. Then the Vikings held sway, and the evidence of many Gallows Hills testifies to their harsh justice.

ESSENTIALS

GETTING THERE   The nearest **rail service** goes to Inverness. From there, the Highland Bus and Coach Company serves the peninsula (nos. 26, 26A, and 126), making stops at North Kessock, Munlochy, Avoch, Fortrose, Rosemarkie, and Cromarty. **Buses** depart from Farraline Park in Inverness (© **01463/233-371** for schedules).

   If you're **driving,** head to Fortrose as your first stop (see below), take A9 north from Inverness. (Follow the signs toward Wick.) Follow A9 for 6.5km (4 miles) until you see the Kessock Bridge. Go over the bridge and take the second road to the right, toward Munlochy. (Fortrose is 13km/8 miles from this turnoff.) Follow A832 through the village of Munlochy and at the junction take the road right, signposted Fortrose. Continue straight on through Avoch to Fortrose.

VISITOR INFORMATION   Ask at the **Inverness tourist office** (see "Inverness: Capital of the Highlands," earlier in this chapter) for details on Black Isle, because the peninsula is often included on a day tour from that city.

FORTROSE ⊕ & ROSEMARKIE

Fortrose is a good place to start. Along the way, you'll pass a celebrated wishing well, or **clootie well,** festooned with rags. Dedicated to St. Boniface, the well has a long tradition, dating back to pagan times. It's said that anyone removing a rag will inherit the misfortunes of the person who placed it there.

   The ruins of **Fortrose Cathedral** stand in this sleepy village. Founded in the 13th century, the cathedral was dedicated to St. Peter and St. Boniface. You can still see fine detailing from the 14th century. If the stones scattered about don't seem to number enough to fill in the gaps, it's because Cromwell's men removed many of them to help build a fort in Inverness. There are no formal hours; you can wander through the ruins at any time.

Fortrose adjoins **Rosemarkie,** up the road. The site has been inhabited since the Bronze Age. A center of Pictish culture, the town saw the arrival of the first Christian missionaries. It's reported that St. Moluag founded a monastery here in the 6th century. Rosemarkie became a royal burgh in 1216. The twin hamlets share a golf course today, and they're the site of the Chanonry Sailing Club, whose annual regatta brings entries from all over Scotland. Right beyond Rosemarkie is the mysterious **Fairy Glen,** signposted at the end of the village. It's one of the loveliest places in the Black Isle for a long walk.

WHERE TO STAY & DINE

Royal Hotel Fortrose   Built in 1865 as a coaching inn, the Royal overlooks the ancient monument of Fortrose Cathedral. The traditional Victorian house has recently undergone extensive renovations, mostly to upgrade the bedrooms. Proprietor Graham Law has left the common areas mostly untouched, preferring to retain the mix of modern and traditional decor. The hotel has two bars and a lounge where pub meals are served. The restaurant serves traditional Scottish fare made from locally produced ingredients.

At the corner of Union and High Sts., Fortrose IV10 8TD. ℭ **01381/620-236.** 14 units, 12 with private bathroom. £55 ($88) double without bathroom; £65 ($104) double with bathroom. Rates include breakfast. DC, MC, V. Free parking. **Amenities:** Restaurant; 2 bars. *In room:* TV, coffeemaker, hair dryer, no phone.

CROMARTY

Cromarty stands at the tip of the peninsula, where the North and South Sutors guard the entrance to the Cromarty Firth, the second-deepest inland waterway estuary in Europe, always of strategic importance to the Royal Navy. Much of the Black Isle invites country walks, but in Cromarty you may want to stay in the village itself, exploring each street with its rows of terraced cottages seemingly hunched against the prevailing north winds. The town has been handsomely restored, and the old merchants' houses are superb examples of domestic architecture of the 18th century.

Once a flourishing port and a former royal burgh, the town gave the world a famous son: Hugh Miller. Born here in 1802, Miller was a stonemason as a young man, but in time he became a recognized expert in the field of geology, as well as a powerful man of letters in Scotland. **Hugh Miller's Cottage,** Church Street (ℭ **01381/600-245**), contains many of his personal belongings and collections of geological specimens. The thatched cottage was built in 1698. From Easter to September, it's open Monday through Saturday from noon to 1pm and 2 to 5pm and Sunday from 2 to 5pm; October Sunday to Wednesday noon to 5pm. Admission is £2.50 ($4) for adults, £1.90 ($3.05) for students and seniors, and £7 ($11) per family.

WHERE TO STAY & DINE

Royal Hotel Cromarty   The only hotel in town sits on an embankment near one of the deepest estuaries in Europe. Around 1940, the British navy combined a series of waterfront buildings into living quarters for sailors. Today, the hotel is a cozy enclave with wood-burning stoves and open fireplaces. The guest rooms are traditionally furnished. The dining room, which spills onto a glassed-in extension opening onto the harbor, features specialties like steaks and stroganoff. You can also enjoy a good bar menu, with a tempting list of burgers, crepes, and salads.

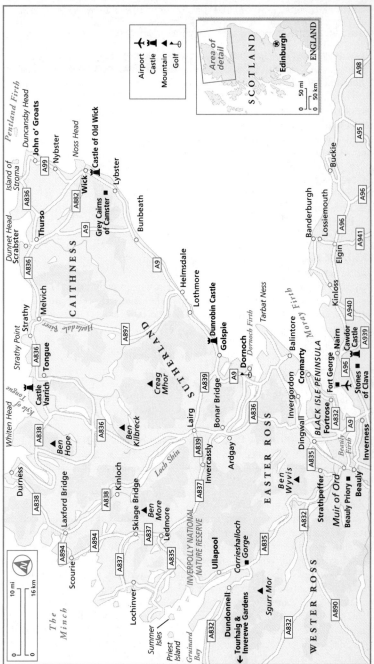

Airport ✈
Castle 🏰
Mountain ▲
Golf ⛳

SCOTLAND

Area of detail

Edinburgh

ENGLAND

0 __ 50 mi
0 __ 50 km

A98

A95

A96

A96

A941

Buckie

Banderburgh

Lossiemouth

Elgin

A940

Kinloss

A939

Nairn

Cawdor Castle

Fort George

Stones of Clava

Cromarty

Balintore

Moray Firth

Tarbat Ness

BLACK ISLE PENINSULA

Fortrose

A832

A9

Beauly Firth

Inverness

Dingwall

Invergordon

Strathpeffer

Muir of Ord

Beauly Priory

Beauly

A835

A832

Ben Wyvis ▲

EASTER ROSS

Ardgay

Bonar Bridge

A839

A9

Dornoch

Dornoch Firth

Golspie

Dunrobin Castle 🏰

A897

SUTHERLAND

Creag Mhor ▲

A839

Lairg

Invercassly

A837

Loch Shin

INVERPOLLY NATIONAL NATURE RESERVE

Ben Kilbreck ▲

Tongue

A836

Castle Varrich 🏰

Kyle of Tongue

Ben Hope ▲

A838

A838

Durness

Laxford Bridge

A838

Kinloch

A838

Ben More ▲

Skiage Bridge

A837

Ledmore

A835

Ullapool

Corrieshalloch Gorge

A835

Sgurr Mor ▲

Dundonnell

← Tourhaig & Inverewe Gardens

A832

A832

WESTER ROSS

A890

Lochinver

Scourie

A894

A894

A837

The Minch

Summer Isles

Priest Island

Gruinard Bay

Helmsdale

Lothmore

A9

CAITHNESS

Melvich

A897

Strathy

Strathy Point

Halladale River

A836

Bunbeath

Grey Cairns of Camster ■

A9

Thurso

Scrabster

Dunnet Head

A836

A836

Penland Firth

Island of Stroma

Duncansby Head

John o' Groats

A99

Nybster

Noss Head

Castle of Old Wick 🏰

Wick ■

Lybster

A882

Whiten Head

10 mi
16 km

0

0

Marine Terrace, Cromarty IV11 8YN. (*C*) **01381/600-217.** Fax 01381/600-813 www.royalcromartyhotel. co.uk. 10 units. £60 ($96) double. Rates include Scottish breakfast. AE, DC, MC, V. Bus: 26, 26A, or 126 from Inverness. Pets. **Amenities:** Restaurant; 2 bars; laundry service. *In room:* TV, coffeemaker, hair dryer, no phone.

9 Sutherland: The Gem of Scotland

Sutherland has more sheep than people (a 20-to-1 ratio). It's genuinely off the beaten track, but if you have time to travel this far, you'll find it perhaps the most beautiful county in Scotland. Adding to the haunting beauty are lochs and rivers, heather-covered moors and mountains—in all, 5,200 sq. km (2,000 sq. miles) of territory. It may not offer many "attractions," but it's a wonderful setting for outdoor pursuits like golf and fishing.

To the northwest of Inverness, Sutherland has three coastlines—on the north and west, the Atlantic, and on the east, the North Sea. Most villages have populations of only 100 or so hearty souls. Sutherland was the scene of the notorious 19th-century Highland Clearances, when many residents were driven out from their ancestral crofts. Many made their way to the New World. In many a deserted glen, you can still see traces of former crofting villages.

DORNOCH ⚐

The ancient cathedral city of Dornoch, 101km (63 miles) northwest of Inverness and 353km (219 miles) northwest of Edinburgh, is Sutherland's major town and the area's most interesting stop. The major sightseeing attraction nearby is **Dornoch Cathedral** (see below). Dornoch is also known for its sandy beaches, but we find that the swimming is best left for polar bears. However, they do make for lovely walks.

A **tourist office** is at the Square ((*C*) **01862/810-400**). It's open daily November to March 10am to 1:30pm; April to May Monday to Saturday 10am to 5pm and Sunday 10am to 4pm; June to July Monday to Saturday 10am to 4:30pm and Sunday 10am to 4pm; August Monday to Saturday 10am to 6pm and Sunday 10am to 4pm; September Monday to Saturday 10am to 5pm and Sunday 10am to 4pm; and October Monday to Saturday 10am to 5pm. From the Inverness bus station at Farraline Park, off Academy Street (call (*C*) **01463/233-371** for schedules), three local companies run daily **buses** to Dornoch: Stagecoach, Scottish CityLink and Highland Country Buses. The trip takes between 60 and 90 minutes and costs £7.50 ($12) one-way.

EXPLORING THE AREA

The village of Dornoch has long been known for its golf club on the sheltered shores of Dornoch Firth, the northernmost first-class course in the world. The turf of the **Royal Dornoch Golf Club,** Golf Road ((*C*) **01862/810-219**), is considered sacred by aficionados. Golf was first played here by monks in 1614. A curious meander of the Gulf Stream as it bypasses northern Scotland keeps the climate balmier than you'd expect. The club itself was founded in 1877, and a royal charter was granted by Edward VII in 1906. Prince Andrew and the duchess of Sutherland are both members today. Its SSS is 73; its par is 70 for an 18-hole yardage of 6,185 (5,628m). Greens fees are from £45 to £76 ($72–$122). Golf club and trolley rentals are £20 to £30 ($32–$48) and £3 ($4.80), respectively. Caddy service is available for £20 to £30 ($32–$48) plus tip.

Dornoch Cathedral, Castle Street, was built in the 13th century and partially destroyed by fire in 1570. It has undergone many restorations, but you can still see its fine 13th-century stonework. The cathedral is famous for its modern stained-glass windows—three are in memory of Andrew Carnegie, the American steel king. The cathedral is open daily from 9am to dusk. The **Plaiden Ell,** found in the cathedral's cemetery where a marketplace used to be, was a medieval method for measuring cloth. (An *ell* was a unit of measure equaling about 96cm/38 in.) The Ell is carved in stone in a flat shape similar to a tombstone's, but with two pieces of metal rising about 5cm (2 in.) above the level of the stone. The distance between those two pieces of metal is an ell. In one of the gardens is the 1722 **witch's stone** marking the spot where the last burning of a so-called witch took place in Scotland.

If the weather is fair, Dornoch is great for country strolls, as the town is flanked by miles of clean sand opening onto chilly waters. You can often see migrant birds on these beaches. At **Embo,** some 5km (3 miles) north of the beaches of Dornoch, you'll come across the remains of two funeral vaults believed to date from around 2000 B.C.

You can drive another 3km (2 miles) north of Embo to the shores of lovely **Loch Fleet,** where there's a meager ruin of **Skelbo Castle.** It's now on a lonely grassy mound, but in the 14th century Skelbo was a powerful fortification.

Shoppers should check out the **Dornoch Craft Centre,** Town Jail, Castle Street (✆ **01862/810-555**), in the center of town opposite the cathedral. You can wander through the selection of crafts, jewelry, and pottery, and then visit the Textile Hall and browse through the range of knitwear, tartans, mohair goods, and tweeds.

WHERE TO STAY & DINE

Carnegie Club at Skibo Castle ★★★   Skibo Castle is as massive a baronial house as you're likely to find in Scotland, an Edwardian pile created from a unique combination of Scottish heritage and one of the most potent fortunes of the Industrial Revolution. Steel magnate Andrew Carnegie, who emigrated from Scotland's woolen mills to America in the mid–19th century, yearned for a return to the land of his birth after he acquired his fortune. After he bought the historic but dilapidated Skibo, 8km (5 miles) east of Dornoch, in 1898 (for the relatively reasonable price of £85,000/$144,500), Carnegie and his second wife, Louise, massively enlarged the place, pouring £2 million ($3.4 million) into its refurbishment. Here they welcomed a stream of distinguished visitors, including Edward VII, during the months they spent in Scotland in their final years.

In 1990, Peter de Savary, the force behind posh semiprivate clubs in London and Antigua, acquired the property and its 2,835 hectares (7,000 acres), installed an 18-hole golf course designed by Donald Steel, and created a resort that's a combination golf mecca and semiprivate club for the celebs, CEOs, and aristocrats who can afford the sky-high rates. Meals are served at a long table in the style of an Edwardian house party. Evenings of Scottish dance are featured every Saturday; other nights, there are dinner performances of Scottish flute, Celtic harp, or piano. Sports opportunities include trap and skeet shooting, falconry, trout and salmon fishing, and golf (on the resort's course or at the nearby Royal Dornoch Course).

Skibo Castle, Dornoch IV25 3RQ. ✆ **01862/894-600.** Fax 01862/894-601. www.carnegieclub.co.uk. 46 units. £475–£595 ($760–$952) double members; £695–£850 ($1,112–$1,360) double nonmembers. Rates include meals, drinks, and sporting activities (including greens fees at the resort's golf course). Membership costs £3,525 ($5,640) per year per family. AE, DC, MC, V. The club will send a car to Dornoch or anywhere in Inverness to meet new arrivals. **Amenities:** Restaurant (guests only); indoor pool; spa; golf course; tennis court; room service (7am–10:30pm). *In room:* TV, hair dryer.

Dornoch Castle Hotel   This unusual hotel, close to the Royal Dornoch Golf Course, occupies what was once the residence of the bishops of Caithness, built of stone in the center of town in the late 15th or early 16th century. Today, its winding stairs, labyrinthine corridors, and impenetrable cellars have been converted into a well-directed hotel and restaurant. The guest rooms are in the original building and an extension overlooking the garden; all tend to be dowdy, however. Most bathrooms contain combination tub and shower. Restaurant specialties include leg of Sutherland lamb with onion marmalade and Highland Estate venison with black currants. Reservations are suggested.

Castle St., Dornoch IV25 3SD. ℂ **01862/810-216.** Fax 01862/810-981. www.dornochcastlehotel.com. 18 units. £86–£130 ($138–$208) double. Rates include Scottish breakfast. AE, MC, V. **Amenities:** Restaurant; bar. *In room:* TV.

GOLSPIE

This family resort town with a golf course sits on A9 and looks out across the water to the Dornoch Firth, with a crescent of sandy beach. Golspie, 367km (228 miles) northwest of Edinburgh and 116km (72 miles) northwest of Inverness, is visited chiefly because of its towering Dunrobin Castle.

Dunrobin Castle 𝄐   Home of the earls and dukes of Sutherland, Dunrobin is the most northerly of the great houses of Scotland and also the biggest in the northern Highlands, dating in part from the early 13th century. Its formal gardens are laid out in the manner of Versailles. On the grounds is a museum containing many relics from the Sutherland family. Some of the castle's 180 rooms are open to the public—the ornately furnished dining room, a billiard room, and the room and gilded four-poster bed where Queen Victoria slept when she visited in 1872.

Golspie, Sutherland KW10 6SF. 1km (½ mile) northeast of Golspie on A9. ℂ **01408/633-177.** Admission £6.50 ($10) adults, £4.50 ($7.20) students, seniors, and children 5–16, £17.50 ($28) per family. Apr–May and Oct Mon–Sat 10:30am–4:30pm, Sun noon–4:30pm; June–Sept Mon-Sat 10:30am–5:30pm. Last entrance 30 min. before closing.

WHERE TO STAY & DINE

Golf Links Hotel   The best place to stay in Golspie dates from the early 1900s, when it was built as the stone rectory for the local minister. Many of the guests are golfers drawn to the nearby Golspie, Royal Dornoch, and Brora courses. The rooms in the main building are well furnished, each with a midsize bathroom. Scottish and Continental cuisine are served in a dining room with a view of Ben Bhraggie.

Church St., Golspie KW10 6TT. ℂ **01408/633-408.** Fax 01408/634-184. www.golflinkshotel.co.uk. 9 units. £55 ($88) double. Rates include Scottish breakfast. MC, V. **Amenities:** Restaurant; 2 bars; tour desk; laundry service. *In room:* TV, coffeemaker, hair dryer, iron/ironing board, no phone.

TONGUE

Heading north along A836, you cross high moors and brooding peaks to Tongue, 414km (257 miles) northwest of Edinburgh and 163km (101 miles) northwest of Inverness. For the nature lover and hiker, there's a lot to see, from the mighty cliffs of **Clo Mor,** near Cape Wrath (known for its large colonies of puffins), to waterfalls like **Eas-Coul-Aulin** (the highest in Britain) and the **Falls of Shin,** where you can see salmon leap. Masses of land, like **Ben Loyal** (known as the queen of Scottish mountains), suddenly rise from a barren landscape. Any of the district's tourist offices, including the one in Dornoch, can provide a map of the local hills, valleys, and trails. The one closest to the above-mentioned trekking sites is the office on Main Street in Bettyhill (ℂ **01641/521-342**), a coastal village about 24km (15 miles) from Tongue.

West of Tongue on a promontory stand the ruins of **Castle Varrich,** said to have been built by the Vikings. Possibly dating from the 14th century, this castle was the Mackay stronghold. This is a great place for a walk.

A rather dramatic walk from the center is to the **Kyle of Tongue,** crossed by a narrow causeway. Protected from the wild and raging sea nearby, this is a long, shallow inlet. At low tide, wearing a pair of boots, you can walk out to Rabbit Island, a little isle lying at the mouth of Kyle of Tongue. You'll pass towering cliffs, sandy bays, odd rock formations, and deserted rocky islets that time has seemingly forgotten.

WHERE TO STAY & DINE

Ben Loyal Hotel   This is a good choice, with everything under the careful attention of Paul and Elaine Lewis. The guest rooms are a bit plain but comfortably furnished in traditional style, with shower-only bathrooms and electric blankets. Several superior rooms have four-poster beds and views over the castle ruins and loch. Home-cooked meals feature local beef and produce grown on the grounds. A fine wine list and an assortment of malt whiskies complement the cuisine. The Ben Loyal incorporates 19th-century stables, a former post office, a shop, and a village bakery.

Main St., Tongue IV27 4XE. ℂ **01847/611-216.** Fax 01847/611-336. www.benloyal.co.uk. 11 units. £50–£64 ($80–$102) double. Rates include breakfast. MC, V. Pets accepted. **Amenities:** Restaurant; bar. *In room:* TV, coffeemaker, hair dryer.

Tongue Hotel ⌾   Since Queen Victoria's day, the best place to stay in town has been the Tongue Hotel, 1.6km (1 mile) north of the village center beside the road leading to Durness. Built of gray stone in the baronial style in 1850, it began as a hunting lodge for the duke of Sutherland. The hotel opens onto the Kyle of Tongue and still possesses much of its original character. Both the public rooms and the guest rooms are decorated in Victorian style, with flowered curtains and well-upholstered furniture. Most of the bathrooms are equipped with combination tub and shower.

The quality of the food is well known locally. A hearty, moderately priced dinner usually includes a choice of game or fresh fish caught in the region. Affordable bar meals are served in the popular pub, with an open fireplace and impressive collection of whiskies, and the more sedate cocktail lounge.

Tongue, Sutherland IV27 4XD. ℂ **01847/611-206.** Fax 01847/611-345. www.scottish-selection.co.uk. 19 units. £70–£120 ($112–$192) double. Rates include Scottish breakfast. MC, V. **Amenities:** Restaurant; 2 bars; laundry service. *In room:* TV, coffeemaker, hair dryer.

10 Caithness: Unspoiled Country

It doesn't look like the Highlands at all, but Caithness is the northernmost county of mainland Scotland, where the ancient landscape is gentle and rolling. Within its 1,820sq km (700 sq. miles) you'll find signs of the Stone Age—the enigmatic **Grey Cairns of Camster** date from 4000 B.C. The county is filled with cairns, mysterious stone rows and circles, and standing stones. The Vikings once occupied this place with its rock stacks, old harbors, craggy cliffs, and quiet coves, and many place names are in Old Norse. It has churches from the Middle Ages, as well as towering castles on cliff tops. The Queen Mother's home, the **Castle of Mey,** dating from 1570, is between John o' Groats and Thurso.

Rich in bird and animal life, Caithness is unspoiled country. Fishing draws people to the area: Wild brown trout are found in some 100 lochs, along with salmon in the Thurso and Wick Rivers. Most people head for Caithness with **John o' Groats** as their final destination. John o' Groats is popularly called the extreme northern tip of the British mainland. Actually, Dunnet Head is farther north by a few kilometers.

Scrabster, a ferry harbor, is the main car-and-passenger service that operates all year to the Orkney Islands (see chapter 12, "The Orkney & Shetland Islands," for more information). There are day trips in summer.

WICK

The famous old herring port of Wick, on the eastern coastline of Caithness, 462km (287 miles) northwest of Edinburgh and 203km (126 miles) northwest of Inverness, is a popular stop for those heading north to explore what's often called the John o' Groats Peninsula. The town has some claim as a holiday resort as well: Robert Louis Stevenson spent part of his boyhood in Wick when his father worked here on an engineering project. Today, a sleepy nostalgia hangs over the town. There's daily bus and rail service from Inverness, from which train connections are possible via Edinburgh, Glasgow, or Stirling.

At **Caithness Glass,** Airport Industrial Estates (*©* **01955/602-286**), you can watch the glassblowing and tour the factory Monday through Friday from 9am to 5pm. The shop and restaurant are open Monday through Saturday from 9am to 5pm (Sat to 5pm from June–Sept). The **Wick Heritage Centre,** 20 Bank Row (*©* **01955/605-393**), has many exhibits pertaining to Wick's herring-fishing industry in days of yore. From Easter to October, it's open Monday through Saturday from 10am to 5pm; last entrance is at 3:45pm. Admission is £2 ($3) for adults and 50p (75¢) for children 5 to 16.

The most important sites in the area are the two megalithic **Grey Cairns of Camster,** 10km (6 miles) north of Lybster on the Watten Road off A9. The ruins of the **Castle of Old Wick** are also worth exploring, and they're always accessible. The location is off A9, 2.5km (1½ miles) south of Wick. Once known as Castle Olipant, the ruined structure dates back to the 14th century. You can still see three floors of the old castle rising on a rocky promontory.

WHERE TO STAY & DINE

Breadalbane House Hotel This 1891 building on the southern outskirts of town, a 5-minute walk from the center, was once the home of a furniture maker. It's now an unpretentious guesthouse with traditionally decorated rooms. You can dine in the restaurant or in the cozy bar. Food offerings vary from curries and steaks to a traditional roast dinner served on weekends.

20 Breadalbane Crescent, Wick KW1 5AQ. *©* **01955/603-911.** Fax 01955/603-911. www.breadalbane. activehotels.com. 10 units, 8 with private bathroom. £47 ($75) double with bathroom. Rates include Scottish breakfast. AE, MC, V. **Amenities:** Restaurant; 2 bars; babysitting (by arrangement). *In room:* TV, coffeemaker, no phone.

Mackay's This recently refurbished hotel on the south shore of the River Wick is the home of the Lamont family, who has welcomed guests for more than 40 years. All bedrooms are tastefully decorated and provide well-maintained, shower-only bathrooms. In the heart of Wick, the hotel is a short walk to the Heritage Center and the swimming pool and leisure center. The restaurant, specializing in traditional Scottish fare, offers fixed-price five-course meals.

Union St. (opposite Caithness General Hospital), Wick KW1 5ED. *©* **800/528-1234** or 01955/602-323. Fax 01955/605-930. www.mackayshotel.co.uk. £80 ($128) double; £110 ($176) family room. Rates include breakfast. AE, MC, V. Closed Jan 1–2. **Amenities:** Restaurant; 2 bars. *In room:* TV, coffeemaker, hair dryer.

JOHN O' GROATS

John o' Groats, 27km (17 miles) north of Wick, is the northern equivalent of Land's End at the tip of the Cornish peninsula in England. The southern tip of England is 1,414km (878 miles) south of John o' Groats. From here, there are views north to the Orkney Islands and the Pentland Firth.

John o' Groats was named after a Dutch ferryman, Jan de Groot. His tombstone can still be seen at Cabisbay Church. The town abounds in souvenir shops, some selling small Arctic cowrie shells once used as decoration by the first settlers in Caithness. You can take interesting walks along the coast to **Duncansby Head,** 3km (2 miles) east—one of the most dramatic coastlines in this part of Scotland. Many species of sea birds, especially puffins, live among the jagged cliffs. A road leads out to a lighthouse suspended on the cliffs; from here you get a panoramic view over Pentland Firth. These turbulent waters have been a nightmare to mariners, with some 400 wrecks reported in the past century and a half.

In summer, there's daily passenger-only ferry service to Orkney. Bus tours of the island are included. The Orkney Islands are just a 45-minute sail from John o' Groats across the Pentland Firth (see chapter 12).

WHERE TO STAY & DINE

Seaview Hotel   The Seaview is a family-run hotel whose severe and streamlined sides rise abruptly from a flat, windswept landscape beside the town's only highway. Built in the 1950s, it's covered with a roughly textured white stucco that locals refer to as pebble dash. Each guest room is rather austere but comfortable, with a shower-only bathroom and electric blanket. Bar lunches and dinners draw an appreciative crowd to the pub. Main courses in the restaurant are moderately priced.

John o' Groats KW1 4YR. (℃) and fax **01955/611-220.** www.johnogroats-seaviewhotel.co.uk. 9 units, 5 with private bathroom. £30–£40 ($48–$64) double. Rates include Scottish breakfast. MC, V. **Amenities:** Restaurant; bar. *In room:* TV, coffeemaker, no phone.

THURSO

Many visitors drive through the northern port of Thurso as they're heading for Scrabster, where ferries leave for the Orkney Islands (see chapter 12). The town, on the River Thurso, is of only mild interest, used mainly as a refueling stop for those who have made it this far north. It remains a big, bustling holiday resort

---

The Arts in John O' Groats

In an old converted country school, the **Lythe Arts Centre** (℃ **01955/ 641-270**) stages year-round performances of innovative and experimental works by small touring companies, from drama and dance to jazz, folk, and new music. There's also a permanent collection of art related to northern Scotland, and July and August bring touring exhibits of contemporary art, photography, and some crafts. Exhibits are open daily from 10am to 6pm; admission is £1.50 ($2.40) for adults, £1 ($1.60) seniors, and 50p ($.80) for students and children. Performances usually start at 8pm. Advance booking is necessary for all shows, so call ahead. Tickets cost £8 ($13) for adults, £6 ($9.60) for seniors, and £4 ($6.40) for students and children. Coffee, tea, and light snacks are available on performance evenings. The arts center is signposted, 6.5km (4 miles) off A99 between Wick and John o' Groats.

with a still-active fishing fleet. In the center, many restored sandstone town houses date from the 1700s.

Once an important and major Viking stronghold, Thurso—meaning "river of the god Thor"—knew its greatest power and prestige in the 11th century, when it was ruled by Thorfinn, who had defeated King Duncan's nephew in 1040. In medieval times, Thurso became the major trading town between Scotland and the Norse countries.

To the west are the cliffs of Holborn Head and Dunnet Head, which boast a lighthouse. Many visitors walk out to the most northern point of mainland Britain for its panoramic views of the southern tier of the Orkneys. The town is 214km (133 miles) northwest of Inverness, 34km (21 miles) northwest of Wick, and 32km (20 miles) west of John o Groats.

If you'd like to explore by bike, head for **Sandra's Back Packer Hostel,** 24 Princes St. (℗ **01847/984-575**). Open daily 9am to midnight. Rental rates are £5 to £6 ($8–$9.60) per day.

For information on Thurso, visit the **tourist office** at Riverside (℗ **01847/ 892-371**), open April to October Monday to Saturday 10am to 5pm and Sunday 10am to 4pm.

WHERE TO STAY & DINE

The Weigh Inn & Lodges ⍟   This is the most modern hotel in the far north of Scotland, overlooking the Pentland Firth with panoramic views that extend (on a clear day) to the Orkney Islands. It's on the outskirts of Thurso, at the junction of the A9 to Scrabster Harbour and the main artery leading to the western coast of the Highlands. Many travelers planning to take the morning car ferry to the Orkney Islands stay overnight here. The wide variety of accommodations includes doubles, twins, singles, and even family rooms. Some bathrooms contain showers only.

Burnside, Thurso. KW14 TUG. ℗ **01847/893-722.** Fax 01847/892112. www.weighinn.co.uk. 58 units. £40–£78 ($64–$125) double. MC, V. **Amenities:** Restaurant; bar. *In room:* TV, coffeemaker, iron/ironing board.

The Park Hotel   With an almost Scandinavian style, this hotel offers comfortable, adequately furnished rooms with small, shower-only bathrooms; eight units can accommodate families. Guests receive a warm reception and friendly service. Both the lounge and restaurant offer reasonably priced meals accompanied by a fine selection of wines, beers, and malt whiskies. High tea is served as well.

Thurso KW14 8RE. ℗ **01847/893-251.** Fax 01847/893-252. www.parkhotelthurso.co.uk. 11 units. £70 ($112) double. Rates include full Scottish breakfast. AE, DC, MC, V. Closed Jan 1–3. Located on the right-hand side of the A9 on approach to the Thurso town center. **Amenities:** Restaurant; 2 bars. *In room:* TV, coffeemaker, hair dryer, iron/ironing board.

ULLAPOOL ⍟

Ullapool is an interesting village, the largest in Wester Ross, 95km (59 miles) northwest of Inverness and 383km (238 miles) north of Glasgow. It was built by the British Fishery Society in 1788 as a port for herring fishers and is still a busy harbor. The original town plan hasn't been changed, and many of the buildings look much as they did at the time of their construction. Ullapool has long been an embarkation point for travelers crossing the Minch, a section of the North Atlantic separating Scotland from the Outer Hebrides.

EXPLORING THE AREA

One of our favorite towns in this region of Scotland, Ullapool was founded on the lovely shores of the salt lake **Loch Broom.** The site of the ferry docks for the island of Lewis, Ullapool remains a bustling fishing station. It's also the best embarkation point for trips to the Summer Isles (see below).

One of the most dramatic and scenic views in the north of Scotland is possible from Ullapool, a 64km (40-mile) run north following the signposts to the village of Lochiner. Take A835 north from Ullapool, enjoying the views of Loch Broom as you go along. You'll pass the hamlet of Armair on Loch Kanaird, then come to the **Inverpolly National Nature Reserve** of some 10,935 hectares (27,000 acres), including lochs and lochans along with the peaks of Cul Mor at 849m (2,786 ft.), Cul Beag at 769m (2,523 ft.), and Stac Pollaidth at 612m (2,010 ft.).

At **Knockan,** 24km (15 miles) north of Ullapool, a signposted nature trail along the cliff offers the most dramatic views in the area and is the best place to observe the regional flora, fauna, and geology.

At the Ledmore junction, take A837 to the left, passing along **Loch Awe,** with the mountain peaks of Canisp at 847m (2,779 ft.) and Ben More Assynt at 984m (3,230 ft.) forming a backdrop. You'll reach the lovely 10km-long (6-mile) **Loch Assynt.** The road along this lake-dotted landscape eventually carries you to **Lochiner,** a hamlet with fewer than 300 souls. It's known for its scenery, sandy coves, and crofting communities. For tourist information, call © **01854/612-135.**

There are a number of day trips you can take from Ullapool, including a jaunt to the **Corrieshalloch Gorge,** 19km (12 miles) southeast, a nature reserve along A835 at Braemore. From this point, the Falls of Measach plunge 45m (150 ft.) into a 1.6km-long (1-mile) wooded gorge. A bridge over the chasm and a viewing platform offer a panoramic way to enjoy this spectacular scenery.

Another interesting excursion is to the **Inverewe Gardens** (© **01445/781-200**). An exotic mixture of plants from the South Pacific, the Himalayas, and South America allows the gardens to have color year-round. They can be reached along A832, 10km (6 miles) northeast of Gairloch. Open daily from 9:30am to 7:30pm. Admission is £5 ($8) for adults, £4 ($6.40) for seniors and children, and £14 ($22) per family.

From either Ullapool or Achiltibuie, you can take excursions in season to the **Summer Isles** ★★, a beautiful group of almost uninhabited islands off the coast. They get their name because sheep are transported here in summer for grazing; the islands are a mecca for bird-watchers. Boat schedules vary, depending on weather conditions. Information is available from the **tourist office** on Argyle Street (© **01854/612-135**).

WHERE TO STAY

Dromnan Guest House *Value*   Mrs. MacDonald is your host at this 1970s stone guesthouse on the southern outskirts of town, a 10-minute walk from the center. The place is very well maintained, and the guest rooms are described by the kindly owner as being decorated in a combination of Marks & Spencer department-store goods and Shand-Kydd wallpapers and fabrics designed by the mother of the late Princess Diana. Each unit is equipped with a small bathroom with shower.

Garve Rd., Ullapool IV26 2SX. © **01854/612-333.** Fax 01854/613-364. www.dromnan.co.uk. 7 units. £40–£50 ($64–$80) double. Rates include breakfast. MC, V. **Amenities:** Access to nearby pool, tennis courts, and sauna; laundry service. *In room:* TV, coffeemaker, hair dryer, no phone.

Royal Hotel   The Royal sits on a knoll on the Inverness side of town, overlooking the harborfront. Graced with curved walls and large sheets of glass, it was reconstructed in 1961 from an older building, with an added east wing. It offers well-furnished guest rooms, half with balconies opening onto views of Loch Broom. All are equipped with shower-only bathrooms. Live entertainment is offered in season. Scottish fare is served in the dining area; afterward, guests sit around a log fire in the well-appointed lounge.

Garve Rd., Ullapool IV26 2SY. ℭ **01854/612-181** Fax 01854/612-951. www.royalhotel-ullapool.com. 52 units. £60–£70 ($96–$112) double. Rates include Scottish breakfast. MC, V. Closed Nov to early Mar. **Amenities:** Restaurant; 2 bars; access to nearby pool; 2 tennis courts; sauna; room service (7am–midnight). *In room:* TV, coffeemaker, hair dryer (on request).

WHERE TO DINE

Mariner's Restaurant SCOTTISH/INTERNATIONAL   Within the simple confines of a somewhat battered building, this restaurant serves food that is both upscale and elegant. Its design (ca. 1970s) might remind you of a roadside motel, if not for the wild and verdant scenery around you. Lunches are rather deceptively promoted as bar snacks, even though they include full-fledged waitress service and elaborate versions of lobster, oak-roasted smoked salmon, and haggis with black pudding. Dinners are in the same price range as lunch, but are served in a separate dining room.

On the premises are 12 motel rooms, clean and unassuming but not particularly distinctive. Doubles go for £50 ($80) and come with TV and phone.

North Rd. ℭ **01854/612-161.** Reservations recommended. Main courses £8–£27 ($13–$43). DC, MC, V. Daily noon–2pm and 5:30–9:30pm.

11

The Hebridean Islands

Once the Hebridean islands were visited only by geologists, bird-watchers, and the occasional fisher or mountain climber. Today, the chain of islands just off the Scottish mainland that makes up the Inner Hebrides is becoming more and more accessible to the general visitor. But what about the Outer Hebrides? One of the lesser-known parts of western Europe, these are a splintered sweep of windswept islands stretching for some 209km (130 miles) from the Butt of Lewis in the north all the way to Barra Head in the south. With rugged cliffs, clean beaches, archaeological treasures, and tiny bays, the Outer Hebrides lure more and more visitors every year.

1 The Inner & Outer Hebrides: An Overview

THE INNER HEBRIDES If you travel to the Inner Hebrides, the chain of islands just off the west coast of the Scottish mainland, you'll be following in the footsteps of Samuel Johnson and his faithful Boswell. The **Isle of Skye** is the largest. **Mull** has wild scenery and golf courses, and just off its shores is the important **Iona,** the isle that played a major part not only in the spread of Christianity in Britain, but also in the preservation of the culture and learning of the ancient world when it was being forgotten all over Europe. Adventurous travelers will also seek out **Coll** and **Tyree** as well as the **Isle of Colonsay** and **Rhum (Rum), Eigg,** or the tiny island of **Raasay,** off Skye.

If your time is limited, we suggest you concentrate on Skye. It offers your best chance for getting the flavor of the Hebrides in a nutshell, all in a 2-day trip. The island's natural beauty ranges from the rugged Trotternish Peninsula to the jagged peaks of the Cuillin Hills. The Cuillins are called both Black Cuillins (the hills encircling the glacial trough of Loch Coruisk) and Red Cuillins (based on the pink granite found in the hills). A favorite of hill climbers, these often harsh mountains make for some of the grandest walks in Skye.

Our favorite drive in all the Hebrides is to the Trotternish Peninsula and northeast Skye, which you can easily tour in a day from Portree. This is only a 32km (20-mile) peninsula but is so fascinating you can easily spend a day enjoying it. The highlight of the drive is 13km (8 miles) north of Portree: the **Old Man of Storr,** a stone pinnacle standing 48m (160 ft.) high. Once at the top, you'll be rewarded with great views of the island.

If you have time for one more Hebridean island, make it **Mull.** From Mull you can also spend an afternoon visiting the ancient ecclesiastical center off the coast at **Iona.** Spend the morning exploring parts of Mull, including a visit to Torosay Castle and Gardens. Have lunch on Mull, and then hop over to the little island of Iona.

THE OUTER HEBRIDES   At first you may feel you've come to a lunar landscape where there's a sense of infinite time. The character of the Outer Hebrides is quite different from that of the Inner Hebrides. This string of islands, stretching for 209km (130 miles), is about 64km (40 miles) off the northwest coast of Scotland, and the main islands to visit are **Lewis** and **Harris** (parts of the same island despite the different names), **North Uist, Benbecula, South Uist,** and **Barra.** The archipelago also takes in some minor offshore islands. Gaelic is spoken here; its gentle cadence is said to have been the language spoken in the Garden of Eden. Presbyterianism is still very strong (in one B&B, watching TV on Sunday is forbidden). Before you go, you might read Compton Mackenzie's novel *Whisky Galore.*

The islands knew 2 centuries of Viking invasions, but today are the retreat of many a disenchanted artist from the mainland. They come here, take over old crofter's cottages, and devote their days to such pursuits as pottery making and weaving. Bird-watchers flock here to see the habitats of the red-necked phalarope, corncrake, golden eagle, Arctic skua, and grayleg goose. Golfers come to play on these far-northern courses, including one at Stornoway (Lewis) and another at Askernish (South Uist). Anglers come to fish for salmon, brown trout, and sea trout.

You can see much of the dim past on these islands, including a version of Stonehenge. A good time to visit is June and July, when adults' and children's choirs compete for honors at festivals celebrating Gaelic music and poetry. Each of the main islands has accommodations, most small, family-run guesthouses and hotels. Many are crofter's cottages that take in B&B guests, mainly in summer. Advance reservations are important.

ESSENTIALS

GETTING THERE   By Ferry   From Gourock, the ferry terminal near Glasgow, **Caledonian MacBrayne** (© **01475/650-100** for information, or 0990/650-000 for reservations) sails to 23 Scottish islands in the Firth of Clyde and the Western Isles, including Skye and Mull, as well as the Outer Hebrides. The company also offers inclusive tours ideal for visiting places well off the beaten track.

For Mull and Iona, Oban is your port. These islands are part of the Inner Hebrides and enjoy fairly good connections with the mainland. From Oban, the ferries to the offshore islands run only twice a day until summer; then there are cruises to Iona from early June to late September. For details about ferry services to Mull, Iona, and the Outer Hebrides, get in touch with Caledonian MacBrayne's Oban office (© **08705/650-000**). It sails to 24 islands, with fares ranging from £18 ($29) per car and £6.30 ($10) per adult passenger for travel to Mull up to £122 ($195) per car plus £33.50 ($54) per adult passenger for travel to Barra. Book in advance, particularly in summer, as the ferries often sell out.

By Car   If you're driving from the mainland, you can take the "Road to the Isles," heading for the Kyle of Lochalsh if your destination is Skye. The more remote Outer Hebrides are linked by car ferries from mainland ports like Ullapool (© **01854/612-358** in Stornoway for schedules). The main islands to visit here are Lewis and Harris.

By Air   Glasgow has **air service** to the airport at Stornoway on Lewis; call British Airways (© **0845/773-3377** in Glasgow) for details.

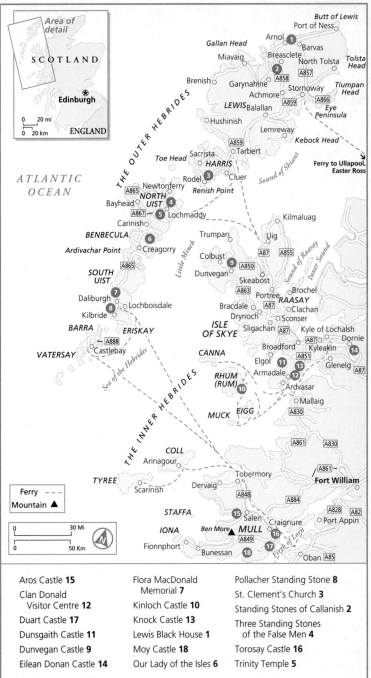

The Hebrides

Area of detail

SCOTLAND

Edinburgh

0   20 mi
0   20 km

ENGLAND

ATLANTIC OCEAN

THE OUTER HEBRIDES

Butt of Lewis
Port of Ness
Arnol **1**
Barvas
Gallan Head
Miavaig
Breasclete
North Tolsta *Tolsta Head*
2 A858 A857
Brenish
Garynahine
Achmore Stornoway *Tiumpan Head*
LEWIS Balallan A859 A866 *Eye Peninsula*
Hushinish
Lemreway
Kebock Head
A859 Tarbert
Toe Head Sacrista
HARRIS
Rodel **3** Cluer *Sound of Shiant*
Newtonferry Renish Point
Ferry to Ullapool, Easter Ross
A865 *NORTH UIST* **4**
Bayhead A867 **5** Lochmaddy
Carinish
Kilmaluag
BENBECULA **6**
Ardivachar Point Creagorry
Trumpan Uig
A87 A855
Colbust
SOUTH UIST A865 **9** A850
Dunvegan
Skeabost *Brochel*
A863 Portree *RAASAY*
Daliburgh **7** A87 Clachan
Kilbride **8** Lochboisdale Bracdale Sconser
Drynoch
BARRA ERISKAY *ISLE OF SKYE* Sligachan A87 Kyle of Lochalsh
A87 A87 Dornie
VATERSAY A888 Broadford **14**
Castlebay A851
CANNA Elgol **11** Glenelg
13 A87
Sea of the Hebrides Armadale **12**
RHUM (RUM) **10** Ardvasar
MUCK EIGG Mallaig
A830
A861 A830
COLL
Arinagour A861
Tobermory **Fort William**
TYREE Dervaig
Scarinish A848 A884
A828 A82
STAFFA Salen **15**
IONA *Ben More* ▲ *MULL* Craignure Port Appin
Fionnphort A849 **16**
Bunessan **18** **17** *Firth of Lorn*
Oban A85

Little Minch
Sound of Raasay
Inner Sound
Firth of Lorn

Ferry – – –
Mountain ▲

0   30 Mi
0   50 Km

N

2 Kyle of Lochalsh: Gateway to the Isle of Skye

329km (204 miles) NW of Edinburgh, 132km (82 miles) SW of Inverness, 201km (125 miles) N of Oban

The popular Kyle of Lochalsh is the gateway to the island of Skye (now reached by toll bridge). You can drive the length of Skye in a day, returning to the mainland by night if you want.

ESSENTIALS

GETTING THERE   Three **trains** per day (one on Sun) arrive from Inverness, taking about 2½ hours and costing £14 ($22) each way and £25.50 ($41) round trip. Call ✆ **08457/484-950** for schedules.

Both **Scottish CityLink** and **Skye-Ways** coaches arrive daily from Glasgow at the Kyle of Lochalsh (trip time: 5 hours), costing £17 ($27) each way. Skye-Ways also operates three buses a day from Inverness (trip time: 2 hours), costing £9.50 ($15) one-way. Call ✆ **08705/808-080** for schedules.

If you're **driving** from Fort William, head north along A82 to Invergarry, where you cut west onto A87 to the Kyle of Lochalsh.

VISITOR INFORMATION   The **tourist office** is at the Kyle of Lochalsh Car Park (✆ **01599/534-276;** www.highlandfreedom.com). It's open April to June, Monday through Saturday from 9am to 5:30pm; July and August, Monday through Saturday from 9am to 7pm and Sunday from 10am to 4pm; September and October, Monday through Friday from 9am to 5pm; and November to March, Monday through Friday from 9am to 5pm and Saturday from 10am to 4pm.

A NEARBY ATTRACTION

Eilean Donan Castle   This romantic castle was built in 1214 as a defense against the Danes. In ruins for 200 years, it was restored by Colonel MacRae of Clan MacRae in 1932 and is now a clan war memorial and museum, containing Jacobite relics, mostly with clan connections. A shop here sells kilts, woolens, and souvenirs.

Dornie. ✆ **01599/555-202.** Admission £4.50 ($7.20) adults, £3.40 ($5.45) seniors, students, and children, £9.50 ($15) per family. Apr–Oct daily 10am–6pm; Mar and Nov daily 10am–3:30pm. Drive 13km (8 miles) east of the Kyle of Lochalsh on A87.

WHERE TO STAY

The lodgings here are limited, just barely adequate to meet the demand for rooms.

Kyle Hotel   This modernized stone hotel in the center of town, a 5-minute walk from the train station, is your best all-around bet in the moderate category. The midsize guest rooms are furnished in a functional style, with neatly kept bathrooms (some with shower only). The hotel serves reasonably priced dinners in the lounge nightly.

Main St., Kyle of Lochalsh IV40 8AB. ✆ **01599/534-204.** Fax 01599/534-932. 31 units. £76–£110 ($122–$176) double. Rates include Scottish breakfast. MC, V. **Amenities:** Restaurant; 2 bars; laundry. *In room:* TV, coffeemaker, hair dryer.

Lochalsh Hotel ⟨€   This landmark hotel is the most refined nesting ground in the area. It was built as a luxury oasis when the British Railway finally extended its tracks in this direction. The hotel's crafted small-paned windows with hardwood and brass fittings will remind you of those on an oceangoing yacht. The comfortable guest rooms have been stylishly overhauled and include state-of-the-art bathrooms. Upscale dinners in the restaurant include the best Scottish cuisine and ingredients, accompanied by a panoramic view.

Ferry Rd., Kyle of Lochalsh IV40 8AF. ℂ **01599/534-202.** Fax 01599/534-881. www.lochalshhotel.com. 38 units. £70–£90 ($112–$144) double. Rates include Scottish breakfast. AE, MC, V. **Amenities:** Restaurant; bar; 24-hr. room service. *In room:* TV, coffeemaker, hair dryer.

WHERE TO DINE

The Seafood Restaurant ☆ SEAFOOD   This blue-and-white clapboard building (1880) was originally a waiting room for rail passengers en route to other destinations, but now it's one of the most frequented restaurants in town. The menu items are flavorful but unfussy, prepared with attention to detail. The best examples are Lochalsh langoustines in herb-flavored butter sauce and local queen scallops in white-wine sauce.

In the Railway Station. ℂ **01599/534-813.** Main courses £6–£12 ($9.60–$19) lunch; £8–£15 ($13–$24) dinner. MC, V. Mon–Fri 10am–3pm; daily 6–9pm. Closed Oct–Easter.

3 The Isle of Skye: Star of the Hebrides ☆☆

134km (83 miles) W of Inverness, 283km (176 miles) NW of Edinburgh, 235km (146 miles) NW of Glasgow

Off the northwest coast of Scotland, the mystical Isle of Skye, largest of the Inner Hebrides, is 77km (48 miles) long and varies between 5km and 40km (3–25 miles) wide. It's separated from the mainland by the Sound of Sleat (pronounced Slate). At Kyleakin, on the eastern end, the channel is only .5km (¼ mile) wide.

Sailing the Hebrides

One of the best ways to visit Scotland's far-flung Hebridean islands is by ship. One company geared for this kind of travel is **Hebridean Island Cruises,** Griffin House, Boughton Hall, Skipton, North Yorkshire BD23 3AN (ℂ **800/659-2648** in the U.S. and Canada, or 01756/704-704; www. hebridean.co.uk). It operates the *Hebridean Princess,* a shallow-draft, much-refitted and -retooled remake (1990) of an older vessel. Outfitted with 30 staterooms and a crew of 38, it can carry up to 50 passengers in cozy circumstances to some of the most remote and inaccessible regions of Scotland. The ship is equipped with beach landing craft, especially useful during explorations of the fragile ecosystems and bird life of the more remote islands.

From March to October, the company offers 12 itineraries that focus on nature and ecology or on the castles, gardens, and archaeology of Scotland. Tours usually depart from Oban and cruise through the Inner and Outer Hebrides and the Orkneys, stopping in places like Saint Kilda's, known for its bird life and tundra. The tours and prices vary enormously depending on the date of travel, but generally range from 4 to 10 nights and cost £1,280 to £6,190 ($2,048–$9,904). All meals and shore excursions are included, but liquor tabs at the well-stocked bar, wine at dinner, and gratuities are extra.

Dominating the land of summer seas, streams, woodland glens, mountain passes, cliffs, and waterfalls are the **Cuillin Hills** ★★★, a range of jagged black mountains that are a mecca for rock climbers. The Sleat Peninsula, the island's southernmost arm, is known as the "Garden of Skye." There are many stories as to the origin of the name *Skye.* Some believe it's from the Norse *ski,* meaning "cloud," and others say it's from the Gaelic word for "winged." There are Norse names on the island, however, as the Norsemen held sway for 4 centuries before 1263. Overlooking the Kyle is the ruined **Castle Maol,** once the home of a Norwegian princess.

On the island you can explore castle ruins, *duns* (hill forts), and *brochs* (prehistoric round stone towers). For the Scots, the island will forever evoke images of Flora MacDonald, who conducted the disguised Bonnie Prince Charlie to Skye after the Culloden defeat.

ESSENTIALS

GETTING THERE   From the Kyle of Lochalsh, drive west along the new toll bridge over the strait to Kyleakin; it costs £5.50 ($8.80) to cross one-way.

VISITOR INFORMATION   The **tourist office** is at Bayfield House in Portree (© **01478/612-137;** www.highlandfreedom.com). It's open April to June, Monday through Saturday from 9am to 5:30pm; July to mid-August, Monday through Saturday from 9am to 8pm and Sunday from 10am to 4pm; mid-August to October, Monday through Saturday from 9am to 5:30pm; and November to March, Monday through Friday from 9am to 5pm and Saturday from 10am to 4pm.

OUTDOOR PURSUITS AROUND THE ISLAND

BIKING   Gently undulating hills, coupled with the good roads and a relative lack of traffic, make the Isle of Skye appealing to cyclists. The island's premier rental outfits are **Island Cycles,** The Green, in the coastal city of Portree (© **01478/613-121**), and **Fairwinds Bicycle Hire,** Elgol Road, Broadford (© **01471/822-270**), farther inland, near the center of the island. Both charge £7 to £12 ($11–$19) a day. Island Cycles is open Monday through Saturday from 9:30am to 5pm; Fairwinds is open daily from 9am to 7pm.

BOATING   The coast of Skye is the most ruggedly beautiful this side of the Norwegian fjords, and several entrepreneurs offer boat trips letting you drink in the scenery. Foremost is **Bella Jane Boat Trips,** The Harbourfront, Elgol (© **0800/731-3089** in Britain, or 01471/866-244). From the piers in the village of Elgol, you'll board a sturdy vessel that sails daily (if there's enough business) between Easter and October into the rock-ringed borders of Loch Coruisk, at the foot of the Cuillin Hills, which are rich in bird life. Most visitors opt for the standard return trip; you're carried to the base of the hills, deposited for 90 minutes of wandering, and then returned over water to Elgol. It lasts 3 hours and costs £18.50 ($30) per person. If you're hardy and really interested in hiking, you can extend this experience to a full day.

GOLF   Golfing on Skye means an almost total lack of supervision, weather that can rain out or dry out a game with almost no notice, and often a lack of players. Whether you find this charming depends on your expectations, but overall, the island's best course is the nine-hole **Isle of Skye Golf Club** (© **01478/650-414**), adjacent to the hamlet of Sconser, on the southeast coast. Maintained by the local municipality, it has a simple snack bar and bar, and an on-again–off-again employee who cuts the grass whenever necessary. Less desirable but still prized for its convenience to residents of the **Skeabost House Hotel** (see "Ske-abost Bridge," later in this chapter) is the 9-hole course associated with the hotel. Nonguests can play if they phone ahead for a reservation. Greens fees at both courses are £16 ($26) for a full day's play.

HIKING Any branch of Skye's tourist office will offer advice on the many hikes available through the heather and glens of the island. For a walking adventure advised only for the stout-hearted and the fit, consider extending a boat trip on the Bella Jane (see above) with an additional 23km (14-mile) overland hike from the Cuillin Hills back to more heavily populated regions of the island. To do this, take the boat trip (one-way only) from Elgol to the Cuillin Hills. From here, brown-and-white signs direct you across an undulating, rock-strewn landscape to the Sligachan Hotel (see below), the premier hotel for trekkers. You can overnight at the hotel or take a bus or taxi the remaining 11km (7 miles) back to Portree.

KYLEAKIN

The seaport community of Kyleakin is the site of the old ferry terminal where the boats from the Scottish mainland used to arrive before Skye became linked by a bridge. Many visitors still prefer to stay here rather than on more remote, less convenient parts of the island.

Kyleakin opens onto a small bay and is dominated by a ruin, **Castle Maol,** on a jagged knoll. For a lovely walk, go from the town center up to this ruin from the 12th century, when it was a fortified stronghold of the Mackinnon clan.

WHERE TO STAY & DINE

The White Heather Hotel   These two connected buildings provide basic accommodations with up-to-date amenities. For more than half a century, this family-run guesthouse has been providing accommodations to wayfarers, opening onto panoramic views with the Torridon mountains to the north. The small guest rooms are simple but well maintained (some with shower only). Moderately priced dinners are served nightly in the dining room. The lounge, licensed only to serve guests, has a pleasant view of the Castle Maol. The hotel is convenient to both the ferry dock and the bus terminals.

The Pier, Kyleakin, Isle of Skye IV41 8PL. © **01599/534-577.** Fax 01599/534-427. www.whiteheatherhotel. co.uk. 10 units. £40 ($64) double. Rates include Scottish breakfast. MC, V. Closed Oct–Feb. *In room:* TV, coffeemaker, no phone.

Crafts on Skye

Edinbane Pottery, on A850, 13km (8 miles) east of Dunvegan (© **01470/ 582-234**), celebrates its 30th anniversary in 2002. The three artists working in this studio produce wood-fired stoneware and salt-glazed pottery, and they can fill custom orders in a wide range of finishes.

Artist Tom Mackenzie's etchings, prints, aquatints, and greeting cards are all inspired by the scenery and day-to-day life of the island. You can find his work at **Skye Original Prints at Portree,** 1 Wentworth St. (© **01478/612-544**).

Since 1974, Stewart John Wilson has been designing and producing silver and gold jewelry, ceramic tiles, cheese boards, platters, and clocks, all featuring intricate Celtic patterns. You can see his work at **Skye Silver,** in the Old School, on Glendale Road (B884), 11km (7 miles) west of Dunvegan (© **01470/511-263**). The selection of tiles is especially vast.

Craft Encounters, in the Post Office building in Broadford (© **01471/ 822-754**), showcases many of Skye's talented artists. You'll find pewter jewelry, stained-glass light catchers, salt-dough bric-a-brac, folk and landscape paintings, tartan ties, and handmade jumpers (sweaters). Celtic patterns show up on glassware, tableware, linens, and pieces of marquetry. The island's musical talent is represented in a selection of traditional Scottish music CDs.

Skye Batik, The Green (© **01478/613-331**), is one of the best crafts shops in Scotland. It sells wall hangings and cotton, tweed, wool, and linen clothing handprinted with Celtic designs from the 6th to the 8th centuries.

In **Harlequin Knitwear,** next to the Duisdale Hotel on Sleat (© **01471/ 833-321**), local knitter Chryssy Gibbs designs men's and women's machine-knit Shetland wool sweaters. Her work is bright and colorful.

For more knitwear, go to **Ragamuffin,** on the pier in Armadale (© **01471/844-217**), featuring quality Scottish, Irish, and British hand-knits for the whole family as well as accessories like hats, gloves, and scarves.

SLIGACHAN

The village of Sligachan sits at the head of a sea loch in a setting of scenic beauty with views of the Cuillin Hills (pronounced *coo*-lin). It's one of the best bases for exploring Skye because of its central location. Visitors enjoy sea-trout fishing, with an occasional salmon caught on the Sligachan River. It's also possible to rent a boat from the hotel below to explore the Storr Lochs, 24km (15 miles) from Sligachan, known for good brown-trout fishing from May to September.

WHERE TO STAY & DINE

Sligachan Hotel *(Kids)*   This family-run hotel nestles at the foot of the Cuillins on the main road between Portree and Kyleakin and is an ideal center from which to explore Skye. It's one of Skye's oldest coaching inns, built sometime in the 1830s. The guest rooms are old and a bit outdated, but still reasonably comfortable, each with a tub and shower. And the food is good, consisting of freshly caught seafood and at least one vegetarian selection served at dinner nightly. The bar also serves simple meals in front of an open fireplace and live music is often presented. Children are welcome and there's separate menu for them, as well as toys to keep them amused. In fact, the hotel is the most kid friendly place on the island.

Sligachan, Isle of Skye IV47 8SW. © **01478/650-204.** Fax 01478/650-207. www.sligachan.co.uk. 22 units. £60–£90 ($96–$144) double. Rates include Scottish breakfast. MC, V. **Amenities:** Restaurant; 2 bars; limited room service; laundry. *In room:* TV, coffeemaker, hair dryer, no phone.

PORTREE *(★★)*

Skye's capital, Portree, is the port for steamers making trips around the island and linking Skye with the 24km (15-mile) long island of Raasay. Sligachan, 14km (9 miles) south, and Glenbrittle, 11km (7 miles) farther southwest, are centers for climbing the Cuillin Hills.

WHERE TO STAY

Bosville Hotel   This well-established hotel stands in the center of Portree and commands panoramic views of the harbor and the Cuillin Hills. It's a bright, welcoming inn known equally for its cuisine (see the Chandlery Restaurant, below) and for its well-decorated and generally spacious bedrooms.

Bosville Terrace, Portree, Isle of Skye IV51 9DG. © **01478/612-846.** Fax 01478/613-434. 15 units. £60–£90 ($96–$144) double. Rates include Scottish breakfast. AE, MC, V. **Amenities:** Restaurant; bar; room service (7am–10pm); laundry/dry cleaning service. *In room:* TV, dataport, coffeemaker, hair dryer.

The Cuillin Hills Hotel *(★)*   This stone-sided manor was built in the 1820s as a hunting lodge for the MacDonald clan. Almost 1km (½ mile) north of Portree's center, the comfortable hotel appeals to hikers and bird-watchers. Views from the guest rooms encompass the unspoiled Cuillin Hills, Portree's harbor, or the sea. Each unit is outfitted with reproductions of old-fashioned furniture against a backdrop of flowered wallpaper. Rather expensive dinners are available to both guests and nonguests who phone in advance.

Portree, Isle of Skye IV51 9QU. © **01478/612-003.** Fax 01478/613-092. www.cuillinhills.demon.co.uk. 28 units. Winter £100–£120 ($160–$192) double; summer £160–£210 ($256–$336). Rates include full Scottish breakfast. AE, MC, V. Pets accepted by prior arrangement. **Amenities:** Restaurant; bar; room service (7am–9pm); laundry. *In room:* TV, coffeemaker, hair dryer, iron/ironing board, trouser press.

The Rosedale Hotel   In one of the more secluded parts of Portree, on the harbor 91m (100 yd.) from the village square, the Rosedale opens directly onto the sea. It was created from a row of fishermen's dwellings dating from the reign of William IV. The midsize guest rooms in this warm and welcoming place are decorated in modern style. The dining room serves expensive Scottish fare with the requisite seafood.

Beaumont Crescent, Portree, Isle of Skye IV51 9DF. ℂ **01478/613-131.** Fax 01478/612-531. www.rosedale hotelskye.co.uk. 23 units. £76–£106 ($122–$170) double. Rates include Scottish breakfast. MC, V. **Amenities:** Restaurant; bar. *In room:* TV, coffeemaker.

The Royal Hotel The Royal stands on a hill facing the water and is said to have extended hospitality to Bonnie Prince Charlie during his 1746 flight. Back in those faraway days, the building that stood here was the old MacNab Tavern. In less dramatic circumstances, you can book one of its comfortable, small-to-midsize guest rooms; the preferred ones open onto the sea. Formal meals and bar snacks are offered.

Bank St., Portree, Isle of Skye IV51 9BU. ℂ **01478/612-525.** Fax 01478/613-198. www.royal-hotel.demon. co.uk. 21 units. £88 ($141) double. Rates include Scottish breakfast. MC, V. **Amenities:** 2 restaurants; 3 bars; exercise room; spa; sauna; room service (10am–9pm). *In room:* TV, coffeemaker, hair dryer.

WHERE TO DINE

The Chandlery Restaurant SCOTTISH/SEAFOOD This restaurant attracts visitors and locals alike. The highly skilled chef creates delicious, innovative dishes such as king scallops with green garlic butter and crispy bacon, rosemary roast loin of venison with fondant potatoes, puy lentils and beans with light port sauce, and a dessert of ripe pear poached in port and flavored with cinnamon, served with a tartlet of whisky, honey, and oatmeal ice cream.

In the Bosville Hotel, Bosville Terrace. ℂ **01478/612-846.** Reservations recommended. Main courses £14.95–£16.90 ($24–$27). AE, MC, V. Daily 6–10pm.

UIG 🏕

The village of Uig is on Trotternish, the largest Skye peninsula. The ferry port for Harris and Uist in the Outer Hebrides, it's 24km (15 miles) north of Portree and 79km (49 miles) from the Kyle of Lochalsh. Many people like to anchor here because it's convenient for early departures. Uig is also one of the most beautiful places in Skye to spend the night, as it opens onto Uig Bay and is known for its **sunrises and sunsets.**

Now a virtual ruin and only of passing interest, **Monkstadt House,** 2.5km (1½ miles) north, is where Flora MacDonald brought Bonnie Prince Charlie after their escape from Benbecula. This famous Scottish heroine was buried in **Kilmuir churchyard,** 8km (5 miles) north.

While on the Trotternish peninsula, you can also visit the **Skye Museum of Island Life** (ℂ **01470/552-206**), at Kilmuir. The old way of island life is preserved here, along with artifacts based on farming on the crofts. Some interiors from the 18th and 19th centuries have been reconstructed. Admission is £2 ($3.20) for adults, £1.50 ($2.40) for seniors and students, and 75p ($1.20) for children. From Easter to October, the museum is open Monday through Saturday from 9:30am to 5pm.

WHERE TO STAY & DINE

Ferry Inn This building was first a bank and later a post office, but today this hotel's main focus is its popular pub, serving affordable meals. There are a handful of cozy guest rooms upstairs, each comfortably furnished. You'll recognize this place in the town center by its roadside design of late-Victorian gables.

The Young Pretender

He was called **Bonnie Prince Charlie,** and he blazed across the pages of British history in his gallant but ill-fated attempt to regain the British crown for the Catholic Jacobite dynasty. Born in 1720 in exile in Rome, Charles Edward Stuart had a direct claim to the throne of Britain but had lost the succession to the German Protestant House of Hanover.

On July 23, 1745, when the prince landed on the Isle of Eriskay from France, islanders advised the 25-year-old pretender to return home. Within 2 days, he crossed to the mainland at Loch nan Uamh in Arisaig to rally support, and on August 19, raised his royal standard at Glenfinnan. Many clans rallied to his call, and backed by 1,200 troops, he marched south, gathering an ever larger army as he went.

Amazingly, he took Edinburgh by stealth on September 17. And on September 21, the prince's army crushingly defeated the English at the Battle of Prestonpans. The prince proclaimed his father as James VIII, king of Scotland, with himself as regent. For a few weeks, he held court at the Palace of Holyroodhouse in Edinburgh.

On November 8, he directed his army south, crossing into England and capturing the town of Carlisle. His invading armies took Kendal, Penrith, Lancaster, and Preston. Even Manchester fell, as the Scots were joined by English Jacobites. By December, they were only 193km (120 miles) from London. There was panic in the streets of the English capital, and King George planned an escape to Hanover.

Charles wanted to press forward, but his military advisers warned him to turn back. Slowly they retreated to Scotland and settled down for the winter in Inverness. In the meantime, the duke of Cumberland's army was moving up to challenge the prince's forces. Charles decided to confront them on the desolate Moor of Culloden, an ill-fated choice. On the morning of April 16, 1746, backed by anti-Jacobite Scots, the English army crushed the Scottish forces and earned for its general the name of "Butcher Cumberland." The Battle of Culloden ended in notorious atrocities, including the burning alive of injured prisoners and the killing of women and children.

The prince began 5 long months of wandering across the Highlands and islands. He had a £30,000 ($51,000) price tag on his head— unbelievable wealth in those days—but no one turned him in. Finally, in the words of the song, he went "over the sea to Skye" disguised as the servant girl of Flora MacDonald, the Highland heroine. On September 20, Bonnie Prince Charlie returned to France secretly on the vessel *L'Heureux.* There he drifted and drank, eventually ending in Rome, where he died, all but forgotten by the world. A piper played "Lochaber No More" outside the window of his death chamber.

His brother assumed the Jacobite mantle, and—believe it or not— there's still a claimant to the throne today. His name is Prince Michael Stuart. He lives in exile in Paris but stays abreast of events in Scotland and even has plans of what he'll do "when [he's] restored to the throne, as [he] inevitably will be."

Uig, Isle of Skye IV51 9YP. ℂ **01478/542-242.** Fax 01478/542-377. 6 units. £52–£62 ($83–$99) double. Rates include Scottish breakfast. MC, V. **Amenities:** Restaurant; 2 bars. *In room:* TV, coffeemaker.

DUNVEGAN

The village of Dunvegan, northwest of Portree, grew up around Skye's principal sight: **Dunvegan Castle** ✸ (ℂ **01470/521-206**), the seat of the chiefs of Clan MacLeod, who have lived here for 800 years. Standing on a rocky promontory and said to be Britain's oldest inhabited castle, it was once accessible only by boat, but now the moat is bridged and the castle open to the public. It holds many relics, like a "fairy flag" believed to have been given to the MacLeods by woodland spirits and reputed to have brought good luck in battle. The castle is open daily: March to October from 10am to 5:30pm and November to February from 11am to 4pm. Admission to the castle and gardens is £6.50 ($10) for adults, £5.50 ($8.80) for seniors, and £3.50 ($5.60) for children. Admission to the gardens only is £4.50 ($7.20) for adults and seniors and £2.50 ($4) for children.

WHERE TO STAY

Atholl House Hotel 𝒦𝒾𝒹𝓈 Opposite the post office and near Dunvegan Castle, this hotel was once the home of a local priest, standing at the heart of the village, .6km (1 mile) from Dunvegan Castle. This well-run little hotel rents well-furnished rooms with tub or shower bathrooms (eight with shower only and one with a shower and tub combo). Two units have four-poster beds along with the best views of the mountain moorland and Loch Dunvegan. The chef prepares quality cuisine using an abundance of locally caught seafood.

Dunvegan, Isle of Skye IV55 8WA. ℂ **01470/521-219.** Fax 01470/521-481. www.athollhotel.demon.co.uk. 9 units. £70–£76 ($112–$122) double; £80–£90 ($128–$144) double with four-poster bed; from £85 ($136) per person family room. Rates include Scottish breakfast. AE, MC, V. **Amenities:** Restaurant; bar; laundry. *In room:* TV, coffeemaker, hair dryer.

WHERE TO DINE

Three Chimneys Restaurant ✸✸ SCOTTISH The Three Chimneys, in a stone crofter's house, is the winner of multiple awards. An exceptionally good starter is the wild duck pâté, with wafer-thin grilled potato scones. Specialties are fresh seafood and Highland game, with examples like roasted wild salmon with warm lime-and-peppercorn vinaigrette and a trio of Highland game (venison, wild hare, and pigeon) with a sauce of beet root and black currants. The dessert menu includes scrumptious treats like marmalade pudding and Drambuie custard. More than 100 vintages from the wine list are available to accompany your meal.

Six luxurious suites are located a few steps away from the restaurant. The House Over-By boasts a panoramic view of the sea, and each suite is fully equipped with amenities such as a TV, VCR, CD player, phone, minibar and hair dryer. The cost is £190 ($304) double; £270 ($432) family room; including breakfast. Both the restaurant and the suites have been given a five-star rating by the Scottish Tourist Board.

Hwy. B884, Colbost, Isle of Skye, IV55 8ZT. ℂ **01470/511-258.** Fax 01470/511-358. www.threechimneys. co.uk. Reservations required for dinner, recommended for lunch. Fixed-price lunch £24 ($38); fixed-price dinner £42 ($67) for 3 courses, £48 ($77) for 4 courses. AE, MC, V. Mon–Sat 12:30–2pm (last order) and daily 6:30–9:30pm (last order). Drive 6.5km (4 miles) W of Dunvegan on B884.

SKEABOST BRIDGE

Eastward from Dunvegan, Skeabost Bridge has an island cemetery of great antiquity. The graves of four Crusaders are here.

WHERE TO STAY & DINE

Skeabost Country House Hotel ⊕   This is one of the most inviting country homes on Skye. Built in 1851 as a private estate, it has been converted into
a lochside hotel boasting dormers, chimneys, tower, and gables. The Skeabost
owns 13km (8 miles) of the bank of the River Snizort, so it attracts many folks
who come to fish. In addition, guests can play the hotel's par-3 golf course. The
comfortable bedrooms come in a variety of shapes and sizes. The main dining
room offers expensive table d'hôte menus focusing on seafood.

Skeabost Bridge, Isle of Skye IV51 9NP. ⓒ **01470/532-202.** Fax 01470/532-454. www.skeabostcountry
house.com. 26 units. £85–£95 ($136–$152) double; £100–£120 ($160–$192) suite. Rates include Scottish
breakfast. MC, V. Closed Dec–Mar. **Amenities:** 2 restaurants; 2 bars; 18-hole golf course; game room; room
service (8am–10:30pm); babysitting; laundry. *In room:* TV, coffeemaker, hair dryer.

SLEAT PENINSULA

A lot of Skye can look melancholy and forlorn, especially in misty weather. For
a change of landscape head for the **Sleat Peninsula,** the southeastern section of
the island. Because of the lushness of its vegetation (the shores are washed by the
warmer waters of the Gulf Stream), it has long been known as the "Garden of
Skye." As you drive along, you'll note the intense green of the landscape and the
well-kept grounds of locals' homes.

A ruined stronghold of the MacDonalds, **Knock Castle** is off A851 some
19km (12 miles) south of Broadford. Another MacDonald stronghold, **Duns-
giath Castle** has some well-preserved ruins open to view. They're found at
Tokavaig on an unclassified road (watch for a sign) at a point 32km (20 miles)
south and southwest of Broadford. You can visit both these evocative ruins for
free, day or night. Inquire at the number given below for the Armadale Castle
Gardens & Museum of the Isle.

Armadale Castle Gardens & Museum of the Isles   You don't have to have
MacDonald as your last name to enjoy a stop at Skye's award-winning Clan
Donald Visitor Centre. From Broadford, travel along a winding seaside road to
the ruins of Armadale Castle and the rebuilt baronial stables. A multimedia
exhibit tells of the lost culture of the ancient Gaelic world under the MacDonalds as lords of the Isles. The countryside ranger service offers a full summer program of guided walks and talks to introduce you to several kilometers of trails
and the history of the Highland estate. A licensed restaurant in the stables offers
good local food, from tea to a full meal. The drive from the ferry at Kyleakin is
about 30 minutes, and the center is along A851 (follow the signs) near the
Armadale-Mallaig ferry.

Armadale. ⓒ **01471/844-305.** Admission £4.50 ($7.20) adults, £3 ($4.80) seniors and children 5–15, £14
($22) per family. Apr–Oct daily 9:30am–5:30pm (last entry at 5pm).

WHERE TO STAY & DINE

Ardvasar Hotel ⊕ *Kids*   The oldest part of this 1800s coaching inn is a stone-
trimmed pub in what was once a stable. In 1990, a major renovation added
bathrooms with tub and shower to each of the guest rooms and a cottage-cozy
decor that includes pastels and chintz. Virtually everyone in the area comes to
the restaurant for a mug of lager and a taste of the fine cuisine. Menu items
include starters like peppered mushrooms with hot brandy sauce, followed by
smoked chicken with cranberry sauce, although seafood is the specialty.

Ardvasar, Isle of Skye IV45 8RS. ⓒ **01471/844-223.** Fax 01471/844-495. www.ardvasarhotel.com. 10 units.
£85 ($136) double; from £90 ($144) family room. Rates include Scottish breakfast. MC, V. Pets accepted at staff
discretion. **Amenities:** Restaurant; 2 bars; limited room service; laundry. *In room:* TV, coffeemaker, hair dryer.

Kinloch Lodge ⭐ The white-stone walls of this manor are visible from across the scrub- and pine-covered hillsides bordering the property. Built in 1680 as a hunting lodge, it's now the elegant residence of Lord and Lady MacDonald. Portraits of the family's 18th-century forebears are a striking feature of the reception rooms, as are the open fireplaces and the scores of antiques. The guest rooms come in various shapes and sizes (some with shower only); from the windows of some, you can occasionally glimpse the sea. In 1998, a new house, also impressive architecturally, was completed 50m (164 ft.) from the main lodge, containing an additional five handsomely furnished bedrooms. Every evening, you can enjoy drinks in the drawing room before dining on one of the upscale meals for which Lady MacDonald is famous. The author of 13 cookbooks, she applies her imaginative recipes to ingredients shot, trapped, netted, or grown on Skye.

Isle of Ornsay, Sleat, Isle of Skye IV43 8QY. (C) **01471/833-333**. Fax 01471/833-277. www.kinloch-lodge. co.uk. 15 units. £170–£270 ($272–$432) double. Rates include dinner and Scottish breakfast. AE, MC, V. **Amenities:** Restaurant; bar. *In room:* TV, coffeemaker, trouser press.

ISLE ORNSAY

Adjacent to Sleat Peninsula, the Isle of Ornsay is also called Eilean Iarmain in Gaelic. Attached to the mainland, it is a lovely, remote islet in a small, rocky bay with mountains of Knmoydfart in the background. Its heyday as Skye's main fishing port is long gone. Today you'll find little whitewashed cottages around the small harbor. The island's landlord is Sir Iain Noble who also owns the hotel below.

WHERE TO STAY

Hotel Eilean Iarmain ⭐⭐ *Finds* Most often called "Isle Ornsay Hotel," this elegant harbor-side retreat is one of the most award-winning hotels in Britain. Sir Iain and Lady Noble welcome guests to their century-old hotel, where original antiques, wood paneling, and chintz fabrics create an aura of a tasteful country house. In winter, the charming atmosphere is enhanced by log fires and the performances by guest musicians. All the accommodations are individually styled, with the suites housed in a former stable block dating back to the 1870s. Of particular note is the Tower Room, with its pine-paneled walls, a great mahogany double bed, and views toward the sea. All the rooms contain tastefully-furnished bathrooms.

Isle of Ornsay, Sleat, Isle of Skye, 1V43 8QR. (C) **01471/833-332**. Fax 01471/833-275. www.eilean-iarmain. co.uk. 16 units. £120–£135 ($192–$216); £200–£220 ($320–$352) suite. Rates include breakfast. AE, V. Pets accepted by prior arrangement. **Amenities:** Restaurant; bar; room service (8am–10pm); babysitting; laundry/dry cleaning service. *In room:* TV, minibar (in suites), coffeemaker, hair dryer.

4 Rhum (Rum)

14km (9 miles) SW of the Isle of Skye

The enticingly named island of Rhum is only about 13km (8 miles) wide and 13 km long. There are those who'll tell you not to go: "If you like a barren desert where it rains all the time, you'll love Rhum," a skipper in Mallaig recently told us. It's stark, all right. And very wet. In fact, with more than 229cm (90 in.) of rainfall recorded annually, it's said to be the wettest island of the Inner Hebrides.

Since the mid-1950s, Rhum has been owned by the Edinburgh-based Nature Conservancy Council, an ecological conservation group. Attempts are being made to bring back the sea eagle, which inhabited the island in Queen Victoria's day. On this storm-tossed outpost in summer, mountain climbers meet challenging peaks and anglers come for good trout fishing. Bird-lovers seek out the Manx shearwaters that live on the island in great numbers. Red deer and ponies, along with the wildflowers of summer, add color to an otherwise bleak landscape.

ESSENTIALS

GETTING THERE   A passenger **ferry** from Mallaig, on the western coast of Scotland, leaves about four times a week. No cars are allowed on the island. For information, contact **Caledonian MacBrayne** (© **01687/462-403** in Mallaig). Sailings are from April to October only, on Monday to Wednesday at 10:30am, Friday at 12:30pm, and Saturday at 6:20am and 12:30pm. A round-trip is £10.30 ($16) for adults. **Arisaig Marine** (© **01687/450-224**) sails from Arisaig to Rhum on Tuesday, Thursday, Saturday, and Sunday at 11am. A round-trip ticket is £19.50 ($31) for adults, £8 ($13) for children 12 to 16, and £4 ($6) for those under 12. Schedules can vary, so it's best to call for confirmations. It takes about 2 hours to reach Rhum from one of these ports.

WHERE TO STAY & DINE

Kinloch Castle ★★ *Finds*   You'll be astonished that in such a forbidding place, you can come across a hotel that has been called "Britain's most intact example of an Edwardian country house." On the seafront in the center of Rhum's biggest hamlet, Kinloch, this mansion was completed in 1901 for Sir George Boullough, a wealthy Lancashire textile magnate. The castle still contains a ballroom, a massive Adam-style fireplace, and monumental paintings and stuffed animals. (This section is now part of an exhibit; to visit these areas, enter the front of the castle for a tour.) The former servants' quarters are now a simple and functional hostel, while the more elegant private rooms are furnished with four-poster beds (these share spacious bathrooms with tubs). Because guests spend their days trekking around the island, all lunches are packed picnics at £4 ($6.40) per person. The restaurant serves breakfasts and hearty dinners at reasonable prices.

> **Tips Before You Go . . .**
>
> Before traveling to Rhum, you must contact **Denise Reed,** the reserve manager at the Scottish Natural Heritage Nature Reserve, by calling © **01687/462-026.** The office will assist you in organizing accommodations on the island.

Kinloch, Isle of Rhum PH43 4RR. © and fax **01687/462-037.** kinloch@highland-hostels.co.uk. 27 units, none with private bathroom; 52 hostel beds. Rooms £60 ($96) double; hostel £12 ($19) per person in rooms with 2–5 beds. No credit cards. **Amenities:** Restaurant. *In room:* No phone.

5 Eigg & Muck

Eigg: 6.5km (4 miles) SE of Rhum; Muck: 11km (7 miles) SW of Eigg

The tiny islands of Eigg and Muck lie in the Sea of the Hebrides, which separates the Inner from the Outer Hebrides. If you're doing the whirlwind tour of Europe, Eigg and Muck will hardly top your agenda. They appeal only to nature lovers seeking a variety of Hebridean scenery and a chance to look at life of long ago. If your time is limited and you can visit only one isle, make it Eigg, which has the most dramatic scenery.

ESSENTIALS

GETTING THERE   Before venturing to either Eigg or Muck, confirm the schedule of the ferry's return. Because service isn't every day, you may find yourself staying at least 2 nights on either island. **Caledonian MacBrayne**

(✆ **01687/462-403** in Mallaig) sails from Mallaig to Eigg on Monday and Thursday at 10:30am and Saturday at 1:40pm. The round-trip ticket is £8.80 ($14) for adults and £4.40 ($7.05) for children. From Arisaig, **Arisaig Marine** (✆ **01687/450-224**) sails to Muck on Monday, Wednesday, and Friday (but departure days and times can vary). Sailings to Eigg are Friday through Wednesday. Most departures are at either 11 or 11:30am (subject to change, based on weather conditions). The round-trip fare for either is £16 ($26).

VISITOR INFORMATION   For assistance in finding accommodations on Eigg or for general information, contact **Mrs. Mairi Kirk,** 7 Cleadane, Isle of Eigg (✆ **01687/482-416**).

EIGG

Eigg, about 7km by 5km (4½ by 3 miles), is some 19km (12 miles) out in the Atlantic. The island is owned by the Isle of Eigg Heritage Trust, which consists of about 70 island residents and the Highland Council and Scottish Wildlife Trust. The farmers, shepherds, fishermen, and innkeepers who live here raised the $2.4 million to buy their island through a worldwide public appeal over the Internet.

The **Sgurr of Eigg,** a tall column of lava, is thought to be the biggest such pitchstone (volcanic rock) mass in the United Kingdom. Climbers on its north side try to attain its impressive height of 394m (1,300 ft.). It's said that the last of the pterodactyls roosted here.

After your arrival at **Galmisdale,** the principal hamlet and pier, you can take an antique bus to Cleadale. Once there, walk across moors to **Camas Sgiotaig,** with its well-known **beach of the Singing Sands.** Since the island is crisscrossed with paths and tracks, and access isn't restricted, you can walk in any direction that captures your fancy.

Visitors come to Eigg for the remoteness and the sense of living in the 19th century. The island is known for its plant, animal, and bird life, including golden eagles and seals. In summer, you can sometimes see minke whales and porpoises in the offshore waters. The island's resident warden leads guided walks of Eigg once a week in summer; call ✆ **01687/482-477** for details.

MUCK

Lying 11km (7 miles) southwest of Eigg, Muck has such an unappetizing name that visitors may turn away. However, the name of this 6.5 sq. km (2½ sq. miles) island was originally a Gaelic word, *muic,* meaning "island of the sow." Naturalists come here to see everything from rare butterflies to otters. Large colonies of nesting seabirds can be viewed in May and June.

Muck is actually a farm, and the entire island is owned by two brothers: the Laird of Muck, Lawrence MacEwan, and his younger brother, Ewen MacEwan. There are hardly more than 30 residents, and all are concerned with the running of the farm. There are no vehicles on the island except for bicycles and tractors.

What's the real reason to come? To see and explore a tiny, fragile Hebridean community that has survived, sometimes at great odds. That it carries on, and that its locals still eke out a living from farmland and sea, is reason enough. The scenery and the solitude are wonderful, as are the cattle, sheep, hens, house cats, and ducks roaming with relative freedom. If you walk to the top of the highest hill, **Ben Airean,** at 137m (451 ft.), you'll have a panoramic view of Muck and its neighbor islands of Rhum and Eigg.

WHERE TO STAY & DINE

Port Mhor House   This solidly weatherproof hotel was built by Ewen Mac-Ewan from 1975 to 1980; most of its building materials were barged in from the mainland. The small guest rooms are functional and well maintained, as are the shared bathrooms. Guests can get a drink in the sitting room, where a log fire blazes during cold weather. The kitchen uses produce from the island's farm for plain and wholesome fare well suited to the brisk climate. Vegetarian dishes are available on request.

Port Mhor (a few steps from the ferry landing), Isle of Muck PH42 4RP. ℂ and fax **01687/462-365.** 8 units, none with private bathroom. £72 ($115) double. Rates include half-board. No credit cards. Closed Sept 15–May 15. **Amenities:** Restaurant; lounge; babysitting; laundry. *In room:* No phone.

6 Coll & Tyree

145km (90 miles) NW of Glasgow, 77km (48 miles) W of Fort William.

If you like your scenery stark and tranquil, try tiny Coll and Tyree. The outer-most of the Inner Hebrides, they're exposed to the open Atlantic and said to have the highest sunshine records in Britain. On Tyree (also spelled Tiree), the shell-sand *machair* (sand dunes) increase the arable area, differentiating it from the other inner isles.

Trees are rare on either island, but that doesn't mean they're bleak. Both are rich in flora, with some 500 species. The islands' roughly 150 bird species, including Arctic skuas and razorbills, make them a bird lover's paradise. Both common and gray seals have breeding colonies on the islands. There are few cars for rent here, but visitors don't seem to mind biking around the islands or catching a ride on Tyree's least expensive method of transport: A mail bus serves most of the island. Boat rentals and sea angling can also be arranged.

GETTING TO THE ISLANDS

British Airways (ℂ **0845/733-3377** in Glasgow) flies directly to Tyree from Glasgow, with about six 90-minute flights per week (none on Sun). A **car ferry** sails from Oban to Coll (a 3-hr. trip, costing £17 ($27) round-trip) and Tyree (an extra 45 min.), but in very rare instances gales may force cancellation of the trip. If the gale is very strong, you might be stranded on an island for a while, waiting for the next departure. Details and bookings, essential for cars, are available from **Caledonian MacBrayne** (ℂ **08705/650-000**).

COLL

Lying in the seemingly timeless world of the Celtic west, the island of Coll, with a population of some 130 hearty souls, is rich in history. Distances from one place to another are small, since the island averages about 5km (3 miles) in breadth; at its longest point, it stretches for some 21km (13 miles).

Coll has a partially restored castle, **Breacachadh,** rising majestically from its southeastern side. A stronghold of the Macleans in the 15th century, it is now a private residence, although on some occasions it's open to the public. Immediately adjacent is the so-called **New Castle,** built for Hector Maclean in 1750. It provided shelter for Samuel Johnson and James Boswell when they were stranded on the island for 10 days because of storms at sea. The castle, still a private home, was altered considerably in the 19th century and embellished with pepper-pot turrets and parapets.

In the western part of the island at Totronald are two standing stones called **Na Sgeulachan** ("Teller of Tales"). The stones pre-date the Druids and are thought to have been the site of a temple. The highest point on Coll is **Ben Hogh** (103m/340 ft.), which you can climb for a panoramic view.

On the road to Sorisdale, at **Killunaig,** stand the ruins of a church from the late Middle Ages and a burial ground. Going on to **Sorisdale,** you'll see the ruins of houses occupied by crofters earlier in this century. Hundreds of families once lived here. Some were chased away in the wake of the potato famine, and many were forced out in Land Clearance programs.

WHERE TO STAY & DINE

Isle of Coll Hotel   This hotel enjoys the dubious honor of having been imme-diately rejected by Samuel Johnson and James Boswell as an inappropriate place to spend the night during their 18th-century tour of Scotland. (They eventually succeeded in securing lodgings with the laird of Coll.) Today, the small-to-midsize guest rooms are far more comfortable, with electric blankets, either shower only or combination tub and shower bathrooms, and simple but func-tional furniture. The dining room serves good but rather expensive dinners. The hotel contains the town's only pub, so you're likely to meet locals over a pint of ale and a platter of more affordable bar food. The hotel sits on a hilltop at the end of the Arinagour estuary, about a 10-minute walk north of town, beside B8071.

Arinagour, Isle of Coll PA78 6SA. ☎ **01879/230-334.** Fax 01879/230-317. 6 units. £60–£80 ($96–$128) double. Rates include Scottish breakfast. MC, V. **Amenities:** Restaurant; bar; children's play area. *In room:* TV coffeemaker, hair dryer, no phone.

TYREE (TIREE)

A fertile island, one of the richest in the Hebrides, flat Tyree has a population of some 800 residents, mostly in farming communities, who enjoy its gentle land-scape, **sandy beaches,** and rolling hills. As you travel about the island, you'll see many 1800s crofter's houses with thatched roofs. In 1886, the duke of Argyll caused a scandal when he sent in marines and police to clear the crofters off the land. Many were sent destitute to Canada.

Most of the population is centered around **Scarinish,** with its little stone har-bor where lobster boats put in. Fishing isn't what it used to be; the appearance of fast and dangerous squalls and storms are said to scatter the fleet as far as the shores of North America.

Bird-watchers are drawn to the shores of **Loch Bhasapoll,** a favorite gather-ing place of wild geese and ducks, and to a cave on the coast at **Kenavara,** where many seabirds can be observed.

Ancient duns and forts are scattered around Tyree. The best of these is a broch at **Vaul Bay,** with walls more than 3.5m (12 ft.) thick. At **Balephetrish,** on the northern rim of the island, stands a huge granite boulder. Locals call it the Ring-ing Stone, because when struck it gives off a metallic sound. In the western part of the island, at Kilkenneth, are the ruins of the **Chapel of St. Kenneth,** dedi-cated to a comrade of St. Columba.

WHERE TO STAY & DINE

Tiree Lodge Hotel   This is the nerve center of the island. Built as a simple hunting lodge around 1790, it was greatly enlarged in the 1970s with a modern addition. About 1.6km (1 mile) east of the island's only ferry landing, the hotel contains one of Tyree's two pubs and attracts a crowd of locals and visitors. The small guest rooms are well maintained and comfortable; most units contain a small, shower-only bathroom (some have shower and tub combinations).

Kirkatol, Isle of Tyree PA77 6TW. © **01879/220-368.** Fax 01879/220-884. 12 units, 9 with private bathroom. £49 ($78) double without bathroom; £54 ($86) double with bathroom. Rates include Scottish breakfast. MC, V. **Amenities:** Restaurant; bar. *In room:* TV, coffeemaker, hair dryer (on request), no phone.

7 Mull ★

195km (121 miles) NW of Edinburgh, 145km (90 miles) NW of Glasgow

The third-largest island in the Hebrides, Mull is rich in legend and folklore, a land of ghosts, monsters, and the wee folk. The island is wild and mountainous, characterized by sea lochs and sandy bars. Mull was known to the classical Greeks, and its prehistoric past is recalled in forts, duns, and stone circles. Be sure to bring a raincoat: Mull is known as one of the wettest islands in the Hebrides, a fact that upset Dr. Johnson, who visited in 1773.

Many visitors consider Mull more beautiful than Skye, a controversy we stay out of because we love them both. Mull has varied scenery with many waterfalls, and the wild countryside was the scene of many of David Balfour's adventures in *Kidnapped,* by Robert Louis Stevenson. Its highest peak is **Ben More,** at 961m (3,169 ft.), but it also has many flat areas. The island's wildlife includes roe deer, golden eagles, polecats, seabirds, and feral goats. Mull is also a jumping-off point to visit Iona and Staffa (see "Iona & Staffa: An Abbey & a Musical Cave," later in this chapter).

> **⌐Tips A Word on Driving**
>
> If you're driving along any of Mull's single-track roads, remember to take your time and let the sheep and cattle have the right of way. Also, a car coming downhill toward you has the right of way, so look for a spot to pull off.

Guarding the bay (you'll see it as you cross on the ferry) is **Duart Castle,** restored just before World War I. In the bay—somewhere—lies the *Florencia,* a Spanish galleon that went down laden with treasure. Many attempts have been made to find it and bring it up, but so far all have failed. To the southeast, near Salen, are the 14th-century ruins of **Aros Castle,** once a stronghold of the Mac-Donalds, lords of the Isles. On the far south coast at Lochbuie, **Moy Castle** has a water-filled dungeon.

At the end of the day, you might enjoy a dram from the **Tobermory Malt Whisky Distillery,** in Tobermory (© **01688/302-647**), which opened in 1823. Tours are given Monday through Friday from 11am to 4pm; the cost is £2.50 ($4) for adults, £1 ($1.60) for seniors, and free for children. Be sure to call in advance, as the distillery seems to shut down from time to time.

ESSENTIALS

GETTING THERE It's a 45-minute trip by **car ferry** from Oban to Craignure, on Mull. For departure times, contact **Caledonian MacBrayne** (© **08705/650-000**). From Oban, there are about five or six sailings per day at a round-trip cost of £6.45 ($10) for adults and £3.23 ($5.15) for children. The cost for a car is £45 ($72) for a 5-day return ticket.

GETTING AROUND Use **Bowmans Coaches Mull** (© **01680/812-313**) to go around the island. Coaches connect with the ferry at least three times per day and will take you to Fionnphort or Tobermory for £9 ($14) or £6 ($9.60) round-trip. Another option is to buy a ticket combining the cost of the ferry with a guided bus tour to Fionnphort and Iona. The tour begins when you board the 10am ferry and ends at about 5:40pm, back at Oban. The cost is £27 ($43) for adults and £14 ($22) for children.

VISITOR INFORMATION   The **tourist office** is on Main Street in Tobermory (© **01688/302-182**). From Easter to October, it's open daily through Friday from 9am to 5pm (to 6pm in July and Aug).

SPECIAL EVENTS   In July, the **Mull Highland Games** feature traditional events such as bagpipes, caber tossing, and dancing. The **Tour of Mull Rally** is held in early October. Ask at the tourist office for exact dates.

OUTDOOR PURSUITS AROUND THE ISLAND

BIKING   Its combinations of heather-clad, rock-strewn moors and sylvan forests make Mull especially appropriate for cycling. To rent a bike, try **On Yer Bike,** The Pierhead, in Craignure (© **01680/300-501**), 35km (22 miles) from Tobermory. In Tobermory itself, consider **Brown's,** High Street (© **01688/302-020**). Both charge £13 to £15 ($21–$24) per day and are open daily from 8:45am to around 5:30pm.

GOLF   Golf isn't exactly as grand out here as on the fabled courses elsewhere in Scotland. The best of the lot is the nine-hole **Western Isles Golf Course,** about .5km (¼ mile) north of Tobermory. You're not likely to even see another player or employee here most times of the year. The course's agent/administrator is **Brown's Hardware Store,** High Street, Tobermory (© **01688/302-020**), where you pay the greens fees of £15 ($24) per day and the rental fee for clubs of £5 ($8) per day. Just over 35km (22 miles) west of Tobermory is the isolated nine-hole **Craignure Golf Course,** with an honesty box into which you deposit the greens fees of £14 ($22) per day. For information about this course, contact its secretary, D. Howitt, at © **01680/300-402.**

HIKING   The island is wonderful for hiking. You'll probably drive off to a trailhead, park your car beside the road (most residents boast they haven't locked their car in decades), and then set off on foot in total isolation. The tourist office sells two books, each costing £3.95 ($6.30): *Walks in North Mull* and *Walks in South Mull.* They provide detailed options for specific routes with historic, ethnographical, scenic, or geological interest. Dress in layers, and wear something waterproof.

(*Moments*   **Close Encounters with Nature**

Several operators will take you out to see whales, dolphins, and seals. Two of the best are **Sea Life Surveys,** Beadoun, Breidwood, Tobermory (© **01688/400-223**), and a hardworking entrepreneur named **Mr. Liverty,** High Street (© **01688/302-048**), who maintains midsize boats for 6 to 12 passengers each. At each, you pay £25 ($40) adults and £20 ($32) for children 12 and under for a half-day excursion that offers sweeping views of the Mull coast and active colonies of seals and sea birds.

Visitors can also experience the wildlife-rich natural habitat with **Island Encounters** (© **01680/300-441**). Guided by a local expert, you can spend the day on a safari, exploring the most remote and scenic areas of the island in a comfortable eight-seat vehicle. The cost for the day is £27 ($43) for adults and £23 ($37) for children under 14. Binoculars and lunch are included in the price, and pick-up can be arranged at all ferry terminals on Mull.

CRAIGNURE

Even passengers who arrive with a car might want to take a 20-minute excursion on the **Mull Railway,** Old Pier Station, Craignure (© **01680/812-494**), the only passenger rail in the Hebrides. It was inaugurated in 1983, but its puffing engine and narrow-gauge tracks are thoroughly old-fashioned. The tracks begin at the Old Pier in Craignure, running 2.5km (1½ miles) to Torosay Castle and its famous gardens. The view is one of unspoiled mountains, glens, and seaside; you can sometimes see otters, eagles, and deer. The trains operate from Easter to mid-October; the most frequent service is from June to mid-September, when daily trips begin around 11am. One-way fares are £2.75 ($4.40) for adults, £1.75 ($2.80) for children, and £6.75 ($11) for families. For details, call the Mull & West Highland Railway Company at © **01680/300-389.**

A good way to see the sights of Mull is to book a ticket for "The Mull Experience," a tour offered by **Caledonian MacBrayne.** For information, call **Torosay Castle** (© **01680/812-421**). The tour begins in Oban, where you board a ferry for Craignure. Once in Craignure, you catch the train to Torosay Castle, where you'll spend a few hours exploring. The next stop is the castle of Duart. You then return to Oban by ferry. The tour is offered from May to September at a cost of £21 ($34) for adults and £11 ($18) for children.

Duart Castle ✿   You can visit both Torosay Castle (see below) and Duart Castle on the same day. Located 5km (3 miles) west of Torosay, this castle dates from the 13th century and was the home of the fiery Maclean clan. A majestic structure, it was sacked in 1791 by the dukes of Argyll in retaliation for the Macleans' support of the Stuarts in 1715 and 1745. It was allowed to fall into ruins until Sir Fitzroy Maclean, the 26th chief of the clan and grandfather of the present occupant, began a restoration in 1911 at the age of 76. It had been his ambition since he was a boy to see his ancestral home restored (he lived until he was 102).

Off A849, on the eastern point of Mull. © **01680/812-309**. Admission £3.50 ($5.60) adults, £3 ($4.80) seniors and students, £1.75 ($2.80) children 3–15, £8.75 ($14) per family. May to mid-Oct daily 10:30am–6pm.

Torosay Castle and Gardens   This is the only privately occupied castle and garden in the western Highlands open daily to the public. The Victorian mansion was built in the mid–19th century by David Bryce, a famous Scottish architect. In his early years, Winston Churchill was a frequent visitor. One writer said a visit here is like returning to the Edwardian age of leisure, and so it is. To the surprise of visitors, the armchairs are labeled PLEASE SIT DOWN instead of PLEASE KEEP OFF. The portraits are by such famous artists as Sargent. You can wander through 4.9 hectares (12 acres) of Italian-style terraced gardens, enjoying extensive views of the Appin coastline from Ben Nevis to Ben Cruachan.

2.5km (1½ miles) S of Craignure on A849. © **01680/812-421**. Admission to castle and gardens £5 ($8) adults, £4 ($6.40) seniors and students, £1.75 ($2.80) children 6–16, £12 ($19) per family. Admission to gardens and tearoom only £4 ($6.40) adults, £3 ($4.80) seniors and students, £1.75 ($2.80) children. Easter to mid-Oct daily 10:30am–5:30pm.

WHERE TO STAY & DINE

Isle of Mull Hotel   This inn stands near the ferry and the meeting point of the Sound of Mull and Loch Linnhe. From the picture windows of its public rooms, you'll have panoramic vistas of mountains and the island of Lismore. The guest rooms are small but handsomely furnished. The chef serves British and Continental food in the attractive dining room.

⎛Moments A Stunning View

Even locals sometimes drive out of their way to catch the sunset over the **Gribun Rock,** a large peninsula midway along the island's western coast, whose centerpiece is the windy uplands of Ben More. The entire stretch of single-lane highway on the western flank of Ben More is a particularly spectacular highlight. To reach it from Tobermory or Craignure, follow the signs to the hamlet of Salen, then drive west to Gribun. En route, you'll pass through the hamlets of Knock, Balnahard, and Balevuin. From dozens of points along the way, views stretch over the clifftops, encompassing the setting sun (if your timing is right) as well as the isles of Staffa, Coll, and Tyree.

Craignure, Isle of Mull PA65 6BB. ℭ **01680/812-351.** Fax 01680/812-462. www.british-trust-hotels.co.uk. 78 units. £95 ($152). Rates include Scottish breakfast. MC, V. Closed mid-Oct to mid-Mar. **Amenities:** Restaurant; bar; 24-hr. room service. *In room:* TV, coffeemaker, hair dryer.

SALEN

Near Salen are the ruins of **Aros Castle,** once a stronghold of the lords of the Isles, the MacDonalds. It dates from the 14th century and was last occupied in the 17th century. Most of the former castle has been carted off, but the site is still visible 18km (11 miles) southeast of Tobermory.

WHERE TO STAY & DINE

Glenforsa Hotel This secluded seaside hotel was built 1968 of Norwegian pine logs. Near the Sound of Mull and the River Forsa 18km (11 miles) southeast of Tobermory, visitors like to come here in late summer to fish for salmon. The guest rooms are well appointed. The bar serves an array of tempting food, with venison, trout, and salmon offered in season for guests and nonguests alike. The hotel has an adjacent grass airstrip, at which private and charter planes can land from dawn to dusk.

Salen, by Aros, Isle of Mull PA72 6JW. ℭ **01680/300-377.** Fax 01680/300-535. www.glenforsa.co.uk. 13 units, 12 with private bathroom. £63–£74 ($101–$118) double. Rates include Scottish breakfast. MC, V. **Amenities:** Restaurant; bar; limited room service. *In room:* Coffeemaker, hair dryer, no phone.

TOBERMORY

Founded as a fishing village in 1789, Tobermory is one of the most sheltered harbors in Scotland and the unofficial capital of Mull. It's a definite photo op with its little buildings in bright pastels opening onto the boat-filled harbor and set against a backdrop of wooded hills. Yachts and ferry boats to and from Kilchoan arrive here in the summer, and Tobermory is a busy little bustling village with its shops, hotels and pubs.

Mull Museum (ℭ **01688/302-208**) exhibits material relating to the island in an old bakery building on Main Street. From Easter to mid-October, it's open Monday through Friday from 10am to 4pm and Saturday from 10am to 1pm. Admission is £1 ($1.60) for adults and 20p ($.30) for children.

Isle of Mull Silver, Main Street (ℭ **01688/302-345**), stocks jewelry made by a number of Scottish designers. Among the unique items made on the premises are traditional Scottish silver *quaich* (drinking vessels) and christening spoons. **Mull Pottery,** Main Street (ℭ **01688/302-057**), features tableware, ovenware, and lamps in seashore, seagull, and turquoise patterns. **Tackle & Books,** Main

Street (© **01688/302-336**), carries fishing gear, bait, and an impressive array of reading materials—especially works by local authors and anything in print about Mull.

The **Western Isle Golf Course** dates from the 1930s and is said to have possibly the best views of any golf course in the world.

WHERE TO STAY

Tobermory Hotel   Even though it's located on the upper end of the town's main street, this hotel offers guests a sense of privacy, having been converted from a row of fisherman's cottages that stood here in the late 18th century. Most guest rooms look out onto the harbor, often dotted with fishing boats; the others have views of the tree-dotted cliff that rises abruptly behind the hotel. The bathrooms are small but neat (some with shower only). The dining room serves dinner nightly.

53 Main St., Tobermory, Isle of Mull PA75 6NT. © **01688/302-091.** Fax 01688/302-254. www.thetobermory hotel.com. 16 units. £76–£96 ($122–$154) double. Rates include Scottish breakfast. MC, V. Parking available on nearby streets. **Amenities:** Restaurant; limited room service; laundry. *In room:* TV, coffeemaker, hairdryer, no phone.

Western Isles Hotel   In a scenic location on a bluff above the harbor, the Western Isles is a large, gray-stone country inn. It was constructed by the Sandeman sherry company in 1883 as a hunting and fishing lodge for top-level staff and customers. The current owners welcome guests to homey rooms decorated in a mix of styles, with small bathrooms. The hotel has a conservatory bar as well as an upscale restaurant.

Tobermory, Isle of Mull PA75 6PR. © **01688/302-012.** Fax 01688/302-297. www.mullhotel.com. 28 units. £99–£120 ($158–$192) double; £143–£210 ($229–$336) suite. Rates include Scottish breakfast. AE, MC, V. Closed Dec 18–28. **Amenities:** Restaurant; bar; limited room service. *In room:* TV, coffeemaker, hair dryer.

WHERE TO DINE

Gannet's Restaurant SCOTTISH   This place enjoys a quayside setting in one of the stone-fronted 200-year-old buildings along Main Street. It's one of the best independent restaurants here. You get fresh seafood, much of it caught locally, along with salads, juicy steaks, and some fine vegetable dishes, finished off by creamy desserts. During the day, you might stop in for sandwiches and fresh coffee.

25 Main St. © **01688/302-203.** Main courses £6–£11 ($9.60–$18). MC, V. Easter–Oct daily 10am–9pm; Nov–Easter daily 10am–3pm.

TOBERMORY AFTER DARK

Macgochan's Pub, Ledaig (© **01688/302-350**), is an old traditional pub that has free Scottish music most nights from 9pm to 1:30am. There's also a game room with a pool table. The **Mishnish Hotel,** Main Street (© **01688/302-009**), is a faux-traditional pub featuring Scottish music nightly. In pleasant weather, you can step into the beer garden for a breath of fresh air.

DERVAIG ⚐

The loveliest village on Mull, Dervaig (Little Grove) is a 13km (8-mile) drive west from Tobermory. The **Old Byre Heritage Centre** (© **01688/400-229**) houses one of the most charming museums you could hope to find. The main exhibit features 25 scale models, painstakingly made by a local historian, showing the history of Mull from the first settlers to the Highland Clearances. A fully licensed tearoom serves light meals. Admission is £3 ($4.80) for adults, £2

($3.20) for seniors and students, and £1.50 ($2.40) for children 5 to 12. From Easter to October, it's open daily from 10:30am to 6:30pm. Take the twice-daily bus from Tobermory.

Just outside Dervaig is the **Mull Little Theater,** founded in 1966, seating 43. According to the *Guinness Book of World Records,* this makes it the smallest professional theater in Great Britain. See "Dervaig After Dark," below, for details.

From Dervaig, you can cruise to the lonely **Treshnish Isles,** a sanctuary for seabirds and seals. From April to September, a local entrepreneur operates the *Turus Mara* (© **01688/400-242**), carrying up to 60 passengers on half-day visits at £15 ($24) or full-day visits at £32.50 ($52). The boat departs from the Ulva Ferry Piers, on the west side of Mull. The Treshnish Isles are murky, muddy, and boggy, so bring dry clothes, boots, and a sense of humor.

WHERE TO STAY

Druimard Country House   In the northwest of the island, this restored Victorian country house opens to views of an idyllic glen and the River Bellart where it flows into Loch Cuin and out to sea. For old-fashioned Scottish comfort and a tranquil atmosphere, this is the place to be. The bedrooms are tastefully furnished and contain small bathrooms. Your hosts, Haydn and Wendy Hubbard, are a font of information about Mull. They'll arrange cruises to remote isles, wildlife expeditions, and even whale-watching jaunts. Even if you don't stay here, consider a visit to their winning restaurant (see below).

Dervaig, Isle of Mull PA75 6QW. © **01688/400-345.** Fax 01688/400-291. www.druimard.co.uk. 7 units. £135–£170 ($216–$272) double. Rates include breakfast and dinner. MC, V. Closed Nov–Mar. Follow signs to Mull Little Theatre. Pets accepted. **Amenities:** Restaurant; bar. *In room:* TV, coffeemaker, hair dryer.

Druimnacroish Hotel   Visitors come here to leave modern life behind. Even though the owners have recently refurbished and upgraded the place, they purposefully left TVs and phones out of the guest rooms, but they're available upon request. Families might be interested in the self-catering apartment, available for weekly stays, on the premises. In the summertime, guests can enjoy a drink and views of the glen in the comfortable conservatory. The moderately priced meals feature simple modern Scottish cuisine, taking full advantage of fresh local produce.

Dervaig, Isle of Mull PA75 6QW. © and fax **01688/400-274.** www.druimnacroish.co.uk. 6 units. £78–£84 ($125–$134) double; £225–£275 ($360–$440) self-catering apt for 1 week. Room rates include Scottish breakfast. MC, V. Closed Nov–Mar. Pets accepted with prior arrangement. **Amenities:** Restaurant; bar. *In room:* Coffeemaker, hair dryer, iron/ironing board, no phone.

WHERE TO DINE

Druimard Hotel Restaurant ∉ SCOTTISH   This acclaimed restaurant offers a varied menu based on local produce and supplies, ranging from the freshest of fish to tender Scottish beef. The cuisine is skillfully prepared, often with unusual sauces. You might begin with a real Scottish creation: creamy smoked haddock soup. The potato pancake topped with spring onion crème fraîche and a basil oil dressing will win you over. Meat-eaters dig into the filet of Aberdeen Angus topped with local oysters and parsley pesto on a bed of celeriac, wild mushrooms, and baby spinach with caramelized shallots and red-wine sauce.

In the Druimard Hotel, Dervaig. © **01688/400-345.** Reservations recommended. Fixed-price 5-course dinner £29.95 ($48). MC, V. Daily 7–8:30pm. Closed Nov–Mar.

DERVAIG AFTER DARK

Located 14km (8½) west of Tobermory, the **Mull Little Theatre,** Tobermory-Dervaig Rd. (© **01688/400-377**), is indeed quite small, with an audience capacity of 43 people for the dramas staged inside a former byre (stable). The season runs from Easter to September, with visiting companies as well as the small-but-capable Mull Theater Company filling the bill. Adult tickets run £6 to £12 ($9.60–$19); seniors; students, and children pay £4 to £9 ($6.40–$14). Tickets should be reserved in advance. There's no seat allocation, so arrive early.

FIONNPHORT

At the western tip of the Ross of Mull, Fionnphort is a tiny port that sees a lot of traffic. This is where the road ends and regular ferry passage is available across the 1.6km (1 mile) Sound of Iona to the Isle of Iona, one of the most visited attractions in Scotland. Less than 3km (2 miles) to the south is the tidal island of Erraid, where David Balfour had adventures in Stevenson's *Kidnapped.*

WHERE TO STAY

Achaban House *Kids*   Its almost indestructible walls (1m/3 ft. thick in places) were built in 1820 of pink granite for the supervisor of the local quarry. Shortly after, the building was converted into the manse (pastor's residence) for the local church. Today, it sits beside the town's only highway, a 10-minute walk east of the ferry landing. All rooms have private bathrooms (some with shower only), though some are across the hall. One family room is available. Fixed-price dinners can be prepared on request and might include excellent poached local salmon wrapped in a sheath of herbs. No smoking is permitted.

Fionnphort, Isle of Mull PA66 6BL. ✆ **01681/700-205.** Fax 01681/700-649. www.achabanhouse.co.uk. 6 units. £50 ($80) double; £65–£75 ($104–$120) family room. Rates include Scottish breakfast. MC, V. *In room:* Coffeemaker, hair dryer, no phone.

WHERE TO DINE

Keel Row SCOTTISH   The undisputed leader in providing food and drink to passengers waiting for a ferry to Iona, this friendly place is in two connected buildings near the pier. Food is served in a cedar-sided building overlooking the waterfront, while drinks are offered in a 19th-century stone cottage whose blazing fireplace adds cheer to many a gray day. Meal options include spicy fried crab with coriander, onions, tomatoes, and spices served with turmeric rice and salad, or the national dish of haggis with neeps and tatties (turnips and mashed potatoes).

At the harborfront, at the end of A849. ✆ **01681/700-458.** Main courses £7–£12 ($11–$19); sandwiches and burgers £3–£6 ($4.80–$9.60). MC, V. Restaurant summer only, daily noon–3pm and 6–9pm; snacks and drinks year-round, daily noon–11pm; meals served in the bar during winter, daily 6–8pm; drinks year-round, daily noon–11pm; meals served in the bar during winter, daily 6–8pm.

8 Iona ⭐ & Staffa ⭐: An Abbey & a Musical Cave

Iona: 20m (⅛ mile) W of Mull; Staffa: 10km (6 miles) NE of Iona

A remote, low-lying, and treeless green island with high cliffs and rolling meadows, Iona is off the southwestern coast of Mull across the Sound of Iona. It's only 1.5km by 5.5km (1 mile by 3½ miles). Staffa, with its famous **musical cave,** is a 30-hectare (75 acre) island in the Inner Hebrides, lying to the west of Mull.

IONA

Iona has been known as a place of spiritual power and pilgrimage for centuries and was the site of the first Christian settlement in Scotland, preserving the learning that was nearly lost in the Dark Ages.

Staying at Iona Abbey

Some people consider a visit to Iona the highlight of their trip to Scotland. Besides being impressed by the unusual historical and archaeological site, many gain a renewed interest in the power of religion. If that's what you're seeking, you can contact the **Iona Community** (© **01681/700-404**), an ecumenical religious group that maintains a communal lifestyle in the ancient abbey and offers full board and accommodation to visitors who want to share in the community's daily life. The only ordained members of the group are its two wardens, who are members of either the Presbyterian Church of Scotland or the Scottish Episcopal Church.

From March to October, the community leads a series of discussion seminars, each stretching from Saturday to Saturday. A recent example focused on the role of the Christian Church in the united Europe of the 21st century. The cost of a week's full board during one of these seminars is £195 ($312) per person. The abbey also opens to guests from late November to mid-December, although no seminars are offered then. The per-week price is the same as in summer. Guests are expected to contribute about 30 minutes per day to the execution of some kind of household chore. The daily schedule involves a wake-up call at 8am, communal breakfast at 8:20am, a morning religious service, and plenty of unscheduled time for conversation, study, and contemplation. Up to 44 guests can be accommodated at one time in bunk-bedded twin rooms without private bathrooms. In addition to the abbey, there's the Iona Community's center for reconciliation, the **MacLeod Centre,** built for youth, people with disabilities, and families. It accommodates up to 50 guests, during summer only. For further details, phone © **01681/700-404.**

The island was owned by the dukes of Argyll from 1695, but to pay £1 million ($1.6 million) in real-estate taxes, the 12th duke was forced to sell it to Sir Hugh Fraser, former owner of Harrods. Fraser secured Iona's future and made it possible for money raised by the National Trust for Scotland to be turned over to the trustees of the restored abbey. The only village on Iona, **Baille Mor,** sits in the most sheltered spot, allowing some trees and garden plots to be cultivated. The best way to get around Iona is to walk.

Iona is accessible only by passenger ferry from the Island of Mull. (Cars must remain on Mull.) Service is informal but fairly frequent in summer. In the off season, transport depends entirely on the weather. The round-trip fare is £4 ($6.40). Call **Caledonian MacBrayne** (© **01688/302-017** in Tobermory) for exact times.

Today, the island attracts nearly 1,000 visitors a week in high season. Most come to see the Benedictine **Iona Abbey** ⚔, part of which dates from the 13th century. People also come to visit relics of the settlement founded here by St. Columba in A.D. 563, from which Celtic Christianity spread through Scotland and beyond to Europe. The abbey has been restored by the Iona Community, which leads tours and runs a coffee shop daily from 10am to 4:30pm; a voluntary contribution of £2 ($3.20) is requested. The community also offers room and board to interested visitors, conducts workshops on Christianity, sponsors a youth camp, and each Wednesday leads a 11km (7-mile) hike to the island's holy and historic spots.

Despite the many visitors, the atmosphere on the island remains peaceful and spiritual. You can walk off among the sheep and cows that wander freely everywhere to the top of **Dun-I,** a small mountain, and contemplate the ocean and the landscape as though you were the only person on earth.

WHERE TO STAY & DINE

Most of the islanders live by crofting and fishing and supplement their income by taking in paying guests in season, usually charging very low or at least fair prices. You can, of course, check into the hotels below, but a stay in a private home may be an altogether rewarding adventure.

Argyll Hotel 🐾 *Finds*   Housed in an 1868 Victorian, this hotel stands 182m (200 yd.) from the ferry dock, overlooking the Sound of Iona and Mull. The small guest rooms are comfortably furnished. The good home cooking includes very fresh fish and baked goods; vegetarian meals are available. The hotel is licensed to serve alcohol to guests.

Isle of Iona PA76 6SJ. 📞 **01681/700-334.** Fax 01681/700-510. www.argyllhoteliona.co.uk. 15 units, 14 with private bathroom. £92–£138 ($147–$221) double with bathroom. Rates include Scottish breakfast. MC, V. Closed early Oct to Mar. Pets. **Amenities:** Restaurant. *In room:* Coffeemaker, hair dryer, no phone.

St. Columba Hotel   This hotel, built of clapboard and white stone, is just uphill from the village about .5km (¼ mile) from the jetty. Built as a manse for Presbyterian clergy in 1846, its guest rooms are rather monastic, but clean and reasonably comfortable for the price. Bathrooms are small and equipped with either a tub or a shower. Try to get a room overlooking the sea, and reserve well in advance in summer. A set dinner is served nightly at 7pm, with hearty and wholesome food. Vegetarian meals are available on request.

Isle of Iona PA76 6SL. 📞 **01681/700-304.** Fax 01681/700-688. www.stcolumba-hotel.co.uk. 18 units. £114–£142 ($182–$227) double. Rates include half-board. MC, V. Closed Oct 18 to mid-Apr. Pets. **Amenities:** Restaurant; bar. *In room:* Coffeemaker, hair dryer, no phone.

STAFFA

The attraction of the island of Staffa, 10km (6 miles) north of Iona, is **Fingal's Cave** 🐾, a lure to visitors for more than 200 years and the inspiration for music, poetry, paintings, and prose. Its Gaelic name, *An Uamh Ehinn,* means "musical cave." It's the only such formation known in the world that has basalt columns; over the centuries, the sea has carved a huge cavern in the basalt, leaving massive hexagonal columns. The sound of the crashing waves and swirling waters (the music) caused Mendelssohn to write the *Fingal's Cave Overture.* Turner painted the cave on canvas, and Keats, Wordsworth, and Tennyson all praised it in their poetry.

Staffa has been uninhabited for more than 170 years, but you can still explore the cave, which is strictly protected by the National Trust from development. Entrance is free, requiring only payment for boat passage from Mull or Iona at £14 ($22) for adults and £7 ($11) for children under 14. The boat runs twice daily from Iona and Mull between March and October. Rubber-soled shoes and warm clothing are recommended. Reservations are important; call **Mrs. Carol Kirkpatrick,** whose husband, David, operates the boat, at *Tigh-na-Traigh* (House by the Shore), Isle of Iona (📞 **01681/700-358**).

9 Colonsay

24km (15 miles) S of the Isle of Mull

The most remote of the islands of Argyll, Colonsay shares some of the same characteristics as Iona, Tyree, and Coll. To the west, it faces nothing but the open Atlantic—only a lighthouse stands between Colonsay and Canada. The island encompasses 52 sq. km (20 sq. miles). It's more tranquil than Mull and Skye because it doesn't accommodate day-trippers.

A ferry, operated by **Caledonian MacBrayne** (✆ 08705/650-000 for schedules), sails between Oban and Colonsay three times a week. The 60km (37-mile) crossing takes 2½ hours.

You can explore all parts of the island along its one-lane roads. Many visitors prefer to rent a bike rather than drive. You can also rent sailing dinghies and rowboats and sail around the island, following in the grand tradition of the Vikings. Go to the **Isle of Colonsay Hotel** (see below), whose staff can rent you a bike (£5/$8 per day or £15/$24 per week) or put you in touch with local fishermen and entrepreneurs; the boat should cost around £15 ($24) per hour.

Wildlife abounds, including golden eagles, falcons, gray seals, otters, and wild goats with elegant horns and long shaggy hair. Prehistoric forts, stone circles, and single standing stones attest to the antiquity of Colonsay, which has been occupied since the Stone Age.

It's estimated there are some 500 species of flora on the island. The gardens of the 1722 **Colonsay House** (not open to the public) are filled with rare rhododendrons, magnolias, and eucalyptus, even palm trees; from April to October, Wednesday from noon to 5pm and Friday from 2 to 5pm, you can visit the gardens for £3 ($4.80). There's also an 18-hole golf course.

The little island of **Oransay** was named for Oran, a disciple of St. Columba. It's joined at low tide by the Strand, and you can wade across the sands during a 2-hour period. The ancient monastic ruins here date from the 6th century.

WHERE TO STAY & DINE

Isle of Colonsay Hotel ⭐ *Finds* This is Great Britain's most isolated hotel and Colonsay's social center. Its 1750 gables and chimneys rise above surrounding herb and vegetable gardens. The bedrooms are small and decidedly informal, with basic but comfortable furnishings. Guests who want to get close-up views of the island's abundant flora and fauna can ask to be dropped off by courtesy car to go on rambles. A meal in the tongue-and-groove-paneled dining room is an event for locals, who appreciate the ambience of the cocktail lounge and bar. The inn serves lunch and rather expensive fixed-price dinners daily, with selections like homemade soup, fresh mussels, and vegetables from the garden.

Isle of Colonsay PA61 7YP. ✆ **01951/200-316.** Fax 01951/200-353. www.colonsay.org.uk/hotel.html. 12 units, 9 with private bathroom. £80–£130 ($128–$208) double. Rates include half-board. MC, V. **Amenities:** Restaurant; bar; scooter rental; laundry service. *In room:* TV, coffeemaker, hair dryer, iron/ironing board, no phone.

10 Lewis ⭐: Island of Heather

336km (209 miles) NW of Edinburgh, 343km (213 miles) NW of Glasgow

The most northerly of the Outer Hebrides and also the largest at 100km (60 miles) long and 29 to 45km (18–28 miles) across, Lewis is easily reached by ferry from Ullapool (see chapter 10, "Inverness & the West Highlands," for more information). The island was once known as Lews, or, more poetically, the "island of heather"—the sweetness of the lamb raised here is said to come from their heather diet. Lewis and Harris (see "Harris," below) form part of the same island, stretching for a total of 153km (95 miles). Filled with marshy peat bogs, Lewis's landscape is relatively treeless, thanks in part to Norse raider Magnus Barelegs. He and his Viking warriors burned most of the trees, leaving Lewis as bare as his shanks.

Even though the whole world has heard of Harris tweed, it might as well be called Lewis tweed, as Stornoway has taken over the industry. On the eastern side of the island and with a population of 5,000, **Stornoway** is the only real town in the Outer Hebrides; it's a landlocked harbor where you can see gray seals along with fishing boats. There are some 600 weavers on the island, and one of the attractions of this rather bleak port is visiting a mill shop or a weaver's cottage.

ESSENTIALS

GETTING THERE   An **airport,** which doubles as an RAF base, is 5.5km (3½ miles) from the center of Stornoway. Stornoway receives flights from Glasgow and Inverness Monday through Saturday, as well as frequent service from Benbecula. Phone **British Airways** (② **0845/733-3377** in Glasgow) to make reservations.

Monday through Saturday, **Caledonian MacBrayne** (② **08705/650-000** at the ferry terminal in Gourock) operates two or three ferries from Ullapool to Stornoway. One-way passage costs £13.70 ($22). Cars can be transported as well. Trip time is 3½ hours.

VISITOR INFORMATION   The **Western Isles Tourist Board,** which has information about all the Outer Hebrides, is at 26 Cromwell St., Stornoway (② **01851/703-088**). It's open April to October, Monday to Friday from 9am to 6pm and Saturday from 9am to 5pm and 8 to 9pm; and October to April, Monday through Friday from 9am to 5pm.

EXPLORING THE ISLAND

The major attraction of the island is the Neolithic temple of Callandish ★★, lying off A858 26 km (16 miles) west of Stornoway. Only Stonehenge in the West Country of Britain equals these 13 standing stones as a site of prehistoric archaeological splendor. The stones are laid out to depict a Celtic cross with a burial cairn at the center. They are approached from either north or south by a road lines with erect stone pillars. The site dates from about 1800 B.C. An old Gaelic legend claims that when the alleged giants of old, who were said to inhabit the island, refused to convert to Christianity, St. Kieran turned them to stone. You can wander among the ruins for free, day or night. The "visitor center" provides historical background and charges £1.75 ($2.80) if you want to see videos on the site. It's open Monday through Saturday from 10am to 6pm (9am–6:30pm in July and Aug). Also here are a gift shop and cafe.

Just west of the harbor at Stornoway, you can visit the grounds of 1818 **Lews Castle** (which uses the old spelling). The castle itself is closed to the public, but you can wander through the garden, which is at its flowery best in May.

At Arnol, 24km (15 miles) northwest of Stornoway off A858, is the thatched **Lewis Black House** (② **01851/710-395**), constructed without mortar and preserved to show what a typical Hebridean dwelling looked like. It's called a "black house" because it was believed the smoke from the open peat fires was good for the thatched roof—the Leodhasach (as the islanders are called) built their houses with no chimneys so the smoke could pass through the thatch. From April to September, it's open Monday through Saturday from 9:30am to 6:30pm (to 4pm Oct–Mar). Admission is £3 ($4.80) for adults, £2.30 ($3.70) for seniors, and £1 ($1.60) for children 5 to 15.

At 6m (19 ft.) tall and 2m (6 ft.) wide, the **Clach an Trushal** at Balan-thrushal, Barvas, is the largest single monolith in northern Scotland. It's sign-posted beside the main highway leading north from Stornoway. Along A858, 32km (20 miles) northwest of Stornoway, stands **Dun Carloway Broch,** a 9m (30-ft.) broch (round-sided stone tower) left over from the Iron Age. You can visit at any time for free.

At Dun Borranish, near the village of Ardroil, the famous **Lewis Chessmen** were dug up in 1831 outside Uig Sands. Made of walrus tusks and reputed to have been carved around A.D. 500, they now form an outstanding exhibit in the British Museum in London. If you're a chess player, you may want to purchase a reproduction set in Lewis.

At Ness, toward that northerly outpost, the Butt of Lewis, is **St. Moluag's Church,** a Scottish Episcopal church, which still holds occasional services. The chapel, known in Gaelic as *Teampull Mhor* ("big temple"), is from about the 12th century, founded by Olav the Black during the Norse occupation.

Borge Pottery, on A857 at Borve, 27km (17 miles) from Stornoway on the road to Ness (© **01851/850-345**), has been in business for more than 20 years, producing hand-thrown stoneware in pink, blue, red, green, black, and cream. Its name is spelled with a *g,* the Gaelic spelling of Borve.

The Isle of Lewis's contribution to the world of golf is the 18-hole **Golf Club,** Willow Glen Road, about 1.6km (1 mile) from Stornoway (© **01851/ 702-240**). It's a windswept, isolated course carved out of the moors. Greens fees are £15 ($24).

If you'd like to rent a bike, head for **Alex Dan's Cycle Centre,** 67 Kenneth St., Stornoway (© **01851/704-025**).

WHERE TO STAY

Cabarfeidh Hotel ★ (Finds) Cabarfeidh is one of the best hotels on Lewis. It stands about 1.6km (1 mile) north of Stornoway, midway between Laxdale and

Newmarket, in a 3.2-hectare (8-acre) garden. Designed as a contemporary arrangement of cubes, it was built by a Mackenzie, who named it after the battle cry of his fighting clan, "stag antlers," and the decor includes a collection of just that. The pleasant guest rooms have small, attached bathrooms. The dining room offers the best local produce, fresh fish and local beef and lamb. The convivial bar is shaped like a Viking longship.

Manor Park, Stornoway, Lewis, Outer Hebrides H51 2EU. ℂ **01851/702-604.** Fax 01851/705-572. www. calahotels.com. 46 units. £92 ($147) double. Rates include Scottish breakfast. AE, DC, MC, V. Free parking. **Amenities:** Restaurant; bar; 24-hr. room service; babysitting; laundry service. *In room:* TV, coffeemaker, hair dryer, trouser press.

Seaforth Hotel   A 5-minute walk from the town center, the Seaforth is one of the most modern hotels—also the largest—in the Outer Hebrides. The public rooms have several full-size snooker tables; there's a bar as well as a basement nightclub open Friday and Saturday. The guest rooms don't have a lot of charm but are well-equipped. The restaurant offers a reasonably priced three-course dinner menu. The fare is rather plain but hearty, a combination of Scottish and Italian dishes.

9 James St., Stornoway, Lewis, Outer Hebrides HS1 2QN. ℂ **01851/706-600.** Fax 01851/703-900. www. calahotels.com. 68 units. £85 ($136) double. Rates include Scottish breakfast. AE, MC, V. Free parking. Closed Jan. **Amenities:** Restaurant; bar; babysitting; laundry service. *In room:* TV, coffeemaker, hair dryer, trouser press.

WHERE TO DINE

Park Guest House SCOTTISH/FRENCH   In a century-old stone house about a 10-minute walk north of the ferry terminal, this is the best dining room in town, with a country-house decor and a fireplace in the style of Charles Rennie Mackintosh. Menu items feature seasonal game, such as venison in port-wine sauce, and seafood choices like oysters raw or au gratin, pan-fried scallops in lemon butter and herbs, and turbot filet grilled with herb butter. The restaurant is fully licensed and at its most elegant between 7 and 9pm.

Nine simple guest rooms go for £72 to £84 ($115–$134) double, including breakfast. Each unit comes with a TV and hair dryer.

30 James St., Stornoway, Lewis, Outer Hebrides H51 2QN. ℂ **01851/702-485.** Reservations required. Main courses £12–£20 ($19–$32); fixed-price 2-course early-bird dinner (5:30–6:45pm) £11.95 ($19). MC, V. Tues–Sat 5–8:45pm.

STORNOWAY AFTER DARK

Most of the pubs lining the waterfront have live music on weekends, usually traditional Celtic or Scottish performers. There's generally no cover. **Clachan Bar,** North Beach Street (ℂ **01851/703-653**), boasts none of the quaintness of a traditional pub, but locals and visitors alike come on Friday and Saturday for live bands downstairs or for the disco upstairs. Another updated bar with live music is **Lewis Bar,** South Beach Street (ℂ **01851/704-567**). On Saturday, the stage might hold anything from a rock band to a traditional Scottish group.

An Lanntair Gallery, Town Hall, South Beach Street (ℂ **01851/703-307**), stages musical and theatrical events with a strong emphasis on Gaelic culture. The center also has jazz, folk, and traditional music concerts, plus classic and contemporary drama, comedy, and children's shows. Tickets are £6 to £10 ($9.60–$16) for adults and £2 to £4 ($3.20–$6.40) for children under 16. Productions take place in either the gallery space, which seats 55, or the town hall, which holds 350.

11 Harris (★)

351km (218 miles) NW of Glasgow, 90km (56 miles) NW of Mallaig, 396km (246 miles) NW of Edinburgh, 55km (34 miles) S of Stornoway

Harris, south of Lewis but really part of the same island, has a different geography. North Harris is full of mountains, dominated by the **Clisham,** which at 789m (2,600 ft.) is the highest peak in the Outer Hebrides. Harris may not have as many ancient relics as Lewis, but most visitors agree that the mountains, beaches, and scenic vistas make up for it. The **beaches** in the west are good for strolling, swimming (if you're hearty), or camping; the bays in the east are ideal for fishing and sailing.

The locals, some 3,000 in all, are called Hearach, and they're different from the people of Lewis, even speaking with a different accent. If you've arrived in Lewis, you can drive to Harris, as the two areas are connected by a small single-lane road. As you go along the rugged terrain, you might meet another car. If you do, "passing places" have been provided. In any case, you should drive slowly, as sheep might suddenly scamper in front of your wheels. The distance from Stornoway, the capital of Lewis, to Tarbert, the capital of Harris, is 55km (34 miles).

Many visitors prefer to take the ferry from the little port of Uig on the Isle of Skye; it heads for Harris Monday through Saturday. Even in the busiest season, Harris isn't overrun. From Harris you can also make connections to Lochmaddy on North Uist (see "North & South Uist," below).

Harris has long been known for its hand-weaving and tweed. Although that industry has now passed to Stornoway (see "Lewis: Island of Heather," above), you can still buy Harris tweed jackets in Harris. In summer, you'll see them displayed on the walls of sheds along the road, selling for very good prices.

The island is bisected by two long sea lochs that meet at Tarbert, the single-street main village. Whatever you need in the way of supplies, you should pick up here—otherwise you'll be out of luck. If you're touring by car, also fill up with petrol (gas) here. Ask at the tourist center about the island bus tours conducted in summer. For an adventure, take the car ferry running regularly across the sound to the little fishing community of **Scalpay,** an offshore island.

ESSENTIALS

GETTING THERE You can take a **ferry** to Tarbert, capital of Harris, from Uig on the Isle of Skye, Monday through Saturday. There are one or two ferries per day; a one-way ticket for the 1¾-hour trip costs £8.95 ($14). Call **Caledonian MacBrayne** (© 08705/650-000) for schedules.

Buses run from Stornoway to Tarbert daily (a 70-min. trip). Call **Harris Coaches** (© 01859/502-441) for schedules. At least five buses per day make the run Monday through Saturday.

If you're **driving** from Stornoway on Lewis in the north, head south along A859 to reach Tarbert.

VISITOR INFORMATION A **tourist office** operates from the port at Tarbert (© 01859/502-011). April to October, it's open Monday through Saturday from 9am to 5pm; November to March, it's open Monday and Friday 11am to 1pm; Tuesday, Thursday and Saturday 11am to 2pm..

EXPLORING THE ISLAND

Because of the lack of roads, it's impossible to take a circular tour of the island. However, using Tarbert as your base, you can set out northwest along the coast of **West Loch Tarbert,** with the Forest of Harris to your north. Or you can go south from Tarbert, hugging the western coast road along the Sound of Taransay, with Rodel as your final destination.

Taking the northwesterly route first, you come to an **Old Whaling Station** at Bunavoneadar. Norwegians set up a whaling station here in the early 20th century, but because of dwindling profits it was abandoned in 1930. Continuing north along B887, you'll arrive at the **Amhuinnsuidhe Estate,** a Scottish baronial castle built in 1868. The river to the left has one of the most beautiful salmon leaps in Scotland. The road beyond the castle continues to **Hushinish Point,** where you can see the little island of Scarp, which was once inhabited.

Returning to Tarbert, you can take A859 south. Some of the South Harris coastline will remind you of Norway, with its sea lochs and fjord fingers. The main road to Rodel is mostly two lanes and well surfaced; however, if you take the east-coast road, you'll find it not only single lane but also winding. Along the way you'll pass the **Clach Mhicleoid** ("standing stone"). Locals call it MacLeod's Stone.

From here you can look out across the Sound of Taransay to the **Island of Taransay,** named after St. Tarran. It has several ancient sites, including the remains of St. Tarran's Chapel. Like Scarp, it was once populated, but now its grazing fields have been turned over to sheep. Continuing on the coastal road along the wild Atlantic—actually the Sound of Taransay—you'll see another ancient stone, the **Scarista Standing Stone.** Before reaching it, you'll pass **Borve Lodge,** the former home of Lord Leverhulme, the soap tycoon.

The road south passes the little promontory of Toe Head jutting into the Atlantic. An ancient chapel, **Rudhan Teampull,** stands about 1.2km (¾ mile) west of Northton, reached by a sand track. Many prehistoric sites were uncovered and excavated on the tiny machair-studded peninsula of Toe Head.

The next village is **Leverburgh,** named after Lord Leverhulme. He's credited with trying to bring the people of the area into the 20th century, but his efforts to rejuvenate the economy largely failed. From here you can take a small passenger ferry to North Uist and Berneray.

Finally, drive east to Rodel, where **St. Clement's Church** ✿ stands high in the village. Overlooking Loch Rodel, this church is one of the most important monuments in the Western Isles. Cruciform in plan, it has a western tower, a nave, and two cross aisles. Some of the masonry work in freestone is similar to that used at Iona Abbey. The church is believed to have been built in the late 15th century or very early 16th century.

In the Sound of Harris, separating Harris from North Uist, lie the islands of **Ensay, Killegray,** and **Pabbay.** They were once populated, but now have been turned over to grazing sheep.

The island has a 9-hole **Golf Club,** Sgarasta (✆ **01859/502-214**), an isolated, windswept course carved into the Hebridean moors. Greens fees are £14 ($22). You can rent clubs for around £7 ($11).

WHERE TO STAY & DINE

Harris Hotel ✿   This 1865 hotel, a landmark since it opened, is one of the most popular places in the Outer Hebrides. The novelist, J. M. Barrie, visited in the 1920s, where he found inspiration for his story, *Mary Rose.* His initials, which he etched, can still be seen on the dining room window. Each room has hot and cold running water and lots of old-fashioned comfort. Some family rooms are available, many overlooking the garden. The pub is the social center for locals. You can order pub grub throughout the day; a more formal restaurant offers moderately priced dinners.

Tarbert, Harris, Outer Hebrides HS3 3DL. © **01859/502-154**. Fax 01859/502-281. www.harrishotel.com. 24 units, 20 with private bathroom. £59 ($94) double without bathroom; £89 ($142) double with bathroom. Rates include Scottish breakfast. MC, V. **Amenities:** Restaurant; bar. *In room:* TV, coffeemaker, hair dryer, no phone.

Leachin House 🌟 *Finds*　On the north shore of the loch, this house was built of Berneray granite (a form of gneiss) with Victorian gingerbread trim. Its original owner was Norman McLeod, the fisherman and entrepreneur credited as the father of the Harris tweed industry. The house is now loaded with antiques and paintings. The comfortable, high-ceilinged guest rooms will make you think you're staying in a friend's home, while the rather pricey dinners have the feel of a private dinner party. The food is based on modern Scottish cuisine.

Tarbert, Isle of Harris HS3 3AH. © and fax **01859/502-157**. www.leachin-house.com. 3 units, 1 with private bathroom. £90 ($144) double with or without bathroom. Rate includes breakfast. MC, V. From Tarbert, follow A859 for 1.6km (1 mile), signposted to Stornoway. **Amenities:** Restaurant; laundry service. *In room:* TV, coffeemaker, hair dryer, no phone.

Scarista House 🌟🌟　Built long ago as a Georgian vicarage, this is now a lovely hotel with handsome guest rooms and two self-catering cottages. Some summer guests enjoy a bracing dip in the icy water of Scarista Beach, while others prefer to read in the well-stocked library. Here you get the best breakfast around: freshly squeezed orange juice, compote of fresh and dried fruits, organic oatmeal porridge with cream, Lewis kippers, Stornoway black pudding, bacon, sausage, fresh eggs, fresh herring rolled in oatmeal, and a variety of baked goods. If you plan to burn off this morning feast on a hike, a packed lunch will be provided. Most guests return for a drink by the fireplace, and then at 8pm enjoy an upscale four-course dinner featuring local shellfish and heather-fed lamb.

Scarista, Harris, Outer Hebrides HS3 3HX. © **01859/550-238**. Fax 01859/550-277. www.scaristahouse.com. 5 units. £134 ($214) double; Room rates include Scottish breakfast. £275–£550 ($440–$880) per week, cottage. MC, V. 24km (15 miles) SW of Tarbert on A859. Pets accepted by prior arrangement. **Amenities:** Restaurant; lounge; babysitting; laundry service. *In room:* Coffeemaker, hair dryer.

12 North & South Uist

145–161km (90–100 miles) NW of Glasgow

Standing stones, chambered cairns, ruins, and fortresses tell of a history-rich past on North Uist and South Uist, connected by the smaller island of Benbecula.

ESSENTIALS

GETTING THERE　British Airways flies Monday through Saturday to **Benbecula Airport** (the nearest connection for North Uist) from Glasgow, a 1-hour trip. Phone © **0141/887-1111** at the Glasgow Airport for flight information.

　Lochboisdale is the site of the ferry terminal providing a link between South Uist and the mainland at Oban, taking 5½ hours. Monday through Saturday, one ferry per day runs from Oban to Lochboisdale, costing £19.70 ($32) one-way. Some of these ferries stop at Castlebay on Barra. Other ferries run from Uig on the Isle of Skye to Lochmaddy, North Uist, once or twice daily. The most popular connection, this ferry trip takes anywhere from 2 to 4 hours and costs £8.95 ($14) one-way. For information, consult **Caledonian MacBrayne** (© **08705/650-000** in Lochmaddy).

North Uist is linked to Benbecula and South Uist by causeways and bridges, so you can **drive** to or from either of these islands along A867, which becomes A865.

VISITOR INFORMATION   Consult the **Western Isles Tourist Board** in Stornoway (see "Lewis: Island of Heather," earlier in this chapter). There's also a **tourist office** at the pier in Lochmaddy, on North Uist (© **01876/500-321**), open Monday through Friday from 9am to 5pm, Saturday from 9:30am to 1pm and 2 to 5:30pm, and Monday, Wednesday, and Friday from 7:30 to 8:30pm. The staff can arrange accommodations if you've arrived without a reservation. On South Uist, the **tourist office** at the pier at Lochboisdale (© **01878/700-286**) is open Easter to October only, Monday through Saturday from 9am to 5pm. It's also open for late ferry arrivals, usually Monday through Thursday and Saturday from 9 to 10pm and Friday from 7:30 to 8:30pm. Accommodations can be arranged through this office as well.

NORTH UIST

A real bogland where hardy crofters try to wrestle a living from a turbulent sea and disappointing ground, North Uist is one of the lesser-known islands in the Outer Hebrides, but it's beautiful nonetheless. Its antiquity is reflected in the brochs, duns, wheelhouses, and stark monoliths, all left by the island's prehistoric dwellers.

The population of North Uist is about 2,000, and the island is about 20km (12 miles) wide by 56km (35 miles) at its longest point. North Uist is served by a circular road, usually a single lane variety with passing places, and several feeder routes that branch east and west.

The main village is **Lochmaddy,** on the eastern shore. Whatever you need, you're likely to find it here (if it's available on North Uist at all), from a post office to a petrol station. Lochmaddy is also the site of a ferry terminal. In addition to the ferries from Oban and Uig, a small private ferry runs from Newton Ferry, north of Lochmaddy, to Leverburgh on Harris. This isn't a car ferry, but it does allow small motorcycles and bikes. A small vehicular ferry will take you to the island of Berneray. In keeping with the strict religious tradition of these islands, the ferry doesn't operate on Sunday—and neither, seemingly, does anything else.

EXPLORING THE ISLAND

North Uist may be small, but its scenery is extremely varied. The eastern shores possess an untamed beauty. The coastline is dotted with trout-filled lochs, and everything is set against a backdrop of rolling heather-clad hills. Nights come on fast in winter; sunsets linger in summer. The western side of North Uist is a land of rich meadows filled with wildflowers. Here you find **long white beaches,** where Atlantic rollers attract the hardier surfers.

Heading northwest from Lochmaddy for 4km (2½ miles), you come to the hamlet of **Blashaval,** where you'll find the **Three Standing Stones of the False Men.** Local tradition has it that this trio of stones, known in Gaelic as *Na Fir Bhreige,* were actual men, wife deserters from Skye turned into stone by a witch.

Continuing along the road for 6.5km (4 miles), you approach uninhabited **Dun Torcuill Island,** rising above the west side of **Loch an Duin.** Access to the island is possible on foot only during low tide; exercise caution. On the island is a ruined but still fine example of a broch (circular fortified tower) that provided defense during the Middle Ages. Most visitors prefer to admire it from across the water.

Turning north on B893, you come to **Newton Ferry.** A 15-minute crossing will take you to the little offshore island of **Berneray,** which has some ancient sites, including the mysterious-looking **Borve Standing Stone.** There's a privately run hostel here. The 140 or so people who live on the island are mainly engaged in crofting and fishing and may regard *you* as a sightseeing attraction.

After you return to Newton Ferry, head south on the same road. A left-hand fork takes you to **Trumisgarry** to see the ruins of an old chapel where an early Christian settlement was founded. **St. Columba's Well** (*Tobar Chaluim Chille* in Gaelic) is named after the saint.

Return to the main road and head west toward Sollas. On both sides of the road are cairns and standing stones, many from 2000 B.C.—some hard to reach, including those on uninhabited islands. Pass through **Hosta,** site of the Highland Games, heading for the **Balranaid Nature Reserve,** 5km (3 miles) northwest of Bayhead. At a reception cottage at **Goulat,** near Hougharty, you can learn more about the birds inhabiting the Outer Hebrides. You can walk through the reserve at any time at no charge, but guided tours (£2.50/$4) are given at 2pm Tuesday and Friday.

Back on the main road, you'll pass through **Bayhead** heading southeast. Again, the area is filled with an astonishing number of ancient monuments. At the junction, take A867 back toward Lochmaddy. You'll see a sign pointing to **Ben Langass.** On the mountain slopes is a chambered cairn thought to be at least 3,000 years old, one of the best preserved on the island. Some historians believe a warrior chieftain was buried here, but others suggest it was a communal burial ground. Bones and pottery fragments removed from excavations were sent to the National Museum in Edinburgh.

Returning to the main road again, retrace your trail and head south for Carinish, a hamlet known for the **Carinish Stone Circle** and the **Barpa Carinish,** the site of the major attraction on the island, **Trinity Temple** (*Teampull na Trionad* in Gaelic), off A865 some 13km (8 miles) southwest of Lochmaddy. Admission is free and it's open at all times. The monastery is said to have been founded in the 13th century by Beathag, the first prioress of Iona, daughter of Somerland, an Irish mercenary and the founding father of the MacDonalds.

WHERE TO STAY & DINE

Langass Lodge 🏔 *Finds* This hotel's spaciousness and comfort come as a welcome surprise after the miles of windswept, barren countryside you traverse before reaching it. The nearby sycamores are cited by the staff as among the few trees on all North Uist. Built as a hunting lodge in 1876, the hotel today attracts hunters, anglers, and nature lovers. The guest rooms were completely refurbished in 1997, with solid furnishings and pleasant decor. Each has a small, shower-only bathroom (some have tubs) and views of the nearby loch.

Locheport, North Uist, Outer Hebrides HS6 5HA. ℭ **01876/580-285.** Fax 01876/580-385. www.langass lodge.co.uk. 6 units. £80 ($128) double. Rates include Scottish breakfast. MC, V. Closed Feb. **Amenities:** Restaurant; bar; laundry. *In room:* TV, coffeemaker, hair dryer.

Lochmaddy Hotel You can't miss the peaked gables of this white-walled hotel a few steps from the ferry terminal. Those who come to fish for the area's brown trout, sea trout, and salmon often stay here. (Guests are welcome to use the hotel's scales to weight the catch of the day.) This is one of the few places on the island where you can buy fishing permits; prices are £6 to £40 ($9–$60) a day, according to what kind of fish you're seeking and the season. The guest rooms are tasteful, each with a small, shower-only bathroom. The bar offers about the best collection of single-malt whiskies in the Outer Hebrides. The dining room serves fresh local produce, lobster, king prawns, venison, and salmon.

Lochmaddy, North Uist, Outer Hebrides HS6 5AA. ℭ **01876/500-331.** Fax 01876/500-210. www. lochmaddyhotel.co.uk. 15 units. £65–£80 ($104–$128) double. Rates include Scottish breakfast. AE, MC, V. **Amenities:** 2 restaurants; 2 bars; watersports. *In room:* TV, coffeemaker, hair dryer.

SOUTH UIST

South Uist holds a rich treasure trove of antiquity. A number of ecclesiastical remains are scattered along its shores, and Clan Ranald left many ruins and fortresses known as *duns.* Ornithologists and anglers are attracted to this island. Part bogland, it's 32km (20 miles) long and 10km (6 miles) wide at its broadest. A main road, A865, bisects the island, with feeder roads branching off east and west.

EXPLORING THE ISLAND

The biggest village in South Uist is **Lochboisdale,** at the head of a deep-sea loch in the southeastern part of the island. It was settled in the 19th century by crofters who had been forced off their land in the notorious Land Clearances. The ruins of a small medieval castle can be seen at the head of the loch on the island of Calvay, one of the many places where Bonnie Prince Charlie hid out.

Leaving Lochboisdale, A865 goes west for 5km (3 miles) to Daliburgh, where you can pick up B888 south to Pollachar on the southern shore, a distance of 10km (6 miles). The village is named for the **Pollachar Standing Stone,** a jagged dolmen rising a few paces from the hamlet's center. Continue east along a minor road for 4km (2½ miles) to the Ludag jetty, where a private ferry goes to Eriskay and Barra.

The next stop is the **Klipheder Wheelhouse,** 3km (2 miles) west of A865, the meager ruins of a circular building from A.D. 200. Back on the main road again, you come to Askernish, site of a nine-hole **golf course.**

About 5km (3 miles) north from Daliburgh, at Airidh Mhuilinn, is a **Flora MacDonald memorial.** West of A865, about 182m (200 yd.) up a little farm track about 1km (½ mile) north of Milton, a cairn atop a little hill marks the spot where this woman, so revered in legend, was born in 1722. Staying on the minor roads, you'll see the dramatic machair-fringed shoreline and pass through the hamlets of Bornish, Ormiclete, and Stoneybridge. At Ormiclete are the ruins of **Ormiclete Castle,** constructed by the Clan Ranald chieftains in the early 18th century.

Rejoin the main road at Howbeg. The part of the island directly north of Howbeg is rich in archaeological remains. Ruins of several **medieval chapels** are all that's left of a major South Uist ecclesiastical center.

Farther north, A865 passes the **Loch Druidibeg National Nature Reserve,** the most significant breeding ground in the country for the native grayleg goose. Attracting the dedicated bird-watcher, it's a setting of machair and brackish lochs. At Drimsdale lie the ruins of a big dun, a fortification in a loch where the villagers retreated when under attack. It continued as a stronghold for the Clan Ranald until the early 1500s.

The road continues past the Royal Artillery Rocket Range. On the flank of Reuval Hill stands **Our Lady of the Isles,** a 9m (30-ft.) statue of the Virgin and Child. Erected in 1957, it's the largest religious statue in Britain. **Loch Bee,** inhabited by mute swans, nearly bisects the northern part of South Uist.

You'll find **Hebridean Jewelry,** Garrieganichy, Iochdar (© **01870/610-288**), signposted on the north end of the Iochdar Road. The shop produces silver and gold pendants and brooches featuring Celtic patterns. The artists here can create custom pieces on request.

If you'd like to explore the island by bike, head for **Rothan Cycles,** 9 Howmore (© **01870/620-283**).

WHERE TO STAY & DINE

Borrodale Hotel   Near the center of the island, 4km (2½ miles) west of Loch Boisdale along A865, this gabled hotel stands in a landscape of freshwater lakes, heather, and gorse. The hotel underwent extensive renovations in 1997, updating the guest rooms and common areas, which include an upscale restaurant. The owners will assist in arranging fishing and golf expeditions.

Daliburgh, South Uist, Outer Hebrides HS8 5SS. © **01878/700-444.** Fax 01878/700-446. www.uistonline. com/borrodalehotel.htm. 14 units, 12 with private bathroom. £90 ($144) double. Rates include Scottish breakfast. MC, V. **Amenities:** Restaurant; 2 bars; babysitting. *In room:* TV, coffeemaker, hair dryer, iron/ironing board.

13 Barra ⟨★⟩: Garden of the Hebrides

190km (118 miles) NW of Edinburgh, 142km (88 miles) NW of Glasgow

Barra lies at the southern end of the Outer Hebrides. Locals claim it has some 1,000 varieties of wildflowers. The island is one of the most beautiful in the Hebridean chain, with heather-clad meadows, beaches, sandy grasslands, peaks, rocky bays, and lofty headlands. Since the days of the conquering Vikings, it has been associated with the Clan MacNeil.

Most of the 200 inhabitants of Barra are centered at **Castlebay,** its capital, a 19th-century herring port and the best place to stock up on supplies. In the background of the port rises **Ben Heaval,** at 379m (1,250 ft.) the highest mountain on Barra. A circular road of 16km (10 miles) will take you around Barra, which is about 6.5 by 13km (4 by 8 miles) in size.

ESSENTIALS

GETTING THERE   At the northern end of Barra is **Cockle Strand,** the airport. A long and wide beach of white sand, it's the only runway in Britain washed twice daily by sea tides. The Scottish airline, **Loganair** (call British Airways at © **0845/777-3377** in Glasgow for flight information), flies here from Glasgow or from Benbecula on Lewis.

From the mainland at Oban, Barra can be reached by **Caledonian MacBrayne** car ferry (© **08705/650-000** for information), which docks at Castlebay. Subject to weather conditions, departures from Oban are on Monday, Wednesday, Thursday, and Saturday, with a return on Tuesday, Thursday, Friday, and Sunday. Sailing time is 5 hours, and a one-way ticket is £19.70 ($32).

VISITOR INFORMATION   The **Castlebay Tourist Information Centre** (© **01871/810-336**) is near the pier where the ferry docks. From Easter to mid-October, it's open Monday through Saturday from 9am to 5pm. The staff will help you locate a room should you arrive on Barra without a reservation.

EXPLORING THE ISLAND

The most important attraction sits on a rocky islet in the bay: **Kisimul Castle** (© **01871/810-313**) was built for strategic purposes on a small islet, the longtime stronghold of the notorious MacNeils of Barra, a clan known for piracy and lawlessness. The oldest part of the castle is an 1120 tower. In 1938, the 45th chieftain, the late Robert Lister MacNeil of Barra, began restoration work on his ancestral home. From April to October, you can visit on Monday, Wednesday, and Saturday afternoons. A boatman will take you over and back from 2 to 4 or 5pm. Entrance is £3 ($4.80) for adults and £1 ($1.60) for children, including the boat ride.

To drive around the island, head west from Castlebay until you reach Kinloch. On the left is **Loch St. Clair,** reached by a tiny track road. In the loch, on an islet, stand the ruins of St. Clair Castle, called **MacLeod's Fort.**

Continuing north to Borve, you'll see the **Borve Standing Stones** on your left. At Borve, the north fork leads to a chambered cairn and the hamlet of **Craigston,** which has a church dedicated to St. Brendan, the Irish navigator who many cite as the discoverer of America. In the area are two interesting ruins: **Dun Bharpa,** a collection of stones encircled by standing stones, and **Tigh Talamhanta,** a ruined wheelhouse.

Continue north to Allasdale. **Dun Cuier** is one of the few excavated Hebridean Iron Age forts, better preserved than most. Opposite Allasdale is **Seal Bay,** a beauty spot where the seals do as much inspection of you as you of them.

At **Northbay** at Loch an Duin, the remains of an old dun protrude from the water. Continue north to Eoligarry, site of a small ferry terminal taking passengers to Ludag on South Uist. Eoligarry's proud possession is **St. Barr's Church,** named after St. Findbarr of Cork (A.D. 550–623), who's said to have converted the islanders to Christianity after finding many of them practicing cannibalism when he arrived. The original 12th-century chapel was restored by Fr. Callum MacNeil.

For bike rentals and advice on scenic routes, head for **Barra Cycle Hire,** 29 St. Brendans Rd. (© **01871/810-284**).

WHERE TO STAY & DINE

Castlebay Hotel   Built around 1890, this gabled hotel overlooks the bay and the ferry terminal where most of the island's visitors disembark. The small guest rooms are simply but comfortably furnished, each with a neat, shower-only bathroom. Its cocktail bar has a quiet corner reserved for dining. Adjacent to the hotel and under the same management is the Castlebay Bar, the island's most popular gathering place.

Castlebay, Barra, Outer Hebrides HS9 5XD. © **01871/810-223.** Fax 01871/810-455. www.castlebay-hotel. co.uk. 14 units. £78 ($125) double. Rates include Scottish breakfast. MC, V. Closed Dec 22–Jan 5. **Amenities:** Restaurant; 2 bars. *In room:* TV, coffeemaker, hair dryer.

Isle of Barra Hotel ★ *(Finds*   This low-slung seashore hotel is architecturally striking, and for the Outer Hebrides, it's a luxury choice. Its brick walls are adorned with nautical paraphernalia, and the hotel is a favorite with the yachting crowd. It commands a view of the tranquil, less-populated western shore of the island, and its pub, the most westerly in Scotland, is widely touted as the "last dram before America." From the dining room and many of the well-furnished guest rooms (most equipped with combination tub and shower), you can see everything that's coming and going at sea. The best food on Barra is served here.

Tangusdale, Castlebay, Barra, Outer Hebrides HS9 5XW. © **01871/810-383.** Fax 01871/810-385. www. isleofbarra.com/iob.html. 30 units. £80–£92 ($128–$147) double with breakfast; £116 ($186) double with half-board. MC, V. Closed Oct 18–Mar 20. **Amenities:** Restaurant; bar. *In room:* TV, coffeemaker, no phone.

The Orkney & Shetland Islands

Northern outposts of civilization, the Orkney and Shetland archipelagos consist of around 200 islands, about 40 of which are inhabited. "Go to Shetland for scenery, Orkney for antiquities"—or so the saying goes. That doesn't mean the Orkneys don't have scenery too. They do, in abundance.

These far-flung and scattered islands are rich in a great Viking heritage. Ceded to Scotland by Norway as part of the 1472 dowry of Princess Margaret when she married James III, the islands were part of the great Norse earldoms. They were a gathering place for Norse fleets and celebrated in the Orkneyinga Saga, which detailed the exploits of the Viking warriors.

Before the Vikings, however, tribes of Stone Age people occupied both the Shetlands and the Orkneys. The Picts came later, and you can still see ruins of their round forts dotting the coastlines. The island chains aren't part of the Highlands and totally differ from both the Inner and the Outer Hebrides. Clans, Gaelic, and kilts were unfamiliar to the Orcadians and the Shetlanders—until the Scots arrived. At first these merchants and newcomer landlords were bitterly resented. Even today, the islanders are fiercely independent. They speak of themselves as Orcadians and Shetlanders rather than Scots. Not only are Orkney and Shetland different from the Highlands, they're different from each other, as you'll soon see.

Change, as was inevitable, has come to the Orkneys and Shetlands by the way of oil and modern conveniences, but tradition is still strong. It has a lot to do with climate and with ancestry.

1 The Orkney Islands: An Archaeological Garden ★★

10km (6 miles) N of John o' Groats (mainland Scotland) across Pentland Firth, 451km (280 miles) N of Edinburgh

To visit the Orkney Islands, an archipelago extending about 81km (50 miles) north and northeast, is to look at 1,000 years of history. Orkney is a virtual archaeological garden. Some 100 of the 500 known brochs—often called the "castles of the Picts"—are found here. Built by Orkney chiefs, they were fortified structures where islanders could find refuge from invaders, and wells inside provided water. The Orkneyinga Saga, written in the 9th or 10th century, is the record of the pomp and heraldry of Orkney's "golden age."

Covering a land area of 978 sq. km (376 sq. miles), the islands lie 10km (6 miles) north of the Scottish mainland. The terrain has lots of rich and fertile farmland but also dramatic scenery: Britain's highest perpendicular cliffs rise to 346m (1,140 ft.). The population of the entire chain is less than 20,000, spread sparsely across about 29 inhabited islands. The people are somewhat suspicious of strangers, and if you meet an Orcadian in a local pub, you'll have to break the ice. The climate is far milder than the location would suggest because of the warming currents of the Gulf Stream. There are few extremes in temperature. From May to July, you'll be astonished by the sunsets, with the midsummer sun

The Orkney Islands

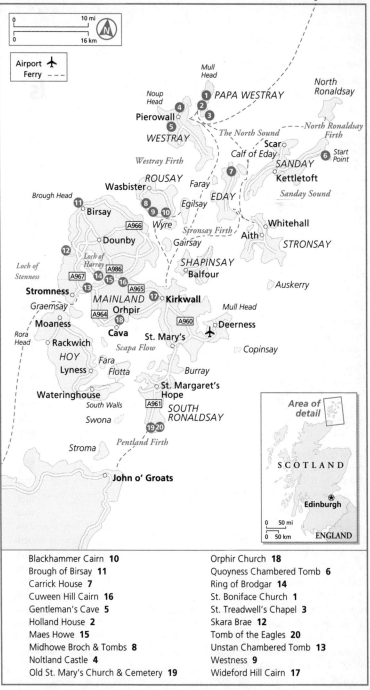

0   10 mi
0   16 km

Airport ✈
Ferry – – –

Mull Head

North Ronaldsay

Noup Head

1 PAPA WESTRAY
2
4
3
Pierowall
5

The North Sound

North Ronaldsay Firth

WESTRAY

Scar
Calf of Eday
6 Start Point

SANDAY
Kettletoft

Westray Firth

ROUSAY
Faray
7

Sanday Sound

Wasbister

EDAY

Brough Head
11
Birsay
8
9 **10**
Egilsay
Wyre

Whitehall

Aith
STRONSAY

A966

Dounby
Stronsay Firth

Gairsay

12

Loch of Harray

SHAPINSAY
Balfour

Loch of Stenness

A986
A967
14 **15** **16**
A965

Auskerry

Stromness
13
MAINLAND
17 Kirkwall

Graemsay
A964
Orphir
18

Mull Head

Moaness
Cava
St. Mary's

A960
Deerness ✈

Rora Head

Rackwich
Scapa Flow
Copinsay

HOY
Fara
Lyness
Flotta

Burray

Wateringhouse
St. Margaret's Hope

South Walls
A961
SOUTH RONALDSAY

Swona

Stroma
19 **20**

Pentland Firth

John o' Groats

Area of detail

SCOTLAND

Edinburgh

0   50 mi
0   50 km

ENGLAND

remaining over the horizon for 18¼ hours a day. The Orcadians call their mid-summer sky "Grimlins" from the Old Norse word *grimla,* which means to twinkle or glimmer. There's enough light for golfers to play at midnight.

Who comes here other than golfers? Archaeologists, artists, walkers, climbers, bird-watchers, and more. Divers are drawn by the remains of the German Imperial Navy warships scuttled here on June 21, 1919, on orders of Rear Adm. Ludwig von Reuter. Most of the vessels have been salvaged, but there are still plenty down in the deep. From mid-March to the first week in October, anglers come in droves. Unlike other parts of Scotland, fishing is free in Orkney because of Old Norse law and ancient Udal tradition. The wild brown trout is said to be the best in Britain.

A large percentage of the world's gray seal population visits the Orkneys to breed and molt. The islanders call the seal a "selkie." Migrating from Iceland and northern Europe in winter are wildfowl such as the goldeneye, the red-throated diver (known locally as the "rain goose"), and the short-eared owl ("cattieface"), as well as such breeding seabirds as kittiwakes, puffins ("tammie-honies"), and guillemots. The resident bird of prey is the hen harrier. Some 300 species have been identified on the islands.

The Orkneys are also known for their flora, including the Scottish primrose, which is no more than 2 inches (5cm) in height and is believed to have survived the Ice Age by growing in small ice-free areas. The amethyst, with a pale-yellow eye, is found only in the Orkneys and parts of northern Scotland.

ORKNEY ESSENTIALS

GETTING THERE   Monday through Saturday, **British Airways** (© 0845/722-2277; www.britishairways.com) offers service to Kirkwall Airport, on Mainland Orkney (the largest Orkney island), from Glasgow, Inverness, and Aberdeen, with connections from London and Birmingham.

Motorists can visit Orkney with their cars by booking passage on one of the **NorthLink ferries** (© 0845/600-0449). The line offers service from Scrabster (near Thurso) on Scotland's north coast to the Orkneys. It's a 2-hour trip made 2 to 3 times Monday to Saturday or twice a day on Sunday. A round-trip ticket, valid for 5 days, is £33 ($53) per person or £112 ($179) per car and driver. If you don't have to transport a car, you can take one of the **John O' Groats Ferries** (© 01955/611-353), which operates May to December only 2 to 4 times a day depending on demand (trip time: 40 min.). Round trip fares are £24 ($38) per passenger.

GETTING AROUND   Island-hopping is common in the north of Scotland. **Loganair** (call British Airways at © 0845/772-2277 for reservations) operates flights from Kirkwall Airport on Mainland to the isles of Sanday, Stronsay, Westray, Eday, North Ronaldsay, and Papa Westray.

Orkney Ferries Ltd. (© 01856/872-044 in Kirkwall; www.orkneyferries.co.uk) operates scheduled service from Kirkwall to Orkney's north and south islands: Eday, Papa Westray, Sanday, Stronsay, Westray, North Ronaldsay, and Shapinsay. From Houton, there's service to the south isles: Flotta, Hoy at Longhope and Lyness, and from Tingwall to Rousay, Egilsay, and Wyre. There's also a private ferry service to take you to Hoy, departing from Stromness. The tourist office will have details on departures.

The Churchill barriers, erected to impede enemy shipping in World War II, have been turned into a road link between the islands of Mainland and South Ronaldsay.

VISITOR INFORMATION   To find out what's going on during your visit, consult the *Orcadian,* a weekly published since 1854. There are tourist offices in Kirkwall and in Stromness (see below). You can also get information at **www. visitorkney.com**.

SPECIAL EVENTS   These sparsely populated islands generate quite a bit of cultural activity, especially in celebrating the region's music. A number of festivals draw both curious visitors and fans of Scottish and, more specifically, Orkney music. Information is available through the Kirkwall tourist office (see below), which publishes the yearly *Orkney Diary,* listing events and dates.

The season kicks off in February with the **Drama Festival,** which hosts traveling companies presenting an array of productions in venues spread across the islands. Ticket prices hover around £5 to £7 ($8–$11). Early May brings the **Country and Irish Festival,** while late May finds the **Orkney Traditional Folk Festival** in full swing. Both feature ceilidhs and concerts of traditional music; tickets to most events are £6 to £8 ($9.60–$13). June brings a change of pace in the form of the **St. Magnus Festival,** which celebrates classical music and the dramatic arts, as well as music and drama workshops. Tickets average £12 to £17 ($19–$27).

TOURS   Bus tours operate throughout the year, but with limited schedules in winter. One reliable choice is **Wildabout Tours,** 5 Clouston Corner, Stenness (© **01856/851-011**). Its full- and half-day minibus tours (of no more than 15 passengers) take in prehistoric and Neolithic monuments and local wildlife. Prices range from £17.50 to £19.50 ($28–$31). The tours are popular, particularly in summer, so it's wise to book seats in advance.

KIRKWALL

Kirkwall, established by Norse invaders on the island called Mainland, has been the capital of the Orkney Islands for at least 900 years. It used to be called Kirkjuvagr ("church bay"), after a church built around 1040 honoring the memory of King Olaf Harraldsson, later the patron saint of Norway. That church no longer stands.

The Old Norse streets of Kirkwall are very narrow, to protect the buildings from galelike winds. But don't get the idea they're pedestrian walkways: That myth is dispelled when a car comes roaring down the street.

The **tourist office** is at 6 Broad St. (© **01856/872-856;** www.visitorkney. com). It's open in April, Monday to Saturday from 9am to 5pm; May to September, daily from 8:30am to 8pm; and October to March, Monday through Saturday from 9:30am to 6pm.

SEEING THE SIGHTS

For the most scenic walk in town, providing views of Kirkwall and the North Isles, head up **Wideford Hill,** about 3km (2 miles) west of town. On the western slope of this hill, 4km (2½ miles) west of Kirkwall, is the **Wideford Hill Cairn,** a trio of concentric walls built around a passage and a megalithic chamber.

The "Pride of Orkney" is **St. Magnus Cathedral** ★★, on Broad Street (© **01856/874-894**). Jarl Rognvald, nephew of the martyred St. Magnus, the island chain's patron saint, founded the cathedral to honor him in 1137, and the remains of the saint and Rognvald were interred between the two large East Choir piers. The cathedral is a "Norman" building, constructed of gray and pinkish rose sandstone. Work went on over centuries, and additions were made in the transitional and very early Gothic styles. It's still in regular use as a church. You can visit from April to September, Monday through Saturday from 9am to 6pm and Sunday from 2 to 6pm; and October to March, Monday through Saturday from 9am to 1pm and 2 to 5pm.

Across from the cathedral are the ruins of a 12th-century **Bishop's Palace,** Broad Street (© **01856/871-918**), with a round tower from the 16th century. King Haakon came here to die in 1263, following the Battle of Largs and his attempt to invade Scotland. The palace was originally constructed for William the Old, a bishop who died in 1168. An easy scenic walk will take you to the impressive ruins of **Earl Patrick's Palace** , on Watergate (© **01856/871-918**). Built in 1607, it has been called the most mature and accomplished piece of Renaissance architecture left in Scotland. Earl Patrick Stewart was the son of the illegitimate brother of Mary Queen of Scots, and the palace figured in Sir Walter Scott's *The Pirate.* Both the Bishop's Palace and Earl Patrick's Palace are open April through September, daily from 9:30am to 6:30pm. Admission covering both palaces is £2 ($3.20) for adults, £1.50 ($2.40) for seniors and students, and 75p ($1.20) for children 5 to 16.

Nearby is the 1574 **Tankerness House** (also known as the **Orkney Museum**), on Broad Street (© **01856/873-191**), an example of a merchant laird's mansion, with crow-stepped gables, a courtyard, and gardens. The museum depicts life in the Orkneys over the past 5,000 years. Exhibits range from the bones of the earliest prehistoric inhabitants and Neolithic pottery to Pictish stone symbols and domestic utensils. It's open Monday through Saturday from 10:30am to 12:30pm and 1:30 to 5pm (10:30am–5pm May–Sept). Admission is free.

Orkney Wireless Museum, Kiln Corner, Junction Road (© **01856/871-400**), is a museum of wartime communications used at Scapa Flow, which was a major naval anchorage in both world wars. Today, this sea area, enclosed by Mainland and several other islands, has developed as a pipeline landfall and tanker terminal for North Sea oil. You can also see a large collection of early domestic radios. It's open from April to September, Monday through Saturday from 10am to 4:30pm and Sunday from 2:30 to 4:30pm. Admission is £2 ($3.20) for adults and £1 ($1.60) for children.

In the environs are the **Grain Earth Houses** at Hatson, near Kirkwall. This is an Iron Age souterrain (underground cellar), with stairs leading down to the chamber. Another Iron Age souterrain, **Rennibister Earth House,** is about 7km (4½ miles) northwest of Kirkwall. This excavation also has an underground chamber with supporting roof pillars.

SHOPPING

The **Longship,** 7–9 Broad St. (© **01856/873-251**), is the retail outlet of Ola Gorie for Orkney jewelry in Kirkwall. This family business has a wide range of high-quality pieces, including some inspired by stone carvings found at archaeological digs and others by the rich flora and fauna of the islands. A collection based on Charles Rennie Mackintosh designs has proved popular. The Longship also offers a variety of gifts, including fashion and furnishing accessories by Orkney-based Tait & Style.

Ortak Jewelry, 10 Albert St. (© **01856/873-536**), is the main shop of the famous jewelry studio that produces a wide range of silver and gold pieces featuring Celtic, traditional Orcadian, Victorian, and Art Nouveau designs. The shop also sells items like pottery, barometers, and crystal made by other local artists. The **Ortak Factory Shop,** Hatson Industrial Estate (© **01856/872-224**), is adjacent to the Ortak factory, and is the only shop that carries the complete Ortak line. A visitor center shows videos on jewelry making, and free factory tours are offered Monday through Friday in July and August. In winter, the shop and visitor center are open by appointment only.

Judith Glue, 25 Broad St. (*©* **01856/874-225**), produces hand- and machine-made knitwear for the entire family. The artisans tend to favor old-fashioned island patterns, handed down over the generations. Also available are wares of other local artists, along with an interesting selection of handmade pottery, jewelry, greeting cards, soaps, and island music.

WHERE TO STAY

You can also rent rooms at the **Foveran Hotel** (see "Where to Dine," below).

Ayre Hotel   Midway between the town's copper-spired church and the harborfront, this hotel consists of a 1792 stone core and a sprawling, uninspired 1970s addition. When it was first built, it was a social center for the town, hosting dances and bridge parties. Today, guests congregate in the popular bar. The small bedrooms are functionally modern and well appointed, each with a shower. The restaurant and bar serve moderately priced meals.

Ayre Rd., Kirkwall, Orkney KW15 1QX. *©* **01856/873-001.** Fax 01856/876-289. www.ayrehotel.co.uk. 33 units. £130–£140 ($208–$224) double. Rates include Scottish breakfast and dinner. AE, MC, V. **Amenities:** Restaurant; bar. *In room:* TV, coffeemaker, hair dryer.

Orkney Hotel   Although this hotel has been fully refurbished and the guest rooms modernized (with shower-only bathrooms), the overall style is traditional. The restaurant offers a moderately priced table d'hôte menu nightly as well as an extensive a la carte selection. There are also two well-stocked bars, both offering affordable food.

40 Victoria St., Kirkwall, Orkney KW15 1DN. *©* **01856/873-477.** Fax 01856/872-767. www.orkneyhotel. co.uk. 30 units. £99 ($158) double; £119 ($190) suite. Rates include Scottish breakfast. MC, V. **Amenities:** Restaurant; 2 bars; room service (7am–10pm); business center; nearby golf. *In room:* TV, dataport, coffeemaker, hair dryer.

West End Hotel   This hotel offers simple comforts but is still among the top three or four places to stay in town. It was built just outside of Kirkwall in 1824 by a retired sea captain and became Orkney's first hospital in 1845. Today, owners Jimmy and Isabelle Currie provide a warm welcome and comfortable guest rooms, each with shower-only bathroom. The property has been refurbished in the past few years and is now fresh and inviting. Cost-conscious meals are served in a small restaurant and bar. The hotel is fully licensed to sell alcohol, attracting both locals and visitors.

14 Main St., Kirkwall, Orkney KW15 1BU. *©* **01856/872-368.** Fax 01856/876-181. www.orkneyisles.co.uk/ westendhotel. 16 units. £59 ($94) double. Rates include Scottish breakfast. AE, DC, MC, V. Free parking. **Amenities:** Restaurant; bar. *In room:* TV, coffeemaker, hair dryer.

WHERE TO DINE

Foveran Hotel *☞* SCOTTISH   Located on 14 hectares (34 acres) overlooking the Scapa Flow, where the German Imperial Fleet was sunk in 1919, the Foveran looks like a modern hotel of Scandinavian design. Fully licensed to sell alcohol, its restaurant offers the best cuisine in the area and emphasizes "taste of Scotland" menus. The catch of the day might turn out to be lobster, grilled salmon, deep-fried squid, giant crab claws (known locally as "partan toes"), or brown trout. Vegetarian meals are also served, as well as succulent portions of Orkney Island beef, lamb, and farm-made cheeses.

The hotel rents eight pleasant guest rooms; doubles go for £75 ($120), which includes breakfast.

St. Ola (3km/2 miles west of Kirkwall), Kirkwall, Orkney KW15 1SF. © **01856/872-389.** Fax 01856/876-430. Reservations recommended. Main courses £10.50–£18 ($17–$29). MC, V. Daily 7–9pm.

EXPLORING MAINLAND FROM KIRKWALL TO STROMNESS

Heading south from Kirkwall along the southern coastal road toward Stromness, you come first to the hamlet of Orphir. **Orphir Church,** along A964, is 10km (6 miles) southwest of Kirkwall. The ruins are of the country's only circular medieval church, built in the first part of the 1100s and dedicated to St. Nicholas. At Orphir, you can see vast tracts of land set aside for bird-watching. This area is also ideal for scenic walks even if you aren't a "birdie." If you're an angler, the fishing is free on Kirbister Loch. Ferries leave the Houton Terminal for Hoy and Flotta five or six times a day.

In the area is the **Cuween Hill Cairn,** along A965, 1km (½ mile) south of Finstown and 10km (6 miles) northwest of Kirkwall. The owner of a nearby farmhouse (look for the signs) has the key that opens a door to reveal a low mound over a megalithic passage tomb, probably dating from the 3rd millennium B.C. Ancient human bones, along with those of their oxen and dogs, were excavated here.

Bypassing Stromness for the moment, you can continue on a circular tour of the island. Near Stromness, lying off A965, is **Maes Howe,** 16km (10 miles) west of Kirkwall. Dating from 2700 B.C., this is a superb achievement of prehistoric architecture, constructed from single slabs more than 5.5m (18 ft.) long and some 1.2m (4 ft.) wide. There's a passageway that the sun shines through only at the winter solstice. It also contains the world's largest collection of Viking rune inscriptions, the work of marauding Norsemen who broke into the chambered cairn in search of buried treasure.

The **Ring of Brodgar** ⊛, between Lochend Stenness and Loch of Harray, is 8km (5 miles) northwest of Stromness. Dated to 1560 B.C., a circle of some 36 stones is surrounded by a deep ditch carved out of solid bedrock. While it has been suggested it was a lunar observatory, like Stonehenge, its exact purpose remains a mystery. In the vicinity, the **Stenness Standing Stones** are a quartet of four upright stones, all that's left of a stone circle from 3000 B.C.

Unstan Chambered Tomb ⊛, 3km (2 miles) northeast of Stromness along A965, 16km (10 miles) west of Kirkwall, is a big (35m/115 ft. in diameter) burial mound dating from 2500 B.C. For its type, it's unsurpassed in western Europe. There's a chambered tomb more than 2m (6 ft.) high. It's open throughout the day, and admission is free. For information, call the **Tankerness House** (© **01856/873-191**). Unstan Ware is the name given to pottery discovered in the tomb.

Last occupied about 2500 B.C., **Skara Brae** ⊛⊛ (© **01856/841-815**), 12km (7½ miles) north of Stromness, was a collection of Neolithic village houses joined by covered passages. This colony, which was believed to have sheltered farmers and herders, remained buried in the sands for 4,500 years, until an 1850 storm revealed the ruins. You can see the remains of six houses and a workshop. The walls were made from flagstone rock and the roofs were skins laid on wooden or whalebone rafters. A fireplace was in the center; beds were placed against the side walls. The bed "linen" was bracken or heather, and the "quilts" were animal skins. This prehistoric village is the best preserved of its type in Europe. It's open from April to September, daily from 9:30am to 6:30pm; and

October to March, Monday through Saturday from 9:30am to 4:30pm and Sunday from 2 to 4:30pm. Admission is £5 ($8) for adults, £3.75 ($6) for seniors, and £1.30 ($2.10) for children.

Brough of Birsay, in Birsay at the northern end of Mainland about 18km (11 miles) north of Stromness, is the ruin of a Norse settlement and Romanesque church on an islet that you can reach only at low tide. You can see a replica of a Pictish sculptured stone. (The original was removed to a museum for safekeeping.) The site is open daily year-round; admission is free. Nearby are the ruins of the **Earls' Palace** at Birsay, a mansion constructed in the 16th century for the earls of Orkney.

Click Mill, off B9057, 3km (2 miles) northeast of Dounby, is the only still-functioning example of an old horizontal water mill on the island.

If you'd like to explore the region described above on two wheels, stop by **Bobby's Cycle Centre,** Kirkwall (✆ **01856/873-097**), with rates of £8 ($13) daily or £50 ($80) weekly. It's open Monday through Saturday from 9am to 5:30pm.

Every Wednesday night, the **Ayre Hotel,** in Kirkwall (✆ **01856/873-001**), hosts the **Accordion and Fiddle Club.** On Thursday nights in winter, locals gather at the Town Hall to enjoy the music of the **Reel and Strathspey Society.** Admission to these events is about £4 to £6 ($6.40–$9.60). Parish halls in the different communities host an erratic schedule of ceilidhs and concerts throughout the year. Check with the Kirkwall tourist office (see above) for details.

WHERE TO DINE

Scorrabrae Inn BRITISH   In an extension attached to a 19th-century grocer's shop, this simple but convenient restaurant also contains the town's only pub. The bar features whiskies distilled in the Orkneys. The menu offers a wide variety of choices, including several fish and chicken dishes, lasagna, salads, and vegetarian meals.

Orphir. ✆ **01856/811-262.** Reservations recommended. Main courses £7.90–£12 ($13–$19). No credit cards. May–Aug Mon–Thurs 6–11pm, Fri 5pm–1am, Sat noon–2pm and 5pm–1am, Sun 12:30–10pm; Sept–April Mon–Sat 6–10pm, Sat noon–2pm, Sun noon–10pm. Bar open year-round to at least 11:30pm.

STROMNESS

Set on the west coast of Mainland against a hill, Brinkie's Brae, Stromness was once known as Hamnavoe ("haven bay") in Old Norse. With its sheltered anchorage, it's the main port of Orkney, and the stone-flagged main street is said to "uncoil like a sailor's rope." Fishing boats find shelter here from storms in the North Atlantic.

With its waterfront gables, nousts (slipways), and jetties, Stromness strikes many visitors as more interesting than Kirkwall. It's an ideal place to walk about, exploring whatever captures your fancy. In the old days, you could see whaling ships in port, along with vessels belonging to the Hudson's Bay Company. Some young men of Orkney left with them to man lonely fur stations in the far outposts of Canada. For many transatlantic vessels, Stromness was the last port of call before the New World. At Login's Well, many ships were outfitted for Arctic expeditions.

Stromness has a **tourist office** in the ferry terminal building (✆ **01856/850-716**), open from April to October, Monday through Friday from 8am to 5pm, Saturday and Sunday from 10am to 3pm (also opens to greet all incoming ferries, too, as late as 9pm; July and Aug, also open Sun from 9am–4pm); and

November to March, Monday through Friday from 8am to 5pm and Saturday from 9am to 4pm.

A small but well-planned bookshop, **Stromness Books and Prints,** 1 Graham Place (② **01856/850-565**), specializes in books about Orkney and has in-stock copies of the Orkneyinga Saga. It's open Monday through Saturday from 10am to 6pm and sometimes during ferry arrival times in the evening.

The **Pier Arts Centre,** Victoria Street (② **01856/850-209**), has dazzled Orcadians with its "St. Ives school" of art, including works by Barbara Hepworth and Ben Nicholson. Admission is free; it's open Tuesday through Saturday from 10:30am to 5pm (closed 12:30–1:30pm in winter).

At the **Stromness Museum,** 52 Alfred St. (② **01856/850-025**), you can see a collection of artifacts relating to the history of the Orkneys, especially a gallery devoted to maritime subjects, such as the Hudson's Bay Company and the sinking of the German Imperial Fleet. The section on natural history has excellent collections of local birds and their eggs, fossils, shells, and butterflies. It's open from May to September, daily from 10am to 5pm; and October to April, Monday through Saturday from 11am to 3:30pm. Admission is £2.50 ($4) for adults, £2 ($3.20) for students, 50p ($.80) for children under 14, and £5 ($8) per family.

If you want to rent a bike, head for **Orkney Cycle Hire,** 52 Dundas St. (② **01856/850-255**), which charges rates of £7 to £9 ($11–$14) daily and £30 to £35 ($48–$56) weekly. Summer hours are daily from 8:30am to dusk.

WHERE TO STAY & DINE

Ferry Inn   As its name implies, this modernized hotel is near the ferry. The small guest rooms are simple and a bit utilitarian. Affordable meals are served at lunch and dinner; look for typical Scottish fare like haggis, smoked salmon, and steak pie. To finish, try a clootie dumpling with cream.

John St., Stromness, Orkney KW16 3AA. ② **01856/850-280.** Fax 01856/851-332. www.ferryinn.com. 12 units, 8 with private bathroom. £36 ($58) double without bathroom; £54 ($86) double with bathroom. V **Amenities:** Restaurant; bar. *In room:* TV, coffeemaker, hair dryer, no phone.

Mill of Eyrland ⭐ *(Finds)*   A water mill from 1861 has been successfully converted into an upmarket B&B. A stay here is like a nostalgic journey into the past, as you can hear the rippling sound of the mill stream from your open bedroom window. Island antiques abound throughout the property, which lies behind white stone walls. Lying 4.8km (3 miles) from Stromness, the property also contains some of the mill's old machinery. But it's hardly an industrial site, as beautiful and well-tended gardens surround the building. Ian and Margo Heddle took over the abandoned mill and spent 20 years restoring it and bringing it back into shape. All the bedrooms are modernized and comfortably furnished. Packed lunches are made for those setting out for a day's exploration of Orkney's archaeological attractions. Good-tasting Scottish dinners can be prepared on request.

Stenness, KW16 3HA. ② **01856/850136.** Fax 01856/851633. www.millofeyrland.com. 5 units, 2 with bathroom. £50–£80 ($80–$128) double without bathroom. £50–£100 ($80–$160) double with bathroom. Rates include breakfast. No credit cards. Free parking. **Amenities:** Laundry. *In room:* TV, coffeemaker, hair dryer, no phone.

Stromness Hotel   Behind an elaborate Victorian facade of symmetrical bay windows and beige sandstone blocks, sits the most important hotel in the Orkneys' second most important community. It was once a bit dowdy, but was extensively renovated in 1997. The small guest rooms are outfitted with old-fashioned furniture and shower-only bathrooms; many offer views of the harbor. Lunch and dinner, simple but hearty, are served in the lounge; the moderately priced restaurant focuses on seafood and steaks from Orkney.

Victoria St., Stromness, Orkney KW16 3AA. ℭ **01856/850-298**. Fax 01856/850-610. www.stromnesshotel. com. 42 units. £84 ($134) double. Rates include Scottish breakfast. MC, V. Free parking. Pets. **Amenities:** Restaurant; 2 bars; bike rental; laundry. *In room:* TV, coffeemaker.

BURRAY

Burray and South Ronaldsay (see below) are two of the most visited of the southeastern isles, lying within an easy drive of Kirkwall on Mainland. Both are connected to Mainland by the Churchill Barriers causeway linking the islands of Glims Holm, Burray, and South Ronaldsay. The Vikings called the island Borgarey ("broch island").

You come to Burray for scenic drives, coastal views, lush pastures, and rugged grandeur. A center for watersports in summer, it also boasts several sandy beaches. You can inquire locally about the possibilities, as everything is casually run. But many Scots come here for canoeing, diving, sailing, swimming, and water-skiing.

The island is an ornithologist's delight, with a **bird sanctuary** filled with a wide range of species, including grouse, lapwing, curlew, and the Arctic tern. Look also for the puffin, the cormorant, and the oystercatcher. You can see gray seals along various shorelines. Their breeding ground is Hesta Head.

Burray is one of the major dive centers of the Orkneys. **Scapa Flow** is the best dive site in the northern hemisphere, for here lay the remnants of the German High Seas fleet scuttled on June 21, 1919. Seven warships range from battleships to light cruisers. Many block ships were sunk before the building of the Churchill Barriers, which were constructed to prevent enemy ships from coming into British waters. Marine life, including some rare sponges, enhances the variety of the dives. If you'd like a diving adventure, call the **European Technical Dive Center,** Garlise, Burray (ℭ **01856/731-269**).

WHERE TO STAY & DINE

Sands Hotel Bar & Restaurant   One of the island's most prominent structures, this building was originally a fish-processing plant. The hostelry sits in the center of Burray Village, 13km (8 miles) north of the passenger ferry at Burwick, on South Ronaldsay. There are four upper-story flats, each containing three rooms and a kitchenette. These can be rented for less than a week if not fully booked (most likely in low season).

The reputable restaurant contains the island's only pub. Lunch and dinner choices may include preparations of local trout as well as other Orkney products.

Burray Village, Burray, Orkney KW17 2SS. ℭ **01856/731-298**. www.thesandshotel.co.uk. 4 units. £300 ($480) per week for 1–6 occupants. MC, V. **Amenities:** Restaurant; bar. *In room:* TV, kitchenette, fridge, coffeemaker, iron.

SOUTH RONALDSAY

Also joined by the Churchill Barriers, the island of South Ronaldsay is unspoiled fertile countryside. The hamlet St. Margaret's Hope was named after the young Norwegian princess, the "Maid of Norway," who was Edward II's child bride. Had she lived, she was slated to become queen of England, which at the time laid claim to Scotland. South Ronaldsay is the nearest Orkney island to mainland Scotland, 10km (6½ miles) north of the port of John o' Groats. It's separated from the British mainland by the waters of Pentland Firth.

The island offers some of the best **sea angling** waters in the world. Record-breaking catches, particularly in halibut and skate, have been caught, and you can hire local boats on a daily basis. There's also excellent shore fishing from local shores and rocks.

Tomb of the Eagles, south of Windwick Bay at the southern tip of the island, is a fine chambered tomb dating from 3000 B.C. Nearby is a recently excavated mound dating from 1500 B.C. Mr. R. Simison of Liddle Farm, who has excavated the area, will be happy to explain the mound and tomb. Please call at the farm before visiting the tomb and mound (© **01856/831-339**). Admission is £3.50 ($5.60) for adults, £3 ($4.80) for seniors, and £1.50 ($2.40) for children under 13. Open daily from 10am to 8pm.

In the southwest corner of the island, on the opposite side from the Tomb of Eagles, stands **Old St. Mary's Church and Cemetery.** This ancient church is stone-carved with the shape of two feet. Other stones of similar type have been found, and they're thought to be coronation stones for tribal chiefs or petty kings.

The Workshop, Front Road (© **01856/831-587**), is a craft producers' cooperative in the center of the village of St. Margaret's Hope. It sells a wide range of locally produced crafts, including pottery, jewelry, baskets, rugs, and fine-quality handknits.

WHERE TO DINE

Creel Restaurant ✿ SCOTTISH   This cozy restaurant overlooking the bay has won the "Taste of Scotland" award. The kitchen uses a large variety of local products. Specialties include Orkney crab soup and roasted monkfish tails with sweet-pepper dressing. The clootie dumpling parfait is a lighter version of the traditional clootie dumpling that you may have sampled elsewhere. The strawberry shortcake, made with homemade shortbread, cream, and fresh Orkney strawberries in season, is also a treat.

The restaurant rents three guest rooms costing £70 ($112) double, which includes a Scottish breakfast.

Front Rd., St. Margaret's Hope, Orkney KW17 2SL. © 01856/831-311. Reservations recommended. All main dishes £16.80 ($27). MC, V. April–Oct daily 7–9pm; open some weekends in winter (call first).

SHAPINSAY

Visitors come here mainly for the **secluded beaches,** the many walking trails, and the wildlife, including seals. Getting here is fairly easy if you're based on Kirkwall, for the **Orkney Ferries Ltd.,** Shore Street (© **01856/872-044;** www. orkneyferries.co.uk), comes here six times a day. The round-trip passage is £17 ($27) for vehicles, £5.70 ($9.10) for adults, and £2.80 ($4.50) for children.

The island was the seat of the Balfours of Trenabie. John Balfour was a nabob, making his fortune in India before becoming the member of Parliament for Orkney and Shetland in 1790. He launched the Scottish baronial castle Balfour. Several Neolithic sites—most unexcavated—are on the island.

WHERE TO STAY & DINE

Balfour Castle ✿✿ *Finds*   There is no more unusual accommodation in all the Orkney Islands, an unexpected discovery billed as "the most northerly castle hotel in the world." The region's most important benefactors were the Balfour family, worldwide shipping magnates. John Balfour began work on this castle in the southwest corner of Shapinsay, but it was completed by his heir in 1847. In the 1950s, when the last Balfour died without an heir, the castle and estate were bought by a former Polish officer, Tadeusz Zawadski, and his Scottish wife, Catherine. Today, the place is run by the widow Catherine and her family. It accepts no more than 12 guests at a time, and the family treats them to conversation and entertainment. The guest rooms boast antique or semi-antique furniture and lots of character.

The estate shelters the only forest in the Orkney Islands, planted in the 19th century by the Balfours and composed chiefly of sycamores. In its center, a 3.5m (12 ft.) stone wall surrounds the kitchen gardens, where greenhouses produce peaches, figs, and grapes; and strawberries, cabbages, and salad greens grow well within the shelter of the wall. The estate is still a working farm, involved with beef cattle, sheep, and grain production. The hosts will take the time to tour the property with guests and also arrange fishing trips or bird-watching tours, as well as photographic and ornithological trips with guide and boat. Between May and July, the bird life is unbelievably profuse. Guests may also be taken to the family's 40 hectare (100-acre) uninhabited island, where colonies of gray seals and puffins like to say hello.

The kitchen relies on such tempting ingredients as local wild duck and fresh scallops, crabmeat, and lobster. Guests who catch their own dinner will have it cheerfully prepared for them.

Balfour Village, Shapinsay, Orkney KW17 2DY. ℂ 01856/711-282. Fax 01856/711-283. www.balfourcastle. com. 6 units. £100 ($160) per person. Rates include 2 meals. Discount of 30% for children under 12. There is a discount of 10% for a 3 or more day stay. MC, V. **Amenities:** Restaurant; bar. *In room:* Coffeemaker, hair dryer, iron, no phone.

ROUSAY

Called the "Egypt of the North," the island of Rousay lies off the northwest coast of Mainland. Almost moon-shaped and measuring about 10km (6 miles) across, the island is known for its trout lochs, which draw anglers from all over Europe. Much of the land is heather-covered moors. Part of the island has hills, including **Ward Hill,** which many people walk up for a panoramic sweep of Orcadian seascape. In the northwestern part of the island is **Hellia Spur,** one of Europe's most important seabird colonies. As you walk about, you can see the much-photographed puffin.

But where does the bit about Egypt come in? Rousay boasts nearly 200 prehistoric monuments. The most significant site, the Iron Age **Midhowe Broch and Tombs** ⭐, is located in the west of the island and was excavated in the 1930s. The walled enclosure on a promontory is cut off by a deep rock-cut ditch. The cairn is more than 23m (75 ft.) long and was split among a dozen stalls or compartments. The graves of some two dozen settlers, along with their cattle, were found inside. One writer called the cairn the "great ship of death." The other major sight, the **Blackhammer Cairn,** lies north of B9064 on the southern coast. This megalithic burial chamber is believed to date from the 3rd millennium B.C. It was separated into about half a dozen compartments for the dead.

Excavation began in 1978 on a Viking site at **Westness,** which figured in the Orkneyinga Saga. A farmer digging a hole to bury a dead cow came across an Old Norse grave site. Three silver brooches, shipped to the National Museum of Scotland at Edinburgh, were discovered among the ruins; the earliest one dated from the 9th century. Die-hard archaeology buffs might like to know that a 1.6km (1 mile) archaeological trail begins here; a mimeographed map (not very precise) is sometimes available from the tourist office. The trail is clearly marked with placards and signs describing the dusty-looking excavations that crop up on either side.

To reach Rousay, you can rely on the service provided by the **Orkney Ferries Ltd.,** in Kirkwall (ℂ **01856/872-044;** www.orkneyferries.co.uk). The trip is made six times daily; round-trip passage is £17 ($27) for vehicles, £5.70 ($9.10) for adults, and £2.80 ($4.50) for children.

EDAY

Called the "Isthmus Isle of the Norsemen," Eday is the center of a hardworking and traditional crofting community that ekes out a living among the heather and peat bogs of this isolated island.

Life isn't easy here, for most of this north isle is barren, with heather-clad and hilly moorlands that often lead to sheer cliffs or give way to sand dunes with long sweeping beaches. Chambered cairns and standing stones speak of ancient settlements. In the 18th and 19th centuries, the island was a major supplier of peat.

Today, most of the population derives its income from cattle and dairy farming, although other products include hand-knit sweaters, cheese, and a highly rated beer brewed in individual crofts by local farmers and their families.

People come to this almost-forgotten oasis today for bird-watching, beachcombing, and sea angling. Others prefer the peaceful scenic walks to the **Red Head cliffs,** likely to be filled with guillemots and kittiwakes. The cliffs rise to a height of 61m (200 ft.), and on a clear day you can see Fair Isle.

On its eastern coastline, Eday opens onto Eday Sound, where pirate John Gow was captured. After a trial in London, he was hanged in 1725; his exploits are detailed in Sir Walter Scott's *The Pirate.* Following his capture, Gow was held prisoner at **Carrick House,** discreetly signposted on the northern part of the island. Carrick House was built in 1633 by James Stewart, the second son of Robert Stewart, who had been named earl of Carrick. It's now the home of **Mrs. Joy** (© 01857/622-260), but if you're polite and have a flexible schedule, she might open her house to a visit. There may or may not be a fee—about £5 ($8) per person "feels right." She's most amenable to visitors between late June and mid-September, and Sundays are an especially good time to test your luck. Despite the sale of various parcels of land to the island's 130 to 140 inhabitants, most of the island is owned by the laird of Eday, Mrs. Rosemary Hebdon Joy, whose link to the island dates to around 1900, when her grandfather bought it from his London club. The circumstances surrounding the island's inheritance have made it one of the few matriarchal lairdships in Scotland—its ownership has passed from mother to daughter for several generations.

Because of limited accommodations, Eday is most often visited on a day trip. **Loganair,** in Kirkwall (call British Airways at © 0845/722-2277 for reservations), offers service to Eday every Wednesday. **Orkney Ferries Ltd.,** Shore Street in Kirkwall (© 01856/872-044; www.orkneyferries.co.uk), crosses to Eday about twice daily. The round-trip fare is £25.40 ($41) for vehicles and £11.50 ($18) for adults.

WHERE TO STAY

There's no formal tourist office in Eday. However, **Mrs. Popplewell** (© 01857/ 622-248) from Little Croft House (see "Where to Dine," below) provides an information service and can assist you with finding accommodations or organizing any activities.

Skaill Farm ☆ *(Finds* Operated by a pair of English expatriates fleeing the congestion of the London suburbs, Skaill is the centerpiece for the island's third-largest farm. Set on 324 hectares (800 acres) of windswept grazing land, midway along the length of the island near its narrowest point, 8km (5 miles) from both Calfsound and Backaland, it's in a stone building whose 18th-century core was constructed on the foundations of Orkney's medieval skaill. (A skaill is the honorific home of an earl, designed to shelter him during his visits from other parts of his realm.) Michael and Dee Cockram welcome you to their home, providing well-prepared dinners and simple but comfortable guest rooms. Meals might include fresh vegetables from the family garden, lobsters, scallops, lamb, and beef.

Skaill, Eday, Orkney KW17 2AA. ✆ and fax **01857/622-271.** 2 units, none with private bathroom. £60 ($96) double. Rates include half-board. No credit cards. Closed April and May. *In room:* No phone.

WHERE TO DINE

Little Croft House ✆ *Value* SCOTTISH   One of the most charming possibilities for a meal on Eday is provided by Emma Popplewell, who, if notified in advance, will prepare fixed-price lunches and dinners. Meals are often served to a loyal following of "off-island" yacht owners enjoying the nautical challenges of the local waters. The setting is a croft cottage whose 76cm (30-inch) -thick stone walls were built around 1900. Its flower and vegetable gardens slope down to the edge of the sea, source of some of the kelp and seaweed Mrs. Popplewell uses to flavor her succulent versions of Orkney lamb. Depending on what's available, menu items may include grilled halibut with scallops and local dill and fennel, salads made with wild greens gathered from the hills, homemade raspberry bramble sorbet, locally made cheeses and beers, and aromatic crusty bread that's freshly baked every morning.

In one of the croft's outbuildings (a former boathouse), Mrs. Popplewell sells sweaters, accessories, and caftans that are handknit on Eday by local women. Also for sale are paintings and sculpture by island artists.

Mrs. Popplewell also rents four comfortably furnished rooms containing TVs; the two doubles are £60 ($96), including half-board.

Isle of Eday, Orkney KW17 2AB. ✆ **01857/622-248.** Reservations required as far in advance as possible. About £9.50 ($15) per person. No credit cards. Time to be arranged when making reservations.

SANDAY

The name of Sanday means "sand island," which is appropriate; the island's long white beaches have grown as tides have changed over the last century. With few residents or visitors, the stretches of seashore are often deserted—perfect for long, solitary walks. One of the largest of the North Isles, some 26km (16 miles) in length, Sanday is part of the eastern archipelago.

On the Elsness Peninsula, jutting southeast from the bulk of Sanday Island, you'll find one of the most spectacular chambered cairns in the Orkneys: the **Quoyness Chambered Tomb** ✆. The tomb and its principal chamber date from around 2900 B.C., reaching a height of some 4m (13 ft.). Access is by key, which is available at the local post office in Lady Village. Other ancient monuments, including Viking burial grounds and broch sites, have been found on Sanday.

You can see rare migrant birds and terns at the **Start Point Lighthouse,** near the extreme tip of Start Point, a tidal peninsula jutting northward from the rest of Sanday. The early-19th-century lighthouse is one of the oldest in the country, but since the 1960s has been on "automatic pilot," without a permanent resident to tend the machinery except for a part-time warden (✆ **01857/600-385**) who may or may not be here at the time of your visit. The number of ships wrecked off Sanday's shore is topped only by North Ronaldsay; you can see the wreck of a German destroyer on the Sand of Langamay. If you want to see this monument, know that only specialized vehicles can drive across the tidal flats and only at low tide. Locals, however, are aware of the times when a trekker can safely walk across the kelp-strewn sandy flats. If you feel adventurous, ask a local how to get here or phone the warden for advice.

Loganair flies in from the Kirkwall Airport (✆ **01856/872-494**) twice a day Monday through Friday and once on Saturday at a cost of £31 ($50). **Orkney**

Ferries Ltd., Shore Street, Kirkwall (© **01856/872-044;** www.orkneyferries. co.uk), crosses to the island about two times daily. Round-trip fares are £16.30 ($26) for adults and £25.40 ($41) for vehicles.

WHERE TO STAY & DINE

Accommodations are extremely limited, so book your room in advance.

Belsair Hotel   This stone and clapboard inn is located in the village of Kettletoft, about 13km (8 miles) northeast of Sanday's roll-on/roll-off ferry pier. Kettletoft consists of about 15 buildings and is the most central of the island's four communities. The functionally furnished guest rooms in this hotel were upgraded and renovated back in 1992, but the original building dates back to 1879, when it was built by ancestors of the Belsair's present owners.

The Belsair is the site of the island's only restaurant. Gardens across the road produce many of the vegetables served in the dining room, where moderately priced dishes include straightforward but flavorful preparations of fish, beef, and lamb.

Kettletoft, Sanday, Orkney KW17 2BJ. © 01857/600-206. emma@white1935.freeserve.co.uk. 3 units. £25 ($40) double without bathroom; £50 ($75) double with bathroom. Rates include full Scottish breakfast. No credit cards. **Amenities:** Restaurant. *In room:* TV, coffeemaker, no phone.

WESTRAY

One of the biggest of the North Isles, Westray is a fertile island with a closely knit community, many of whom are said to have Spanish blood, owing to shipwrecks of the Armada off its stormy shores. The western shoreline is the steepest, rising in parts to some 61m (200 ft.), from which you can enjoy panoramic vistas. The island is a bird-watcher's paradise, who can see seabirds like guillemots around Noup Head, with its red-sandstone cliffs. Along the lochs are many **sandy beaches.**

Below the cliffs is the so-called **Gentleman's Cave.** A Balfour of Trenabie is said to have found refuge in this cave, along with his comrades, after the defeat at Culloden in 1746. As winter winds howled outside, they drank to the welfare of the "king over the water," Bonnie Prince Charlie. A hike to the remote cave is recommended only for the hardy and only after you've talked to locals first about how to access it.

At **Pierowall,** the major hamlet, you can see **Pierowall Church,** a ruin with a chancel and a nave. There are also some finely lettered grave slabs.

The most famous attraction is **Noltland Castle,** a former fortress overlooking Pierowall. A governor of the island, Thomas de Tulloch, had this castle built in 1420. Eventually it was occupied by Gilbert Balfour of Westray, who had it redesigned as a fortress in a "three-stepped" or Z plan. This would have provided complete all-around visibility against attack—but it was never finished. The castle's present ruins date from around the mid-1500s. It was destroyed in part by a fire in 1746. A kitchen, a stately hall, and a winding staircase are still standing.

Orkney Ferries Ltd. (© **01856/872-044** in Kirkwall; www.orkneyferries. co.uk) sails to Pierowall, Westray, two to three times daily. Bookings are required for cars; the cost is £25.40 ($41) round-trip. Adult passengers pay £11.30 ($18). **Loganair** flies to Westray one to two times Monday through Saturday at a cost of £35 ($56). Phone © **01856/872-494** in Kirkwall for information; for reservations, call British Airways at © **0845/722-2277.**

WHERE TO STAY & DINE

Because accommodations are very limited, make reservations in advance.

Pierowall Hotel   Built a century ago as a manse (clergyman's residence) for a nearby Presbyterian church, this cozy hotel, 12km (7½ miles) north of the roll-on-roll-off ferry terminal, is the domain of Mrs. Jean Fergus. The pub offers affordable food and drink to anyone who stops in.

Pierowall Village, Westray, Orkney KW17 2BZ. ℭ **01857/677-472.** Fax 01857/677-707. www.orknet.co.uk/pierowall. 5 units, 2 with private bathroom. £40 ($64) double without bathroom; £52 ($84) double with bathroom. Rates include Scottish breakfast. MC, V. **Amenities:** Restaurant; 2 bars. *In room:* TV, coffeemaker, hair dryer, no phone.

PAPA WESTRAY

Both bird-watchers and students of history are drawn to Papa Westray, which was believed to have been settled by at least 3500 B.C. One of the most northerly isles in the Orkneys, it's rich in archaeological sites. In the fertile farmland around Holland, the **Knap of Howar** was discovered, the earliest standing dwelling house in northwestern Europe, dating from before 3000 B.C.

On the eastern shore of Loch Treadwell, on a peninsula jutting southeast from the bulk of Papa Westray, you can visit the ruins of **St. Treadwell's Chapel,** believed to have marked the arrival of Christianity in the Orkney Islands. The chapel, now in ruins, was dedicated to Triduana, a Celtic saint. When a Pictish king, Nechtan, admired her lovely eyes, she is said to have plucked them out and sent them by messenger to the king—she hoped he'd learn it was foolish to admire physical beauty. For many decades, the chapel was a place of pilgrimage for those suffering from eye problems.

On the island's western edge, about 3km (2 miles) from St. Treadwell's Chapel, north of the airport, is **St. Boniface Church,** also a Celtic site. Stone Celtic crosses were found here, as well as a series of much-eroded grave slabs carved from red sandstone. This is believed to have been a Christian Viking burial ground, now exposed to the howling winds and bleak sunlight of this rocky peat-clad island.

A major attraction here is **Holland House,** formerly the home of the Traills of Holland. Dating from the 17th century, the house is a fine example of a circular "Horse Engine House," which was driven by 11 horses and a dovecote. The house is now owned by farmer John Rendall (ℭ **01857/644-251**); you might be able to see inside if you're polite and Mr. Rendall is feeling sociable.

The northern end of the island has been turned into a **nature reserve,** which is the best place to go for scenic walks. Along with colonies of guillemots and kittiwakes, **North Hill** is the site of one of the largest breeding colonies of the Arctic tern.

Twice-daily flights to Papa Westray from Kirkwall on Mainland are offered by **Loganair** (ℭ **01856/872-494,** or call British Airways at ℭ **0845/772-2277** for reservations). **Orkney Ferries Ltd.,** Shore Street, Kirkwall (ℭ **01856/872-044;** www.orkneyferries.co.uk), sails to Papa Westray direct on Tuesdays and Fridays; on other days, the ferry stops at Westray, where you catch a smaller ferry service to Papa Westray. Round-trip fares are £25.50 ($41) for vehicles and £11.30 ($18) for adult passengers.

WHERE TO STAY & DINE

Beltane House   Built in 1983 about 3km (2 miles) from the island's main pier, this all-purpose accommodation is run by the local farm cooperative. A row of stone-sided farmworkers' cottages was renovated to form a complex of shops, a guesthouse, and a bare-bones youth hostel containing two dorms (male and female) with bunk beds. June and July are the busiest months, requiring advance reservations. No meals are provided in the hostel, but there's a self-catering kitchen. Hostel guests sometimes choose to join the guests of the main house for the affordable nightly dinner.

Papa Westray, Orkney KW17 2BU. ① **01857/644-267**. 4 units in guesthouse. £80 ($128) double. Rates include Scottish breakfast and dinner. For youth hostel: £9.50 ($15) per adult; £8 ($13) per child under 18 (Rates are set by the Scottish Youth Hostel Association and change frequently.) MC, V. **Amenities:** Restaurant; bar. *In room:* No phone.

2 Fair Isle ⍟

43km (27 miles) S of Lerwick, Shetland Islands

Called the "most isolated inhabited part of Britain," Fair Isle lies on the same latitude as Bergen, Norway. It measures only about 1.6km by 6km (1 mile by 3½ miles) and sits about midway between the Orkneys and the Shetlands, administered by the latter. Relentless seas pound its 32km (20 mile) coast in winter and powerful westerly winds fling Atlantic spray from one side of the island to the other. It's home to fewer than 100 rugged, self-reliant souls.

An important staging point for migrating birds, Fair Isle is even better known for its patterned pullovers, which greatly aid the island's economy. In stores around the world, you'll see these intricately patterned garments retailing at high prices. The homegrown product is sold on Fair Isle at half the price. Fair Isle knitting is even a part of the curriculum at all primary schools, and many jobless men have turned to knitting.

Originally the fame of the sweaters was spread in the 1920s by the prince of Wales. The pattern is of mysterious origin. Some suggest it was derived from Celtic sources, others that it came from the island's Viking heritage. A more daring theory maintains the themes were Moorish, learned from Spanish sailors shipwrecked off Fair Isle from the Armada in 1588.

In 1954, the island was acquired by the National Trust for Scotland. The **bird observatory** installed here is the most remarkable in the country. Since work began in 1948, some 200 species have been ringed. Fair Isle is an important breeding ground for everything from the puffin and the Arctic skua to the razorbill and the storm petrel.

GETTING THERE

Loganair operates scheduled service in a seven-seat "Islander"; flight time is 25 minutes. From Sumburgh Airport, there's a flight on Saturday only, which links with incoming Loganair flights from both Glasgow and Edinburgh. From Lerwick Airport, flights are once or twice a day from Monday to Saturday. Call Loganair at ① **01856/872-494** or British Airways at ① **0845/722-2277** for more information.

The mailboat *Good Shepherd* sails on Tuesday, Thursday, and Saturday from Grutness Pier, Sumburgh Head, on Shetland. It's advisable to check sailing times from Grutness by phoning before 9:30am on the morning of the scheduled departure for Fair Isle, in case of weather delay. Bookings for the trips to Fair Isle can be made through **J. W. Stout,** Skerryholm, Fair Isle (① **01595/760-222**). A one-way fare is £2.40 ($3.85); the trip takes 2½ hours.

WHERE TO STAY & DINE

Fair Isle Lodge and Bird Observatory ⍟ *Finds*   Even if you're not a birdwatcher, you might want to stay at this low-slung, big-windowed building in the shelter of treeless hillsides. Located near the sea at the northern end of the island, the lodge was the dream of a well-respected ornithologist, George Waterston, who bought it in 1948 and created the observatory. It's now administered by the Fair Isle Bird Observatory Trust. Adjacent accommodations were constructed to provide housing for visitors. There are 33 beds for rent. It's also possible to stay in a dorm room, with four to six beds.

The place is most popular during the spring and autumn bird migrations. It's always wise to reserve well in advance, especially during those seasons. Sometimes the wardens will take guests on before-breakfast tours of bird traps, which, for tagging purposes, are placed in strategic points along the stone dikes surrounding the island.

Fair Isle, Shetland ZE2 9JU. ℭ and fax **01595/760-258**. www.fairislebirdobs.co.uk. 14 units, none with private bathroom. £74 ($118) double; £30 ($48) dorm bed. Rates include full board. MC, V. Closed Nov to late-April. **Amenities:** Bar. *In room:* no phone.

3 The Shetland Islands: A Land of Stark Beauty ⋆

97km (60 miles) N and NE of the Orkneys

The northernmost part of the British Isles, the archipelago of the Shetland Islands includes some 100 islands that make up 130 sq. km (50 sq. miles) of land. Many are merely islets or rocks, but 17 are inhabited. The major island is called Mainland, as in the Orkneys. This island, on which the capital, Lerwick, is located, is about 89km (55 miles) long and 32km (20 miles) wide. It has been turned into what some critics have called "a gargantuan oil terminal." The Shetlands handle about half of Britain's oil.

The islands also have been called "that long string of peat and gneiss that stands precariously where three seas—the Atlantic Ocean, the North Sea, and the Arctic Ocean—meet." Shetland's fjordlike voes (sheer rock cliffs) make the islands beautiful in both seascape and landscape. But it's a stark beauty, wild and rugged, with windswept moors. Because there are few trees, the landscape at first looks barren. After a while, it begins to take on a fascination, especially when you come on a typical Shetlander, in his sturdy Wellington boots and thick woolen sweater, cutting peat along a bog as his ancestors did before him. Shetlanders are proud, warm, and often eager to share the treasures of their island chain with you. At no point in Shetland are you more than 5km (3 miles) from the sea—the coastline stretches for some 4,830km (3,000 miles).

The major airport is at **Sumburgh,** on the southern tip of the southernmost island of Mainland. The far-northern outpost is **Muckle Flugga Lighthouse,** an advanced achievement of engineering. Standing poised on near-vertical rock, it's the "last window on the world" through which Great Britain looks out to the north. It's not as cold here as you might think: The Shetland archipelago benefits from the warming influence of the Gulf Stream, but even in summer the weather tends to be chilly. Shetland has less than half the annual rainfall recorded in the western Highlands. In summer, there's almost continuous daylight. The Shetlanders call it "Simmer Dim." In midwinter, there are no more than 5 hours of daylight.

Civilization here dates back some 5,000 years. The Shetlands were inhabited more than 2,000 years before the Romans, who called them "Ultima Thule." These islands paraded Neolithic people, followed by the people of the Iron and Bronze Ages, who gave way to the Picts and the Celts. But the most enduring influence came from the Vikings, who ruled the Shetlands until some 500 years ago. The Norse established an influence that lasted for centuries and is still evident today in language, culture, and customs.

The Vikings held the islands from A.D. 800 until they were given to Scotland in 1469 as part of the wedding dowry of Princess Margaret of Norway when she married James III. Scotland's takeover of the Shetlands marked a sad period in the life of the islanders, who found themselves under the sway of often cruel and unreasonable feudal barons. One of the most hated of rulers was Earl Patrick Stewart, who was assigned the dubious task of imposing Scottish customs on a people who had known only Viking law. His son matched him in cruelty, and eventually both earls were executed in Edinburgh for their crimes. Shetlanders still think of themselves as separate from Scots.

The impact of the North Sea oilmen on this traditionally straitlaced community is noticeable, in overcrowding and other ways. However, away from all the oil activity, life in the Shetlands goes on much as it always did, except for the profusion of modern conveniences and imported foodstuffs. Speaking of food, you'll notice that food on Shetland tastes better when it's from Shetland—try the distinctive salted and smoked Reestit mutton to see what we mean.

The islands are famous for their ponies and wool. **Shetland ponies** roam freely among the hills and common grazing lands in the island chain. Some are shipped south to England, where they're popular as children's mounts. The Shetlands also have 10% of all the seabirds in the British Isles, and several of the smaller islands or islets have nature reserves. Seals are protected and welcomed here—you can see them drifting among the waves, sliding down in pursuit of a fish dinner, or lounging about on the rocks and beaches. You'll recognize most of them as the Atlantic gray seal, with its big angular head. The common seal, with a dog-shaped head, is most often found on the islet of Mousa. And if you want to see otters, you have a better chance in Shetland than anywhere else in Britain.

Anglers find some 200 freshwater lochs in Shetland, and deep-sea angling makes for a memorable sport. Many world fishing records have been set in Shetland. "Ton-up" fish are common.

The island craftspeople are noted for their creativity, reflected in their handcrafts, jewelry, and knitware. In some places, you can watch these items being made in the workshops of the artists. **Hand-knitted sweaters** are still produced in great numbers, and anyone contemplating a visit might want to return with at least one.

Note: It's imperative to have advance reservations if you're considering a trip to the Shetlands, especially in midsummer.

SHETLAND ESSENTIALS

GETTING THERE   Shetland is a 2½-hour flight from London. By air or sea, Aberdeen is the major departure point from Scotland. **British Airways (© 800/ 247-9297** in the U.S., or 0845/772-2277) flies from Aberdeen four times per day Monday through Friday, with reduced service on Saturday and Sunday. The flight takes less than an hour.

Roll-on–roll-off car ferries operate from Aberdeen to Shetland Monday through Friday, carrying up to 600 passengers and 240 cars. For information, contact **NorthLink, (© 0845/6000-449**). The trip takes about 14 hours and costs £53 to £63 ($85–$101) per person. On-board facilities include restaurants, cafeterias, bars, lounges, and gift shops.

NorthLink offers year-round ferry service once a week, departing on Sunday at noon and Tuesday at 10pm from Stromness, Orkney, heading for Lerwick in the Shetlands. For information, call © **0845/772-2277** in Stromness.

The Shetland Islands

Area of detail

SCOTLAND

⊛ Edinburgh

0 20 mi
0 20 km

ENGLAND

0 10 mi
0 16 km

N

Muckle Flugga Lighthouse — Lamba Ness
Herma Ness — UNST
Haroldswick
Baltasound
A968
Cullivoe
Belmont
Point of Fethaland
Gutcher
YELL HASCOSAY
FETLAR
A968
Mid Yell
A970
Yell Sound
Colgrave Sound
Burravoe
Stenness
Hillswick
OUT SKERRIES
Esha Ness
Saint Magnus Bay
A970
WHALSAY
Brae
A968
MUCKLE ROE
Voe Laxo
Vidlin
PAPA STOUR
PAPA LITTLE
Symbister
A970
Kergord
Melby Ho
MAINLAND
North Sea
A971
Bridge of Walls
Wats Ness
A971
Walls
Whiteness
VAILA
Lerwick
ISLE OF NOSS
FOULA
The Deeps
BRESSAY
Ham
Scalloway
Bard Head
Hamnavoe
WEST BURRA
Ferry to Bergen →
Kettle Ness
MOUSA
Sandwick
ST. NINIAN'S ISLAND
A970
Ferries to Fair Isle & Aberdeen
Ferry to Westray Fitful Head (Orkney Islands)
Sumburgh

Broch of Mousa 5
Clickhimin Broch 4
Jarlshof 8
Kirk of Lund 1
Muness Castle 2
Shetland Crofthouse Museum 7
St. Ninian's Island 6
Staneydale Temple 3

Airport ✈
Ferry - - -

GETTING AROUND If you have a problem with transportation either to or around the islands, you can always check with the tourist office in Lerwick (see below).

Loganair (☏ **01595/840-246**) provides daily and weekly service to the islands of Whalsay, Fetlar, Foula, and Out Skerries. Although flying is a bit more expensive than taking a ferry, the bonus is that you can go and return on the same day as opposed to spending 2 or possibly 3 days on a rather small island.

Most of the inhabited islands are reached from the Shetland Mainland, and passenger fares are nominal because they're heavily subsidized by the government. Service is 13 to 16 times a day to the islands of Unst, Yell, Whalsay, Fetlar, and Bressay. Passenger and cargo vessels service the islands of Fair Isle, Foula, the Skerries, and Papa Stour. Scheduled services to the little-visited places operate only once or twice a week, however. Boat trips to the islands of Mousa and Noss can be arranged in summer. Call the **Shetland Islands Tourism office** (☏ **01595/693-434**) for more information.

In summer, buses travel around Mainland to all the major places of interest. Call the leading bus company, **John Leask & Son** (© **01595/693-162**), or pick up a copy of the *Inter-Shetland Transport Timetable,* costing £1 ($1.60) at the Shetland Islands Tourism office (see below).

It's easier to drive around the Shetlands than you'd think, as there are some 805km (500 miles) of passable roads—no traffic jams, no traffic lights. Many of the islands are connected by road bridges, and for those that aren't, car ferries provide service. Renting a car might be the best solution if you want to cover a lot of ground in the shortest time. You can either bring a car from mainland Scotland or pick one up in Lerwick. No major international car rental firm as yet maintains an office in the Shetlands. However, Avis and Europcar have as their on-island agents **Bolts Car Hire,** 26 North Rd., Lerwick (© **01595/693-636**); a competitor is **Grantsfield Garage,** North Road, Lerwick (© **01595/692-709**).

If you want to pedal your way around, **Grantsfield Garage,** North Road (© **01595/692-709**), rents bikes for £7.50 ($12) per day and £30 ($48) per week. If you're planning on renting a bike for several days, reserve at least a day in advance.

VISITOR INFORMATION   The **Shetland Islands Tourism office** is at the Market Cross in Lerwick (© **01595/693-434;** www.visitshetland.com). The helpful staff does many things, such as arranging rooms and providing information on ferries, boat trips, car rentals, and local events—they even rent fishing tackle. It's open from April to September, Monday through Friday from 8am to 6pm and Saturday from 8am to 4pm (May to Aug, also Sun from 10am–1pm); and October to March, Monday through Friday from 9am to 5pm.

SPECIAL EVENTS   Festivals and a festive atmosphere surround the communities of these remote islands, where the slightest excuse will kick off music and revelry. Pubs and community centers regularly schedule music and dancing, and on most weekend nights, all you have to do is go in search of a pint of beer to find live traditional music.

The **Shetland Folk Festival** (© **01595/694-757** for information; www.sffs.shetland.co.uk) takes place at Lerwick around the end of April and the beginning of May. Young fiddlers on the island take part, and international artists fly in for 4 days of concerts, workshops, and informal jam sessions, climaxed by what is called the "Final Foy." Concerts, usually incorporating dinner and dancing, and are held in local halls throughout the islands, with most events costing about £20 to £30 ($32–$48). Often festival entertainers will convene at the pubs and join local performers.

January also finds Lerwick hosting **Up Helly Aa,** its famous **Fire Festival,** on the last Tuesday of the month, when a thousand locals, torches held high, are cheered on as they storm an effigy of a Viking longboat and set it aflame. These heroes and their witnesses follow this with a long night of eating, drinking, playing music, and dancing. The celebrations spread out from here, and more remote communities hold their local versions of the event over the next 3 months (see "Up Helly Aa!," below).

Summer weekends bring regularly scheduled local **regattas,** in which different communities compete in sailing and rowing competitions. Afterward, there are celebratory dinners, music, and dancing in local venues.

LERWICK

The capital of the Shetlands since the 17th century, Lerwick, on the eastern coast of Mainland, is sheltered by the little offshore island of Bressay. In the 19th century, it was the herring capital of northern Europe, and before that, a haven for smugglers. The fishing fleet of the Netherlands put in here after combing the North Sea. Even before Victoria came to the throne in 1837, Lerwick had a bustling, cosmopolitan atmosphere. That's even truer today, with the influx of foreign visitors.

Believe it or not, Lerwick is sometimes the sunniest place in Britain, experiencing some 12 hours of sunshine a day in early summer. Commercial Street is the town's principal artery, and it's said that beneath the steep and narrow lanes runs a network of passages used by smugglers. Lerwick today is the main port and shopping center of Shetland.

EXPLORING THE TOWN

Your first stop should be at the Shetland Islands Tourism office (see above). The helpful staff members are used to unusual requests: Sometimes visitors from Canada or the United States drop in here wanting their ancestors traced.

Shetland Library and Museum, Lower Hillhead Road, a 5-minute walk west of Lerwick's center (© **01595/695-057;** www.shetland-museum.org.uk), has, in addition to a reading room, four galleries devoted to exhibits covering art and textiles, shipping, archaeological digs, and oil exploration. Admission is free. It's open Monday, Wednesday, and Friday from 10am to 7pm and Tuesday, Thursday, and Saturday from 10am to 5pm.

Entered via both Market Street and Charlotte Street, pentagonal **Fort Charlotte** (© **01595/693-434**), built in 1665, contains high walls with gun slits pointing, naturally, at the sea. Eight years after it was constructed, it was burned by the Dutch. Restoration came in 1781. It's open daily from 9:30am to sunset; admission is free.

Clickhimin Broch, about .4km (¼ mile) southwest of Lerwick beside A970, was fortified at the beginning of the Iron Age. Excavated in the 1950s, the site revealed 1,000 years of history. It was at one time turned into a broch, rising 5m (17 ft.) and built inside the fort. Admission is free; it's open daily with no set hours. It's a great place to go for a scenic walk.

A 12m (40-ft.) replica of a Viking longboat, **Dim Riv** ("Morning Light"), is available for a tour of the harbor on summer evenings. The boat was constructed by Lerwick craftsmen in 1980. Ask at the tourism office (see above).

Of the many shops in Lerwick, you may want to drop in at **Anderson & Co.,** Shetland Warehouse, Commercial Street (© **01595/693-714**), which sells handmade crofter and designer sweaters as well as other cottage-industry goods. **G. Rae,** 92 Commercial St. (© **01595/693-686**), sells silver and gold jewelry featuring Celtic motifs and images based on Norse mythology and Shetland legends. Gold- and silversmith Rosalyn Thompson produces the jewelry sold at **Hjaltasteyn,** 161 Commercial St. (© **01595/696-224**), where you'll find a selection of sterling silver and gold items, some of which are set with garnets and amethysts.

WHERE TO STAY

Glen Orchy House   Near the top of a brae (gently sloping hill) and not far from a nine-hole golf course that's free to the public, Glen Orchy House is a 4-minute walk from the center of town. The building was constructed in 1904 as an Episcopalian nunnery; the most recent modifications to it were in 1997, when a new wing was added. In addition to singles and doubles, there are now four family rooms. The hosts will provide an affordable evening meal to those who request it.

Up Helly Aa!

The farther north you travel in Scotland, the stronger are the undercurrents of pagan myth and pageantry, culminating in the vivid Norse traditions of the Shetlands. On the moss-covered rocky surface of the 100 or so islands, the collective unconscious of the locals is sometimes startlingly revealed as something other than Anglo-Saxon or Celtic.

Ask anyone in a local pub, and he or she will tell you the islands are Scottish only because of the fiscal embarrassment of a Norwegian king who sold the Shetlands to the Scottish monarchs in 1469 with the tacit understanding they'd eventually be returned to Scandinavia. Although for many generations the Shetlanders retained their Norse dialect and allegiance to Viking ways, the switch back to Norway never happened. Perhaps in reaction to their medieval role as bartered chattel between the two northern kingdoms, the Shetlands remained dourly outside Scottish culture, with a populace who, for many generations, used "the mainland" to refer to the provincial capital of Lerwick and not to the mainland of Scotland.

How do the Shetlanders celebrate their Nordic heritage? By brightening up the midwinter darkness with the Up Helly Aa festival, held—in fair weather, snow, or storm—every year on the last Tuesday in January. The festival's centerpiece is a meticulously crafted re-creation of a Viking longboat. The people of Lerwick parade by torchlight through the streets in Viking costume, and the highlight of the evening comes when the longboat is set alight and its dragon-head prow is engulfed in flames. Presiding over the ritual is an elected master of ceremonies, the Guizer Jarl (a significant honor bestowed only on a longtime resident male of proven civic worth and integrity).

This ancient ritual celebrates the death of winter and the return of the sun and the earth's rebirth with the coming of spring. The ceremony is based on an ancient Viking death ritual when the body of a dead earl (Jarl) would be set ablaze at sea. An essential part of the ritual is the almost immediate removal of all traces of the burned-out hulk of the longboat after the cremation is over. The morning after the ceremony, even the ashes of the celebration have been carted off, and Lerwick resumes its outwardly Christian and Scottish demeanor—until the Viking tradition of the Up Helly Aa is revived again the following year.

20 Knab Rd., Lerwick, Shetland ZE1 0AX. ℂ and fax **01595/692-031**. www.guesthouselerwick.com. 22 units. £72 ($115) double. Rates include Scottish breakfast. MC, V. Pets accepted. **Amenities:** Bar. *In room:* A/C (some rooms), TV, coffeemaker, hair dryer.

Grand Hotel ✪   A grander hotel would be hard to find anywhere in Shetland. With pointed turrets, weather vanes, crow's-step gables, and solid stone walls, it lies a block from the waterfront, in the town center. The guest rooms are conservative yet comfortable, each with a shower-only bathroom. The extensively modernized hotel has two lounge bars, a dining room, and a nightclub open

Wednesday, Friday, and Sunday. The Grand shares its reservations facilities and some of its staff with the Queens Hotel (see below).

149 Commercial St., Lerwick, Shetland ZE1 0AB. ℂ **01595/692-826.** Fax 01595/694-048. www.kgq hotels.co.uk. 24 units. £23 ($37) double; £120 ($192) family room. Rates include Scottish breakfast. AE, DC, MC, V. Free parking in nearby public lot. **Amenities:** Restaurant; 2 bars; room service (7am–11pm). *In room:* TV, coffeemaker, hair dryer.

Lerwick Hotel ⚐   This is one of the biggest and most up-to-date hotels in the Shetlands, sprawling beside a gravel- and kelp-covered beach. Its simply furnished guest rooms offer various amenities and small, shower-only bathrooms; half have views over the water toward Bressay. The upscale restaurant offers at least one seafood and one vegetarian choice as well as chicken or wild game. In summer, dinner dances that combine hearty meals with traditional Scottish fun are frequently held.

15 South Rd., Shetland ZE1 0RB. ℂ **01595/692-166.** Fax 01595/694-419. www.shetlandhotels.com. 35 units. £89.95 ($144) double; £115 ($184) suite. Rates include Scottish breakfast. AE, DC, MC, V. Take Scalloway Rd. west from the center for 5 min. **Amenities:** 2 restaurants; bar; room service (10am–9:30pm); laundry service. *In room:* TV, coffeemaker, hair dryer, trouser press.

Queens Hotel ⚐   Its foundations rise directly from the sea at the harborfront, so on blustery nights, fine sprays of saltwater sometimes coat the windowpanes of the lower floors. Built of natural stone around 1860, the Queens rivals the nearby Grand Hotel (see above) as the most prestigious hotel in Lerwick. They share the same reservations staff. The small guest rooms are conservatively and comfortably furnished, each with shower. Inexpensive bar lunches are offered in the cocktail lounge, and more formal dinners with Shetland cuisine are served in the dining room (see "Where to Dine" below).

24 Commercial St., Lerwick, Shetland ZE1 0AB. ℂ **01595/692-826.** Fax 01595/694-048. www.kgqhotels. co.uk. 26 units. £90 ($144) double; £120 ($192) family room. Rates include Scottish breakfast. AE, DC, MC, V. **Amenities:** Restaurant; bar; 24-hr. room service. *In room:* TV, coffeemaker, hair dryer.

Shetland Hotel   Built in 1984, this four-story brick, stone, and concrete structure is one of the most modern hotels in the Shetlands. It's opposite the ferry terminal, with a good view of the harbor. The good-size guest rooms are well furnished. The two on-site restaurants offer local fish and vegetarian items. It has been upgraded and much improved in the wake of the Shetland oil boom, when oil executives often filled up its rooms

Holmsgarth Rd., Lerwick, Shetland ZE1 0PW. ℂ **01595/695-515.** Fax 01595/695-828. www.shetland hotels.com. 65 units. £92 ($147) double; £99 ($158) suite. Rates include Scottish breakfast. AE, DC, MC, V. **Amenities:** 2 restaurants (see Oasis Bistro, below); 2 bars; 24-hr. room service; laundry service. *In room:* TV, coffeemaker, hair dryer.

WHERE TO DINE

Golden Coach CHINESE   One of the two Chinese restaurants in the Shetlands, this intimate place is softly lit and contemporary in decor. Try the barbecued Peking duck or deep-fried shredded beef in sweet-and-sour sauce. Malaysian chicken comes in a peanut sauce, or you can order king prawns Peking with garlic sauce.

17 Hillhead. ℂ **01595/693-848.** Reservations required Sat–Sun. Main courses £7.50–£9.20 ($12–$15); fixed-price lunch £8 ($13); dinner menu £20 ($32). MC, V. Mon–Fri noon–2pm and 5:30–11pm; Sat–Sun noon–11pm.

Oasis Bistro SCOTTISH   This eatery is a good choice for a light snack at odd hours; salads and sandwiches are served all day. The restaurant also offers hot meals at lunch and dinner. Emphasis is on fresh fish and vegetarian fare straight from Shetland gardens.

In the Shetland Hotel, Holmsgarth Rd. ℂ **01595/695-515.** Main courses £9–£16.95 ($14–$27). AE, DC, MC, V. Daily 11am–9:30pm; hot meals noon–2pm and 5–9:30pm.

Queens Hotel *Kids* BRITISH   On the lobby level of this previously recommended hotel, this pink-and-white dining room overlooks the sea, the wharves, and the many fishing boats bobbing at anchor. It caters to families, many of whom seem to arrive in groups as part of reunions. Many locals consider it the best restaurant in Lerwick, a staple on the island's culinary scene. Specialties include goujons of haddock with tartar sauce, roast beef sirloin with Yorkshire pudding, chicken Caribbean with pineapple sauce, braised lamb cutlets, and conservative preparations of fish dishes.

24 Commercial St. ℂ **01595/692-826.** Reservations recommended. Main courses £11–£15 ($18–$24); fixed-price 3-course dinner £20 ($32). AE, DC, MC, V. Daily noon–2pm and 6–9:30pm.

LERWICK AFTER DARK

From May to September, the **Islesburgh Community Centre,** King Harold Street (ℂ **01595/692-114**), hosts dancing to Shetland fiddle music called the Summer Exhibition on Wednesdays and Fridays from 7 to 9:30pm. Admission is £3.50 ($5.60). The **Lounge Bar,** Mounthooly Street (ℂ **01595/692-231**), hosts an informal evening of traditional fiddle music on Wednesdays, usually starting around 9:30pm. There's also live music on Friday nights and often on Saturday afternoons. There's no cover.

SOUTH MAINLAND

This part of Shetland, reached by heading south from Lerwick along A970, is both ancient and modern. On the one hand, there's the gleaming **Sumburgh Airport,** which has played a major role in the North Sea oilfields development and services many of the offshore rigs today. On the other hand, you'll stumble on the ruins of **Jarlshof** (see below), which may have been inhabited for some 3,000 years.

EXPLORING THE AREA

As you go down the "long leg" of Shetland, as it's called, heading due south, passing a peaty moorland and fresh meadows, the first attraction is not on Mainland at all but on an offshore island called Mousa: the famous **Broch of Mousa** ✦✦, a Pictish defense tower that guarded the islet for some 2,000 years. It reached the then-incredible height of some 12m (40 ft.) and was constructed of local stones, with two circular walls, one within the other. They enclosed a staircase leading to sleeping quarters. It's the best-preserved example of an Iron Age broch in Britain. The village of **Sandwick,** 11km (7 miles) south of Lerwick, is the ferry point for reaching Mousa. There's daily bus service between Lerwick and Sandwick. A local boatman, Mr. Jamieson, will take you across to Mousa; it takes about 15 minutes. From April to September only, you can visit Mousa Monday through Saturday. The cost is £7.50 ($12) for adults and £3.50 ($5.60) for children. For boat schedules, call the tourist office in Lerwick at ℂ **01595/693-434.**

South of Sandwick, you reach the parish of Dunrossness. At Boddam is the **Crofthouse Museum** (ℂ **01595/695-057**), east of A970 on an unmarked road 40km (25 miles) south of Lerwick. Rural Shetland life comes alive here in this thatched croft house from the mid-1800s. The museum also has some outbuildings and a functioning water mill. It's open from May to September. Admission is free.

Continuing south, you reach the outstanding man-made attraction in Shetland, **Jarlshof** ⚐, Sumburgh (© **01950/460-112**), near the Sumburgh Airport. It has been called the most remarkable archaeological discovery in Britain. A violent storm in 1897 performed the first archaeological dig. Washing away sections of the large mound, it revealed huge stone walls. Excavations that followed turned up an astonishing array of seven distinct civilizations. The earliest was from the Bronze Age, but habitation continued at the site through the 1500s, from wheelhouse people to Vikings, from broch builders to medieval settlers. A manor house was built here in the 16th century by the treacherous Patrick Stewart, but it was sacked in 1609. The site is open April through September, daily from 9:30am to 6:30pm. Admission is £3.20 ($5.10) for adults, £2.50 ($4) for seniors, and £1.25 ($2) for children.

Also nearby is the **Sumburgh Lighthouse,** one of the many Scottish lighthouses constructed by the grandfather of Robert Louis Stevenson. The lighthouse is now fully automated. The property offers a self-catering four-bedroom cottage, costing £350 ($560) per week. Built in 1821, it can be visited by the public, but you must phone the Lerwick tourist office (© **01595/693-434**) for an appointment; reservations for the cottage can also be made with the owner, Catrina Canter, at © **01595/694-688.** Reserve at least 3 months in advance.

On the coast at the tip of Scatness, about 1.6km (1 mile) southwest of Jarlshof at the end of the Mainland, is the **Ness of Burgi,** which was a defensive Iron Age structure related to a broch.

Heading back north toward Lerwick, you can veer west for a trip to **St. Ninians Island** in the southwestern corner of Shetland. It's reached by going along B9122. The island is approached by what's called a *tombolo* (bridging sandbar). An early monastery once stood on this island, but it wasn't uncovered until 1958. Puffins often favor the islet, which has a pure white sandy beach on each side. The island became famous in 1958 when a group of students from Aberdeen came upon a rich cache of Celtic artifacts, mainly silverware, including brooches and other valuable pieces. Monks are believed to have hidden the treasure trove, fearing a Viking attack. The St. Ninian treasure is in the National Museum of Scotland at Edinburgh.

WHERE TO STAY & DINE

Sumburgh Hotel   This is an old favorite. Its turrets and towers were built in 1857 for the laird of Virkie, the Victorian descendant of Robert the Bruce. Set on 4.9 barren hectares (12 acres) of land jutting dramatically out to sea, it lies at the southernmost end of the Shetland Islands, at the end of A970. A modern addition completed in the 1960s doubled the size of the place, which contains the Voe Room restaurant (offering affordable dinners nightly) and two popular bars. Recent refurbishments have made the bedrooms more inviting.

Sumburgh Head, Virkie, Shetland ZE3 9JN. © **01950/460-201.** Fax 01950/460-394. www.sumburgh-hotel. zetnet.co.uk. 32 units. £65 ($104) double. Rates include Scottish breakfast. AE, MC, V. **Amenities:** Restaurant; 2 bars; limited room service; laundry service. *In room:* TV, coffeemaker, hair dryer, trouser press.

SCALLOWAY

On the western coast, 10km (6 miles) west of Lerwick, Scalloway was once the capital of Shetland. This town was the base for rescue operations in Norway during the darkest days of World War II. Still an important fishing port, Scalloway has been changed by the oil boom. New businesses have opened, attracting more and more people to the area, which has emerged after a long slumber into a prosperous and lively place in this remote corner of the world.

Dominating the town are the ruins of corbel-turreted medieval **Scalloway Castle** (© **01595/880-243**), commissioned by the dreaded Earl Patrick Stewart at the beginning of the 17th century and built with forced (slave) labor culled from the island's residents. After it was built, he imposed exorbitant taxes and fines on the islanders. In 1615, the Earl and all his sons were executed in Edinburgh, partly as a means of placating the islanders, partly because he rebelled against the powers of the central Scottish-British government. Admission is free; hours are those of the Shetland Woollen Company (see below), from which you must get the key to enter.

The **Shetland Woollen Company** (© **01595/880-243**) is open Monday through Friday from 9am to 5pm (in summer, also Sat 9am–5pm). You can see the processing and finishing of Shetland knitware, and then visit the showroom where a selection of garments is sold.

To escape to a beautiful area, ideal for long walks or drives, follow B9075 east off A970 to the top of a small sea inlet that will lead you to the surprisingly lush **Kergord.** This green valley contains forests ideal for long strolls.

WEST MAINLAND

It's said you can see more of Shetland from the **Scord of Weisdale** than from any other vantage point in the archipelago. This is a hill or plateau lying west of Weisdale that offers a dramatic and panoramic view of the Shetland. This vista changes constantly, depending on the time of the day, the weather, and the season, of course.

Shetland's only stone-polishing business operates at **Hjaltasteyn,** Whiteness, 14km (9 miles) west of Lerwick. Here gemstones are turned out from raw materials in fetching hand-wrought silver settings. Alas, the workshop isn't currently open to visitors. You can, however, visit the showroom at 161 Commercial St., Lerwick (© **01595/696-224**). It's open in summer only, Thursday through Saturday, Monday, and Tuesday from 9:15am to 4:45pm, and Wednesday from 10am to 4pm (closed daily 1–2pm for lunch).

Continuing north, you can watch high-quality jewelry being made at **Shetland Jewelry,** Soundside, Weisdale (© **01595/830-275**), where the artisans base many of their designs on ancient Celtic and Viking patterns. It's open Monday through Friday from 9am to 1pm and 2 to 5pm.

You can continue your tour of West Mainland by heading west along A971 toward Walls. You come first to **Staneydale Temple,** 4.5km (2¾ miles) outside Walls. This early Bronze Age (perhaps Neolithic) hall once had a timbered roof. It's called a temple because it bears a remarkable resemblance to similar sites on Malta, lending support to the theory that the early settlers of Shetland came from the Mediterranean.

Continuing past several lochs and sea inlets, you come to **Walls,** a hamlet built on the periphery of two voes (a local term for inlet). Its natural harbor is sheltered by the offshore islet of Vaila.

WHERE TO STAY & DINE

Burrastow House 🌟🌟 *(finds*   This is the most tranquil, idyllic retreat in the Shetlands. About 5km (3 miles) southwest of Walls, a 40-minute drive northwest of Lerwick, this simple but comfortable building was constructed in 1759 as a *haa* (home of the farm manager of a laird's estate) and has been a guesthouse since 1980. Set amid lands still used for grazing sheep, it lies at the widest section of a windswept peninsula with views of a cluster of rocky and sparsely inhabited islands. The well-furnished guest rooms evoke country-house living. There's one family suite, consisting of a double room and a twin room connected by a bathroom.

The food is the best on the island. The daily menu in the oak-paneled dining room is likely to include nettle-and-oatmeal fritters, mussel brose (a stew of mussels thickened with oatmeal), and monkfish with anchovy stuffing, lamb, and Scottish beef. Lunch, high tea, and upscale dinners are served daily. The proprietors ask that you call ahead if you want a hot meal, but they'll accommodate you with fresh-baked bread, cheese, and homemade soup if you just drop in. They offer a good vegetarian selection. The restaurant is closed Sunday and Monday to nonguests.

Walls, West Mainland, Shetland ZE2 9PD. © **01595/809-307.** Fax 01595/809-213. www.users.zetnet. co.uk/burrastow-house-hotel. 6 units. £130 ($208) double; £86 ($138) per person in family room. Rates include half-board. AE, DC, MC, V. Closed Jan–Mar. Pets accepted at staff discretion. **Amenities:** Restaurant. *In room:* TV (on request), coffeemaker, no phone.

SIDE TRIP TO PAPA STOUR

The "great island of priests," in the shape of a large starfish, Papa Stour lies off the west coast of Mainland, 40km (25 miles) northwest of Lerwick. As its name indicates, it was an early base for monks. Two centuries ago there was a leper colony here on the little offshore islet of Brei Holm.

Legend has it that its profusion of wildflowers had such a strong scent that old fishermen could use the perfume—borne far out on the wind—to fix their positions. Papa Stour is very isolated, and once it was feared the island might be depopulated, but about 26 settlers live here now.

In the darkest days of winter, bad weather can cut it off for days. But if you see it on a sunny day, it's striking. Encircled by pillars of rock and reefs, its sea caves, sculpted by turbulent winds and raging seas, are among the most impressive in Britain. The largest of these is **Kirstan's Hole,** extending some 73m (80 yd.).

Boats go to Papa Stour about seven times per day, 5 days a week, from West Burrafirth on Mainland, at a cost of £4.80 ($7.70). Call **Mr. Clark** at © **01595/810-460** for information on these constantly changing details.

WHERE TO STAY & DINE

Northouse *Finds* Within walking distance of the island's only pier, just outside Housa Voe (the only hamlet, with seven buildings), this stone croft is an unusual building. The foundations are Viking, and Dutch coins from the 1620s have been unearthed here. It's the domain of Andrew and Sabina Holt-Brook, who moved from the mainland of Scotland more than 20 years ago. Now owners of 12 hectares (30 acres) of windswept peninsula, they offer the only accommodations and meals on the island. The rooms are comfortable and inviting, and the "garden room" has its own entrance. Meals are served to both guests and nonguests, but for just a meal, call in advance. The working farm supplies the Holt-Brooks with free-range eggs and fresh vegetables. The inexpensive lunches are brown-bag affairs (homemade sandwiches and cakes) to be taken along while you enjoy the island's wild landscapes.

North-house, Papa Stour, Shetland ZE2 9PW. © **01595/873-238.** 4 units, 1 with private bathroom. £38–£40 ($61–$64) double. Rates include breakfast. No credit cards. Pets by arrangement. **Amenities:** Dining room; lounge. *In room:* Coffeemaker, hair dryer, no phone.

SIDE TRIP TO FOULA

This tiny, remote island is only 5km (3 miles) wide by 8km (5 miles) long, with five high peaks. Called the "Island West of the Sun," Foula may have been the Romans' legendary Thule. In local dialect, *foula* means "bird island"—and the name fits. Uncountable numbers of birds haunt the isle. Its towering sea cliffs include the second-highest cliff face in Britain, the **Kame,** at 370m (1,220 ft.). About 3,000 pairs of the world's great skuas, known as "bonxie," live here. You'll hear many stories about the rock-climbing prowess of locals who go in search of gulls' eggs.

The island lies 43km (27 miles) west of Scalloway on the west coast of Mainland, and the locals are vastly outnumbered by sheep. Until the beginning of the 19th century, Old Norse was the language spoken. Its 400 people remain very traditional. If you're lucky, you might see them dance the Foula reel, a classic dance in Shetland.

If the weather's right, a weekly mailboat sails to Foula from Walls on Mainland. Even in summer, the seas are likely to be turbulent, and in winter, Foula has been known to be cut off from the rest of Britain for weeks. The trip takes 2½ hours. **Loganair** also operates a summer service from Tingwall on Monday, Wednesday, and Friday; trip time is 15 minutes.

WHERE TO STAY & DINE

Because of the interest by visitors in recent years, some islanders have taken to offering accommodations that include half-board.

Mrs. Marion Taylor   Owners Bryan and Marion run this cozy modern farmhouse near the geographical center of the island, within walking distance of everything. The comfortable rooms in the main house have easy access to the large kitchen, whose brick hearth is the focal point of the farm. The cottage has two bedrooms, a sitting room, and a kitchen. There are no food shops on the island, so you'll have to bring your own supplies, as the rates for the cottage don't include meals. The Taylor's 2.8 hectares (7 acres) are a sheep farm, and they extend their income by knitting and spinning—you can order a custom-made, handknit sweater.

Leraback, Isle of Foula, Shetland ZE2 9PN. ℂ 01595/753-226. 3 units, none with private bathroom; 1 cottage. £55 ($88) double; £30 ($48) per day in cottage (sleeps up to 4). No credit cards. *In room:* TV, fridge, microwave, no phone.

NORTH MAINLAND

The most rugged scenery Shetland has to offer is in the northern part of the island of Mainland. Some visitors have found the area reminds them of Norway, and we agree. That's especially true in the tiny village of **Voe,** with its little wooden houses.

Heading north from Voe along A970, you'll reach the eastern junction of B9071, which will take you to **Vidlin,** where the **Lunna Kirk,** one of the oldest churches in the archipelago, is still used by its congregation. Construction began in 1753. The church has a "leper hole," from which the poor victims could listen to the sermon without being seen.

Heading west back to A970, continue north to **Mavis Grind,** a narrow isthmus marking the point where the North Mainland is at its most narrow. The touristy thing to do in North Mainland is to pause at Mavis Grind, take a couple of stones, and throw one to your right into the North Sea and the other to your left into the Atlantic Ocean.

Near the villages of **Brae** and **Busta,** you'll find some of the best food and hotels in Shetland. Oil contractors, helicopter pilots, and shipping executives sent by mainland companies to service the nearby Sullom Voe, site of the largest oil terminal in Europe, often stay in this area.

If you head north along A970, we suggest you take the secondary road going west to **Esha Ness** ★★, where you'll come upon the most dramatic cliff scenery not only in Shetland but in all Britain. This is a simply gorgeous area for **hiking.** On the way, 24km (15 miles) northwest of Brae, you'll pass the little fishing hamlet of **Hillswick,** opening onto the bay in Ura Firth.

WHERE TO STAY & DINE

Brae Hotel   Built in 1979, this modern building lies in the center of Brae, 45km (28 miles) north of Lerwick beside A970 about 1.6km (1 mile) south of the narrow isthmus that separates North from South Mainland. The small, pastel-toned guest rooms are reassuringly warm. Each comes with a small, shower-only bathroom. The restaurant serves affordable meals.

Brae, North Mainland, Shetland ZE2 9QJ. (C) **01806/522-456.** Fax 01806/522-026. 36 units. £79 ($126) double. Rates include Scottish breakfast. Discounts offered for stays of 4 or more days. AE, MC, V. **Amenities:** Restaurant; bar; billiard room. *In room:* TV, coffeemaker.

Busta House ★★   Busta House is the oldest continuously inhabited house in the Shetlands. Built in 1580, with ample extensions added in 1714 and 1983, it was the original *busta* (homestead) of the medieval Norwegian rulers of the island. Later inhabited by the island's laird, it once welcomed Elizabeth II at tea during her tour of the Shetlands on the royal yacht *Britannia.* The estate's long and tormented history includes episodes of multiple drownings, a handful of resident ghosts, and some of the most famous lawsuits in Britain. Some literary enthusiasts claim the house in all its drama was the inspiration for Dickens's *Bleak House.*

In recent times, the important economic agreement that paved the way for the construction of the massive Sullom Voe oil terminal (the Busta House Agreement) was signed here between the local government and Britain's multinational oil companies.

Rising above its own small harbor a short drive from A970, a 10-minute drive south of the village of Sullom, 2.5km (1½ miles) from Brae, the hotel has crow's-foot gables, stone walls measuring 2m (6 ft.) thick, and an appearance of a fortified manor house. The proprietors maintain the antique charm of the public rooms and the chintz-filled guest rooms, and prepare upscale dinners as well. (There's also a more affordable bar menu.)

Busta, near Brae, North Mainland, Shetland ZE2 9QN. (C) **01806/522-506.** Fax 01806/522-588. www.bustahouse.com. 20 units. £100 ($160) double. Rates include Scottish breakfast. Discounts offered for stays of 4 or more days. AE, DC, MC, V. **Amenities:** Restaurant; bar; business center; room service (6:30am–11:30pm); laundry service. *In room:* TV, dataport, coffeemaker, hair dryer.

SIDE TRIP TO YELL & UNST

The second largest island in the Shetlands, Yell measures 9.6km (6 miles) north to south, with a population that has shrunk to 1,000, down from its all-time high of 2,600 in 1841 shortly after Victoria came to the throne. This is the least cultivated of Scottish Islands because most of it lies under a peat blanket 3m (10 ft.) deep. The Yell Ferry, often making stormy crossings, is one of the "roll-on, roll-off" ferries sailing between Toft, near Mossbank on the mainland, to Ulstra at the southwesterly corner of Yell. The crossing from Toft to Ulstra takes about

25 minutes, with ferries generally leaving throughout the day at half-hour intervals. A car, driver, and adult passenger pays £4.60 ($7.35) 1 way, and booking for the ferry is possible Monday to Saturday 8:30am to 5pm by calling © **01957/722-259.**

From Yell, the northernmost point of Britain, remote and beautiful Unst is easy to reach. Drive along A968 to the little harbor at Gutcher, northeast of Yell. The **Shetland Island Coastal Marine Operations** (© **01957/722-259** for schedules) operates a ferry crossing from here fairly frequently every day. The cost is £3.50 ($5.60) for a car and driver, £1.50 ($2.40) for each extra adult, and 50p ($.80) per child. **Loganair** (© **01595/840-246**) flies to Unst from both Lerwick and Sumburgh, once a day from Monday to Friday.

Robert Louis Stevenson stayed on Unst for a time. His father, Alan Stevenson, was designing and building the Muckle Flugga Lighthouse on an outermost skerry, which is even farther north than Labrador.

Unst is steeped in folklore and legend. An **Old Norse longhouse,** believed to date from the 9th century, was excavated at Underhoull. The best beach is at **Skaw,** set against the backdrop of **Saxa Vord,** legendary home of the giant Saxi. A drive to the top will reward you with a view of the Burra Firth. Visitors go to Haroldswick to mail their cards and letters in the northernmost post office in the British Isles.

The roll-on/roll-off car ferry from Yell comes into Belmont. Nearby is **Muness Castle,** constructed in 1598 by Laurence Bruce, a relative of the notorious Earl Patrick Stewart who ruled Shetland so harshly. Adam Crawford, who designed Scalloway Castle for the ruling earls on Mainland, also drew up the plans for Muness. Built with rubble and known for its fine architectural detail, the castle was inhabited for less than a century. Normally it's open April through September, daily from 9am to 7pm. If it's closed, ask for the key at Mrs. Peterson's cottage across the way. For information, call © **01957/755-215.**

The ruins of the **Kirk of Lund,** dating from the Middle Ages, can also be seen on Unst. Like Lunna Kirk in Vidlin, it, too, had a "leper hole" through which victims could hear the service.

Unst is home of the **Hermaness Bird Reserve** ⟨, one of the most important ornithological sites in Britain. Ideal for scenic walks, its 182m (600-ft.) cliffs are filled with kittiwakes, razorbills, guillemots, and the inevitable puffins.

WHERE TO STAY & DINE

Baltasound Hotel *Finds*   Built 150 years ago for the local laird and converted into a hotel in 1939, this granite house sits in isolation beside the sea about .5km (¼ mile) from the hamlet of Baltasound. Many of the guests are bird-watchers and geologists. The simple, uncluttered bedrooms are in what locals call a "Scandinavian extension" jutting out to the building's side, sheathed with blackened wood siding. In 1992, the hotel was enlarged with a series of motel-like "chalet" rooms attached to the main building. The bar serves lunch and inexpensive dinners; the restaurant offers moderately priced dinners, which you should book in advance.

Baltasound, Unst, Shetland ZE2 9DS. © **01957/711-334.** Fax 01957/711-358. www.baltasound-hotel. shetland.co.uk. 25 units. £68 ($109) double. Rates include Scottish breakfast. MC, V. **Amenities:** Restaurant; bar. *In room:* TV, coffeemaker, hair dryer (on request).

Appendix:
Scotland in Depth

A small nation ("Tis a wee country, aye—but a bonny one"), Scotland is only 443km (275 miles) long and some 242km (150 miles) wide at its broadest. No Scot lives more than 65km (40 miles) from saltwater. But despite the small size of their country, the Scots have extended their influence around the world. And in this land of bagpipes, clans, and kilts, you'll find some of Europe's grandest scenery.

Inventor Alexander Graham Bell and explorers Mungo Park and David Livingstone came from Scotland. This country gave the world entrepreneur Andrew Carnegie, poet Robert Burns, novelist Sir Walter Scott, actor Sean Connery, singer Sheena Easton, and comedian/actor Billy Connolly. But, curiously, for a long time its most famous resident has been neither man nor woman but Nessie, the Loch Ness Monster.

The border is just a line on a map; you'll hardly be aware of crossing out of England into Scotland. Yet even though the two countries have been joined constitutionally since 1707, Scotland is very different from England and is very much its own country. (In fact, on July 1, 1999, Scotland was granted greater independence when a reform instituted by Prime Minister Tony Blair brought back regional government and a new Scottish Parliament was opened by Queen Elizabeth in Edinburgh.)

In Scotland, you'll discover mountains and glens, lochs and heather-covered moors, skirling bagpipes and twirling kilts, and rivers and streams filled with trout and salmon. Lush meadowlands are filled with sheep, and rocky coves and secret harbors wait for the adventurous. You can hear the sounds of Gaelic, admire the misty blue hills, and attend a Highland Gathering. You can schedule quiet contemplation or an activity-filled calendar. And in Scotland, you'll find one of Europe's biggest welcomes.

1 History 101

Much of the history of the Scots has been shaped by their country's location in a remote corner of northwestern Europe. Amazingly, Scotland encompasses 787 islands (although only about a fourth are inhabited). Its 10,004km (6,214 miles) of coastline are deeply penetrated by the Atlantic Ocean on the west and the often turbulent North Sea on the east. Most places lie only 97km (60 miles)

Dateline

- 6000 B.C. The earliest known residents of Scotland establish settlements on the Argyll Peninsula.
- 3000 B.C. Celtic tribes invade, making the use of Gaelic widespread.
- A.D. 82 Roman armies directed by Agricola push into southern Scotland; the Roman victories, however, are short-lived.

continues

inland. In fact, the sea has shaped Scotland's destiny more than any other element and bred a nation of seafarers, many of whom still earn their living on the water.

Scotland is a world apart, a distinctly unique nation within the United Kingdom. Just more than half the size of England, with only a tenth of England's population, it boasts more open spaces and natural splendor than England ever did. The Scots are hard to classify: They're generous yet have a reputation for stinginess, eloquent yet dour at times, and romantic at heart yet brutally realistic in their appraisals (especially of the English). Even the Romans couldn't subdue these Caledonians, and they remain Braveheart proud and fiercely independent.

But how did it all begin?

EARLY HISTORY   Scotland was a melting pot in its early history. Standing stones, *brochs* (circular stone towers), cromlechs, cairns, and burial chambers attest to its earliest occupation, but we know little about these first tribes and invaders. When the Roman armies decided to invade in A.D. 82, the land was occupied by a people the Romans called the Picts (Painted Ones). Despite spectacular bloodletting, the Romans were unsuccessful, and the building of Hadrian's Wall effectively marked the northern limits of their influence.

Parts of Hadrian's Wall still stand, but in England, not Scotland. The wall extends for 118km (73 miles) across the north of England, from the North Sea to the Irish Sea, its most interesting stretch consisting of 16km (10 miles) west of the town of Housesteads. If you're driving north from England into Scotland, you might want to stop and see the remains of this wall before penetrating the Border Country of Scotland.

By A.D. 500, the Picts were again attacked, this time by the Dalriada

A.D. 90 Romans abandon the hope of conquering Scotland, retreating to England and the relative safety of Hadrian's Wall.

500 Newcomers from Ireland, identified as Scots, invade from the west, mingling their bloodlines with Norse, Pictish, Celtic, and Teutonic tribes.

563 St. Columba establishes a mission on Iona, accelerating the movement established by earlier ecclesiastics to Christianize Scotland.

843 Kenneth MacAlpin unifies the Picts and the Scots.

1005–34 Malcolm II unites the four major tribes of Scotland into one roughly cohesive unit.

1124–53 David I builds monasteries, consolidates royal power and prestige, and imports clearly defined Norman values.

1266 The Hebrides and the coast of western Scotland are released from Norse control; the Donald clan consolidates power here into a semi-autonomous state within Scotland.

1272 Edward I of England embarks on an aggressive campaign to conquer both Wales and Scotland but is deflected by Robert the Bruce, among others.

1314 The victory of the Scots over the English armies at Bannockburn leads to the Treaty of Northampton (1328), formally recognizing Scotland's independence from England.

1468 The Orkney and the Shetland Islands are given to Scotland as part of the marriage dowry of a Norse princess to a Scottish king.

Late 1400s The Auld Alliance with France, a cynical arrangement based mostly on mutual distrust of England, is born.

1535 At the urging of Henry VIII of England, Parliament officially severs all ties with the Catholic Church, legally sanctioning the Reformation.

1559–64 John Knox lays out the rough outline of the Scottish Presbyterian Church.

1561 Queen Mary returns to Scotland from France.

1568 Mary is defeated and flees to England.

1572 John Knox dies; his work is continued by Andrew Melville.

Irish called Scots, who were successful. They established themselves on the Argyll Peninsula and battled and intermarried with the Picts. Britons emigrated from the south and Norsemen from the east, creating new bloodlines and migratory patterns. Druidism, a little-understood mystical form of nature worship whose most visible monuments are runic etchings and stone circles, flourished at this time. Languages of the era included a diverse array of Celtic and Norse dialects with scatterings of Low German and Saxon English.

The power of the Scotians, entrenched in western Scotland, was cemented when a missionary named Columba (later canonized) arrived from Ireland in 563. The rocky Hebridean island of Iona became the base for his Christian mission. Christianity, already introduced by Sts. Ninian and Mungo to Strathclyde and Galloway, became widespread.

If you have an interest in this early part of Scottish history, visit remote Iona, part of the Hebrides (see chapter 11, "The Hebridean Islands," for more information). More than any dull recitation of history, a visit here, especially to Iona Abbey, can recapture some of this land's dim, often unrecorded history.

THE MIDDLE AGES The Scots and the Picts were united in 843 under the kingship of an early chieftain named Kenneth MacAlpin, but it was the invasionary pressures from England and Scandinavia and the unifying force of Christianity that molded Scotland into a relatively coherent unit. Under Malcolm II (1005–34), the British and the Angles, who occupied the southwest and southeast of the Scottish mainland, merged with the Scots and the Picts. Malcolm's son and heir, Duncan, was murdered by Macbeth of Moray, and this event fueled the plotline of Shakespeare's famous "Scottish play."

- 1587 Mary Queen of Scots is executed.
- 1603 Mary's son, James VI of Scotland, accedes to the throne of England as James I and unifies the two countries.
- 1689 Parliament strips the uncompromising Catholic James II of his crown and imports the Protestant William and Mary from Holland to replace him.
- 1746 Bonnie Prince Charlie's attempt to reclaim his grandfather's throne ends in defeat at the Battle of Culloden, destroying any hope of a Stuart revival.
- 1750–1850 England and Scotland experience rapid industrialization; the Clearances strip many crofters of their farms, creating epic bitterness and forcing new patterns of Scottish migrations.
- 1789 The French Revolution ignites; British monarchists tighten their grip on civil unrest in Scotland.
- Late 19th century An astonishing success in the sciences propels Scotland into the role of arbiter of industrial know-how around the globe.
- Mid–20th century The decline of traditional industries, especially shipbuilding, painfully redefines the nature of Scottish industry.
- 1970 The discovery of North Sea oil deposits brings new vitality to Scotland.
- 1973 Scotland, as part of the United Kingdom, becomes a member of the Common Market.
- 1974 The old counties or shires are reorganized; many regions are renamed.
- 1979 Scots vote on devolution (separation from England): 33% vote yes, 31% vote no, and 36% don't vote at all.
- 1981 The largest oil terminal in Europe is launched at Sullom Voe in the Shetland Islands.
- 1988 Scottish nationalism revives under the marching cry of "Scotland in Europe"; Pan Am Flight 103 from London crashes at Lockerbie, killing all passengers, including some locals.

continues

Glamis Castle, outside Dundee, contains Duncan's Hall, where the Victorians imagined Macbeth killed Duncan. See chapter 9, "Aberdeen & the Tayside & Grampian Regions," for details on Glamis.

Malcolm III's marriage to an English princess, Margaret, furthered the Anglicization of the Scottish Lowlands. A determined woman of strong ideas, she imported English priests into Scotland and carried out church reforms that soon replaced St. Columba's Gaelic form of Christianity. Her Anglicization efforts and introduction of the English language as a teaching tool laid important groundwork for making Scotland into a potential English kingdom. She led a life of great piety and was canonized as St. Margaret in 1251.

While Europe's feudal system was coming to full flower, Scotland was

- **1992** The Scots continue to express dissatisfaction with English rule: Polls show one out of two favor independence.
- **1996** A psychopath guns down 16 kids and a teacher in one of Britain's worst mass-murder sprees.
- **1997** A sheep is cloned for the first time; Scotland votes to establish a legislature of its own for the first time since 1707.
- **1999** British Prime Minister Tony Blair holds off threats from the Nationalist Party as his own Labour Party triumphs in national elections; on July 1, Queen Elizabeth opens a new Scottish Parliament for the first time in 300 years.
- **2001** Scottish Parliament opens to a bad press—goes from the so-called "silly season to the totally absurd."
- **2003** Scotland joins England in sending troops to Iraq.

preoccupied with the territorial battles of clan allegiances and the attempt to define its borders with England. Cultural assimilation with England continued under David I (1081–1153), who made land grants to many Anglo-Norman families, providing Scotland with a feudal aristocracy and bringing in ancient names like Fraser, Seton, and Lindsay. He also embarked on one of the most lavish building sprees in Scottish history, erecting many abbeys, including Jedburgh, Kelso, Melrose, and Dryburgh. You can still see these abbeys or their ruins.

In 1266, after about a century of Norse control, the foggy and windswept Western Isles were returned to Scotland following the Battle of Largs. Despite nominal allegiance to the Scottish monarch, this region's inhabitants quickly organized themselves around the Donald (or MacDonald) clan, which for nearly 100 years was one of the most powerful, ruling its territory almost as an independent state. The honorary title of their patriarch, Lord of the Isles, is still one of the formal titles used on state occasions by Britain's Prince of Wales. To learn more about what may be the most important clan in Scottish history, you can visit the Clan Donald Visitor Centre at Armadale on the Isle of Skye (see chapter 11).

In the meantime, real trouble was brewing in the south. Edward I, ambitious Plantagenet king of England, yearned to rule over an undivided nation incorporating England, Scotland, and Wales. Successful at first, he set up John de Balliol as a vassal king to do homage to him for Scotland. Many of Scotland's legendary heroes lived during this period: Sir William Wallace (1270–1305), who drove the English out of Perth and Stirling; Sir James Douglas, the Black Douglas (1286–1330), who terrorized the English borders; and Robert the Bruce (1274–1329), who finally succeeded in freeing Scotland from England. Crowned Robert I at Scone in 1306 in defiance of the English, Robert the Bruce decisively defeated Edward II of England at the 1314 Battle of Bannockburn.

Scotland's independence was formally recognized in the 1328 Treaty of Northampton, inaugurating a heady but short-lived separation from England.

For more legend and lore about those towering Scottish heroes William Wallace and Robert the Bruce, see chapter 8, "Fife & the Central Highlands." You can also visit Stirling Castle, which loomed so large in Scottish history. If you'd rather see where the crucial Battle of Bannockburn took place, you can visit the Bannockburn Heritage Centre outside Stirling (see chapter 8).

In 1468, the Orkneys and the Shetlands, Norse to the core, were brought into the Scottish web of power as part of the marriage dowry of the Norse princess Margaret to James III. This acquisition was the last successful expansion of Scottish sovereignty during the period when Scottish power and independence were at their zenith. It was at this time the Scots entered with the French into an alliance that was to have far-reaching effects. The line of Stuart (or Stewart) kings, so named because the family had become powerful as stewards of the English king, were generally accepted as the least troublesome of a series of potential evils. Real power, however, lay with Scotland's great lords, patriarchs of the famous clans. Jealous of both their bloodlines and their territories, they could rarely agree on anything other than their common distrust of England.

THE REFORMATION   The passions of the Reformation burst on an already turbulent Scottish scene in the person of John Knox, a devoted disciple of the Geneva Protestant John Calvin and a bitter enemy of both the Catholic Church and the Anglican Church. Knox became famous for the screaming insults he heaped on ardently Catholic Queen Mary and for his absolute lack of a sense of humor. His polemics were famous—in his struggle against Queen Mary, he wrote his *First Blast of the Trumpet Against the Monstrous Regiment of Women*. His was a peculiar mixture of piety, conservatism, strict morality, and intellectual independence that's still a pronounced feature of the Scottish character.

Knox's teachings helped shape the democratic form of Scottish government and set the Scottish Church's austere moral tone for generations to come. He focused on practical considerations as well as religious ones: church administration and funding, and the relationship between church and state. Foremost among the tenets were provisions for a self-governing congregation and pure allegiance to the Word of God as contained in meticulous translations of the Old and New Testaments. In Edinburgh, you can still visit the John Knox House, where the reformer lived (see chapter 4, "Edinburgh & the Lothian Region," for more information).

On Knox's 1562 death, his work was continued by Scots-born, Geneva-trained Andrew Melville, who hated ecclesiastical tyranny even more (if that were possible) than Knox himself. Melville reorganized the Scottish universities and emphasized classical studies and the study of the Bible in its original Hebrew and Greek. Under his leadership emerged a clearly defined Scottish Presbyterian Church whose elected leaders were responsible for practical as well as spiritual matters.

Later, the Church of Scotland's almost obsessive insistence on self-government led to endless conflicts, first with the Scottish and then, after unification, with the British monarchs.

MARY QUEEN OF SCOTS   When Mary Stuart, Queen of Scots (1542–87), took up her rule, she was a Roman Catholic of French upbringing trying to govern an unruly land to which she was a relative newcomer. Daughter of Scotland's James V and France's Mary of Guise, she became queen when 6 days old. She was sent to be educated in France and at age 15 married the heir to the French throne; she returned to Scotland only after his death. Mary then set out on two roads that were anathema to the Scots—to make herself absolute monarch in the French style and to impose Roman Catholicism. The first alienated the lords who held the real power, and the second made her the enemy of John Knox and the Calvinists. After a series of disastrous political and romantic alliances and endless abortive episodes of often indiscreet intrigue, her life was ended by the headsman's ax in England. The execution order was reluctantly issued by her cousin Elizabeth I, who considered Mary's presence an incitement to civil unrest and a threat to the stability of the English throne.

Of all the towering figures in Scottish history, only Mary Queen of Scots left an extensive trail of palaces and castles that you can still visit. Begin in the Borders at Mary Queen of Scots House (see chapter 5, "The Borders & Galloway Regions," for more information) and go on to the Palace of Holyroodhouse in Edinburgh (see chapter 4), where her Italian secretary, David Rizzio, was stabbed 56 times in front of her. The queen used to come to Falkland Palace for hunting and hawking and lived at Stirling Castle as an infant monarch for the first 4 years of her life (see chapter 8).

The power of the great lords of Scotland was broken only in 1603, when Mary's son, James VI of Scotland, assumed the throne of England as James I, Elizabeth's heir. James succeeded where his doomed mother had failed. He was the first of the Stuarts to occupy the English throne, and his coronation effectively united England and Scotland.

UNION WITH ENGLAND   Despite the hopes for peace that accompanied the union, religion almost immediately became a prime source of discontent. From their base in England, the two Stuart kings attempted to promote a Church of Scotland governed by bishops, in opposition to the Presbyterian Church's self-ruling organization. So incensed were the Scots that in 1638 they signed the National Covenant, which not only reasserted the Reformation's principles but also questioned the king's right to make laws, a role the Covenanters believed should be filled by Parliament. However, the monarch was still allowed a role, unlike the position the Puritans took in England.

Charles I, king of England from 1625 to 1649, believed strongly in the divine right of kings. When Parliament stripped away much of his authority in 1642, Charles fled north to organize an army against the Parliamentary forces centered in London. A civil war ensued, and the forces of Parliament were led to victory by Oliver Cromwell (1599–1658). Charles fled to Scotland, but the Scots turned him over to Parliament, and in 1649 he was convicted of treason and beheaded. Under the Commonwealth setup, Cromwell assumed a dominant political role and became Lord Protector in 1653. King in all but name, he ruled England until his death.

But trouble brewed in Scotland. The death of Charles I led to deep divisions in the country, which finally openly defied Cromwell, proclaiming Charles II

Tips **A Scot Is Not a Scotch**

Remember one thing: Scotch is a whisky and not the name of the proud people who inhabit the country. They're called **Scots,** and the adjective is **Scottish.** Don't worry—if you forget and call them Scotch, they'll forgive you. What they won't forgive is calling them English.

king. The Scots even launched abortive invasions of England. Cromwell's forces finally defeated the Scots at Dunbar in 1650. For nearly 9 years (1651–60), Scotland was under Commonwealth military occupation, although the result of that invasion had virtually nothing to do with what you'll see as a visitor today. Religious friction continued, however, after the restoration of Charles II to the English throne.

THE JACOBITES   In 1689, when the English Parliament stripped Catholic James II of his crown and imported Protestant monarchs William and Mary from Holland, the exiled ex-king and then his son James Edward (the Old Pretender) became focal points for Scottish unrest. The Jacobites (the name comes from *Jacobus,* the Latin form of James) attempted unsuccessfully in 1715 to place the Old Pretender on the English throne and restore the Stuart line. Although James died in exile, his son Charles Edward (the Young Pretender), better known as Bonnie Prince Charlie, carried on his father's dream. Charismatic but with an alcohol-induced instability, he was the central figure of the 1745 Jacobite uprising. For more legend and lore about Bonnie Prince Charlie, see chapter 11.

Although the revolt was initially promising because of the many Scottish adherents who crossed religious lines to rally to the cause, the Jacobite forces were crushed at the Battle of Culloden, near Inverness, by a larger English army led by the duke of Cumberland. Many supporters of the Pretender's cause were killed in battle, some were executed, and others fled to the United States and other safe havens. Fearing a rebirth of similar types of Scottish nationalism, the clan system was rigorously suppressed; clans that supported the Jacobite cause lost their lands, and, until 1782, the wearing of Highland dress was made illegal. Ten kilometers (6 miles) southeast of Inverness, you can still visit the historic battlefield at Culloden (see chapter 10, "Inverness & the West Highlands," for more information).

The Young Pretender himself was smuggled unglamorously out of Scotland, assisted by Flora MacDonald, a resident of the obscure Hebridean island of South Uist. One of the era's most visible Scottish heroines, she has ever since provided fodder for the Scottish sense of romance. The Bonnie Prince dissipated himself in Paris and Rome, and the hopes of an independent Scotland were buried forever.

ECONOMIC GROWTH & THE INDUSTRIAL REVOLUTION   During the 18th century, the Scottish economy underwent a radical transformation of growth and diversification. The British government, fearing civil unrest, commissioned one of its most capable generals to build roads and bridges throughout the country, presumably to increase military access from London in the event of a revolt—however, they actually encouraged business and commerce.

As trade with British overseas colonies, England, and Europe increased, the great ports of Aberdeen, Glasgow, and Leith (near Edinburgh) flourished. The merchants of Glasgow grew rich on a nearly monopolistic tobacco trade with Virginia and the Carolinas, until the outbreak of the Revolution sent American tobacco elsewhere. Other forms of commerce continued to enrich a battalion of shrewd Scots.

The 1789 outbreak of the French Revolution engendered so much Scottish sympathy for the cause that a panicked government in London became more autocratic than ever in its attempts to suppress antimonarchical feelings.

The infamous Clearances (1750–1850) changed forever Scotland's demographics. Small farmers, or crofters, were expelled from their ancestral lands to

The Stone of Destiny, Home at Last

After a rocky journey, the Stone of Scone or Stone of Destiny has finally been returned to Scotland. The stone is physically only a block of sandstone, measuring 26 inches long and 16 inches wide and weighing 336 pounds. But it's not just a stone: Revered for centuries as a holy relic, it allegedly came from the Middle East, and in biblical times Jacob is said to have used the stone as a pillow.

The stone was used at Dunadd, Iona, and Dunstaffnage for enthroning the Dalriada Irish Monarchs called Scots. Later it was moved to Scone, and in 1292 John Balliol became the last king to be crowned on the stone in Scotland. So powerful was its legend that Edward I took it to England in 1296, believing possession of the stone gave him sovereignty over Scotland. There it stayed, under the coronation chair in Westminster Abbey. In 1328, the Treaty of Northampton, recognizing Scotland's independence, returned the stone to Scotland, but the English reneged on the promise and the stone never moved from Westminster Abbey.

On Christmas Day 1950, the stone was taken from the abbey by a group of Scottish Nationalists. No one knows where it went then, but it was found about 4 months later in Arbroath Abbey and returned to Westminster. A rumor went around that the found stone was actually a replica and that the replica was carted back to London, but this has never been proved.

In 1996, the Stone of Destiny left Westminster Abbey by Land Rover, crossing from England into Scotland at the border town of Coldstream, where a small but moving ceremony was held. On November 30 of that year, the stone proceeded with pomp and circumstance up the Royal Mile in Edinburgh to its permanent home beside the Scottish Crown Jewels in Edinburgh Castle, where you can see it today (see chapter 4).

Scots hailed the return of the stone after 700 years in English captivity. Yet not all are pleased with the return of the stone. Some have denounced it as a "cheap political ploy," especially as the Queen claims she's "lending" it to her Scottish subjects—the idea is that after 7 centuries, possession is nine tenths of the law, and it can be called back to London for a future coronation.

Some Scots want to see the stone returned to Scone. "Edinburgh has no claim, legally, morally, or whatever, to the Stone of Scone," said Andrew R. Robinson, administrator of Scone Castle. "It's not called the Stone of Edinburgh, is it?"

make way for sheep grazing. Increased industrialization, continued civil unrest, migration into urban centers, and a massive wave of emigration to the United States, Canada, Australia, South Africa, and New Zealand all contributed to a changing national demographic and a dispersal of the Scottish ethic throughout the world.

Meanwhile, rapid progress in the arts, sciences, and education and the new industrial age meshed neatly with the Scottish genius for thrift, hard work, shrewdness, and conservatism. The 19th century produced vast numbers of prominent Scots who made broad and sweeping contributions to all fields of endeavor. Many of the inventions that altered the history of the developing world were either invented or installed by Scottish genius and industry.

THE 20TH CENTURY   Scotland endured bitter privations during the Great Depression and the two world wars. In the 1960s and 1970s, Scotland found that, like the rest of Britain, its aging industrial plants couldn't compete with more modern commercial competition from abroad. The most visible decline occurred in the shipbuilding industries. The vast Glasgow shipyards that once produced some of the world's great ocean liners went bankrupt. The companies that produced automobiles were wiped out during the 1930s. Many commercial enterprises once controlled by Scots had been merged into English or multinational conglomerates.

However, all wasn't bleak on the Scottish horizon. The 1970 discovery of North Sea oil by British Petroleum boosted the economy considerably and provided jobs for thousands of workers. Oil has continued to play a prominent role in the Scottish economy. In 1981, the largest oil terminal in Europe opened at Sullom Voe in the remote Shetland Islands.

As part of the United Kingdom, Scotland became a member of the European Common Market in 1973, although many Scots—perhaps owing to their long-time isolationism—opposed entry. Some voters expressed a fear that membership would take away hunks of their rights of self-government and determination. In 1974, Scotland underwent a drastic revision of its counties, and many regions were renamed. Tayside, for example, was carved out of the old counties of Perth and Angus.

A landmark scientific breakthrough occurred in 1997. The Scots had always contributed almost disproportionately to the world's sciences and technology. Now the land that gave us Sir Alexander Fleming, a Nobel Prize winner for discovering penicillin, gave us the first cloned sheep. The issue of *Nature* for February 27, 1997, reported the event, the work of scientists in Roslin. Dolly was the first lamb to be produced by cloning the udder cells of an adult sheep. In the summer of 1997, another major step was taken, and Polly was created, a lamb that has a human gene in every cell of its body. The work was hailed as a milestone. Animals with human genes (at least in theory) could be used to produce hormones or other biological products to treat human diseases or even to produce organs for human transplant.

In 1999, under Prime Minister Tony Blair's reforms, Scotland was allowed to elect its own legislature for the first time since its 1707 union with England. A total of 129 Scots were elected to this newly formed Parliament. Unlike the Welsh Parliament, the Scottish Parliament, centered at Edinburgh, has taxing powers and can make laws and can pursue such matters has health, education, public transportation, and public housing. Scotland is still represented in the main British Parliament in London. Scotland, however, must bow to the greater will of Britain in matters of foreign policy.

The Scottish Parliament got off to a bad start in 2000, with Scotland's 21 robustly competitive newspapers writing of "the silly season" or the "totally absurd." The press noted that members of Parliament awarded lawmakers with commemorative medals before they had done anything, granted bonuses, and fretted about parking spaces and vacation grants instead of tackling some of the country's more serious problems, such as a feudal landowning system. Some lawmakers found themselves heckled in the streets, and they had to endure the bite of such popular comics as Billy Connolly, who dismissed the body "as a wee pretendy Parliament." This characterization was most dramatically illustrated in 2003 when Scotland, in spite of widespread opposition on the homefront, along with England and Wales, sent soldiers and equipment to do battle in Iraq, toppling the dictator Saddam Hussein.

On a more optimistic front, Scotland is turning a strong face to the world, with its abundant natural resources in oil, water, gas, and coal. Its high-tech industries have played an important role in the technological revolution, and today the country produces 13% of Europe's personal computers, 45% of Europe's workstations, and 50% of Europe's automated banking machines. Everything in the country is loosening up—blue laws are giving way, later hours are being kept, nightlife is looking up, and ecotourism is being developed. Scotland's time-tested crafts (woolen tweeds and knitwear) are thriving, the market for Scotch whisky has burgeoned all around the world, and tourists are visiting in record numbers.

As Scotland goes deeper into the 21st century, there's a new esprit in the land. Scots are on a roll, declaring that their country is not a mere tartan theme park.

And speaking of tartans, nothing has shaken up the identity of Scotland more than the new kilts designed by Howie Nicholsby of Edinburgh. To model his new kilt design, Howie secured tough rugby star Chris Capaldi. The kilt is transparent—and in pink, no less.

Is nothing sacred?

2 A Portrait of the Scots

LANGUAGE   In Scotland's earliest history, its prevailing tongue was the Celtic language, Gaelic, along with a smattering of Norse dialects. When English was introduced and Scottish English developed, it borrowed heavily not only from Gaelic but also from Scandinavian, Dutch, and French. In the 15th and 16th centuries, when Scotland had close ties to France, French was a literary language of precision and grace, and it was the language of Mary Queen of Scots, who spoke no Gaelic at all. After the Scottish court moved to England in 1603, Scottish English was looked on as a rather awkward dialect.

As the centuries progressed, the ancient and complex Gaelic diminished in importance, partly because the British government's deliberate policy was to make English the language of all Britain. By the 1980s, less than 2% of the Scottish population understood Gaelic. Most of those who still speak it live in the northwestern Highlands and in the Hebridean Islands—especially the Isle of Skye, where about 60% of the population still use Gaelic.

Scottish English never developed the linguistic class divisions that exist so strongly in England among upper-, middle-, and lower-class speech patterns. Throughout most of its English-speaking history, the hardships of Scotland were suffered in common by a society that was well knit and had few barriers between the classes. Social snobbery was relatively unknown and the laird (estate owner) and his man conversed as equals.

At the end of the 20th century, the great leveling effects of TV and radio had begun to even out some of the more pronounced burrs and lilts of the Scottish tongue. However, the dialect and speech patterns of the Scots are still rich and evocative. Today, after years of struggle, Scottish students are rewarded with approval by pro-Scots educators when they say, "Whos all comin tae the jiggin?" ("Who's coming to the dance?"). This increasing pride in the Scottish language is in direct contrast to what happened in classrooms back in, say, the 1950s. At that time, students were under a constant threat of a whack from a tawse (leather strap) if they blurted out a single *aye*.

HIGHLAND GAMES & GATHERINGS Highland Gatherings or Games have their origins in the fairs organized by the tribes or clans for the exchange of goods. At these gatherings, there were often trials of strength among the men, and the strongest were selected for the chief's army.

The earliest games were held more than 1,000 years ago. The same tradition is maintained today: throwing hammers, putting rounded stones found in the rivers, tossing tree trunks, and running in flat races and up steep hillsides. Playing the bagpipes and performing dances have always been part of the gatherings. The Heavies, a breed of gigantic men, draw the most attention with their prowess. Of all the events, the most popular and most spectacular is the tossing of the caber (the throwing of a great tree trunk).

Queen Victoria, who had a deep love for Scotland (which was dramatized in the film *Mrs. Brown*), popularized the Highland Games, which for many decades had been suppressed after the failure of the 1745 rebellion. In 1848, the queen and her consort, Prince Albert, attended the Braemar Gathering and saw Duncan, her *ghillie* (a term that originally meant a male attendant or a Scottish Highland chief, today it is mainly used to mean a fishing and hunting guide; Duncan was said to have been the queen's lover), win the race up the hill of Craig Choinnich, as she recorded in her journal.

The most famous gathering nowadays is at Braemar, held in late August or early September and patronized by the royal family. When that chief of chiefs takes the salute, Queen Elizabeth is fulfilling a role assumed by a predecessor of hers in the 11th century.

Other major games are held at Ballater (Grampian), Aberdeen, Elgin, and Newtonmore.

CLANS, TARTANS & KILTS To the outsider, Scotland's deepest traditions appear to be based on the clan system of old with all the familiar paraphernalia of tartans and bagpipes. However, this is a romantic memory, and in any case, a good part of the Scots—the 75% of the population who live in the central Lowland, for example—have little or no connection with the clansmen of earlier times.

The clan tradition dates from the tribal units of the country's earliest Celtic history. Power was organized around a series of chieftains who exacted loyalties from the inhabitants of a particular region in exchange for protection against exterior invasions. The position of chieftain wasn't hereditary, and land was owned by the clan, not by the chieftain. Clan members had both rights and duties. Rigidly militaristic and paternalistic—the stuff with which Scottish legend is imbued—the clan tradition is still emphasized today, albeit in a much friendlier fashion than when claymores and crossbows threatened a bloody death or dismemberment for alleged slights on a clan's honor.

Chieftains were absolute potentates, with life and death power over members and interlopers, although they were usually viewed as patriarchs actively engaged in the perpetuation of the clan's bloodlines, traditions, and honor. The entourage of a chieftain always included bodyguards, musicians (harpers and pipers), a spokesman (known as a tatler), and—perhaps most important to latter-day students of clan traditions—a bard. The bard's role was to sing, to exalt the role of the clan and its heroes, to keep a genealogical record of births and deaths, and to compose or recite epic poems relating to the clan's history.

How the Scots Say It

aber   river mouth
ach   field
aird   promontory
alt   stream
auch   field
auld   old
baillie   magistrate
bal   hamlet or tiny village
ben   peak, often rugged
birk   birch tree
brae   hillside, especially along a river
brig   bridge
broch   circular stone tower
burn   stream
cairn   heap of stone piled up as memorial or landmark
ceilidh   Scottish hoedown with singing, music, and tall tales
clach   stone
clachan   hamlet
close   narrow passage leading from the street to a court or tenement
craig   rock
creel   basket
croft   small farm worked by a tenant, often with hereditary rights
cromlech, dolmen   prehistoric tomb or monument consisting of a large flat stone laid across upright stones
dram   ⅛ fluid ounce
drum   ridge
dun   fortress, often in a lake, for refuge in times of trouble
eas   waterfall
eilean   island
factor   manager of an estate
fell   hill
firth   arm of the sea reaching inland

Most of the clans were organized during two distinctly different eras of Scottish history. One of the country's oldest and largest is Clan Donald, whose original organization occurred during the early mists of the Christianization of Scotland and whose headquarters has traditionally been Scotland's northwestern coast and western islands. The fragmentation of Clan Donald into subdivisions (which include the Sleat, the Dunyveg, the Clanranald, and the Keppoch clans) happened after the violent battles of succession over control of the clan in the 1400s. These feuds so weakened the once powerful unity of the MacDonalds that a new crop of former vassal tribes in northwestern Scotland declared their independence and established new clans of their own. These included the Mackintoshes, the Macleans, the MacNeils, the Mackinnons, and the MacLeods.

gait   street (in proper names)
gil   ravine
glen   a small valley
haugh   water meadow
how   burial mound
howff   small, cozy room or meeting place
inver   mouth of a river
kil, kin, kirk   church
kyle   narrows of ancient or unknown origin
land   house built on a piece of ground considered as property
larig   mountain pass
links   dunes
loch   lake
machair   sand dune, sometimes covered with sea grass
mon   hill
muir   moor
mull   cape or promontory
ness   headland
neuk   nose
pend   vaulted passage
provost   mayor
reek   smoke
ross   cape
schist   highly compact crystalline rock formation
strath   broad valley
tarbert   isthmus
tolbooth   old town hall (often with prison)
uig   sheltered bay
uisge   water
uisge beatha   water of life, whisky
way   bay
wynd   alley

Meanwhile, the giant Celtic earldoms of eastern Scotland disintegrated and Norman influences from the south became more dominant. Clans whose earliest makeup might have been heavily influenced by Norman bloodlines include Clan Frasier (from the French *des fraises*, because of the strawberry leaves on the family's coat of arms), de Umfraville, and Rose. Other clans adapted their Celtic names, like Clan Robertson (Celtic Clan Donnachaidh) and Clan Campbell (Celtic Diarmid).

Simultaneously, in the Borders between England and Scotland, families and clans with differing sets of traditions and symbols held a precarious power over one of Britain's most heavily contested regions, enduring or instigating raids on their territories from both north and south. But despite the rich traditions of the

Garb o' the Gods

A memorable photograph from the handover of Hong Kong may spare the First Battalion of the Black Watch from having to answer the question most frequently put to men in kilts. As the flags were being lowered at the Cenotaph, a rush of wind lifted the tartan fabrics from the backside of Lance Cpl. Lee Wotherspoon and revealed nothing at all but his backside. He received a lot of mail and an admiring review from a gay publication in France.

—Warren Hoge, *New York Times* (1998)

Although not every visitor to Scotland is descended from a clan, almost all are familiar with plaids and the traditions associated with them. Over the centuries, each clan developed a distinctive pattern to be worn by its members, presumably to better identify its soldiers in the heat of battle. (Today, *tartan* is used interchangeably with *plaid,* but the word *tartan* originally referred specifically to a mantle of cloth draped over the back and shoulders.)

Kilts enjoy an ancient history. Checkered tartans were first mentioned in a 1471 English inventory. The clans developed special dyeing and weaving techniques, with colors and patterns reflecting their flair and imagination. The craft of dyeing was raised to an art that was a point of pride for the clan: Alder bark, steeped in hot water, produces a black dye; gorse, broom, and knapweed produce shades of green; cup moss produces purple; dandelion leaves produce magenta; bracken and heather produce yellow; white lichens produce red; and indigo had to be imported for blue.

When Bonnie Prince Charlie launched his abortive rebellion in 1745, he used tartans as a symbol of his army, and this threatened the English enemy so much that public display of tartans was banned for a period after his defeat. Tartans came into high fashion in Queen Victoria's day,

Lowland and Border clans, it's the traditions of the Highland clans (with their costumes, bagpipes, speech patterns, and grandly tragic struggles) that have captured the imagination of the world.

The clans had broken down long before Sir Walter Scott wrote his romantic novels about them and long before Queen Victoria made Scotland socially fashionable. The clans today represent a cultural rather than a political power. The best place to see the remnants of their tradition in action is at any traditional Highland gathering, although battalions of bagpipers seem to show up at everything from weddings and funerals to political rallies, parades, and civic events throughout Scotland.

3 A Taste of Scotland

FROM ANGUS BEEF TO HAGGIS   For many years, restaurants in Scotland were known mainly for their modest prices, watery overcooked vegetables, and boiled meats. But you need no longer expect a diet of oats, fried fish, and greasy chips—in the past 20 or so years, there has been a significant improvement in when she and her kilt-wearing German consort, Albert, made all things Scottish popular.

Today, there are at least 300 tartans, each subtly distinct from its neighbor and all available for sale in Scotland's shops and markets. If you're not fortunate enough to be of Scottish extraction, Queen Victoria long ago authorized two Lowland designs as suitable garb for Sassenachs (the English and, more remotely, the Americans).

Few people realize that from 6.3m to 9m (7 yd.–10 yd.) of tartan wool cloth goes into the average kilt. Even fewer non-Scots know what's actually worn beneath those folds strapped over the muscular thighs of a parading Scotsman. For a Highlander, the answer to that question is nothing, an answer that goes along with such defenders of ancient tradition who hold that only a Stewart can wear a Stewart tartan, only a Scotsman looks good in a kilt, and only a foreigner would stoop to wearing anything under it.

Alas, commercialism has reared its head with the introduction of undershorts to match the material making up bagpipe players' kilts. A story is told of a colonel who heard a rumor that the soldiers of his elite Highland Light Infantry regiment were mollycoddling themselves with undershorts. The next day, his eyebrows bristling, he ordered the entire regiment to undress in front of him. To his horror, half a dozen of his soldiers had disgraced the regiment by putting on what only an Englishman would wear. He publicly ordered the offending garments removed, and when he gave the order the next day to drop your kilts, not a soldier in the regiment had on the trews (close-cut tartan shorts).

Even in today's general decline of standards, the mark of a man in the Highlands is still whether he can abide the drafts up his thighs and the feel of wool cloth against his tender flesh.

Scottish cookery. There was a time when the Scot going out for dinner would head for the nearest hotel, but independent restaurants are now opening everywhere, often by newly arrived immigrants, along with bistros and wine bars.

More and more restaurants are offering "Taste of Scotland" menus of traditional dishes prepared with the freshest local ingredients, a culinary program initiated by the Scottish Tourist Board. Scotland's culinary strength is in its fresh raw ingredients, ranging from seafood, beef, and game to vegetables and native fruits.

One of Scotland's best-known exports is pedigree **Aberdeen Angus beef.** In fact, ye olde roast beef of England often came from Scotland. Scottish **lamb** is known for its tender, tasty meat. A true connoisseur can taste the difference in lamb by its grazing grounds, ranging from the coarse pastureland and seaweed of the Shetlands to the heather-clad hills of the mainland.

Game plays an important role in the Scottish diet, ranging from woodcock, red deer, and grouse to the rabbit and hare in the crofter's kitchen. And **fish** in this land of seas, rivers, and lochs is a mainstay, from salmon to the pink-fleshed

Impressions

It is not exactly true that you have to have grown up eating haggis—sheep's offal cooked in a sheep's stomach—to enjoy it. Not when it has been taken out of the sheep's stomach (the major turnoff) and turned into a tiny layer cake with puréed turnips and mashed potatoes and given the hilariously over-the-top name of gateaux of haggis, neeps, and tatties with whisky butter sauce. I licked my plate.

—Marian Burros, *In Britain* (1997)

brown trout to the modest herring that's transformed into the elegant kipper (the best are the Loch Fyne kippers). Scottish smoked salmon is, of course, a delicacy known worldwide.

The good news is that the word "eclectic" now describes many restaurants in Scotland. To cite only an example or two, fresh salads are often given a Thai kick with lime leaves and chile, and stir-fries and chargrill are standard features. Scots today can eat better than ever before. Robert Burns would be shocked at some of the new taste sensations creative chefs are devising. But he would be happy to learn that alcohol—especially whisky—is still a favored ingredient in many dishes and sauces.

Of course, it takes a wise chef to leave well enough alone, and many Scottish cooks know the simplest dishes have never lost their appeal, especially if that means **Lismore oysters** or **Loch Etive mussels.** The Scots have always been good bakers, and many small tearooms still bake their own **scones** and buttery **shortbread.** Heather honey is justly celebrated, and jams make use of Scotland's abundant harvest of soft fruit. Scottish raspberries, for example, are said to be among the finest in the world.

You'll most definitely want to try some of Scotland's excellent **cheeses.** The mild or mature cheddars are the best known. A famous hard cheese, Dunlop, comes from the Orkney Islands as well as Arran and Islay. One of the best-known cheeses from the Highlands is Caboc, creamy and rich, formed into cork shapes and rolled in pinhead oatmeal. Many varieties of cottage cheese are flavored with herbs, chives, or garlic.

And, yes, **haggis** is still Scotland's national dish—it's perhaps more symbolic than gustatory. One wit described it as a "castrated bagpipe." Regardless of what you might be told facetiously, haggis isn't a bird. Therefore, you should turn down invitations (usually offered in pubs) to go on a midnight haggis hunt. Cooked in a sheep's paunch (nowadays more likely a plastic bag), it's made with bits and pieces of the lung, liver, and heart of sheep mixed with suet and spices, along with onions and oatmeal. Haggis is often accompanied by single-malt whisky—then again, what isn't?

SINGLE MALT OR BLEND? "It's the only liquor fit for a gentleman to drink in the morning if he can have the good fortune to come by it . . . or after dinner either." Thus wrote Sir Walter Scott of the drink of his country—**Scotch whisky.** Of course, if you're here or almost anywhere in Britain or Europe, you don't have to identify it as *Scotch* whisky when you order. That's what you'll get. In fact, in some parts of Scotland, England, and Wales, they look at you oddly if you order Scotch as you would in the States.

The true difference in the Scotch whiskies you may have become accustomed to seeing in bars or liquor stores at home is whether they're blends or single-malt

Impressions

Despite the beauty of the land and the indomitable spirit of its people, take whisky away from Scotland and you take away the heart.
—Laura Latham, *In Britain* (1997)

whiskies. Many connoisseurs prefer single malts, whose tastes depend on their points of origin: Highlands, Lowlands, Islay, or Campbeltown on Kintyre. These are usually seen as sipping whiskies, not to be mixed with water (well, maybe soda) and not to be served with ice. Many have come to be used as after-dinner drinks, served in a snifter like cognac.

The blended Scotches came into being both because the single malts were for a long time too harsh for delicate palates and because they were expensive and time-consuming to produce. A shortcut was developed: The clear and almost tasteless alcohol produced in the traditional way could be mixed with such ingredients as American corn, Finnish barley, Glasgow city tap water, and caramel coloring with a certain percentage of malt whiskies that flavored the entire bottle. Whichever you prefer, both the single malts and the blends must be made within the borders of Scotland and then aged for at least 3 years before they can legally be called Scotch whisky.

Two after-dinner drinks are Scotch-based liqueurs—**Drambuie** and **Glayva.** The recipe for Drambuie, better known to Americans than Glayva, is supposed to have been given to its first producers, the Mackinnons of Strath on the Isle of Skye, by an impecunious guest, Bonnie Prince Charlie. The name of the drink is derived from the Gaelic *an dram buidheach,* meaning "a dram that satisfies."

The making of Scottish **beer**—the ales drunk by the common folk in earlier days—almost died out when palates became more adapted to Scotch whisky and when a malt tax was levied in the 18th century, followed in the 19th century by beer duty. The brewing industry has made a comeback in the last quarter of a century, and Scottish beer, or Scotch ale, is being produced. Real **ale** is beer made from malted barley, hop flowers, yeast, and water, with a fining process (use of an extract from the swim bladders of certain fish) to complete the brewing. Ales are fermented in casks in a series of steps. Scottish ale, either dark or light, is malty and full of flavor.

Index

HIT THE ROAD WITH
FROMMER'S DRIVING TOURS!

Frommer's Britain's Best-Loved Driving Tours
Frommer's California's Best-Loved Driving Tours
Frommer's Florida's Best-Loved Driving Tours
Frommer's France's Best-Loved Driving Tours
Frommer's Germany's Best-Loved Driving Tours
Frommer's Ireland's Best-Loved Driving Tours
Frommer's Italy's Best-Loved Driving Tours
Frommer's New England's Best-Loved Driving Tours
Frommer's Northern Italy's Best-Loved Driving Tours
Frommer's Scotland's Best-Loved Driving Tours
Frommer's Spain's Best-Loved Driving Tours
Frommer's Tuscany & Umbria's Best-Loved Driving Tours

Available at bookstores everywhere.

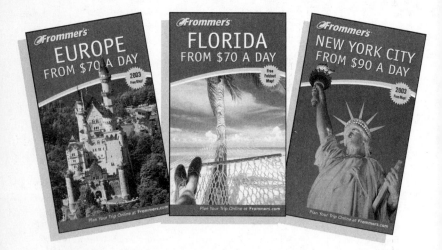

FROMMER'S® COMPLETE TRAVEL GUIDES

FROMMER'S® DOLLAR-A-DAY GUIDES

FROMMER'S® PORTABLE GUIDES

FROMMER'S® NATIONAL PARK GUIDES

FROMMER'S® MEMORABLE WALKS

Chicago	New York	San Francisco
London	Paris	

FROMMER'S® WITH KIDS GUIDES

Chicago	Ottawa	Vancouver
Las Vegas	San Francisco	Washington, D.C.
New York City	Toronto	

SUZY GERSHMAN'S BORN TO SHOP GUIDES

Born to Shop: France	Born to Shop: Italy	Born to Shop: New York
Born to Shop: Hong Kong, Shanghai & Beijing	Born to Shop: London	Born to Shop: Paris

FROMMER'S® IRREVERENT GUIDES

Amsterdam	Los Angeles	San Francisco
Boston	Manhattan	Seattle & Portland
Chicago	New Orleans	Vancouver
Las Vegas	Paris	Walt Disney World®
London	Rome	Washington, D.C.

FROMMER'S® BEST-LOVED DRIVING TOURS

Britain	Germany	Northern Italy
California	Ireland	Scotland
Florida	Italy	Spain
France	New England	Tuscany & Umbria

HANGING OUT™ GUIDES

Hanging Out in England	Hanging Out in France	Hanging Out in Italy
Hanging Out in Europe	Hanging Out in Ireland	Hanging Out in Spain

THE UNOFFICIAL GUIDES®

Bed & Breakfasts and Country Inns in:	Southwest & South Central Plains	Mexio's Best Beach Resorts
California	U.S.A.	Mid-Atlantic with Kids
Great Lakes States	Beyond Disney	Mini Las Vegas
Mid-Atlantic	Branson, Missouri	Mini-Mickey
New England	California with Kids	New England & New York with Kids
Northwest	Central Italy	New Orleans
Rockies	Chicago	New York City
Southeast	Cruises	Paris
Southwest	Disneyland®	San Francisco
Best RV & Tent Campgrounds in:	Florida with Kids	Skiing & Snowboarding in the West
California & the West	Golf Vacations in the Eastern U.S.	Southeast with Kids
Florida & the Southeast	Great Smoky & Blue Ridge Region	Walt Disney World®
Great Lakes States	Inside Disney	Walt Disney World® for Grown-ups
Mid-Atlantic	Hawaii	Walt Disney World® with Kids
Northeast	Las Vegas	Washington, D.C.
Northwest & Central Plains	London	World's Best Diving Vacations
	Maui	

SPECIAL-INTEREST TITLES

Frommer's Adventure Guide to Australia & New Zealand

Frommer's Adventure Guide to Central America

Frommer's Adventure Guide to India & Pakistan

Frommer's Adventure Guide to South America

Frommer's Adventure Guide to Southeast Asia

Frommer's Adventure Guide to Southern Africa

Frommer's Britain's Best Bed & Breakfasts and Country Inns

Frommer's Caribbean Hideaways

Frommer's Exploring America by RV

Frommer's Fly Safe, Fly Smart

Frommer's France's Best Bed & Breakfasts and Country Inns

Frommer's Gay & Lesbian Europe

Frommer's Italy's Best Bed & Breakfasts and Country Inns

Frommer's Road Atlas Britain

Frommer's Road Atlas Europe

Frommer's Road Atlas France

The New York Times' Guide to Unforgettable Weekends

Places Rated Almanac

Retirement Places Rated

Rome Past & Present